Ultimate Agile Administration with Jira (2nd Edition)

Administer Jira Cloud, Streamline Agile Workflows, and Build AI Agents with Rovo

Yogita Chhaya

www.orangeava.com

First Published: April 2026

Published By: Orange Education Pvt Ltd, AVA®

Address: 9, Daryaganj, Delhi, 110002, India

275 New North Road Islington Suite 1314 London,
N1 7AA, United Kingdom

ISBN (PBK): 978-93-49887-95-4
ISBN (E-BOOK): 978-93-49887-02-2

Scan the QR code to explore our entire catalogue

www.orangeava.com

Get a Free eBook

We hope you're enjoying your recent book purchase! Your feedback is incredibly valuable to us and helps other readers discover books that truly make a difference.

If you found this book useful or enjoyable, we'd greatly appreciate it if you could leave a short review with a 5-star rating on Amazon. Your review supports our work and allows us to reach more learners worldwide.

As a thank-you, we're happy to offer you a **free digital copy of this book** plus a **30% discount code** for your next purchase on our official websites:

www.orangeava.com

www.orangeava.in (For the Indian Subcontinent).

✅ **How it works:**

Leave your review on Amazon, take a screenshot of the confirmation or use the following link to submit the claim and email it to **info@orangeava.com.** Once received the required detail, we will send your rewards within 24 hours, **along with one month free subcription to the book on AVA SkillShelf!**

Claim Form
https://rebrand.ly/4d2477

Thank you for your support–it truly means a lot to us.

Colored Images

Please follow the links or scan the QR codes to download the *Images* of the book:

You can find code bundles of our books on our official Github Repository. Go to the following link to and QR code to explore the further:

https://github.com/orgs/ava-orange-education/repositories

Please follow the link to download the Colored Images of the book: ***https://rebrand.ly/jo2lcu7***

In case there's an update to the code, it will be updated on the existing GitHub repository.

Errata

We take immense pride in our work at **Orange Education Pvt Ltd,** and follow the best practices to ensure the accuracy of our content to provide an indulging reading experience to our subscribers. Our readers are our mirrors, and we use their inputs to reflect and improve upon human errors, if any, that may have occurred during the publishing processes involved. To let us maintain the quality and help us reach out to any readers who might be having difficulties due to any unforeseen errors, please write to us at:

errata@orangeava.com

Your support, suggestions, and feedback are highly appreciated.

Dedicated To

My Beloved Parents,

Family Members,

And

My Mentors.

About the Author

Yogita Chhaya is an Engineer, Educator and Certified Jira Administrator (ACP-120) with over 20 years of cross-functional industry experience. She helps professionals and teams work smarter by combining deep expertise in Atlassian Jira, Agile practices and practical workplace skill development.

As an independent Atlassian tools trainer and author of "*Ultimate Agile Administration with Jira (2nd Edition)*," Yogita has designed and delivered hands-on Jira training programs that go beyond tool usage to ensure real-world adoption and performance improvement. She has trained more than 3500 professionals, ranging from end users to administrators, across tools including Jira, Jira Service Management (JSM), Jira Product Discovery, Confluence and Rovo.

In addition to technical training, Yogita conducts impact-driven soft skills workshops focused on communication, professionalism, collaboration, adaptability, and managing workplace challenges. Her sessions are known for being practical, engaging and tailored to real professional environments.

Her diverse background spans telecom manufacturing, systems testing, Agile transformation, product evaluation, academia and corporate training, giving her a rare ability to bridge tools, processes and people effectively.

During her tenure at Tata Telecom Ltd., she served as the single point of contact for Y2K evaluation and certification of EPABX products and applications, and was honoured with both an Individual and Team Excellence Award for her contributions.

Yogita is also recognized as an Atlassian Community Champion, an Atlassian Certification SME who has contributed to certification exam development and a Lifetime Member of the Indian Society for Training & Development (ISTD).

About the Technical Reviewer

Nehaa Bansal is a trailblazing thought leader and data scientist driven by a relentless passion for early innovation. With experience across banking, finance, telecom, and insurance, she has developed a strong expertise in building predictive models that deliver meaningful, measurable impact. Her ability to thrive both as an independent contributor and as a collaborative team player distinguishes her in the field.

Academically accomplished, Nehaa topped in her class graduating in computer science, establishing a solid technical foundation. She further advanced her expertise by earning a master's degree in data science from BITS Pilani, sharpening her analytical and strategic capabilities.

Passionate about solving real user problems, Nehaa combines analytics, product strategy, and leadership to design innovative, scalable solutions. She approaches challenges with dedication and resilience, constantly pushing boundaries to unlock new possibilities.

Beyond her professional achievements, Nehaa is committed to lifelong learning and staying ahead of emerging industry trends. She is also a strong advocate for diversity and inclusion, fostering collaborative, empathetic environments where individuals can thrive.

Acknowledgments

I am grateful for the support I received from my parents when I started learning Atlassian products. They were always with me in this journey of learning, and supported me at every step I took. In fact, it would not have been possible to write this book without their inspiration.

I am also thankful to my family members for supporting and encouraging me throughout this incredible writing journey of mine. I am grateful to all the organizations that provided support when I was a beginner, and later as a trainer. Writing this book would not have been possible without their support.

Above all, I would like to thank the editorial team at Orange Education Pvt. Ltd. that guided, supported, and helped me immensely in writing this book. I also extend my heartfelt gratitude to the technical reviewer who guided me throughout the writing process. Their input has made this book more insightful and invaluable for readers seeking practical understanding and real-world applications.

Preface

This book covers the fundamentals of Agile, including Agile values and principles. It also introduces the Scrum and Kanban frameworks, important terms in Jira, and how to create a Jira site. It also includes project templates in Jira, and explains the importance of creating the right project. Additionally, the book covers all the concepts related to Jira administration and customization with examples.

The book includes both types of projects, whether they are managed by administrators or teams. It explores all the concepts related to Agile project management, reporting, and tracking Agile metrics. The content includes backlog management, sprint operations, insights provided by Jira, and harnessing the power of Jira filters. It highlights the importance of Automation in Jira and the concept of using smart values in Automation rules.

The book also provides use cases and step-by-step guides for administrator tasks. Additionally, it covers an advanced roadmap including program boards, useful for capacity planning and tracking cross-project work in large organizations. Furthermore, it explains the significance of adding plugin applications to expand the functionality of Jira, and how to purchase such software from the Atlassian Marketplace. It also covers how to get started with Rovo, creating agents to enhance productivity, and utilizing them through automation.

This book has been divided into 13 chapters, and they cover all the Agile fundamentals, Jira Cloud basics, complete Jira Administration with examples, Atlassian Intelligence and Rovo, multiple use cases, and step-by-step processes. Thus, after going through these chapters, learners will be able to use Jira more efficiently, and will find administration easier and more interesting. The following paragraphs contain a chapter-wise summary.

Chapter 1: The book starts with an introduction to Agile, providing an overview of Agile frameworks, followed by the difference between Agile and waterfall methodology, and explaining the basics of Scrum and Kanban frameworks. It then takes you through Jira concepts, various products in the Atlassian ecosystem, Jira Terminology, and explains why it is so popular..

Chapter 2: This chapter covers the understanding of project definition, creating various projects using standard templates in Jira. It also provides detailed information about the differences between team-managed and company-managed projects. Additionally, the chapter offers details on customizing a template, and providing an overview of the available templates.

Chapter 3: It covers user creation, groups and permissions from the administrator's perspective. The chapter also includes use cases, adding users, project roles in company-managed projects, and details about various permissions in Jira. These permissions are helpful for creating and customizing permission schemes.

Chapter 4: This chapter covers the creation of issues, creating product backlog, sprint boards, and all related operations and customizations. It also encompasses all the features of Agile boards, sprint operations, creating epics, and versions. The chapter includes understanding Jira Insights on backlog and board.

Chapter 5: This covers how to add issue types and issue type schemes as an Administrator. It includes information about issue status, resolutions, priority, and issue type hierarchy levels. The chapter also guides you to create sub-task issue types, issue operations, associating an issue type with a project, and understanding issue type schemes.

Chapter 6: This chapter focuses on creating new custom fields, ways to customize fields on the screen, and details about the types of custom fields available in Jira. It also explains how to add context to the fields, locked custom fields, and field configuration schemes with examples. Lastly, it covers creating screens, screen schemes, issue-type screen schemes, and use cases, providing step-by-step explanations with examples for each topic.

Chapter 7: The chapter begins with an understanding of workflows and their components. It covers the steps to create, edit, and delete workflows, including global transitions, adding screens to set resolution, advanced workflow features, and a comparison between active and inactive workflows. Each concept in this chapter is explained with examples, highlighting common mistakes to avoid, while creating workflows and providing relevant use cases.

Chapter 8: This chapter starts by explaining basic and advanced search methods, and how to create as well as save filters. It provides insights into Jira's built-in filters, managing subscriptions, various filter operations, and JQL with examples. The chapter then covers dashboards, explaining how to add gadgets, customize dashboards according to your needs, and use the wallboards feature. It covers the types of reports available in Jira, and provides detailed explanations of all Agile reports. Finally, it gives an overview of Atlassian Analytics.

Chapter 9: This begins with an understanding and accessing of Automation rules in Jira, including various elements of Automation rules. It covers the usage of automation templates, the automation playground, and the performance insights on automation rules executed. The chapter guides you through various steps to create automation rules, and provides multiple examples of these rules. Finally, it discusses a few use cases of these rules.

Chapter 10: This chapter begins with understanding team-managed projects, their salient features, and how to set them up. It includes information on adding people, roles, access levels, and Agile features. The chapter then covers issue types in team-managed projects, creating custom issue types, configuring workflows, defining statuses, transitions, and transition properties. It also discusses adding/removing workflow rules, Agile board features, managing backlogs, understanding insights, and the Timeline view. Lastly, it addresses reports, migrating from team-managed to company-managed projects and vice versa, and provides use cases related to team-managed projects.

Chapter 11: This starts with tips for Product Owners, Scrum Masters, and Software Developers. It covers creating projects with sample data, creating a project with multiple boards, and importing issues in Jira. Additionally, it discusses various Administrator roles in Jira, understanding advanced roadmap, viewing a sample plan, creating a plan, Time-line View, Dependency Report, setting up teams, creating releases, creating cross-project releases, adding filters, and configuring issue hierarchies above Epics in Advanced Roadmap. Finally, it provides an overview of JIRA Product Discovery with use cases.

Chapter 12: This chapter begins with an introduction to the Atlassian Marketplace, guiding readers on selecting plugins, and explaining the key terms of the applications listed on the marketplace. It also covers how to install plugins, and provides an overview of Admin-tools plugins. Lastly, it offers an overview of popular plugins and important use cases.

Chapter 13: This chapter introduces Rovo as Atlassian's modern AI-powered teammate, and explains why teams struggle when information is scattered across tools. It compares Atlassian Intelligence with Rovo, highlighting their key capabilities and features for streamlining workflows. Readers will learn essential admin configuration settings, how to enable or disable AI and Rovo, and how the Teamwork Graph powers smarter collaboration. The chapter also explores Rovo connectors, ready-to-use agents, and step-by-step guidance to build, duplicate, share and optimize no-code Rovo Agents through real-world automation examples and best practices.

DID YOU KNOW

Did you know that Orange Education Pvt Ltd offers eBook versions of every book published, with PDF and ePub files available? You can upgrade to the eBook version at **www.orangeava.com** and as a print book customer, you are entitled to a discount on the eBook copy. Get in touch with us at: **info@orangeava.com** for more details.

At **www.orangeava.com**, you can also read a collection of free technical articles, sign up for a range of free newsletters, and receive exclusive discounts and offers on Print Books and eBooks.

PIRACY

If you come across any illegal copies of our works in any form on the internet, we would be grateful if you would provide us with the location address or website name. Please contact us at **info@orangeava.com** with a link to the material.

ARE YOU INTERESTED IN AUTHORING WITH US?

If there is a topic that you have expertise in, and you are interested in either writing or contributing to a book, please write to us at **business@orangeava.com**. We are on a journey to help developers and tech professionals to gain insights on the present technological advancements and innovations happening across the globe and build a community that believes Knowledge is best acquired by sharing and learning with others. Please reach out to us to learn what our audience demands and how you can be part of this educational reform. We also welcome ideas from tech experts and help them build learning and development content for their domains.

REVIEWS

Please leave a review. Once you have read and used this book, why not leave a review on the site that you purchased it from? Potential readers can then see and use your unbiased opinion to make purchase decisions. We at Orange Education would love to know what you think about our products, and our authors can learn from your feedback. Thank you!

For more information about Orange Education, please visit **www.orangeava.com**.

Table of Contents

Chapter 1
Getting Started with Agile, Jira, and Jira Terminologies

Introduction

This chapter will cover the basics of Agile methodology, including the history of Agile, and how it differs from the waterfall approach. We will then understand Scrum and Kanban, which are two popular methodologies of software development. This will help build a strong foundation for understanding modern software practices.

We will explore Jira, different Jira products, and reasons why Jira is being used by different industries. At the end of the chapter, we will cover Jira terminology commonly used in the field. This will give you a practical understanding of how Jira is applied in real-world scenarios.

Structure

In this chapter, we will cover the following topics:

- History of Agile
- Difference between Waterfall and Agile
- Agile Mindset
- 4 Values and 12 Principles of Agile
- Various Agile Frameworks
- Defining Scrum
- Creating User Stories and Product Backlogs
- Defining Kanban
- Estimating and Prioritizing Work in Agile

- Agile Metrics and Performance Tracking
- About Jira
- Step-by-Step Guide to Create a Jira Site
- The Popularity of Jira
- Terminologies

History of Agile

Back in the 1990s, products were not solely dominated by software applications. They were a combination of hardware and software products. It is important to note that software was becoming increasingly complex and important in its own right. This is one of the factors that led to the need for a new way of developing software. It used to take more than a few years to complete the development cycle and launch a product. By the time it was handed over to the customer, their requirements had changed due to the long lead time and the products had already entered the market. In addition to that, some of the features were of no use to the customers. In software development, there were many processes to be followed, and a lot of documentation was required to be done as a part of the process.

As years passed, software projects were becoming more important, and it was felt that a new process or new way of developing software was required by everyone. The same thing was experienced in other industries such as automotive, aerospace, healthcare, and many others.

Many industries, beyond software development, faced challenges with long project cycles. Issues such as change in customer requirements, late feedback, increasing cost, time spent on documentation, and most importantly, how to deliver continuously concerned the project teams. The need for a more responsive and iterative approach became evident as businesses sought to stay competitive in rapidly evolving markets.

The introduction of the Toyota Production System (TPS) by Toyota, which revolutionized manufacturing, was the beginning of the foundations of Agile. It was founded between 1945 and 1975 by Japanese industrial engineers. TPS prioritized flexibility, waste minimization, and ongoing improvement. To encourage flexibility and effectiveness in software development, agile techniques drew inspiration from TPS and adopted its ideas. While Agile drew inspiration from TPS, it was not directly founded during that period; instead, it was formalized in 2001 with the Agile Manifesto.

Evolution toward the Agile Manifesto

The Agile Manifesto was not created suddenly. It was developed over time as people looked for better ways to build software. Traditional methods were rigid and slow, so developers began looking for more flexible and collaborative approaches. These ideas eventually came together in 2001 as the Agile Manifesto.

- **1980s:** In the early 1980s, the seeds of Agile methodology were sown with the emergence of lightweight software development approaches. The Waterfall model, a sequential and document-heavy methodology, dominated the scene. However, cracks begin to show as projects face delays, scope changes, and poor communication.
- **1990s - Iterative and Incremental Practices**: As the 1990s dawned, software practitioners started experimenting with iterative and incremental practices.
- **Late 1990s - Crystal and DSDM**: Towards the late 1990s, two notable methodologies, Crystal and Dynamic Systems Development Method (DSDM), emerged.
- **1990s - Extreme Programming (XP)**: In the late 1990s, Kent Beck introduced Extreme Programming (XP).
- **2001- The Agile Manifesto Takes Shape:** In 2001, 17 people from the software industry met at a place, and they agreed upon a way of working which is known as the Agile Manifesto. There were people from the software industry who were following Scrum, XP, FDD, and many different methodologies. They did not like the word **Lightweight** for this new methodology and agreed and decided to name it **Agile,** meaning responding to change.

Implementing an Agile way of working organization-wide is known as Business Agility. It refers to the ability of an organization to adapt quickly to market changes, seize opportunities, and deliver value to customers. It enables businesses to respond quickly to changing customer needs. It is implemented by many organizations worldwide to stay ahead in the currently dynamic business environment.

Difference between Waterfall and Agile

Agile and waterfall project management strategies are two separate approaches to project management. In the waterfall model, the next phase starts only after the earlier phase is completed. In waterfall methodology, requirements gathering, design, development, testing, and deployment phases are accomplished in sequence. It emphasizes extensive planning, documentation, and a fixed scope, making it suitable for projects with well-defined requirements and limited changes. It is therefore considered to be rigid and not able to manage unplanned changes.

Agile, on the other hand, is a flexible and iterative strategy that emphasizes adaptive planning and collaboration. It divides work into discrete sprints or iterations, allowing for continual feedback and adjustments. Agile values change and encourage client participation throughout the project. It encourages self-organizing teams and frequent communication, and focuses on providing incremental value. Agile teams use documentation to communicate and collaborate, but they do not produce as much documentation as waterfall teams.

Table 1.1 illustrates the difference between Waterfall and Agile Methodology:

Aspects	Waterfall Methodology	Agile Methodology
Project Phases	Distinct phases – requirements, design, development, and more	Continuous cycles - sprints
Development Approach	Sequential and linear	Iterative and incremental
Project roles	Specific roles are assigned for each phase (for example, Business Analyst, Designer, Developer, Tester, Project Manager)	Product owner, Scrum Master, Development teams
Quality Assurance	Testing at the end of the cycle	Continuous testing and quality assurance
Team Structure	Hierarchical with predefined roles	Cross-functional self-organizing teams
Communication	Less customer involvement	Close collaboration with customers
Documentation	Extensive documentation throughout	Documentation as needed
Flexibility	Limited flexibility to changes in requirements	Welcomes changes in requirements throughout the project
Feedback	Limited customer feedback during development	Regular customer involvement and feedback
Delivery time	Longer delivery time	Shorter delivery time
Change Implementation	Difficult to accommodate changes	Welcomes changes, even in later stages of development
Risk Management	Addressed in early planning, may not handle unforeseen risks well	Ongoing risk management
Project outcome	Well-defined scope and deliverables	Evolving scope and adaptable deliverables
Suitability	Projects with stable and known requirements	Projects with dynamic or evolving requirements

Table 1.1: *Waterfall versus Agile Methodology*

Agile Mindset

Being agile is more about beliefs, values, attitudes, and behaviors. For example, in a game of Rugby, the entire team works towards achieving a goal by adapting to the situation, collaborating, and with the "everyone is equal" attitude. It can be applied to any industry and any functional group, such as marketing, human resources, operations, and more. It is a way of working in which one must co-create, explore new ideas, experiment and experience, innovate, and remain adaptable.

4 Values and 12 Principles of Agile

In the 1990s, there was a period when projects were frequently delayed due to lengthy processes and sequential approaches to software development. The released products did not meet customer expectations due to the time lag, resulting in numerous order cancellations. These frustrations led to the creation of the Agile Manifesto by 17 leaders. This manifesto includes 12 principles and 4 values, which we will cover in this section.

4 Agile Values

There are multiple Agile methodologies, each of which applies the four values of the Agile Manifesto in different ways to guide teams in developing good quality software.

1. **Individuals and Interactions over Processes and Tools:** In the waterfall model, more importance was given to rigid processes. Even after spending a lot of time following these processes, the final software products were not of the best quality and error-free. It is possible to design and develop innovative software products if more importance is given to smart and competent people who can sit together, discuss, share, and solve problems. Processes should be followed, but they need to be simplified. Tools have to be customized to follow processes easily and make the development faster.

2. **Working Software over Comprehensive Documentation:** There was a time when very detailed documents were prepared for the features, requirements, test cases, diagrams, and releases. This was not helpful to provide value to the customer, and it used to delay the product releases. Delayed releases and obsolete features were the cause of the loss of business. More significance is given to working software, which is provided to the customer, and based on the feedback, further development is done. As per Agile Manifesto, providing value first is of more importance than creating outdated documents.

3. **Customer Collaboration over Contract Negotiation:** In the old ways of project development, customers used to come into the picture at the beginning,

once during the development cycle, and finally at the end. The products were developed based on what is written in the contract documents. In an agile way of working, customers come into the picture to provide feedback on a small piece of software, and based on the feedback and their actual needs, further development is carried out. This way it is possible to do immediate corrections if it is going in the wrong direction with the help of a customer. Continuous interaction with the customer is helpful to find out the right needs than what is written in the legal documents.

4. **Responding to Change over Following a Plan:** Traditionally, plans were prepared well in advance. However, it was not possible to incorporate any changes in that plan. Even a small change in the requirement was considered impossible. When a plan is made with agility in mind, it provides direction initially. Based on a rough plan, product development is started and then there is a scope for change. A small change in specification is discussed by all the stakeholders and taken up as an opportunity rather than an obstacle.

Agile Principles

The 12 principles act as guiding principles for the Agile methodologies. They outline a culture that embraces change and emphasizes customer-centric product development. These principles emphasize the importance of aligning new products with business needs:

1. **Customer Satisfaction through Early and Continuous Delivery:** By iteratively delivering working software, the customer is satisfied as he is getting some valuable features early in the cycle. At the same time, in every release cycle, he is going to receive something new which makes the customer happy.

2. **Welcome Changing Requirements, Even Late in Development:** In this dynamic world, everything changes continuously. Similarly, by incorporating changes in the requirements during the entire software development life-cycle, people can create the right products. By doing so, the final released software application is aligned with the actual and evolving requirements of the customer. Agile allows scope for changes even late in the development process.

3. **Deliver Working Software Frequently:** This principle recommends delivering new versions in a shorter time span, as opposed to the earlier longer time span. By doing this, the number of bugs per release is significantly reduced, leading to an overall improvement in the success of the software release. The release cycles are measured in the number of days rather than months.

4. **Collaborate Daily between Business People and Developers:** In the Agile way of working, there are no barriers to communication between business

teams and developers. Business teams must communicate about the business requirements, any changes from the side of the customer, and also whether these changes can be managed or not by the developers. By collaborating with developers, any misunderstandings can be avoided. Business analysts have to convert any business language to a language that developers can understand. Even if the teams are geographically far from each other, providing feedback on a daily basis helps in getting good outcomes.

5. **Motivated Individuals:** It is about creating a conducive work culture and keeping the workforce motivated. Every member is allowed, trusted, and encouraged to give new ideas and find better ways of designing new products. If the team members are motivated, they can eventually create innovative architectures, designs, and products.

6. **Face-to-face Conversations:** Communication is the key to success. The same thing is emphasized in Agile. It could be physical meetings in the office or video conference meetings where people can communicate efficiently. Developers and teams must communicate daily to understand the initial and evolving requirements.

7. **Measure of Progress through Working Software:** Customers want a working and good quality product. It is the measurement of the overall performance of the team. The software is considered to be of good quality based on the feedback from the end-user.

8. **Promote Sustainable Development:** The teams should work at the same pace irrespective of the number of changes introduced. Any member or employee should not be burdened by the work more than his/her capacity. Otherwise, it can result in burnout of the teams and hence, can affect the quality of the product.

9. **Continuous Attention to Technical Excellence:** Agile emphasizes on the good design of the product. This is a must-have for each and every team. It ensures that the software application is adaptable, maintainable, and scalable for future enhancements.

10. **Simplicity:** This principle suggests keeping the processes simple. Simplicity does not mean skipping important processes but it means avoiding complexity in design and coding. A working software product with less number of features is better than a problematic product having multiple features.

11. **Self-organizing Teams:** If the teams are empowered and autonomous, they can get better results. The agile teams consider themselves accountable and are ready to take responsibility for their work. Teamwork, Commitment collaboration, and Competency are the core skills to become more agile. The teams require a coach or a mentor but not a manager.

12. **Regularly Reflect on Continuous Improvement:** During the meeting, teams reflect on how they can improve the processes, productivity, and performance by making small changes. It is a continuous process to create a culture of continuous learning and working on improvement areas.

Various Agile Frameworks

We have covered Agile Scrum and Kanban in this chapter, among the many Agile frameworks listed as follows:

- **Kanban**: We have covered the details of this framework in the next section.
- **Scrum**: We have covered the details of this framework in the next section.
- **Feature-driven Development (FDD)**: FDD is a software development methodology that follows an iterative and incremental approach. In FDD, the development process is broken down into manageable pieces – features – and then it is built incrementally. In this process, an overall model is developed, followed by creating a feature list, feature-wise planning, features-based design, and features development.

  In FDD, the development process is structured around feature teams. Each of these teams is assigned the responsibility of delivering specific features. This way, the development effort is divided into smaller, more manageable tasks, making it easier to track progress and ensure that each feature is developed effectively. It maintains the iterative approach.

  One of the important characteristics of FDD is its emphasis on collaboration. It promotes close interaction among team members, stakeholders, and clients. It helps to understand the project requirements correctly.

  It also emphasizes well-defined processes. To summarize, it is a structured and flexible approach to software development.
- **Extreme Programming**: Extreme Programming (XP) is an Agile software development methodology that promotes collaboration, adaptability, and high-quality code. It emphasizes practices like continuous testing, pair programming, and frequent releases. With a focus on customer involvement and iterative development, XP makes sure that software remains responsive to changing requirements. By fostering teamwork, automation, and streamlined processes, XP enables developers to deliver reliable software efficiently while maintaining a sustainable work pace. Extreme Programming is suitable for teams working on dynamic projects with evolving requirements.
- **Adaptive Software Development (ASD)**: ASD is a software development approach that embraces change as an inherent part of the process. ASD involves three distinct phases: speculation, collaboration, and learning. Speculation includes creating a preliminary plan based on what is known,

while collaboration encourages open communication and active participation from both the development team and stakeholders. The learning phase emphasizes adapting the plan based on new information and insights gained throughout the process. ASD recognizes that software projects often encounter unexpected shifts and encourages a flexible and iterative approach to development, ensuring that the end result aligns closely with evolving needs and requirements.

- **Dynamic Systems Development Method (DSDM)**: It is an Agile methodology that focuses on delivering functional solutions within a fixed timeframe and budget. DSDM divides development into specific time-bound phases, promoting regular user involvement and feedback. It encourages collaboration between developers, users, and business representatives to ensure that the software aligns with business needs. DSDM emphasizes the importance of delivering the most valuable features first, and it provides a set of principles and practices to guide teams in building high-quality solutions while accommodating changes. Overall, DSDM provides a structured framework for Agile software development, aiming to strike a balance between fixed constraints and adaptability.
- **Scrumban**: Scrumban is a hybrid approach that combines the practices of both Scrum and Kanban methodologies. In Scrumban, teams use the structured framework of Scrum but add elements from Kanban to enhance flexibility and continuous improvement. This allows teams to transition smoothly between planned iterations (sprints) and a more flow-based approach. Scrumban is especially useful for teams that are already familiar with Scrum and want to introduce the focus of Kanban on optimizing workflow and minimizing bottlenecks. Scrumban can be implemented when a company wants to allow more flexibility to the teams or for a team facing problems implementing scrum.

Defining Scrum

Scrum is an Agile project management framework to create solutions for complex problems. It can be compared to the game of Rugby in which the goal is set and achieved by working on the principles of collaboration, teamwork, transparency, and agility. In scrum, work is divided into small time intervals called sprints, which can last for 1-4 weeks. The work items are also divided into small chunks called stories, tasks, and more. Each sprint begins with a planning meeting where the priority of the tasks to be taken is decided. The team meets daily to discuss the tasks done, tasks to be taken up, and to report any obstacles in completing the tasks planned to achieve the sprint goal. The teams are empowered, motivated, and work collaboratively to adapt to changing requirements at the same pace.

Scrum Roles, Ceremonies, and Artifacts

This section explains scrum roles, ceremonies, and artifacts.

In scrum methodology, there are three defined roles: scrum master, product owner, and the development team, which collaborate with each other:

- **Scrum Master:** Scrum Master is a facilitator and a scrum expert. He makes sure that everybody in the team understands how the team has to collaborate, set the sprint goal, and achieve the same. He helps the team to remove any impediments and leads the scrum meetings.
- **Scrum Team:** The scrum team is a team of developers and testers working together, collaborating, and working towards achieving the sprint goal. Team members can communicate with the product owner to understand the product specifications and task priorities. The team follows the guidance provided by the scrum master in case of any obstacles such as resources, server availability, or any other problems faced during the sprint.
- **Product Owner:** Product owner is the single point of contact between the customer/end user and the scrum team. He manages the product backlog, helps in sprint planning, and participates in scrum meetings. He is also responsible for product backlog grooming and deciding the priorities of the user stories.

Scrum ceremonies provide opportunities for planning, tracking, and feedback. During these ceremonies, scrum teams interact with each other to understand the requirements, plan sprints, communicate about the obstacles, demonstrate the working software, and move forward with the lessons learned and action plan.

- **Sprint Planning:** It is a collaborative planning done by the product owner, scrum master, and development team. They discuss the priorities and decide which tasks to be included in the sprint backlog. During this ceremony, the team decides the sprint goal, which means deciding what they will deliver/develop in this sprint. The team estimates the effort required for each task and creates a plan to achieve the sprint goal.
- **Daily Stand-up:** It is conducted daily in which team members and the scrum master discuss the progress done.

  Points to discuss in Daily Scrum are as follows:

  - What did I do yesterday as per the current sprint plan?
  - What will I do today to meet the Sprint goal?
  - Share about any impediment that prevents me/team towards completing the ongoing task in the sprint.

  The members discuss the work done on the tasks, which task they will be taking up next, and share any impediments with the scrum master. It builds a culture of transparency, collaboration, and accountability among the team.

- **Sprint Review:** It is done at the end of the sprint. In this ceremony, team members demonstrate the features and functionality developed to the stakeholders. Based on the feedback from the stakeholders, improvements can be made in the next sprint.
- **Sprint Retrospective:** This ceremony is held to reflect on the completed sprint. In this ceremony, what went well, what could be improved, and actions to be taken are discussed. The team and developers identify the areas for improvement. A culture of continuous improvement and learning is created by conducting this ceremony.

There are three main artifacts in Scrum: Product backlog, Sprint backlog, and Increment.

- **Product Backlog:** Product backlog is a list of features, bugs, and any other type of requirements to develop a product and is managed by the product owner.
    - It is a complete list of items to design and develop the product.
    - It is an ordered list and evolves continuously.
    - The product owner is fully responsible for this artifact.
    - It includes features, functionalities, fixes, and any other details required.
- **Sprint Backlog:** Sprint Backlog is a complete list of tasks to be taken up in the next sprints and is managed collectively by everyone on the team.
    - It is a complete list of work items to be taken up in a sprint.
    - It is a detailed list that includes estimation and who will work on what details.
    - It is updated or maintained by the developers.
- **Increment:** In Scrum methodology, increment is the combination of the software developed earlier plus the software developed in the recent sprint, which is integrated, tested, and ready to be released.
    - It is work that is complete and meets the definition of done.
    - It must be a working feature/functionality that can be used by the customer.
    - An increment does not necessarily equal a release.

Agile scrum artifacts are the details used by the team and stakeholders. It is generated during the planning, breaking the tasks, working on the sprints, and at the end of the sprint. There are also other artifacts such as the definition of Done and the Burndown Chart.

Creating User Stories and Product Backlogs

User stories are a way of writing customer requirements in a simple language that anyone can understand. The number of such user stories, along with other tasks and features, are added to create the product backlog. The product backlog can be visualized and prioritized in a project management tool and is regularly updated by product owners to meet new business needs.

User Stories:

- It is a document that contains information about the product requirements of the end-user in an understandable format.
- It contains information such as a description of the user, what exactly the user wants from that feature/functionality, and how the user will benefit from that feature.
- For example: As a user, I can find important items on the board by using the customizable "Quick Filters" so that I don't have to search for those work items every time and work efficiently.
- For each and every user story, there is an acceptance criterion written, which makes sure the specific conditions are met. Based on the criteria, it is accepted as a working functionality or else it gets rejected.
- User stories can be divided into sub-tasks to simplify the work by the developers.
- It is user-centric and a new way of writing requirements in Agile methodology.
- User stories will evolve based on received feedback, providing clear specifications for both technical and non-technical team members.

Product Backlog:

- A product backlog is a prioritized list of features, functionalities, improvements, suggestions, and bugs in detail.
- It is a bucket of tasks from which one can take up tasks and create a sprint backlog based on the priority decided by the scrum team.
- It is continuously refined during the development cycle and tasks can be added and modified based on the change in the requirements and other conditions.
- Priority of the work items is decided based on the value it provides to the customer.
- It is created and maintained by the product owner and is updated to meet the final objective of the product to be developed.

- The team and product owner estimate the tasks in the product backlog and break them down based on the complexity of the tasks.
- In a project management tool, it can be viewed on boards and then moved to the sprint backlog based on priority.

Defining Kanban

Kanban, derived from the Japanese word for **signboard**, was originally implemented by Toyota in Japan as part of their manufacturing processes. This innovative system served as a signaling mechanism, effectively enhancing the efficiency of their manufacturing units by visualizing bottlenecks within the system.

Kanban is a **Pull system**. In this method, work is done when there is a demand. Known as Just in Time (JIT), Kanban methodology employs a board where tasks or work items progress from left to right as the work unfolds. This concept has been embraced not only by manufacturing but also by software development teams. On a Kanban board, tasks are categorized into three main statuses: **To do**, where prioritization occurs before moving on to design, coding, testing, and release tasks in progress; and finally, tasks are moved to the **Done** status, signifying completion.

Here are some of the Kanban practices, principles, benefits, and disadvantages:

- **Core Practices:**
  - Visualize the workflow
  - Limit WIP (Work in Progress)
  - Manage flow
  - Make process policies explicit
  - Take feedback
  - Improve collaboratively, evolve experimentally
- **Principles:**
  - Start with what you know
  - Agree to pursue incremental, evolutionary change
  - Respect the current process, roles, responsibilities, titles
  - Encourage acts of leadership at all levels in your organization
- **Benefits:**
  - Identifying issues
  - Flexibility
  - It can save time
  - It empowers teams

- Balance productivity
- Increased customer satisfaction
- **Disadvantages:**
  - Cannot be used independently
  - May be difficult where dependencies are involved
  - Inability for an iteration
  - Too simple board
  - Lack of time representation

Approaching Kanban

The Kanban approach should be selected in the following situations:

- When the teams are new to the Agile way of working and the team is very small.
- When the nature of work varies continuously, such as changing priorities, task durations, and inflow of new requirements.
- Optimizing flow is more important than fixed timeframes.
- When work items cannot be easily broken down into sprints.
- When there is a need to be flexible and adapt to changes in requirements, market conditions, and customer feedback.
- When there is a need for managing work in progress to identify bottlenecks and manage capacity.
- When there is a need for continuous improvement in processes and more visibility of task status and progress through Kanban boards.

Comparison of Scrum and Kanban Frameworks

Scrum and Kanban frameworks are similar; however, there are some distinctions, as mentioned in *Table 1.2*:

Factors	**Scrum**	**Kanban**
Planning	Done at the beginning of the sprint/iteration	JIT Planning means - no planning is done
Sprint	It can be of 1-4 weeks time	There are no sprints/iterations
Roles	PO, SM, and team	No Roles defined: There might be an Agile Coach
Boards	Indicates the workflow steps	Indicates the workflow steps and WIP limits

Commitment	Team commits for each sprint: Sprint may fail if capacity is not measured	Commitment is based on Capacity: WIP limits help team members working on multiple tasks
Workload	Workload: Limits WIP per iteration	Workload: Limits WIP per status
Modifications	Once the sprint begins, not allowed to add tasks in the iteration...scope creep	You can add tasks in the backlog and take up based on the priorities
Industries	Software Development, Construction, Data Analytics, Advertising, Pharmaceuticals	Marketing, Content creation, Manufacturing, Healthcare, Fashion

***Table 1.2**: Comparison of Scrum and Kanban Frameworks*

Estimating and Prioritizing Work in Agile

Estimating and deciding the priority of tasks is an important aspect of Agile planning. The task estimation is done with the help of techniques such as story points, t-shirt sizing, Fibonacci sequence, and many more. In these techniques, estimation is done based on the complexity of the tasks and not on the time taken. Tasks are moved to the sprint after deciding the priority. Priority may change throughout the cycle and the decision is taken by the team based on the value it provides to the customer. The most important features are delivered first to the customer. This way, it is a value-driven approach that takes into account the feedback provided by the customer.

Agile Metrics and Performance Tracking

Agile metrics are a quantitative measurement of the agile project life cycle used to track and improve performance. We have defined some must-learn Agile metrics as follows:

- Agile metrics are used to track the project and improve the performance of the team and develop better products.
- Burndown charts and burn-up charts measure the amount of work remaining and completed, respectively. It helps to understand the progress towards the sprint -goal.
- Cycle-time is a measurement of the time it takes from start to finish the project. It helps to understand the speed and efficiency of the teams.
- Lead-time is a measurement of the time it takes a feature to enter the backlog, then design-coding-release, and finally reach the customer.
- Velocity is a measurement of how much work a team can complete in a given time frame. It is measured in story points or number of stories completed.
- Epic and release burndown charts track the progress over an epic or release, which is the larger body of the work.

- There are many other metrics and charts such as Control chart, Cumulative flow diagram, No. of defects, Customer support requests, Customer retention rates, and many more. These are used to measure the performance of the Agile project life cycle.

About Jira

Jira is a robust project management tool used by Agile teams worldwide. It was designed by an Australian software company - Atlassian in 2002. It has evolved as a unique tool, which has many variants and can be customized for all types of projects and teams. Jira offers features to plan, track, and release software and collaborative platforms for teams. It is used for work item management, bug tracking, agile project management, and IT service management with the help of customizable workflows and integration with other add-ons. Jira is a popular tool for many other tasks, such as requirements gathering, test case management, and documentation.

A Step-by-Step Guide to Create a Jira Site

We will learn how to set up Jira on Cloud.

These are the steps to create a Jira site free for 10 users:

1. Go to :https://www.atlassian.com/software/jira/pricing

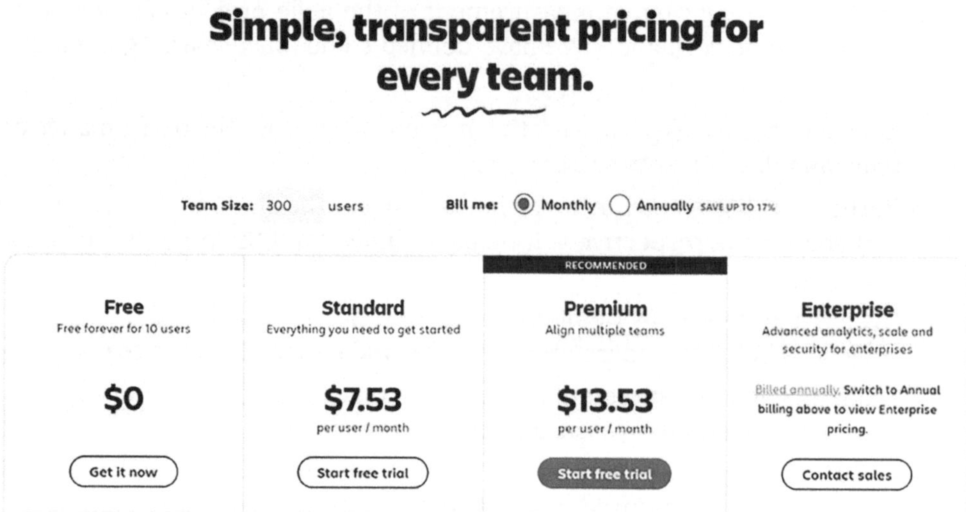

Figure 1.1: *Step 1 to Create a Jira Site*

2. Choose the free version and click on "**`Get It now`**"
3. Enter your work email or other email ID
4. Follow the prompts to sign up for an Atlassian account

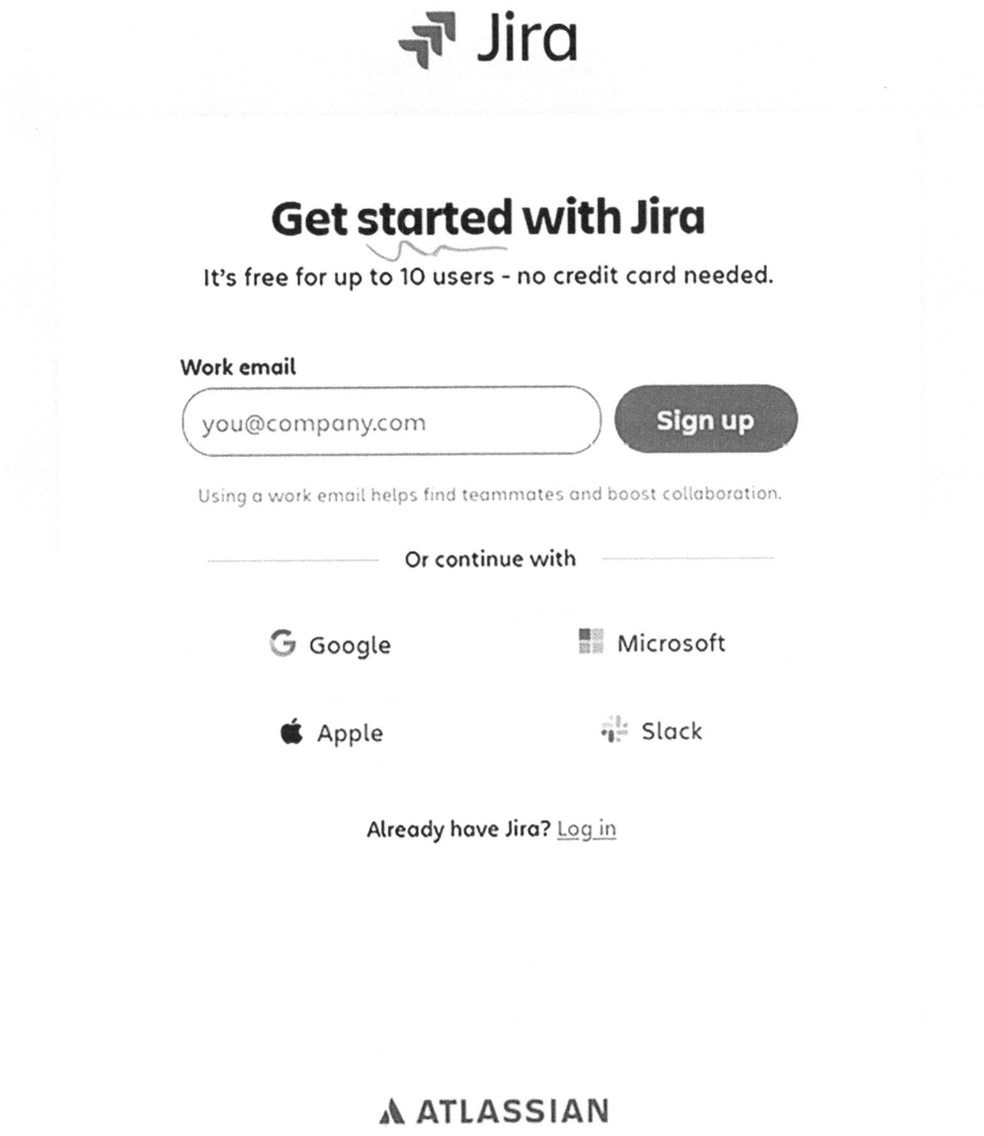

Figure 1.2: *Step 2 to Create Jira Site*

5. After signing up, login to your Jira Cloud Account
6. Insert the site name for your site to be created

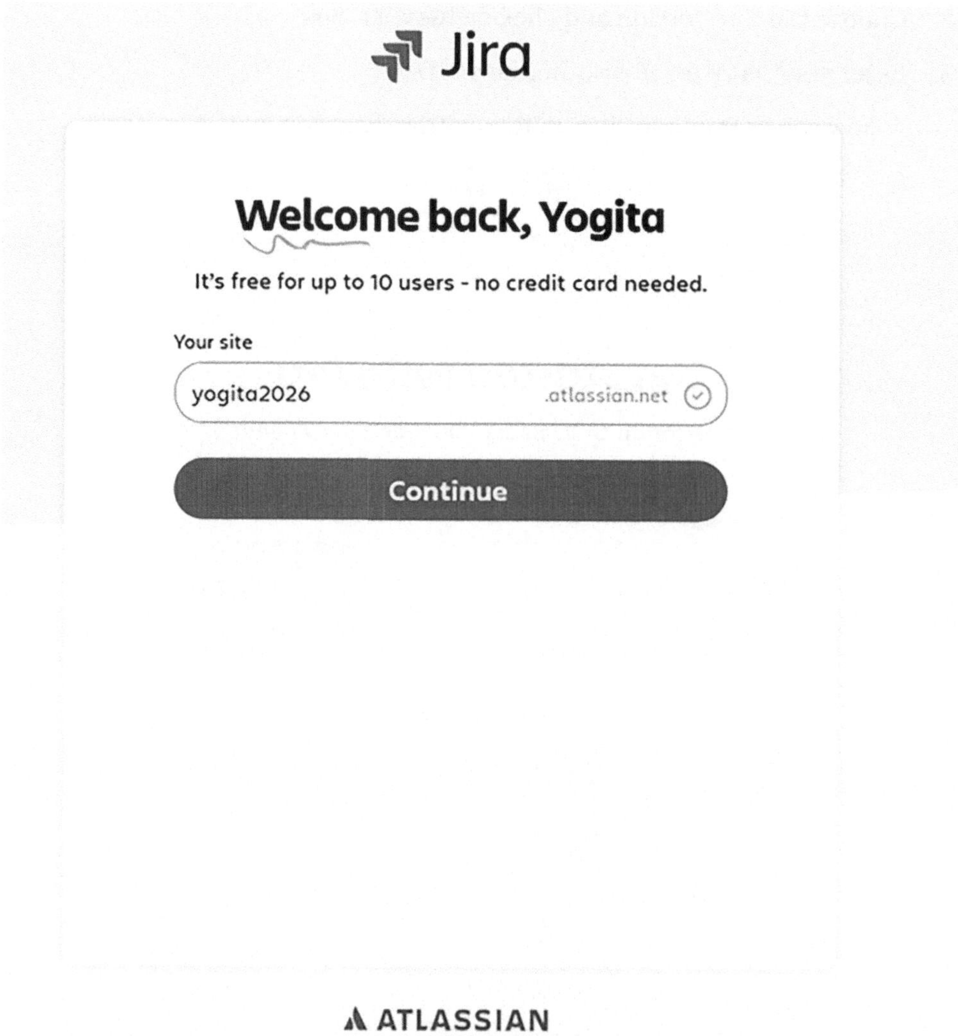

***Figure 1.3**: Step 3 to Create Jira Site*

7. Click **`Continue`**
8. Jira will create your site and your Jira site is ready.

Different Atlassian Products

Let us explain some Jira products as follows:

- **Jira**: A tool used worldwide to manage projects for software teams, featuring agile development, time tracking, work management, program management with the help of features like customizable templates, artificial intelligence and agentic AI. Jira is a solution designed for business teams in marketing, sales, HR and finance. It is a friendly tool built for cross team collaboration and coordination for all types of teams.

- **Jira Service Management**: It is a Service desk and ITSM solution with ticketing, incident management, problem management, and self-service features.
- **Jira Align**: It is an Enterprise Agile Planning platform that helps improve visibility, strategic alignment, and enterprise adaptability to accelerate your digital transformation.
- **Jira Product Discovery**: A tool for product teams to organize and prioritize ideas, share product roadmaps, and connect business and tech teams, all in Jira.

Additionally, there are other Products that are used for version control repository, code review, team collaboration, and incident management:

- **Bitbucket**: A source-code management and version control repository with code collaboration and CI/CD capabilities.
- **Opsgenie**: Incident management and alerting tool for prompt response and resolution of critical issues.
- **Statuspage**: Communication tool for real-time status updates, incident notifications, and customizable incident response pages.
- **Trello**: Visual project management tool using boards, lists, and cards for organizing tasks and projects.
- **Sourcetree**: Sourcetree is a free Git client for Windows and Mac, which simplifies how you interact with your Git repositories.
- **Bamboo**: Bamboo is a continuous delivery pipeline that offers resilience, reliability, and scalability for teams of any size.
- **Fisheye**: Fisheye makes it easy to search, track, and compare code changes.
- **Crucible**: Crucible is a collaborative code review platform that helps you find bugs and improve code quality.
- **Confluence**: Team collaboration software for creating, organizing, sharing documents, project plans, and knowledge bases.
- **Loom**: Loom makes it easy to create and share videos directly within Atlassian apps like Jira, Confluence and Bitbucket, helping teams communicate visually. The app includes AI-powered features and simple editing tools for quick and professional videos.
- **Rovo**: Rovo is the AI-powered digital assistant of Atlassian that helps teams find, learn and act on information across Atlassian and connected apps faster.

- **Focus**: Atlassian Focus is a strategic planning hub that connects goals, work, teams and funds in real time to align execution with organizational priorities.
- **Talent**: It is an app that helps leaders plan, align and manage their workforce with real-time insights.

The Popularity of Jira

Jira is a very famous and customizable tool that has been used by Agile teams and other teams for 20 years. Here are some features and functionalities of Jira as follows.

- **Designed for All Types of Teams:** It is a unique tool that is the right fit for software development and various other teams, such as HR, marketing, sales, service, and more. It was originally designed for bug tracking in software development, but it has evolved for all types, sizes, and industries.
- **Pricing and Plan:** Jira products are available in a free plan for 10 users and three different variants. There are three variants available based on the pricing, number of users, features, and other criteria.
- **Customizable Space Templates:** Jira provides built-in space templates for various purposes, such as:
    - Scrum
    - Kanban
    - Bug Management

  Each space can be of two types:
    - Company-managed space, and
    - Team-managed space.

In addition to this, there are many other templates to manage various processes and projects. We will understand the same in *Chapter 2*, "*Working with Space Templates*".

- **Time Tracking:** Jira has a time tracking feature that shows the time estimated, time spent, and time left for a task.
- **Bug Management:** In Jira, a template for bug management is readily available. It can be customized easily to manage the bugs for agile software development teams. Users can add fields available to customize the process in more detail.
- **Work Management:** Users can create work item types/task types as per the requirements of the spaces. Work items can be created, edited, and managed based on permissions and roles.

- **Search Filters:** The searching feature in Jira is helpful to find out any work items by setting criteria to filter work items. There is a basic search and an advanced search. Basic search helps filter work items based on task types, spaces, assignees, status, and more, while advanced search uses Jira Query Language (JQL), which consists of a set of keywords, functions, operators, and values.
- **Timeline:** Jira has a feature called Timeline View that has been used for planning, tracking, and creating tasks and map dependencies. In this view, one can create parent and child work items and schedule the same. The linking is done automatically between the tasks created in the timeline view. So, all the tasks created are child work items under an epic, which is the parent task.
- **Advanced Roadmap:** Advanced Roadmap is a feature of planning across multiple teams and spaces. It is an inbuilt feature in Premium and Enterprise versions. You can plan based on capacity, priorities, set dependencies, and explore different scenarios in the Advanced roadmap.
- **Automation in Jira:** Jira has rich templates for automation rules. Automation rules help teams automate the repetitive tasks and simplify the processes. There is an automation library for beginners to learn and implement the rules. The rules are of two types: space-specific and Global rules.
- **Community Support:** Atlassian community is a group of users of Atlassian products and Community Champions. It is a very big community where users can ask questions and clear doubts. Beginners can get help from community champions and other people in the group as and when it is required. By collaborating with experienced people, anyone can learn everything about Atlassian products.
- **Boards:** Jira boards are powerful tools used for visualizing, updating, and tracking purposes. There are two types of boards: Scrum and Kanban boards. Jira boards can be customized for sorting the work items based on priority and other criteria. One can also match the statuses in Jira workflow and Jira boards. It also provides insights about the epics, sprints, and work items to be worked on. Users can move tasks between statuses as per the customized workflow.
- **Dashboards and Reporting:** Jira is a rich project management tool with customizable dashboards and reporting features. One can add gadgets and create their own dashboards, making it easy to present critical information to management during meetings. The reporting functionality of Jira provides Agile metrics, such as burndown charts and cumulative flow diagrams, allowing teams to track project progress and identify bottlenecks. Jira offers reports for time tracking, workload, and resolution time, enabling teams to make data-driven decisions and optimize their processes.

- **Atlassian Intelligence and Rovo:** Jira became richer with the introduction of AI features and Rovo Agents. AI helps teams generate Work Breakdown Structures, refine work item descriptions and summarize updates instantly. Users can create no code/low code Agents. With Rovo Agents, everyday tasks get automated, tickets are managed smoothly and right information can be found easily. Together, they make Jira easier to use and free up your time for real work.

Conclusion

We had started by learning about the necessity of a new way of working in various industries to manage projects. We explored the importance of adaptability and collaboration through the values and principles of Agile. We also discussed when to use Scrum and Kanban, including practices such as user stories, backlogs, estimation, and prioritization. Finally, we covered Agile metrics for performance tracking.

We are now familiar with the Agile manifesto and concepts of Scrum and Kanban methodologies in Agile software development. We also learned about the various Jira products and other product solutions offered by Atlassian including the incorporation of Artificial Intelligence and Agentic AI. We now know the reasons behind the popularity of Jira and also its terminologies.

In the next chapter, we will learn how to create the first space in Jira, configure different spaces, and explore a few examples of space templates in Jira.

Terminologies

- **Attachment**: A file attached to a Jira work item.
- **Backlog**: A list of user stories, bugs, and features for a sprint or a product to be worked upon.
- **Board**: It is the place from where information about the work items can be read and updated. It provides status-based information, and the tasks can be moved from one status to another on the board.
- **Burndown Chart**: It shows the amount of total work estimated and remaining in a sprint.
- **Component**: It is a subcategory of the space; for example, Modules of a space.
- **Field**: Jira provides its own system fields and other customizable fields. The custom field is a field used by the users to capture additional information about the work item.
- **Control Chart**: It provides information about the lead-time and cycle-time for a space or sprint.

- **Dashboard**: Using this feature, one can present information about the key metrics of a space.
- **Dependency**: A relationship between two or more work items when they rely on each other to get completed.
- **Epic:** A large task that has to be broken down into smaller tasks or stories.
- **Fix Version**: A version of a software application in which a bug is fixed.
- **Group**: A collection of users/Administrators in Jira who have common permissions and responsibilities.
- **Work Item**: It is a unit of work, which is also named as a task. It can be based on the work a person is supposed to do. For example, tasks, bugs, epic, story, and more, which can be tracked through workflow.
- **Impediment**: An obstacle that can prevent work on a work item.
- **JQL (Jira Query Language)**: It is the own language of Jira used to search and display a work item.
- **JSM**: It stands for Jira Service Management.
- **JWM**: It stands for Jira Work Management.
- **Key**: A unique identifier for each and every work item in Jira.
- **Label**: A tag that can be used to search and sort the work items in Jira.
- **Notification**: An email sent from Jira to notify events like create, edit, delete work items, and many other events.
- **Space**: A combination of work items, components, workflow steps, and other resources in Jira to work towards achieving a goal.
- **Priority**: It defines the level of importance assigned to the work items used to decide its order in the backlog.
- **Parent Work Item**: A work item in Jira, which is related to one or multiple child work items.
- **Release:** A version of a software application that is delivered to the customer.
- **Resolution**: The way of fixing or completing a work item in Jira and sending it to the resolved status.
- **Screen**: It is the combination of fields that creates a form to accept information about a work item.
- **Story**: It is the task type in Agile project management, which is used to describe the needs of the end user.
- **Sprint**: It is the time span during which the software development teams design, develop, and implement the small working piece of software. It is also called an iteration and can be 1-4 weeks.

- **Story Point**: It is a unit of estimation used by Agile teams. It is the measurement of the relative complexity of a story.
- **Swimlane**: It is the way to categorize the work items. Based on the categorization, teams can see which work items to work on.
- **Sub-task**: It is the child work item of task, story, and more, which is smaller than the parent task.
- **Task**: A piece of work in Jira that needs to be done to complete a process.
- **Time-tracking**: The way of logging and tracking the time spent on different tasks in Jira.
- **Transition**: When a task moves from one status to another in Jira, it is called transition.
- **User**: Any person who works to manage and track work items in Jira.
- **Version**: A release of a software application, which is a set of work items and bug-fixes.
- **Velocity**: It is the measure of how much work a team can take up in a sprint. It could be based on story points, work item counts, value, and more.
- **Work-flow**: It is the process-steps to complete a task from the start to resolution.
- **Work-log**: A record of the time spent while working on a work item in Jira.

CHAPTER 2
Working with Space Templates

Introduction

In this chapter, we will learn about spaces in Jira. We will cover the types of spaces, types of space templates and how to configure the spaces for your specific business needs. We will understand how to enable or disable specific features within a space.

Additionally, we will understand the difference between team-managed and Company-managed spaces along with tips on when to select the appropriate space type based on your requirements. We will understand how to migrate data between team and company managed spaces and what are the limitations in each case. By the end of this chapter, you will understand important aspects of implementing space templates and configuring Jira to support your processes.

Structure

In this chapter, we will cover the following topics:

- Defining a Space in Jira
- Definition and Purpose of Space Templates
- Benefits of Using Space Templates in Jira
- A Step-by-Step Guide to Create a Space
- Choosing the Right Space Type: Team-Managed versus Company-Managed Spaces
    - The Difference between Company-Managed and Team-Managed Spaces
- Exploring Different Space Template Types and Their Purposes
- Examples of Successful Space Template Implementation
    - Agile Scrum Software Development Space Template
    - IT Service Management Space Template

- Important Use-Cases

Defining a Space in Jira

A space comprises tasks that a team works on to achieve a specific goal. In Jira, a space can be seen as a container for organizing, tracking, and accessing these tasks as required. The team collaborates on these tasks to accomplish a predetermined objective.

Definition and Purpose of Space Templates

Space templates are a combination of standardized process flows, task types, and individuals involved in the space, among other elements. They serve as a tool for standardization that can be applied to multiple spaces. A proper template selection is crucial for Jira administrators or Space administrators as it saves time during project execution. The settings and configurations can be shared across multiple spaces, allowing team members to consistently focus on the actual work. It is also essential for all members of the organization to be aware of which space template to use.

Benefits of Using Space Templates in Jira

We will cover the following five benefits of using space templates in Jira:

- **Time Saving**: The project manager does not need to create spaces from scratch every time, resulting in significant time saving.
- **Error Reduction**: Standardized templates minimize the risk of overlooking crucial steps, leading to fewer errors.
- **Improved Efficiency**: Streamlining space management processes and reducing manual work enhances overall efficiency.
- **Standardization:** Space managers can easily apply standardized workflows, work item types, and custom fields using space templates, eliminating the need to create them repeatedly for new spaces.
- **Scalability:** Space structures and settings can be replicated effortlessly, reducing the workload for space management.

Step-by-Step Guide to Create a Space

To create a space, you can follow these step-by-step instructions as mentioned below:

1. **Login to your Jira account**: Open the browser and navigate to the Jira login page and enter your credentials to login to your Jira account.
2. Navigate to Spaces and Select `Createspace`.

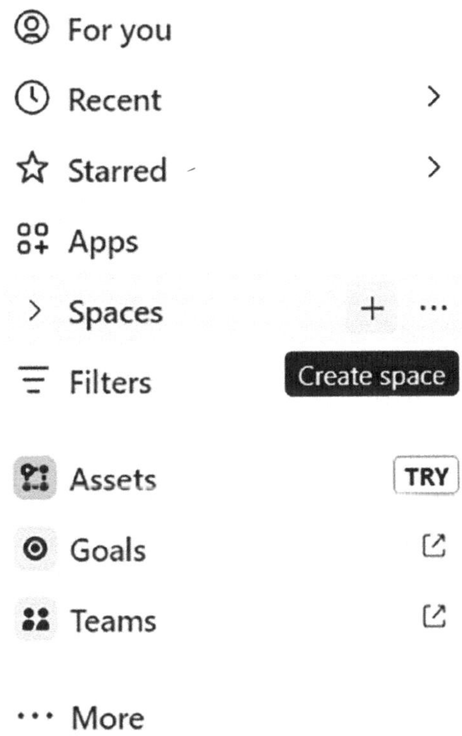

Figure 2.1: *How to Create Space in Jira Step-2*

3. Select **`Software development`** from the sidebar.

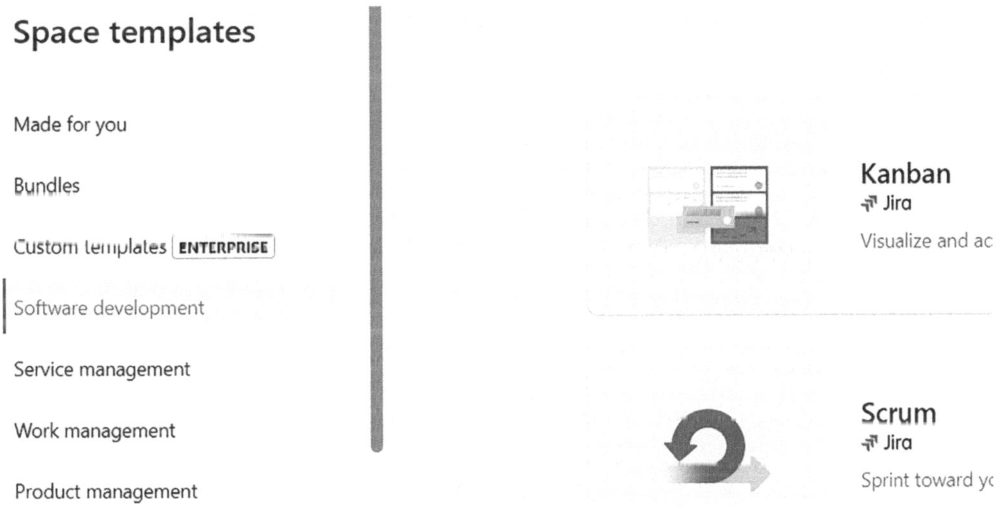

Figure 2.2: *How to Create Space in Jira Step-3*

4. Select **`Scrum, Kanban`**, **`Bug tracking`** or other relevant software space.

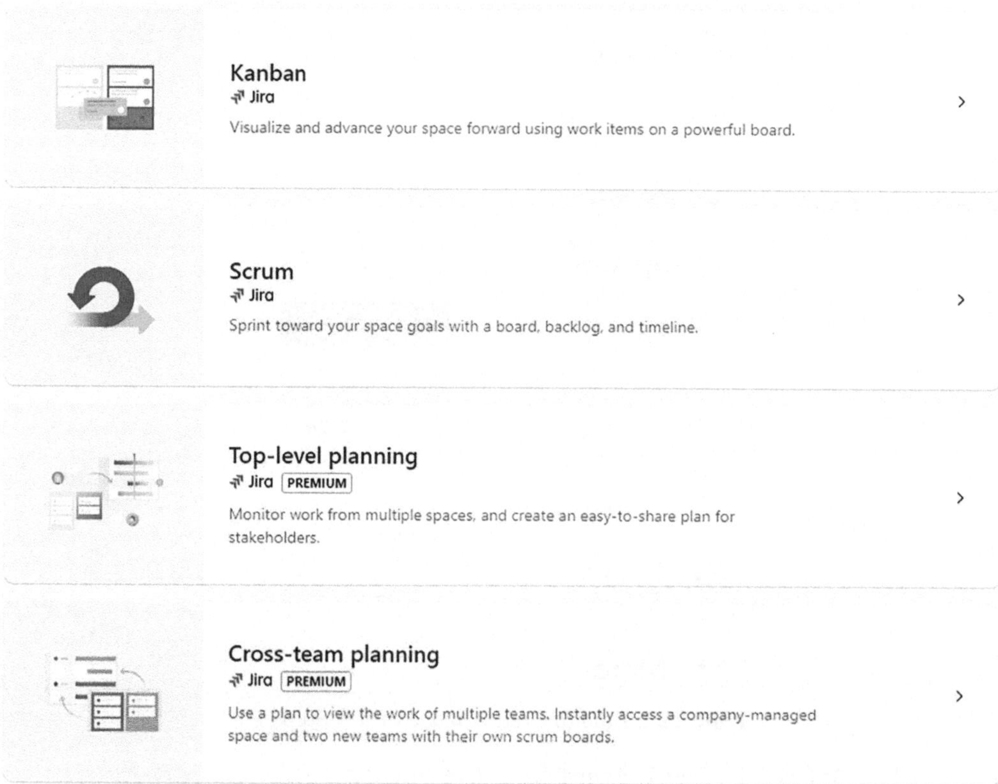

Figure 2.3: *How to Create Space in Jira Step-4*

5. Select **`Use template.`**

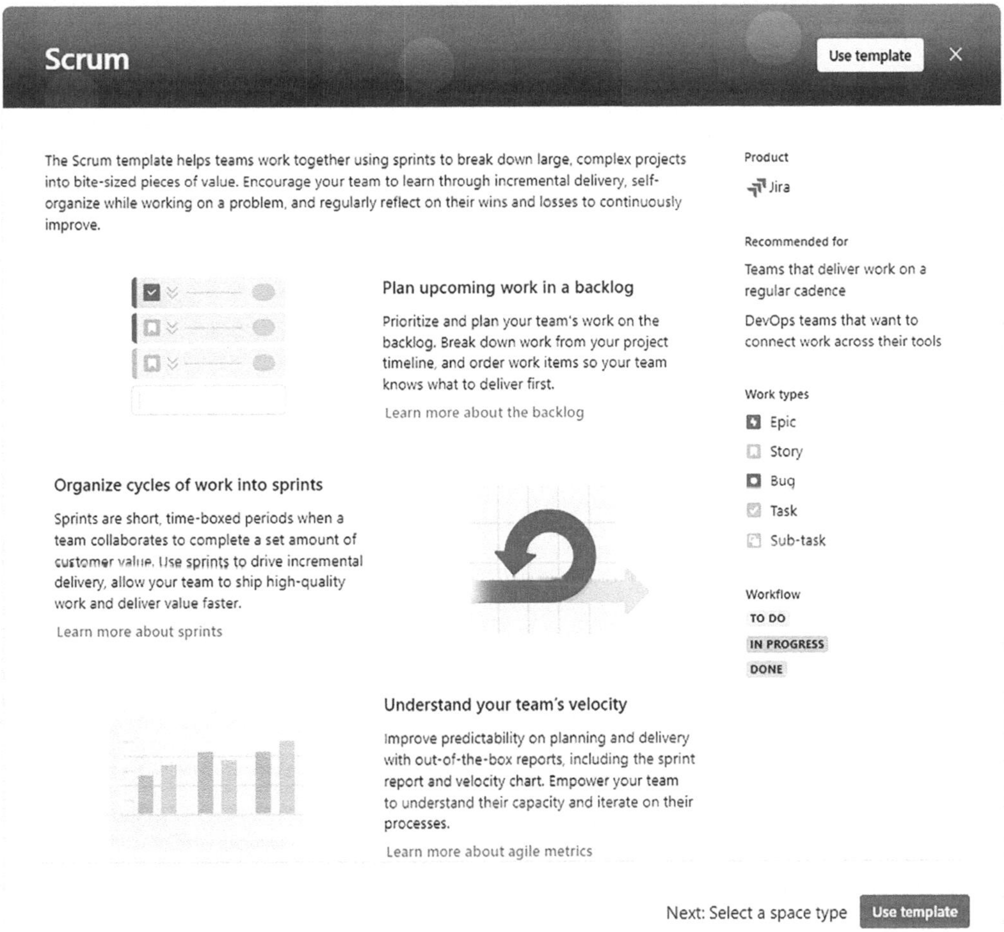

Figure 2.4: *How to Create Space in Jira Step-5*

6. Now select **`company-managed space`** or **`team-managed space`** as per your requirement.

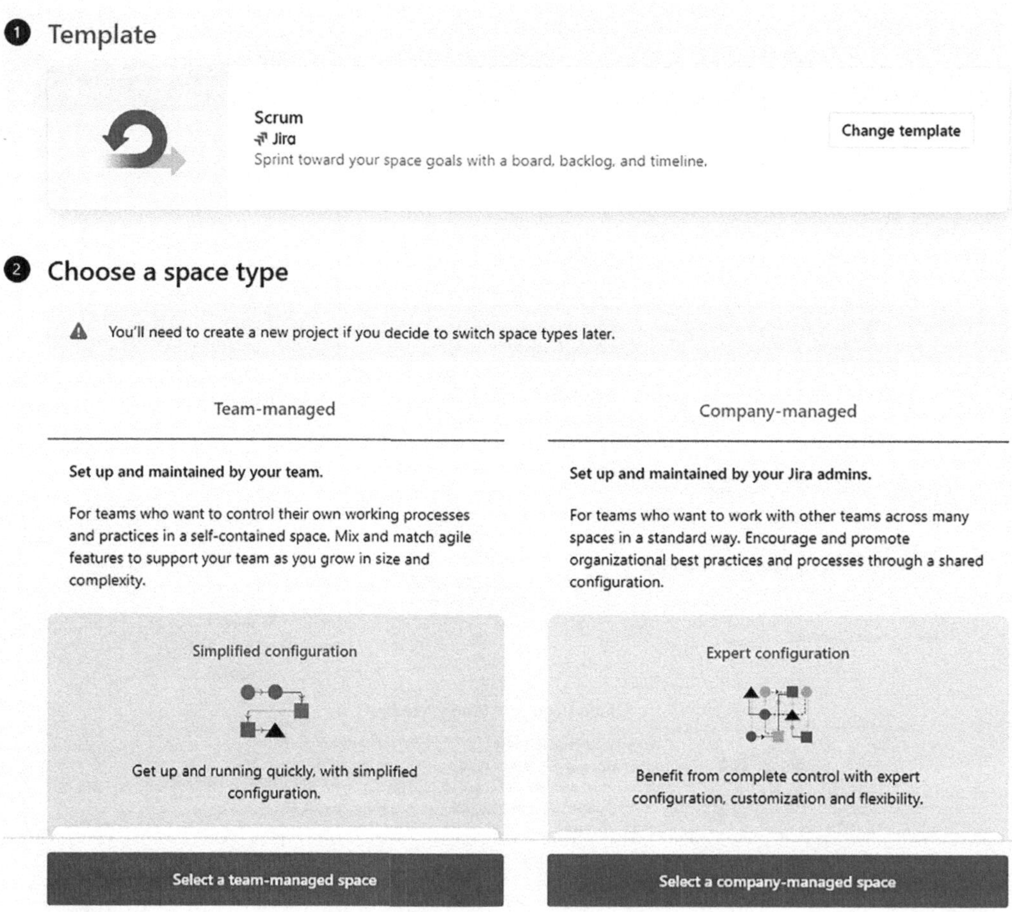

Figure 2.5: *How to Create Space in Jira Step-6*

7. Add the name of the space and it will generate the key of the space. You can also connect with other development tools at this stage.
8. Now click **`Create space.`**

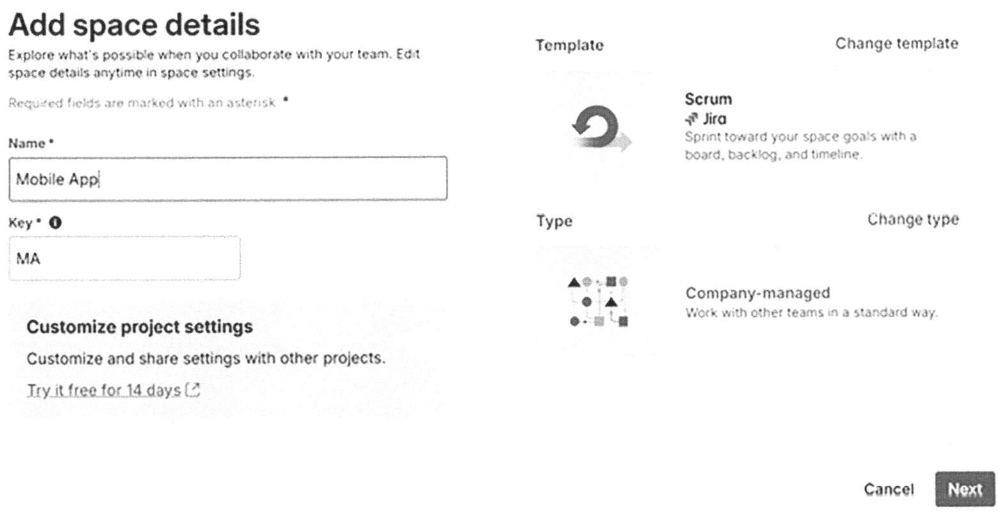

***Figure 2.6**: How to Create Space in Jira Step-7*

9. You have successfully created a new space in Jira.

Once the space is created, you can start to customize and work on the same.

Choosing the Right Space Type: Team-Managed versus Company-Managed Spaces

While selecting the space type, you must select either a team-managed space or company-managed space in Jira. The space type can be decided as per your business requirements and the current process you follow. We will guide you to select the right type of space in this section.

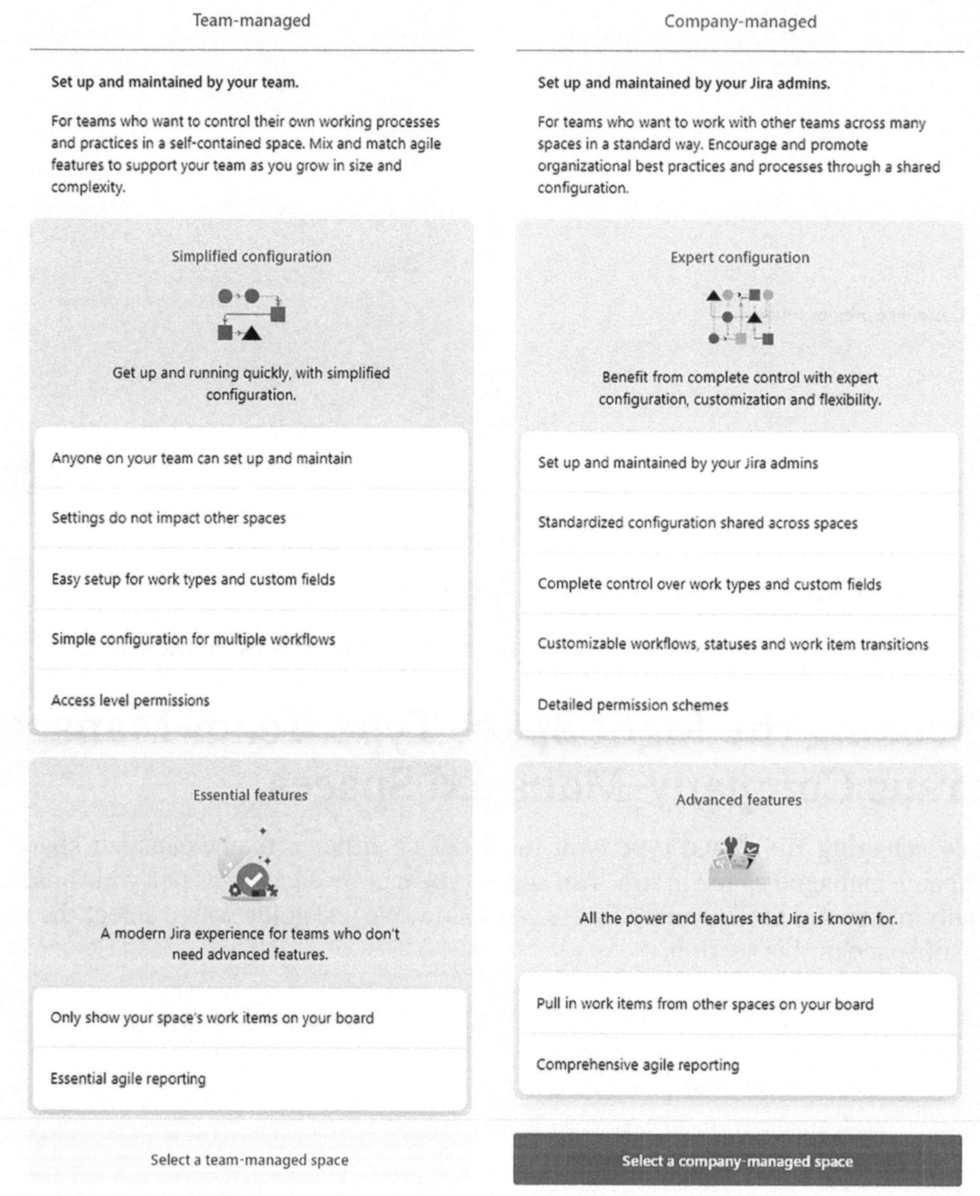

Figure 2.7: *Choosing the Right Space Template – Team- versus Company-Managed Space*

The Difference between Company-Managed and Team-Managed Spaces

There are some factors which differentiate the two types of spaces in Jira. It will help in choosing the right type of space template.

	Team-managed Space	**Company-managed Space**
Who can manage	Team members	Administrators
Set-up and Customization	Can set up easily and faster. Space administrator or anyone can do it without getting help from the Administrators	Its customization requires an experienced Administrator
Add/remove work types, priority, fields	Can be added and applicable to a specific space without affecting others	Can be added and applicable and used by all the spaces with the same configuration
Workflows and Screens	It can be set-up by anyone in the team and is applicable to that space only	It can be customized by Jira Administrators and applies to all the spaces with the same schemes
Permission schemes	Simplified (Access-level) permissions	Advanced permissions
Roadmaps	Basic Timeline and Plans/ Advanced Roadmap with few limitations and (Only available in Premium and Enterprise versions of Jira)	Basic Timeline and Plans/ Advanced Roadmap (Only available in Premium and Enterprise versions of Jira)
Space Boards	Cannot show the other space's work items on a single board	Can combine the tasks from multiple spaces on a single board

Table 2.1: *Company-Managed versus Team-Managed Space in Jira*

Factors to Consider while Choosing Team-Managed Spaces

As a Jira Administrator/Space administrator, you must consider the factors as listed below while selecting the team-managed spaces:

- The team is small and prefers not to customize everything.
- The team aims for a quick and straightforward setup to start promptly.
- Basic timeline features or Plans with some limitations are adequate for planning.
- You want to work at your own pace and in your own space without collaborating with other teams.
- The organization is too small.

If your team size and customization requirements are as mentioned in this section, then you should go for a Team-managed space.

Factors to Consider while Choosing Company-Managed Spaces

As a Jira Administrator/Space administrator, you must consider the factors as listed below while selecting the company-managed spaces:

- You have a dedicated Jira Administrator and want to customize across spaces.
- A large organization wants to streamline processes through complex configuration of workflows and screens.
- Jira Plans/Advanced roadmaps are necessary for planning.
- Detailed permissions are required.
- An advanced workflow editor is needed, providing access to conditions, validators, and post-functions.
- You want to customize different screens for creating, viewing, and editing work items based on the work type.
- Different work types require separate workflows.
- Customized schemes shared across spaces for:
  - Work type
  - Workflow
  - Screen
  - Fields
  - Permission
  - Notification
  - Work item security

If your team size and customization requirements are as mentioned in this section, then you should go for Company-managed space.

Exploring Different Space Template Types and Their Purpose

There are primarily three different categories of space templates available in Jira: Software Development, Service Management and Work Management. Additionally, there is a separate category called Product Management. Each of these categories offers various templates tailored to specific processes and products within Jira.

When selecting space templates, you can choose based on the Jira products you are using and the specific processes you wish to follow. It is important to note that different versions of Jira may have their own unique space templates. In this chapter, we have focused on space templates available in Jira Cloud.

For more comprehensive information and the latest details, it is recommended to refer to the Atlassian documentation.

There are different space templates to manage various processes, teams, and spaces. A detailed list of the templates with their purpose is mentioned in *Table 2.2*.

Product Name	**Space Template**	**Purpose of the Template**
Jira for Software Development	Kanban	Use this template to reduce bottleneck, planning flexibility, and recommended for teams that control work volume from backlog
	Scrum	Prioritize and plan your team's work on the backlog. Break down work from your space timeline, work in sprints, and order work items so your team knows what to deliver first
	Bug Tracking	Manage a list of development tasks and bugs
Jira Service Management	General Service Management for IT teams	This template offers IT teams a centralized platform to capture, assess, and handle requests effectively. It streamlines the process for employees to submit their requests, ensuring prompt responses and enabling them to find the information they need quickly. Additionally, it empowers employees to self-serve by providing access to relevant articles linked to the request forms
	General Service Management for Business teams	This template helps business teams with a central place to collect, prioritize, and manage requests. It simplifies the process for employees to submit their requests while enabling your team to respond to them using workflows that support their processes
	HR Service Management	This template helps HR teams manage service demands by consolidating requests from multiple channels (email, chat tools, request portal), providing full visibility of payroll, onboarding, change requests, and general HR inquiries
Work Management	Project Management	From simple to complex projects, this template provides a simple way of coordinating multiple deadlines, teams and stakeholders involved. Rally all involved parties within a single source of truth and see projects from start to execution

	Performance Review	Simplify and alleviate the stress of performance reviews for both employees and managers. Prepare your employees by providing clear expectations and involving them in ongoing conversations throughout the process. Emphasize outcomes and effectively measure job performance to ensure readiness for the next review cycle
	Sales Pipeline	This template is ideal for sales teams to manage their leads. Track opportunities throughout the sales cycle, forecast revenue, and nurture relationships from lead to customer, all in one convenient place
Jira Product Discovery	Product Management	The product discovery template provides your product team with a special place to understand customer problems and create effective solutions. It helps your team work together by collecting and prioritizing ideas, aligning everyone on product plans, and improving communication between business and tech teams, all within Jira

Table 2.2: *Important Space Templates and their Purpose*

In addition to the above-mentioned templates, there are other templates in Jira cloud such as Top-level planning, Cross-team planning, process control, web design, Content management, personal task planner, budget creation, procurement, and so on.

Configuring Spaces

Once you have created the space, you can configure it as per the requirements of your team. You can use it to track the tasks, for managing bugs, or as a helpdesk for the HR department.

Examples of Successful Space Template Implementation and Configuration

We will learn about two important space template implementations in Jira as follows:

- Scrum template in software development, and
- IT Service Management space template in Jira service Management.

Agile Scrum Software Development Template

In this section, we will learn all the customization features for an agile scrum software development template. We will cover topics such as workflows, add people, screens, fields, Agile scrum boards, and metrics.

Important Permissions

In order to create the space and perform all the configurations, you should login as a Jira Administrator and have Administer Jira Global permission.

Managing Spaces

Select ⚙>**spaces**. You can create spaces, add space categories, and move the space to trash from this as shown in *Figure 2.8*.

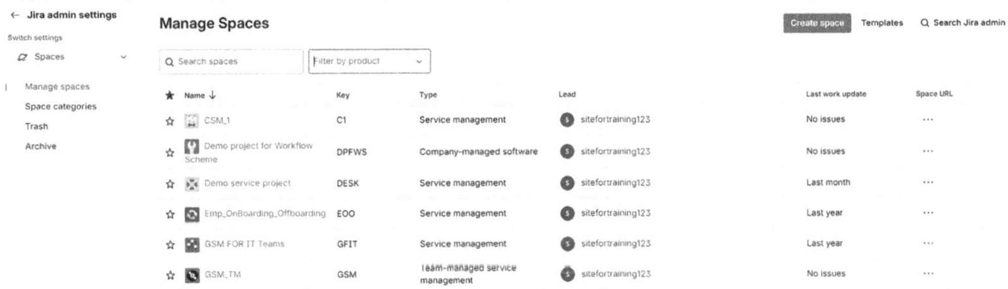

***Figure 2.8**: Manage Spaces from Administration*

Select a space and navigate to **space settings**. We will understand various configurations in Jira to customize everything in a **Company-managed** space.

People

Add people to your spaces as users and assign the roles for a space as shown in *Figure 2.9*. For example, people who are assigned the role of **Scrum Masters** will have all the permissions given to the Scrum Master role. These roles are defined in the general system administration, which are applicable to all the spaces in Jira.

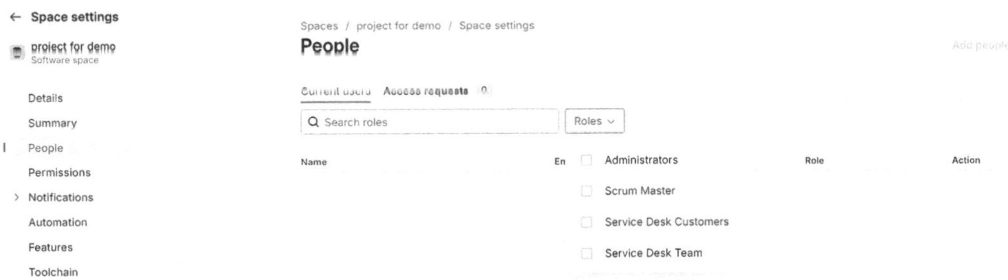

***Figure 2.9**: Adding People in a Space*

Permissions

Space permissions define who can access a space and what they can do (create and comment on work items, for example).

- Space permissions are defined based on users/groups/role. These are customized permissions, and it is called a **`permission scheme`**.
- The other type of permissions is set from system administration, which are known as **`Global permissions`**.
- The permissions can be edited and/or a different scheme can be assigned to a space.

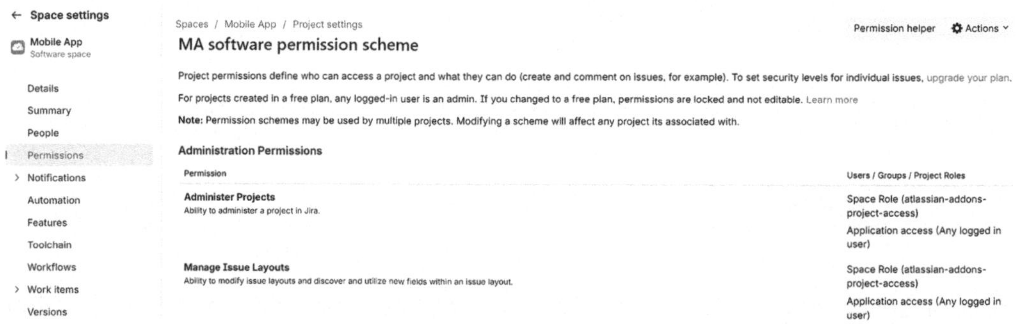

Figure 2.10: *Space-Based Permissions*

Notifications

Jira has the capability to inform the relevant individuals about specific events that occur within your space, such as when a work item is commented on. You have the flexibility to choose the specific people, groups or roles who should receive these notifications. The way these notifications are set up for your space is determined by the notification scheme. If you wish to alter the notifications, you can either select a different notification scheme or make modifications to the currently selected scheme.

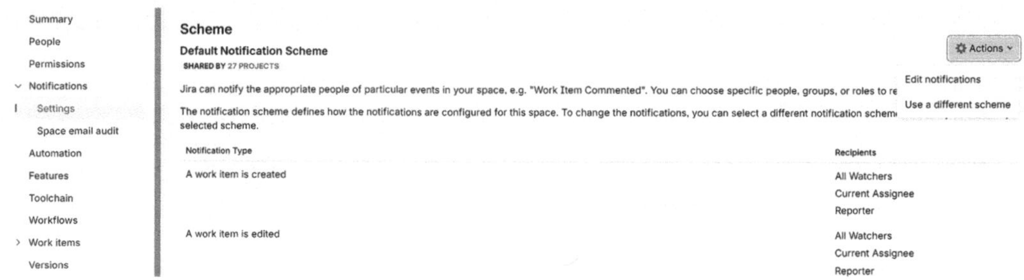

Figure 2.11: *Notification Scheme*

Automation

Space Administrators can create Automation rules, which can be applied to a specific space only. For example: **`When all stories are completed-> then close epic`**. We will explore more about automation rules in *Chapter 9: Jira Automation Rules*.

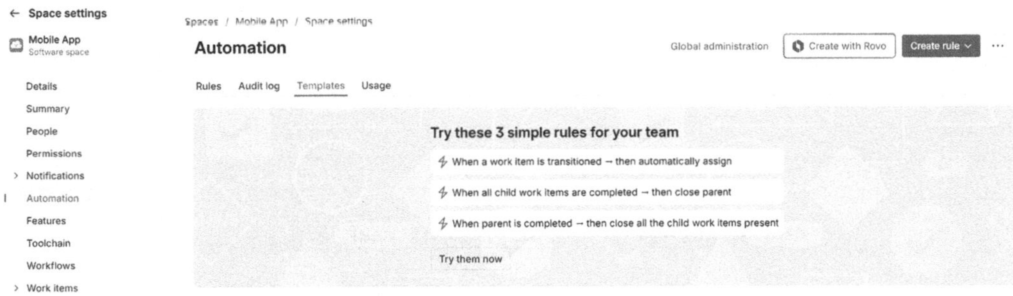

***Figure 2.12:** Create Space Specific Automation Rules*

Features

In the features section, various features can be enabled or disabled. For instance, Summary, Calendar, List, tool integration, product backlog, reports and components are some examples. Jira offers a set of default features that are already enabled based on the type of space team or company management.

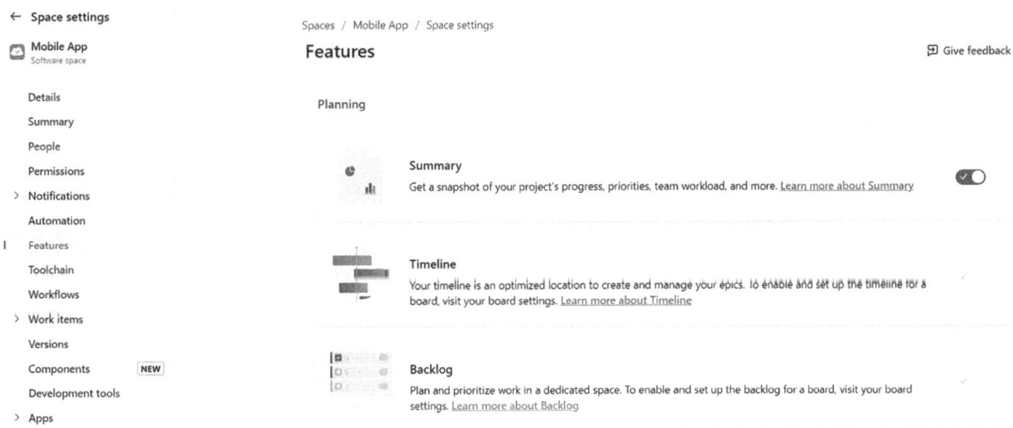

***Figure 2.13:** Enabling Features in Scrum Space*

Workflows

In the workflows section, Jira administrators have the ability to perform several actions. They can add an existing workflow and associate it with a specific work type or switch workflow schemes. *Chapter 7: Configuring Workflows in Jira for Agile spaces* will provide further insights and details on this topic.

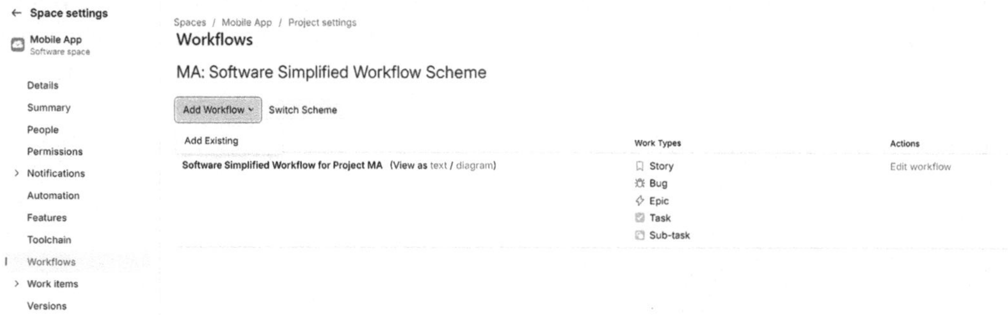

Figure 2.14: *Associating Workflow with Space*

Screens

There are three types of screens in Jira: **`Create`**, **`Edit`**, and **`View`**. All three types of screens can be customized using fields. These screens can be customized on a per-work item basis. **`Screen schemes`** are combinations of screens designed for various work types. Finally, screen schemes can be assigned to a space.

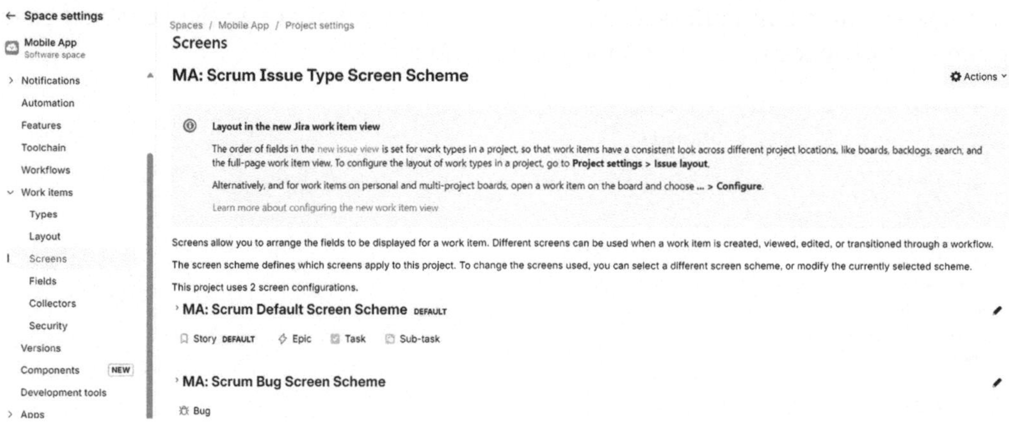

Figure 2.15: *Screens and Screen-Schemes in Jira*

Fields

Jira provides two types of fields: system (standard) fields, which are predefined and should not be modified, and user defined fields, which can be added by users. User defined fields can include options such as text fields, multi-select fields, and many more. By adding these fields to screens, users can create screens that meet their specific process requirements.

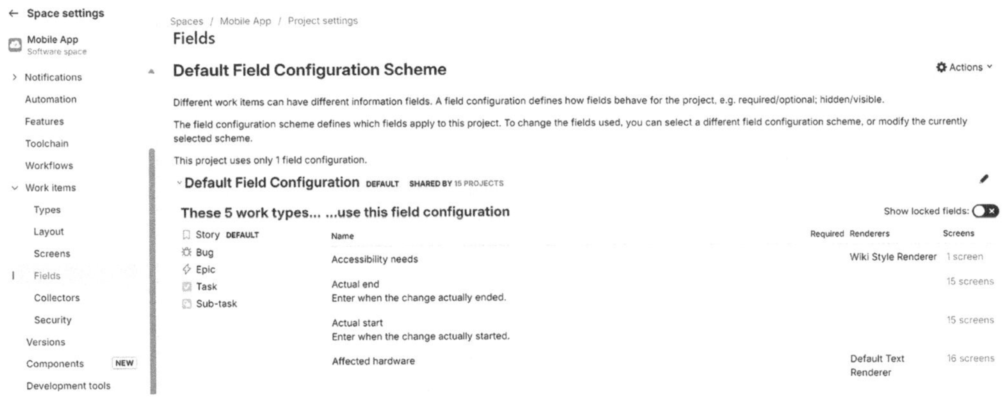

Figure 2.16: *Field Configuration*

Components

`Components` are subsections of a space. They are used to group work items within a space into smaller sets. For example, items of group work that describe work on specific data objects, services, plug-ins, or APIs within their space.

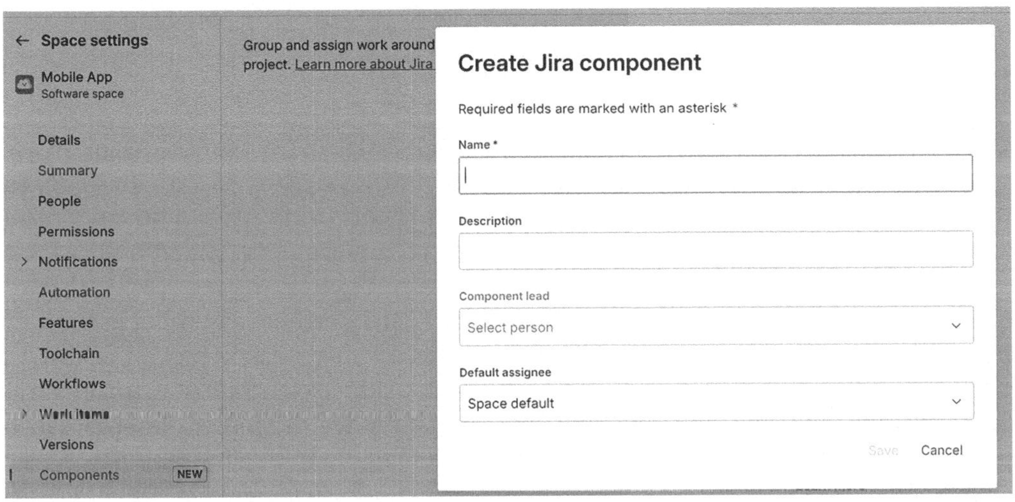

Figure 2.17: *Creating Components*

Development Tools

In a Scrum space template, Jira is connected with different development tools to make collaboration and work more efficient. Some common tools that are used with Jira are as follows:

- **Version Control Systems (VCS)** like Git or SVN, which help track code changes and connect with Jira.

- **Continuous Integration (CI)** tools such as Jenkins or Bamboo, which automate the building and testing of code triggered by Jira events.
- Code review tools like **`Crucible`** or **`Bitbucket`**, which allow team members to review each other's code and work together with Jira.
- Agile space management tools like **`Confluence`**, which are linked with Jira to create space documentation and make it easy to share knowledge.

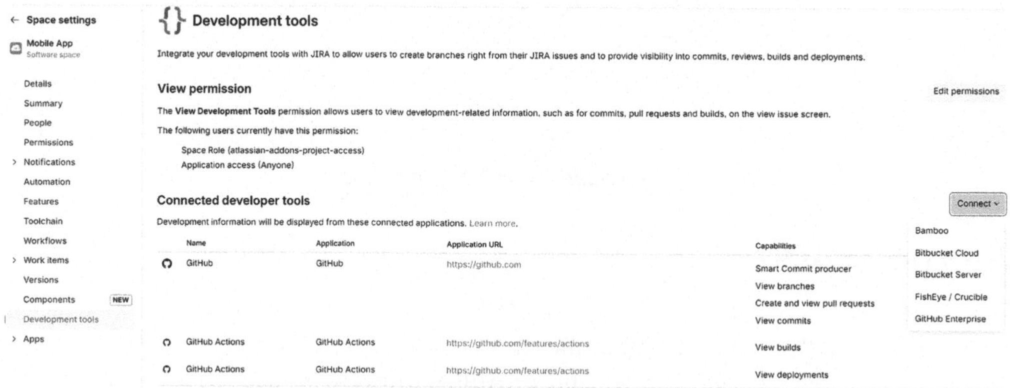

Figure 2.18: *Development Tools*

Scrum Boards

Scrum boards in Jira provide a simple way to track tasks and progress. Scrum boards consist of columns representing different stages of work, such as **`To Do, In Progress`** and **`Done.`** Jira provides three statuses by default. The workflows can be customized as per the process followed by the team and the columns can be added on the board as per the workflow. Scrum boards show the tasks, bugs, and user stories that the team has committed to complete during a sprint. The board usually reflects the work planned for a single sprint. The tasks on the board can be easily moved across the columns as it progresses. It makes it easier to plan, prioritize and track work, ensuring that everyone is on the same page and the space stays organized. Boards can be customized by categorizing the work items for viewing them in a better way.

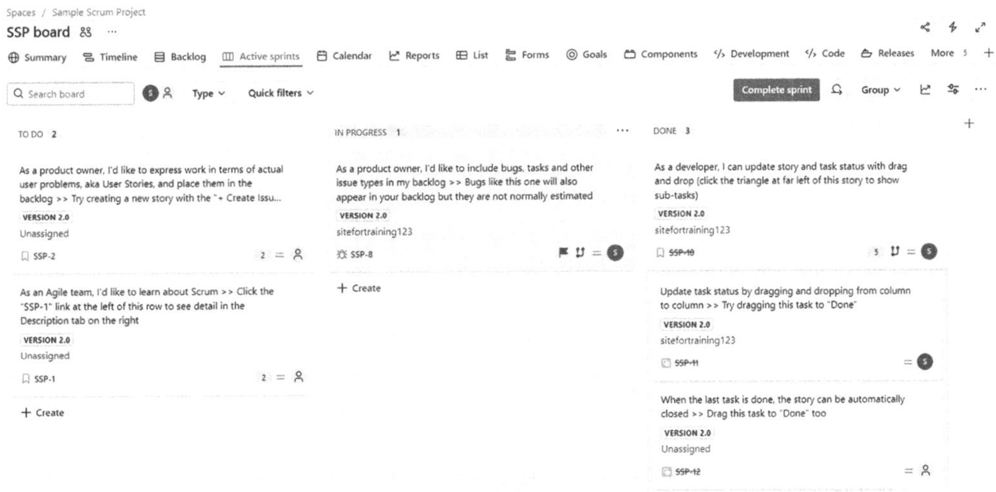

Figure 2.19: *Customizing Scrum Board*

Agile Metrics

The Scrum space template in Jira provides a way to measure Agile metrics, which help teams understand their progress and performance. Some of the key metrics that can be measured using Jira are as follows:

- **Velocity:** Jira calculates the velocity metric automatically based on the amount of work completed in each sprint. It shows how much work the team can accomplish on average, allowing them to plan future sprints more effectively.
- **Burndown Chart:** Jira generates a burndown chart that visually represents the progress of work throughout the sprint. It helps the team track if they are on track to complete all the planned work by the end of the sprint.
- **Lead Time:** Jira captures the time it takes for a user story or a task to move from the backlog to completion. This metric helps identify bottlenecks and optimize the flow of work within the team.
- **Cycle Time:** Jira also tracks the time it takes for an item to move through the different stages of the workflow. By analyzing cycle time, teams can identify areas where improvements can be made to increase efficiency.

By using the Scrum space template in Jira, teams can easily access these Agile metrics, enabling them to evaluate their performance, make data-driven decisions, and continuously improve their processes.

IT Service Management (ITSM) Space Template

Implementing an **IT Service Management (ITSM)** space template in Jira helps organizations to efficiently manage their IT services and support operations. By following the steps below, you can successfully implement an ITSM space template in Jira.

Creating an ITSM Space

Create a new space by selecting the `ITSM` space template in Jira. Provide a space name and key to uniquely identify the space within the Jira instance. Assign a space lead who will manage the implementation of space.

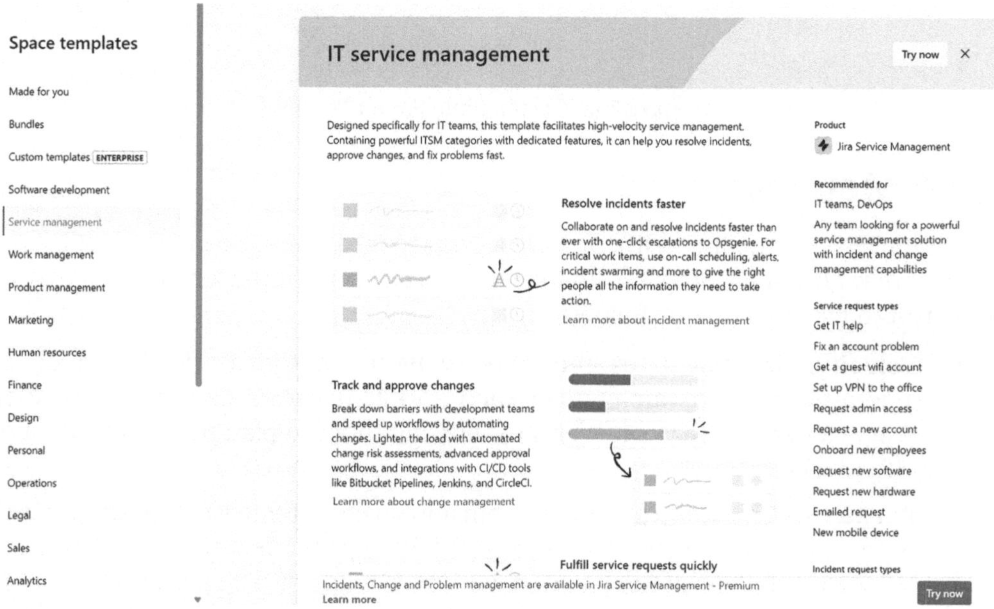

Figure 2.20: *IT Service Management Space Template*

Configuring Space Settings

Decide the space settings according to the requirements of the organizations. Customize the space description, lead, and permissions to ensure proper access control. Set up the notification scheme, ensuring that the relevant stakeholders receive timely updates and notifications.

Defining Request Types and Forms

Service requests are specific tasks or actions that users or customers request from a service desk or IT department. These requests can vary widely depending on the organization's services, such as software installation, access requests, hardware repairs, password resets or general inquiries.

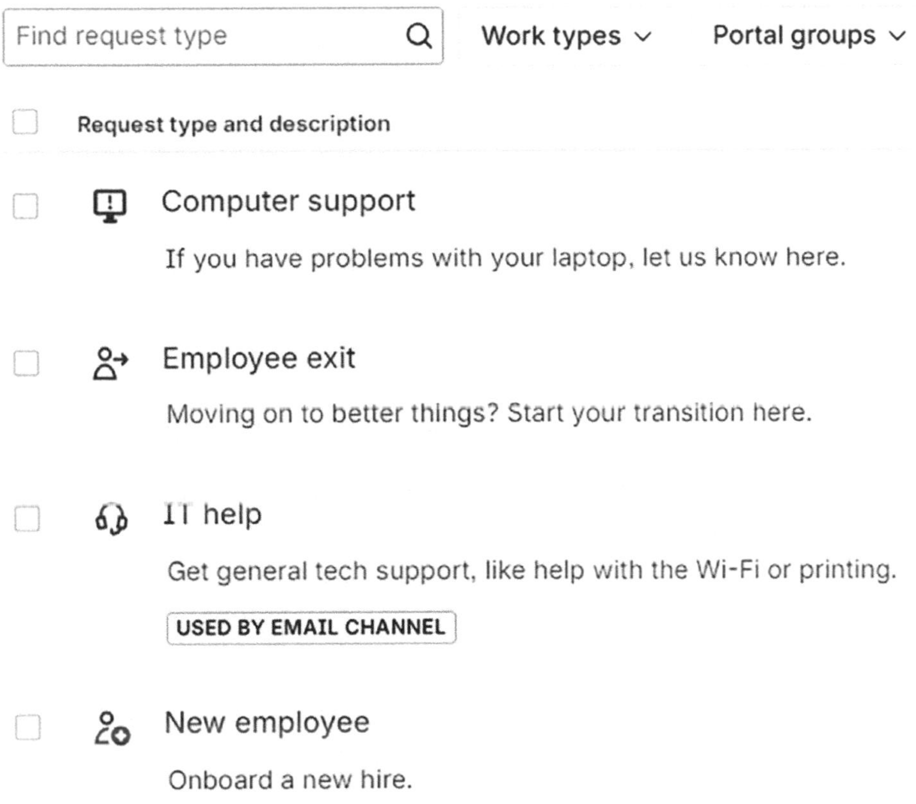

Figure 2.21: *Request Types in Jira Service Management*

`Request types` are predefined categories or templates that represent different types of service requests. They help categorize and streamline the process of handling different types of customer inquiries or tasks. For example, you might have request types like password reset, software installation, or hardware work item.

- Customize the request types to align with the organization's ITSM processes.
- Define the various types of IT service requests, such as incidents, service requests, or changes.
- Modify the request forms to capture essential information from users, such as category, impact, urgency, and detailed descriptions.

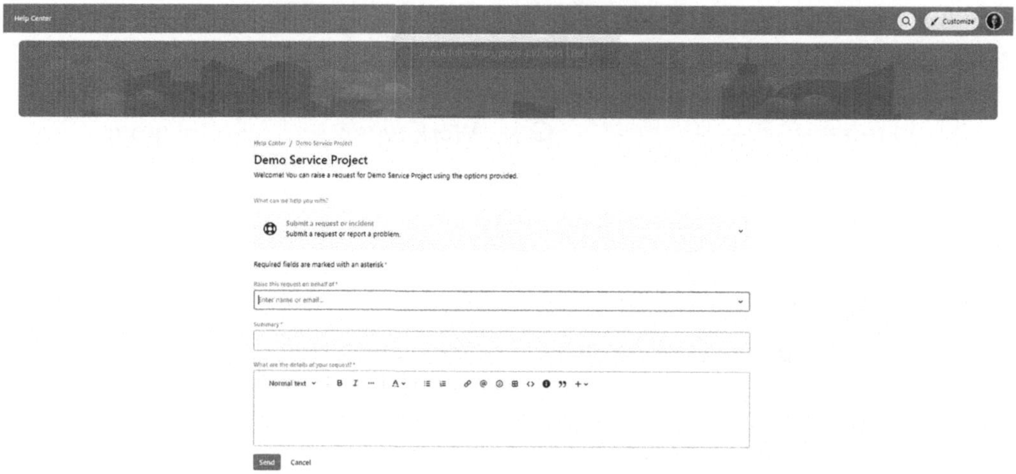

Figure 2.22: *Service Space Portal*

Establishing Service Level Agreements (SLAs)

SLA is an agreement or commitment between a service provider and a customer that defines the expected level of service regarding response and resolution times for service requests. SLAs help set performance expectations, prioritize work, and ensure timely delivery of services. Jira Service Management allows you to define SLAs based on different parameters like request type, priority, or customer segment.

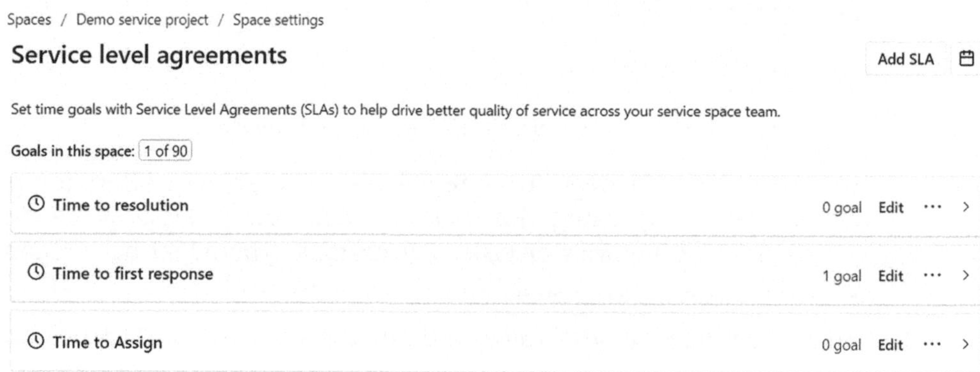

Figure 2.23: *Service Level Agreements in ITSM Space*

- Establish SLAs to ensure timely response and resolution of IT service requests.
- Define SLA metrics, including response time and resolution time, based on organizational goals and customer expectations.
- Associate the SLAs with the corresponding request types to enable automatic monitoring and tracking.

Creating Custom Queues and Workflows

Queues in Jira Service Management are lists or collections of service requests that share a common characteristic or need attention. They help service agents or teams organize and prioritize their work by grouping requests based on different criteria, such as request type, SLA breach, assignee, or priority. Agents can easily view and manage the requests in their assigned queues to ensure timely response and resolution.

- Create the queues and workflows to match the ITSM processes and stages of the organization.
- Configure the stages and statuses that represent the lifecycle of IT service requests.
- Customize the workflow transitions, conditions, and validators to streamline the request handling process.

Assigning and Managing Tickets

Agents in Jira Service Management are the individuals or teams responsible for handling and resolving service requests from customers or users. They play a crucial role in delivering great customer service and ensuring efficient service delivery. Agents are assigned to specific queues or groups based on their expertise and workload. They review incoming requests, categorize them accurately, and prioritize them based on urgency. Agents work closely with customers/users, gathering necessary information, troubleshooting work items, and providing regular updates on request progress. They utilize Jira Service Management's tools to track, assign, and manage requests, ensuring that service level agreements are met and customers are satisfied. Agents in Jira Service Management are the front-line representatives who work diligently to provide high-quality support.

- Assign incoming IT service requests to the appropriate team members or support agents.
- Leverage the built-in features of Jira to track the progress of each ticket.
- Utilize internal collaboration tools within Jira to facilitate communication and collaboration among team members for efficient work item resolution.

Integrating Jira Service Management with Confluence

Connecting Jira Service Management with Confluence makes life easier for both agents and users. Teams can use Confluence to create and update articles, HR policies or other helpful documents and those resources are directly available in Jira Service Management.

With the help of a smart search tool called **Smart Graph**, Jira service management automatically suggests the right articles or request types when users look for answers. This means customers can often solve their own problems quickly, which keeps them happy and reduces the number of requests agents need to handle.

For agents, it shows recommended articles right on the request page, so that they can respond faster. And since teams can keep adding and organizing content in Confluence, the knowledge base grows stronger over time. It helps all teams to make support smoother and more efficient.

Monitoring and Report Generation

Jira Service Management Cloud offers default reports and custom reports. Default reports can be utilized to measure essential functions within service spaces. While these reports cannot be modified, they offer valuable insights into assessing the compliance of your team with SLAs. It also offers custom reports such as Time to resolution, SLA success rate, created versus resolved, and the like.

- Utilize the reporting and monitoring capabilities of Jira to gain valuable insights into IT service performance.
- Generate reports and metrics on request volume, response times, SLA compliance, and overall performance.
- Set up personalized dashboards to monitor key performance indicators and identify areas for improvement.

By following these steps, organizations can successfully implement an ITSM space template in Jira, enabling them to streamline their IT service management processes, deliver prompt customer support, and achieve higher efficiency and customer satisfaction levels.

Important Use Cases

In this section we will learn about different use cases of Jira spaces in which we will include how to create a space with sample data, how to change the space, how to move work items from team manage to company manage spaces, how to migrate work items from team manage to company managed and vice versa.

1. **Create Spaces in Jira with Sample Data**: Jira allows you to create a Scrum and Kanban space with some sample data. It is helpful to evaluate and understand features in Jira.

   This feature is extremely helpful for those who are new to Jira and want to explore the features and functionality. We will learn the step-by- step process to create spaces.

i. Login to Jira as Jira Administrator.

ii. Tap the search bar in the top navigation menu. Select **`Boards`** section. Select **`Create board from the Boards`** page.

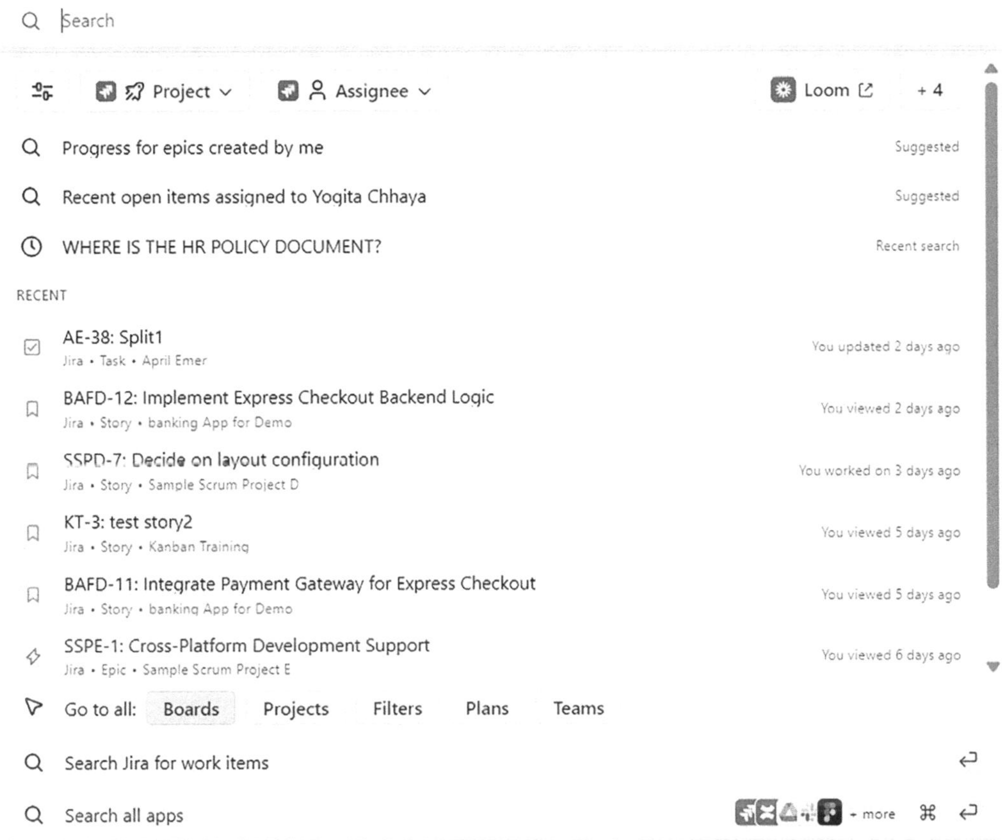

Figure 2.24: *Selecting Boards from the Search Bar*

iii. Jira provides you two options to create a **`Scrum`** or **`Kanban board with sample data`**. Select to create a board with sample data. Enter all the required details and it will create a space with a board.

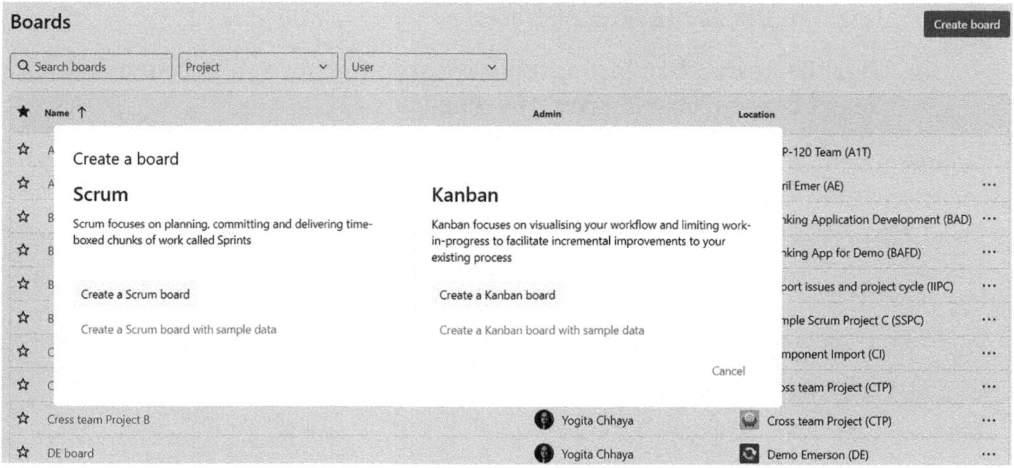

Figure 2.25: *Creating a Board with Sample Data*

iv. The Scrum board looks like this in *Figure* 2.26. Similarly, you can create a Kanban board.

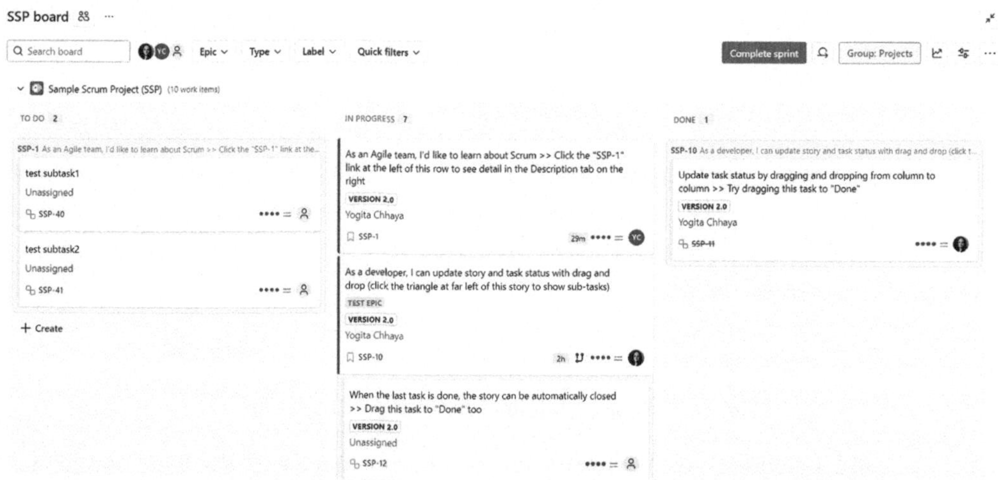

Figure 2.26: *Scrum Board*

Important link for reference:

https://community.atlassian.com/t5/Jira-Software-questions/Sample-spaces-to-practice-and-develop-skills/qaq-p/1747661

2. **Change Space-type in Jira or Migrate between Spaces (Team-managed to Company-managed and Vice-versa)** : A team currently works in one type of Jira space or a specific template like the company-managed Scrum space of Jira and you want to migrate to a different space type or template like the team-managed Kanban space or Scrum space of Jira.

You can follow these steps to Bulk-change work items.

(Only Users with Global permission `Make Bulk Changes` can do this)

i. Go to **`spaces>Create space`**

ii. Create a new space in which you want to migrate all the work items from the old space

iii. Select the **`team-managed`** or **`company-managed`** space and create a new space after confirming the type of space. Enter all the required details such as **`space-name`**, **`space-key`**, and so on.

iv. You have created a new space to migrate all the work items.

v. Select the filter for a space which you want to migrate to another space

vi. In the top-right corner, select **`More>Bulk change all`**.

vii. Navigate to **`spaces >Create space`**.

viii. Generate a new space where you intend to transfer all work items from the previous space.

ix. Select either a **`team-managed`** or **`company-managed space`**. After confirming the space type, proceed to create a new space. Provide all necessary details, including **`space Name`** and **`space Key`**.

You have successfully established a new space for work item migration.

x. Choose the appropriate filter for the space that you wish to migrate to another location.

xi. In the upper-right corner, click on **`More>Bulk change work items.`**

***Figure 2.27**: Selecting Bulk-Change All Work Items*

xii. Choose **`Bulkchange all work items`**. Select all work items and hit **`Next`**.

xiii. Select **`Move work items to new spaces`**.

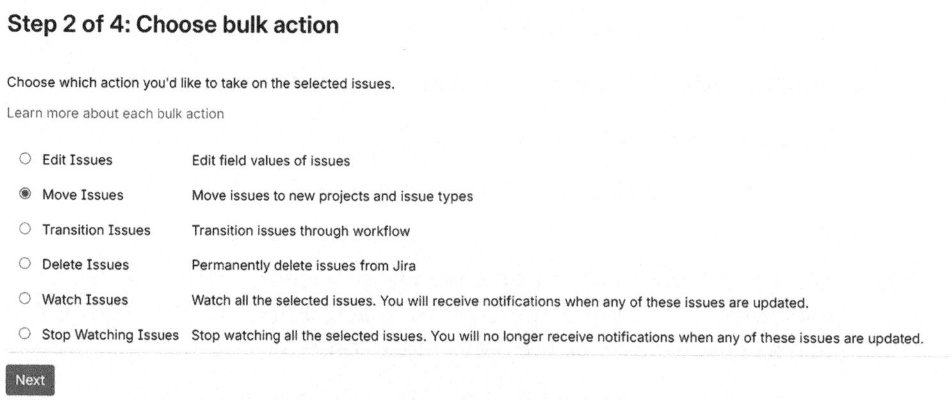

Figure 2.28: *Selecting Move Work Items*

xiv. Select the right space to move to and map all work types.

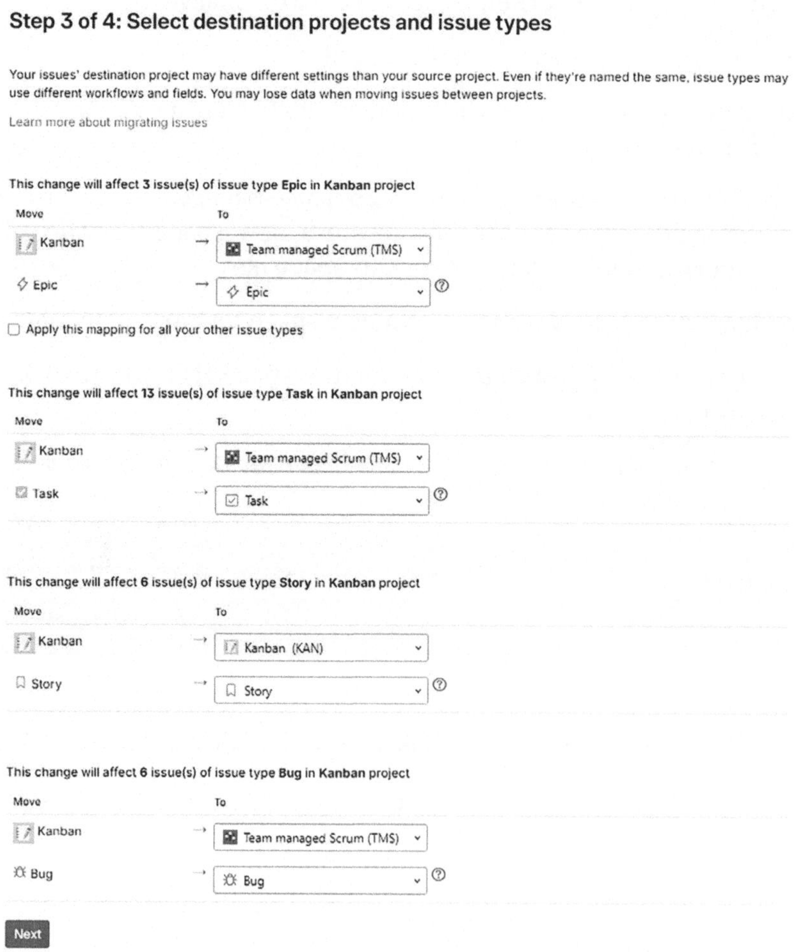

Figure 2.29: *Selecting Spaces and Mapping of Work Items*

xv. Select **Next** in the final step.

xvi. On the final screen, click **Confirm.**

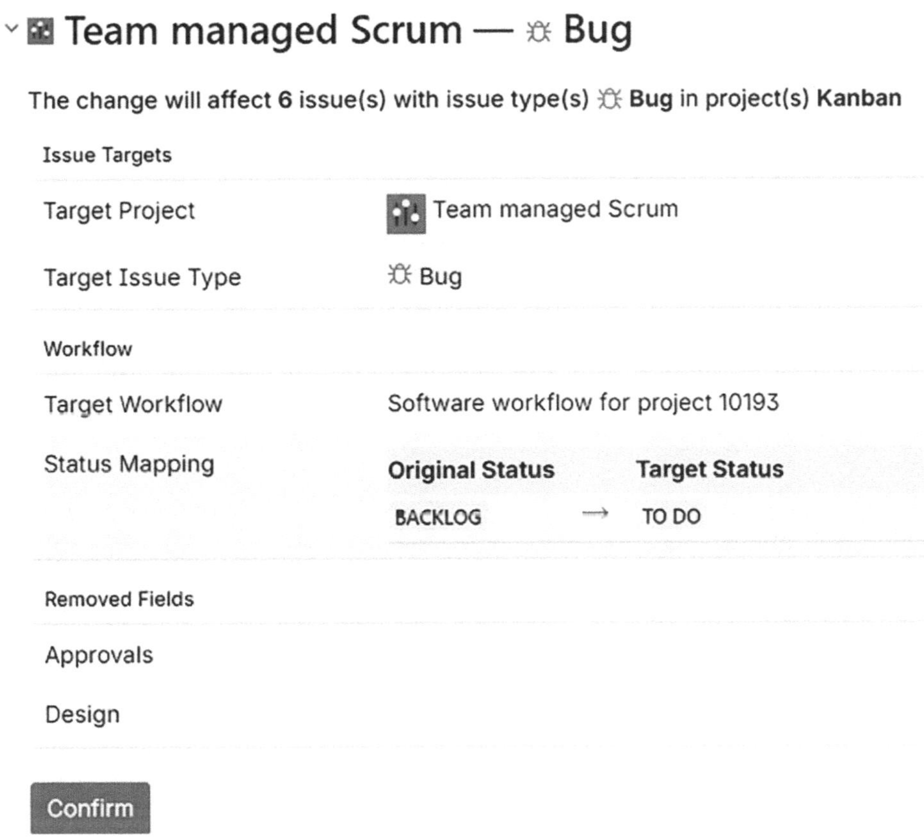

Figure 2.30*: Confirming Move/Migrate Work Items*

xvii. All the work items will be migrated to the new space. However, you need to check for mapping statuses and workflow schemes in both the spaces.

Conclusion

We started by understanding what spaces are and how to standardize them as per the requirements using templates. We learned how to decide whether to use a team-managed space or a company-managed space. We learned how to activate and deactivate features in spaces. We also learned how to create a space with sample data and how to move work items between team-managed and company-managed spaces.

We are now familiar with how to create a space and select the right type of space template as per the size of the team/organization and the business process. We also understood important space template implementation and how to configure Jira for the same.

In the next chapter, we will learn about how to add users, creating groups, space roles, and permissions.

Reference Links

1. https://support.atlassian.com/jira-software-cloud/docs/migrate-between-team-managed-and-company-managed-spaces/
2. https://support.atlassian.com/migration/docs/perform-a-cloud-to-cloud-migration-for-jira/

Chapter 3
Creating Users, Groups, Roles, and Understanding Permissions

Introduction

When working with Jira, creating users, groups, space roles, and permission schemes is essential for efficient project management and collaboration. Users can be added and assigned specific roles, granting them appropriate access and responsibilities within the system. Groups allow for easy management and assignment of permissions to multiple users simultaneously. Space roles help define different levels of involvement and responsibilities for team members. Lastly, permission schemes determine what actions and operations each user or group can perform within Jira. Together, these elements form the foundation for organizing and controlling access to project resources, ensuring smooth teamwork and effective project execution.

Structure

In this chapter, we will cover the following topics:

- Creating Users
    - Invitation Statuses in Jira

- Creating Groups
- Creating Space Roles
    - Example of Creating a Space Role
- Groups versus Space Roles
- Understanding Service Accounts, Managed Accounts, and Domains
- Understanding Permissions and Access Control
    - Global Permissions and Its Examples
    - Space Permissions and Its Examples
    - Jira Admin Helper to Troubleshoot Permissions
    - Work Item Security Permissions
- Understanding Permission Scheme
    - Associating a Permission Scheme with Space

Creating Users

Whenever a person joins the organization, it is required to add/invite users to the Jira. To do this, log in to your Jira instance as an administrator. You need administrative privileges to create new users.

1. Log into your Jira instance with administrative privileges.
2. Navigate to the **`User management`** section by selecting the gear icon and clicking on **`User Management`**. This will redirect you to the **`admin.atlassian.com`** page, where new users can be added.

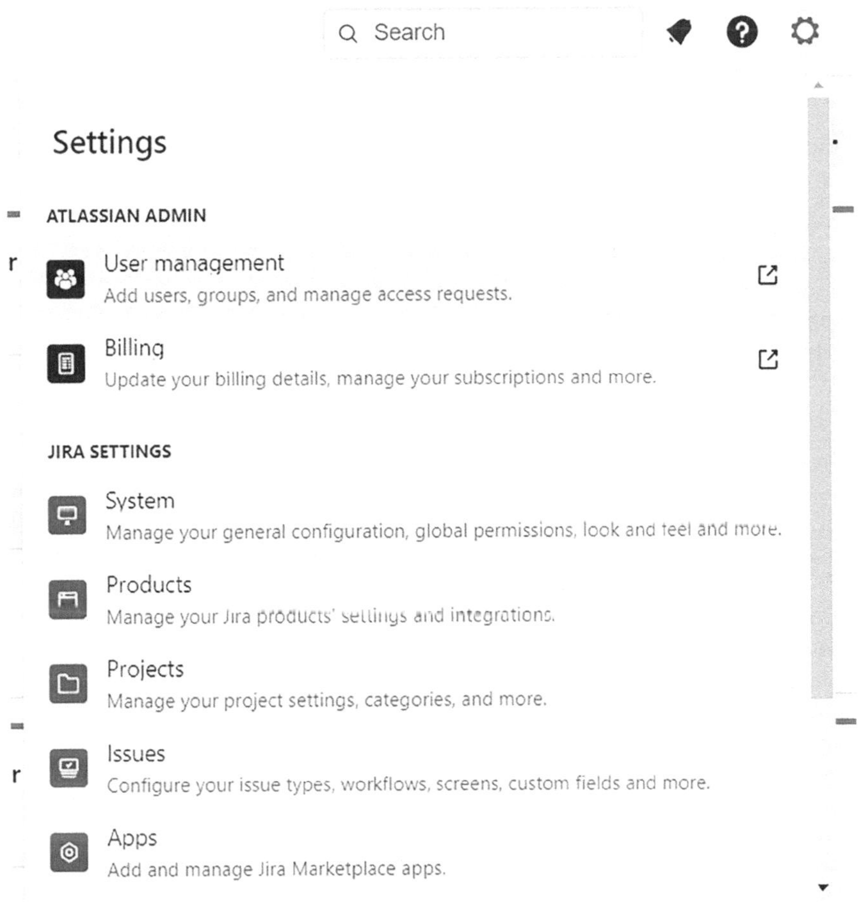

Figure 3.1: *Selecting User Management*

3. From the top right corner, click on **`Invite users.`** Start by adding the email addresses of the users.

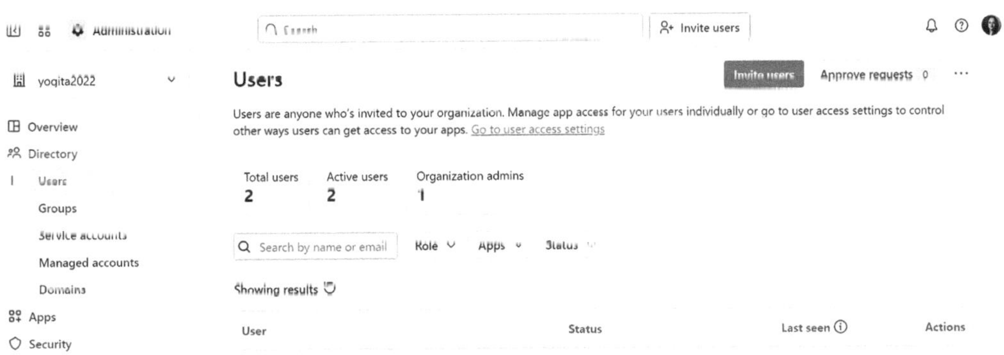

Figure 3.2: *Page to Invite Users*

4. For Jira Cloud, enter the email address of the user to add them as a new user.
5. If you need to add multiple users, simply enter their email addresses separated by commas.
6. Once the email address is entered, you can choose the role of the user from the dropdown menu.

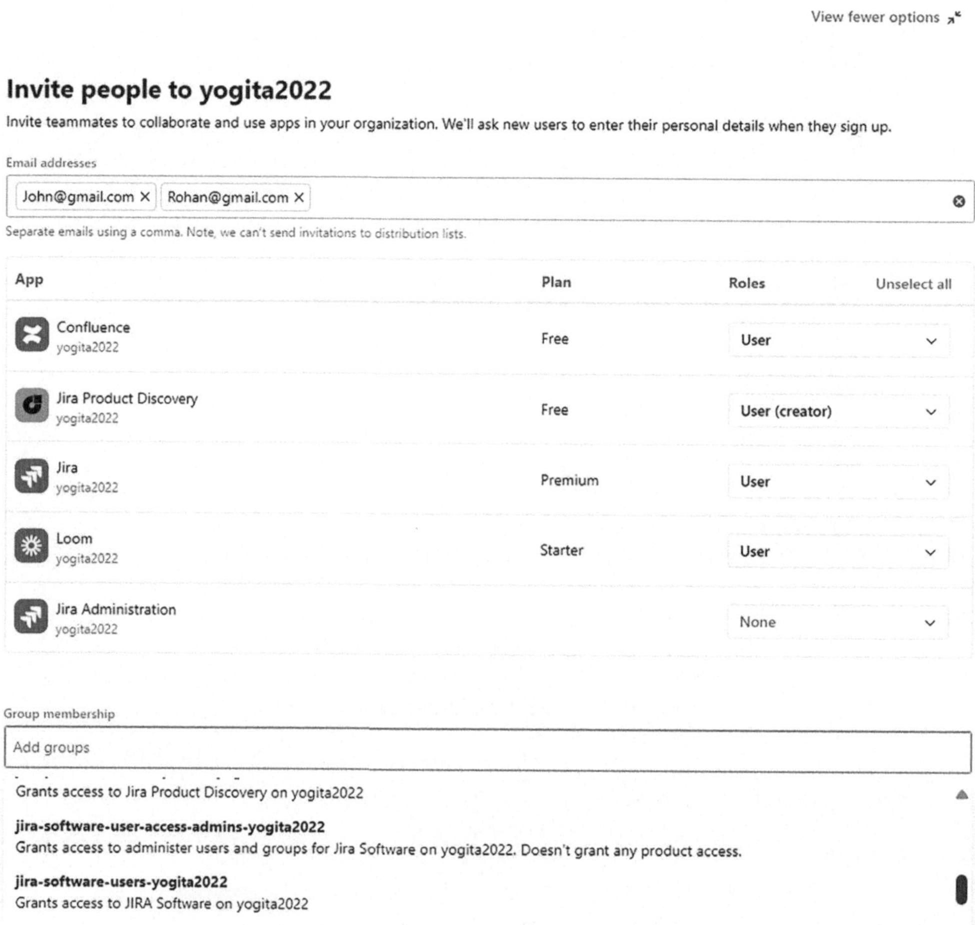

Figure 3.3: *Inviting Users and Adding to Groups*

7. After entering the email address, you can proceed to select the **app access** and **role** for that specific user. The role of the user determines what permissions they have in Jira.
8. Below the **app access** list, you will find the option to assign groups to the user. Choose the relevant group for each user.

9. The groups that the user is a member of determines which permissions they have in addition to their role permissions.
10. If you wish to send a personalized message to the user, you can do so. If not, deselect the personalized message option.

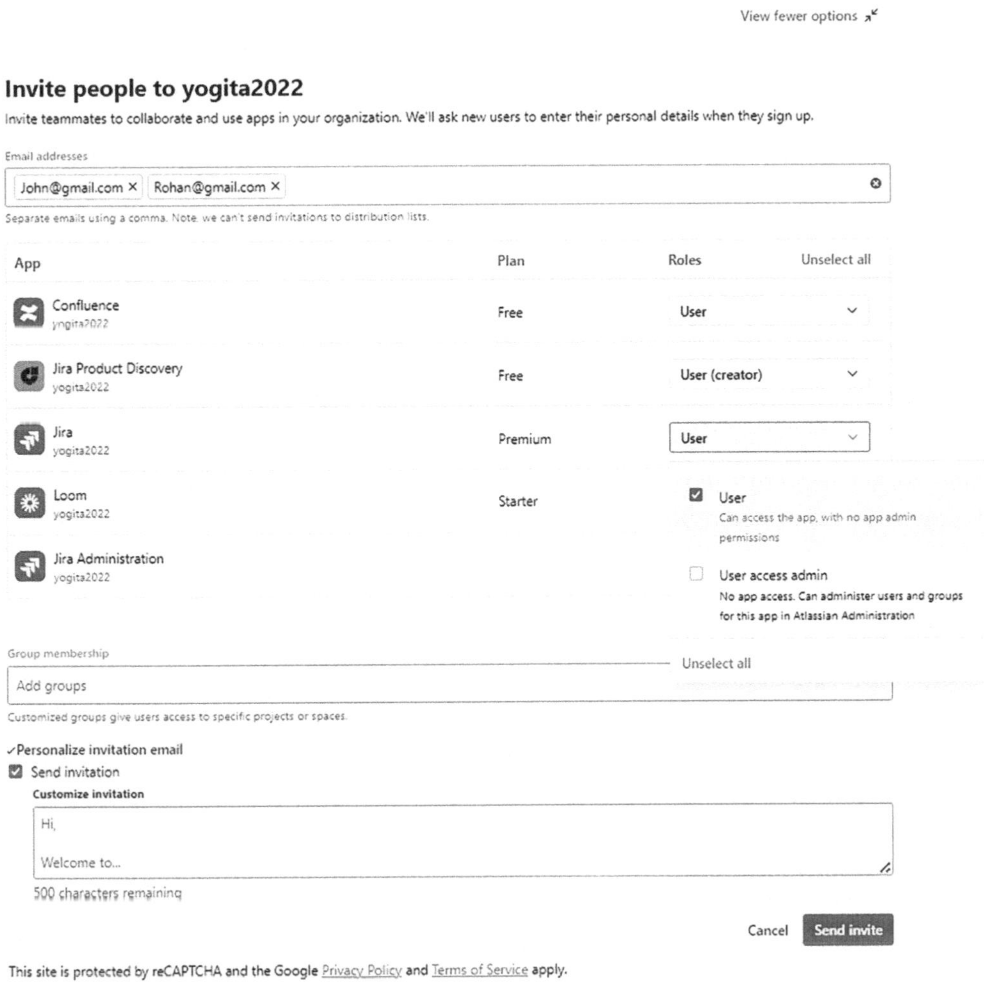

Figure 3.4: *Inviting Users, Adding App Role, and Sending Personal Invitation*

11. Below the personalized message section, click **`Invite users`**. This completes the user invitation process successfully.

Invite Statuses in Jira

We have listed the following examples of the different invite statuses you will see in your User Management screen:

- `Invited` **(Invitation Not Sent)**: This status indicates that the user has been created by the administrator, but no Email has been sent to invite them.
- `Invited`: This status indicates that the user has been created and an Email invitation has been sent to them. Their status will change to active if they access one of the apps.
- `Active`: The user is actively using at least one of the apps they have access to within your organization.
- `Suspended`: This app access of the user has been temporarily revoked within your organization. However, their access can be reactivated at any time. It is possible that they still have access to other apps in different organizations.
- `Deactivated`: This user has been deactivated by the organization administrator and they cannot log in to any Atlassian apps.

From the list page of the user, click a user name to view its details. From this page, administrators can perform the following operations as listed and as shown in *Figure* 3.5:

- **Assign organization role**: This allows the administrator to assign an organization role to the user. Organization roles define the permissions of the user across all apps in the organization.
    - **Can prompt to reset passwords**: This allows the administrator to prompt the user to reset their password. This can be useful if the user has forgotten their password or if the administrator suspects that their password has been compromised.
    - **Suspend access**: This allows the administrator to temporarily revoke the access of the user to all apps in the organization. This can be useful if the user is violating the policies of the organization or if they are suspected of malicious activity.
    - **Remove user**: This allows the administrator to permanently delete the user from the organization. This should only be done as a last resort, as it will delete all of the data of the user in the organization.
    - **Grant access to an app**: This allows the administrator to grant the user access to a specific app in the organization. This can be useful if the user needs to access an app that they do not currently have access to.

- **Add the member to a group**: This allows the administrator to add the user to a group in the organization. Groups can be used to assign permissions to users more easily.

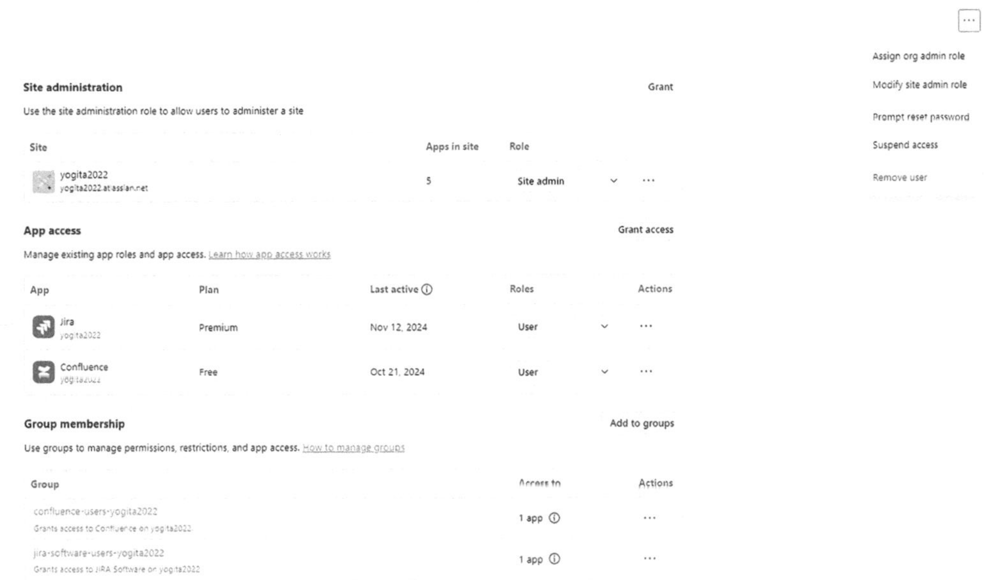

***Figure 3.5:** Options for Administrator to Add a User to Groups and Apps Access Role*

We are now confident about how to add/invite users, add the users to a group, and many other operations. We will learn to create groups in the next section.

Creating Groups

When you have multiple users in your organization who need to be grouped based on criteria other than roles but require the same permissions or restrictions, you can create a group of users. Follow the outlined steps to create groups:

1. Log in as a Jira administrator.
2. Go to **`admin.atlassian.com`** to create groups.
3. Select **`Groups`** from the left navigation bar.
4. Select the **`Create group`** from the right-hand side.

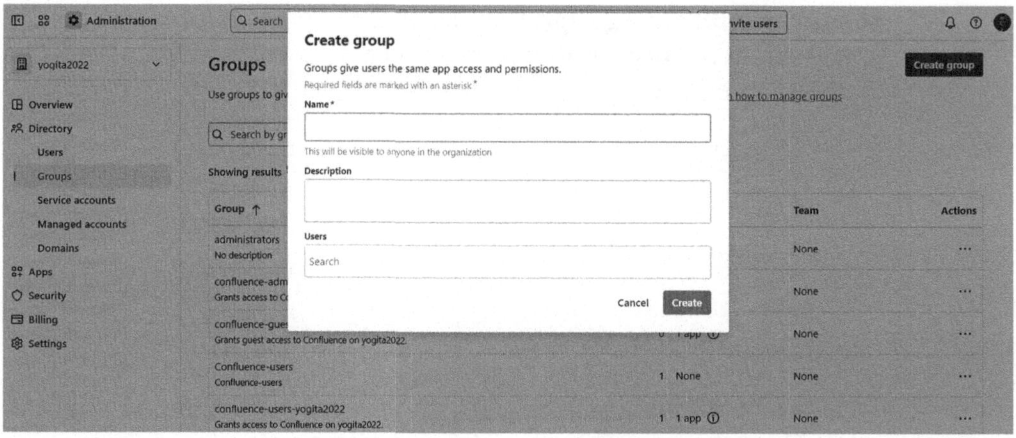

Figure 3.6: *Creating Group and Adding Details*

5. Enter all the details such as group name, members name and description of the group.

Jira creates some default groups, which are listed as follows:

- Jira Administrators,
- Jira software users,
- Site-admins.

In addition to these, Organization admin can create and add groups such as Hardware group, Developers, Design group, Marketing group, and the list continues.

On the Groups page, click a group to view its details. Organization admin can perform the following actions from this page:

1. Add group members.
2. Edit group name.
3. Delete group.
4. Edit group description.
5. Grant app access.
6. Connect the existing team or new team.

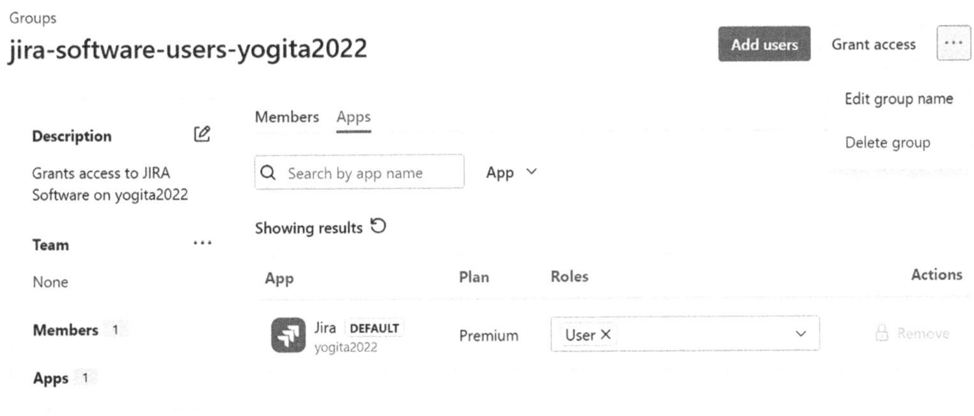

Figure 3.7: *Adding/Editing Group Detail*

We have created a group and now we will learn to create space roles in Jira. Groups are for global and space roles are specific to a space.

Creating Space Roles

Space roles in Jira are specific to a space and are created to customize permissions based on a role in an organization. For example, permissions for creating sprints, managing scrum boards, access to reports and dashboards, and so on. These may be different for each and every space, organization, and they can be customized with the help of permission schemes.

Now we will understand the following step-by-step process to add a space role:

1. Select ⚙ >**`System`**.
2. Select **`space roles`** under security on the left navigation bar.
3. On this page, it displays a list of all space roles.
4. Under **`Add space Role`** at the bottom of the page, enter your new role's **`Name`** and a **`Description.`**

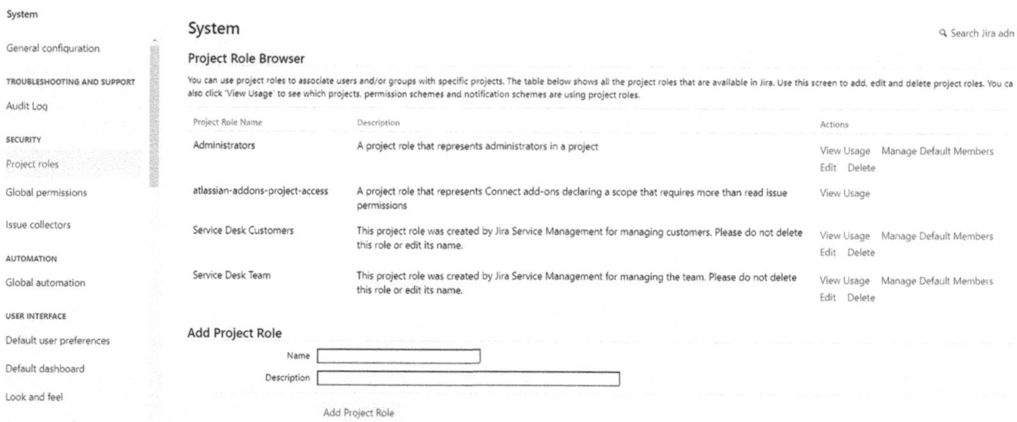

Figure 3.8: *Space Role Browser*

5. Select the **`Add space Role`** button.
6. Space administrators can assign members once a new space role is created.

Example of Creating a Space Role

If you want to create a scrum master role so that all the sprint and board operations can be managed by him, follow the provided steps to create the role and associate the same with the permission scheme and space:

1. Create a space role called **`Scrum Master`**.

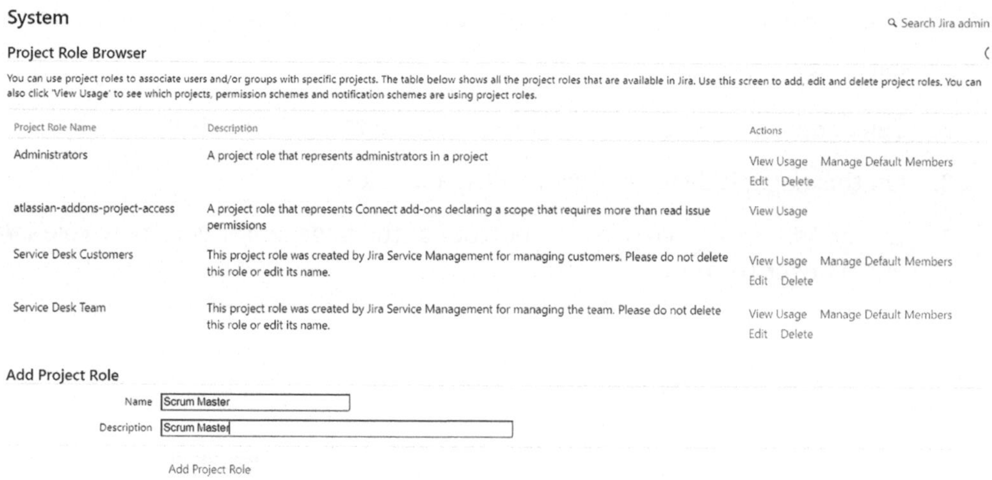

Figure 3.9: *Adding Scrum Master Space Role*

2. Create a permission scheme called the **Agile scrum permission scheme**. In this scheme, you assign the **Manage sprints** permission to the **Scrum Master** space role.
3. For a Scrum Master role, permissions required are **Manage sprints**, **Schedule work items**, **Create work items**, **Edit work items**, **Browse spaces**.

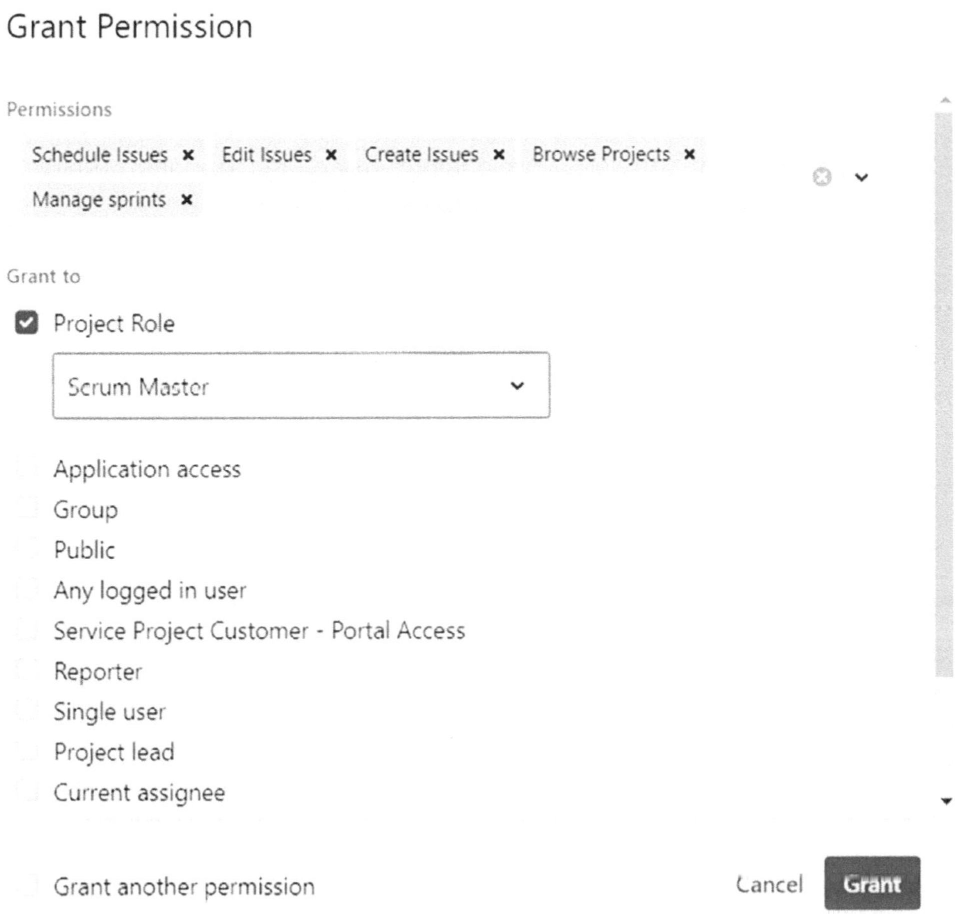

Figure 3.10: *Granting Permissions to a Space Role Scrum Master in Agile Permission Scheme*

4. Associate the Agile scrum permission scheme with all scrum software development spaces. To change the permission scheme, Select **spaces** > **space settings** > **Permissions** > **Actions** > **Use a different scheme.**

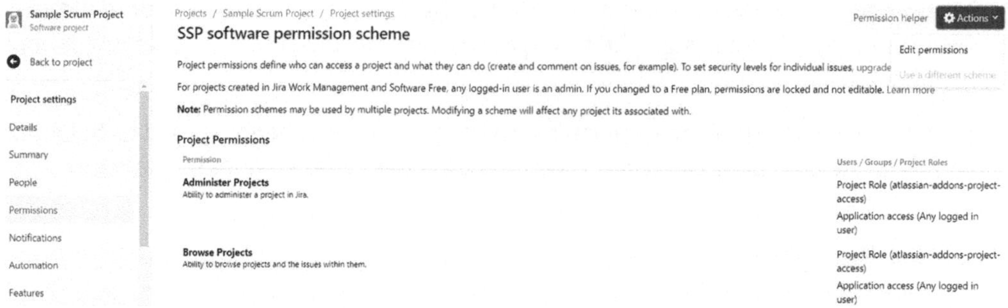

Figure 3.11: *Associating a Permission Scheme with a Space*

5. For each scrum software development space, add the appropriate Scrum Master to the **`Scrum Master`** space role.

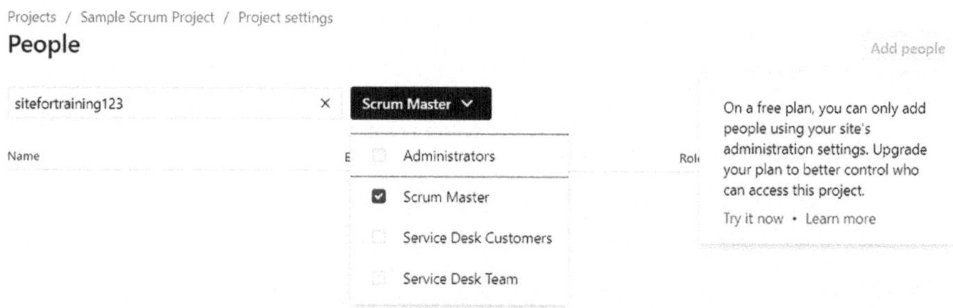

Figure 3.12: *Adding People to Scrum Master Space Role*

Adding Default Members: On the space role browser, select default members. On that page, people can add default users/groups for that space role. Those users or groups are added to each space by default whenever a new space is created.

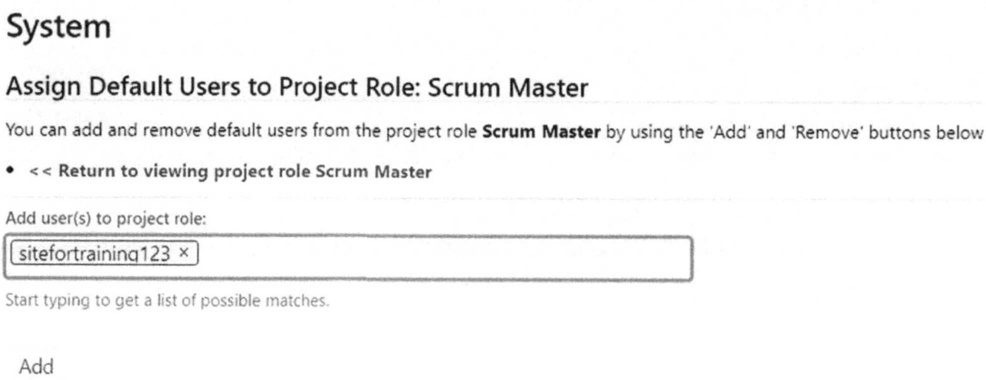

Figure 3.13: *Assigning Default Users to Space Role*

View Usage: Select **`View Usage`** on the space role browser. This page shows which workflows, permission schemes, notification schemes, and work item security schemes are currently using that particular space role. This page also shows which spaces are associated with each scheme.

Space roles can be used in:

- Permission schemes
- Comment visibility
- Workflow conditions
- Email notification schemes
- Work item security levels
- Space roles can also be given access to:
    a. Dashboards
    b. work item filters

Jira creates the following default space roles:

- Administrators
- Atlassian-add-ons-space-access

Groups versus Space Roles

In Jira, there are two distinct concepts related to user and access management: groups and space roles. In the following sub-section, the difference between the two concepts is explained.

Groups

- Groups in Jira are collections of users who share common access permissions and can be assigned to spaces and work items.
- They are primarily used for simplifying user management and applying consistent permissions to multiple users at once.
- Groups can be created and managed within the User Management section of Jira by administrators.
- Users can be added or removed from groups, and permissions can be granted to or revoked from groups, affecting all users within that group.
- Groups can be assigned specific permissions to control access to Jira spaces, boards, and work items.

Space Roles

- Space roles in Jira are predefined sets of permissions that can be assigned to users or groups within a specific space.
- They provide a flexible way to control and manage access to space-related functions and actions.
- Jira offers default space roles such as `Administrators`, `Atlassian-addons-space-access`. Administrators can also create custom roles such as `scrum master`, `product owner` to fit their specific needs.
- Space roles can be assigned to individuals or groups at the space level, allowing for fine-grained control over who can perform certain actions within a space.
- For example, the Developers role may have permissions to create and work on work items, while the Administrator's role may have full control over the space configuration.

In summary, groups simplify user management and permission assignment, and space roles provide granular access control within specific spaces. These concepts can be used together to effectively manage users and permissions in Jira.

Understanding Service Accounts, Managed Accounts and Domains

Service Accounts: In Jira Cloud, a service account is a dedicated account used by apps, integrations or automation tools instead of a real user. These accounts allow external systems to connect to Jira securely without needing the personal login of a user. For example, if a reporting tool needs to pull Jira data, it can use a service account.

Managed Accounts: Managed accounts in Jira Cloud are accounts that your organization can fully control. This means you can update them, deactivate them or make other changes when needed. To manage an account, your organization must first verify its email domain. If an account is not claimed or the domain is not verified, the account is treated as an **external account**. External accounts belong to people outside your organization, such as a customer working with you on a contract.

Domains: A domain in Jira Cloud is the email domain (like company.com) used by an organization. When an admin verifies a domain, they can claim all users with that email address as managed accounts. This helps organizations control which user belongs to them, apply security policies and manage access centrally.

Understanding Permissions and Access Control

Permissions are settings in Jira applications, which control the users to create, view, and delete. It can allow users to create spaces, create work items, view work items, delete spaces/work items, create sprints, and much more similar functions. There are three types of permissions in Jira. In this section, we will learn about all three types of permissions.

Global Permissions

These are the permissions applied globally, which means they are common for all spaces. For example, people can set permissions to browse users and groups, share dashboards and filters, and so forth. To set the Global permissions, it is necessary to log in as Jira Administrator and navigate to System settings. Follow the provided steps:

1. Log in as a Jira Administrator.
2. Navigate to the **`System settings`** by clicking on the **`Settings`** icon.
3. Choose **`System`** from the dropdown menu.
4. Select **`Global Permissions`** in the left side panel.
5. Set the desired permissions based on your requirements.

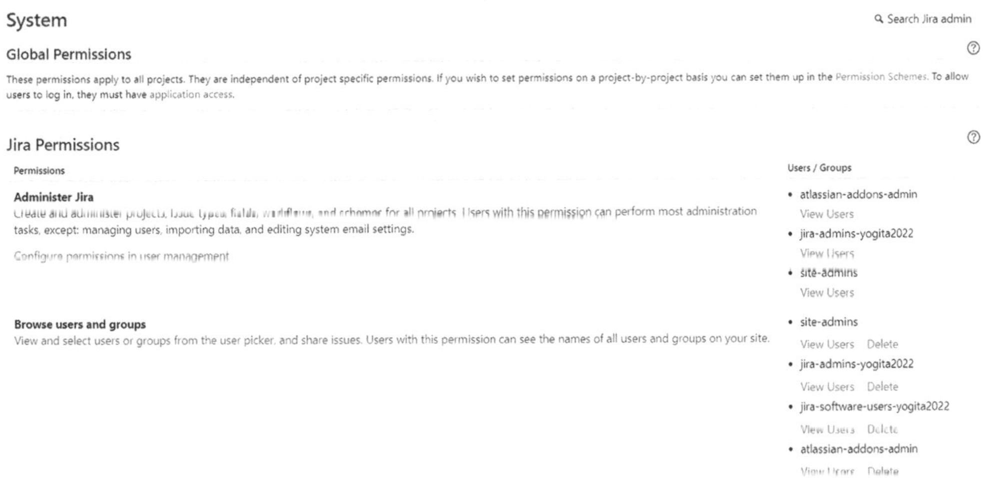

Figure 3.14: *Global Permissions Page*

Examples of Global Permissions

In this section, we have covered a few global permissions, which can be used for system administration. Global permissions in Jira provide various capabilities and access levels to users.

- **Administer Jira**: Create and administer spaces, work item types, fields, workflows, and schemes for all spaces. Users with this permission can perform most administration tasks, except managing users, importing data and editing system Email settings.
- **Share Dashboards and Filters**: Users with this permission can share their customized dashboards and filters with other users, enabling collaboration and information sharing across the organization.
- **Manage Group Filter Subscriptions**: Create and delete group filter subscriptions.
- **Make Bulk Changes**: This permission allows users to perform bulk updates and modifications to multiple work items simultaneously, which helps improve efficiency.
- **Browse Users and Groups**: View and select users or groups from the user picker and share work items. Users with this permission can see the names of all users and groups on your site.
- **Create Team-managed Spaces**: Create spaces separate from shared configurations and schemes. Team-managed spaces don't affect existing spaces or shared configuration like workflows, fields or permissions. Only licensed users can create team-managed spaces.

We have covered all the global permissions in this section. These global permissions play a crucial role in ensuring effective administration, collaboration, and customization within Jira, empowering users to effectively utilize the capabilities of the platform.

Administration Permissions

- **Administer Spaces**: Permission to administer a space which covers the ability to edit space details, components, space role membership, and space versions. Any logged-in user on your Jira site can be granted this permission.
- **Manage Issues Layout:** This permission allows people to edit work item layouts in their company-managed space. While Jira Admins have this ability by default, it can also be granted to any user or role. It allows teams the flexibility to directly manage and add fields (including existing global custom fields) to the layout of work items in the project.
- **Edit Workflows:** This permission allows users to modify existing isolated workflows in their company-managed project (for example, by changing

statuses and transitions). While Jira Admins have this ability by default, it can also be granted to any user or role. This allows teams to directly manage and customize their workflows of the project. This permission is best suited for experienced, trusted Jira users. Workflows can only be edited by non-admins if the workflow is not shared with other projects.

Space Permissions

Permission schemes in Jira are used to organize and control access to spaces. They determine who can view, create, edit, and assign work items within a space. These permissions are related to work items, time-tracking, attachments, and so forth. Space administrators can assign users to a space, but they cannot customize the permission schemes specific to that space. There are some space-level permissions available that allow you to fine-tune and manage what actions users can perform within a space.

Examples of Space Permissions

In this section, we have covered a few space permissions, which can be used from the system administration section and can be applied to `company-managed spaces.`

- **Browse Spaces**: Permission to browse spaces and view work items in Jira spaces, except work items with work item-level security.
- **Manage Sprints**: This permission is to grant people to create, start, and complete sprints in a space. A person having this permission can adjust the sprint duration and goal. If a board contains sprints from multiple spaces, then a user should have to manage sprints permission for all the spaces.
- **Manage Versions (Releases):** Versions (or releases) are specific points in a project, helping organize and track work items toward a planned milestone such as new features, bug fixes etc. It grants people to create, edit, release, merge, archive and delete versions. If you are a project manager having Administer space permission, you can still manage versions irrespective of Manage Versions permission. If someone with this permission is not a space admin, they will only have access to the Versions (Releases) tab in space settings and will not be able to view other settings.
- **View Aggregated Data**: This permission helps view insights on the backlog, boards and deployments view. It allows users to view other aggregated data like results of JQL filter queries, reports, etc. It includes average estimations, work item-count, team cycle time. Disabling it will prevent users from viewing all types of aggregated data.
- **View Development Tools**: This is the permission to view the development tool in which the status of the build data of the work item can be viewed.

- **View (Read-only) Workflow**: It provides a link to view the workflow. You can grant this permission to any logged in user.

Work Item Permissions

These permissions are effective only if the users, groups, and roles are granted to browse spaces.

- **Assign work items:** It allows people to assign work items to users in Jira. This permission is different from an assignable user. In software spaces, the user should have space access to apply for this permission.
- **Assignable user:** This permission grants individuals the capability to be assigned work items, enabling their usernames to populate the Assignee field across any work items within your space. However, it does not confer the authority to assign work items to other users on your site.

  By possessing this permission, users gain the capacity to actively engage with work items. When an individual is assigned to a work item, Jira promptly notify them to review the associated details. This permission plays a pivotal role for core team members involved in any space.
- **Close work items**: It allows the user to set the resolutions field to a closed state, which is based on the workflow conditions of the work item. A user needs the Transition work items and resolve work item permission to close work items. App access is required to close work items in Jira.
- **Create work items**: This permission allows users to create tasks and sub-tasks. Having this permission allows users to see the spaces while creating work items. If this permission is granted to any logged-in user, it is helpful to create suggestions, bugs, etc. However, for security reasons, a few teams may not grant this permission to everyone.
- **Delete work items**: This permission allows users to delete work items and related items like comments, field data, work log entries, and the list continues. In Jira, this permission is dependent on app access permission. To maintain the cleanliness of the Jira instance, it is recommended to transition the work item to done status. Deleting work items should not be a common practice to delete work items unless it is necessary.
- **Archive issues**: This permission is helpful to keep spaces clean, improve site performance and provides a better way than using the Delete permission for work items. This permission may be assigned to any role and it allows users to archive work items in a space, along with their related comments and field values.
- **Edit work items**: This permission allows people to modify fields like Summary, description, and other editable fields. This permission also grants the ability to

convert tasks to subtasks and vice versa. In Jira, this permission is dependent on app access permission. Organizations with strict compliance measures restrict this permission for team members.

- **Link work items**: This permission enables people to link work items within the same or different spaces. They need the same permission in other spaces to view the link. It functions when work item-linking has been enabled. In software spaces, people must have app access to use this permission.
- **Modify reporter**: This permission allows users to modify the default reporter field on any of the work items. By default, the reporter field is pre-set to the creator of the work item. In software spaces, people must have app access to use this permission.
- **Move work items**: This permission allows people to move work items to another space or change the work item-type. This permission requires the create work item permission in the target space.
- **Resolve work items**: This permission allows the users to set or clear the resolution field and see the Fix version field. It doesn't include the ability to close the work item. In Jira, this permission is dependent on app access permission. It is required to have transition work item permission to be useful.
- **Schedule work items**: This permission allows people to set or modify the Due date of the work items. It also allows to rank (or, reorder) the work items on the backlog or board. They must have app access to Jira to use this permission.
- **Set work item security**: It allows users to set the security levels of the work items. It allows or restricts who can view the work items. The users must have app access to Jira to use this permission.
- **Transition work items**: This permission allows users to view the workflow of the space and update the status. The users can move any work item through the workflow triggering post functions. It doesn't allow the users to close the work item or set the resolution field. The users must have app access to Jira to use this permission.

Voters and Watchers Permissions

These permissions are effective only if the users, groups, and roles are granted to browse spaces. First, allow users, groups, and roles to browse those spaces and then only these permissions can work.

- **Manage Watcher List**: This permission is for adding or removing people from the watch list of a work item. It works on the basis of app access permission. In software spaces and service spaces, people must have app access to Jira and Jira Service Management, respectively, to use this permission.

- **View Voters and Watchers**: This allows people to see who is watching a work item. It does not depend on specific app access permissions to be useful.

Comments Permissions

These permissions are only applicable to those who can view the space. To make comments permissions applicable, grant users to browse the space first.

- **Add Comments**: This permission allows people to comment on any work item in your software and business spaces or add internal notes to requests in your service spaces. In software spaces, it is necessary to have app access to Jira to use this permission.
- **Delete all Comments**: This permission allows people to delete any comments added by anyone in any space. In software spaces, users must have app access to Jira. It is recommended to preserve all the comments to ensure a comprehensive understanding of the space.
- **Delete own Comments**: This permission allows people to delete their own comments in any space. It is not dependent on app access permissions. It is helpful to modify any erroneous comments.
- **Edit all Comments**: This permission allows people to edit all the comments done by anyone. Organizations with strict compliance policies do not encourage editing comments. Whereas open organizations encourage teams to make corrections.
- **Edit own Comments**: This permission allows people to edit their own comments. This permission can be granted to any logged-in user. Organizations with strict policies restrict the editing of comments.

Time Tracking Permissions

These permissions are effective only if the users, groups, and roles are granted to browse spaces. First, allow users, groups, and roles to browse those spaces and then only these permissions can work.

- **Work on work items:** It allows people to utilize the features related to the time tracking field on any of the spaces' work items. A user can enter a work log, which includes time spent and time remaining and a description of the work dated on that work item.
- **Delete all work logs:** This permission is to remove any work log added by anyone in spaces' work items. This permission is specifically for team leaders, management roles, or other senior people.

- **Delete own worklogs**: This permission allows people to delete the work logged, description, and estimated time entered by themselves. This permission is required to delete their own worklog in case of data entry errors.
- **Edit all worklogs**: This permission allows people to edit the time logged, description of the work, estimated time, and to perform similar functions. It is helpful for team leaders or management roles, who can modify the entries.
- **Edit own worklogs**: This permission allows users to alter the time logged, estimated time, description of the work log or any data entry errors due to changes of the scope of the work.

Attachments Permissions

These permissions are effective only if the users, groups, and roles are granted to browse spaces. First, allow users, groups, and roles to browse those spaces and then only these permissions can work.

- **Create Attachments**: This permission does not require space access. Any logged-in user can be granted to add files as attachments. It helps people working on spaces to add some information related to the work they are doing.
- **Delete all Attachments**: This permission allows any user to remove attachments, which are attached with any of work items of your space. To delete attachments in Jira and Jira Service Management, it is essential to have space access.
- **Delete own Attachments**: This permission allows people to remove their own attachments. It is not dependent on app access permissions. Organizations with strict compliance policies may restrict team members from deleting their own attachments.

We have covered all the space permissions which can be customized to create a new permission scheme as per the requirement of an organization.

Jira Admin Helper to Troubleshoot Permissions

Whenever a user can or cannot see a certain work item or facing some problems to take action on work items, Jira admin helper can help. Follow the provided steps:

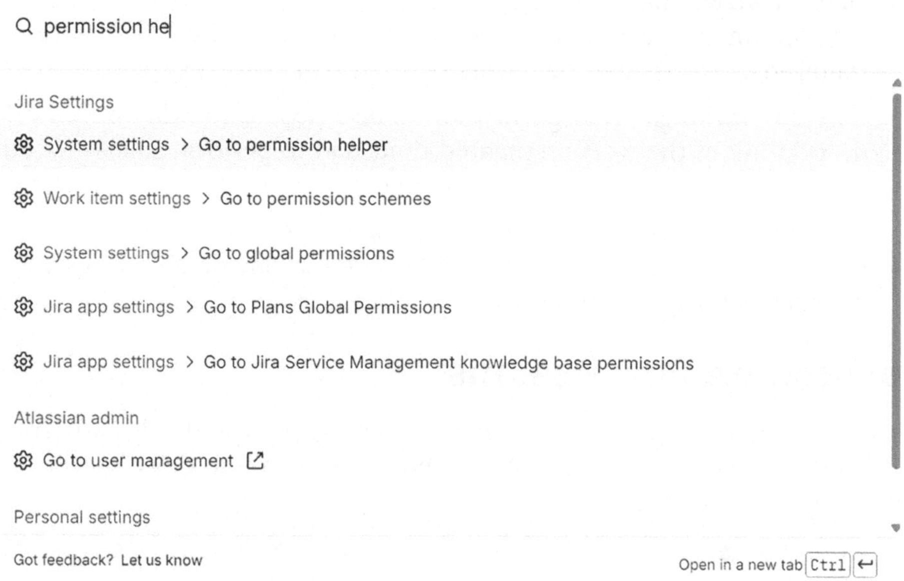

Figure 3.15: *Selecting Permission Helper*

You must be a Jira admin to use the permission helper. The steps are as follows:

1. Choose search **`Jira Admin`** on any page in the right upper corner.
2. Under **`Admin helper`**, select **`Permission helper`**.
3. Enter a username or leave it blank.
4. Add a work item key (for example, work item key - the user can or can't see) and the permission to check.
5. Click **`Submit.`**

Work Item Security Permissions

Security schemes in Jira provide a way to adjust the visibility of individual work items within the constraints of the permissions of the space. They allow you to control who can see certain types of work items based on work item security permissions. For instance, you can configure work item security to limit visibility to space administrators or users belonging to specific groups. This helps you to create different levels of access and confidentiality for different types of work items within your space.

Permission Schemes

Jira Administrators can assign specific permissions for different work item operations, sprint operations, commenting, time tracking, and so on. Whenever a space is created, a default permission scheme is associated with it. Ideally, an administrator should create a copy of the default permission scheme and then can update the new permission scheme as per the roles and requirements of an organization. An administrator can customize the permission scheme by doing this and associate it with all the similar spaces in an organization. Updating and removing permissions to customize the scheme can be done as shown in *Figure* 3.11.

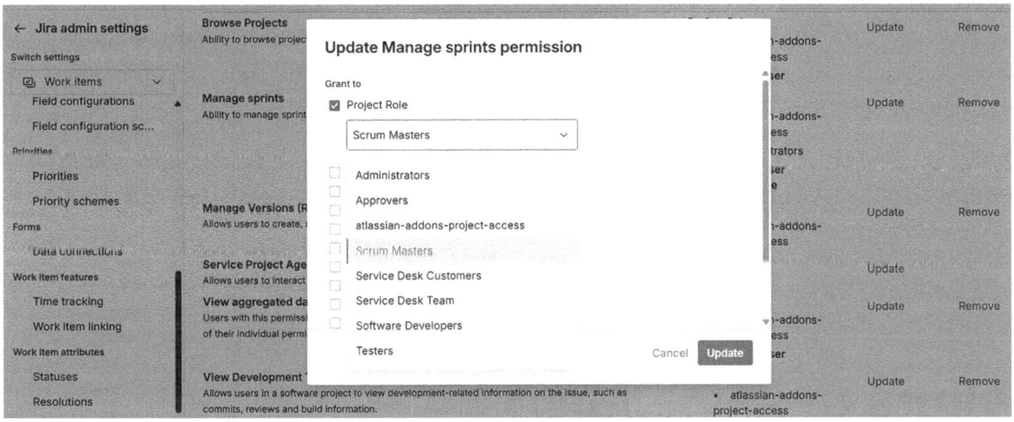

Figure 3.16*: Copying a Permission Scheme and Updating*

We have listed below the steps to copy a permission scheme and associate it with the space.

Associating a Permission Scheme with a Space

After deciding the space permissions for your organization/space, you can implement the scheme by linking it to the spaces.

To associate a permission scheme with a company-managed space, follow these steps:

1. Choose **`spaces`** from the navigation bar.
2. Select the specific space.
3. From the sidebar, select **`space settings`**.
4. Choose **`Permissions`** from the sidebar. It displays the current permissions scheme.
5. Select the **`Actions`** dropdown menu and choose **`Use a different scheme`**.

6. On the **`Associate Permission Scheme`** to **`space page`**, select the permission scheme you want to associate with the space.
7. Click the **`Associate`** button to associate the space with the permission scheme.

The permissions of your space are now updated and the space now follows your permission scheme. Any changes you make in the scheme apply immediately to the space associated with the scheme.

Conclusion

We are now familiar with how to invite users, create groups, and space roles. We also understood the Global and space-specific permissions and how to customize the permission schemes and associate them with a space.

Creating well-structured user management, groups, space roles, and permission schemes in Jira contribute to efficient collaboration, data security, and successful space outcomes.

In the next chapter, we will learn about how to manage backlog, sprints, and Agile boards.

Points to Remember

When creating users, groups, space roles, and permission schemes in Jira, here are a few points to keep in mind:

- **User Management**: Make sure that each user has a unique Email ID and appropriate access privileges based on their role and responsibilities within the space.
- **Group Classification**: Group users based on common characteristics, such as department, team, or space, to easily manage permissions and streamline collaboration.
- **Space Roles**: Define specific roles for users, such as administrators, developers, or stakeholders, to assign different levels of access and responsibilities within the space.
- **Role-Based Permissions**: Assign appropriate permissions to each space role, allowing them to perform specific actions and access relevant space resources.
- **Permission Granularity**: Determine the level of access required for each user or group, balancing security and collaboration needs to prevent unauthorized actions or information exposure.

- **Consider Space Requirements**: Understand the specific needs of the space and align user roles and permissions accordingly to ensure smooth workflows and information flow.
- **Regular Review**: Periodically review user access rights and roles to maintain data security, accommodate organizational changes, and remove unnecessary permissions.
- **Too Many Administrators**: Never give Jira Administrator permissions to too many people. Check it regularly and if not required by the person, revoke it.
- **Not Customizing Permission Scheme**: Default permissions scheme may have less permissions, which are not required by your organization. Make sure to delete and update permissions and customize them for your specific requirement.
- **Communication and Training**: Clearly communicate the roles and permissions assigned to each user or group, providing proper training to ensure understanding and adherence to Jira usage guidelines.
- **Documentation**: Maintain comprehensive documentation of user roles, groups, and permission schemes for future reference and easy troubleshooting.
- **Testing and Validation**: Before deploying the permission schemes, thoroughly test them to validate that users and groups have the expected access and perform necessary adjustments if needed.

Use Cases with Reference Links

These links are from the Jira knowledge base or the Atlassian community. It will be helpful to understand some use cases.

1. How to change the permission scheme on a space: https://community.atlassian.com/t5/Jira-questions/how-to-change-the-permission-scheme-on-a-space/qaq-p/1955536
2. Understanding how space permissions affect space visibility in Jira cloud: https://confluence.atlassian.com/jirakb/understanding-how-space-permissions-affect-space-visibility-in-jira-cloud-1267074303.html
3. How to restrict the creation of an work item based on work item-type: https://confluence.atlassian.com/jirakb/how-to-restrict-the-creation-of-an-work item-based-on-work itemtype-1267761379.html

CHAPTER 4
Managing Backlog, Sprints, and Boards

Introduction

It is important to handle the backlog, sprints, and boards well for a successful Agile project. Backlog management means arranging and deciding which tasks to do first, so we work on the most important stuff. Sprints are like short periods where we plan and finish tasks quickly. Boards show our work visually, helping the team work together better. By mastering these things, we can develop smoothly, deliver faster, and meet the needs of our customers better.

Structure

In this chapter, we will cover the following topics:

- Steps to Create a Work Item
- Different Ways to Create Work Items and Product Backlog
- Creating and Refining Scrum Product Backlog
- Creating and Refining the Kanban Product Backlog
- Creating Epic and Version
- Sprint Operations
- Product Backlog versus Sprint Backlog
- Creating and Customizing scrum and Kanban board
- View settings on Backlog and Boards
- Scrum board versus Kanban board
- Use cases with References

Steps to Create a Work Item

Work types in Jira: In software development spaces, you can create the work types as mentioned below.

- Epic
- Story
- Task
- Bug
- Sub-task

In this section, we will learn about how to create a work item in Jira from any page. This process will also help you to create a work item while creating a backlog or adding work items to the backlog.

1. Select the **`Create`** button as shown in the following figure.

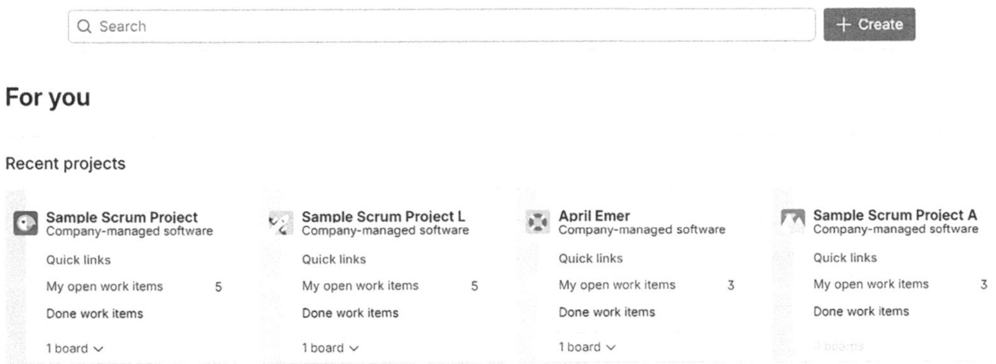

Figure 4.1: *Step-1 to Create a Work Item*

2. Enter the details of the **`Space`**, **`Work type`** and **`Summary`** field.

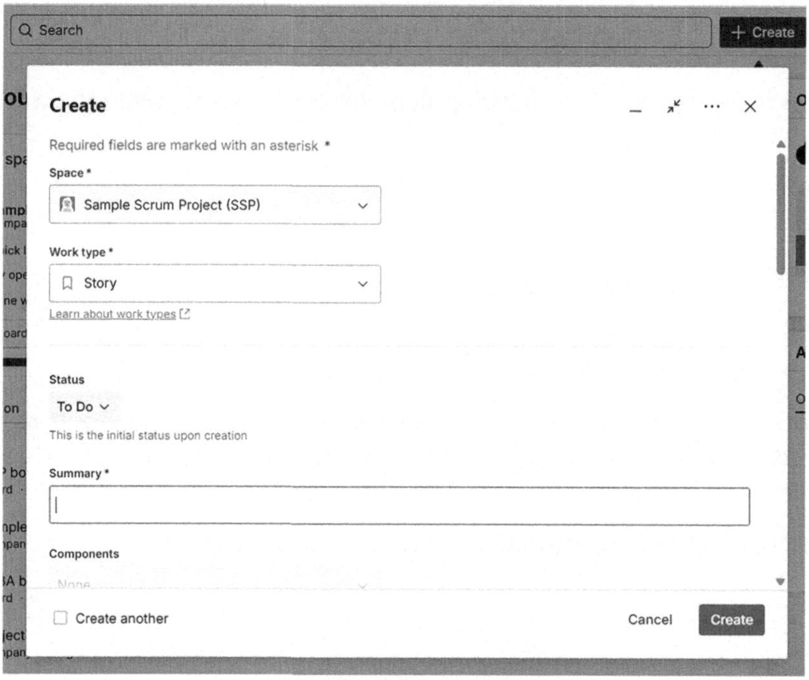

Figure 4.2: *Step-2 to Create a Work Item*

3. Enter all the details about the required fields and other details. Select **`Create`** button. A work item has been created.

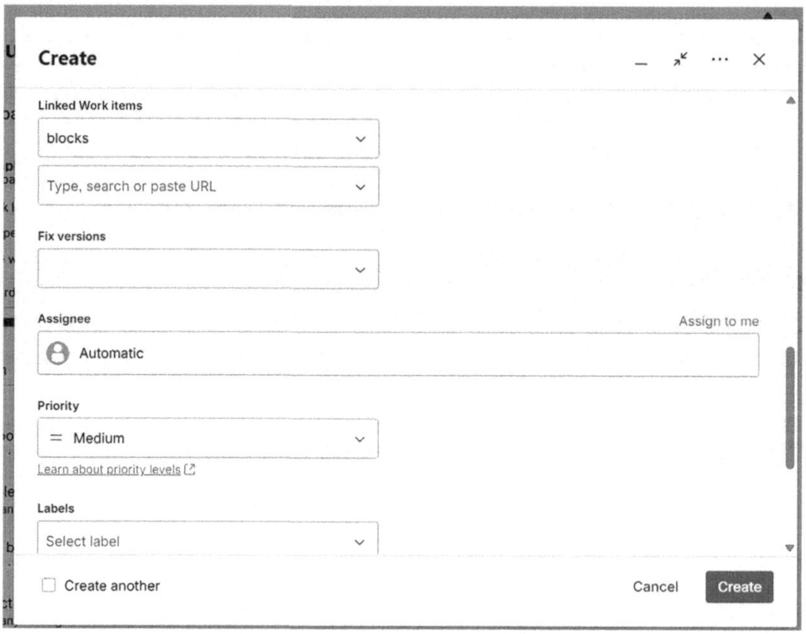

Figure 4.3: *Step-3 to Create a Work Item*

Different Ways to Create Work Items and Product Backlog

You can create work items in four different ways as follows. The created work item goes to the product backlog in Scrum/Kanban spaces.

1. **Creating a work item from the Navigation Bar:** Click on the `Create` tab in the navigation bar and start creating a work item.

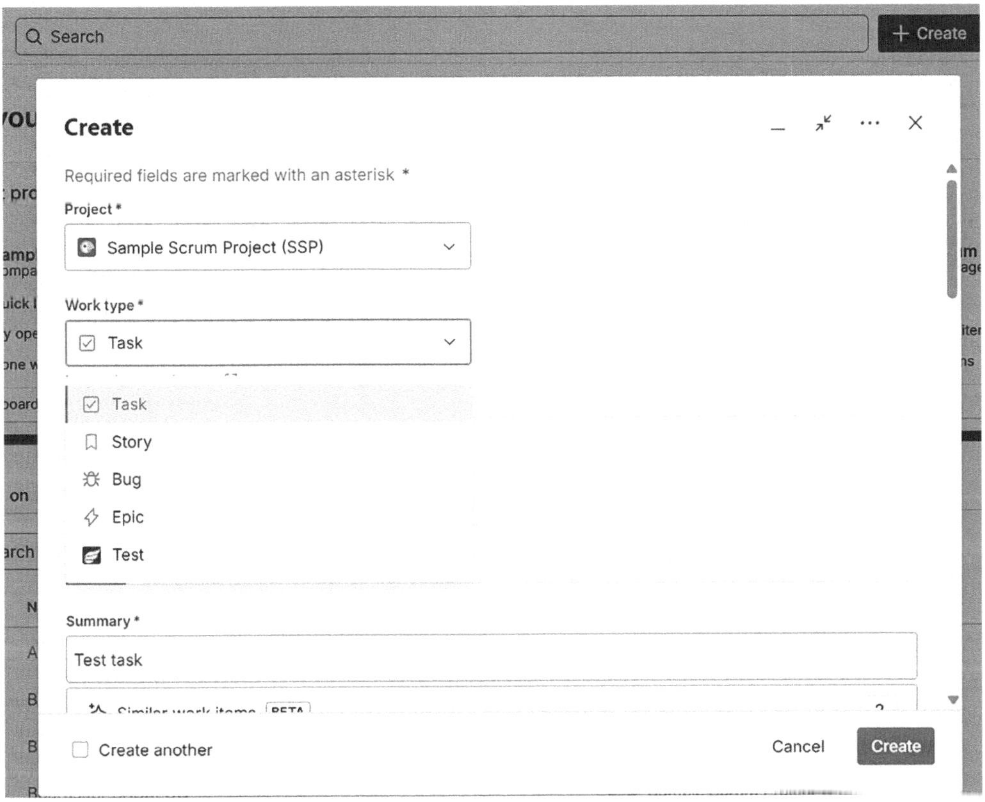

Figure 4.4: *Creating a Work Item from the Navigation Bar*

2. **Creating a work item from Timeline View:** The other way to create a work item is from the timeline view as shown in *Figure* 4.5. You can create an epic, story and task from a timeline view.

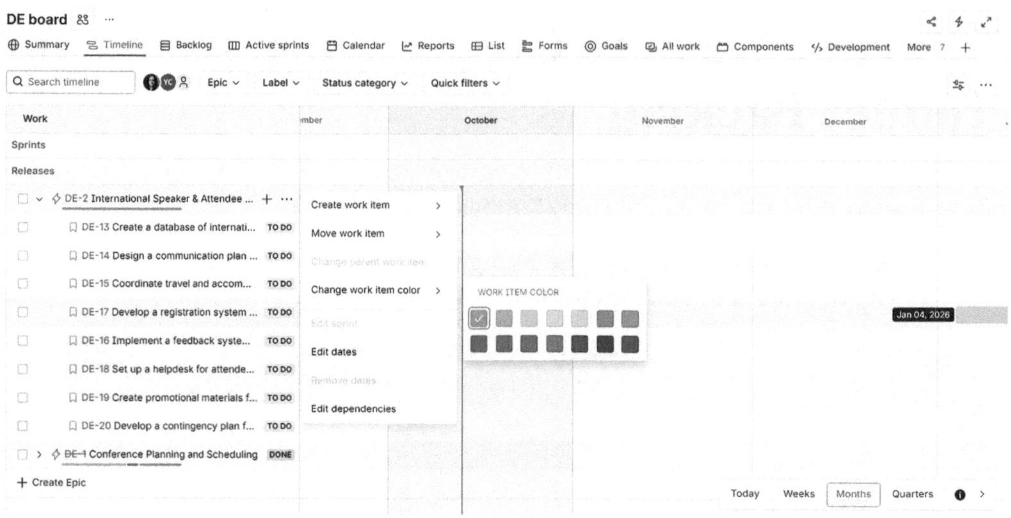

Figure 4.5: *Creating a Work Item from the Timeline View*

3. **Creating a work item from Backlog:** You can also create a work item from the backlog view page. Select **+** sign and create work items such as **Bug**, **Task** and **Story**.

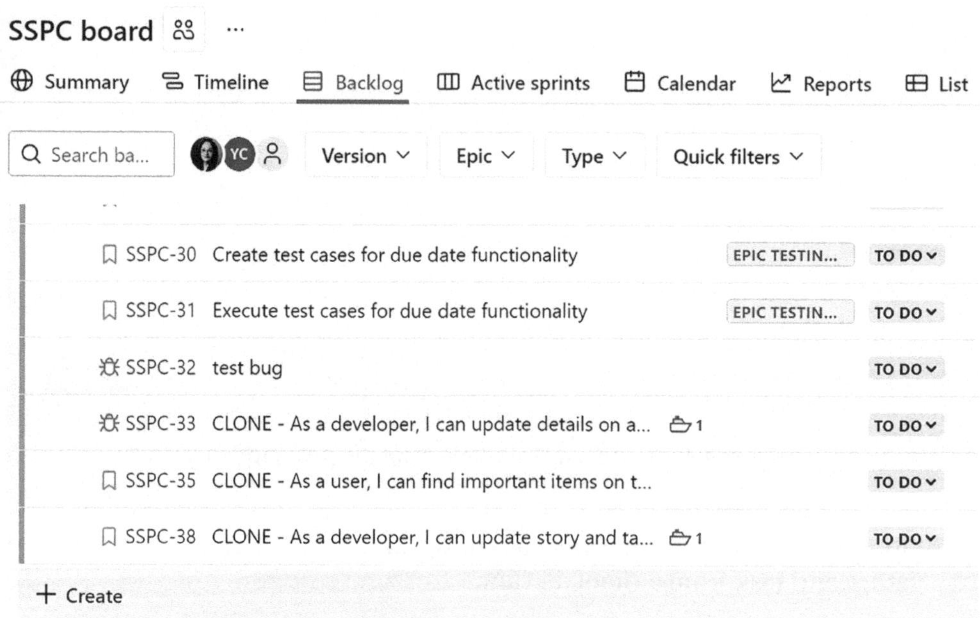

Figure 4.6: *Creating a Work Item from the Backlog*

4. **Creating a work item from Agile Board:** Work items can also be created directly from the Agile board. When a new work item is added from a specific column, it is automatically assigned the status associated with that column

(such as Selected for Development, To Do, or In Progress). To create a work item, simply hover over the desired column and click the **Create** button.

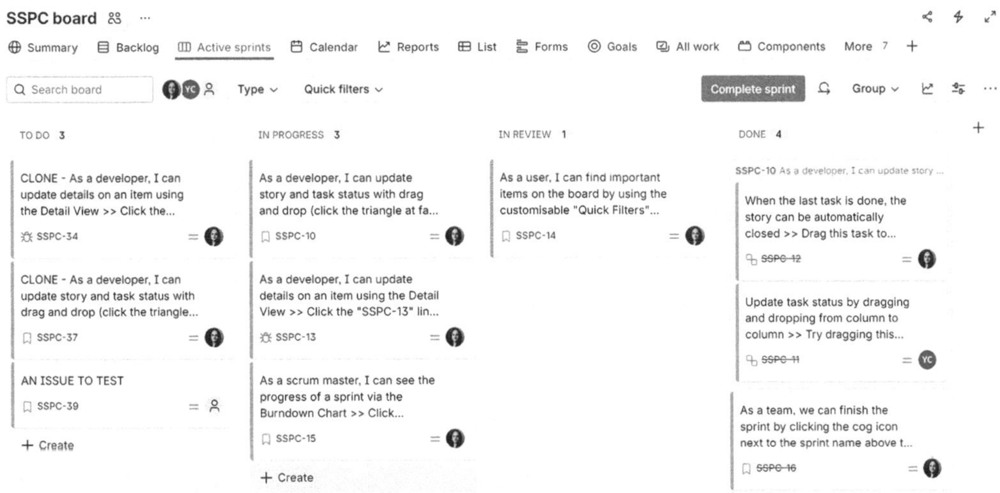

Figure 4.7: *Creating a Work Item from Agile Board*

Additionally, AI-powered capabilities allow users to generate multiple child work items under a parent work item, following the predefined hierarchy. We will explore this functionality in detail in *Chapter 13: Atlassian Intelligence – Getting Started with Rovo and Creating Agents.*

We learned about how to create stories, bugs and tasks. This way we have created a list of work items which makes a product backlog. Now we will learn important things about scrum product backlog and Kanban product backlog.

Creating and Grooming Scrum Product Backlog

The product backlog is a prioritized list of tasks such as features, tasks, stories, bugs and many more. As explained in this chapter, you can create work items from the backlog page. This way there are many stories, tasks and the like in the product backlog to achieve a product goal. In this section, we will understand a few must-be conditions for a work item to appear on the board, how to estimate the product backlog items and grooming the backlog.

Important things about scrum product backlog are:

- Subtasks cannot be viewed directly; however, they can be accessed in the Scrum product backlog by expanding the parent task dropdown.
- If the work item matches the filter of the board, then only it will appear on the board.

- Work item status maps to one of the statuses of the status of the board.
- If the work item status does not match with the board's statuses, then it should be mapped to the right status- for example in review status can be mapped to in progress.

The following example shows a scrum product backlog and work item details on the right side.

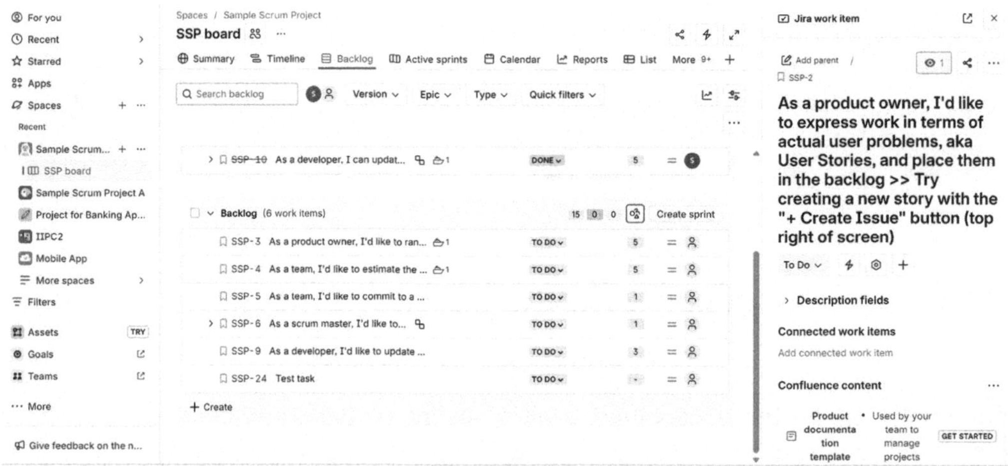

Figure 4.8: *Scrum Product Backlog with Work Item Details*

Important features on the product backlog page are:

- You can add work items to the product backlog.
- You can prioritize the work items. Go to the work item, right click and select **`send to Top of Backlog.`** You can also drag and drop the work item to the top of the backlog, which will change the rank of the work item.
- Click More (the three dots under the sprint name) to view the sprint workload by assignee. You can also see an individual team member's workload by hovering over their avatar.
- Enter the details of Estimates on the work items. Enter the Estimate either in the field **`Original Estimate`** and/or **`Story Points`**.
- Click a work item to open it on the right-hand side, where you can edit its details.
- To bulk edit work items in the backlog, select them using checkboxes, *Ctrl/Command*, or *Shift* for adjacent items. Then, choose **`Edit`** > **`Fields`** from the toolbar to open the bulk edit sidebar. From there, you can edit the details by choosing the required option such as **`Keep as is`**, **`Remove/Replace all`**, **`Add new`**, and the list continues.

- Click on the work item. The work item will open on the right-hand side. Now you can edit the work item details.
- You can transition the work item to the sprint. For transitioning the work item, you should have the transition work item permission. You can also transition multiple work items with the help of the *Shift* or *Ctrl* keys.
- Split a work item is a functionality used when the work item is very big.
    - When a work item is split, you can enter the estimates for both work items.
    - When you split a work item, all the fields are not inherited. However, fields such as priority, label and component remain the same. You can enter a summary for the new work item created by splitting the work item. Worklog, links, comments and history will not be copied to the new work item created.
    - Now there are two parts to the work item. The other work item will go to the backlog.
- To Flag an work item, right-click and flag an work item. Flagging means that a work item is of importance and can be taken on priority. To find the flagged work items, use the query **`Flagged = Impediment`**. Priority is replaced by the Flag symbol.

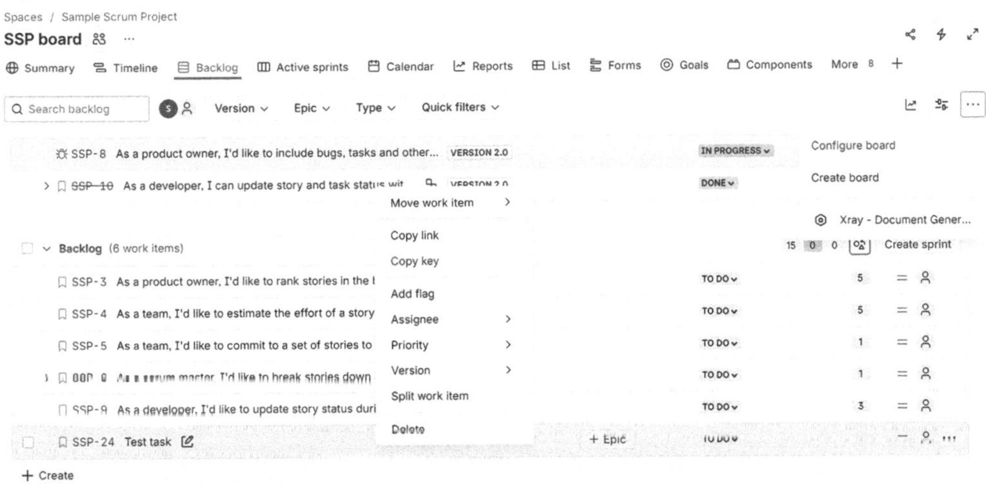

Figure 4.9: *Features on the Scrum Product Backlog Page*

Creating and Refining the Kanban Product Backlog

It can be utilized only if it has been enabled by Jira Administrator or board administrator.

When you have only a few work items in your backlog, it is relatively simple to manage them in the first column of your Kanban board. However, as your backlog expands, it can become challenging to navigate and scroll through all these work items.

The Kanban backlog presents a solution to streamline the work planning process of your team. It offers an improved list view that enhances the prioritization and organization of work items. With this view, you gain access to a larger backlog, enabling you to create and rank tasks with greater efficiency. This helps team members to actively work on a Kanban space to focus on their work-in-progress on the Kanban board, without being overwhelmed by the presence of planning items.

The following example shows a scrum product backlog selected for development work items. It also shows the provision to select the no. of work items on the backlog.

Important things about the Kanban product backlog are:

- If the work item matches the filter of the board, then only it will appear on the board.
- Work item status maps to one of the statuses of the board's status- Kanban backlog column or any other next column.

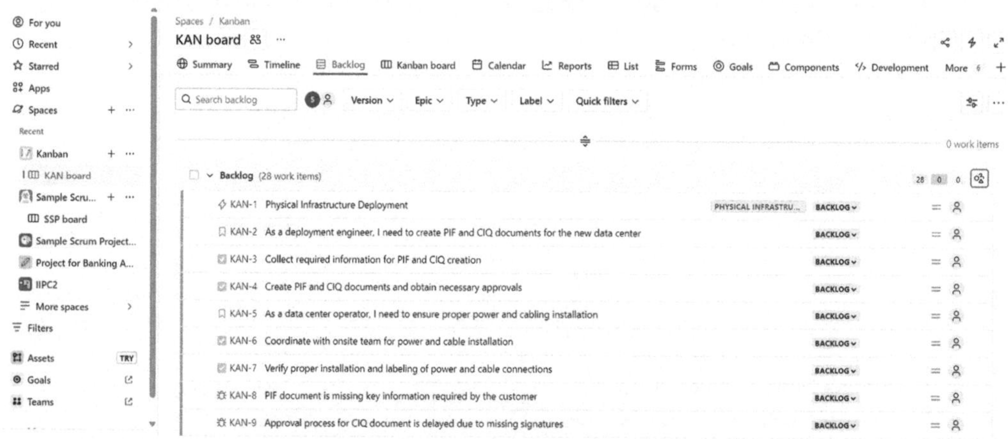

Figure 4.10: *Kanban Product Backlog Page*

Important features on the product backlog page:

- You can add work items to the product backlog.
- You can prioritize the work items. Go to the work item, right click and select **`send to Top of Backlog`**. You can also drag and drop the work item to the top of the backlog.
- Enter the details of **`Estimates`** on the work items. Enter the Estimate either in the field **`Original Estimate`** and/or **`Story Points`**.
- To bulk edit work items in the backlog, select them using checkboxes, *Ctrl/Command*, or *Shift* for adjacent items. Then, choose **`Edit`** > **`Fields`** from the

toolbar to open the bulk edit sidebar. From there, you can edit the details by choosing the required option such as **`Keep as is`**, **`Remove/Replace all`**, **`Add new`**, and so on.

- Click on the work item. The work item will open on the right-hand side. Now you can edit the work item details.
- You can transition the work item to the next status. For transitioning the work item, you should have the transition work item permission. You can also transition multiple work items with the help of *Shift* or *Ctrl* keys.
- Split a work item is a functionality used when the work item is very big.
  - When a work item is split, you can enter the estimates for both work items.
  - When you split a work item, all the fields are not inherited. However, fields such as priority, label and component remain the same. You can enter a summary for the new work item created by splitting the work item. Worklog, links, comments and history will not be copied to the new work item created.
  - It is possible to split work items from the Kanban backlog view and not from the board. After splitting the work item, the other work item will go to the backlog.
- To Flag a work item: Right-click on the work item and flag a work item. Flagging means that a work item is of importance and can be taken on priority. To find the flagged work items, use the query **`Flagged = Impediment`**. Priority is replaced by the Flag symbol.

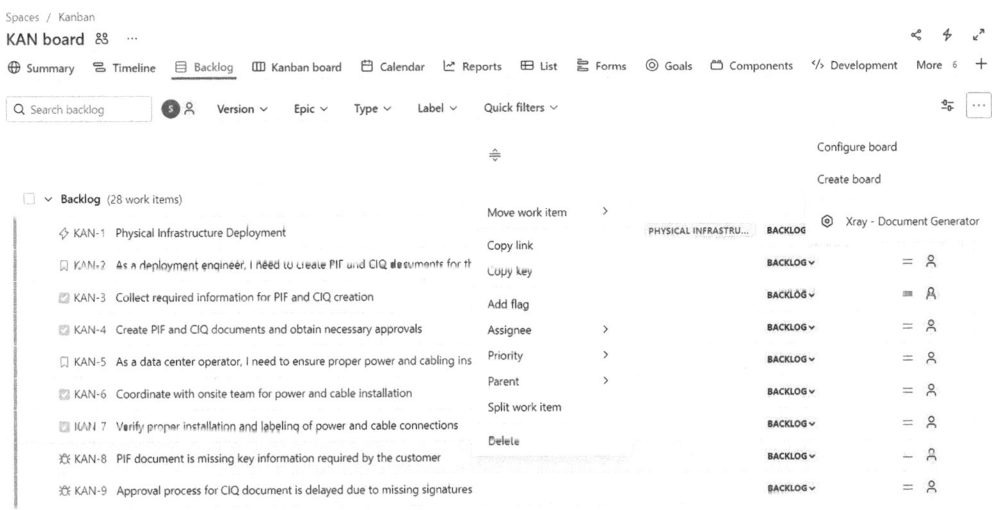

***Figure 4.11:** Features on Kanban Product Backlog Page*

Creating Epic and Version

Epic can be created from three different places:

- From timeline view;
- From create button; and,
- From the backlog view page (as shown in *Figure* 4.11).

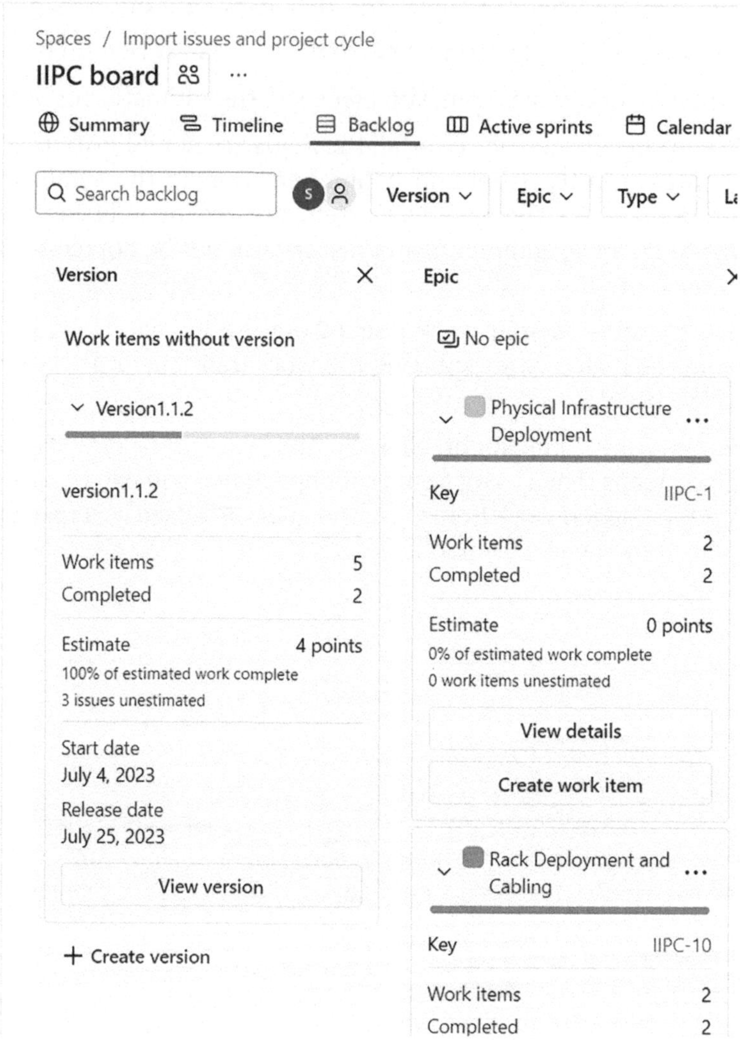

***Figure* 4.12:** *Creating Epic and Version*

To create versions, first enable the feature in your space settings: navigate to **`Space`** > **`Space Settings`** > **`Features`**, and activate **`Releases`**.

1. Under the **`Planning`** section, you can create versions from **`Backlog.`**

2. Under the **Development** section, you can create versions from **Releases**.

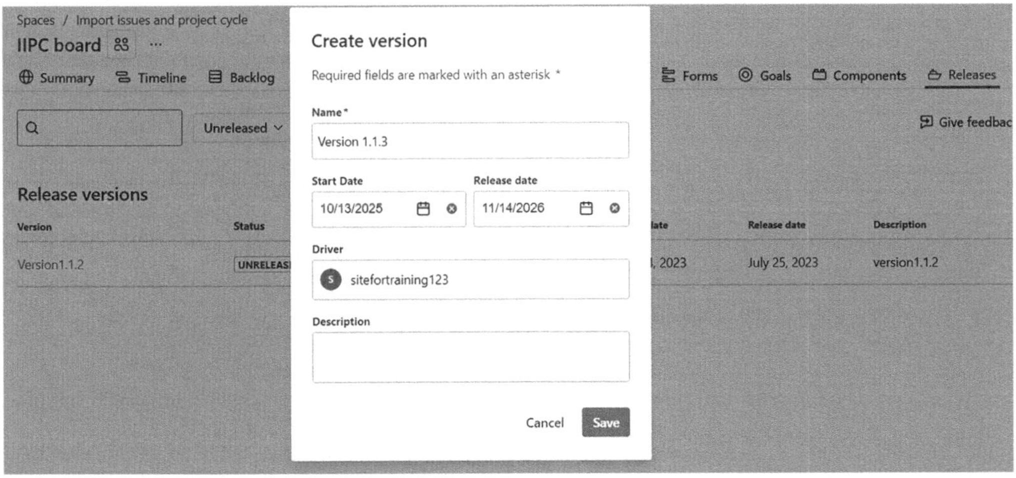

Figure 4.13: *Creating Version Window*

Product Backlog versus Sprint Backlog

Product Backlog	**Sprint Backlog**
A product backlog is a prioritized list of features, functionalities, improvements, suggestions and bugs in detail	It is a complete list of work items to be taken up in a sprint
It evolves continuously and is maintained by the product owner.	It is a detailed list which includes estimation and who will work on what details.
It provides a big picture of the product	It focuses on the small activity related to the sprint

Table 4.1: *Product Backlog versus Sprint Backlog*

Sprint Operations

In this section, we will learn about how to create a sprint, edit a sprint, reopen a sprint and delete a sprint.

Creating sprint

Sprint: It is a predefined time interval during which a scrum team does the development work. It can last from 1 week to 4-week time.

Go to the **Product Backlog** page and create a sprint as shown in the *Figure* 4.13:

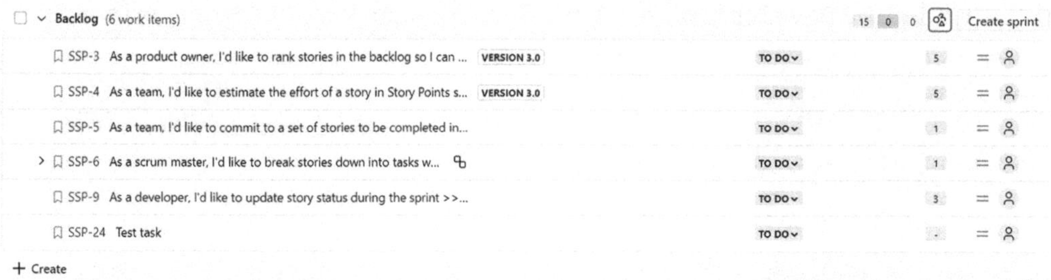

Figure 4.14: *Creating Sprint from the Backlog Page*

`Edit sprint:` Using this option, you can enter the details of the sprint.

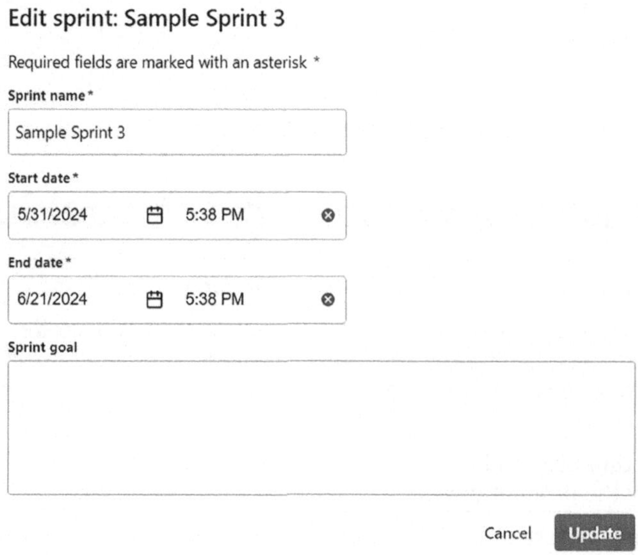

Figure 4.15: *Edit Sprint Window*

You can start the sprint once all the details are entered.

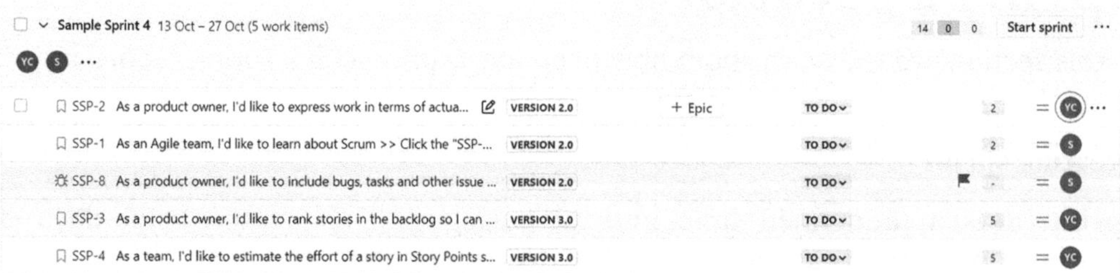

Figure 4.16: *Starting a Sprint from the Product Backlog Page*

The following figure shows the **`Delete sprint`**, **`Edit sprint`** and **`Move sprint up`** options. You can move up and down when there are two parallel sprints.

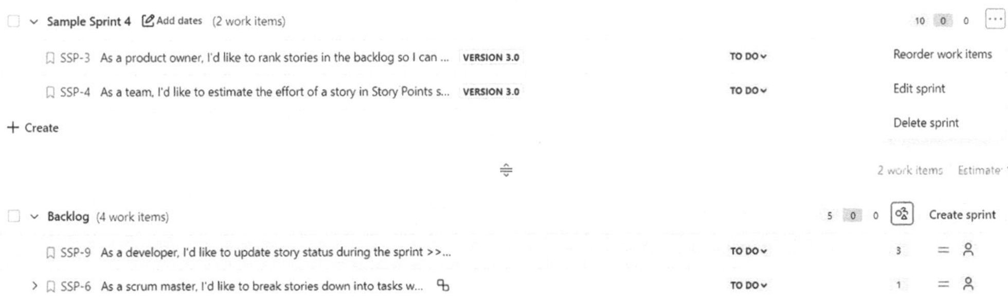

Figure 4.17: *Various Sprint Operations*

Creating and Customizing Scrum and Kanban Boards

Boards in Jira are to track the status of tasks/work items, sprint. It is a simple and detailed representation of the status whether it is in Open, InProgress or Done status. There are two types of boards - scrum board and Kanban board. These boards can also be customized so that you can sort/group work items based on set criteria. In the next section, we will learn about how to customize the board in Jira for a company-managed space.

Customizing Scrum Board

In Jira, by configuring the boards you can do general settings, set swim lanes, set card colors, set filters, set the option for timeline view and map the workflow status with board columns.

To configure the boards, you must be either a space administrator or a board administrator.

The board offers the following customization options:

- General Settings and Filter
- Column Management
- Swim lanes
- Quick filters
- Card colors
- Card layout
- Estimation

- Working days
- Timeline
- Insights

Navigate to the board, click **`More actions`**, and then select **`Board settings`** to customize it.

General Settings and Filter:

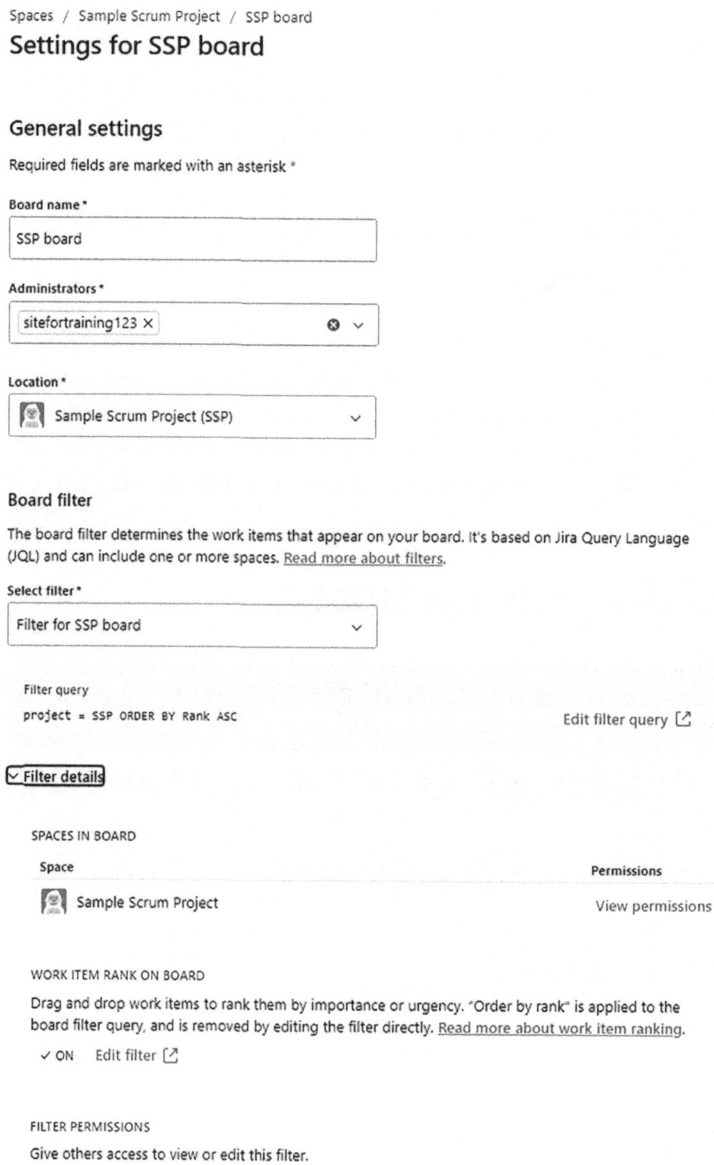

Figure 4.18: *General Board Settings*

You can rename a board by editing its name as needed.

By default, the person who creates a board becomes its administrator. If you are a board administrator or a Jira administrator, you can also update the board's administrators.

Enabling ranking allows you to reorder work items on a board using drag-and-drop and create sprints on Scrum boards. Ranking helps organize tasks by arranging them in order of importance or urgency.

To create a board that shows only the work items based on criteria, you can create a board work item filter based on a JQL query. For example, you may create a board that includes work items from multiple spaces, one space or a particular component of a space.

Columns: Columns are mapped to the statuses of the workflow and they can be added, removed and reordered. Minimum and maximum constraints based on work item count can be set for each column.

In the board view, if column limits are broken, the column header changes color:

- **Red** color indicates too many work items (limit exceeded).
- **Yellow** color indicates not enough work items (below minimum).

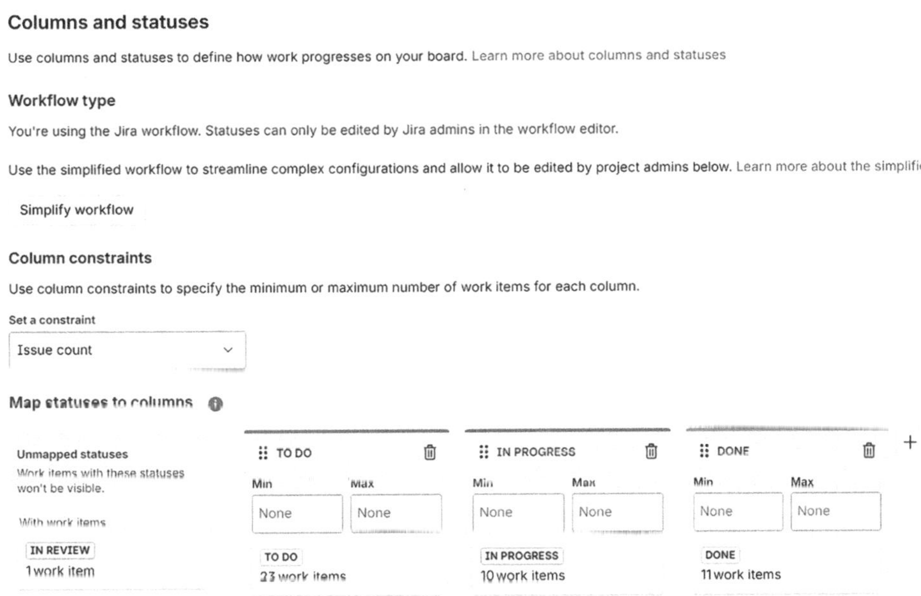

Figure 4.19: *Column Management on Board*

As shown in *Figure* 4.19, the columns display work item counts aligned with the constraints defined in the board settings. Users have the flexibility to incorporate columns onto the board according to the defined process workflow. In this example, the **IN REVIEW** status is not currently mapped. To address this, you can include an **In Review** column, as shown.

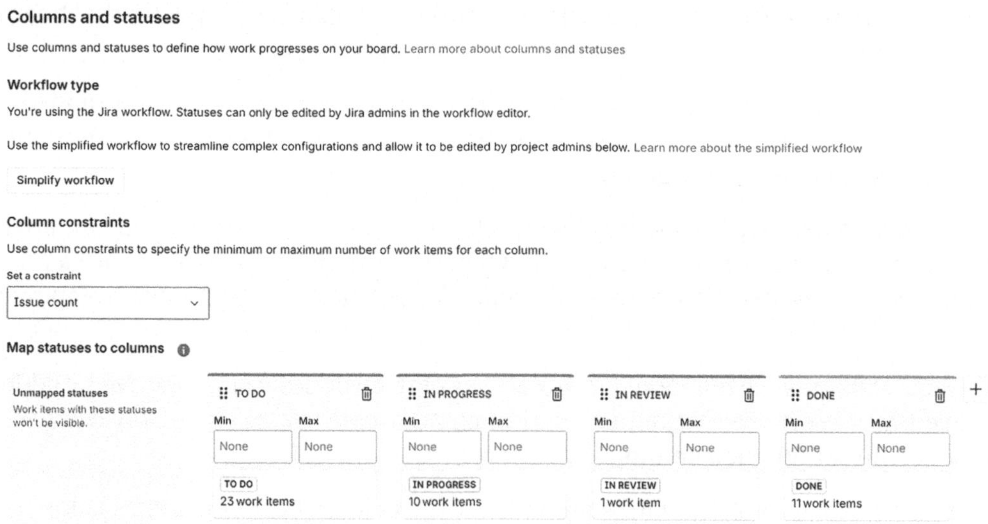

Figure 4.20: *Adding Column in Review on Board*

Swim lanes: It is a row on the board to group the work items. The criteria to sort could be **Assignees**, **Epics**, **Stories**, Spaces or **Queries**.

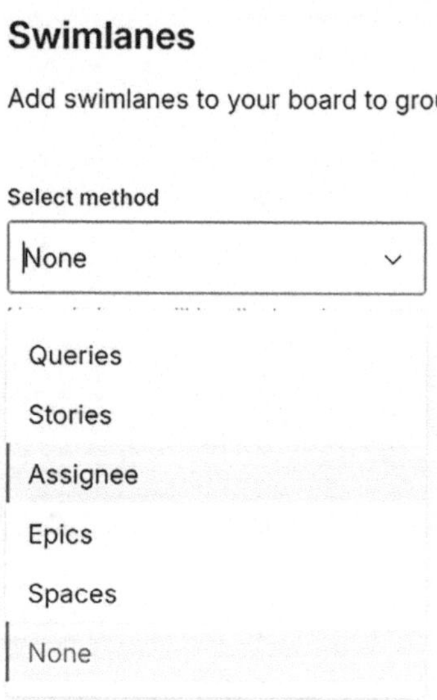

Figure 4.21: *Options for Swimlanes*

As illustrated in *Figure* 4.21, swim lanes have been configured based on the assignee. Users have the flexibility to switch between work items assigned to different team members.

Figure 4.22: *Swimlanes Example*

Quick Filters: It can be used to filter the work items further based on added JQL query.

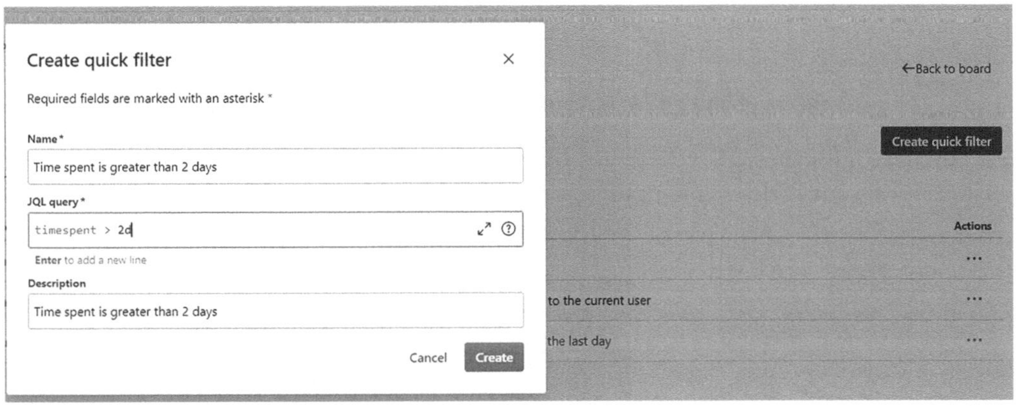

Figure 4.23: *Adding Quick Filters on the Board*

Card Colors: Card colors can be selected based on **`work item types`**, **`Priority`**, **`Assignees`**, and **`Queries`**. You can also set it as **`None`**. The card colors will change based on the methods selected.

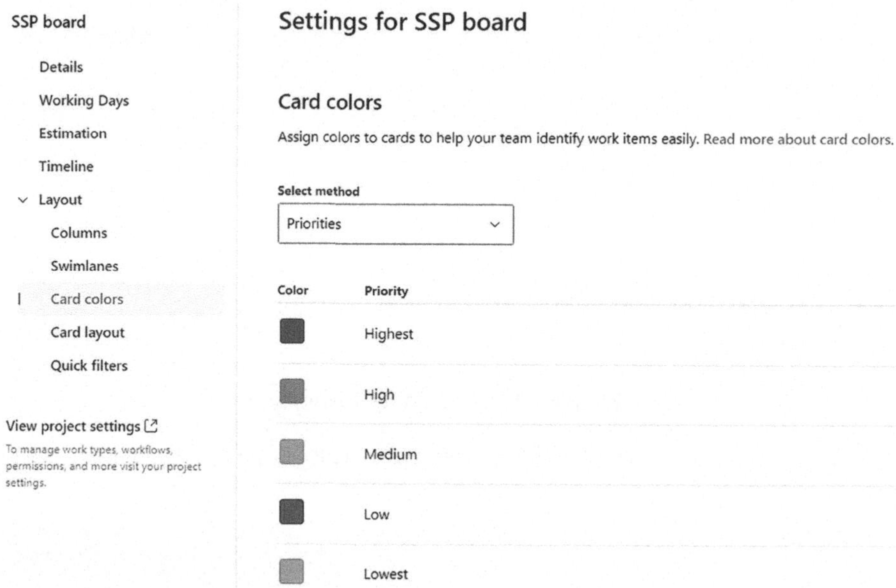

Figure 4.24: *Methods for Adding Card Colors*

As shown in *Figure* 4.24, when configuring card colors based on **`Priority`**, five distinct colors are evident, which represent the five distinct priorities.

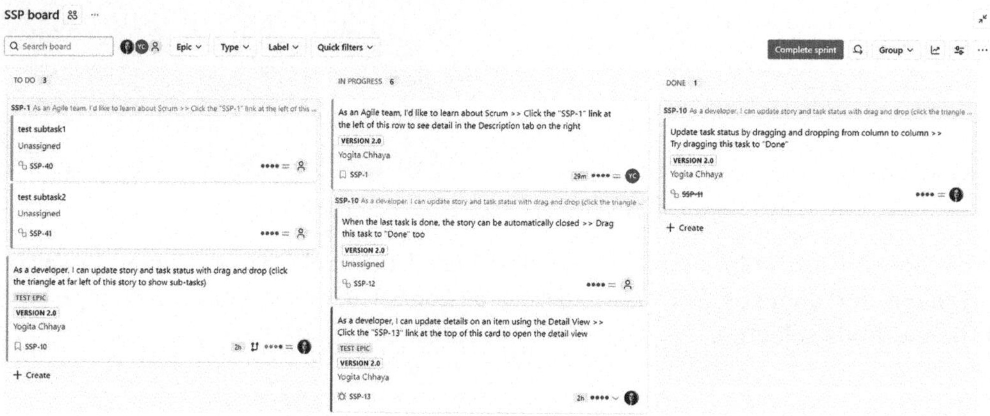

Figure 4.25: *Card Colors Based on Priority*

Card Layout: Cards can be configured to show additional fields on the backlog and active sprints pages. For example, if you want to see the version of the work item you can select it for **`Backlog`** and **`Active sprints`** pages. You can also identify slow-moving work items based on the no. of days spent in the column which can be enabled as shown in *Figure* 4.26.

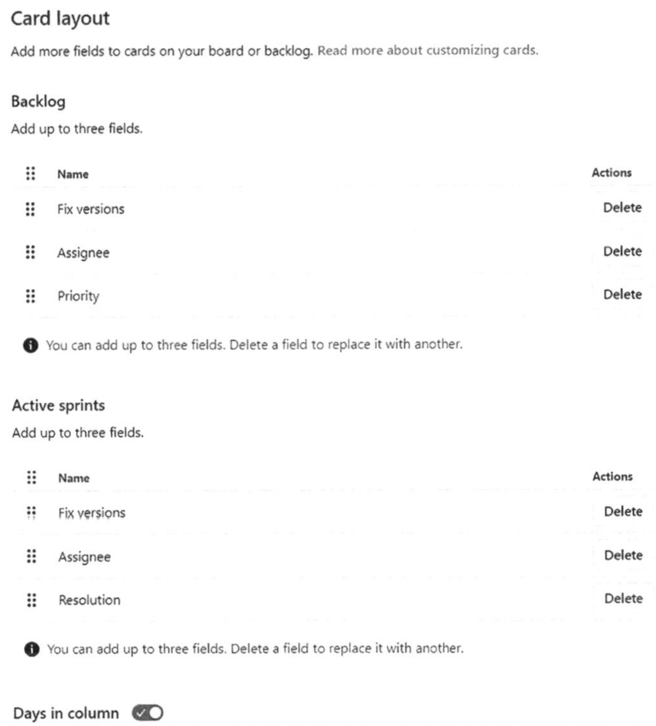

Figure 4.26: *Configuring Card Layout on the Board*

In this example, we have configured the **`Priority`**, **`Assignee`**, and **`Fix Versions`** fields for the backlog view. This setup is visible in *Figure* 4.27, showcasing how **`Resolution`**, **`Assignee`** and **`Fix Version`** fields are prominently displayed on each individual work item.

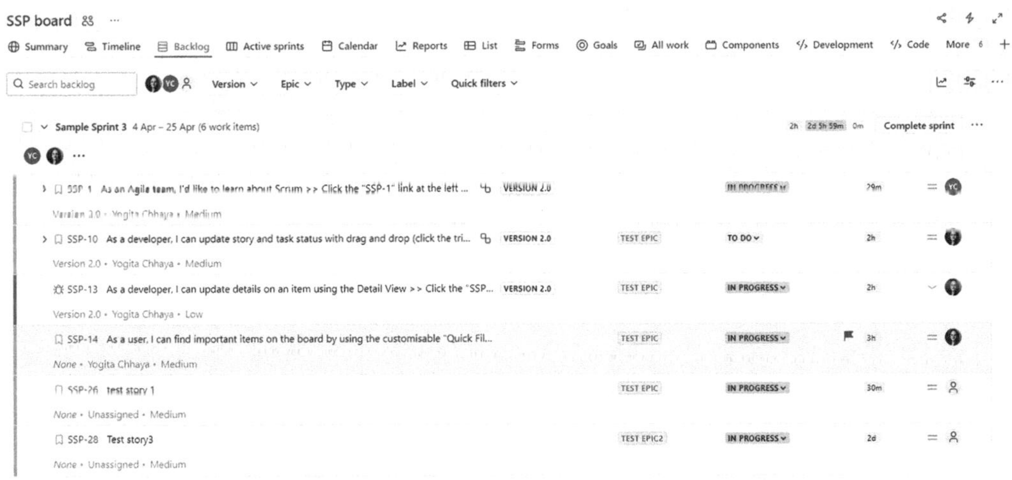

Figure 4.27: *Backlog Page Using Card Layout on the Board*

We have selected the **`Resolution`**, **`Assignee`**, and **`Fix Version`** fields for the active sprints view. This can be viewed in *Figure* 4.28 as well, illustrating how the chosen fields—**`Resolution`**, **`Assignee`**, and **`Fix Version`**—are shown on each work item, aligned with the selections made in the board settings.

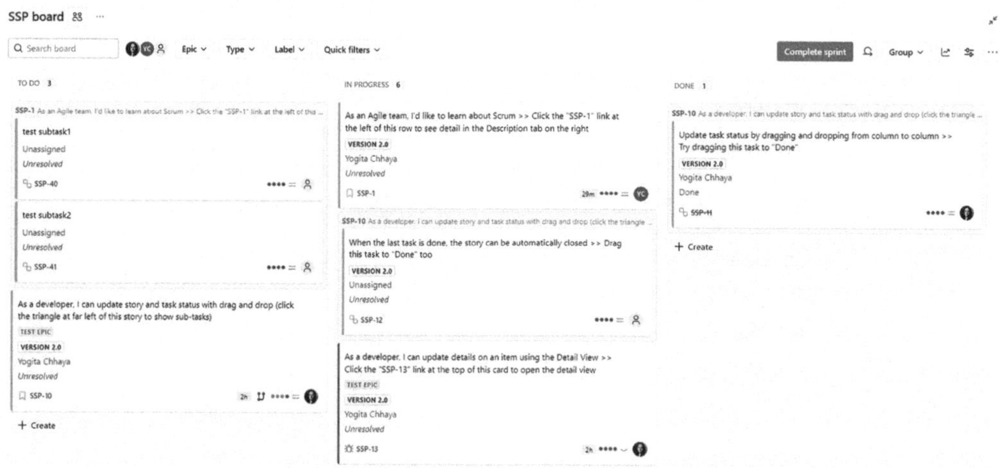

Figure 4.28: *Scrum Board Using Card Layout on the Board*

Estimation: You can set the estimation criteria based on story points, original time estimate, and work item count. The velocity will be calculated based on these criteria.

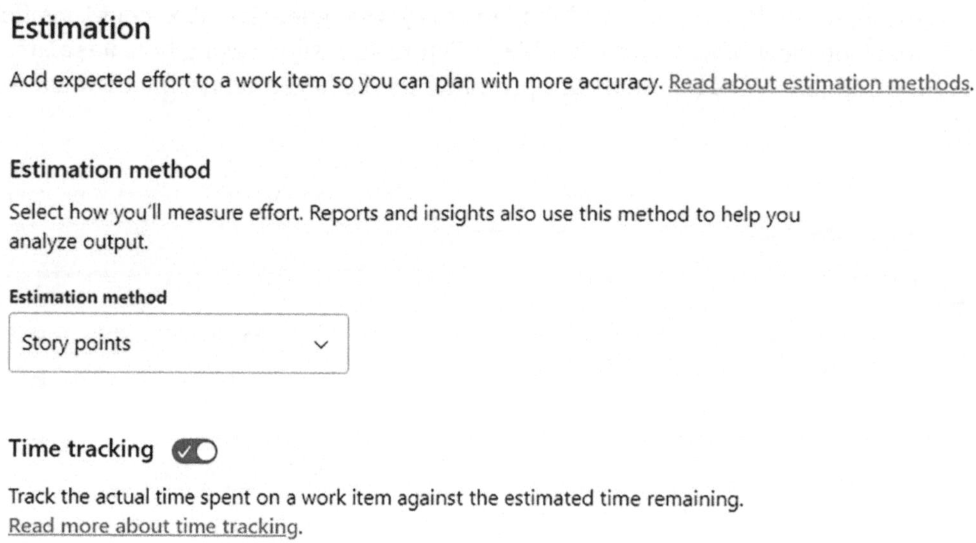

Figure 4.29: *Setting the Estimation Technique*

Working Days: You can set the **`Region`**, **`Time zone`**, **`working days`**, and **`non-working dates`** from this setting.

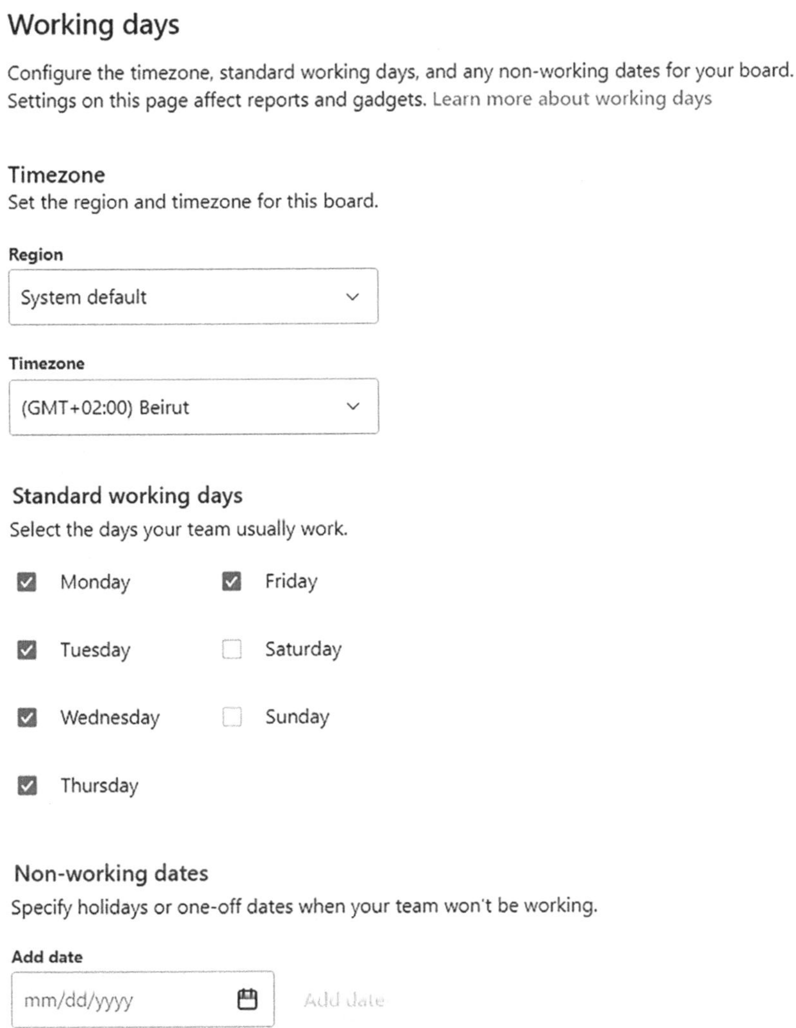

Figure 4.30: *Setting Working/Non-Working Days on the Board*

Timeline: You can enable the **`Timeline`** and set child level work item scheduling from this setting. From the timeline page, you can create, manage and visualize the epics, track the team's progress and map dependencies.

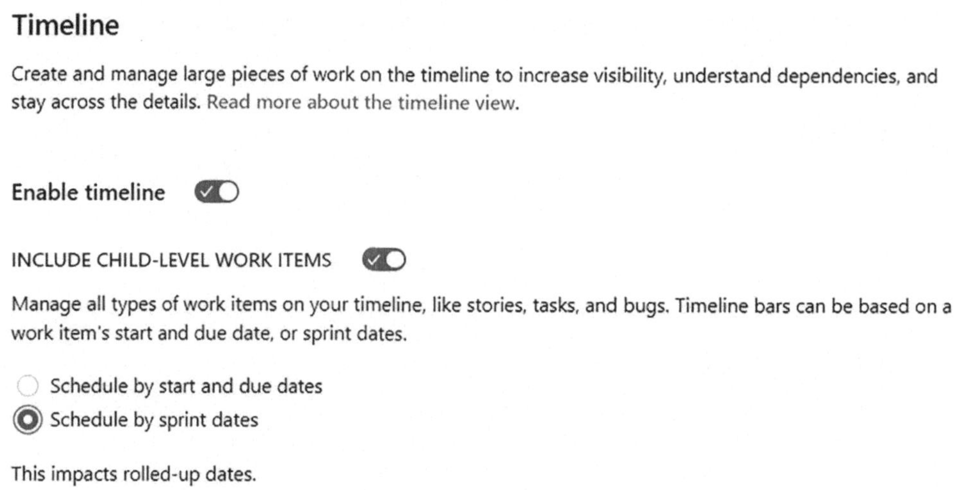

Figure 4.31: *Enabling Timeline Settings from Board Configuration*

Through the activation of the timeline feature in Jira, teams can plan their tasks using the timeline view, create and schedule both parent and child work items, and define interdependencies. Enabling work item-linking is a prerequisite for utilizing the dependencies feature.

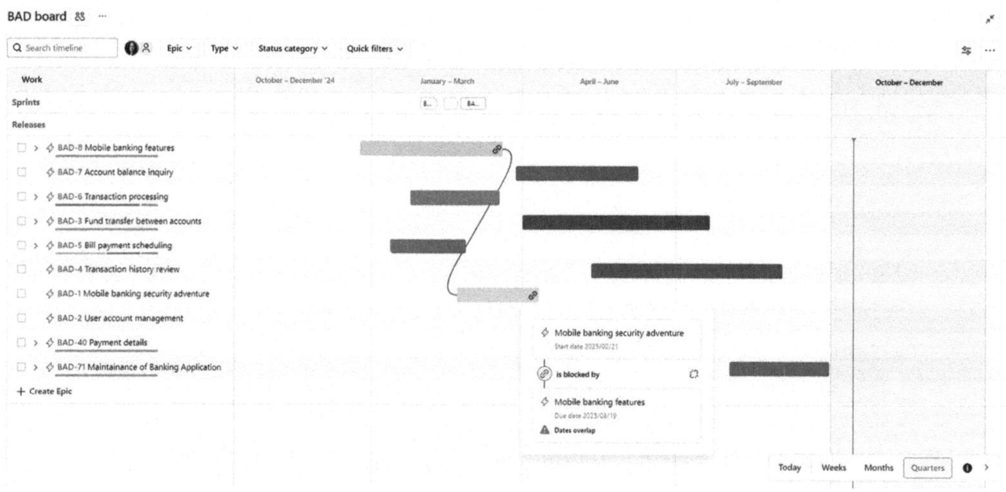

Figure 4.32: *Time Line View in Scrum Space*

Insights: The **`Insights`** button is located in the top-right corner of the Backlog and Board views. By clicking it, you can view different data that will help you plan and track your work. Users can access various parameters, such as work items requiring attention(for example, due in the current sprint, stuck, blocked, flagged), **`Sprint progress`**, and **`Epic progress`**, as shown in *Figure* 4.33. This capability helps the Scrum Master and the team in making informed decisions guided by data-driven insights on the board.

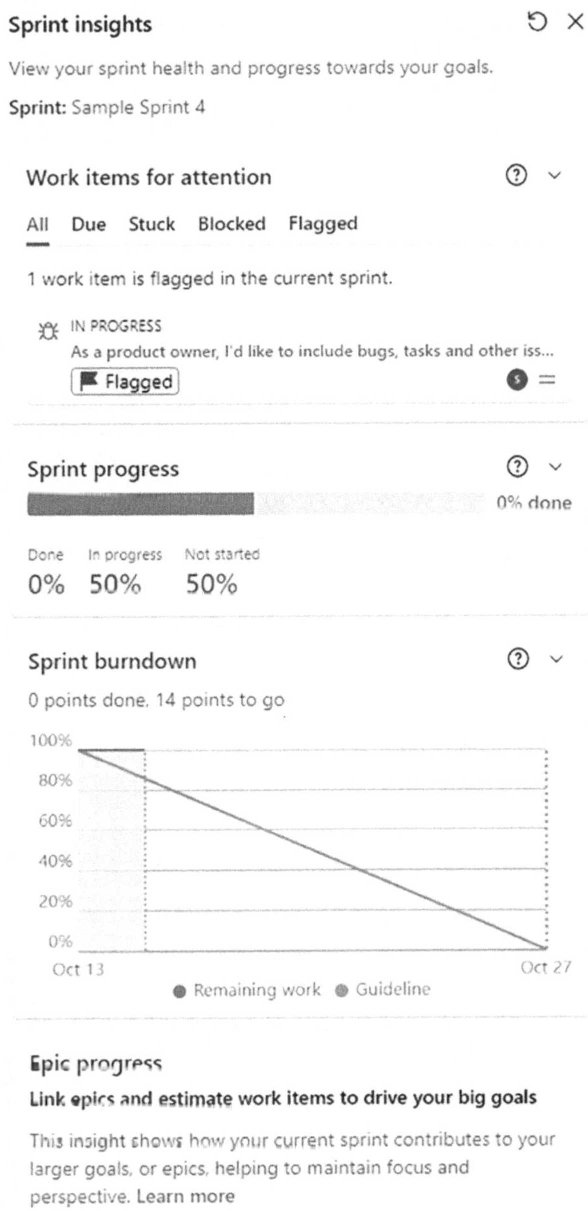

Figure 4.33: *Insights Feature on the Board*

Jira also provides insights in the backlog view. These include details such as how much work is planned for a sprint and the types of work items in it. Such information helps teams plan the next sprint better by learning from past work and deciding where to put more effort. For example, work item type breakdown shows whether the team is working only on bugs or defects.

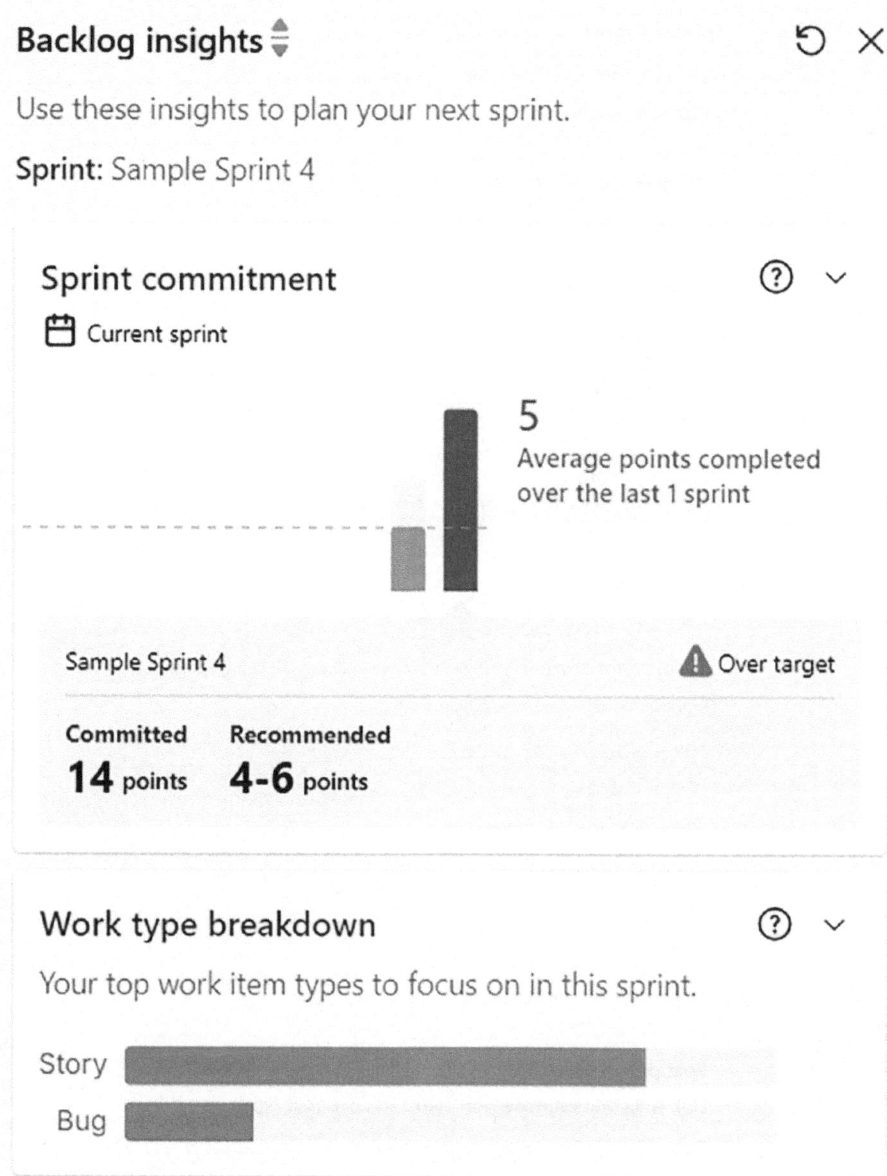

Figure 4.34: *Insights Feature on the Backlog View*

View Settings on Backlog and Board

`View settings` apply only to a specific user. Any changes you make will only affect your own board and backlog, not those of other team members.

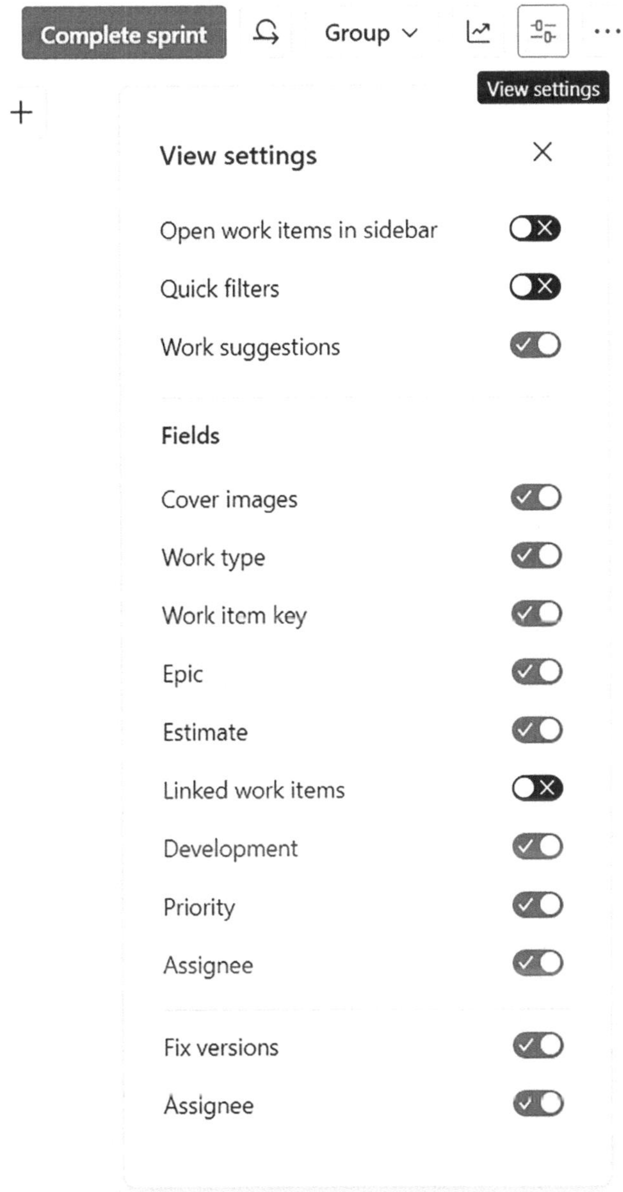

Figure 4.35: *View Settings on Backlog*

Since boards and backlogs are where the work of your team takes place, it can sometimes be difficult to manage so many work items as they can quickly become crowded. View settings help you create a more streamlined and personalized workspace by displaying only the information you need. You can choose the toggles to open work items in the sidebar, view quick filters, work suggestions and select your preferred fields(For example- **`Priority`**, **`Assignee`**, **`Fix Versions`** and more).

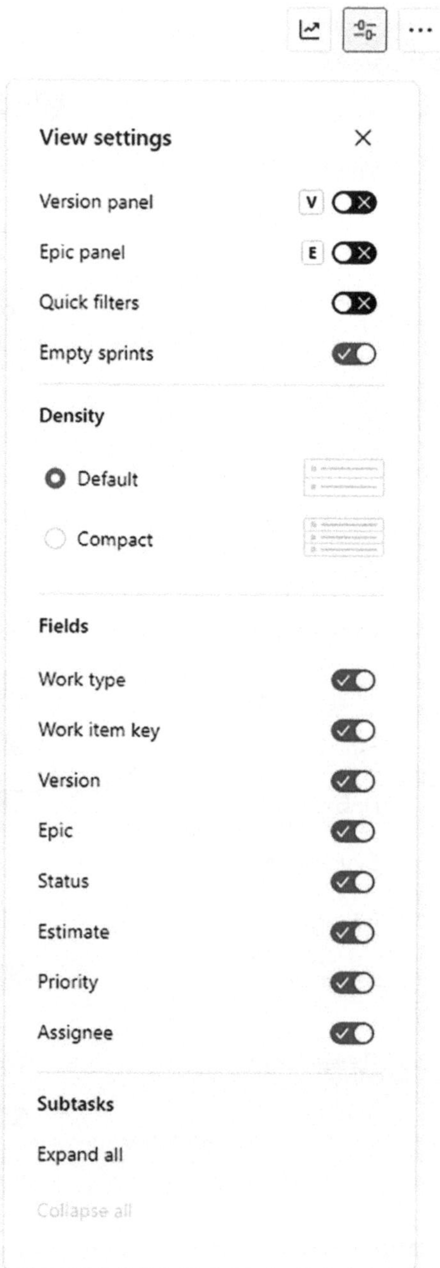

Figure 4.36: *View Settings on the Board*

While on the board, you can enable the epic and version panels to plan future work, use quick filters for faster navigation and select which work item fields are most relevant to you. You can also adjust the density to control how many work items are displayed, allowing you to make the view more compact if needed.

Customizing Kanban Board

From the customization perspective, Scrum and Kanban boards have similar features. All the features which are discussed in customizing the scrum board are applicable to the Kanban board. We will discuss the difference between scrum and Kanban boards in the next section.

Scrum Board versus Kanban Board

The differences between Scrum and Kanban boards in Jira are listed in the following table:

	Scrum board	**Kanban board**
Planning	The work item created goes to the product backlog. Then after entering the details about estimation, priority, and so on, it goes to the 1st. sprint.	Each and every work item entered goes to the backlog column.
Sprints	The board view is for sprints and the work items in the active sprints appear on the board.	In Kanban, there are no sprints and all the work items entered appear on the board.
Commitment and priority	The team commits to completing a set of user stories within the sprint.	No commitment to specific items; priorities can change at any time.
Columns	Columns represent stages like "To Do," "In Progress," "Testing," and "Done." Any change in the workflow has to be reflected on the board by mapping the columns appropriately.	It is simpler to map the columns on Kanban Board.
Reports	There are many reports such as Burndown reports, Burn-up reports, Velocity reports and many more.	It also has similar kinds of reports. One of the important reports in Kanban is the Control chart.
Maintaining and updating Boards	It is a little demanding to maintain as there are time estimates involved.	Kanban boards are easier to maintain comparatively

Table 4.2: *Scrum Board versus Kanban Board*

Both Scrum and Kanban boards in Jira serve different purposes and cater to different team preferences and project management approaches. The choice between them depends on the requirements of the team and the nature of the project.

Conclusion

We are now familiar with how to create a work item, various ways to create work items and product backlog, Product backlog refining, and creating Epics, versions, stories, tasks, sprints and sprint operations. We also understood about creating scrum/Kanban boards and customizing boards.

By learning these skills, teams can manage their work more effectively, prioritize tasks based on business value and make collaboration easier. The backlog and boards of Jira not only support Agile practices but also help in delivering results.

In the next chapter, we will learn about work types and work type schemes.

Points to Remember

- **Backlog Management**
  - Writing correct user stories and including all the details is crucial.
  - If necessary, user stories can be split into multiple tasks.
  - Ensure that all work items are planned, estimated, and completed according to the plan.
  - Estimation is done considering time, complexity, risk, and required effort.
  - Prioritize the stories that offer the highest business value to the customer and then only take it for development.
  - If you are uncertain about the details of user stories, ask the product owners for clarification.
  - Group the stories in an epic to organize and track them.
  - You can add new tasks, user stories, bugs, and features to the backlog based on changes in requirements and feedback received. This way, the backlog is a continuously evolving artifact.
- **Sprint Operations**
  - Once all the tasks are estimated and included in the sprint, plan the sprint for a duration of 2-4 weeks.
  - Conduct daily stand-up meetings to plan daily work and address impediments with the help of the Scrum Master.
  - Hold sprint planning and sprint review meetings to plan and review the work.
  - At the end of each sprint, conduct a review meeting to demonstrate the completed work to stakeholders. Follow it up with a retrospective to identify areas for improvement in the next sprint.

- **Boards in Jira**
  - Use Kanban boards if you want to keep work flowing continuously. With the Kanban way of working, new tasks are taken up as soon as there's space for them.
  - Use Scrum boards if your team works in fixed-length sprints. Scrum boards show the progress of each sprint on the board.
  - Make sure to customize the boards to match the workflow of your team. You can have stages like "To Do," "In Progress," "Review," and "Done."
  - To organize and see the backlog items better, use filters and swim lanes. You can sort tasks based on who's working on them, their importance, or other criteria.
  - Keep the boards always up-to-date. Team members should regularly update the status of their tasks. This way, everyone can see how things are going and if there are any work items.

Use Cases with Reference Links

1. **How to hide sub-tasks on Kanban Board:** To hide the sub-tasks on Kanban board, you can formulate a JQL (Jira Query Language) query that encompasses all work types except for the 'sub-task' work type within your space.

   https://community.atlassian.com/t5/Jira-Software-questions/Subtasks-on-kanban-board/qaq-p/2323195

2. **Can I use both kinds of boards (Kanban, Scrum)**: Users have the capability to create both Scrum and Kanban boards within a single space. With a Scrum board, the option to generate sprints is available, whereas a Kanban board does not offer the ability to create sprints for work planning.

   https://community.atlassian.com/t5/Jira-questions/Can-I-use-both-kinds-of-boards-Kanban-Scrum/qaq-p/2019485

3. **Can I convert the created Kanban Board to Scrum Board**: The kanban board cannot be directly converted into a scrum board. You have to create a new scrum board.

   https://community.atlassian.com/t5/Jira-Software-questions/Kanban-board-to-scrum-Board/qaq-p/2187868

4. **When the story moves to the next sprint, the story presents two sprints:** When a story moves to the next sprint, it can be searched by using a function called opensprints().

https://community.atlassian.com/t5/Jira-Software-questions/When-the-story-move-to-next-sprint-the-story-present-two-sprints/qaq-p/2450047

5. **Spillover user story to next sprint:** When closing a sprint, Jira will prompt you to either transfer all incomplete stories to the next sprint or reassign them to the backlog. If chosen to move to the next sprint, the stories will retain their respective rankings.

   https://community.atlassian.com/t5/Jira-Software-questions/Spill-over-user-story-to-next-sprint/qaq-p/1539800

6. **How to enable sprints in Jira:** Sprint can be created when you create a scrum space.

   https://community.atlassian.com/t5/Jira-Software-questions/how-to-enable-sprints-in-our-project/qaq-p/2452632

7. **Creating boards spread across spaces:** There is an option in Jira to create a board from multiple spaces.

   https://community.atlassian.com/t5/Jira-Software-questions/Multiple-projects-sharing-sprints/qaq-p/2141167

8. **2 Jira Scrum Boards with same filter cannot start sprint on second board:**

   https://community.atlassian.com/forums/Jira-questions/2-Jira-Scrum-Boards-with-same-Filter-Cannot-start-sprint-on/qaq-p/2910736

9. **Allow anonymous view access to boards:**

   https://community.atlassian.com/forums/Jira-questions/Allow-anonymous-view-access-to-boards/qaq-p/3117892

10. **Cannot find where to edit Quick Filter on Kanban Board:**

    https://community.atlassian.com/forums/Jira-questions/Can-t-find-where-to-edit-Quick-Filter-on-Kanban-board/qaq-p/3070566

CHAPTER 5

Understanding Work Types and Work Type Schemes

Introduction

In Jira, work items are like the building blocks of project management. Work items represent different tasks, bugs, or things you want to work on. Each work item has a specific type, such as bug, task, or story, which tells you what it is about. The good thing is that you can customize these types as per your space requirements. The work type schemes of Jira are helpful to organize and manage these work types in a way that makes sense for your team. You can customize a list of tasks/work items for a particular space or multiple spaces. You can perform move work items, link work items, clone work items, and log work on work items. Furthermore, you can set up workflows, control what information to fill in, and decide who can do what with each type of work item. It is like having the ability to keep your spaces organized and running smoothly. So, with the simple and flexible system of Jira, you can manage your work easily and get things done faster.

Structure

In this chapter, we will discuss the following topics:

- Understanding Work Items
- Work Item Status, Priorities and Resolutions
- Understanding Parent and Child Work Items and Work Type Hierarchy
- Creating Work Type Hierarchy Levels
- Examples of Jira Products Work Types
- Understanding Work Types with an Example

- Configuring Work Types
- Creating Sub-Task Work Type
- Understanding Work Type Schemes
- Associating a Work Type Scheme with a Space
- Configuring Work Item Layout
- Understanding Work Item Operations
- Components
- Work Item Management Best Practices

Understanding Work Items

Work items are tasks on which the teams have to work. For example, a work item could be a task, bug, or story. Work items can be created, edited, deleted, and linked to other work items in Jira. Work items can be used to track progress, manage dependencies, and communicate about work. A work item key is a number to identify a work item within a space. All work items in the same space will have the same work item-key with different nos. For example, a work item in the Sample Scrum space has a work item-key SSP-1, SSP-2, SSP-3, and so on. Work item keys are unique and cannot be reused. This way, we can consider work items as building blocks of the space.

Work Item-Status, Priority and Resolutions

You can manage work item Statuses, Priorities and Resolutions as a Jira Administrator. In this section we have covered how to add or modify work item-status, priority and resolutions in Jira.

Work item-Status: Statuses represent the various steps within a workflow, each of which can be mapped to one of the workflow steps. A workflow has multiple statuses. Jira provides default statuses when you create a space from a space template. As a Jira Administrator, you can create, edit and delete statuses within the workflow to align with your defined processes. Jira has statuses such as **`Open`**, **`In Progress`**, **`Reopened`**, **`Resolved`**, **`Closed`**, and so on, depending on the type of spaces you have created. *Figure 5.1* shows some of the statuses along with their descriptions.

Steps to Add, Edit and Delete Statuses in Jira:

1. Log into your Jira instance with administrative privileges.
2. Navigate to the work item section by selecting gear icon and click on **`work items.`**
3. Select **`Statuses`** and click on **`Add Status/Edit`**.
4. Add the **`Name`**, **`Description`**, **`Category`** and icon **`URL`** of the image.
5. Select **`Add`**.

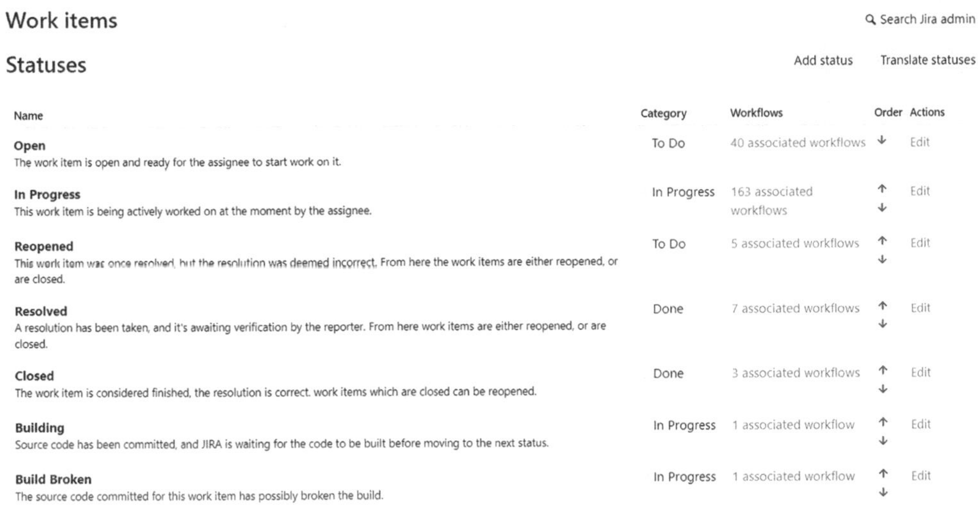

***Figure 5.1**: Work Item Statuses in Jira*

Work item-Priority: The priority of a work item reflects how important it is. Organizations can define and describe priority levels according to their needs. Jira has default priority levels: **`Lowest`**, **`Low`**, **`Medium`**, **`High`** and **`Highest.`**

Steps to add priorities in Jira:

1. Log into your Jira instance with administrative privileges.
2. Navigate to the work item section by selecting gear icon.
3. Select **`Priorities > Add Priority`**.
4. Add the **`Name`**, **`Description`** of the priority, **`URL`** of the image and priority color.
5. Select **`Add`**

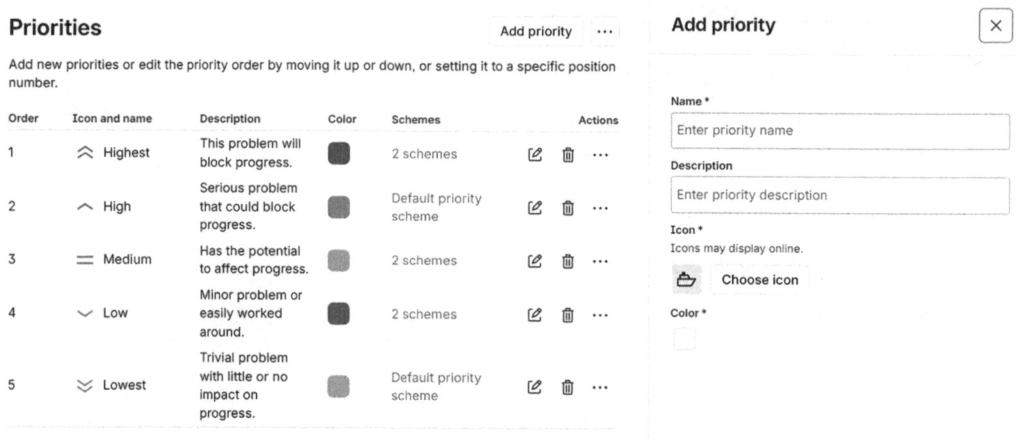

Figure 5.2*: Work Item Priorities in Jira*

Work Item-Resolutions: A work item can be considered resolved or closed in various ways. Resolutions are the available methods in which a work item can be marked as closed.

These methods include options such as **`Done`**, **`Won't fix`**, **`Duplicate`** and more.

Steps to add resolutions in Jira:

1. Log into your Jira instance with administrative privileges.
2. Navigate to the work item section by selecting gear icon and click on **`work items`**.
3. Select **`Resolutions`**.
4. Add the **`Name`** and **`Description`** of the resolutions and then select **`Add`**.

***Figure 5.3**: Work Item Resolutions in Jira*

Understanding Parent and Child Work Items and Work Type Hierarchy

Parent and child work items are used to relate bigger work items with smaller ones. For example, a story is a parent work item with some sub-tasks created under it. The sub-tasks are called child work items. Parent work items are larger or more complex work items, while child work items are smaller or less complex work items that are related to the parent work item. All work items can be a parent work item as well as a child work item. Sub-tasks cannot be created as a parent work item.

Let us understand the work type hierarchy with an example.

If the work type hierarchy is:

- Epic
- Story
- Task
- Sub-task
- Bug

Then,

- Sub-tasks can be created as child work items under any of the higher-level work items: **`Epic`**, **`Story`**, **`Bug`**, or **`Task`**.
- **`Story`**, **`Bug`**, **`task`**, and **`Sub-task`** can be created under Epic.
- **`Sub-task`** cannot be created as a parent work item, because sub-tasks are always related to a parent work item.

Creating Work Type Hierarchy Levels

Select ⚙> **`work items`**. Select **`work type`** hierarchy. By default, the **`Epic`** work type will be associated with the Epic hierarchy level (level 1). You can create new levels by selecting **`Create level`**, as shown in *Figure* 5.4. Change the level names of the work type hierarchy and save the changes. It is only possible to change and add hierarchy levels as part of Jira Cloud Premium and Enterprise.

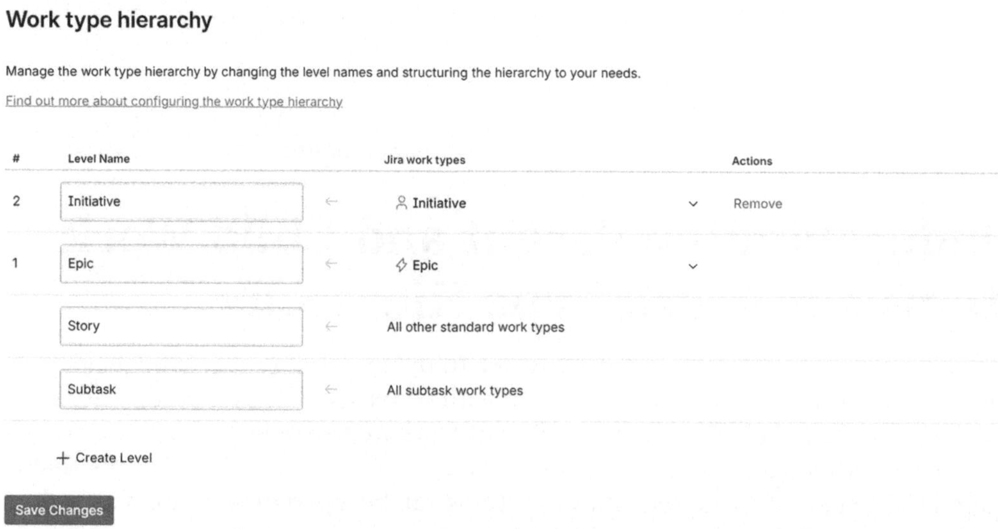

***Figure 5.4**: Understanding Work Type Hierarchy Levels*

Examples of Jira Products Work Types

In this section, we will learn about important work types in Jira and Jira Service Management. Similarly, Jira work management also has various types of work items.

Jira-Software spaces	Work Type	
	Epic	It represents a big amount of work, such as a feature It is required to break it down into smaller work types such as story, Bug, task, and so on

	Bug	It is a problem in software products, which prevents its working
	Story	A user story is the unit of work that is worked upon and completed in the same sprint
	Task	It is a piece of work that needs to be done
	Sub-task	It is a child work type that can be created under standard work types like bug, story, and task
Jira Service Management	IT help	It is a task to create a request for IT-related help
	Incident	Reporting an incident or IT service outage
	Service Request	Request to get help from the internal or external customer service team
	Service Request with Approval	Request to get help from customer service with approval from the Manager

Table 5.1: *Examples of Jira Products Work Types*

Understanding Work Types with an Example

Epic: It represents a large amount of work. It is required to break it down into smaller work types such as story, Bug, task, and so forth.

In this example, we have created a scrum space in Jira to develop an app for Banking Application. We have created an Epic-User Interface for Banking Application Development, which involves a large amount of work. *Figure* 5.5 shows various child work items, such as **`Stories`**, **`Tasks`**, and **`Bugs`**, created under the Epic. By default, an Epic in Jira has the fields like **`Assignee`**, **`reporter`**, **`story points`**, **`priority`**, and so on, and it is possible to customize the fields on the **`Epic`** screen.

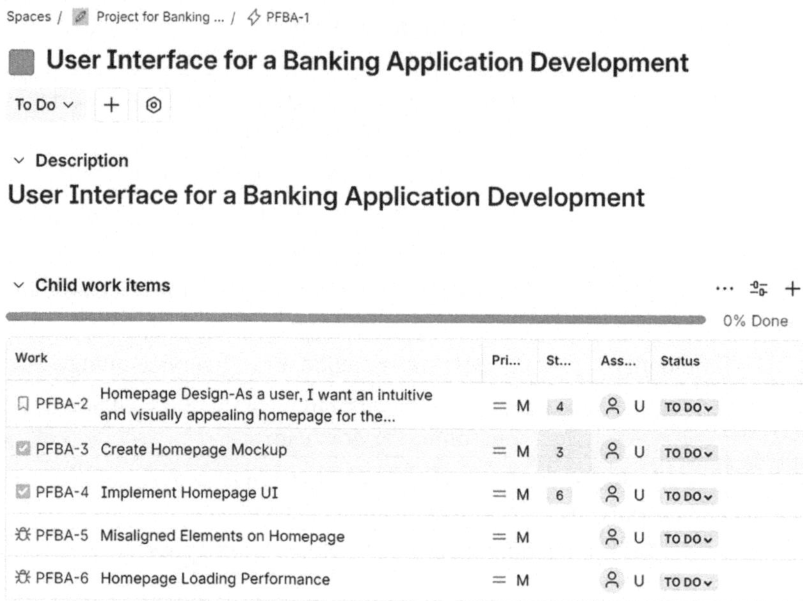

Figure 5.5: *Example of a Work Type Epic with Child Work Items*

Story: A story is a smaller task that can be completed in a single sprint. It is written in non-technical language to describe the requirements of the customer. You can create a sub-task under a story. The story has been written in a standard format and mentions the requirement as a user in the bank application. *Figure* 5.6 illustrates the creation of three sub-tasks under a story. By default, a story in Jira has fields like **`Assignee`**, **`reporter`**, **`story points`**, **`sprint`**, **`priority`**, and the like, and it is possible to customize the fields on the **`Story`**.

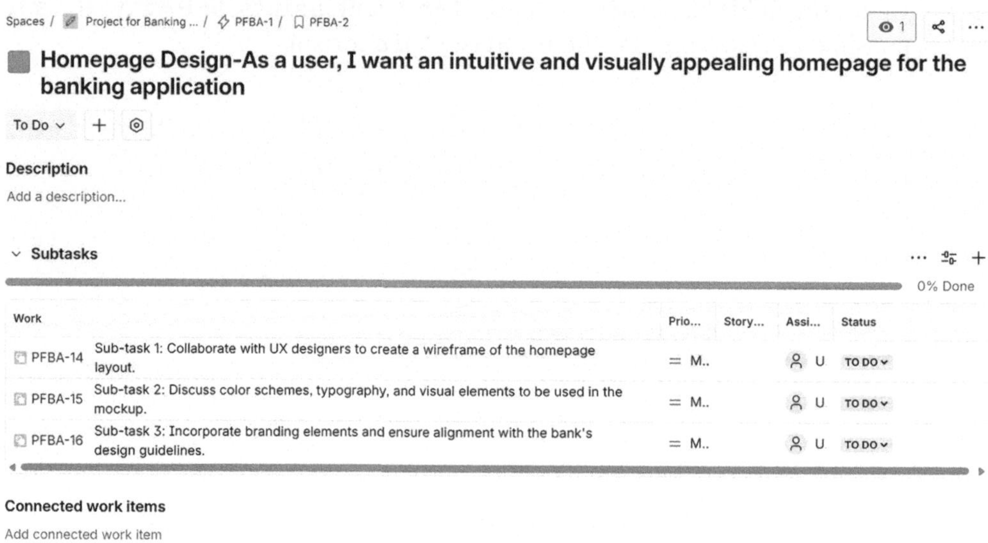

Figure 5.6: *Example of a Work Type Story with Sub-Tasks*

Bug: It is a problem within a software product that prevents its workings.

In this example, we have created a bug **`Misaligned Elements on Homepage`**. If necessary, you can also divide the bug into sub-tasks, as shown in *Figure 5.7*.

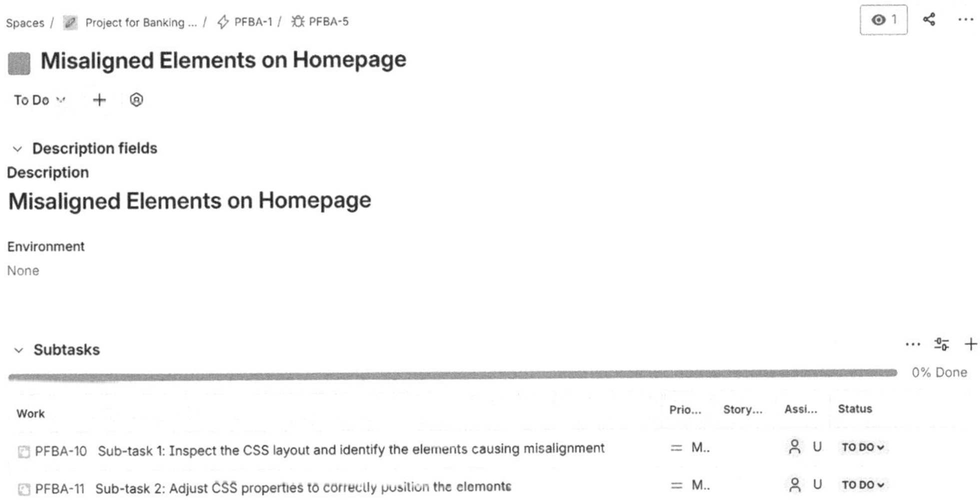

***Figure 5.7**: Example of a Work Type Bug with Sub-Tasks*

Task: It is a piece of work that needs to be done. It can be a technical or non-technical task. However, it has to be completed in the same sprint.

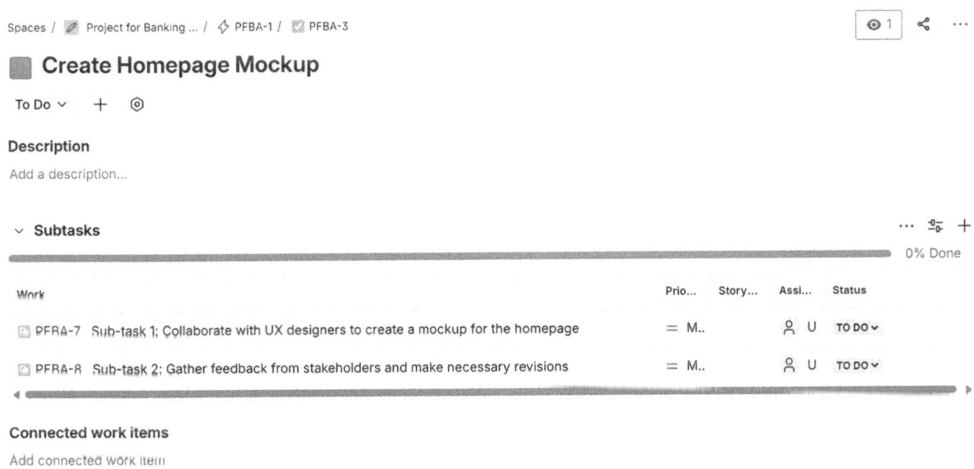

***Figure 5.8**: Example of a Work Type Task with Sub-Tasks*

Configuring Work Types

To add and Configure work types, you must be a Jira Administrator with Administer Jira permission.

Each Jira product has a predefined set of work items as per the need of your team and space requirements. In software development spaces, examples of work types include **`Bug`**, **`Story`**, and **`Tasks`**. Similarly, in IT service spaces in Jira service Management, examples of work types include IT Help, task, and service request. Upon creating a work item, you can view various options for work types.

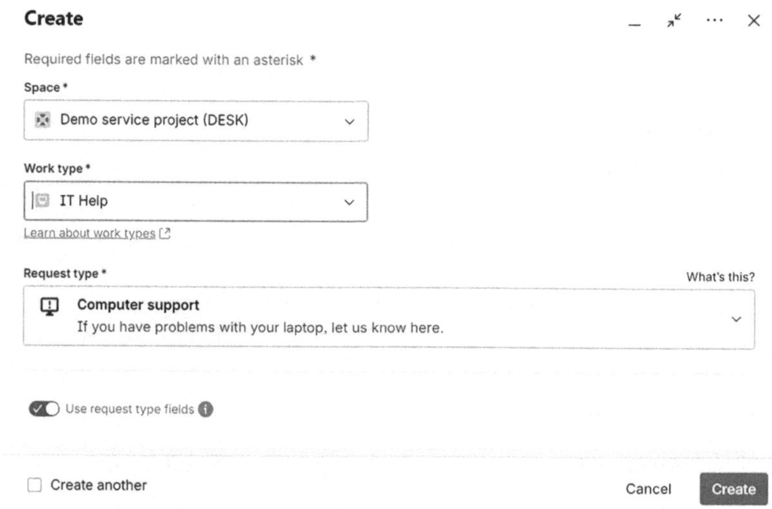

Figure 5.9: *Creating Work Items in JSM*

In *Figure* 5.10, you can view the work types: **`Bug`**, **`Story`**, **`Epic`**, and **`Task`**. These are the work types in Jira.

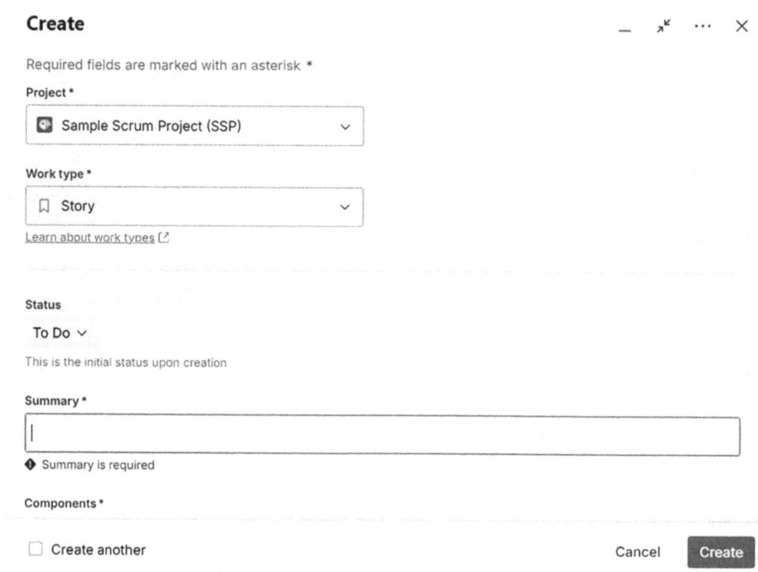

Figure 5.10: *Creating Work Items in Jira*

Steps to add a work type in Jira:

1. Select > **`work items`**. Select **`Add work type`**.

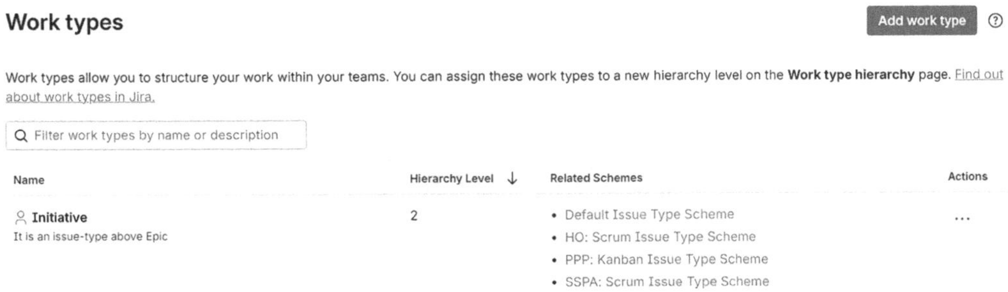

***Figure 5.11**: Step-1 of Adding New Work Types in Jira*

2. Now you can add work types as per your space requirement. For example, you can add a work type like **`Suggestion`**. Work types can be either **`Standard work type`** or **`Sub-task work types`**. Select the **`standard work type`** and then click on **`Add.`**

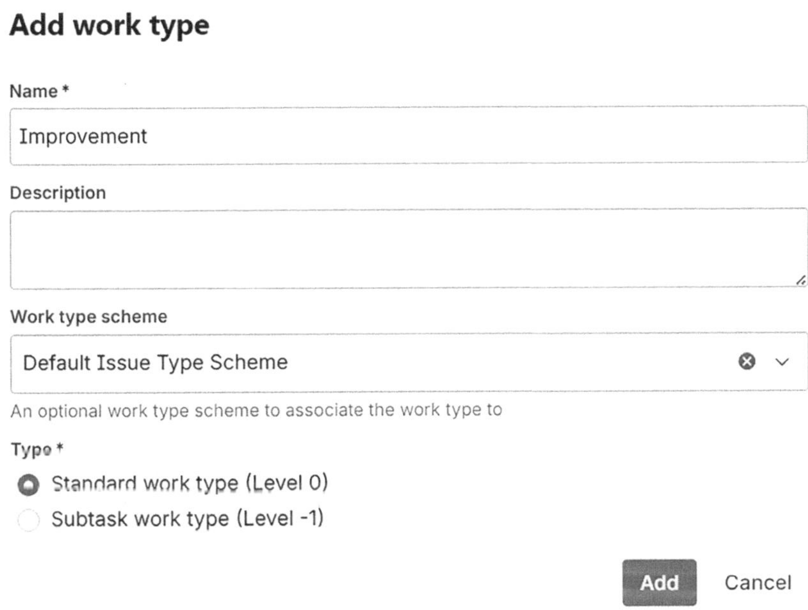

***Figure 5.12**: Step-2 of Adding New Work Types in Jira*

You can edit, delete, and translate work types as follows:

- **Editing:** By editing the work types, you can change the name of the work type, description, and avatar.

- **Deleting**: By deleting a work type, it is permanently deleted. So, make sure to change all the existing work items to other work types. Then you can delete any work type.
- **Translating**: Using this page, you can add work type translations for the installed languages. It is possible to add a name and description for the other languages.

Creating Sub-Task Work Type

Jira has a feature to create generic sub-tasks, which are usually created as a child work item. In addition, you can also customize subtask work items in Jira.

For example, a software team has to create Design, Coding, Testing, and Release tasks for each software development task. You can add all these subtasks as a sub-task work type as follows:

1. Select ⚙ > **`work items`**.
2. Select **`Sub-task`** from the left navigation bar.
3. Select **`Add sub-task work type`**.

   In this manner, you can create multiple sub-tasks under a main task, such as story or task.

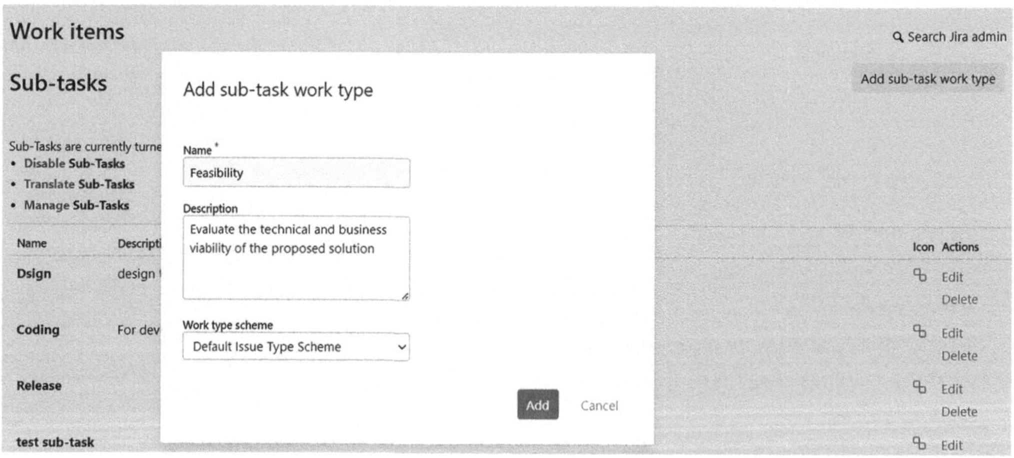

Figure 5.13: *Adding New Sub-Task Work Types in Jira*

Enabling/Disabling Sub-Task

By default, sub-tasks are enabled. You can Enable or Disable subtasks as explained in the following steps. You cannot disable subtasks if there are a few sub-tasks already created.

- Select ⚙ **`>work items`**.
- Select **`Sub-Tasks`**.
- **`Enable/Disable Sub-Tasks`**.

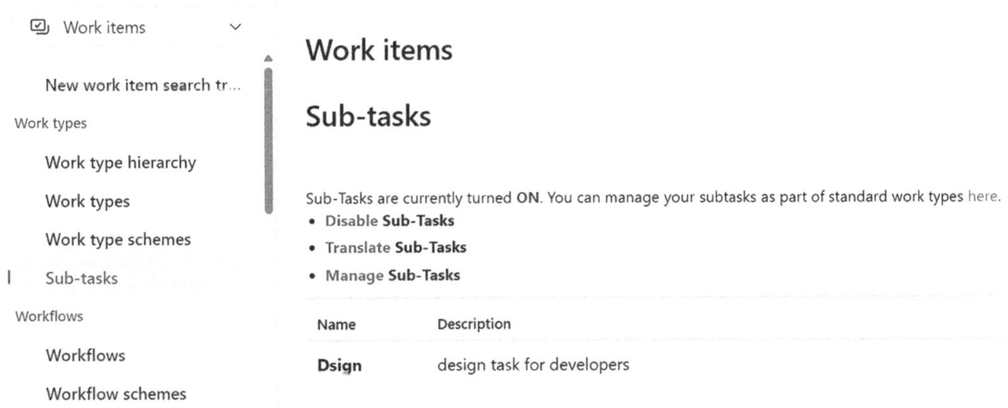

***Figure 5.14**: Enable/Disable/Manage Sub-Task Work Types in Jira*

Adding Conditions on Workflow Based on a Sub-Task Status

You can create a workflow with a condition based on the status of the sub-task. This condition can be added to the work item transition. It will not allow the parent task to be resolved until all the sub-tasks are resolved. The steps to implement this condition are as follows:

1. Select ⚙ **`>work items`**.
2. Select `Workflows`.
3. Select the workflow and go to **`Edit`**.
4. Select a transition to resolve and click **`Conditions`**.
5. Select **`Add Condition`**, **`Sub-task Blocking Condition`**, and then **`Add`** the condition.
6. Select the sub-task statuses (**`Resolved`**, **`Done`**) and then select **`Add`**.

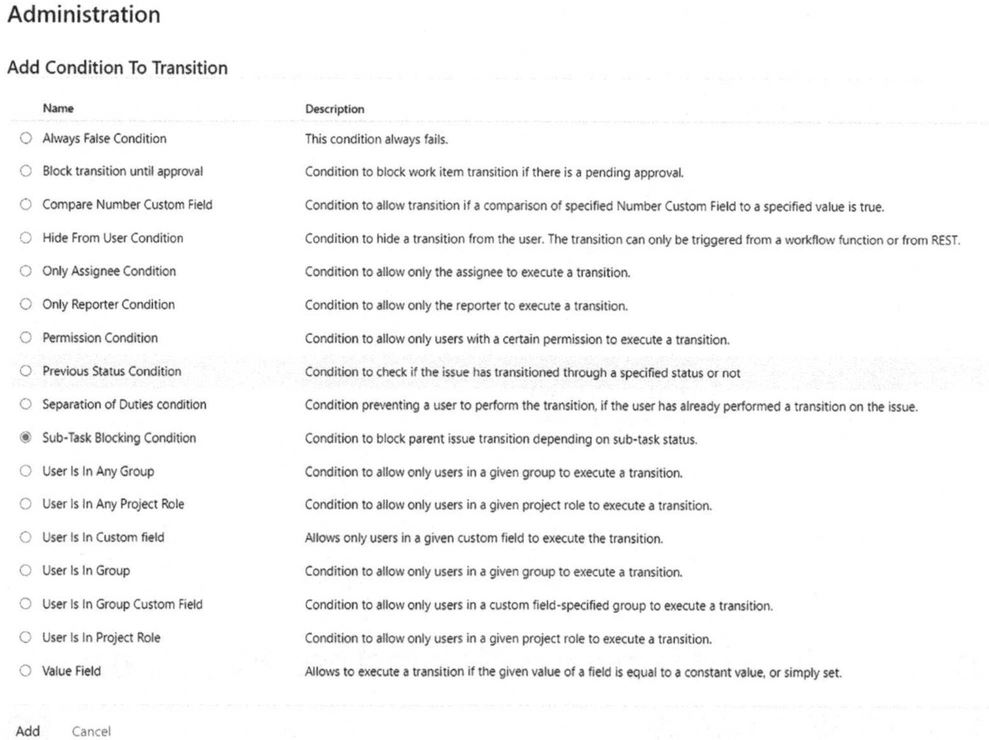

***Figure 5.15**: Adding Sub-Task Blocking Condition in Jira Workflow*

We will understand the workflows in detail in *Chapter 7, Configuring Work-Flows in Jira.*

Understanding Work Type Schemes

Work type schemes allow you to create a list of work types that are applicable to a space. This list of work types will be available while creating a work item and is referred to as a work type scheme.

The advantages are as follows:

- Select the right type of work items in a space.
- Select the default work types and set a sequence of work types while creating a work item.
- Share the same list of work types across the same type of spaces.
- Helpful to Administrators to maintain the work types with respect to spaces.

You can set up a work type scheme having a standard set of work types and then associate it with a space. Subsequently, you can also add some work types and then use the same scheme. This provides flexibility to add work types as and when it is required.

Associating a Work Type Scheme with a Space

A Jira administrator can associate a work type scheme with a space. It can also be selected by a space administrator. In the following steps, we will learn how to associate a work type scheme with a space:

1. Select ⚙ > **`work items`**.
2. Select **`work type scheme`**. And select **`Add work type Scheme`**.

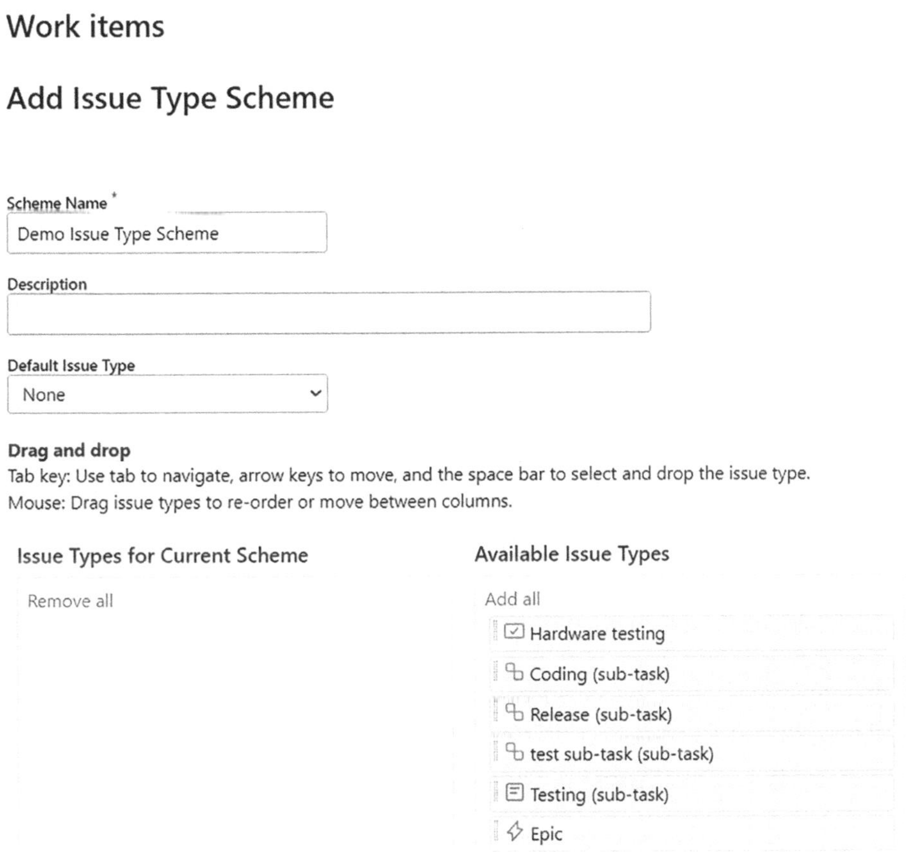

***Figure 5.16**: Creating a New Work Type Scheme*

3. You can drag and drop the available work type into the list of work types for the current scheme.
4. Select **Save**.
5. Now you are ready with the new work type scheme.

6. You can also select the default work type on this page.
7. The default work type can be seen while creating a new work item.

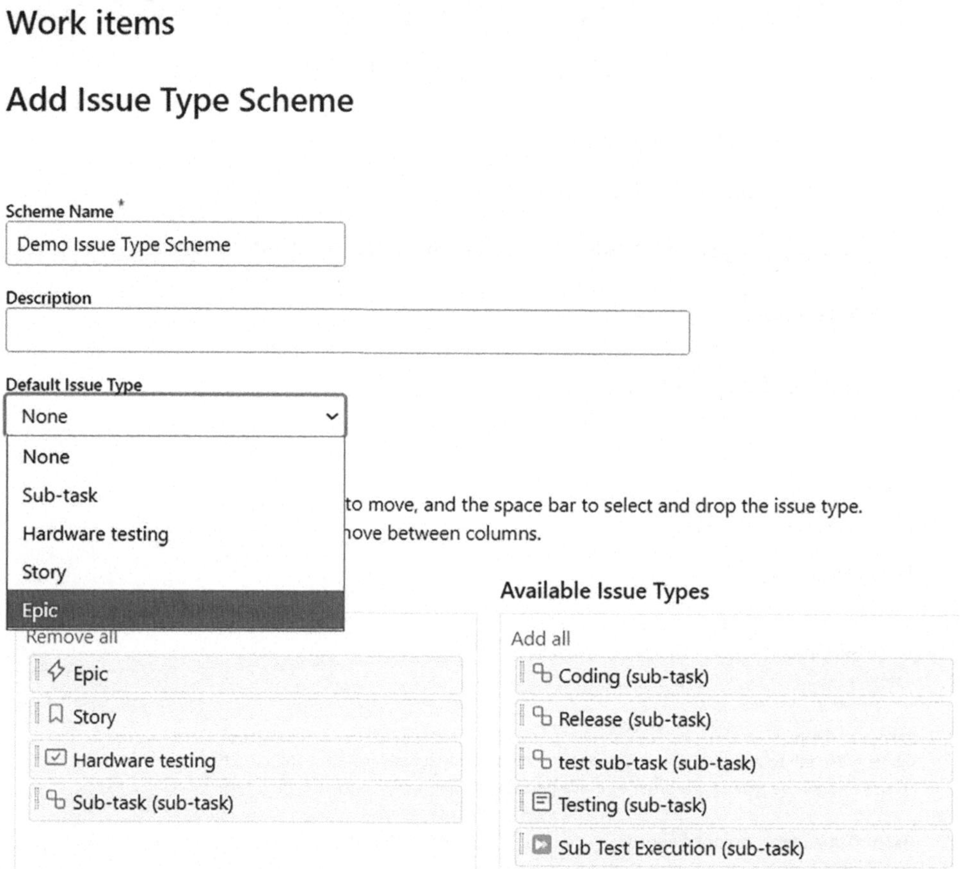

Figure 5.17: *Setting Default Work Types and Adding New Work Types in a Scheme*

Once a work type scheme is created, Jira Administrator can associate it with a space.

Steps to associate a work type scheme with a space:

1. Select > `work items`.
2. Select `work type scheme`.
3. Select **`Associate`** from the on the right-hand side.
4. Select the space from the list, as shown in *Figure* 5.18, and associate it.

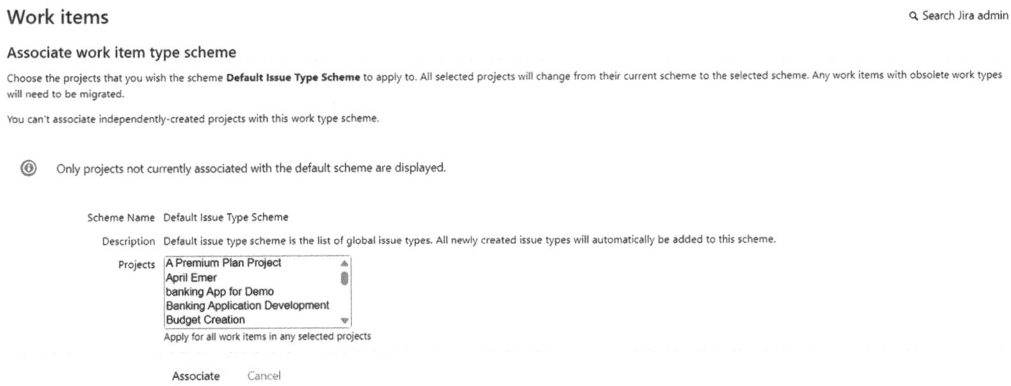

Figure 5.18: *Associating a Work Type Scheme with a Space*

Associating a Work Type Scheme from Space-Settings:

The work type scheme can also be associated with a space from the space settings, as mentioned in the following steps:

1. Select a space.
2. Select **`Space Settings`**.
3. Select **`work items`** and select **`Actions`** on the right-hand side.
4. Select use a different scheme.

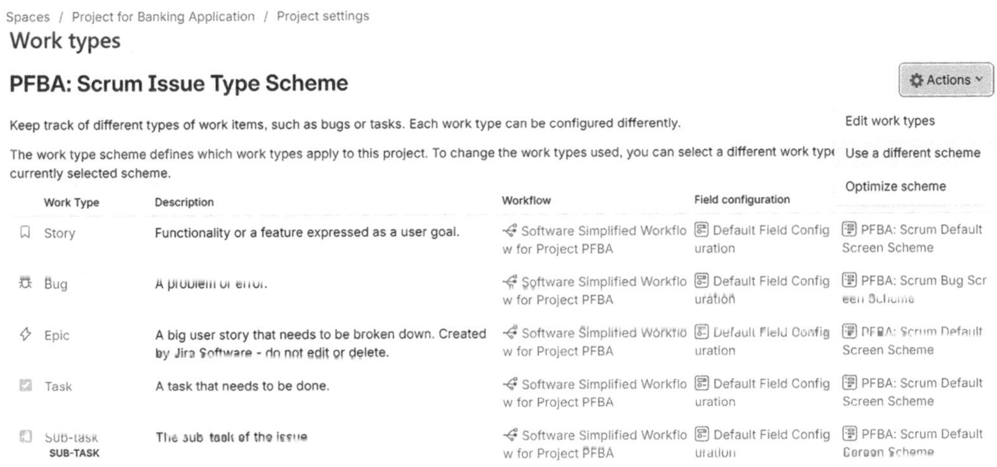

Figure 5.19: *Associating a Work Type Scheme with a Space from Space Settings*

Configuring Work Item Layout

To add or configure a work item layout, you must be a Space Administrator.

In Jira, every piece of work is represented as a work item. Each work item follows a structured layout designed to help teams stay organized. A layout is a predefined set of fields, arranged in a clear and consistent way.

At the top, you will see the summary, which provides a quick overview of the task. Just below it is the description area, where more details can be added, such as what needs to be done or why it matters. On the right-hand side, fields like assignee, reporter, and priority appear, indicating who is responsible, who created the task, and how urgent it is. You may also find fields for estimates, start dates and due dates. Together, these elements ensure that everything related to the work item is kept in one place. This simple layout makes it easy for the team to understand the work and track its progress.

Jira administrators can create new fields, while **Space Administrators** can add these fields to the relevant work item layouts. Work item layouts are unique to each space and can be set up by Space Administrators. Although layout settings can be copied to other spaces that use the same screens, they cannot be shared across different spaces.

The layout configuration consists of three main sections:

- **Description Fields:** Displayed on the left side of a work item, this is the first section users see when opening one. For this reason, the most important fields such as `Summary` and `Description` should be placed here. If the screen layout includes multiple tabs, they will also appear in this section. Only Jira administrators can configure tabs.
- **Context Fields:** Typically shown on the right side of a work item, these fields appear in the Details group if they are placed above the hide when empty divider in the configuration. Each user can also personalize their view by pinning key fields into the `Pinned fields` group. This helps quick access to the most relevant information and makes the workspace feel tailored to the user's needs.
- **Hidden Fields:** Located below the Details group, this section holds fields without values. Once a field is given a value, it automatically moves up to the `Details` group, making it part of the visible information.

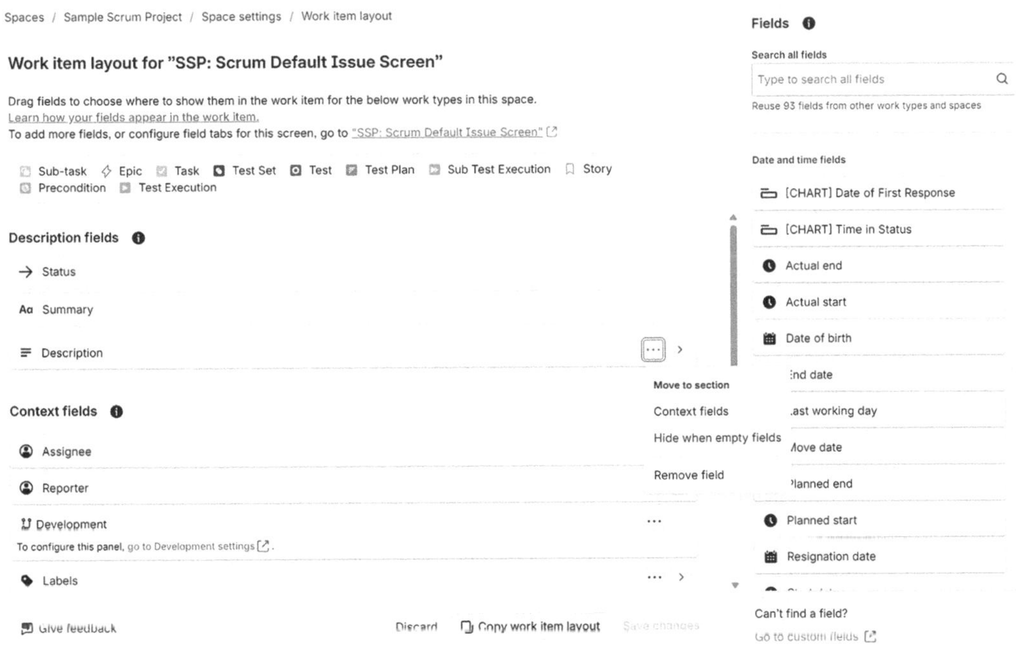

Figure 5.20: *Editing Work Item Layout*

Steps to configure a work item Layout:

1. Open a work item.
2. Select **`Configure`** below the **`More fields`** section in the work item view.
3. In the search bar, type the name of the field you want to add and press **Enter**.
4. Modify the layout by adding, removing, or dragging fields as per your requirement.
5. Once satisfied, click **Save changes** to update the layout.

You can also configure the work item layout by navigating to:

`Space > More > Space settings > Work items > Edit work item layout`.

Understanding Work Item Operations

In this section, we will learn about some basic work item operations such as work item-linking, cloning a work item, logging work on a work item, and moving a work item.

- **Work item-linking:** When creating a work item, you can define relationships between work items, such as is blocked by, is cloned by, duplicate work items, and so on.

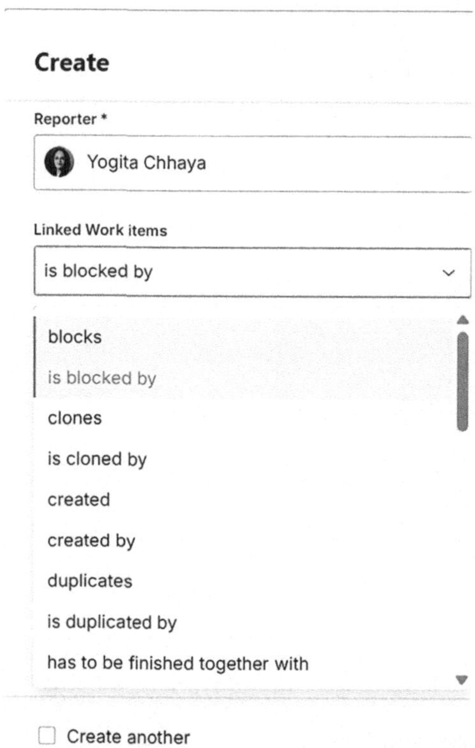

Figure 5.21: *Understanding Work Item-Linking*

- **Moving work items:** It is featured in Jira to move work items from one space to another space. Moving work items should be done only if it is required in some situations, such as work items created in the wrong space. It is better to give **`move work item permission`** to specific individuals, as moving work items randomly can create problems for everyone.

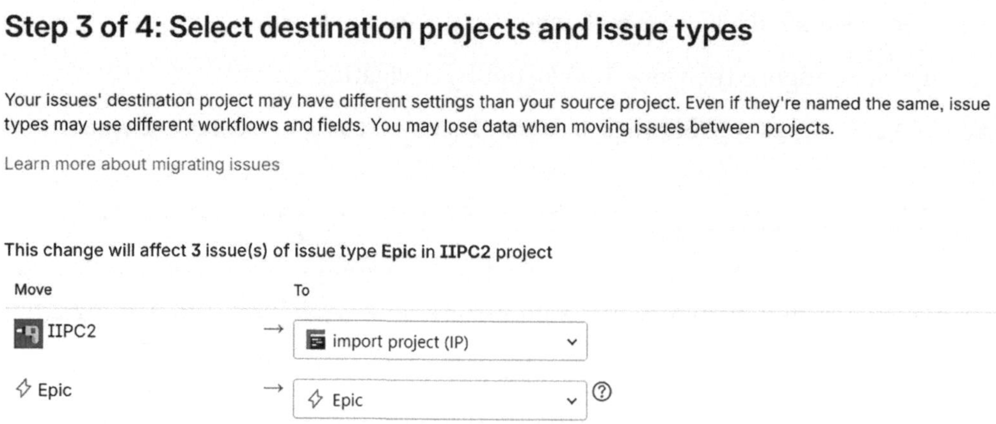

Figure 5.22: *Understanding Moving Work Items*

- **Cloning work items:** Cloning helps you to duplicate a work item within the same space, copying most information from a work item, like the **`Summary`** and **`Description`** fields and more. Cloned work items are created as separate work items from the original work item.

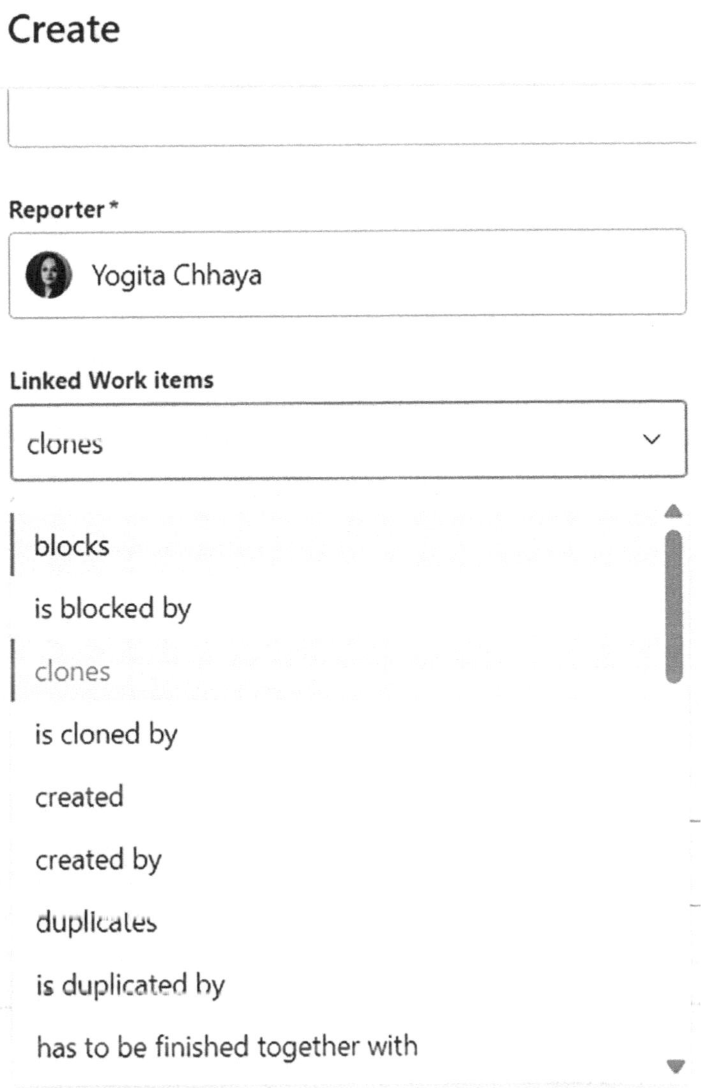

***Figure 5.23**: Understanding Cloning Work Items*

- **Logging work on work items**: As shown in *Figures* 5.24 and 5.25, you can select **`Log work`** from the ••• icon on the right-hand side. And then enter the time in a standard format (2w4d3h40m).

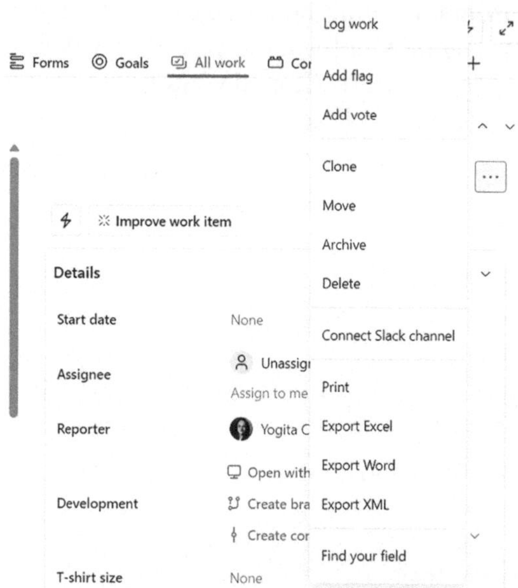

Figure 5.24: *Selecting Log Work*

After selecting **`Log work`**, as shown in *Figure* 5.25, you can enter the details.

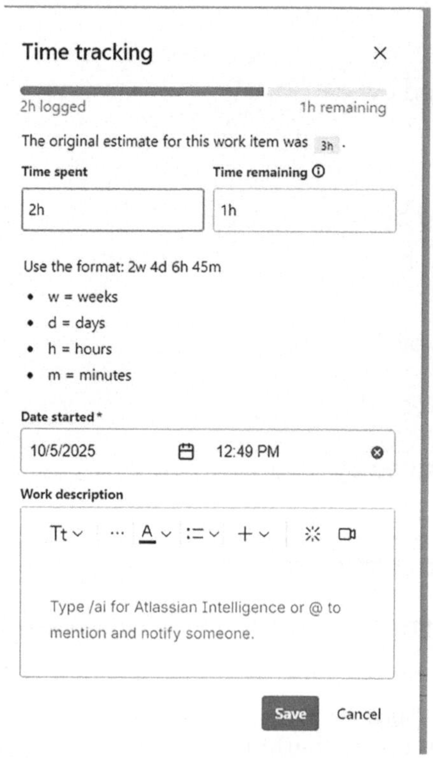

Figure 5.25: *Logging Work on Jira Work Item*

You can comment on a work item, enter an estimation, label a work item, and assign a work item to the assignee.

Components

Components are used to define sub-modules in a space. For example, for a Banking application, User Authentication, Reporting and Analytics, Mobile Banking are sub-modules. You can create components as a Jira Administrator.

To create components,

1. Navigate to space sidebar, select **`space Settings`** > **`Components.`**
2. Click on **`Create Component`**.
3. Enter the details such as **`Name, Description, Component Lead`** and **`Default Assignee.`**

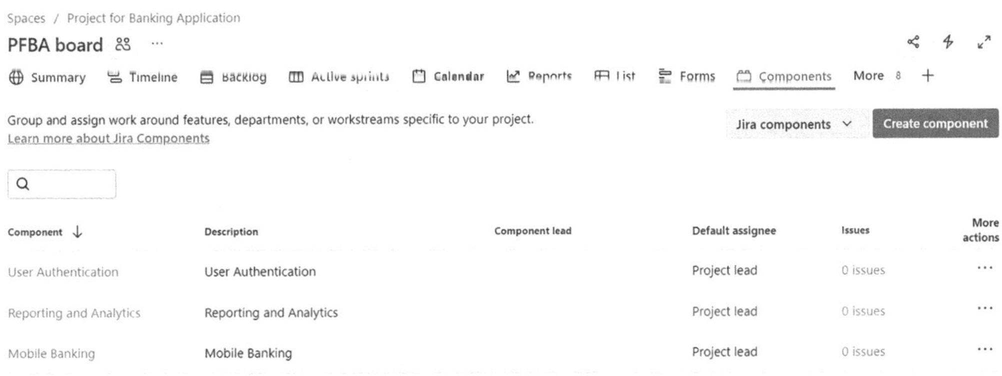

Figure 5.26: *Components in Jira*

To Edit or Delete components,

1. Navigate to the ••• icon on the right side.
2. Click on ••• and select **`Edit`** or **`Delete`**.

Work Item Management Best Practices

Jira has been used by many organizations for many years. Here are the best practices for work item management in Jira:

1. Choose the appropriate work type (**`Story`**, **`Bug`**, **`Task`**, and so on) that accurately represents the work item.
2. Provide a clear description of the task to ensure a common understanding among team members. Include details like estimation and due date.

3. Assign tasks to the relevant team members and fill in the reporter field.
4. Set the priority field based on the task's urgency and importance.
5. Avoid adding excessive details in Jira that might confuse teams. Provide concise and relevant information about the task.
6. Utilize labels to categorize work items and components to assign work items to specific parts of the space.
7. Develop a habit of commenting on work items to share progress updates, challenges, and solutions. Comments also enhance collaboration.
8. Enter all necessary details such as Story Points, work item-links, Fix versions wherever applicable.
9. Enable time tracking and ensure regular work log entries. This helps in generating reports and metrics analysis.
10. Utilize the attachment feature in Jira but avoid attaching excessively large files. Attach important files that provide essential work item details.
11. Integrate Jira with third party add-ons to access advanced features for project management, source code management and documentation.
12. Utilize bulk-editing whenever necessary to manage multiple work items efficiently.

Conclusion

We are now familiar with how to create a work type, examples of work types in Jira and Jira Service Management, child and parent work items, important work item operations, creating a new work type scheme, and associating a work type scheme with a space.

In the next chapter, we will learn about customizing screens and screen-schemes.

Points to Remember

- Work types are the work items in Jira such as Task, Bug, Story, and so on.
- There are two types of work items in Jira: Standard work types and Sub-task work types.
- While customizing work types, do not add too many work types to avoid confusion.
- There are some custom work types provided in Jira. Utilize these as per the requirement of your team or space.

- If you want to create new work types, analyze the workflow and process of the organization and then create new work types.
- Sub-tasks are for very small pieces of work. Use sub-tasks to divide the bigger tasks into very small tasks. Sub-tasks are child work items and do not create them as individual tasks.
- Work type schemes are a combination of multiple work items and are used to associate a group of work types with a space.
- Review the work type schemes regularly and update the same.
- Communicate with everyone in the team about the right usage of the tasks and sub-tasks.
- To add and Configure work types and work type schemes and to associate it with a space, you must be a Jira Administrator with "Administer Jira" permission.

Use Cases with Reference Links

1. What are the work type schemes best practices while associating a new work type scheme with a space- Refer the link to understand in detail.

   https://community.atlassian.com/t5/Jira-Software-questions/work type-schemes-best-practices/qaq-p/2283656

2. If I remove a work type from a Workflow Scheme, will the past work items be deleted? -Read all the details on the link provided

   https://community.atlassian.com/t5/Jira-Software-questions/If-I-remove-an-work type-from-a-Workflow-Scheme-will-the-past/qaq-p/2324428

3. Is there any effect if we remove the "work type Schemes" that are not associated with any space in Jira cloud. - You can delete work type Schemes" that are not associated with any space in Jira cloud.

   https://community.atlassian.com/t5/Jira-Software-questions/work type-scheme-deletion/qaq-p/1599984

4. Default work types - bug work type missing. If bug work type is missing, it has to be created once again.

   https://community.atlassian.com/t5/Jira-Software-questions/Default-work types-bug-work type-missing/qaq-p/2425067

5. How to separate a work type scheme and field scheme which are shared between spaces? (Refer the link to understand in detail.)

https://community.atlassian.com/t5/Jira-questions/How-to-separate-an-work types-scheme-and-field-scheme-which-are/qaq-p/2203767

6. Can we set up a work type "xyz" above work type "Epic"? (Refer the link to read detailed answer.)

   https://community.atlassian.com/t5/Jira-Software-questions/Can-you-please-advise-how-we-can-set-up-an-work type-quot-xyz/qaq-p/2283828

7. When I have selected an Epic, I can create one or many sub work items (Task or Stories) but when I have a Feature (the new work type) I can add one or many sub work items but only of work type task, can I change that so that I can add one or many sub work items (Task or Epics) – It is only possible to change and add hierarchy levels as part of Jira Cloud Premium and Enterprise. It is possible to add the work item level above Epic in Jira Advanced Roadmap. - Refer to the link to read a detailed answer.

   https://community.atlassian.com/t5/Jira-Software-questions/work types/qaq-p/1939411

8. Why are work types missing from Backlog `+ Create work item` mini-dropdown- Refer the link to read detailed answer.

   https://community.atlassian.com/t5/Jira-Software-questions/Why-are-work types-missing-from-Backlog-Create-work item-mini/qaq-p/2253730

9. Associating a work type Screen scheme to a space- Refer the link to read a detailed answer.

   https://community.atlassian.com/t5/Jira-questions/Associating-an-work type-Screen-scheme-to-a-project/qaq-p/2431392

10. Unable to comment on Jira work items

    https://community.atlassian.com/t5/Jira-questions/Unable-to-comment-on-Jira-work items/qaq-p/1922904

CHAPTER 6

Customizing Fields, Field Configuration Schemes, Screens, and Screen Schemes

Introduction

Jira is a project management tool in which you can add fields, customize screens, and create custom screen schemes as per the requirements of your project. In this chapter, we will learn about how to add a field to create different screens. It can be of different types, such as Text fields, Numeric Fields, and many more. A screen is made up of system fields and fields. It is used to enter data from the users. A combination of screens to create, edit, and view issues are known as Screen Schemes. These screen schemes can be associated with an issue and with a space.

Structure

In this chapter, we will cover the following topics:

- Understanding and Creating Fields
- Types of Fields in Jira with Examples
- Adding Context to a Field
- Locked Fields
- Understanding Field Configuration
- Field Configuration Scheme with an Example
- Understanding Screens

- Creating Screen Schemes, Work Type Screen Schemes, and Associating Them with a Space
- Use-cases of Screens and Screen Schemes
- Conclusion
- Points to Remember
- References

Understanding and Creating Fields

Fields are an important part of Jira, as it allows users to enter information and generate reports based on it. Let us understand how you can create new fields and associate the same with screens.

Note: *To customize all the fields and screen schemes, you have to log in as a Jira Administrator with Administer Jira Global Permission in Company-managed Space.*

Creating fields in Jira:

1. Select ⚙ > **Issues**.
2. Under **FIELDS**, select **Fields**.
3. Select **Fields** and click on **Create new field**.
4. In this **example**, we will create a field named severity. **Severity** has 4 levels: **Blocker**, **Critical**, **Major**, and **Minor**.
5. Select a field type such as **Select List** - single choice, as shown in *Figure* 6.1.

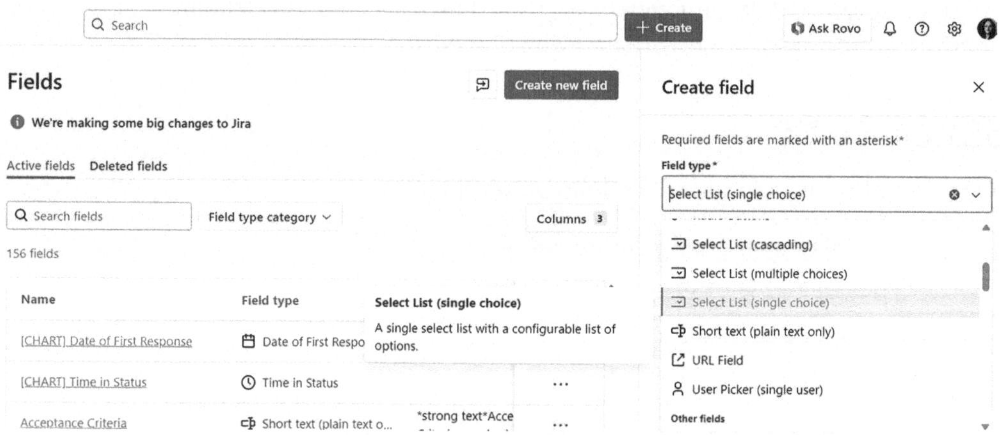

***Figure 6.1**: Creating Custom-Field Select-List (Single-Choice)*

6. Enter the levels as **Blocker**, **Critical**, **Major**, and **Minor**, and then select **Create**.

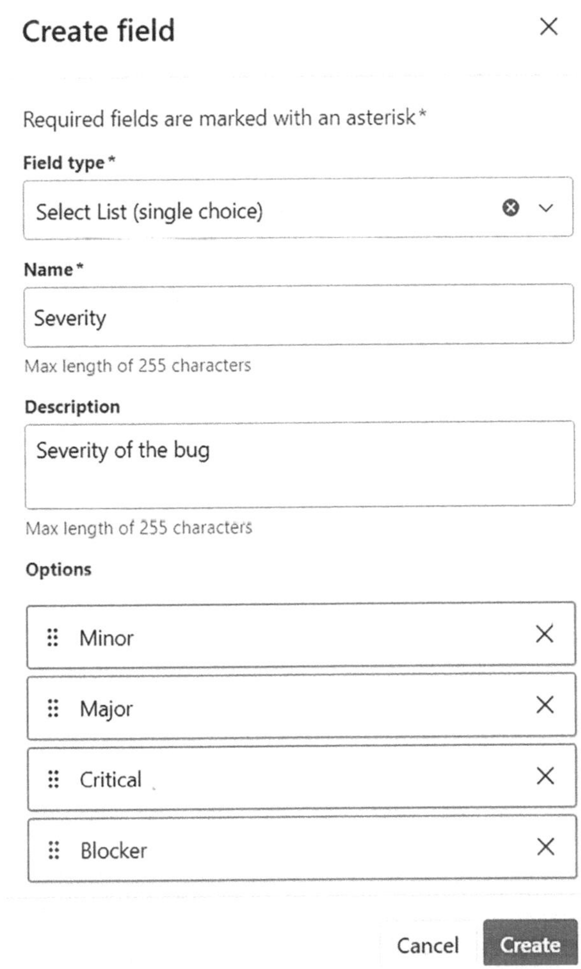

***Figure 6.2**: Entering Values for Severity Field*

7. You can associate it with **`Bug Screens`**, as shown in *Figure* 6.3.

   To add the **Severity** field to a screen, follow these steps:

   i. Navigate to the **`Severity` field.** Locate the field within your project configuration or issue layout settings.

   ii. Click **`More`** under the **`Actions`** menu. This will expand additional configuration options for the selected field.

   iii. Select **`Add Field to Screen`.** Choose the desired screen where you want the **Severity** field to appear, and confirm your selection.

   Now the severity field will appear on the screens, which are associated with the field.

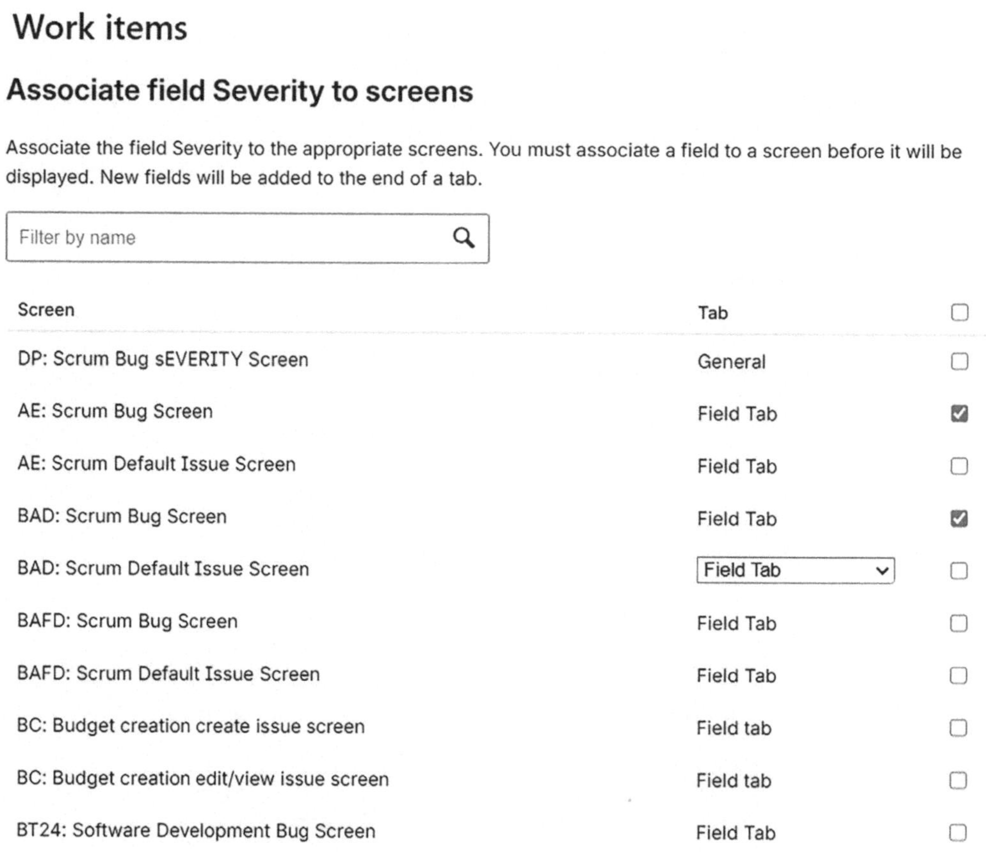

***Figure 6.3**: Associating Severity Field to Screens*

Types of Fields in Jira with Examples

There are mainly two types of fields in Jira as follows:

- Standard field
- Advanced field

Table 6.1 lists both the types of fields and how they can be used.

	Types of field	**How it is used**
Standard field	Checkboxes	Choose multiple values using checkboxes. Checkboxes allow people to select multiple options for a list to complete the field. Checkbox fields help with data entry by reducing entry errors that could appear in free-form text fields, for example. They also increase correct completions by limiting the options a person has to complete the field.

	Date Time Picker	A field that stores dates with a time component. Like date picker fields, date time picker fields allow people to provide time of day information using a calendar and dropdown time selector to complete the field. Time fields have two input areas: one to specify the date, and one to specify the time.
	Labels	Add labels to issues. Label fields allow people to tag issues with reusable text snippets entered as free form text. Jira suggests existing labels to help reduce entry errors. People can also create new labels by typing into the label field.
	Numeric Field	A field that stores and validates numeric input. Number fields allow people to provide numerical information as free-form text. A single line text box allows people to complete the field with a number. People can safely enter numbers between -1 trillion and 1 trillion (100,000,000,000,000). **Note:** Jira rounds decimals to the nearest 1000th place. For example, 5.555555 will be rounded to 5.556. People can enter large numbers using scientific notation. For example, the number 5,000 can be entered as 5e3.
	Radio Buttons	A list of radio buttons. Radio buttons allow people to select a single option from a list to complete the field. Radio buttons help with data entry by reducing entry errors that could appear in free-form text fields, for example. They also increase correct completions by limiting the options a person must complete the field.
	Select list (Cascading)	Choose multiple values using two select lists. Cascading select fields allow people to narrow their selection list by branching select fields into parents and children options. People select an option from the parent dropdown list and are presented with that options sub-list to select from. Cascading select fields help categorize options in a select list and reduce the number of choices needed to complete the field correctly.
	Select list (multiple choice)	Choose multiple values in a select list.
	Select list (single choice)	A single select list with a configurable list of options.
	Short text (plain text only)	The short text (up to 255 characters) field is commonly used to add context, organize the issues, or to provide information to the team. For more complex formatting, use the paragraph field.

	URL Field	People use this field to input a single URL.
	User Picker (Single User)	Choose a user from the user base via a pop-up picker window.
	Paragraph ()	This field is used for longer text. It is a multiline text field which supports rich text format, such as URLs, bold, underlined, and the like.
Advanced field		
	Date of first response	The date of the first comment on an issue by anyone other than the reporter.
	Days since last comment	Date/time since last comment (restricted comments are considered on a per user basis). This field is not searchable or sortable.
	Domain of Assignee	The domain name of the Assignee.
	Domain of Reporter	The domain name of the Reporter.
	Global Rank	Global rank field for Jira Software use only.
	Global picker (multiple groups)	Select multiple user groups using a popup picker window.
	Global picker (Single group)	Select a user group using a popup picker window.
	Last commented by a User Flag	Shows "true" if the latest commenter is not a member of the Jira developer group (Jira-developers).
	Last public comment date	Date and time of the most recent public comment (excluding restricted comments). This field is searchable and sortable.
	Message field (for edit)	A field whose default value will be displayed as HTML or as rendered wiki markup in OnDemand on an 'Edit' screen.
	Message field (for view)	A field whose default value will be displayed as HTML or as rendered wiki markup in OnDemand on the 'View' screen.
	Number of attachments	A specialized field that stores the count of attachments linked to an issue.
	Number of comments	A field designed to hold the count of comments associated with an issue.
	Participants of an issue	Shows the reporter, current assignee, and everyone who has commented on the issue.

	Project picker (single project)	Select from spaces accessible to the user within the system.
	Team	Link issues with a particular team.
	A read-only text label	A text label that is view-only, allowing values to be generated programmatically (Used internally for imports from Mantis). Maximum of 255 characters.
	Time in status	Store statistics about the number of time/times an issue has spent/been in its statuses. This field generates the Average Number of Times Spent in Status and Average Time Spent in Status charts.
	User Picker (multiple users)	Select multiple users from the user base using a popup picker window.
	User Property Field (<255 characters)	A read-only custom-field that displays a user property.
	Name of last updater or commenter	Show the name of the most recent updater or commenter depending on the latest activity.
	Version Picker (multiple version)	Select a version from the options accessible within the space.
	Version Picker (single version)	Select one version from the options provided within the space.

Table 6.1: *Types of Fields (Source – https://support.atlassian.com/jira-cloud-administration/docs/custom-fields-types-in-company-managed-projects/)*

Examples of Adding Fields

In this section, we will learn about how to add fields in Jira and how they can be helpful.

1. **Adding Date-time picker field:**

   i. Select ⚙ > **`Issues`.**

   ii. Select **`Fields`** and click **`Create new field`**.

   iii. Select the standard option: **`Date Time Picker`.**

   iv Add the field and associate it with screens as per the space's requirement.

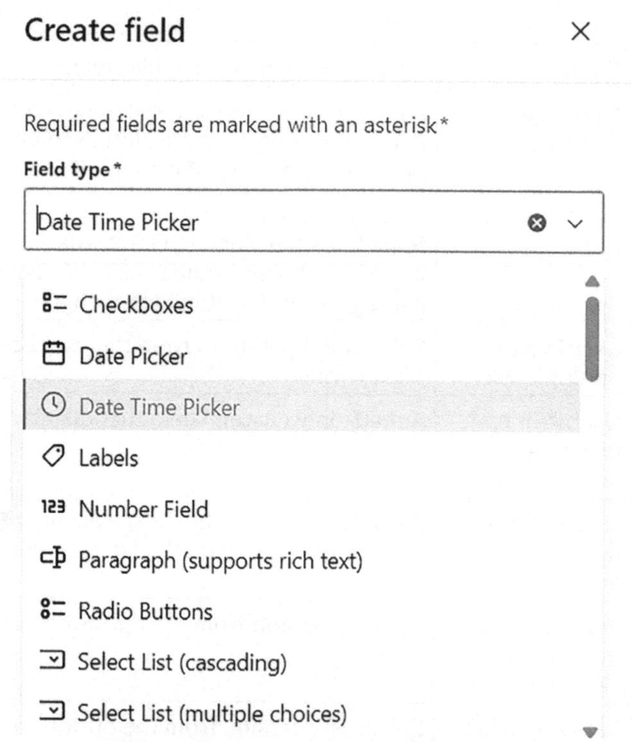

Figure 6.4: *Adding Date Time Picker Field*

After adding the field, check for the functionality of the field. This field is used to select both date and time.

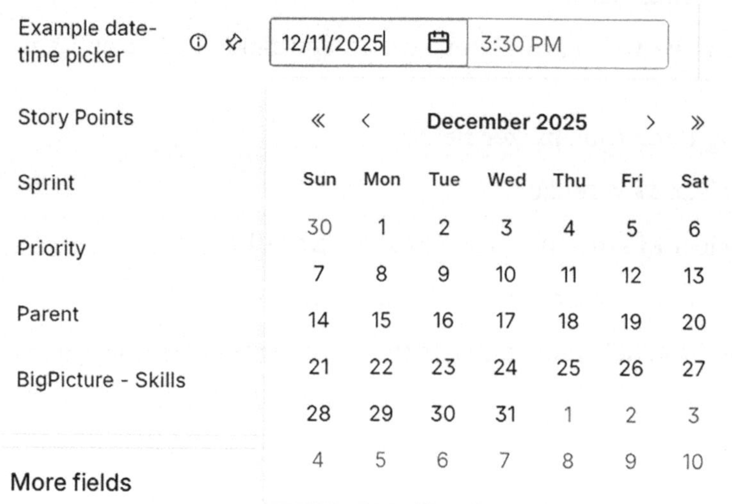

Figure 6.5: *Example of Date and Time Picker Field View*

2. **Adding Username of Last Updater/Commenter Field**

    i. Select ⚙ > **`Issues`**.

    ii. Select **`Fields`** and click on **`Create new field.`**

    iii. Go to the **`Other`** option on the left-hand side and select **`Date Time Picker`**.

    iv. Add a field and associate it with screens as per your requirement.

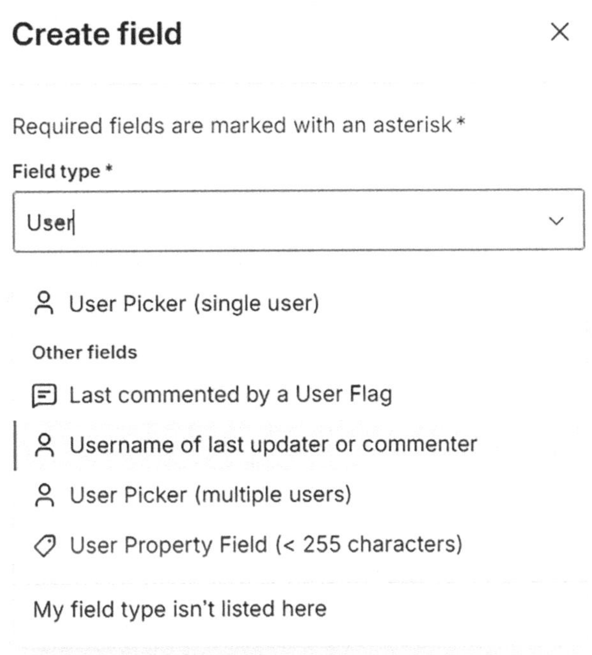

***Figure 6.6**: Adding Advanced Field*

After adding the field, check for the functionality of the field. This field is used to check the username who updated or commented on an issue.

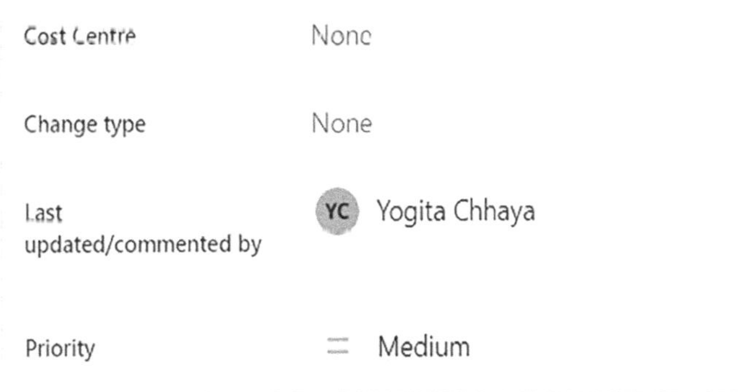

***Figure 6.7**: Last Updated/Commented by Field*

Adding Context to a Field

In Jira, fields allow you to capture and store additional information beyond the default fields provided by the system. Adding context to Jira fields means providing extra information or specifying the purpose of the field, which helps users understand how to use and interpret the field's values. Contextual information can include descriptions, examples, guidelines, and explanations that help users in filling out the field correctly.

Let us understand the concept of adding context to a Jira field using the example of a **Change Type** field.

Example: Field-Change Type

Context: The **Change Type** field is used to classify the nature and significance of changes being made to a space or system. It helps in understanding the purpose and impact of the change.

Description: This field indicates the type of change being introduced. Please select the appropriate change type based on the definitions provided.

You can create a new field context if it is required to associate different default values and options with different spaces or work types.

The step-by-step process to add context is as follows:

1. Select ⚙ > **Issues**.
2. Select **Fields** under **Fields**.
3. Select the field to which you want to add a new context. On the same page, go to ⋯ on the right side under **Action** column and select **Contexts** and default value > **Add new context**.
4. Enter a label and description for the new context. These are not for the end-users but it is for the reference of the administrator only.
5. When selecting the applicable work types, choose the work types that you want this field to appear in.
6. In the section for applicable contexts, choose either a global context or specific spaces that you want this field to appear in. The field will only appear on issues types you have selected.
7. Select **Add.**

After configuring a field, you will have to specify on which screens it should be displayed.

In *Figure 6.8*, we have added a new context for the **`Change Type`** field.

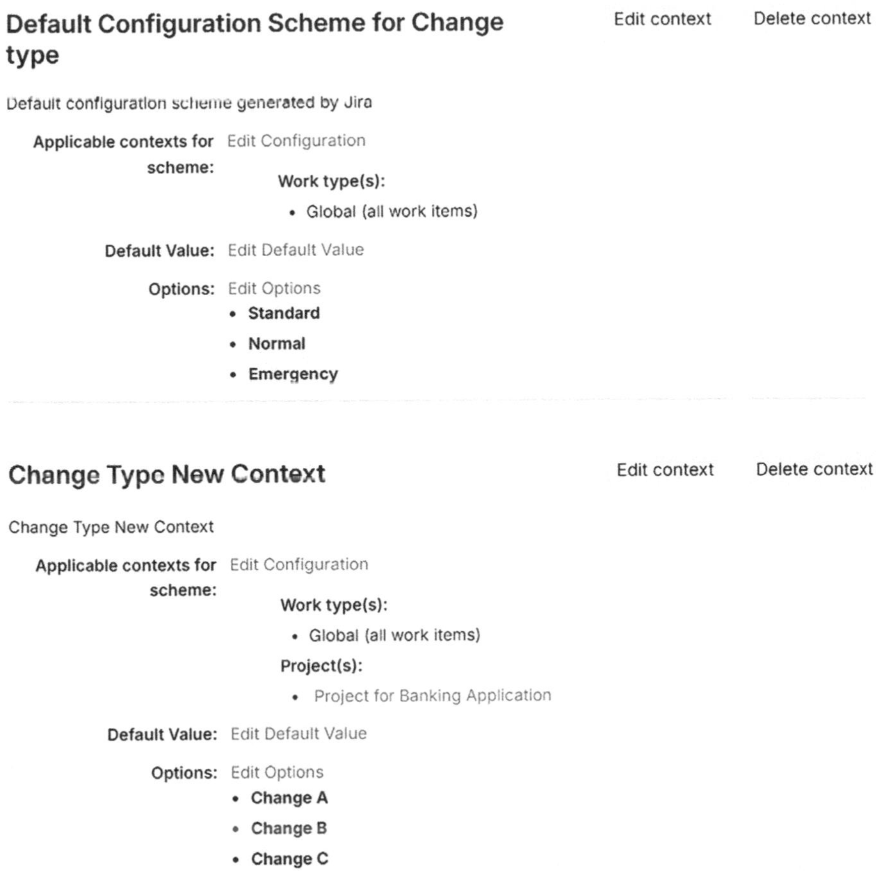

***Figure 6.8**: Adding Context to Field Change Type*

In this example, the field **`Change Type`** is provided with context to help users understand its purpose and how to select the appropriate value.

The **`Change Type`** can be viewed on the create screen as per the issues and spaces selected while setting the contexts. If it is set for **`Global Context`**, it is applied to all issues in Jira.

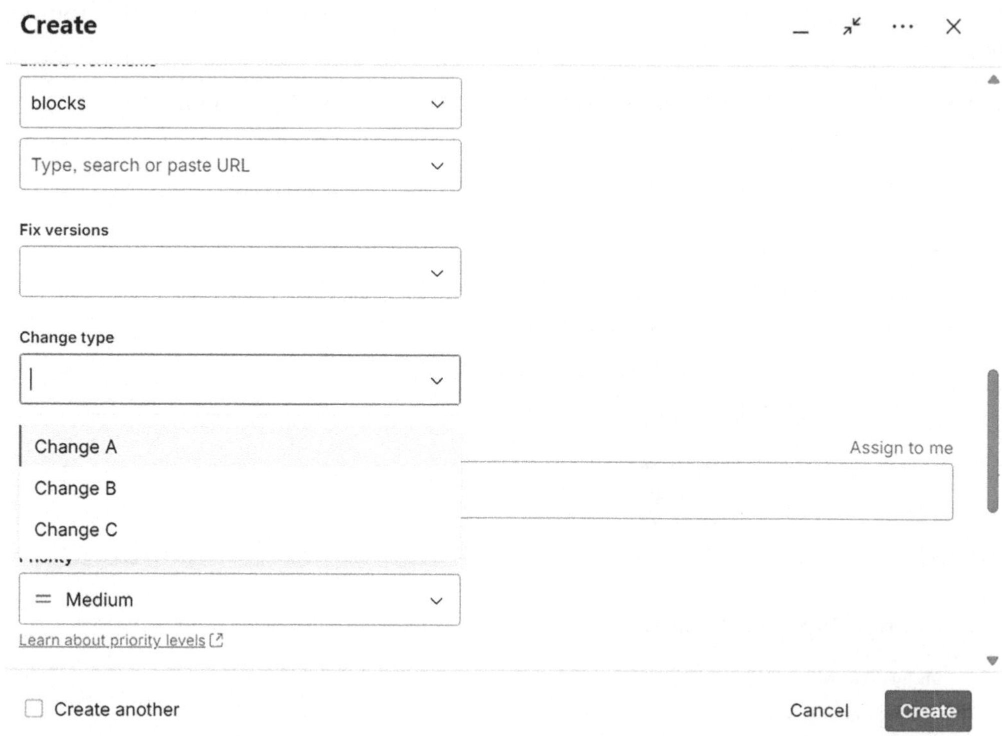

***Figure 6.9**: Change Type Field on Create Screen*

Locked Fields

Some specific fields are created when Jira products are installed. These fields are also created while Jira add-ons are installed. For example, a Sprint field is created when Jira software is installed. These specific fields are locked. It cannot be configured, but you can add these fields to screens and view the field details.

To view field information or associate them with screens:

1. Select ⚙ > **`Issues`**.
2. Select **`Fields`** under **`Fields`**.
3. Go to ⋯ on the right side and select the right option.

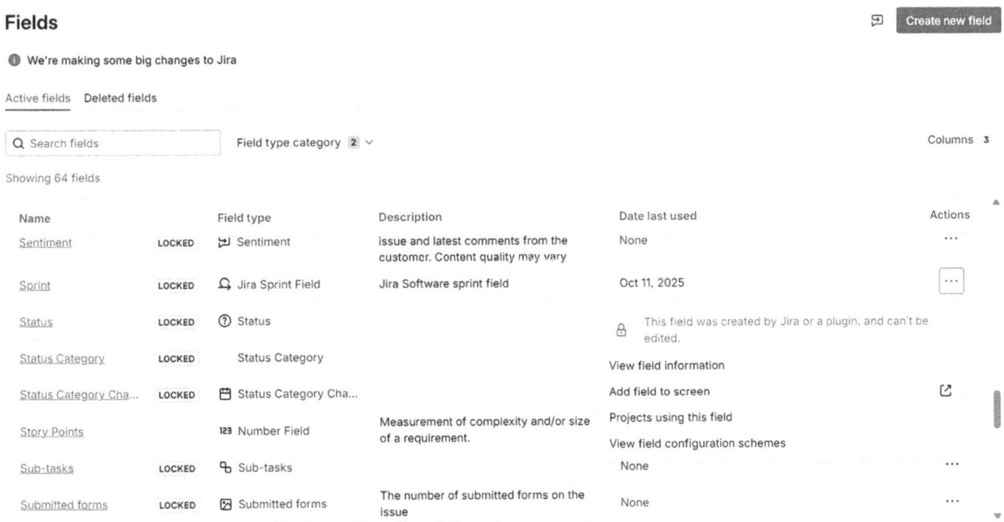

***Figure 6.10**: Locked Fields in Jira*

In *Figure* 6.10, some fields are locked, whereas others such as Story Points are not locked.

Understanding Field Configuration

In Jira, a field configuration allows you to set the behavior of the field. You can set this for both issue fields and fields.

It allows you to set:

- The description of the field that appears at the time of editing.
- Make the field required or optional.
- Decide the renderer to use for text fields.

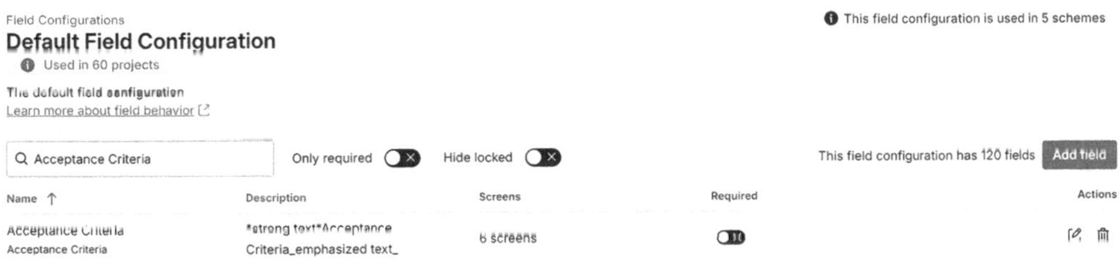

***Figure 6.11**: Configuring Fields*

Required option: If the field is set as the required field, the user has to enter some value while creating it. So, if that field is not there on the space's screen, it may create problems for you.

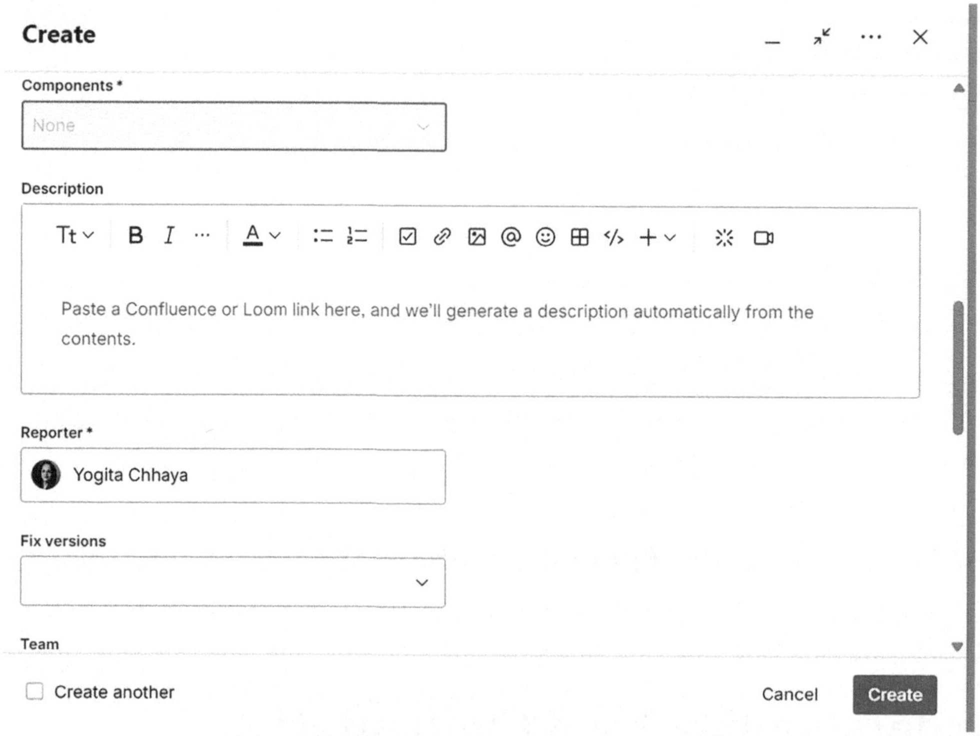

Figure 6.12: *Effect of Making a Field Mandatory*

As shown in *Figure* 6.12, if the **`Components`** field is made required, it has to be entered when creating any type of issue.

To overcome this problem, you can set field configurations that are different for different issues (Epics, Stories, Tasks, and so on.)

Renderers: It affects how the value of a field is viewed. It is installed as a plugin. If you change the renderer, its view is changed. Changing the renderer does not affect the issue data.

For example: There are two types of text renderers as follows:

- **Default Text Renderer**: It looks like a normal text field.
- **Wiki Style Renderer:** It looks like a field where you have all the options to format the text (similar to the Description field in Jira).

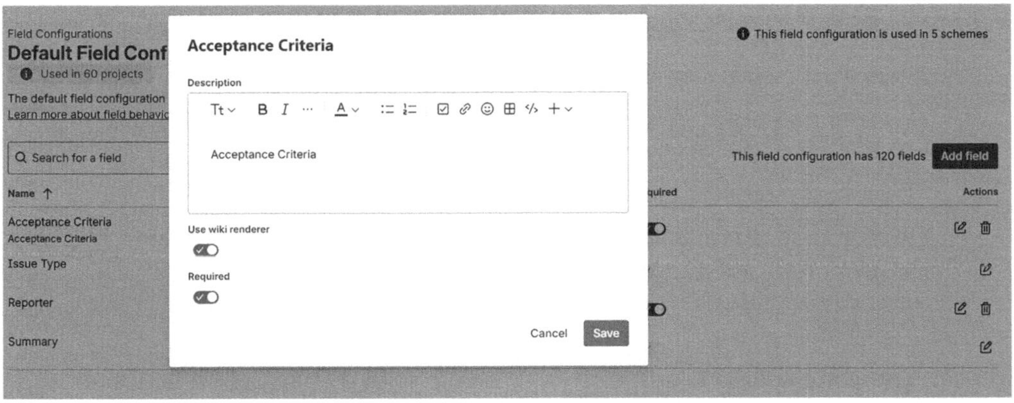

***Figure 6.13**: Editing Field Renderer for the Field Acceptance Criteria*

To see and set the field configurations:

1. Select ⚙ > **Issues**.
2. Select **Field Configurations**.
3. Select **Configure**.
4. On this screen, you can set various fields as per requirement.

***Figure 6.14**: Adding Field Configuration*

Field Configuration Scheme with an Example

Issue field configuration schemes allow you to apply a field configuration to all issues of a specific work type. For example, when you want to change the fields that appear on all story work types in a certain space, you can do it by configuring the field configuration schemes. The same field configuration can be used for multiple spaces.

Steps to associate a Work Type with a Field Configuration:

1. Access the issues section by clicking the gear icon and choosing **`Issues`**.
2. Under the **`Fields`** section, select **`Field configuration schemes`**.
3. Pick the desired field configuration scheme and click **`Configure`**.
4. Opt for **`Associate and work type with a field configuration`**, then select the work type and field configuration to link with this scheme.
5. Click **`Add`**.

Steps to associate a Field Configuration Scheme with a Space:

After establishing a link between a field configuration and a work type within a field configuration scheme, you can integrate the scheme with a space to apply your changes.

1. Navigate to **`Spaces`** > **`space settings`** > **`Fields`**.
2. Click **`Actions`** > **`Use a different scheme`**.
3. Choose the scheme you wish to associate with this space.
4. Click **`Associate`**.

Example:

We will create a field configuration, associate it with a work type, and then associate it to a space.

To do this:

1. Go to **`Default field Configuration`** in Jira Administration, and then select **`Copy`**.

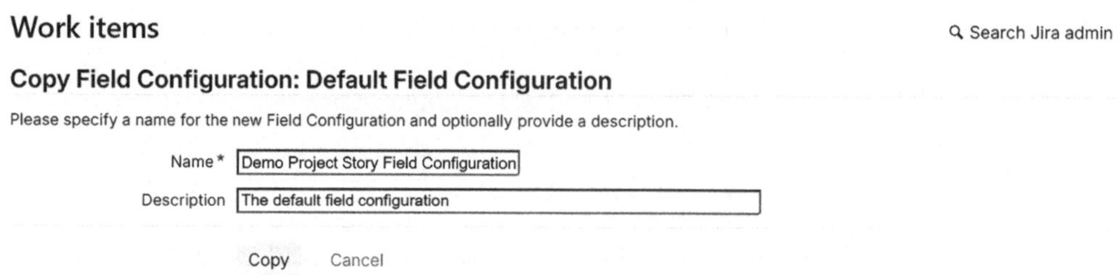

Figure 6.15: *Creating a New Field Configuration*

2. We have created a new Field configuration named **`Demo Space Story Field Configuration`**. Now we can configure it by selecting **`Configure`**.

3. In this step, you can make fields required, change the renderers, and add context to the fields.

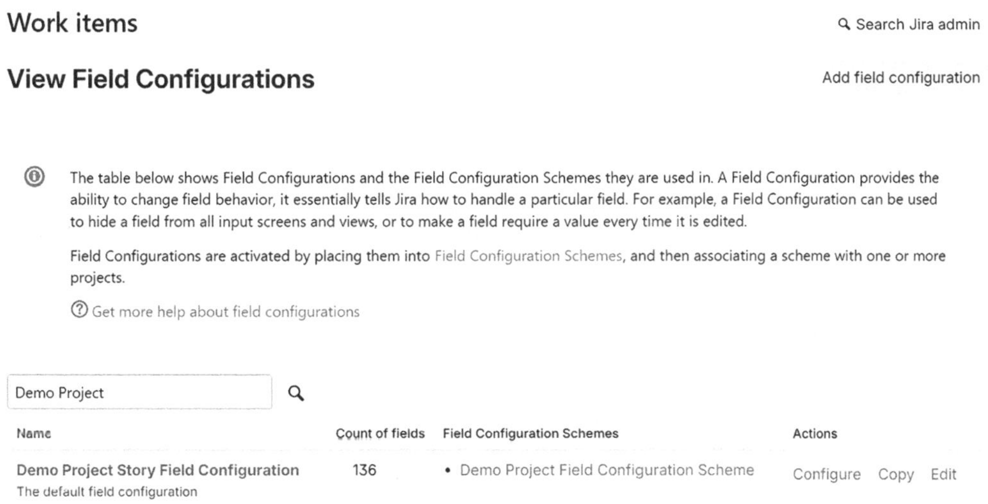

Figure 6.16: *Configuring Fields of Demo Field Configuration*

4. Once the fields are configured, we can associate them with a work type. To do that, we have to add a **`Field Configuration Scheme`**.

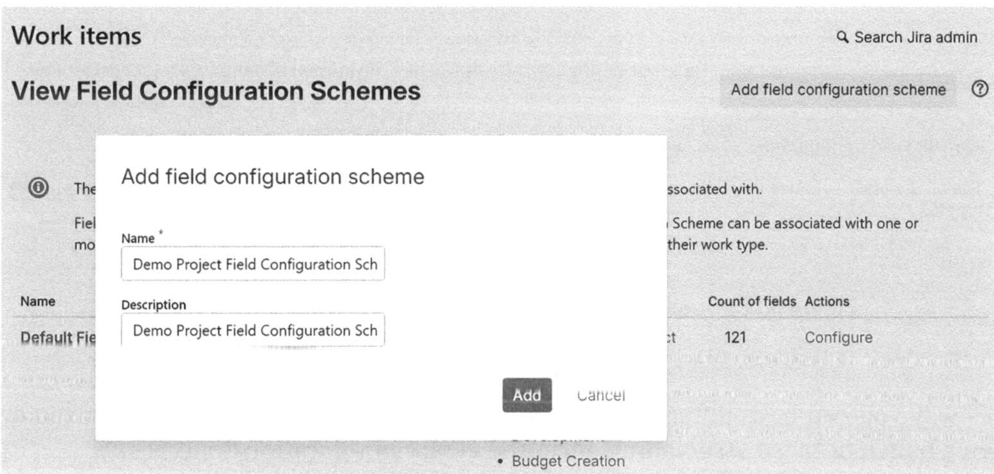

Figure 6.17: *Adding New Field Configuration Scheme*

5. After adding the scheme, associate it with a work type story.

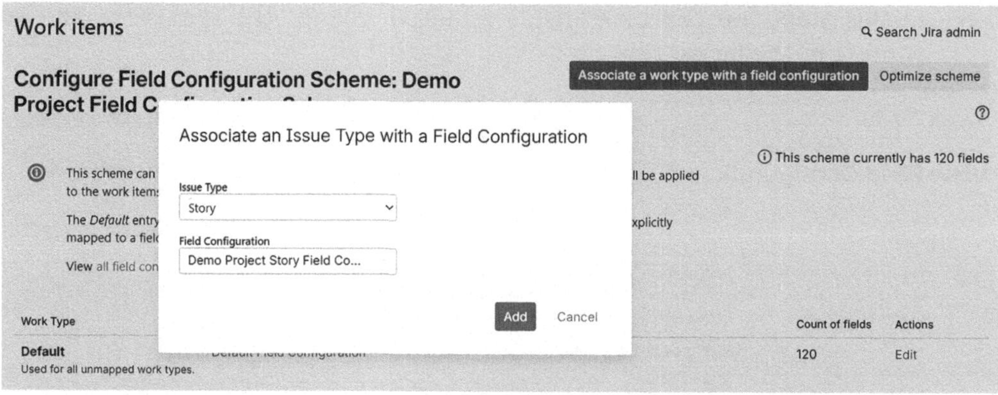

***Figure 6.18**: Associating a Work Type with a Field Configuration*

6. Once it is associated with a work type, associate it with a space.
7. You can customize different field configurations for all the work types.
8. Go to the space settings of a space.
9. Now select **`Issues`** > **`Fields.`**
10. Go to the Actions drop-down and select **`Use a different scheme.`**

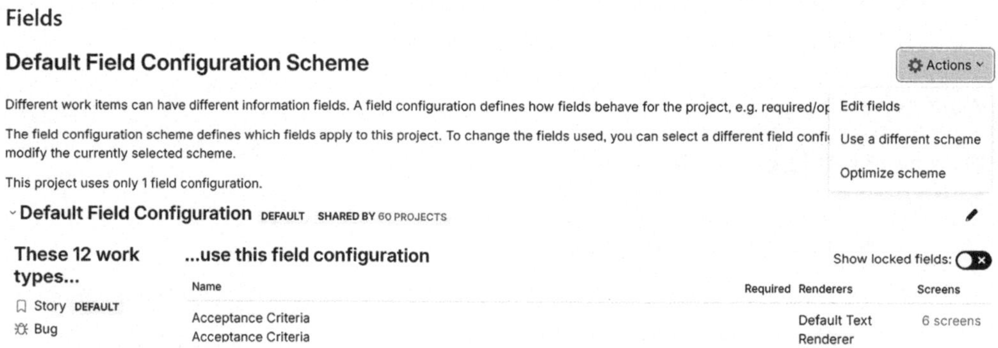

***Figure 6.19**: Associating a Field Configuration Scheme with a Space*

11. Once it is done, select the scheme and associate it with the space.

This way you can have different fields for different issues. It can be customized and then a bunch of these associations form the Field Configuration Schemes.

Understanding Screens

In this section, we will understand about screens provided by Jira. Jira has three types of screens as follows:

- **Default screen**: This screen is used to customize the screens for create, edit, and view operations.

- **Resolve issues screen**: This screen is used while transitioning an issue from open /in progress to close or resolve the issue while resolving an issue. A user can enter details about the resolution.

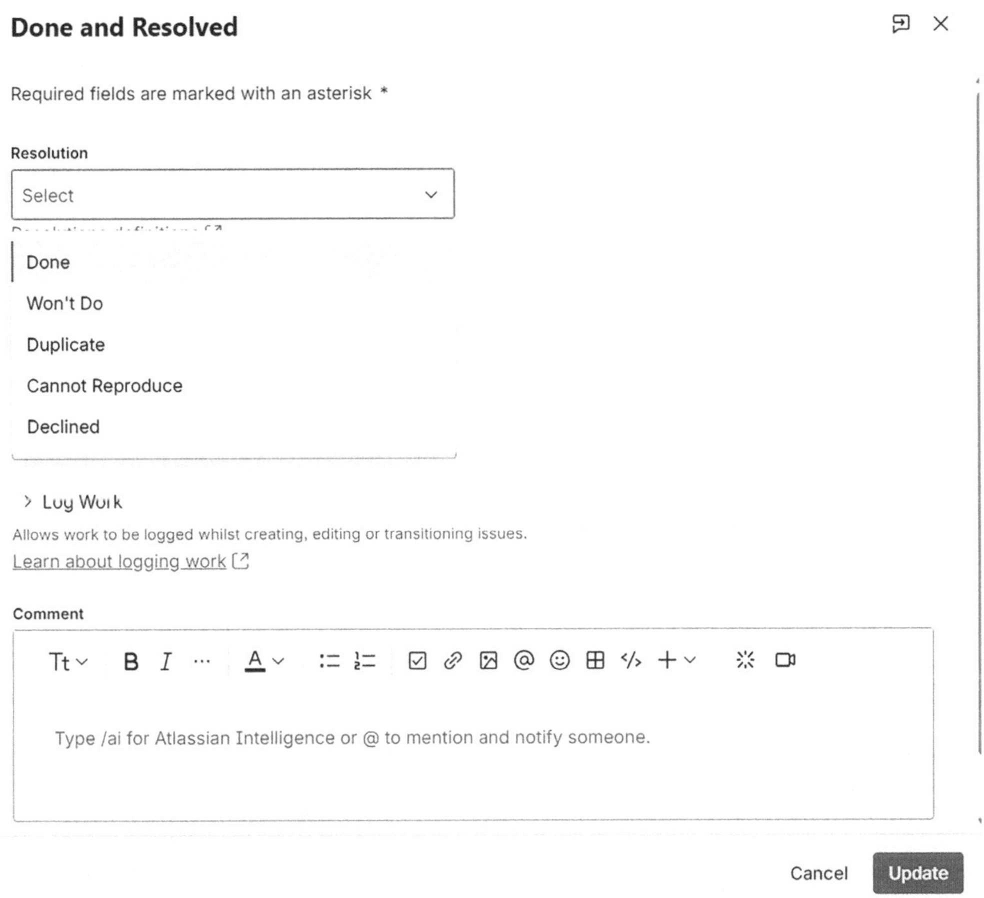

***Figure 6.20**: Resolve Issue Screen*

- **Workflow screen:** This screen is used for:
  - Reopen transitions from `Resolve and closed`.
  - Close transition from resolved step. This screen has a smaller number of fields than the Resolve issues screen.

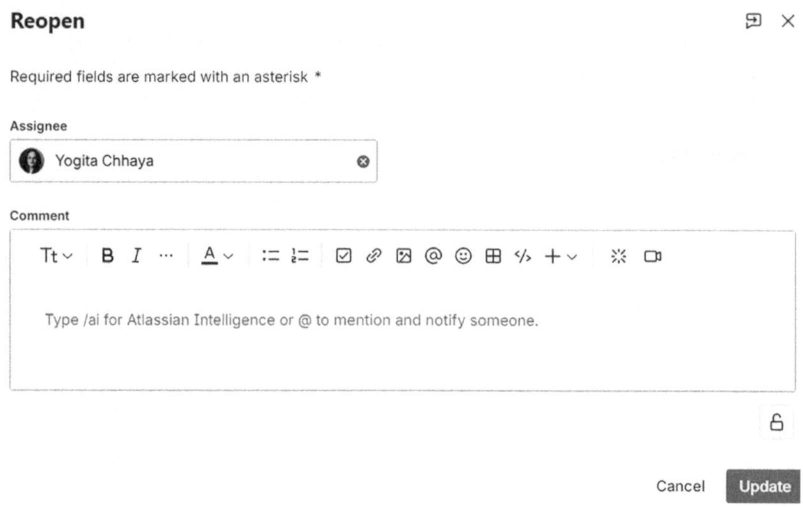

Figure 6.21: *Workflow Transition Screen*

How to Create or Configure Screen:

1. Select ⚙ > **Issues**.
2. Select **Screens** > **Add Screen**.
3. Add a **Name** of the screen and a ***Description*** that describes when this screen should be used.
4. Select **Add.**

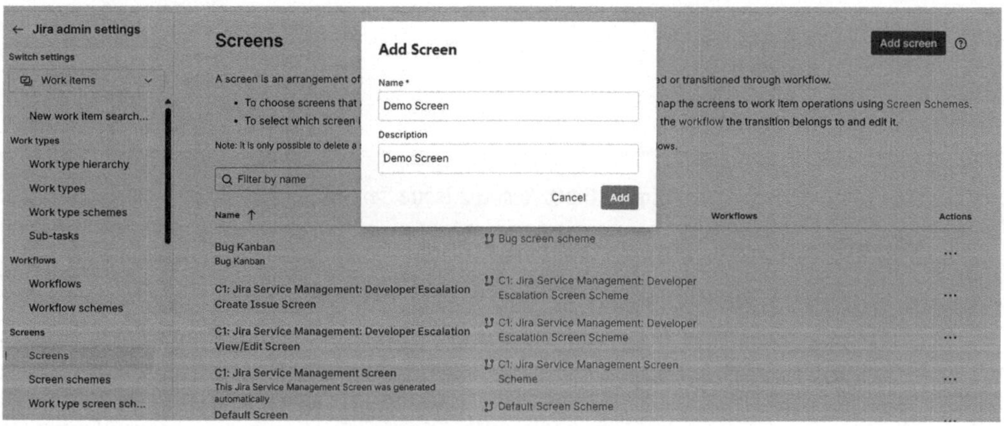

Figure 6.22: *Adding a Screen*

We will learn how to add fields to configure a new screen.

A Summary field is mandatory on any Jira screen. So, the summary field cannot be kept empty when creating an issue in Jira.

Example: You can add tabs to the screen in Jira.

Let us understand how to add multiple tabs and what it looks like. We have added tabs on the screen for the bug work type.

1. Select a screen you want to configure.
2. Select **`Add tab`** and **`Add Test Tab to`** create a new Tab.

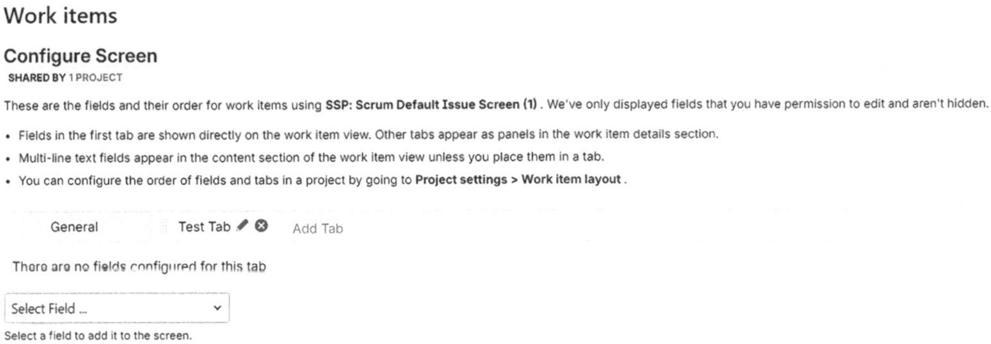

Figure 6.23: *Adding a Field on the New Tab*

3. Now, you can add the **`Acceptance Criteria`** and a few more fields to this tab.

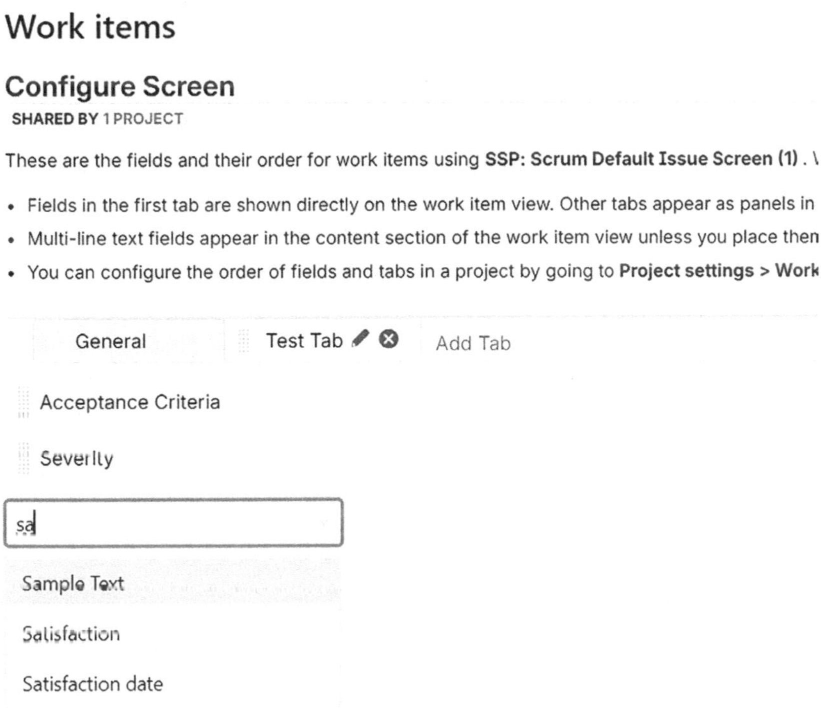

Figure 6.24: *Adding Fields to a Screen*

4. By following the same process, you can add more tabs and add fields to the tabs. The new tab will appear when creating a new issue, and they will get added to the issue screen.

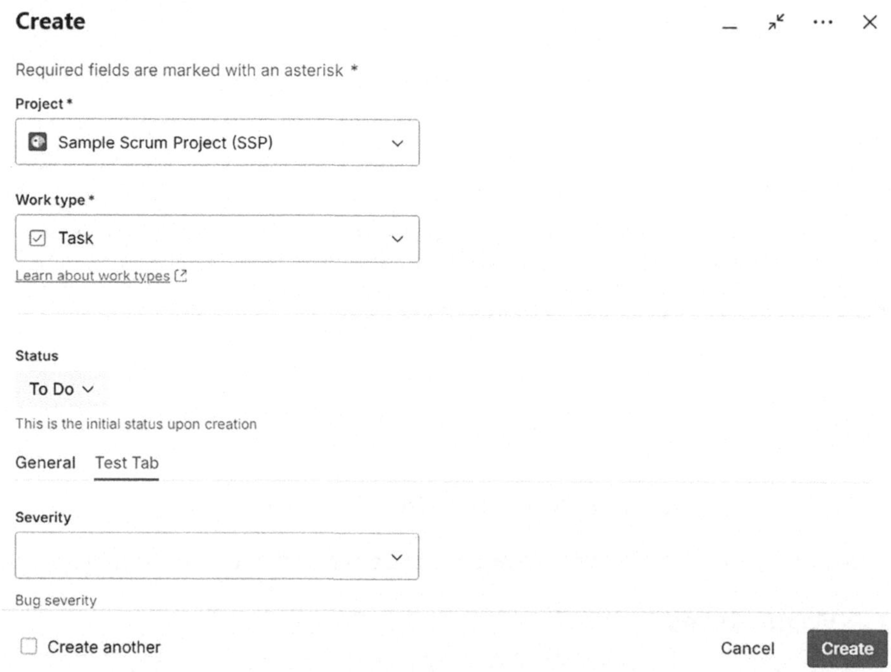

Figure 6.25: *New Tab on the Create Screen*

The other tab for **`Acceptance Criteria`** can be viewed in *Figure 6.25*.

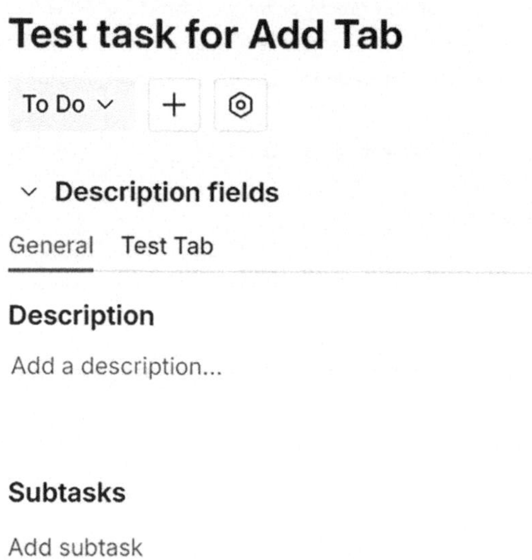

Figure 6.26: *Newly Created Tab on the Work Item View*

You can Edit, Copy, and Delete a screen as follows:

Editing a Screen:

1. Access the issues section by clicking the gear icon and choosing Issues.
2. Select **`Screens.`**
3. Choose the relevant screen, select **`Edit`** to update the name or description.

Copying a Screen:

1. Access the issues section by clicking the gear icon and choosing **`Issues.`**
2. Select **`Screens.`**
3. Choose the relevant screen, select **`Copy`**.

Deleting a Screen:

1. Access the issues section by clicking the gear icon and choosing Issues.
2. Select **`Screens.`**
3. Choose the relevant screen, Select **`Delete`** a screen.

The delete screen option can be seen only if the screen is not associated with a space or it is not related to a workflow.

***Figure 6.27**: Options to Customize Screens*

Creating Screen Schemes, Work Type Screen Schemes, and Associating Them with a Space

We have learned how to create a screen in Jira, and now we will learn how to create a screen scheme. Let us first understand what a screen scheme is in Jira. A screen scheme is a combination of three types of screens for various issues.

Create, Edit, and View Issue Screens

To understand this, select any space, and then go to **`space settings`** and select **`screens`** under issues. You can view the page for screens.

In the sample space **Scrum space A**, two screen combinations are used. One set of screens is used for the Bug work type and another set of screens is used for all other work types (**Story, Epic, Task, Sub-task**).

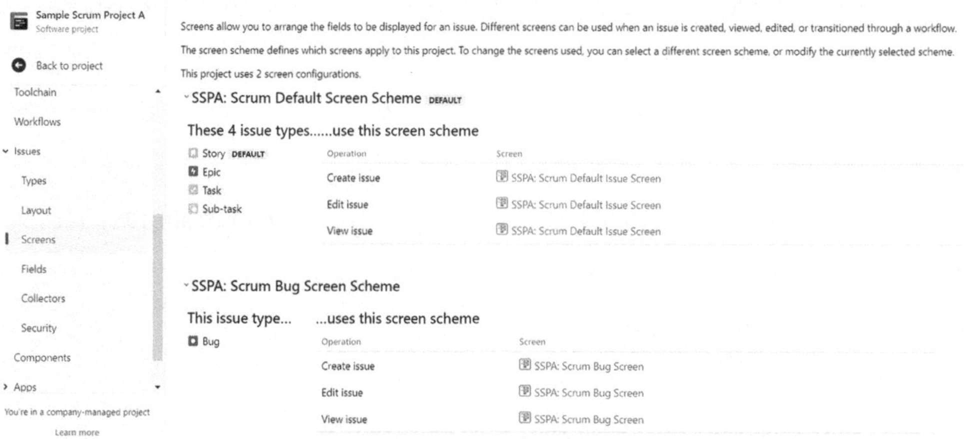

***Figure 6.28**: Create, Edit, and View Screens*

Now, we will learn the steps to create a new screen scheme in Jira software as follows:

1. Select ⚙ > **Issues**.
2. Select **Screen schemes** under **Screens** on the left navigation bar.
3. Select **Add Screen Scheme**.
4. Add the **Name** of the screen scheme, **Description**, and default screen. You can edit all the information later on.
5. Select **Add**.

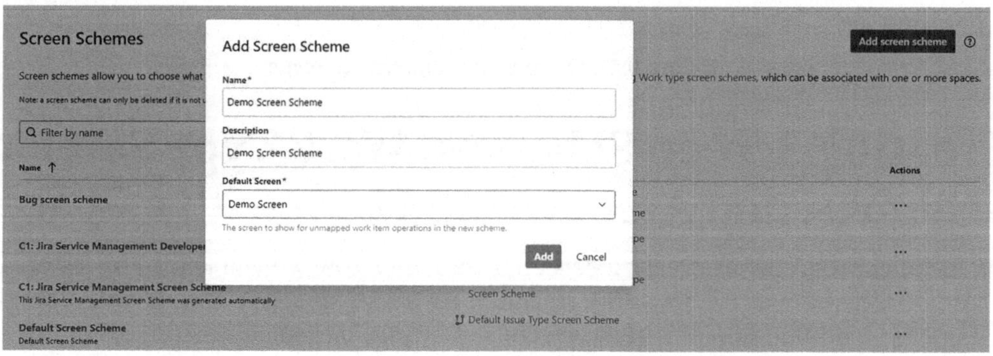

***Figure 6.29**: Adding a Screen Scheme*

Steps to Create a Work type Screen Scheme:

1. Access the issues section by clicking the gear icon and choosing **`Issues`**.
2. Choose **`Work type screen schemes`** under the screen schemes on the left navigation bar.
3. Click **`Add Work type Screen Scheme`**.
4. Add a **`Name`** of the Work type screen scheme, **`Description`**, and default screen scheme. You can edit all the information later on.
5. Select **`Add.`**

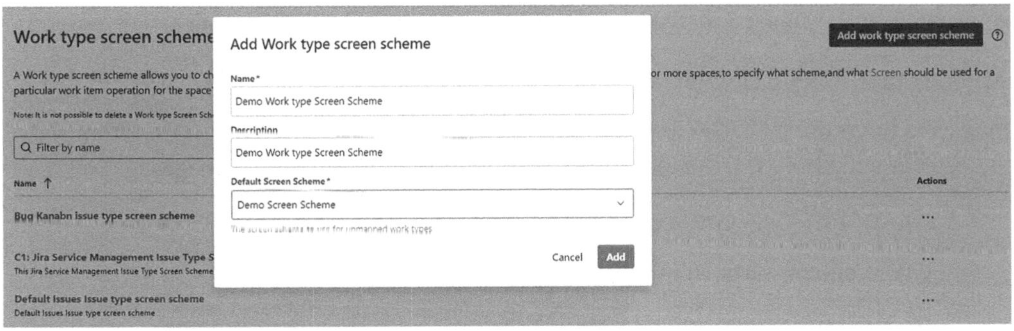

***Figure 6.30**: Adding Work Type Screen Scheme*

Associating a Work Type with a Screen Scheme:

In a screen scheme, each issue operation - **`Create, View`**, and **`Edit`** - can be associated with a single screen. By default, it gets associated with the default screen.

1. Select ⚙ > **`Issues`**.
2. Select **`Screen Schemes`** from the left navigation bar.
3. Click on **`Configure`** next to the relevant screen scheme.
4. Choose **`Associate`** an issue operation with a screen.
5. Click the required issue operation (for example, **`Create`**, **`Edit`**, **`View`**) and the desired screen.
6. Select **`Add.`**

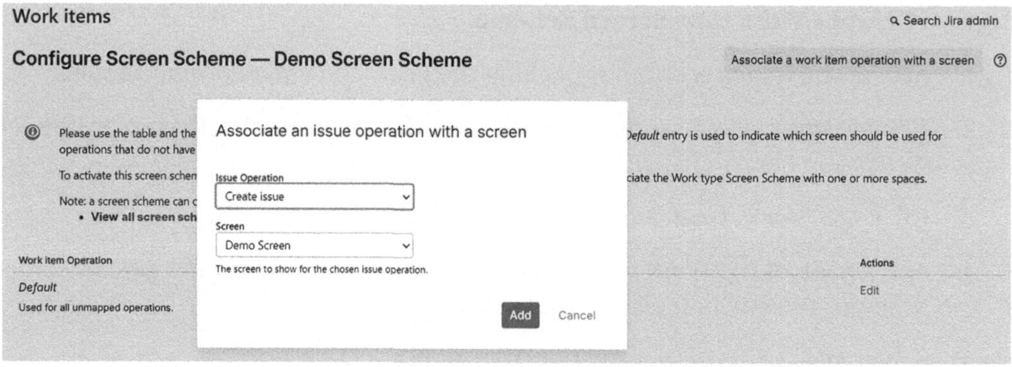

Figure 6.31: *Associating an Issue Operation with a Screen*

Associating a Work Type Screen Scheme with a Space:

Once you have created the Work type screens, you can now associate them with a space. This will apply the screen scheme to all the work types in the space.

1. Go to the space you want to configure.
2. Go to **`space settings`**.
3. In the left navigation bar, select **`Issues`**, and then select **`Screen`**.
4. On the right side, select **`Actions`**, and from the **`Actions`** dropdown, select **`Use a different scheme`**.
5. Now you can select and associate a screen scheme for the selected space.

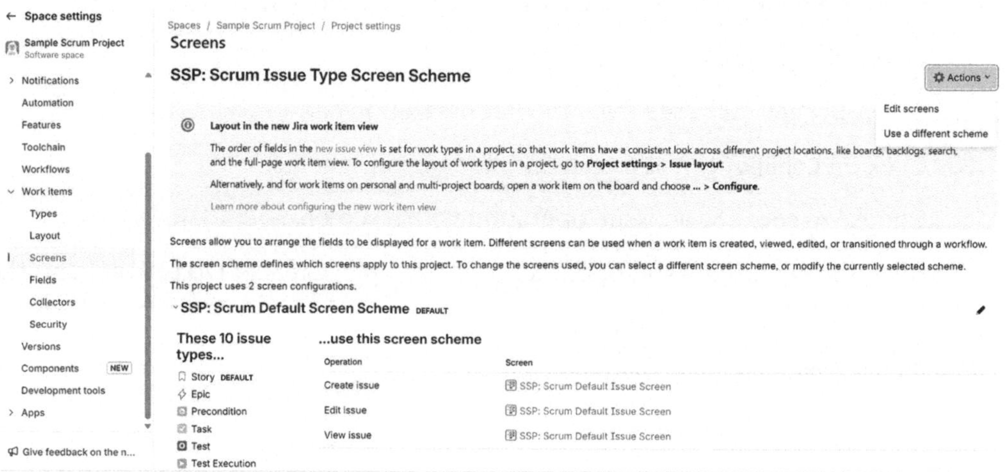

Figure 6.32: *Associating a Work Type Screen Scheme with a Space*

Use Cases of Screens and Screen Schemes

We will learn about a few use cases for screens and screen schemes in Jira as follows:

- **Customized Issue Creation**: A software development team wants to capture specific information during issue creation, such as priority, components, and environment details.

  Solution: They create a custom screen with the relevant fields and associate it with a screen scheme. This screen scheme is then linked to the **`Create Issue`** operation, so that the desired fields are displayed when a new issue is created.

- **Sensitive Information Segregation**: An organization handles both internal and external spaces, and they need to manage sensitive information separately for security reasons.

  Solution: By utilizing screen schemes, they can configure different screens for internal and external spaces. This ensures that sensitive fields are shown only in the internal space context, helping maintain data confidentiality.

- **Workflow Transition Data Gathering**: During the **`Code Review`** workflow transition, a development team wants to gather code review details for each issue.

  Solution: They design a dedicated screen with fields like reviewer's comments and approval status. This screen is associated with a screen scheme that's linked to the **`Code Review`** workflow transition. Thus, every time an issue is sent for review through this transition, the relevant screen with code review fields is presented.

- **Global Template Implementation:** An organization wants to ensure consistency across different spaces by customizing a standardized set of fields for all issues.

  Solution: They set up a default screen scheme that includes a predefined screen with mandatory fields applicable to all spaces. When new spaces are created, this default screen scheme is automatically applied, streamlining the process of ensuring consistent data capture.

Conclusion

We are now familiar with how to create and add fields, customize the screens, and associate a screen with issue operations and spaces. We also understood the sequence to follow to create new work type screen schemes.

In the next chapter, we will learn about workflows and workflow schemes.

Points to Remember

- Choose appropriate fields so that the right information can be captured as per the process you follow.
- Fields can be of different types, such as Text fields, select lists, URL fields, and many more. You can select as per your requirements.
- Create different screens for different work types and keep only the required fields.
- Create screen schemes and assign them to the issues to control which screen appears during create, edit, and view operation.
- The same screen scheme may not be useful for all the work types as it may create confusion.
- A default screen having all the necessary fields can be used while creating an issue.
- Reuse the screens across multiple screen schemes so that it becomes easy to maintain.
- Arrange fields on the screen logically and set them as per the requirements of the user.
- Test and validate screens and screen schemes so that the users can enter data easily.
- Keep a minimum number of fields on the screen and do the maintenance to remove the screens/fields that are not required.
- Jira provides many fields; however, try to customize it to simplify the process.

Use Cases with Reference Links

1. The description field is not visible.

   https://community.atlassian.com/t5/Jira-Software-questions/Description-field-not-visible/qaq-p/2204554

2. Is it Possible to Change a Space Screen Scheme or Workflow for a Subset of space work items?

   https://community.atlassian.com/t5/Jira-Software-questions/Is-it-Possible-to-Change-a-Project-Screen-Scheme-or-Workflow-for/qaq-p/2409599

3. Effect of changing screens, screen schemes and work type screen schemes on existing data

   https://community.atlassian.com/t5/Jira-Software-questions/Affect-of-changing-screens-screen-schemes-and-issue-type-screen/qaq-p/2281608

4. How to set multiple work type screen schemes for a single space?

   https://community.atlassian.com/t5/Jira-questions/How-to-set-multiple-issue-type-screen-schemes-for-a-single/qaq-p/287303

5. Do I need a Workflow scheme, an issues scheme, and a screen scheme for my one space?

   https://community.atlassian.com/t5/Jira-Software-questions/Do-I-need-a-Workflow-scheme-an-issues-scheme-and-a-screen-scheme/qaq-p/2255115

CHAPTER 7
Configuring Workflows in Jira in Agile Spaces

Introduction

Workflows play an essential role in every process as they represent the path a task follows from its creation to its completion. Jira workflows combine statuses and transitions within a process, applicable to various teams like business, Agile, and others. You have the ability to define and execute your processes using Jira workflows. For Agile teams, Jira offers predefined workflows, which can be customized by adding new statuses and transitions. Jira provides default workflows that you can duplicate and modify to fit your space's needs. You can create a workflow on your own or import a workflow from the marketplace.

You can link a workflow to a specific type of task, creating what is called a workflow scheme in Jira. This scheme can be linked to an entire space. By utilizing Jira workflows, you can incorporate conditions, validators, post-functions, and triggers to ensure a streamlined process.

Structure

In this chapter, we will cover the following topics:

- Understanding Workflows in Jira
- Components of Workflow
- Creating a Workflow with an Example
- Editing, Viewing, and Deleting Workflows

- Global Transitions
- Adding a Resolve Issue Screen to the Workflow Transition
- Active versus Inactive Workflows
- Transitions, Conditions, Post-functions, and Triggers
- Workflow Schemes
- Agile Boards and Workflows
- Understanding New Workflow Editor
- Classic Editor versus New Workflow Editor
- Building a Workflow with the New Workflow Editor
- Mistakes to Avoid while Creating Workflows
- Use Cases with References

Components of Workflow

Workflow is a pictorial presentation of any process. It includes statuses, transitions, and resolutions. Jira has a unique feature that allows customization of the workflow steps to match the needs of the spaces. Jira provides its built-in workflow with standard steps. You can also import a workflow from the Atlassian Marketplace. In this chapter, we will be covering topics applicable only to **company-managed spaces**.

Jira workflows mainly consist of three components:

- **Statuses**: They provide information about the current position of a work item or issue. For instance, an issue can progress through stages like Open, In Progress, Resolved, Closed, and Done. These stages are referred to as statuses in Jira.
- **Transitions**: When a work item or issue shifts from one status to another, it is termed as a transition. Transitions can either move in a single direction or go back and forth between two statuses.

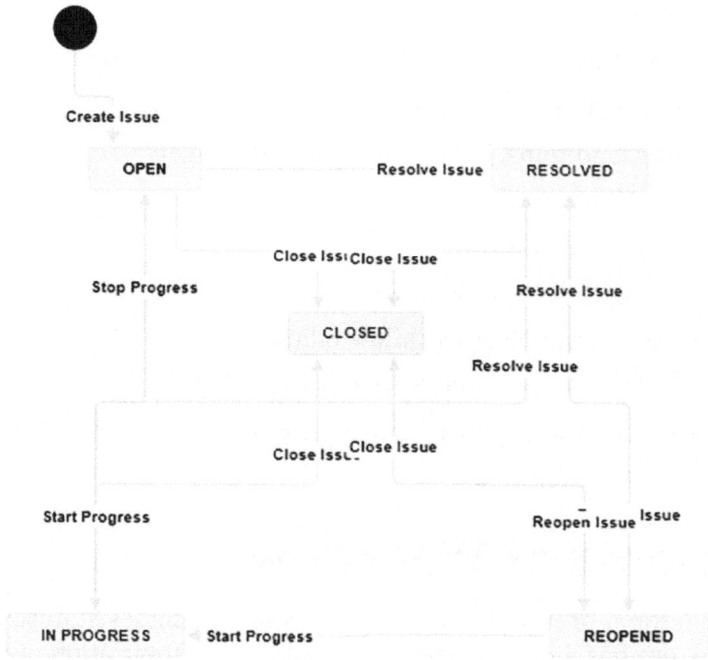

***Figure 7.1**: Classic Default Workflow*

- **Resolutions**: These differ from statuses as they serve to indicate whether an issue has been resolved. If an issue remains unresolved, it can be categorized with statuses like **`abandoned`**, **`won't fix`**, or **`incomplete`**. Resolutions help the team in making informed decisions and effectively managing tasks. Jira also offers a built-in screen for transitioning issues to a resolved state.

Creating a Workflow with Example

In this section, we will learn to create, copy, import, and delete a workflow. Once a workflow is created, we can associate it with a workflow scheme.

Permissions required: Only Jira administrators who have the global permission to Administer Jira can create, edit, and delete workflows in Jira. Members who are not Jira admin with the Edit Workflows permission can modify workflows, if the workflows are not shared with other spaces.

Here are the steps to create a new workflow:

1. Log into your Jira instance with administrative privileges.
2. Navigate to the Issue section by selecting the gear icon and then click on **`Workflow`**.
3. Select **`Workflows`** > **`Add workflow`**.

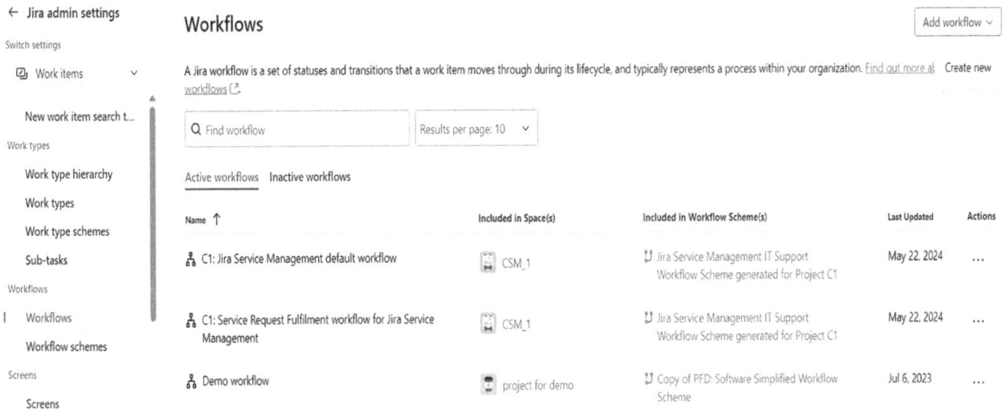

***Figure 7.2**: Adding Workflow*

4. Enter a **Name** and **Description** of the workflow, and then click **Create**.

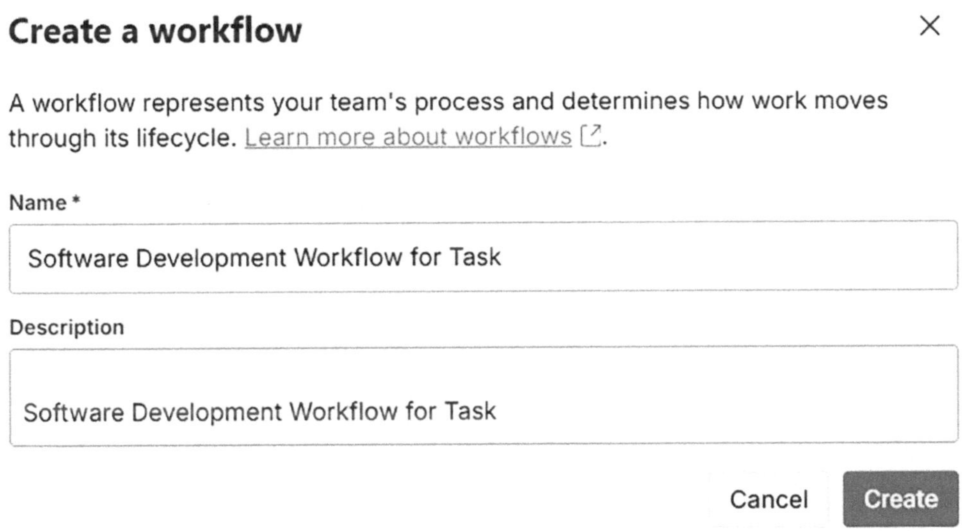

***Figure 7.3**: Adding Name and Description of Workflow*

5. You can then use the workflow editor to add statuses and transitions.

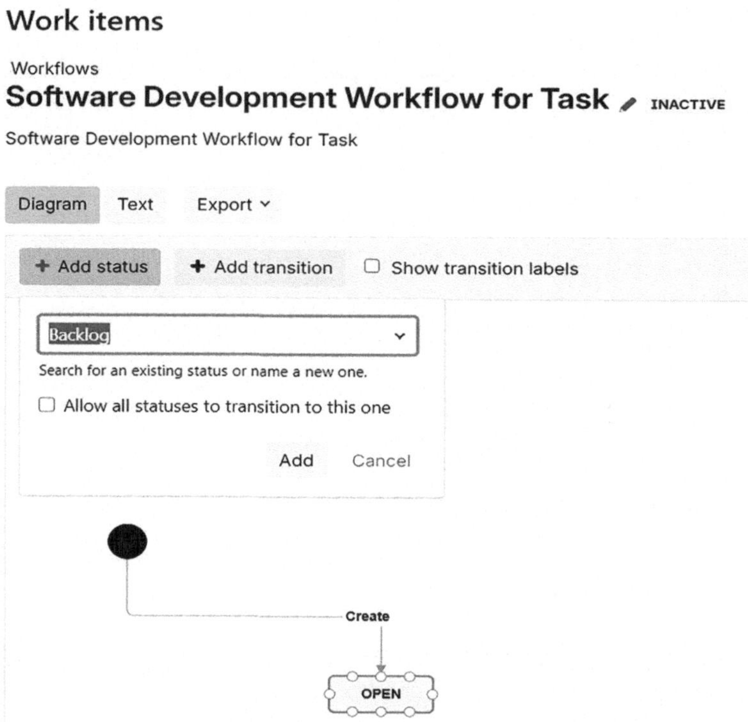

Figure 7.4: *Adding Status*

6. Add all the required statuses as shown in *Figure* 7.5.

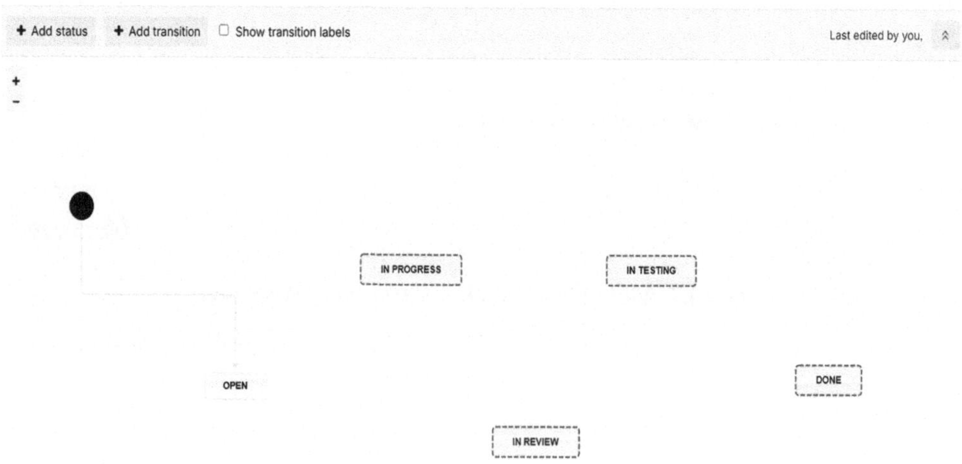

Figure 7.5: *Adding Different Statuses*

7. Now, click on **Add Transition** and enter all the details: From **status, To status**, **Name, Description**, and **Screen**. It is not mandatory to enter the name of the Screen for each transition.

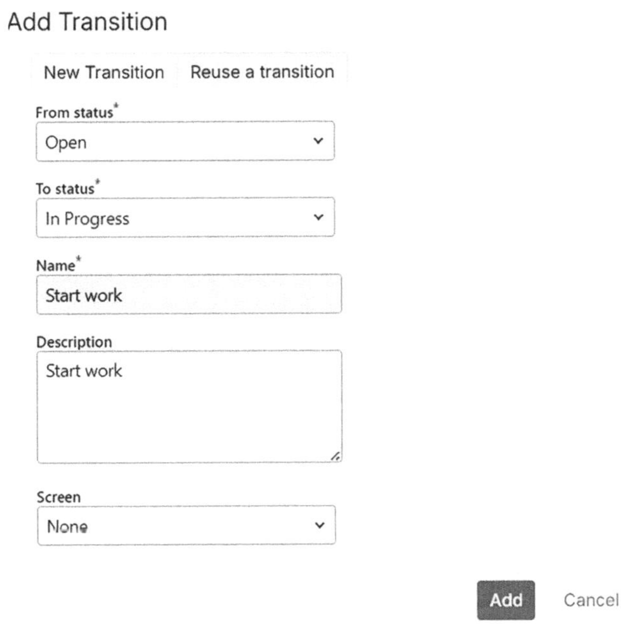

Figure 7.6: *Adding Transitions*

8. Repeat the preceding process for all (forward and backward) the transitions.
9. The workflow has been created.

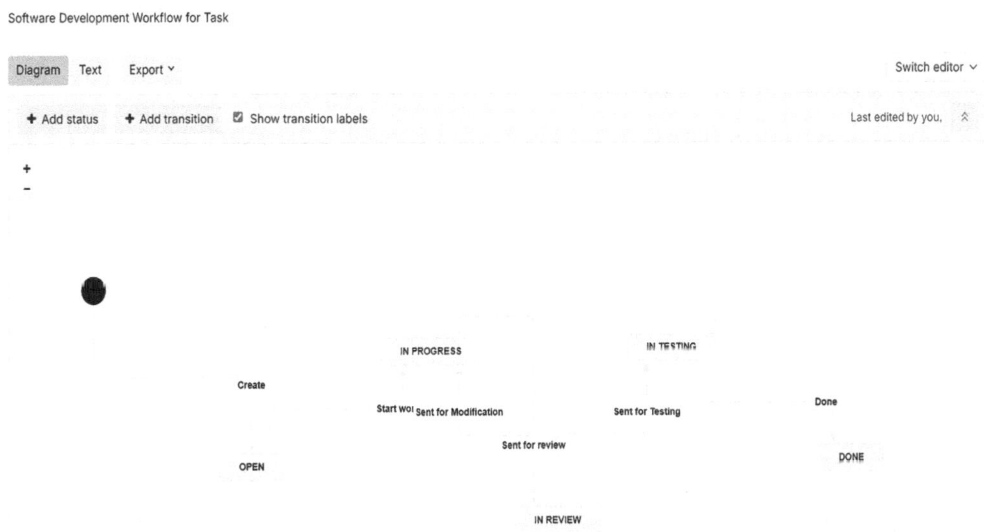

Figure 7.7: *Software Development Workflow for Task*

10. Click on the **`Text`** next to **`Diagram`** to view the workflow in Text mode. You can also edit the workflow in text mode.

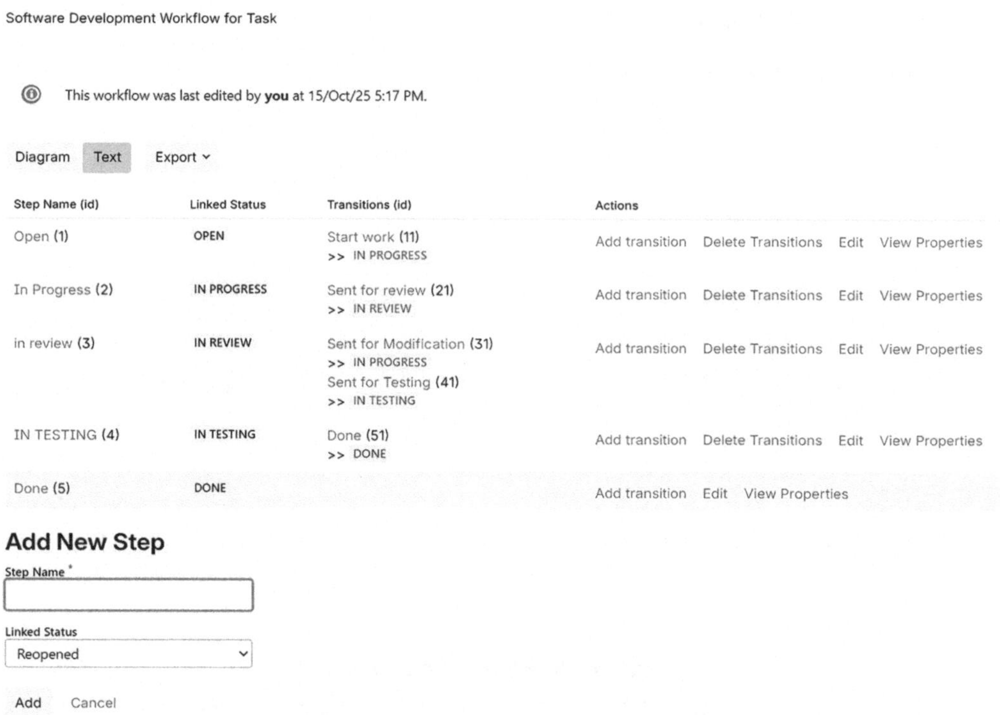

Figure 7.8: *Editing Workflow in Text-mode*

We have created a workflow for software development work type tasks.

Editing, Viewing, and Deleting a Workflow

In this section, we will learn how to Edit, View, or Delete the workflow.

Here are the steps to Edit/View/Delete a workflow:

1. Log into your Jira instance with administrative privileges.
2. Navigate to the **`Issue`** section by selecting the gear icon, and then clicking on Workflow.
3. Select **`Workflows`**.
4. Select **`Active workflows`** or **`Inactive workflows`**.
5. Select the workflow that you want to **`Edit/Delete/Copy`**. Click on the required operation **`(Edit/Delete/Copy)`**.

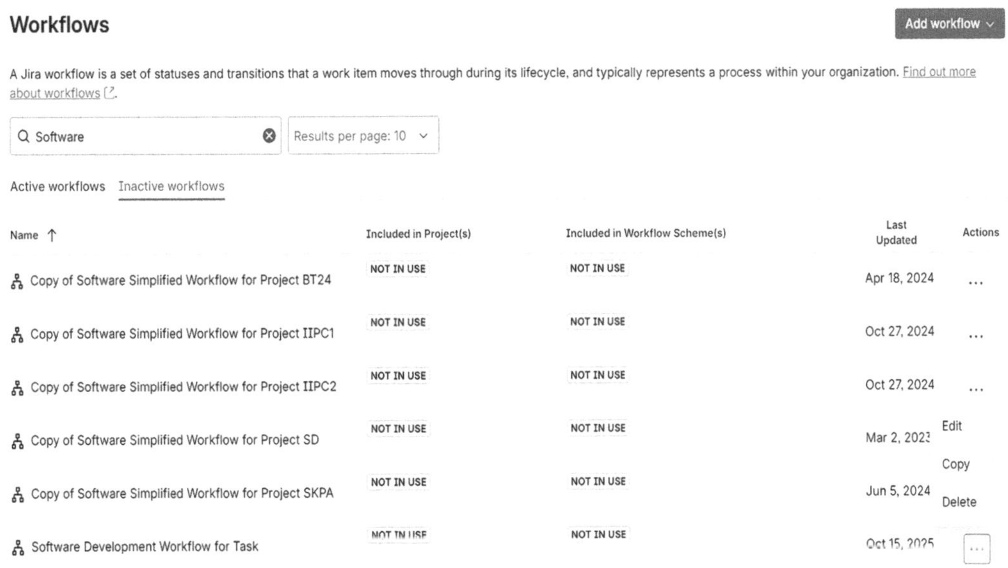

***Figure 7.9**: Edit/Copy/Delete Options for Workflow*

The Delete option can be seen only for those workflows that are not in use (not associated with workflow scheme/space).

Global Transitions

Global transition allows any step in the workflow to transition to a particular workflow step.

Here are the steps on how to add a global transition in a workflow:

1. Log into your Jira instance with administrative privileges.
2. Navigate to the **`Issue`** section by selecting the gear icon, and then clicking on
3. Select **`Workflows`.**
4. Select **`Inactive workflows`.**
5. Select any status in the workflow.
6. Check the **`Allow all statuses to transition to this one`** in the window.
7. You can uncheck it to remove the global transition.

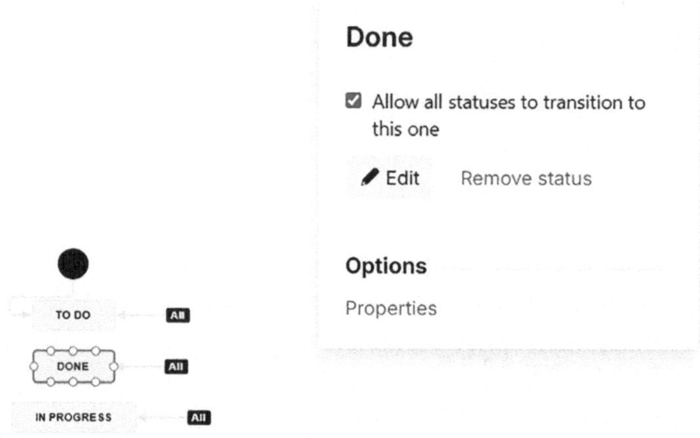

***Figure 7.10**: Adding Global Transitions to a Status*

Associating a Workflow with a Work Type

In Agile spaces, you have different work types such as **`Epic`**, **`Story`**, **`Task`**, **`Bug`**, and so on. **`Story`** can have steps such as **`Open`**, **`In Progress`**, and **`Done`**, while **`Bug`** can go through steps such as **`Open`**, **`In Progress`**, **`In Testing`**, and **`Done`**. You can define **`Workflow 1`** for Story and **`Workflow 2`** for **`Bug`**, new workflow for other work types, and so on. This allows you to have different workflows for various work types.

Example: Here are the steps to associate a `Workflow for Bug` with a work type Bug in a space:

1. We have created a **`Workflow for Bug`**, as shown in *Figure 7.11*.

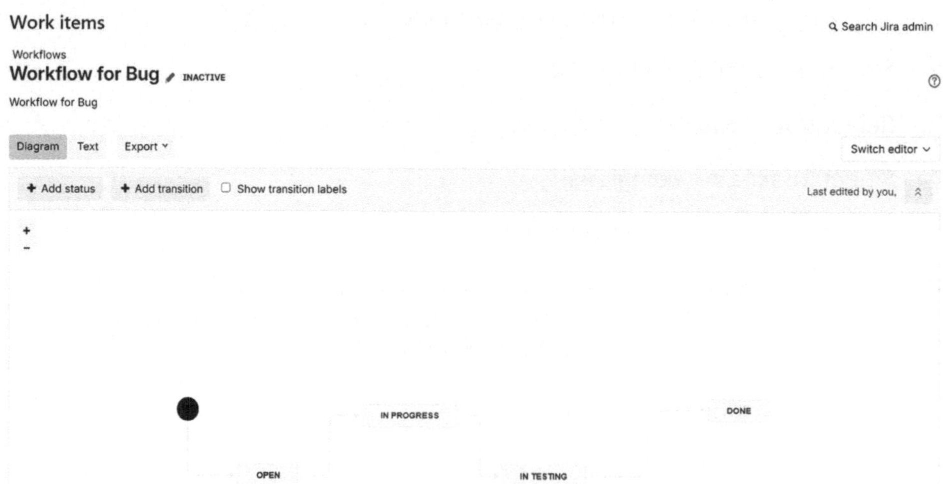

***Figure 7.11**: Workflow for Bug*

2. Navigate to **`All spaces > space > space settings`**.
3. Click on **`Workflows`**.
4. Select **`Add Existing`**.

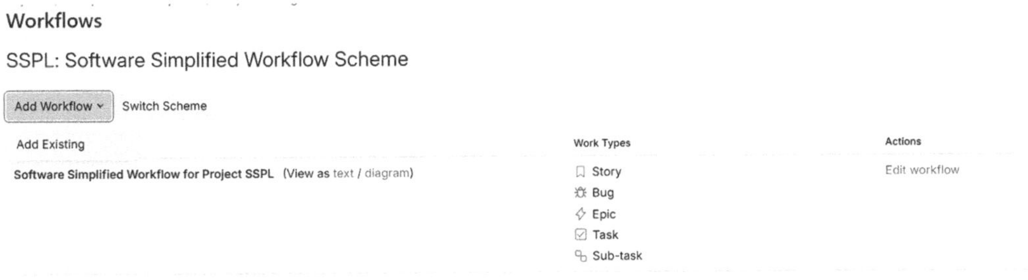

***Figure 7.12**: Adding a Workflow for a Work Type Bug*

5. Select the **`Workflow for Bug`**, and click **`Next`**.

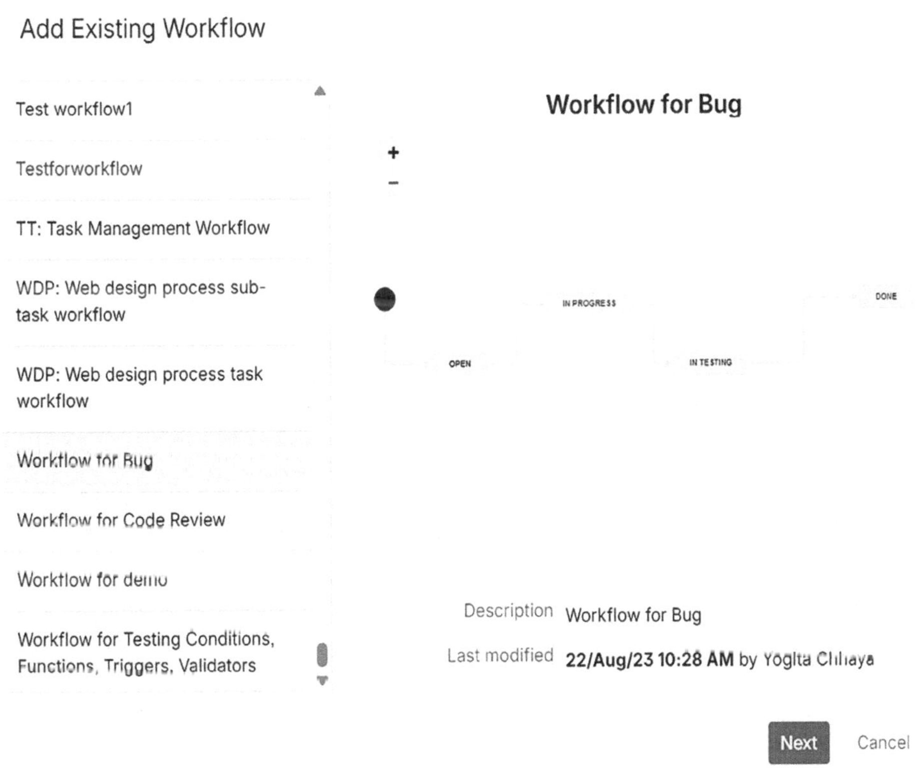

***Figure 7.13**: Associating Bug Work Type with Workflow*

6. Select the work type as **`Bug,`** and click on **`Finish`**.

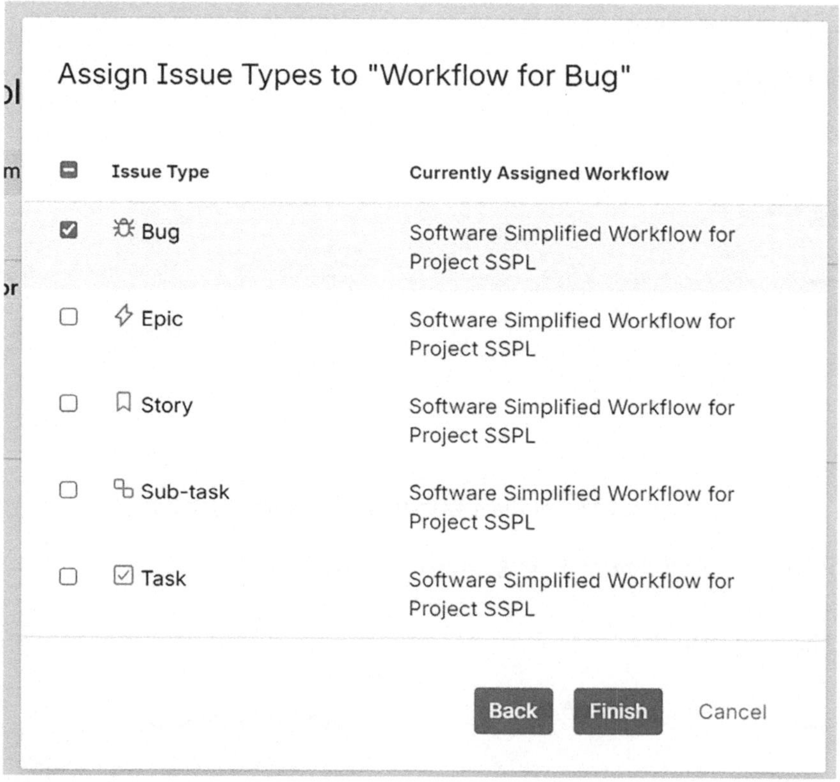

***Figure 7.14**: Associating Bug Work Type*

7. The **`Bug`** work type has been associated with the new workflow for Bug.
8. Click on **`Publish`** to publish the changes in the workflow scheme.

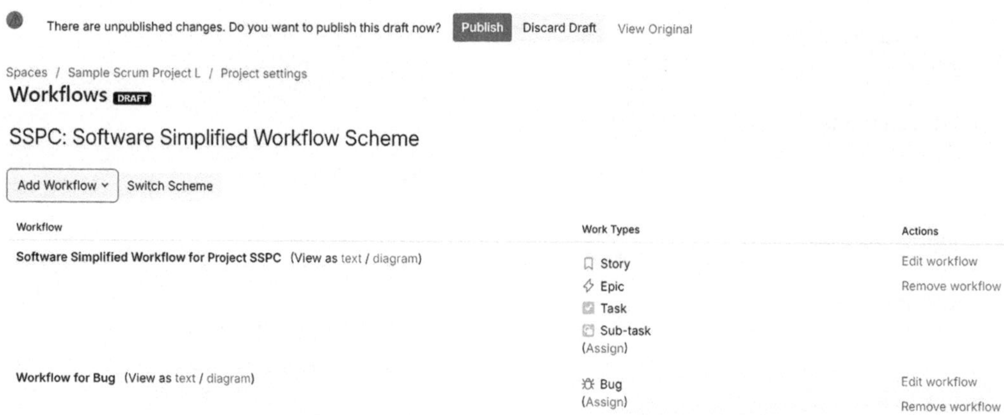

***Figure 7.15**: Publishing Changes in a Workflow Scheme*

Jira creates a draft workflow when we make any changes to the existing workflow. It is necessary to publish the changes so that those changes become permanent.

In this example, we have associated a Bug work type with a new workflow for Bug. All the other work types are associated with the Software Simplified Workflow for space IIPC1.

Adding a Resolve Issue Screen to Workflow Transition

We will learn how to add a resolution screen when the Bug is transitioned to the Done status and add the details.

Jira provides inbuilt screens that can be added to workflow transitions for setting the resolution. In the workflow for Bug, the last transition is Done and Resolved.

Follow these steps to add the Resolve Issue screen on the Done transition:

1. Log into your Jira instance with administrative privileges.
2. Navigate to the **`Issue`** section by selecting the gear icon and then clicking on **`workflow`**.
3. Select **`Workflows`**.
4. Select **`Workflow for Bug`** and select **`Edit`**.
5. Select **`Add Transition`** and add the details for the transition from **`IN TESTING`** to **`DONE`**.
6. Add the transition name as **`Done and Resolved`**.
7. Select the **`Resolve Issue screen`** from the dropdown.
8. Click **`Save`**.

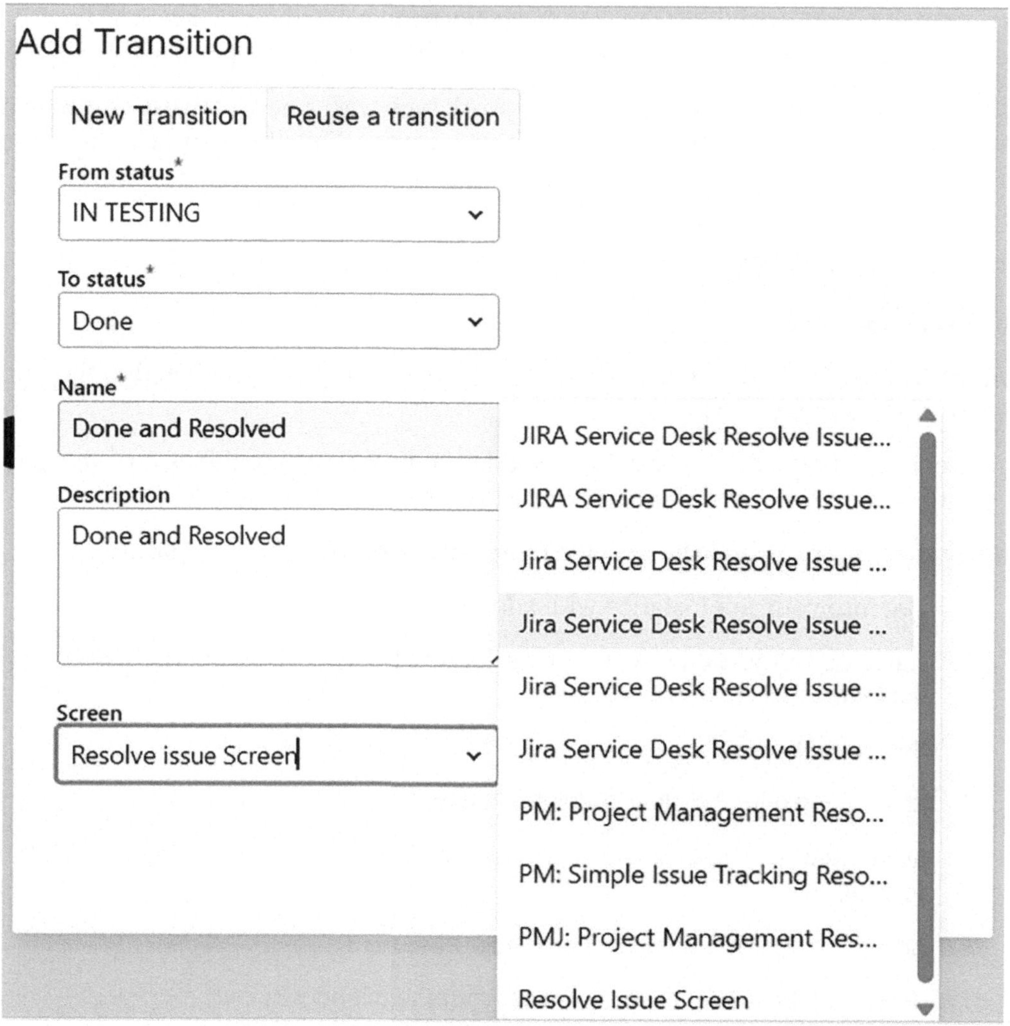

***Figure 7.16**: Adding a Resolve Issue Screen on the Done and Resolved Workflow Transition*

9. We have added the **`Resolve Issue Screen`** on the **`Done and Resolved`** transition.
10. To test this transition, `Open any Bug` in the same space. Do all the transitions as defined in the workflow.
11. In the transition from **`In Testing`** to **`Done`**, you will be prompted to enter the details on the resolve issue screen.
12. Add the details such as **`Resolution`** and **`Time spent`**, and then click on **`Update.`**

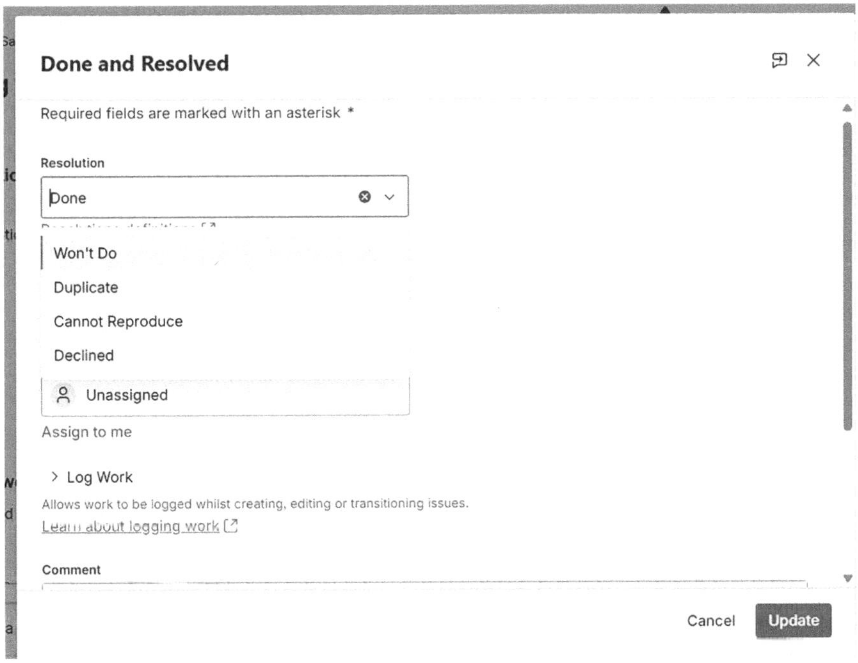

Figure 7.17: *Resolve Issue Screen*

Workflow Schemes

Workflow schemes are like a bunch of different workflows associated with different work types.

For example, space A has work types such as **`Epic`**, **`Story`**, **`Task`**, **`Sub-task`**, and **`Bug`**. You can create a Workflow Scheme A containing different workflows for each work type, which is exclusively for space A.

Space B has work types such as **`Story`**, **`Task`**, and **`Bug`**. You can create a Workflow Scheme B containing different workflows for each work type, which is exclusively for space B.

These schemes can be associated with spaces. It helps organizations to save time by customizing schemes and utilizing the same for multiple spaces.

In this example, we will copy a workflow scheme, and then associate it with a space.

You can also create a new workflow scheme by selecting "Add a workflow scheme".

Here are the steps:

1. Log in as a **`Jira Administrator`**.

2. Navigate to **Workflow Schemes** under **Workflows** in the Jira Administration section.
3. Select a workflow scheme from the **Active workflow** scheme, and click on **Copy.**

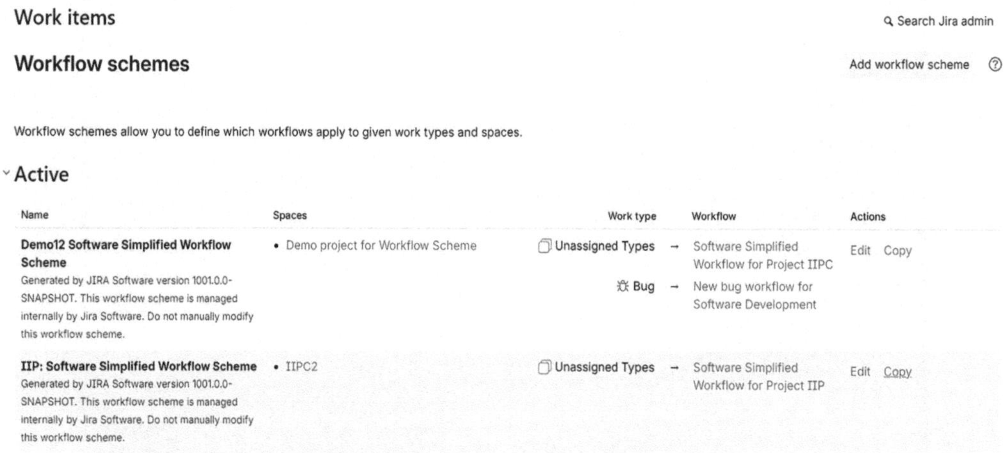

Figure 7.18: *Copying a Workflow Scheme*

4. Jira provides **Active** and **Inactive** workflow schemes. Go to **Inactive** workflow schemes. The copied workflow scheme has been added to the inactive workflow scheme. Click on **Edit.**

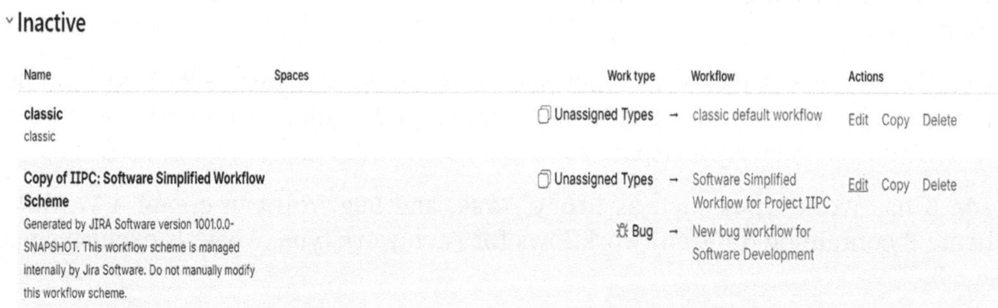

Figure 7.19: *Editing a Copy of Workflow Scheme*

5. Edit the name of the copied scheme as **Demo Software Simplified Workflow Scheme.** Click to save the changes. Now, the newly created workflow scheme is ready to be associated with a space.

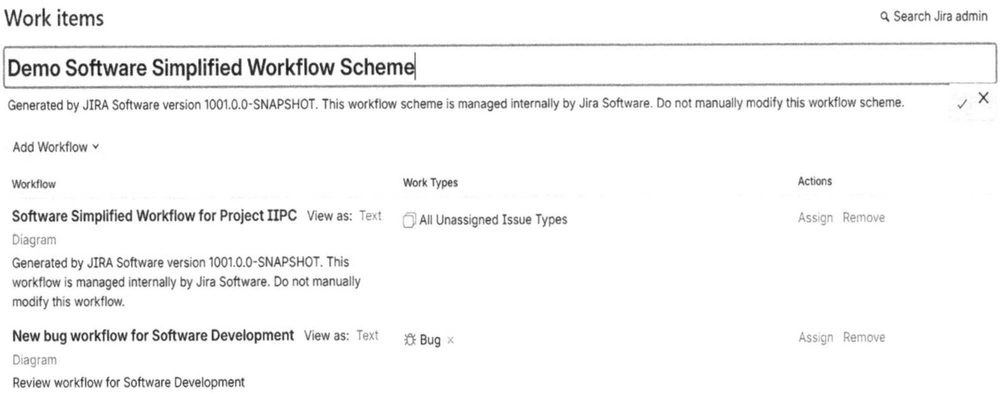

Figure 7.20: *Adding a Name of a New Workflow Scheme*

6. Navigate to **`spaces`** > select **`space`** > **`space Settings`**. Select the space name that you want to associate with the Demo workflow scheme.
7. Select **`Workflows`**, and then click on **`Switch Scheme`**.

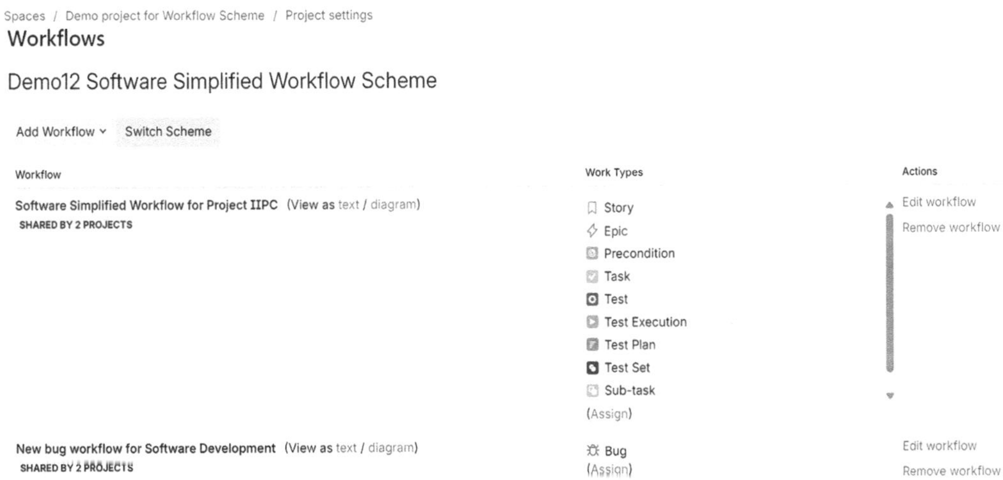

Figure 7.21: *Switch Scheme to Associate with Other Workflow Schemes*

8. Click on **`Associate`**.

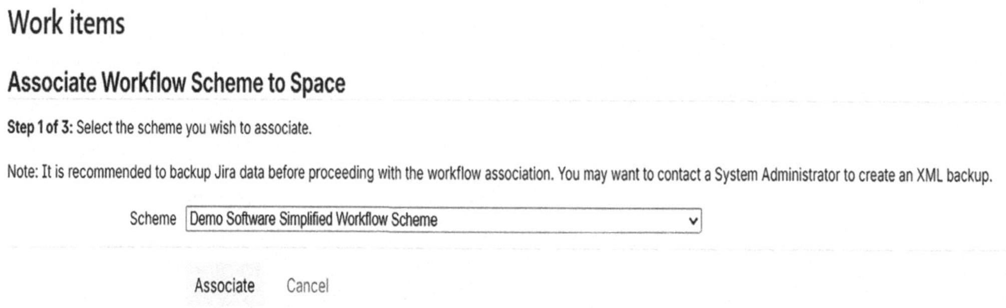

***Figure 7.22**: Associating New Workflow Scheme*

9. The **`Demo Software Simplified Workflow Scheme`** has been associated with the **`Demo space for Workflow Scheme`**.

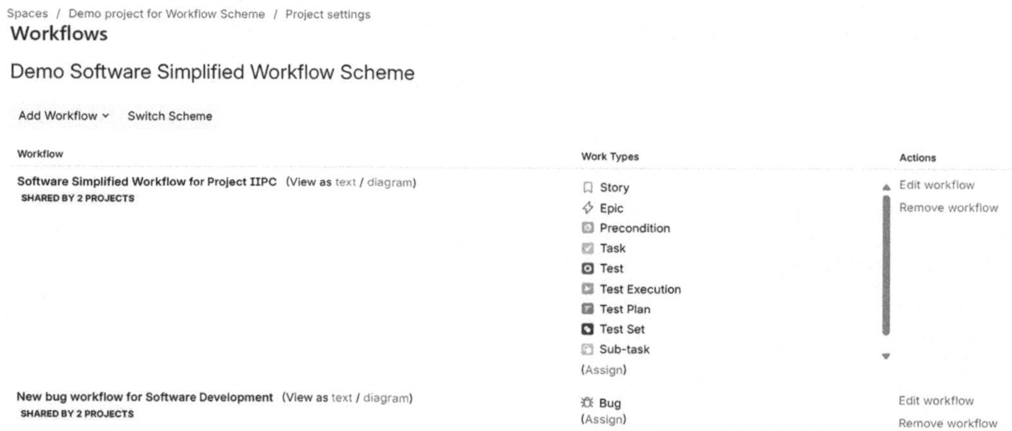

***Figure 7.23**: New Workflow Scheme Association with a Space*

As shown in *Figure* 7.23, the **`Bug`** work type has been associated with the New Bug Workflow for Software Development. All other work types have been associated with Software Simplified Workflow for space IIPC. To summarize, a workflow scheme is a combination of work type and workflow associations, and it can be finally associated with multiple spaces in Jira.

Conditions, Post-Functions, Validators, and Triggers

Conditions: Conditions specify a few essentials for a transition to take place. If the requirements are not met to fulfill the condition, the transition is not allowed.

For example, a user must be in a **Developer** role to start the development task. Conditions control the transitions. A user cannot Start Work on the task until he is assigned a task.

Example: We will add a few conditions on transitioning of an issue. To do this, follow these steps:

1. Log in as a **Jira Administrator**.
2. Navigate to **Workflow** under **Workflows** in the Jira Administration section.
3. Select **Inactive workflows** and open the workflow in **Diagram** mode.
4. Select the transition **Start work** and click on **Conditions** to add a condition.

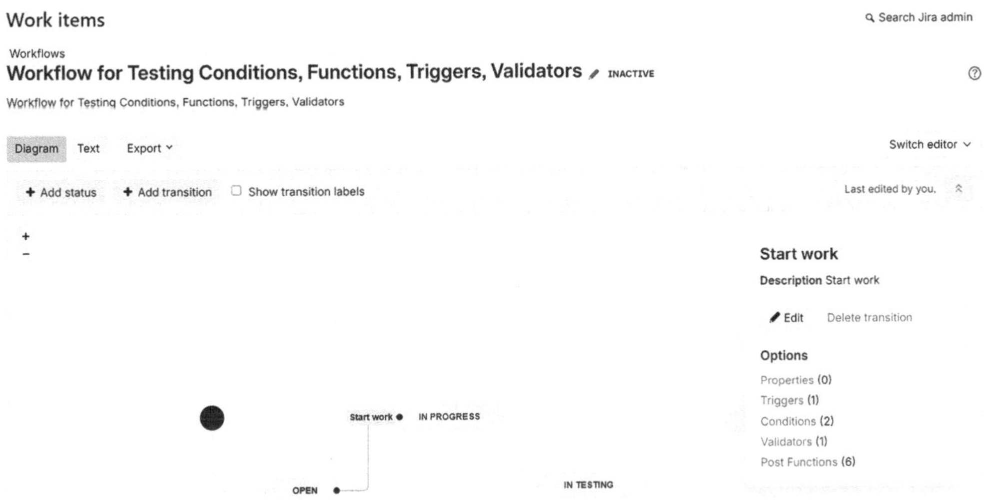

***Figure 7.24**: Adding Conditions on Start Work Transition*

5. Select the condition **User is in space Role** and click **Add.**

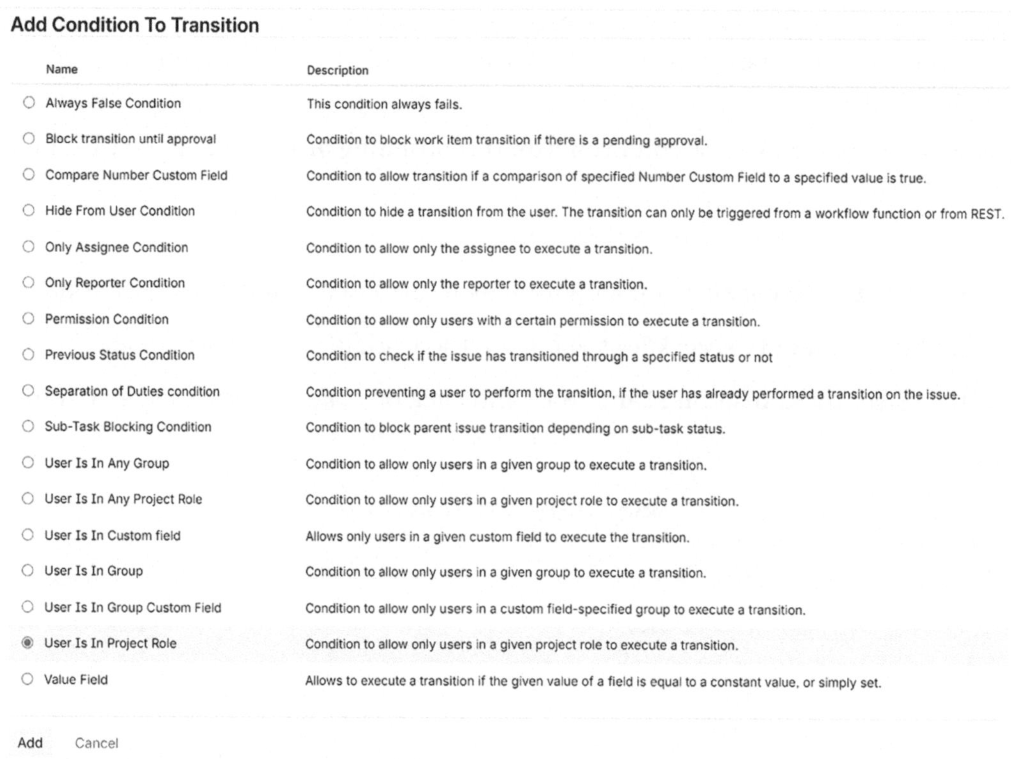

***Figure 7.25**: Condition Based on User Space Role*

6. Select the User Role as **`Scrum Masters`**.

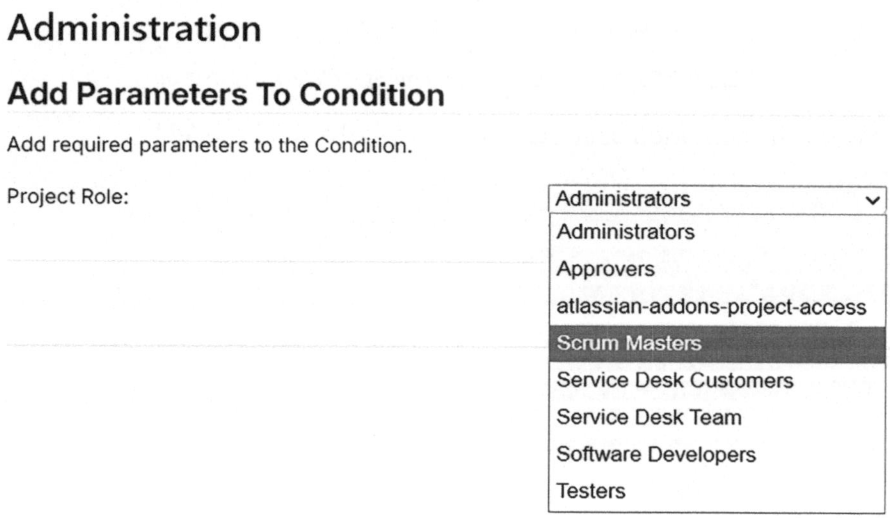

***Figure 7.26**: Selecting Space Role for Adding Role-based Condition*

7. Select another condition, **`Only the assignee of the issue can execute the transition`** and click **Add**. We have now added two conditions.

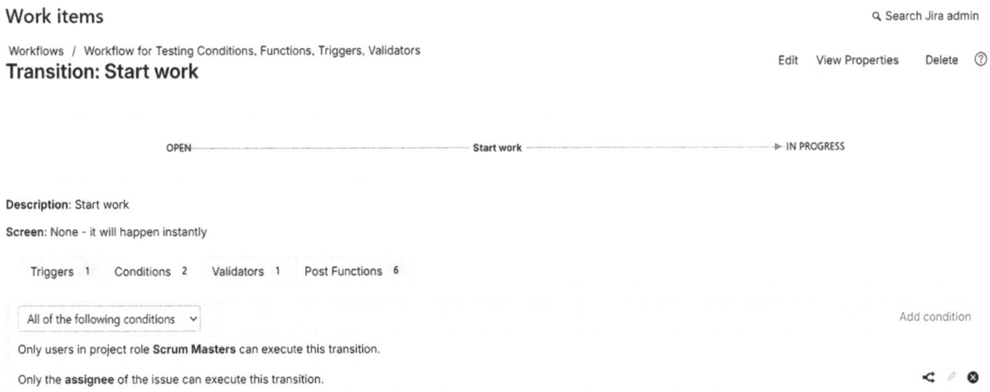

***Figure 7.27**: Multiple Conditions on a Transition*

8. Select the **`Any of the following conditions`** option, as shown in *Figure* 7.28. It allows the assignee of the task or scrum master to close the task.

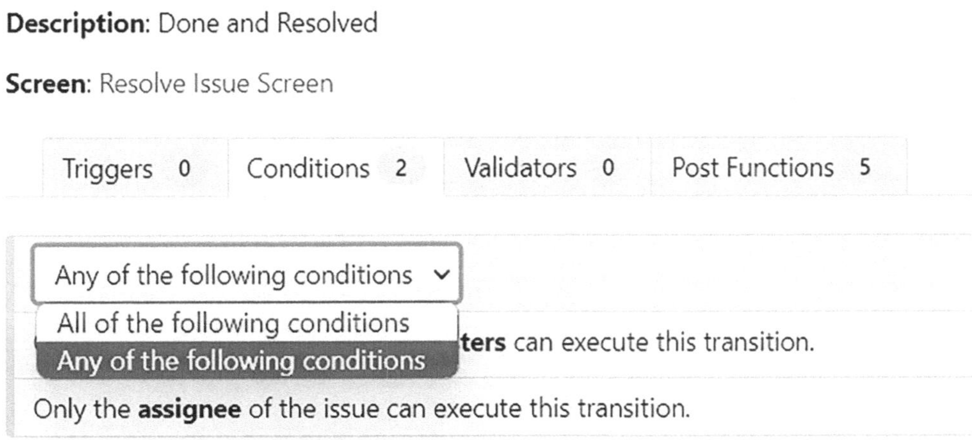

***Figure 7.28**: Selecting Any of the Following Conditions*

There are many other conditions, which can be used to control the transition.

Post-function: Post-functions allow users to add extra functions after a transition has occurred. For example, setting or clearing a field value after a transition has occurred.

In this example, we will learn how to assign a task to the current user when an issue is created. Here are the steps:

1. Log in as a **`Jira Administrator`**.

2. Navigate to **`Workflow`** under **`Workflows`** in the Jira Administration section.
3. Select `Inactive workflows` and open the workflow in Diagram mode.
4. Click on **`Post-Functions,`** and select the **`Create`** transition.

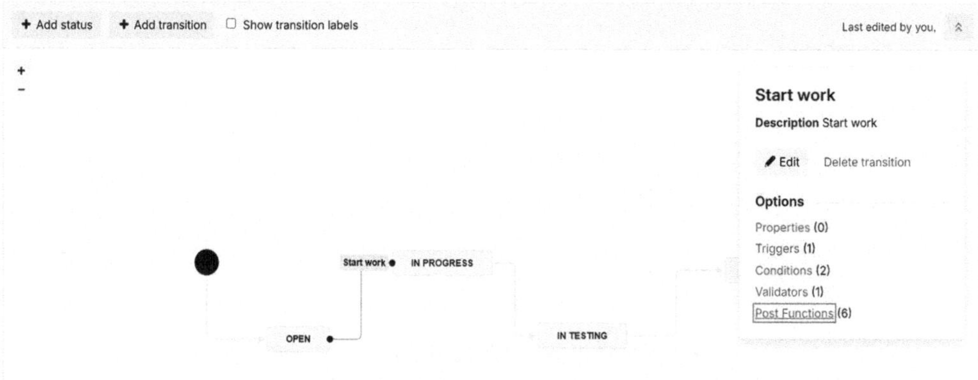

***Figure 7.29**: Adding Post-function*

5. Select the **`Post-function Assign`** to the current user, and click **`Add`**.

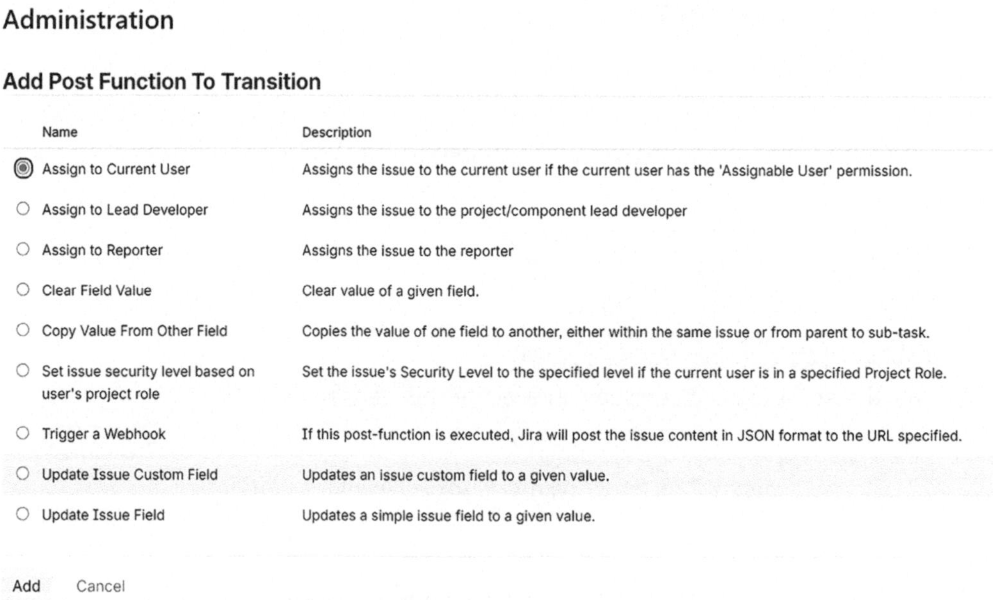

Administration

Add Post Function To Transition

Name	Description
Assign to Current User	Assigns the issue to the current user if the current user has the 'Assignable User' permission.
Assign to Lead Developer	Assigns the issue to the project/component lead developer
Assign to Reporter	Assigns the issue to the reporter
Clear Field Value	Clear value of a given field.
Copy Value From Other Field	Copies the value of one field to another, either within the same issue or from parent to sub-task.
Set issue security level based on user's project role	Set the issue's Security Level to the specified level if the current user is in a specified Project Role.
Trigger a Webhook	If this post-function is executed, Jira will post the issue content in JSON format to the URL specified.
Update Issue Custom Field	Updates an issue custom field to a given value.
Update Issue Field	Updates a simple issue field to a given value.

Add Cancel

***Figure 7.30**: Post-function Selection*

Users can change the sequence of the post-functions by clicking on the up and down arrows. Additionally, users can also select to fire a generic event for an issue created, issue updated, and so on.

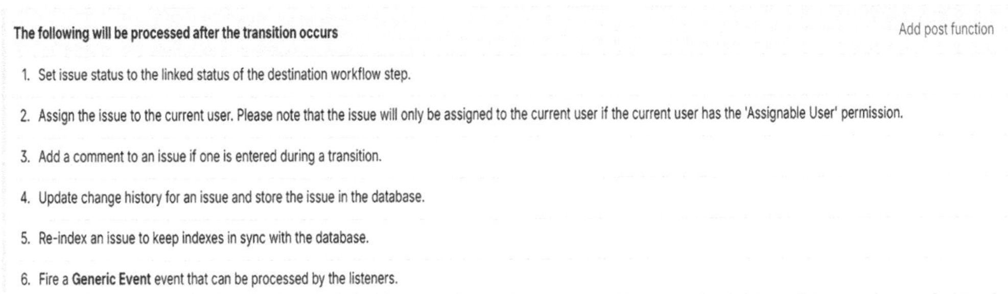

***Figure 7.31**: List of Post-functions after the Transition Occurs*

We have added a post-function on the **`create`** transition.

Validators: These serve as checkpoints to validate values. For instance, they can verify values within required custom fields or assess the presence of necessary permissions.

In this example, we will add a validator to check for manage sprints permissions on the Start Work transition. Here are the steps:

1. Log in as a **`Jira Administrator`**.
2. Navigate to **`Workflow`** under **`Workflows`** in the Jira Administration section.
3. Select `Inactive workflows` and open the workflow in **`Diagram`** mode.
4. Select the **`Start work`** transition, and click on **`Validators.`**

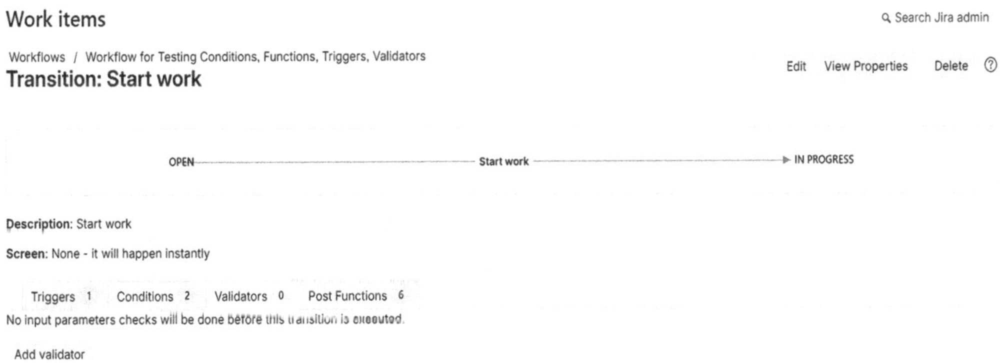

***Figure 7.32**: Adding Validators on Start Work Transition*

5. Select **`Permission validator`** that validates the user permission.

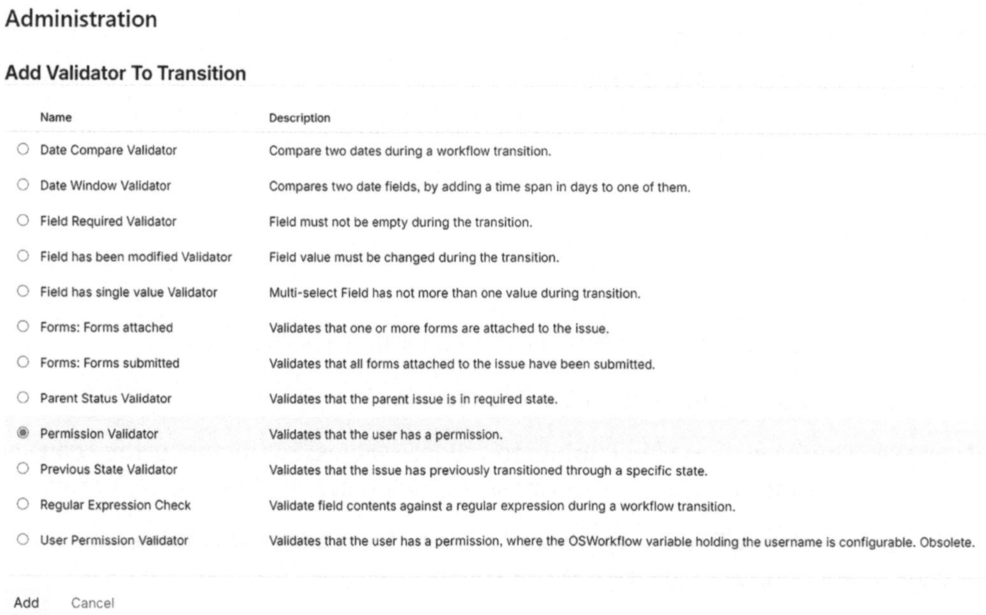

Figure 7.33: *Selecting Permission Validator*

6. Select **`Add`** and the **`Manage sprints`** permission. A user with this permission is allowed to start work in a sprint.

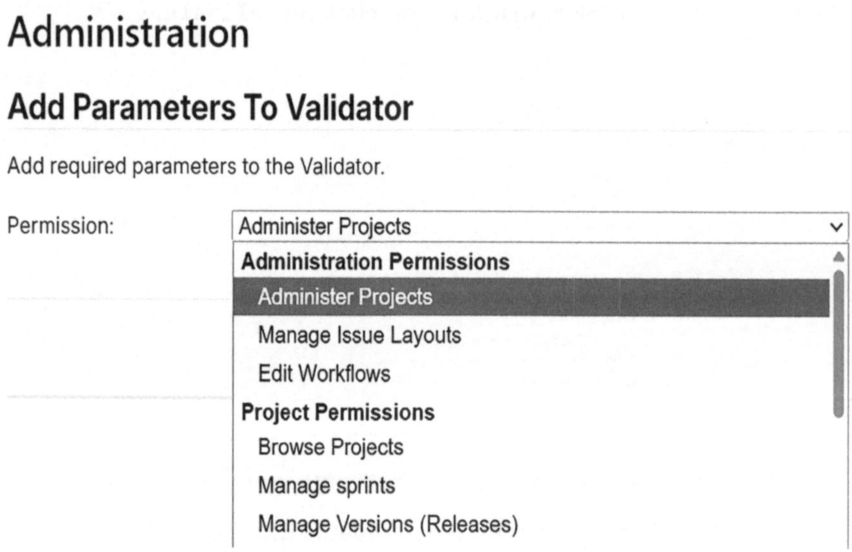

Figure 7.34: *Selecting Manage Sprints from the List of Permissions*

We have added the validator to check for the "Manage Sprints" permission. Similarly, users can add other validators such as parent status validator, date comparison, required field, and so on.

Triggers: The triggers help automate transitions as and when specific events occur in other systems. For example, Code review in the code repository. By doing so, triggers remove the necessity for your team to manually alter the process status when conditions are fulfilled.

Example: Here are the steps to add a `commit created` trigger on the `Start progress` transition:

1. Log in as a **`Jira Administrator`**.
2. Navigate to **`Workflow`** under **`Workflows`** in the Jira Administration section.
3. Select **`Inactive workflows`** and open the **`Workflow for Code Review`** in **`Diagram`** mode.
4. Select the transition **`Start Progress`** and click on **`Triggers`**.

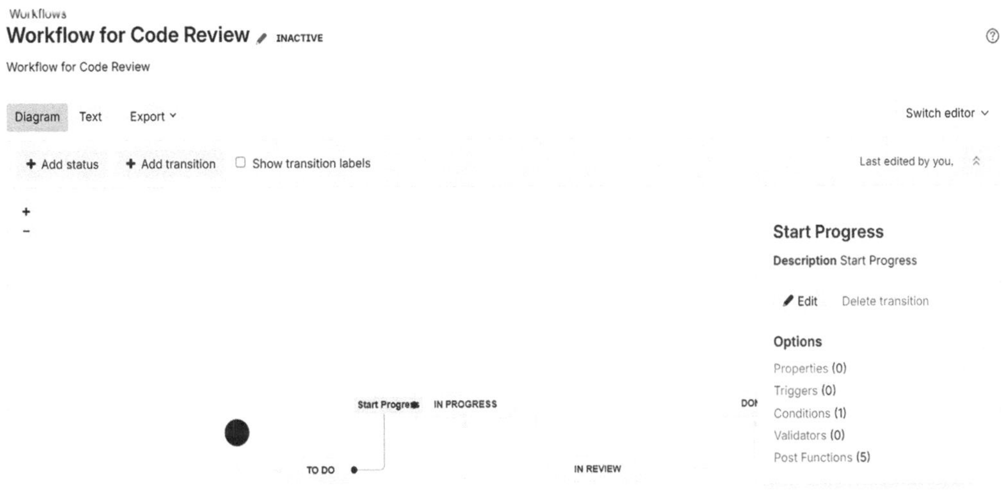

Figure 7.35: Adding Triggers on Start Work Transition

5. Click on **`Add trigger`**.

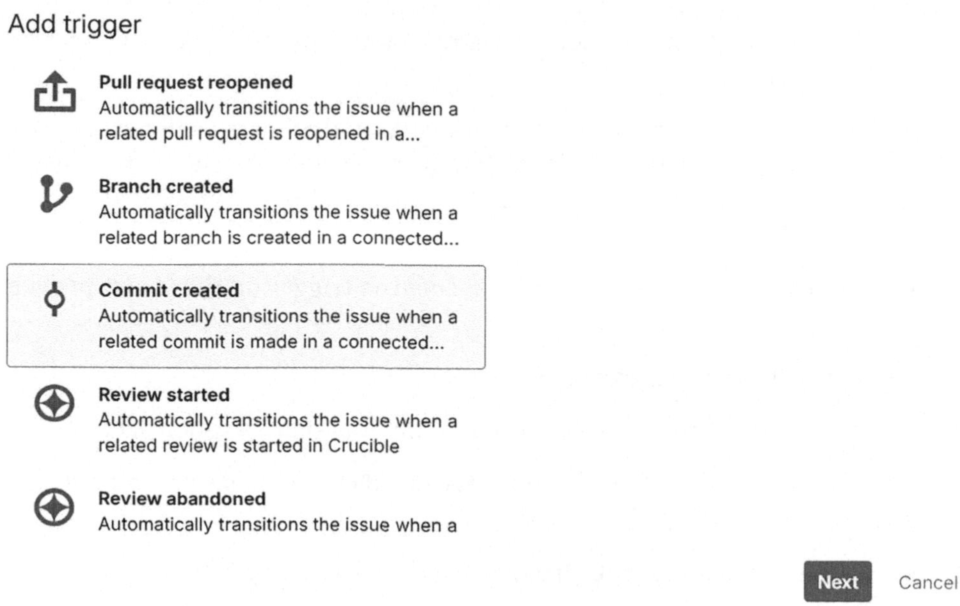

***Figure 7.36**: Adding Commit Created Trigger*

6. Click on **`Next,`** and then click **`Add trigger`**.

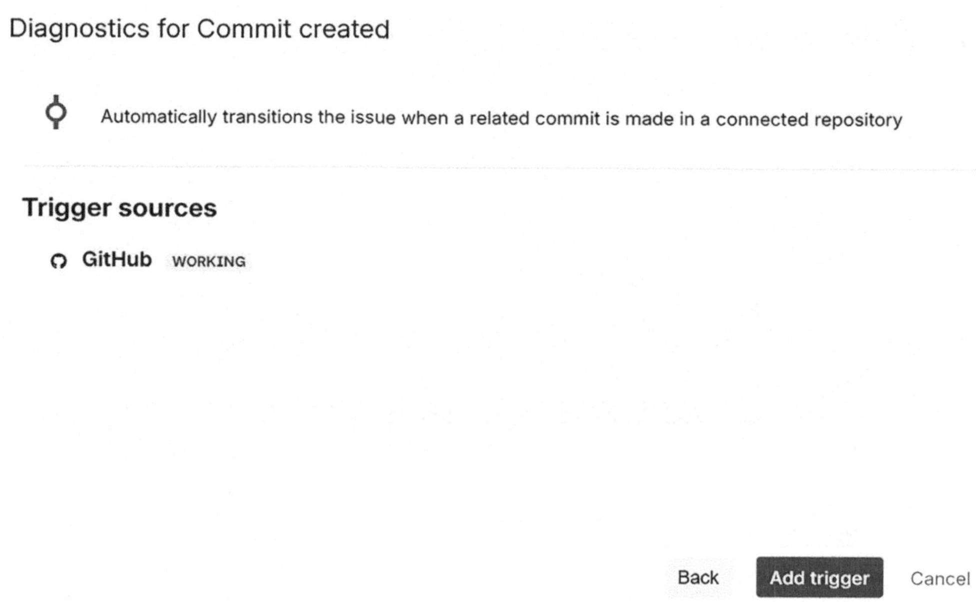

***Figure 7.37**: Adding Trigger to Automate Transitions*

7. Adding this trigger will automatically transition the issue when a pull request is created in a connected repository.

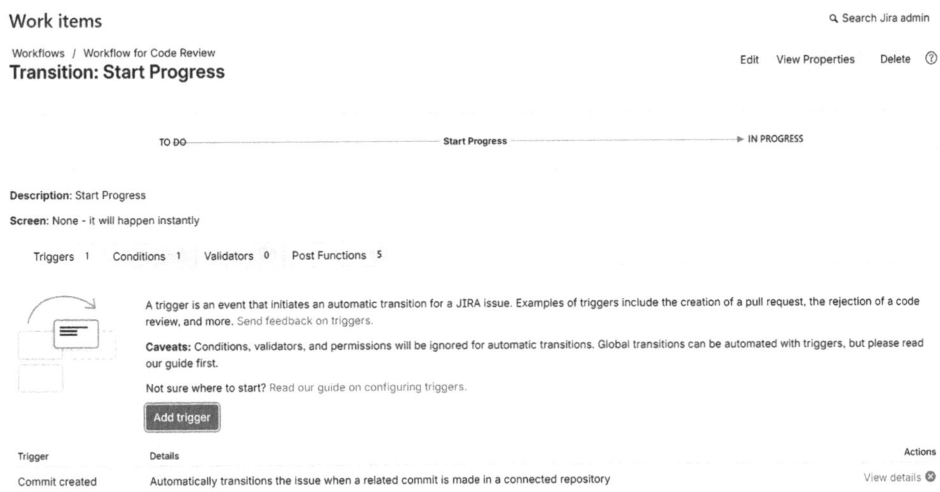

Figure 7.38: Commit Created Trigger

A trigger Commit created has been added. Similarly, triggers such as **Review Started**, **Review Abandoned**, and **Review Closed** can be added to the transitions **Start Review**, **Restart Progress**, and **Done transitions** in Crucible.

The names of the **Development Tools** that can be integrated with Jira for managing code reviews are as follows:

- Fisheye/Crucible
- Bitbucket
- GitHub
- GitHub Enterprise

Publish the Draft workflow after adding Conditions, Post-Functions, Validators, and Triggers, if you are Editing an active workflow.

Do not add triggers on Global transitions. Instead, add the issue key in code-commit, branch, pull request, or review messages. There are many triggers that can be added, such as Review started, Review closed, and so on. Test the triggers, while you are doing it for the first time by integrating them with the development tools.

Active versus Inactive Workflows

Active Workflow: A workflow is considered active when it is presently in use by one or multiple spaces. When you make changes to an active workflow, Jira initially generates a draft version of it. Once you have completed your edits, you can finalize your draft by publishing it and, if desired, retain the original workflow as an inactive backup.

There are limitations while editing a draft of an active workflow in Jira as follows:

- Existing workflow steps cannot be deleted.
- The associated status cannot be edited.
- Step IDs for the existing steps cannot be changed.
- You can modify the workflow description, but you cannot modify its name.

Inactive Workflow: An inactive workflow is one that is presently not being utilized by any spaces. Since there are currently no issues undergoing transitions within an inactive workflow, you have the ability to directly modify the steps and transitions of the workflow.

To convert the inactive workflow into active workflow, associate it with a work type, add the workflow to a workflow scheme, and finally associate the scheme with a space.

Workflows and Agile Boards

Jira has two types of workflows for software spaces:

- Software Simplified Workflow
- Jira (Customized) Workflow.

In this section, we will understand the difference between these two types of workflows.

Software Simplified Workflow:

- It is a straightforward and minimalistic workflow process designed for small teams or simple spaces.
- It involves only three steps: **`To Do, In Progress`**, and **`Done`** for the Scrum board. For the Kanban board, it has four steps: **`Backlog, Selected for Development, In Progress, and Done.`**
- Setting up the Software Simplified Workflow is quick and easy, making it suitable for teams without complex process requirements.
- There is less administrative work as the workflow involves a lesser number of transitions and statuses.
- Issues can be moved easily between columns.
- No transition screens will appear, while moving the issues, and it sets the resolution automatically when the issues move to the final Done status.

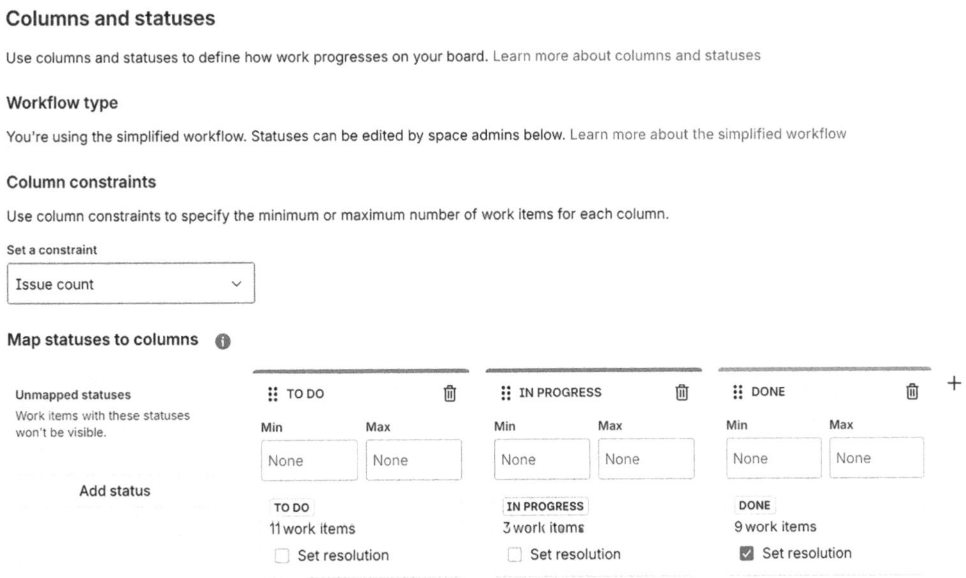

***Figure 7.39**: Software Simplified Workflow*

Jira Workflow:

- It is a highly customizable and adaptable workflow suitable for complex spaces and teams of varying sizes.
- Jira workflows can have multiple steps, statuses, transitions, and conditions to customize the complex space process.
- Jira workflows support automation through conditions, validators, and post-functions, streamlining processes and reducing manual work.
- It can accommodate many workflow steps that are typically needed on a board.
- It has workflow conditions that do not allow issues to be moved between all columns.
- It displays screens on transitions, such as Resolve Issue, Close Issue, and Reopen Issue.
- Jira workflow can only be edited via workflow configuration.

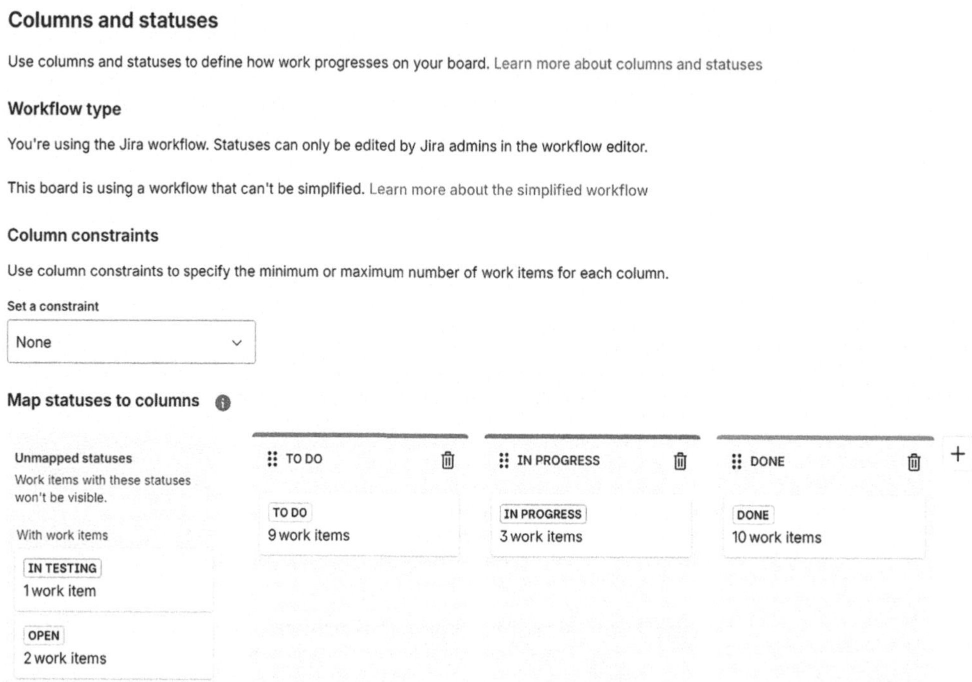

Figure 7.40: *Customizable Jira Workflow*

Understanding New Workflow Editor

We learned everything about the old workflow editor in Jira. Atlassian has introduced a new workflow editing experience known as the new workflow editor. In this section, we will understand what the new workflow editor in Jira is, and explore its benefits and limitations.

The goal of the new editor is to help admins with a better user interface and enable them to make changes without navigating across multiple tabs. Instead, the new editor provides a single-pane, visual canvas that allows you to manage statuses, transitions and rules (conditions, validators, and post-functions) within one unified experience.

However, this update also has some downsides. Some features from the classical editor are still missing or limited in the new editor. As an administrator, you must understand both the advantages and the current limitations so you can choose wisely and manage your workflows easily.

In the next section, we will compare the old vs new editors, walk through step-by-step how to create and configure a workflow in the new editor and then understand triggers, events and tips to overcome these limitations.

Classic Editor versus New Workflow Editor

We will cover a side-by-side comparison of how the old editor differs from the new workflow editor in Jira Cloud.

Differences:

Draft vs Live Editing

- In the old editor, when you modify a workflow that is active, changes are saved in a draft version until you publish them. You must copy the workflow, edit the copy and then associate.
- In the new editor, edits are made directly to the published workflow. You can update immediately or discard changes; there is no separate draft mode.

Editing Active Workflows

- In the old editor, many changes are prohibited on active workflows: you cannot delete statuses, or if a status has no outgoing transitions, you cannot add new ones, etc. You must copy and replace via workflow schemes.
- The new editor does not have many of those restrictions: For example, you can delete a status in an active workflow (you will be prompted to remap issues) or add outgoing transitions to a status with no outgoing transitions.

Unified View and Navigation

- The old editor requires switching between multiple tabs (diagram, text, transitions, conditions, post-functions) and pages to manage parts of the workflow.
- In the new editor, you have a single interface: a toolbar, diagram canvas, and a sidebar for editing details. Everything (statuses, transitions, rules) is available in a single view.

Shared Transitions / Reuse across Statuses

- In the old editor, reuse of transitions required you to define a transition and then manually "`add transition`" or "`reuse transition`" across statuses.
- In the new editor, when creating or editing a transition you can select multiple "`From`" statuses, thus sharing a single transition instance (with its rules) across them.

Terminology Shift / Rule Reorganization

- The classic editor has separate tabs for Conditions, Validators, and Post-Functions, each concept being separate.

- The new editor uses a consolidated concept called Rules, with sub-categories: Restrict transition (conditions), Validate details (validators) and Perform actions (post-functions).

Feature Support Differences / Missing Features

- Some advanced conditions, validators, or post-functions available in older editor (or via apps) are not yet supported in the new editor.
- Some rule types (e.g. certain permission validators, custom field conditions, date window, parent status validator) may not yet be available.

Trigger Support

- The new editor currently has limited or missing support for *triggers* (that is, automatic transitions based on external events) in different contexts.

Building a Workflow with the New Workflow Editor

1. Navigate to **`Cog icon`** > **`Work items`** > **`Workflow`**. Click **`Add workflow`** > **`Create new`**.

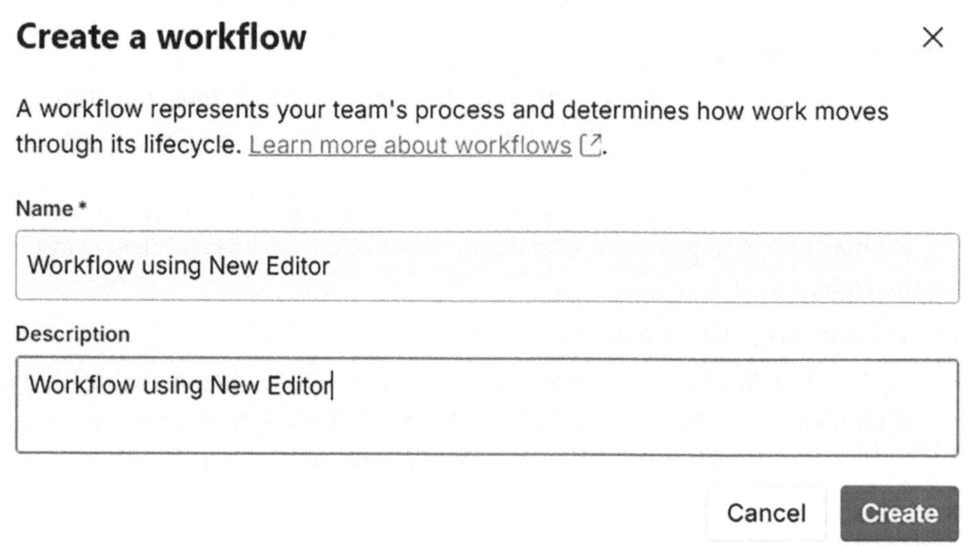

Figure 7.41: *Creating Workflow in New Editor*

2. When the workflow window opens, click **`Switch`** to the new editor.

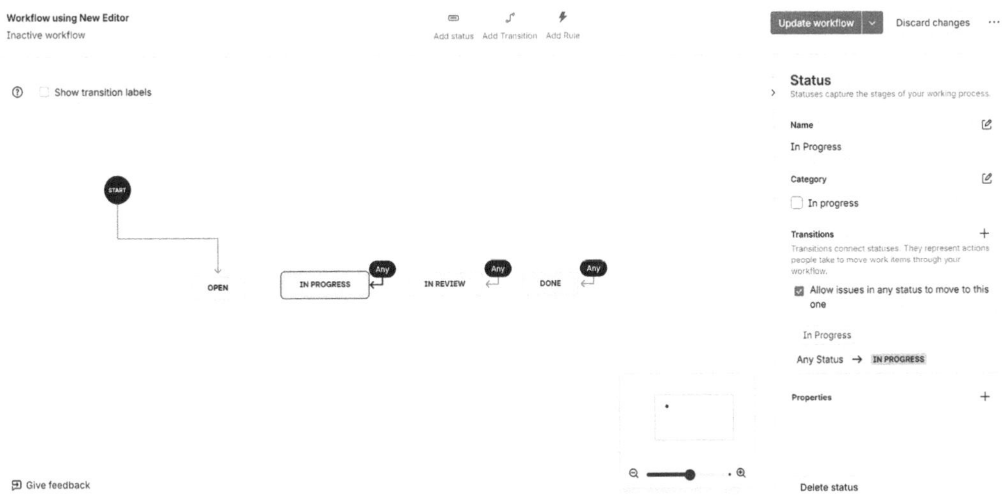

Figure 7.42: *New Workflow Editor*

3. In the new editor, click **`Add status`** to create or add required statuses.

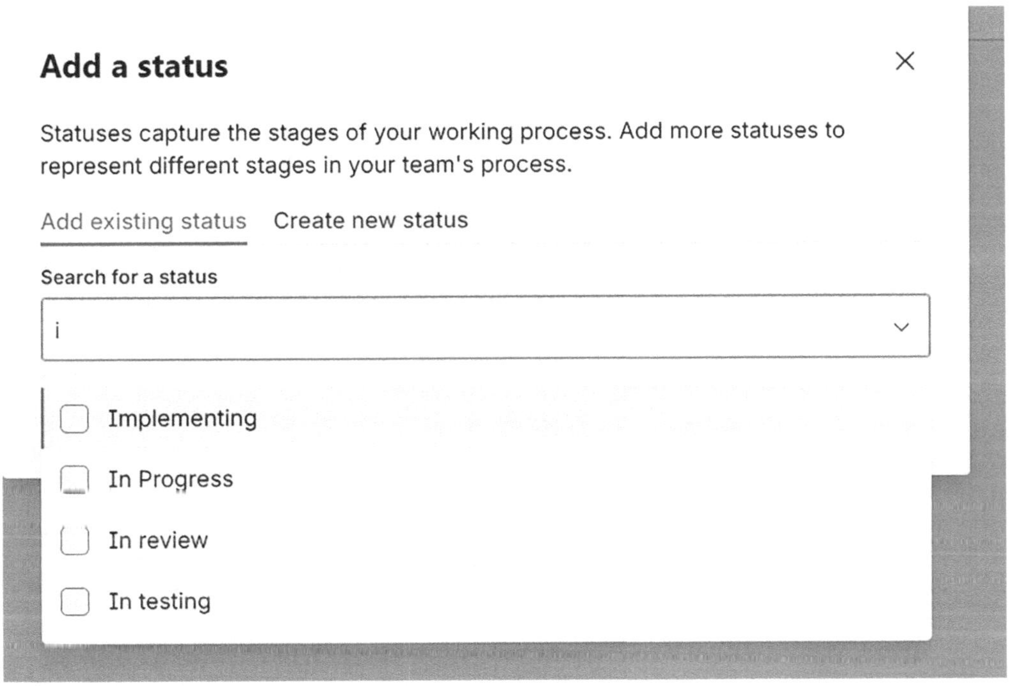

Figure 7.43: *Adding Status*

4. Click **`Add transition`**, enter details and click **`Create`**.

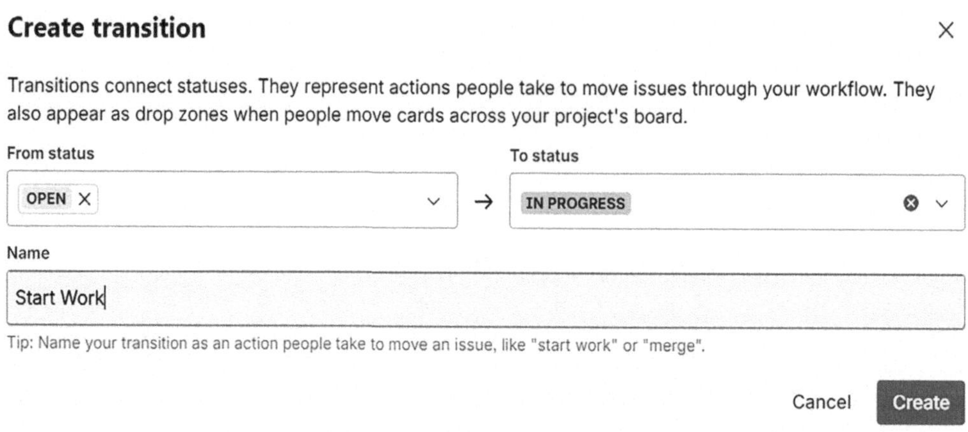

Figure 7.44: *Adding Transitions*

5. To add rules, select **`Add rule`**, and choose one of the following:

   i. **`Restrict transitions`**: For example, allow only certain users or groups.

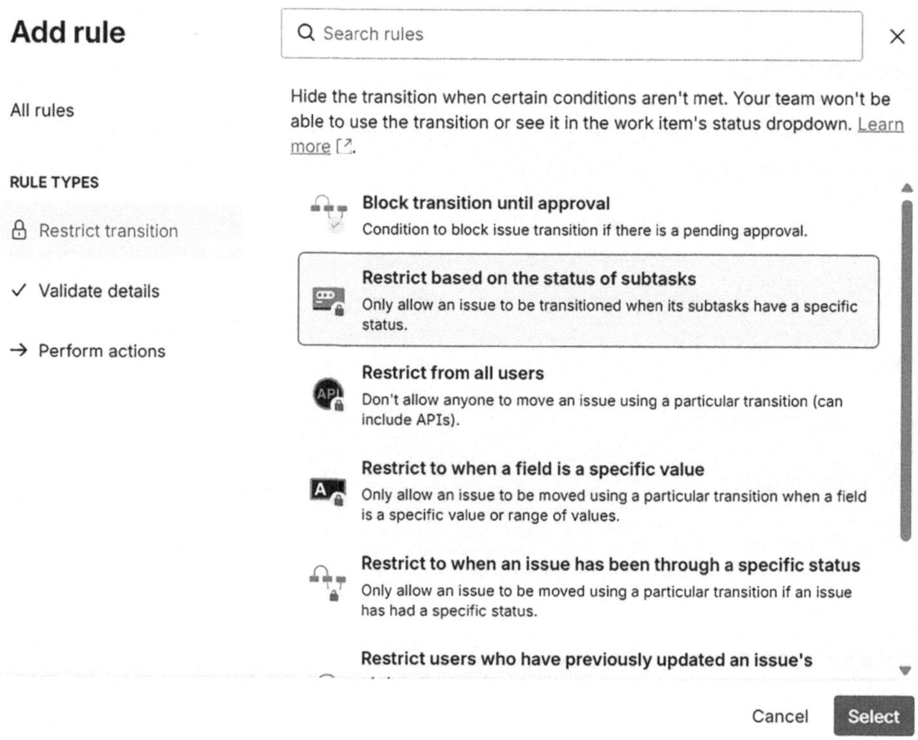

Figure 7.45: *Restrict Transition*

This is similar to Adding Conditions in old editor.

   ii. **Validate details**: For example, block transition until a field has a value.

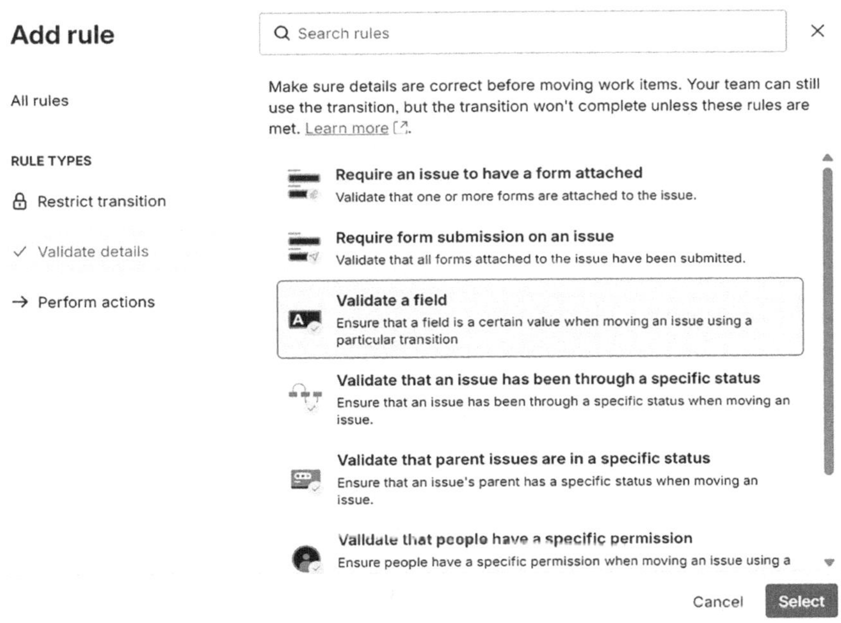

Figure 7.46: *Validate Details*

This is similar to adding Validators in the old editor.

iii. **Perform action**: For example, auto-assign, copy fields or update status.

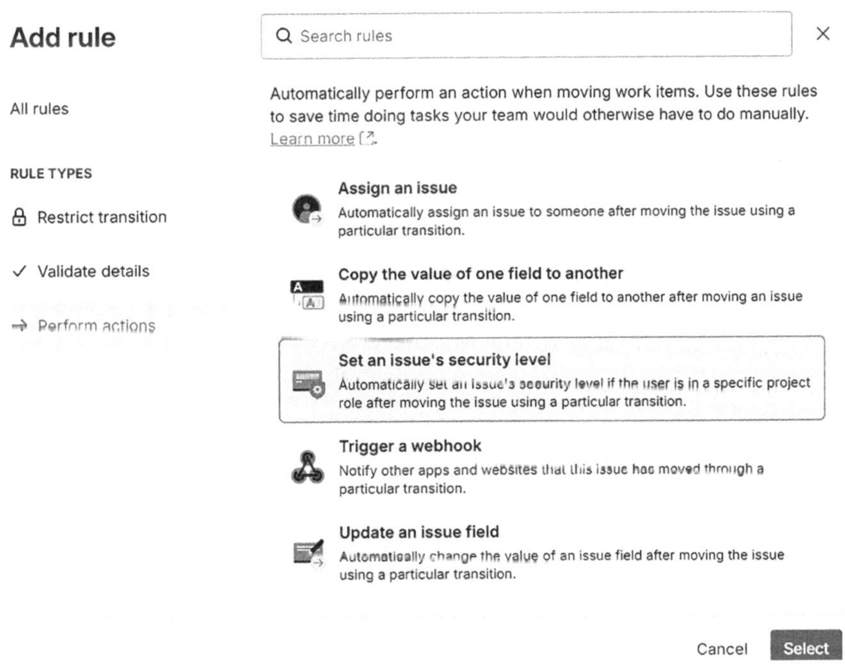

Figure 7.47: *Perform Actions*

This is similar to adding Post functions in old editor.

6. Review your workflow, and click **`Update Workflow`** or **`Discard Changes`**.

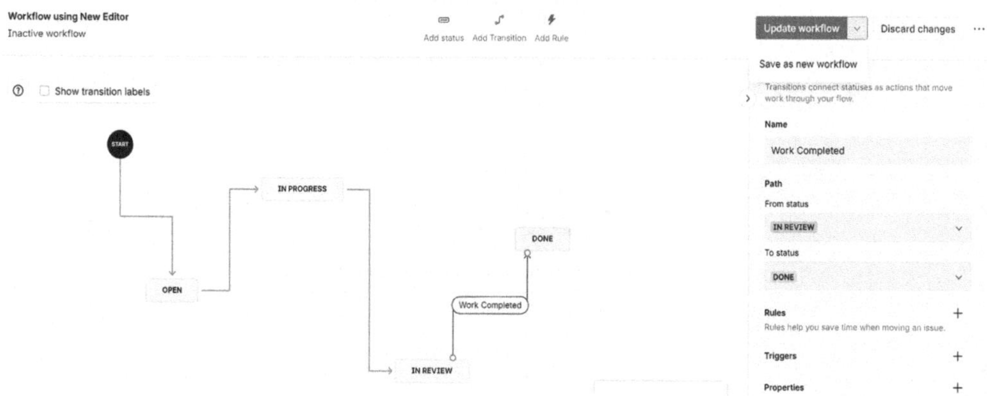

Figure 7.48: *Updating Workflow*

In the new workflow editor, you can also show a screen on transition, add properties, and utilize events generated.

Mistakes to Avoid while Creating Workflows

Here are some of the mistakes to avoid, while creating workflows:

- **Avoid overcomplicating the workflow**: When designing the workflow, refrain from adding excessive steps, conditions, and validators. Additionally, ensure that adding required fields doesn't negatively impact other stakeholders. Strive for simplicity.
- **Consider the team's requirements**: Discuss any planned changes to the workflow with the team to understand their actual needs before implementing changes.
- **Involve all stakeholders during workflow creation**: Gather input from stakeholders, assess the feasibility of proposed changes, and then proceed with creating or modifying the workflow. Workflow changes can affect multiple individuals if schemes are shared across the organization.
- **Maintain relevant status names**: Utilize the provided statuses in Jira, adding new names that appropriately align with "To Do, In Progress, and Done" statuses.
- **Test the workflow and gather feedback**: Conduct thorough testing of the workflow and solicit feedback. Utilize a sandbox environment for testing or create a separate Jira space for testing purposes, inaccessible to others, to ensure smooth workflow testing and maintenance.

Conclusion

We are now familiar with how to create and add status, transitions, global transitions, workflows, and workflow schemes. We have also understood active and inactive workflows, as well as how to associate a workflow with a work type, and how to associate a workflow with a space.

In the next chapter, we will learn about Jira Filters, Dashboards, Reports, and Analytics.

Points to Remember

- Workflows are the steps required to complete a process.
- In Jira, workflows can be created in both Diagram and Text modes.
- Design workflows with simplicity to minimize confusion.
- Maintain clear naming conventions for statuses and transitions.
- Utilize descriptive transition names to provide user guidance.
- Regularly review workflows to ensure alignment with current space practices.
- Harness features like Conditions, Validators, and Post-functions to automate processes and reduce manual effort.
- Conditions check for Transition viability, Validators ensure input validity, and Post-functions manage actions after transitions.
- Workflow schemes are associated with spaces, allowing distinct workflows for different spaces.
- Reusing workflow schemes across spaces promotes consistency and efficiency.
- Changes to a workflow scheme can impact multiple spaces; make modifications thoughtfully and communicate changes effectively.
- Two types of workflows exist: Software Simplified for smaller teams and less complex processes, and Customizable for intricate processes with lesser flexibility.
- Integrating Jira with other development tools enhances efficient code review management.

Use Cases with Reference Links

1. How can I build a new workflow without affecting the existing workflows, screens, and issues?

   https://community.atlassian.com/t5/Jira-Software-questions/How-can-I-build-a-new-workflow-without-affecting-existing/qaq-p/2414148

2. How to define different statuses for specific work types, create a workflow, and add to the workflow scheme?

   https://community.atlassian.com/t5/Jira-Software-questions/Different-statuses-for-specific-issue-types-Workflow/qaq-p/2432098

3. If I remove a work type from a Workflow Scheme, will the past issues be deleted?

   https://community.atlassian.com/t5/Jira-Software-questions/If-I-remove-an-issue-type-from-a-Workflow-Scheme-will-the-past/qaq-p/2324428

4. Adding Workflows for a new work type to Workflow Schemes.

   https://community.atlassian.com/t5/Jira-questions/Adding-Workflows-to-Workflow-Schemes/qaq-p/2265392

5. Can I build a workflow in Production without affecting the existing issues?

   https://community.atlassian.com/t5/Jira-Software-questions/Can-I-build-a-workflow-in-Production-without-affecting-existing/qaq-p/2354907

6. How to activate the workflow I created?

   https://community.atlassian.com/t5/Automation-questions/Workflow/qaq-p/2280162

7. How to activate a workflow?

   https://community.atlassian.com/t5/Jira-questions/How-to-activate-the-inactive-workflow/qaq-p/1198597

8. How do I edit the copied workflow scheme in the cloud?

   https://community.atlassian.com/t5/Jira-Software-questions/Editing-a-copied-Workflow-in-the-cloud/qaq-p/1566531

9. Is it possible to give extended permissions to a user (space lead and space admin), so that they can change the edit workflow on their space, without being site admin?

   https://community.atlassian.com/t5/Jira-questions/Edit-workflows-jira-cloud/qaq-p/946087

10. What is the right way to handle the Close Issue screen? Is it supposed to stand alone, without being associated with a scheme?

    https://community.atlassian.com/t5/Jira-questions/A-screen-for-quot-Close-Issue-quot-transition/qaq-p/2352435

11. Jira workflow conditions are not applying for a specific user group with the All of the conditions option.

    https://community.atlassian.com/t5/Jira-Software-questions/Jira-workflow-condition-not-applying-for-specific-user-group/qaq-p/2339693

12. I have created a Kanban board and want to change the workflow scheme.

    https://community.atlassian.com/t5/Jira-Software-questions/Modifying-workflow-scheme/qaq-p/1867224

13. I want to copy a workflow scheme from space 1 to space 2. And afterwards, I should be able to alter the workflows in space 2 without affecting space 1.

    https://community.atlassian.com/t5/Jira-Software-questions/How-do-I-copy-a-workflow-scheme/qaq-p/1956132

14. Software Simplified Workflow vs. Custom workflow.

    https://community.atlassian.com/t5/Jira-questions/Software-Simplified-Workflow-v-Custom/qaq-p/1860651

15. How to gain permission to edit Software Simplified Workflow?

    https://community.atlassian.com/t5/Jira-Software-questions/How-to-gain-permission-to-edit-Software-Simplified-Workflow/qaq-p/1624932

Chapter 8
Filters, Dashboards, and Agile Reporting

Introduction

In the dynamic world of developing software applications and project management, Jira is a helpful tool comprising three important parts: Filters, Dashboards, and Agile reports. These features help us to organize features, see how things are going, and understand how our team is doing.

Filters are like special tools designed for both basic search and advanced search. They help us to find the exact information from a big database created with spaces. Dashboards help us to show important statistics in one place, much like a dashboard in a car shows speed, fuel, and more. Agile reports are helpful if we work in a certain way called 'Agile'. These reports tell us how fast we are working, what we have finished, and what is left, and get an idea about the obstacles. Jira also provides general reports that can be used by every kind of team.

In this chapter, we will learn about filters, dashboards, and agile reports. We will see how to use them to find important data, keep an eye on our projects, and work better together.

Structure

In this chapter, we will cover the following topics:

- Understanding Basic search and Advanced search in Jira
- Creating Jira filters
  - Step-by-step guide to creating and saving a Jira filter
  - Jira's built-in filters
  - Managing subscription, editing permissions, updating, copying, and deleting filters
- Working with search results

- Creating filters using advanced search
  - Step-by-step process to create a filter using advanced search
  - Understanding JQL Functions, Fields, Keywords, and Operators
- Examples of important JQL queries for everyone
- Understanding the importance of Dashboards
- Step-by-step process to create a Dashboard, and add Gadget
- Choosing a Dashboard Layout
- Copying, Sharing, and Deleting a Dashboard
- Adding and Customizing Gadgets to a Dashboard
- Example Dashboards and Gadgets
- Creating a Wallboard
- Introduction to Reports
- Steps to Accessing Reports in Jira
- Understanding Agile Reports
  - Reports for Scrum Teams
  - Reports for Kanban Teams
- Introduction and Overview of Atlassian Analytics

Understanding Basic Search and Advanced Search in Jira

Jira provides several ways in which you can search for a work item. Primarily, there are two methods: **Basic search** and **Advanced search**. Basic search works by selecting the search bar or navigating to work items, and then setting the criteria to search for work items. On the other hand, advanced search involves writing queries in Jira Query Language (JQL). Basic search has some limitations that can be overcome by using advanced search. In this chapter, we will learn both types in detail.

Creating Jira Filters

In this section, we will learn to create Jira filters using basic search options.

To find specific work items, follow these steps:

1. Navigate to the Main search bar, click **`Search`** > view **`All work items`**.

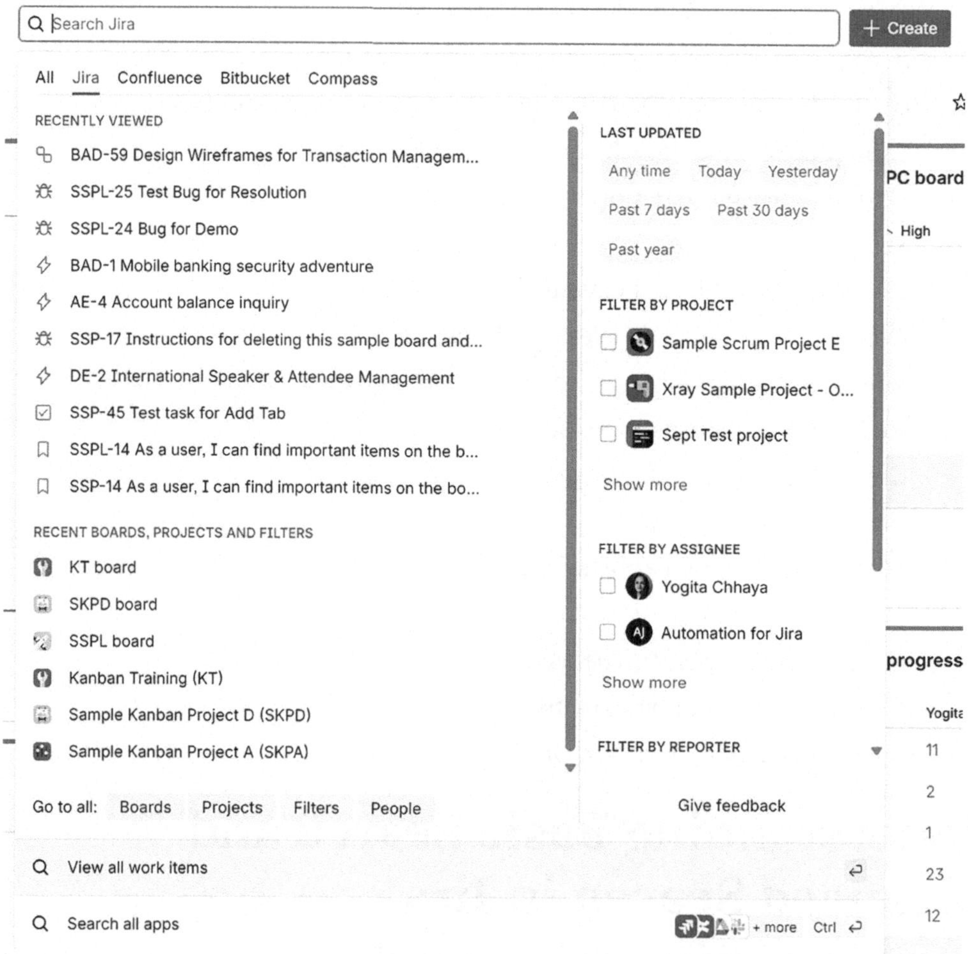

Figure 8.1: *Searching Work Items from the Main Search Bar*

2. Set the criteria for searching: **`Type`**, **`space`**, **`Assignee`**, **`Status.`**
3. Enter the text to search for and click **`More+`**. Post clicks on **`More+`**, the user can choose any number of work item fields from the available list of work item fields.
4. Select **`Search.`**

Jira will provide you with the work items based on the set criteria for the search.

If you want to search for work items in a specific space, start by navigating to **`Space`** > **`All Work Items`** and follow the same steps mentioned above. This will display the work items from that specific space in Jira.

Step-by-step Guide to Create and Save a Jira Filter

Permission required: All Jira Users can create and save their own filters.

To create a filter in Jira, follow these steps:

1. Navigate to **`Filters`** in the side navigation bar, and select **`View all filters.`**

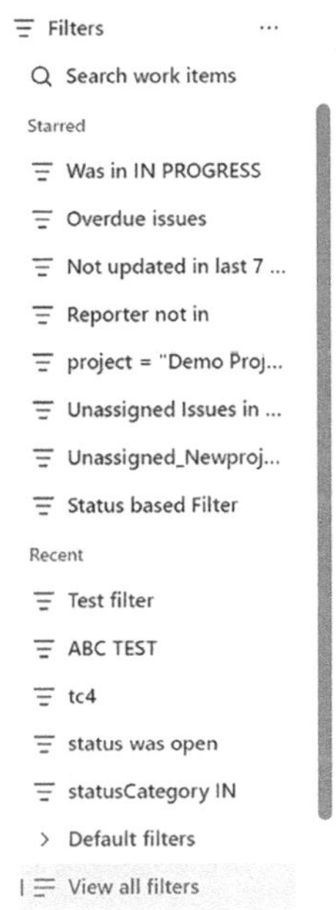

Figure 8.2: *Creating Filters Step- 1*

2. Select **`Create filter.`**

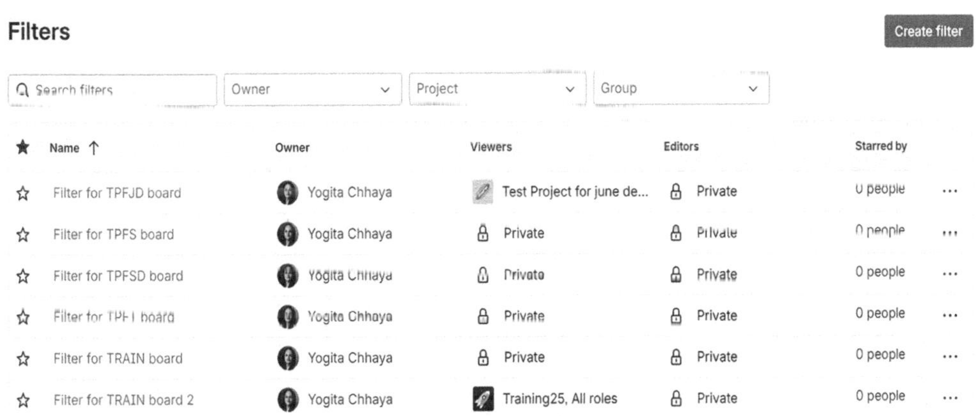

Figure 8.3: *Creating Filters Step-2*

3. Set the criteria for searching: **Type**, **Space**, **Status**, **Assignee**. You can toggle between basic and advanced search:

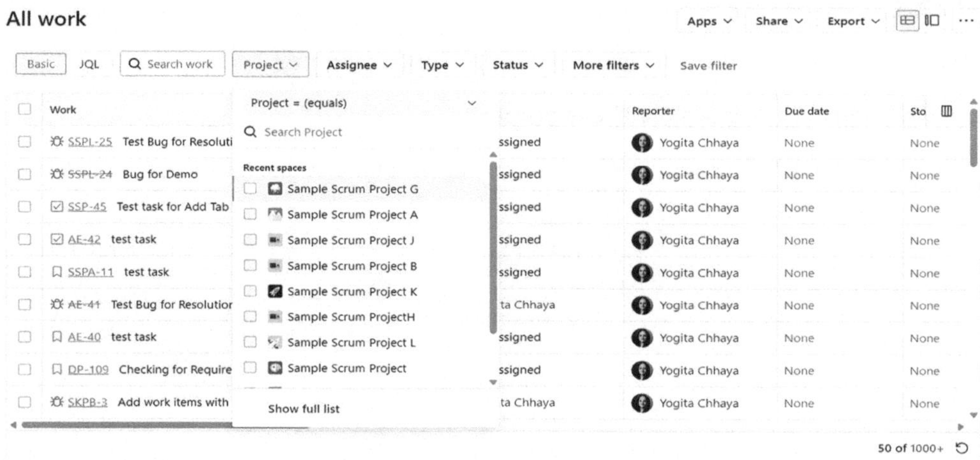

Figure 8.4: Creating Filters Step-3

4. Select **Search**, click **Save Filter**, enter the details like **Name**, **Description**, **Viewers** and **Editors** of the filter, and click **Save.**

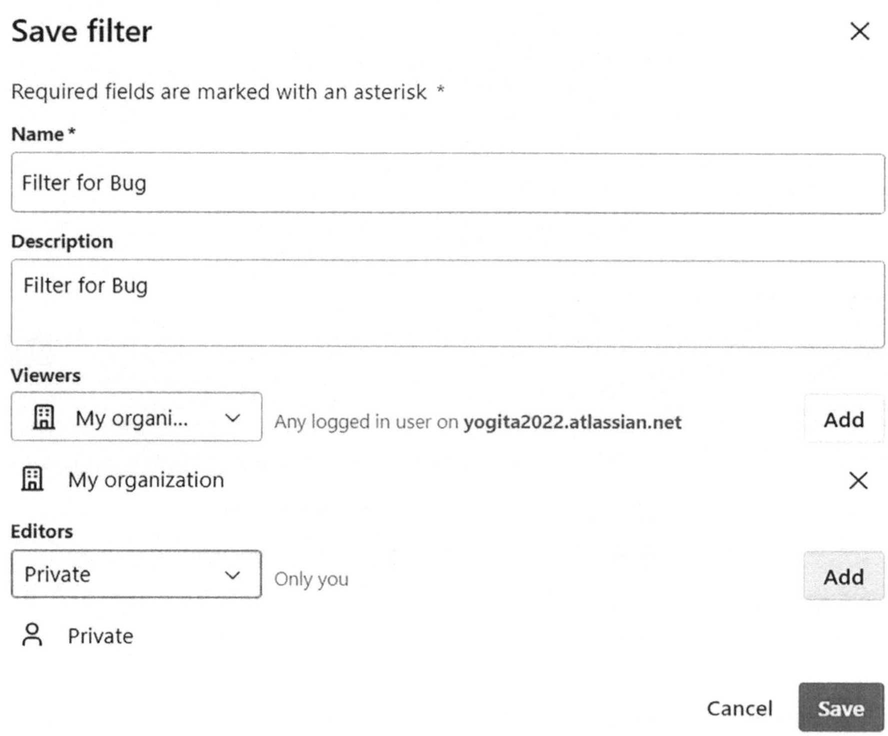

Figure 8.5: Creating Filters Step-4

The filter has been created and saved.

Jira's Built-in Filters

Permission required: All Jira users can access default filters.

Jira provides a few ready filters. You can access these filters from the left navigation bar. The filters that users can access are listed as follows:

- My open work items
- Reported by me
- All work items
- Open work items
- Done work items
- Viewed recently
- Created recently
- Resolved recently
- Updated recently

To access the built-in filters in Jira, follow these steps:

- In the side Navigation bar, navigate to **`Filters`** > **`Default Filters`**. Select the filter you want to access under Default filters.
- In the following built-in filter, you can click **`View all filters`** to access all saved filters.

Managing Subscription, Editing Permissions, Updating, Copying, and Deleting Filters

In this section, we will learn how to edit, delete, and alter permissions, subscribe, as well as mark filters as favorite.

Permissions required: To change the ownership of a filter and delete a filter, you must log in as a Jira Administrator with Administer Jira Global permission.

From the main Navigation bar, select **`Filters`** > **`View all filters`**.

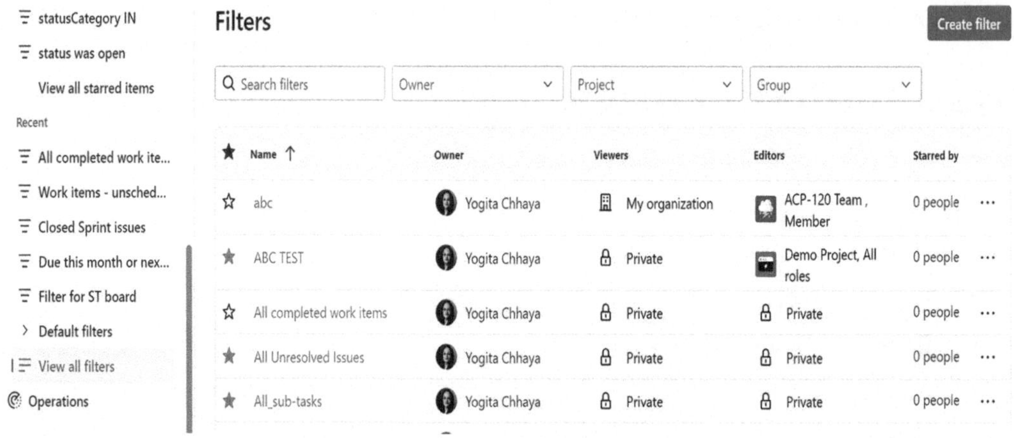

***Figure 8.6**: Viewing All Filters*

On this page, Jira provides a list of all filters - private and shared by others.

Search for filter: You can enter the name of owners, spaces, or groups to search for filters.

By selecting/clicking the name of the filter, it displays all work items of the selected filter.

On the same page, you can:

1. Open the search in Excel and Google Sheets.
2. Share the search by entering an Email address.
3. Export the search in different formats, such as Excel, CSV, and other formats.
4. Change the search criteria and then save it.
5. Mark as favorite by clicking the star symbol. Starred filters are your favorite filters.
6. Click on `Details` to view the owner and edit permissions, and then add details to subscribe to the filter.

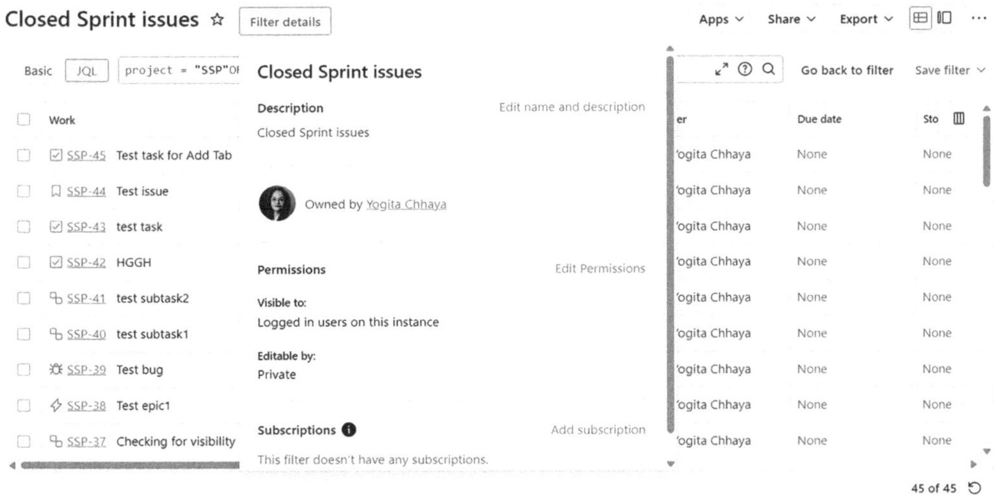

***Figure 8.7:** Options on a Selected Filter Page*

Edit: On the **`Filters`** page, select the three dots, and then select **`Edit`** to edit the name and description of the filter. Then change who can edit and view the filter.

Permissions Required: Individuals with Administer Jira Global permission can see the Edit option.

Steps to Edit Filter:

1. Navigate to **`Filters`** > **`View All Filters`**. Find the filter you want to update.

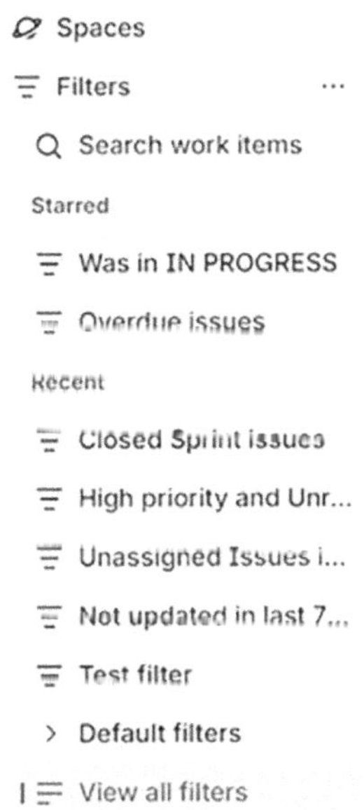

***Figure 8.8:** Viewing All Filters*

2. Navigate to **More** on the right corner and select the same.

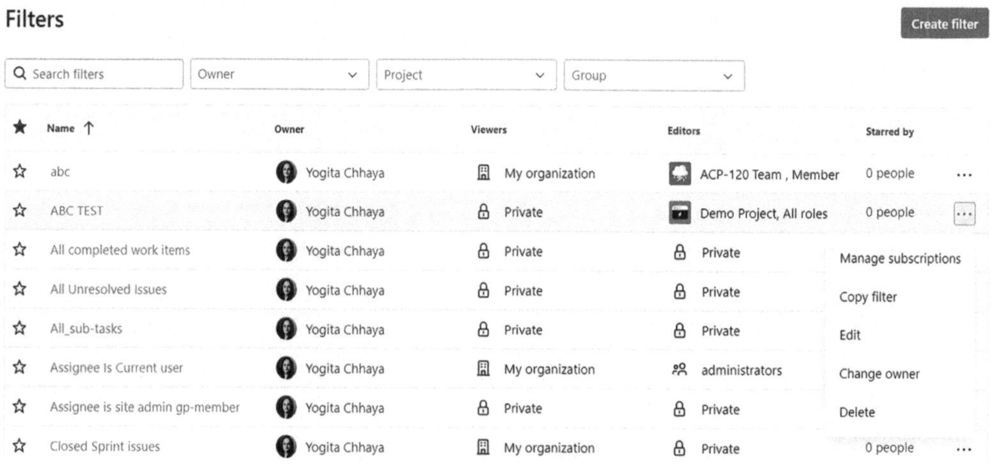

***Figure 8.9**: Selecting to Edit Filter*

3. Select **Edit.**

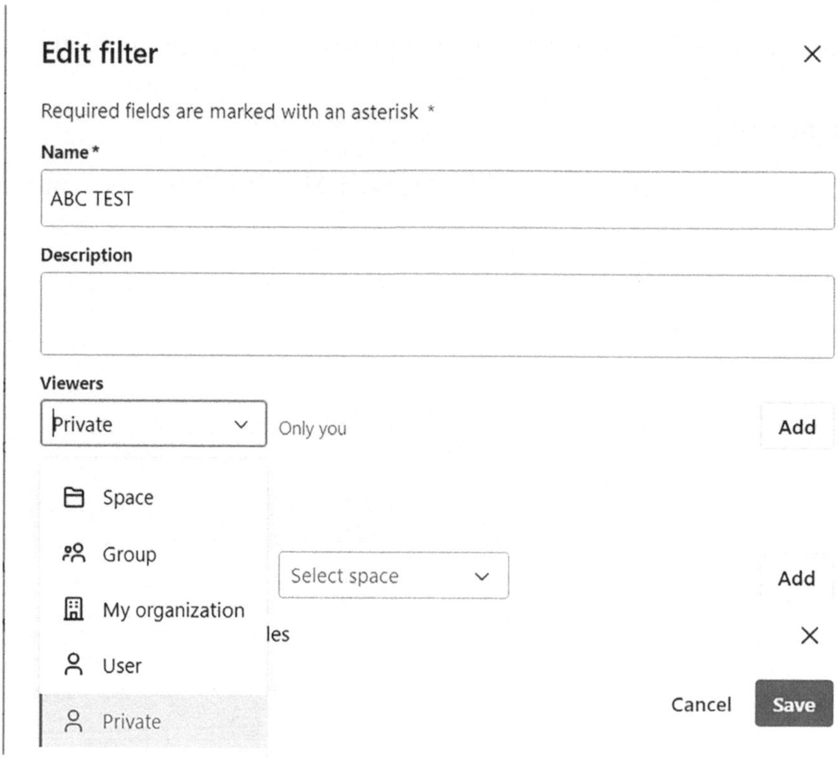

***Figure 8.10:** Editing Viewers, Editors, and Other Details of a Filter*

You can share a filter with:

- **Space**: All members working on a specific space.
- **Group**: It is a group defined in Jira.
- **User:** A user whose name can be specified.
- **Private**: It is a private filter for you, and others cannot view it.

Copy and Delete: Select the three dots, and you will have options to copy or delete the filter:

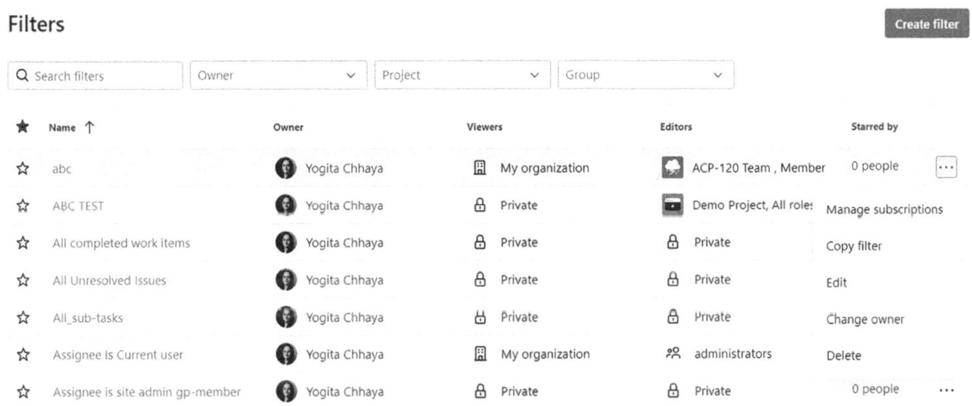

Figure 8.11: *Editing, Deleting, Copying, and Other Options of a Filter*

Working with Search Results

After conducting your work item search, you can take various actions as listed:

- Choose either the **List view** or **Detail view** of the work items according to your preference.
- Select and configure the columns that are visible or hidden.
- Sort the work items based on a column.
- Perform bulk edits on work items.
- Share your search results in different formats.
- Add the search results, that is, Jira filters, as a dashboard gadget.

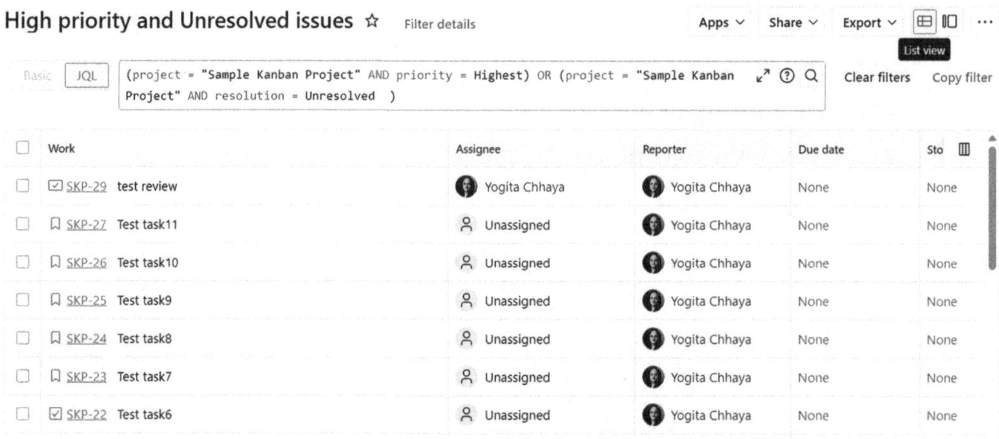

Figure 8.12: *Working with Search Results*

Creating Filters Using Advanced Search

The steps for performing advanced searches in Jira are similar to those for basic searches. Any basic search can be converted into an advanced search by clicking **`Switch to JQL`**. However, not all advanced searches can be converted back into basic searches.

With Jira's advanced search, you can specify search criteria, and create structured queries using JQL. This advanced search feature utilizes keywords, operators, fields, and functions. For example, you can search for specific text or filter work items based on date and time criteria, among other options.

Step-by-Step Process to Create an Advanced Filter

Permission required: All Jira Users can create advanced filters.

To create an advanced filter in Jira, follow these steps:

1. Navigate to **`Filters`** in the side navigation bar, and select **`View all filters`**:

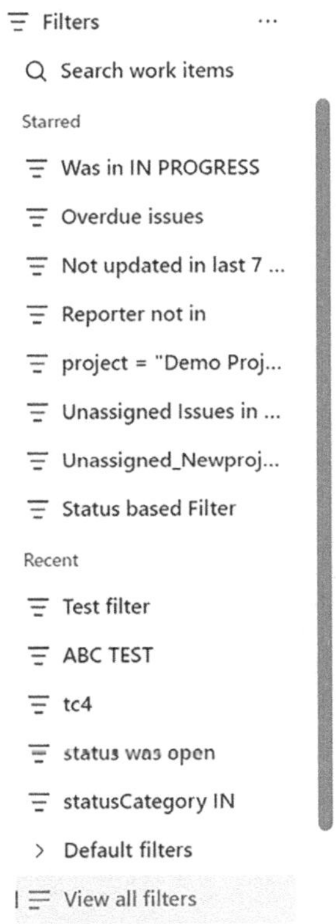

***Figure 8.13**: Creating Filter Using Advanced Search Step-1*

2. Select **`Create filter`**:

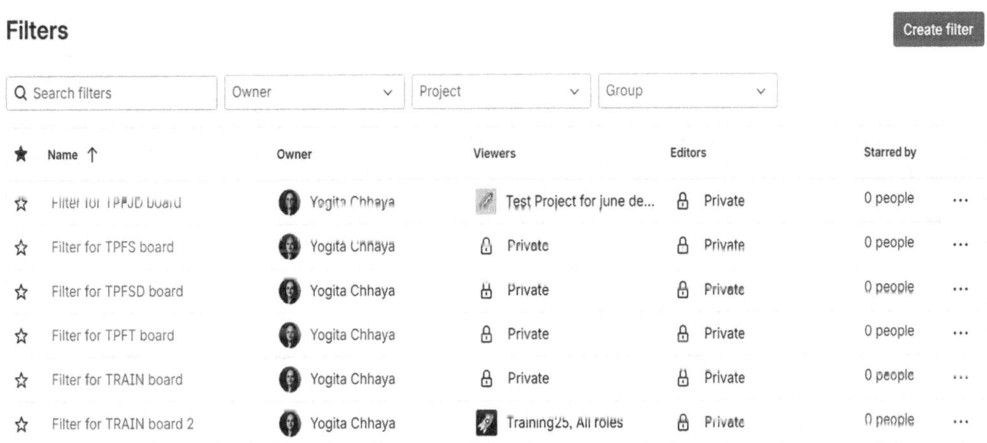

***Figure 8.14**: Creating Filter Using Advanced SearchStep-2*

3. Set the criteria for searching - **`Type`**, **`Space`**, **`Status`**, **`Assignee.`** You can toggle between basic and advanced search. Select **`Switch to JQL`**:

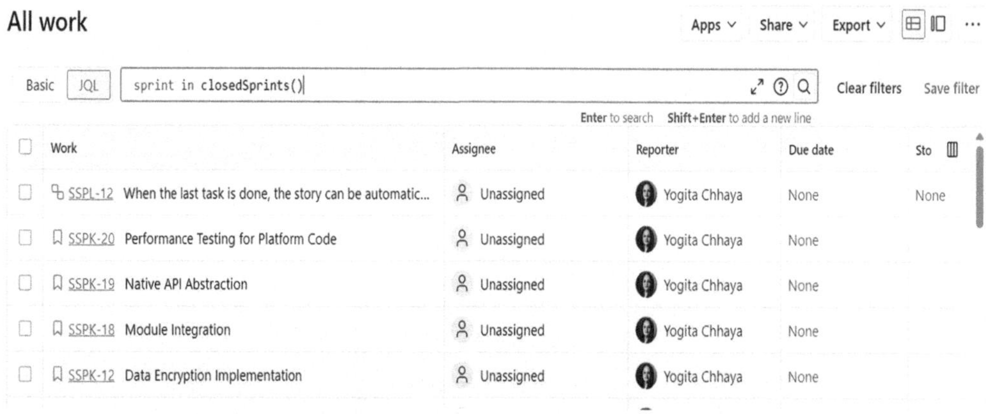

***Figure 8.15**: Creating Filter Using Advanced Search Step-3*

4. Select search, click **Save**, enter the **Name** of the filter, and click **Save.**

***Figure 8.16**: Creating Filter Using Advanced Search Step-4*

The filter for Advanced search has been created and saved. You can modify new search criteria before saving the filter with the help of Jira Query Language.

Understanding JQL Functions, Fields, Keywords, and Operators

Any JQL query is written using specific Keywords, Operators, Functions, and Fields. In this section, we will understand these with the help of examples.

Keywords: These perform the following tasks:

- Combines multiple clauses to construct a query.
- Changes the logic of multiple clauses.
- Adjusts the logic of operators within the query.

JQL Keywords: Here are a few keywords in Jira: **AND**, **OR**, **NOT**, **EMPTY**, **NULL**, **ORDER** and **BY**.

Examples

1. **AND**: It is used to combine multiple clauses of a query. Parenthesis can be used to control the order of the execution in a query.

   Example: Find all the work items of space SSP that belong to closedSprint:

   ```
   project = "SSP" AND sprint IN closedSprints()ORDER BY created DESC
   ```
2. **OR**: It is used to combine multiple clauses. Parenthesis can be used to control the order of the execution in a query.

   Example: Find all work items of the type Bug or defect:

   ```
   issuetype = bug OR issuetype = Defect
   ```

Operators: These are the signs or words that compare the values on both sides of the expression. Only true results are used in the query after comparing the values. Examples of operators are Equals, Not Equals, and Greater than Equals.

Examples:

1. **Equals** (=)

   Example: Find all work items in which the assignee is the current user.

   ```
   Query:  ASSIGNEE = currentUser()
   ```
2. **Not Equals** (!=)

   Example: Find all work items in which a space is not equal to the Sample Kanban space:

   ```
   Query:  project != "Sample Kanban Project"
   ```

3. **NOT IN**

   Example: Find all the work items that are not of the type Bug or defect:

   `Query:  issuetype not in (Bug,Defect)`

Fields: It allows you to search for the values of the fields. Examples of fields are **`Assignee`**, **`Affectedversion`**, **`CreatedDate`**, **`Description`**, **`Due`**, **`Epic link`**, **`Fix version`**, **`work itemKey`**, and many more.

1. **`Assignee`**

   Example: Find all work items where the assignee was the current user.

   `Query: assignee was currentUser()`

2. **`Description`**

   Example: Find all work items where the description contains the word sprint.

   `Query: description ~ "sprint"`

3. **`Due`**

   Example: Find all work items where the due is not empty.

   `Query: due is not EMPTY`

Functions: A function is written using a word followed by parentheses. Parentheses may or may not contain some data. A function does calculations on Jira data or the numbers in parentheses. Function returns some values that are used in a query for searching work items.

Example Function: **`openSprints()`**, **`componentsLeadByUser()`**, **`currentLogin()`**, **`earliestUnreleasedVersion()`**, **`endOfMonth()`**, **`parentepic()`**, and many more:

1. Find work items that are assigned to future sprints.

   `Query: sprint in futureSprints()`

2. Find work items that do not belong to a released version.

   `Query: fixversion in unreleasedVersions()`

3. Find work items that are sub-tasks.

   `Query: issuetype in subtaskIssueTypes()`

4. Find work items that were created before 150 days.

   `Query: createdDate <150d`

Examples of Important JQL for Everyone

Here are some examples of important JQL queries:

1. Find all work items in a space that belong to the **`closedSprint.`**

   `project = "SSP" AND sprint IN closedSprints()ORDER BY created DESC`

2. Find work items in **`openSprints`** where the Status is not equal to done.

   ```
   Sprint in openSprints() and statusCategory != Done
   ```

3. Find out high-priority, unresolved work items, and work item status backlog.

   ```
   project = "Sample Kanban Project" AND priority = Highest AND
   resolution = Unresolved  and status = backlog
   ```

4. Find all work items in the next version to be released.

   ```
   fixVersion = earliestUnreleasedVersion(SSPA)
   ```

5. Find all work items for which time spent is equal to 1 day, and work items are in unresolved status.

   ```
   timespent = 1d and resolution in (Unresolved)
   ```

6. Find all work items in which the current user is an assignee or reporter, and the version is an unreleased version.

   ```
   (reporter= currentUser() or assignee = currentUser()) AND (fixVer-
   sion in unreleasedVersions())
   ```

7. Search all work items that are Created before 150 days, and the status is not equal to "**`To Do`**".

   ```
   createdDate <=150d and status != "To Do"
   ```

8. Select all Bugs assigned to me in a space, where the fixed version is either empty or not released.

   ```
   project = "Demo Project" AND work itemtype = Bug AND assignee
   = currentUser()  AND (fixversion in unreleasedVersions() or
   fixVersion is EMPTY)
   ```

9. Search all work items that are of medium priority and in **`openSprints`**, sort by spaces.

   ```
   sprint in openSprints() AND priority = Medium ORDER BY project
   ```

10. Find all flagged items.

    ```
    "Flagged" IS NOT EMPTY
    ```

11. Find all issues that were resolved in the last month.

    ```
    resolved > startOfMonth("-1") AND resolved <= startOfMonth()
    ```

12. Find all unresolved issues for which the due date is over.

    ```
    resolution = Unresolved AND due < now()
    ```

13. All work items unresolved, and link is blocked by

    ```
    resolution = Unresolved AND issueLinkType = "is blocked by"
    ```

14. Find all work items where the summary contains the word, "**kanban**".

    ```
    project = "SKP" and summary ~ kanban ORDER BY created DESC
    ```

15. Setting precedence by using parentheses.

    Find all work items in Done status that belong to the space "**DemoProject**" OR **assignee** is the current user.

    ```
    status= Done and (project = "Demo Project" OR  assignee
    = currentUser() )
    ```

The users can also write JQL queries in natural language with the help of AI features in Jira. We will cover this topic in Chapter 13, *Atlassian Intelligence*, getting started with Rovo and Creating Agents.

Understanding the Importance of Dashboards

Dashboards are crucial for any project management tool. Jira dashboards help display space statistics and metrics. You can create dashboards, and add gadgets to generate charts and other statistical analysis to track work items and spaces. When you log into Jira, you can first view the dashboard.

A user can create multiple dashboards specific to their requirements, such as different dashboards for various teams or spaces. Jira dashboards provide statistics based on Jira filters. Therefore, it is essential to create the right filters, and then add the appropriate gadgets to create dashboards. You can create dashboards, and display them during daily stand-ups, retrospective meetings, or presentations to the top management. Jira also offers a feature called wallboard, which can be useful for displaying statistics on a TV screen, and keeping everyone informed throughout the space.

Step-by-Step Process to Create a Dashboard and Add Gadget

Follow these steps to create a dashboard:

1. Log into Jira as admin, and navigate to **Dashboards** in the top navigation bar.
2. Select dashboard, and then select **Create** dashboard.

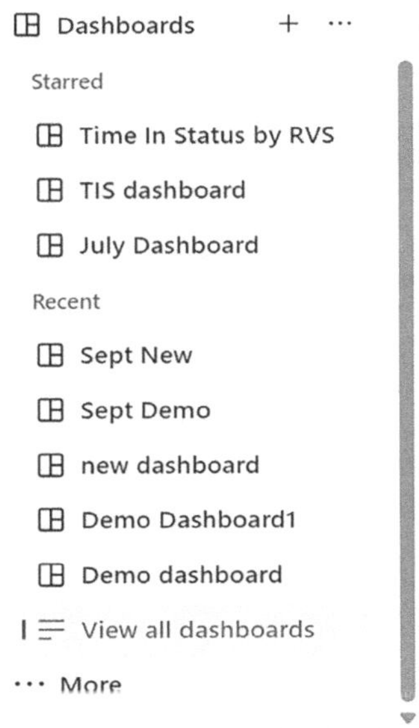

Figure 8.17: *Creating Dashboards*

3. Enter all the details, such as **Dashboard** **`Name,`** **`Description,`** **`Viewers`**, and **`Editors,`** and then click **`Save`**.

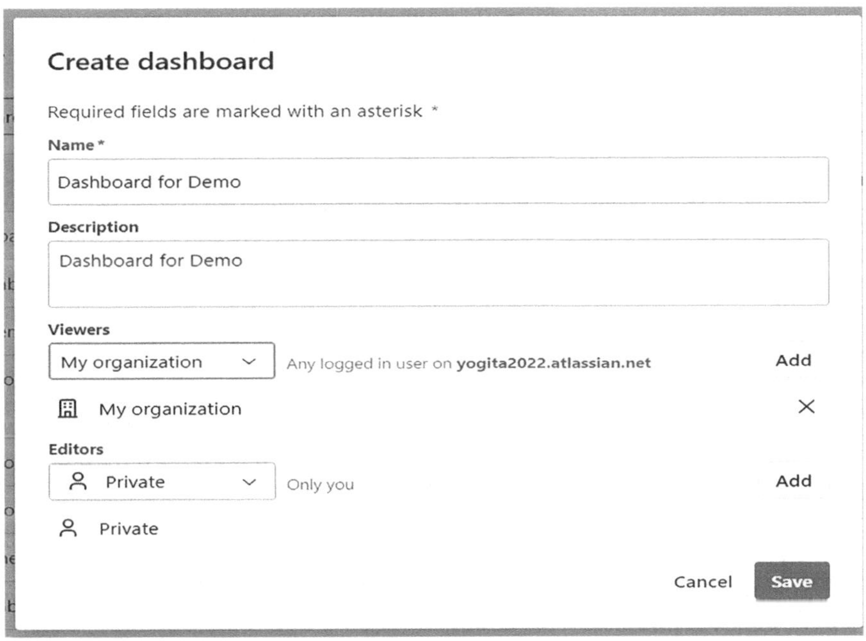

Figure 8.18: *Entering the Details of a Dashboard and Saving It*

4. The dashboard has been created. You can change the layout, add gadgets after searching, and then click **`Done`**.

5. Click on **Add** after searching for the gadget. You can search for the gadget by typing the name of the gadget in the search gadget.

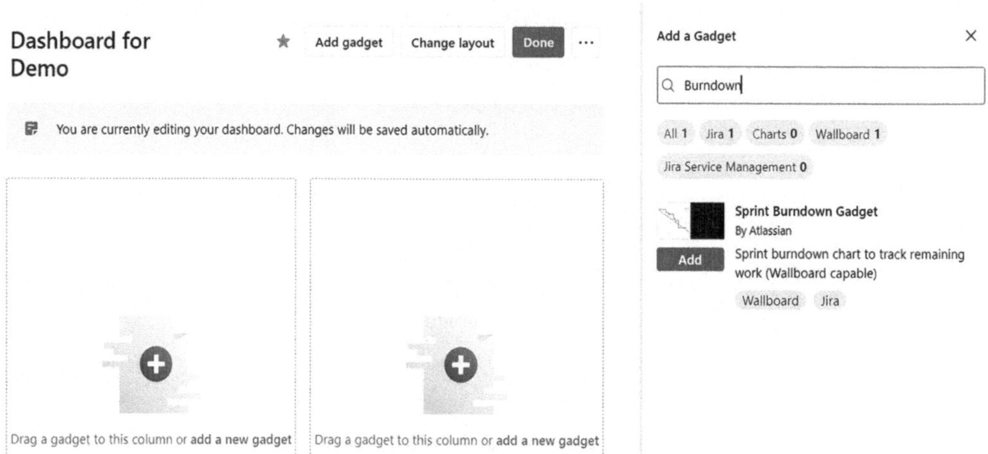

Figure 8.19: *Adding a Gadget on a Dashboard*

Choosing a Dashboard Layout

Follow these steps to choose a dashboard layout:

1. Navigate to the top navigation bar, and select **Dashboards.**
2. Select the dashboard.
3. Click on **Edit,** and then select **Change layout.**
4. Select the layout as per your preference.

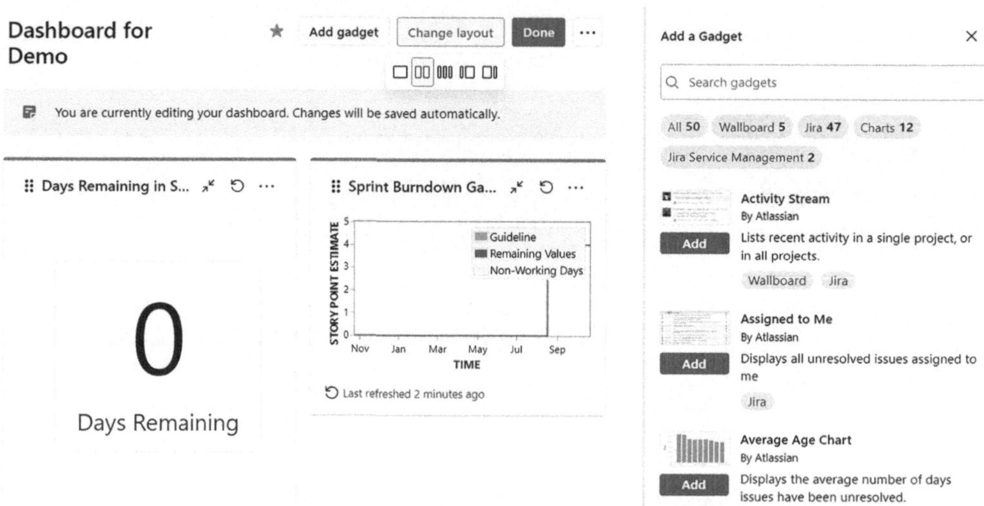

Figure 8.20: *Choosing a Dashboard Layout*

Copying, Sharing, and Deleting Dashboard

Follow these steps to copy, share, and delete a dashboard:

1. Navigate to the top navigation bar, and select **`Dashboards.`**
2. Select **`View all dashboards`**.
3. Select the dashboard and click **More** on the right side.
4. You can copy the dashboard, rename, or share the dashboard, and delete the dashboard by selecting the required option.

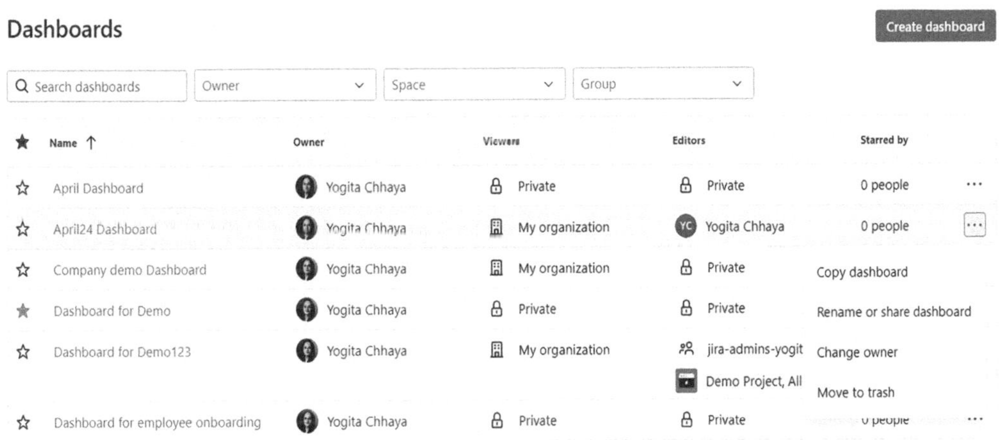

Figure 8.21: *Choosing an Option for a Dashboard*

Jira provides some standard Dashboard Gadgets. If you integrate Jira with an add-on, respective gadgets for that add-on get added and can be added to the dashboard.

Adding and Customizing Gadgets to a Dashboard

Follow these steps to add gadgets:

1. Navigate to the top navigation bar, and select **`Dashboards`**.
2. Select the dashboard.
3. Select **`Edit`** on the right side. It will provide a list of multiple gadgets.

4. You can search for the gadgets by typing in the search bar. Select the preferred gadget and add the required details such as space/filter name, fields details, and save the gadget by clicking on **Done**.

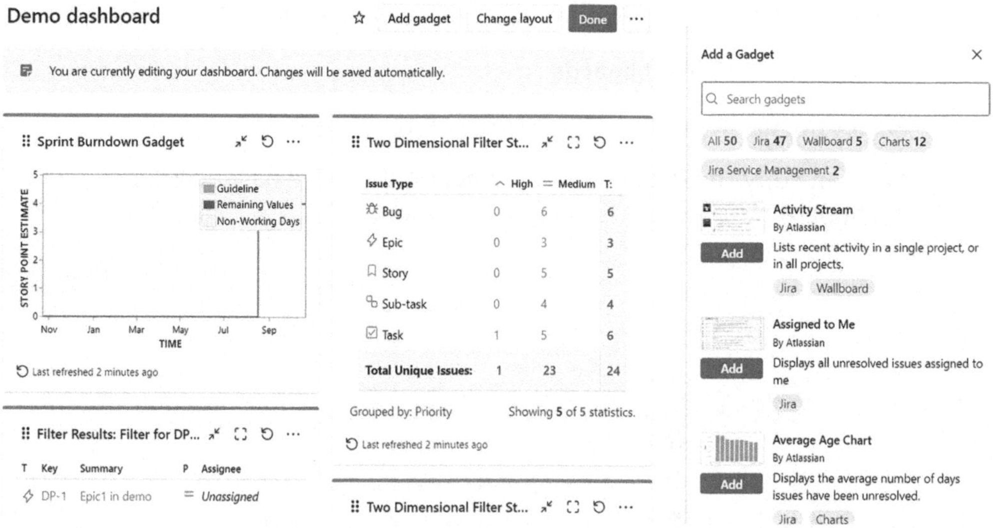

Figure 8.22: *Adding and Customizing Gadgets*

Example Dashboards and Gadgets

Examples of dashboards and gadgets include:

- **Starred Filters**: This gadget lists the current user's favorite filters.
- **Two-Dimensional Filter Statistics**: It displays the data in table form. You can select x-axis and y-axis fields, while configuring the gadget. This gadget can be used to keep track of the workload of a team, keep track of work items v/s priority, and so on.
- **Sprint Health Gadget**: It provides the overall statistics about the sprint such as time elapsed, work completed, scope change in percentage, story point statistics, and name of the assignees in the sprint.

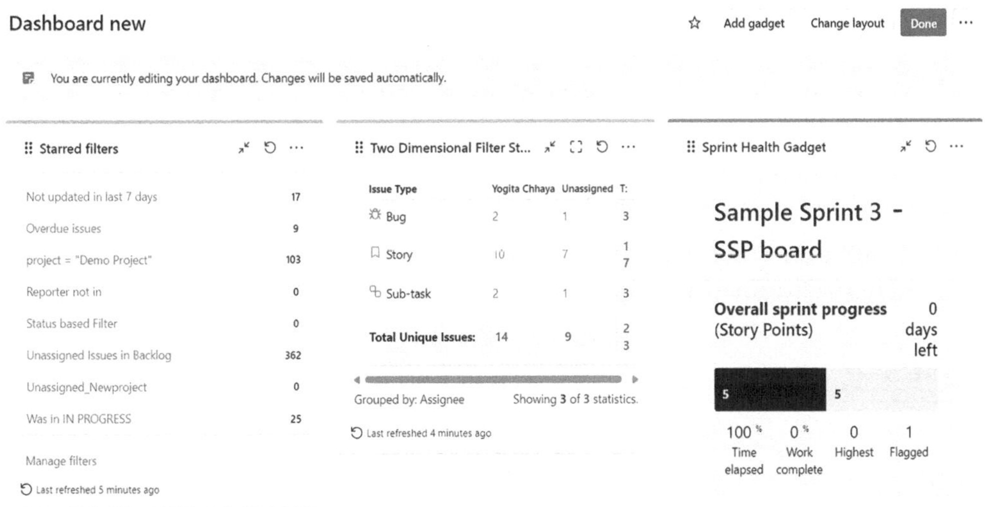

Figure 8.23: *Example Dashboard-1*

- **Issue Statistics**: It provides the percentage of different work types for a selected space.
- **Pie Chart**: This displays a pie chart for a filter or a space. You can select which type of statistics to display. For example, you can select fields such as priority, assignee, labels, work type, and so on.
- **Sprint Burndown Gadget**: It displays the amount of remaining work in a sprint.
- **Workload Pie Chart**: This displays the matching work items based on the selected fields. You can select a filter or a space, and it displays data in the form of a pie chart.

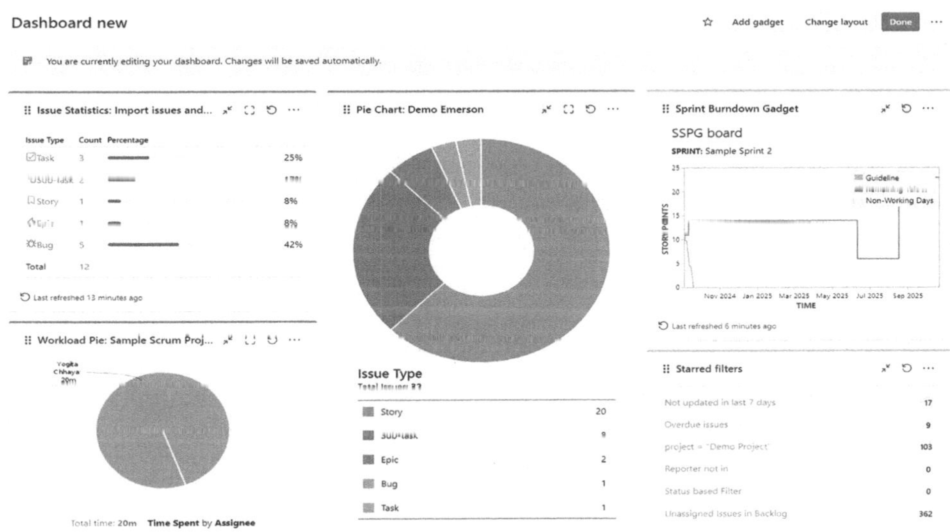

Figure 8.24: *Example Dashboard-2*

- **Spaces Gadget**: It displays the information about all the spaces and filters of each space.
- **Assigned to me**: This displays all work items assigned to the current user in all spaces.
- **Jira Road Map**: It displays the upcoming versions of the space, and a summary of the work items for that version.
- **Resolution Time Gadget**: This displays the average number of days the work items were open for the selected period. It also displays data in bar chart format.

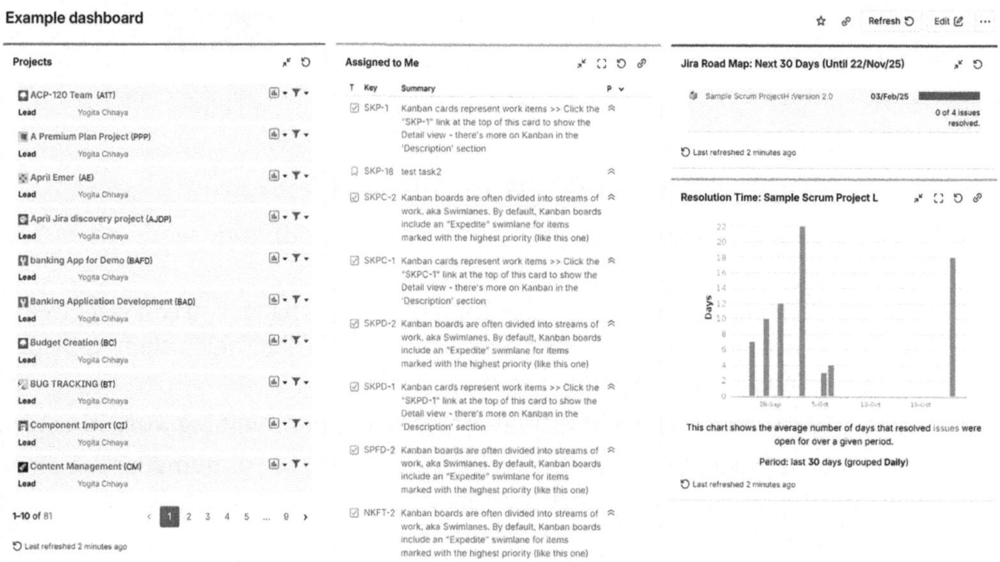

***Figure 8.25:** Example Dashboard-3*

Creating a Wallboard

Wallboard is a full-screen display of the Jira dashboard that can be done on a TV screen. It displays all the gadgets one-by-one, and does not have any navigation menu on it.

Here are the steps:

1. Log into Jira, and navigate to **`Dashboards`** in the top navigation bar.
2. Select **`View all dashboards`**, and the dashboard that is required.
3. Select **`More`** and click **`View as wallboard`**.

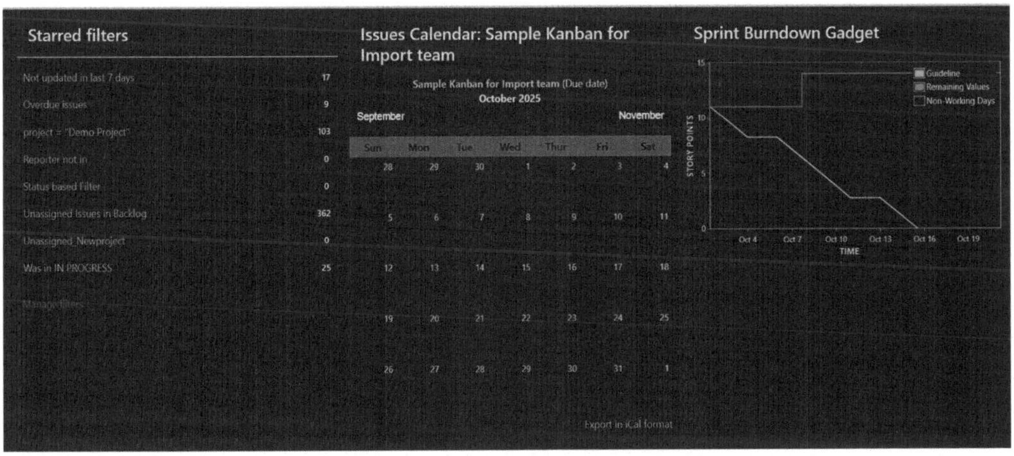

Figure 8.26: *Example Wallboard*

Introduction to Reports

Reports are an important feature in any project management tool. Jira provides a reporting feature for individuals, teams, and spaces. Jira reporting helps teams manage time tracking, project management, and measuring agile metrics. By utilizing these parameters, project managers and teams can plan work in advance, track progress, and make data-driven decisions based on forecasts. You can also add plugins to get more detailed reports.

Steps to Accessing Reports in Jira

Follow these steps to access the Jira reports:

1. Navigate to **`All spaces`**, and then select one space.
2. Click **`Reports`** on the left navigation bar.
3. You will be able to select various kinds of Jira reports.
4. Click the required report, and select the parameters to view.

Jira provides different kinds of reports, and we will learn about Agile reports in detail.

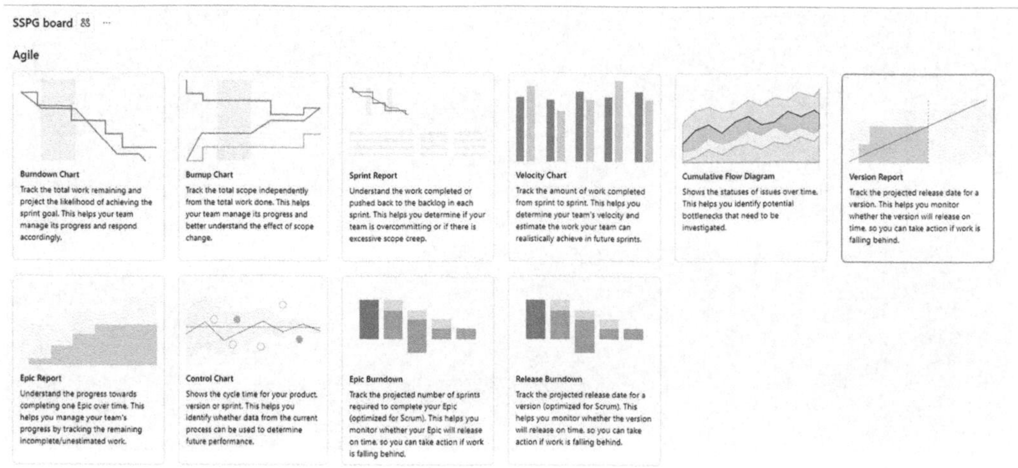

Figure 8.27: *Agile Reports in Jira*

Understanding Agile Reports

In this section, we will understand all the reports for Agile teams in detail.

Reports for Scrum Teams

There are eight reports for Agile Scrum spaces as follows:

- **Burndown Chart**: This report is applicable to sprints within a space. It displays how much work is left in a sprint and provides an idea about achieving the sprint goal. By tracking the remaining work throughout the sprint, teams can manage changes in priority and plan the work to achieve the sprint goal. Users can select the sprints to view and also have the option to choose estimations in the board settings and on the reports page. The Burndown chart will only include the work items in the filter for the board. The Red line shows the remaining values, whereas the gray line is used to display the guideline.

The following is a chart that shows details about work items and information related to those work items, such as sprint start, work item burndown, sprint end, and scope changes. This helps in understanding the overall pattern of iteration, and its progress.

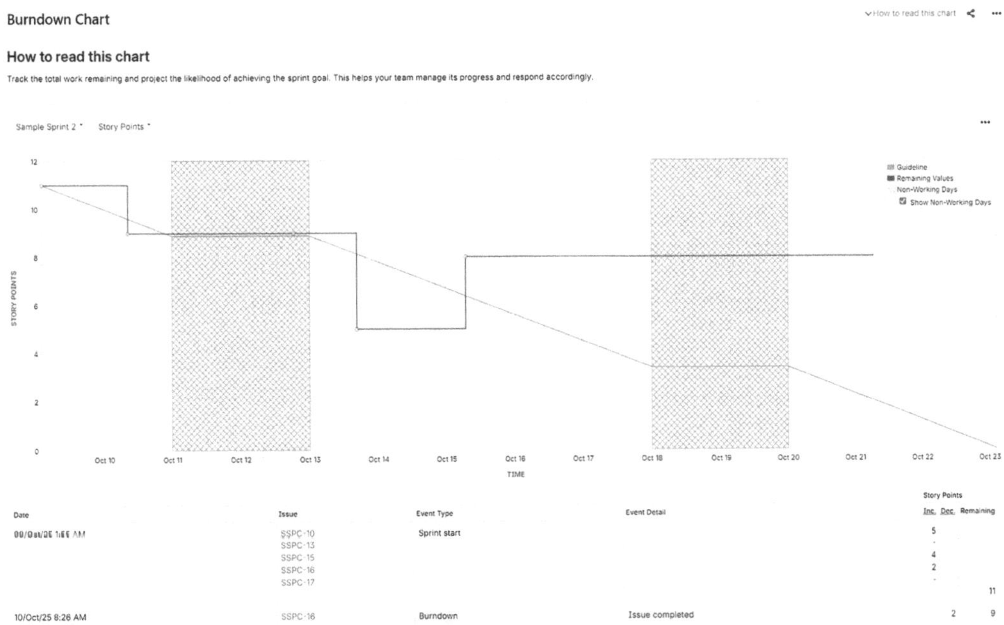

Figure 8.28: *Burndown Chart*

- **Burnup Chart:** This report is applicable to sprints within a space. It displays the sprint's completed work compared with its total scope.

The chart uses a vertical axis to measure the amount of work, which can be selected using various metrics like story points, work item count, or estimates. The horizontal axis represents time, measured in days. The gap between the lines on the chart indicates the remaining workload. When the space reaches completion, these lines will converge.

Thus, by closely observing the **`Work scope`** line, you can spot any instances of scope creep.

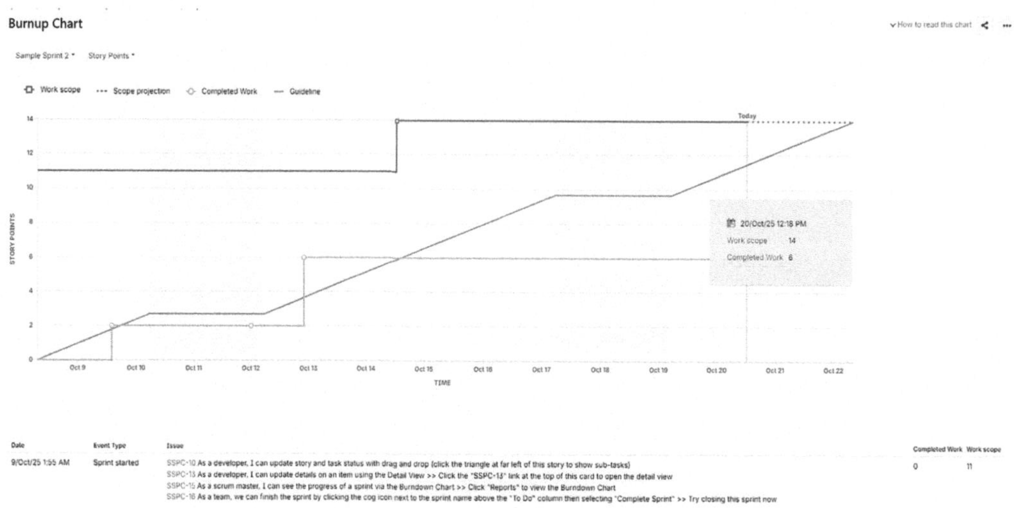

Figure 8.29: *Burnup Chart*

- **Sprint Report:** This report is applicable to sprints in a space. It displays the statistics regarding the completed and not completed work items, priority, status, and story points. This data can assist teams in understanding whether the teams are overcommitting or there is scope creep. The red line indicates the actual work done, whereas the gray line indicates the guideline based on the estimation entered before the start of the sprint. Users can select the sprints to view, and also have the option to select estimations in the board settings. The Sprint Report will only include the work items in the filter for the board.

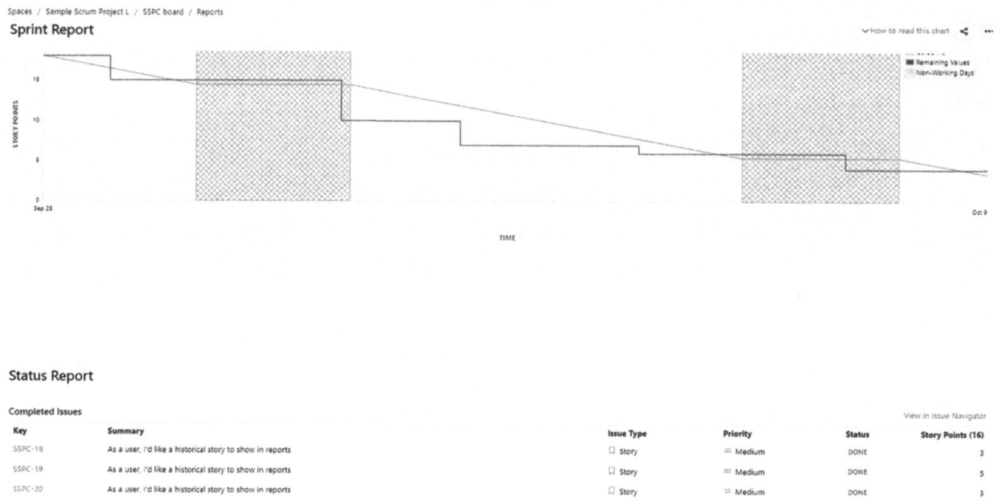

Figure 8.30: *Sprint Report*

- **Velocity Chart:** This report is applicable to sprints within a space. The velocity report is used to know the average amount of work a team can complete in a sprint. You can measure this in different ways, such as counting the number of tasks, measuring time in minutes, hours, days, or using the story points.

Jira keeps track of this over time, and shows it in reports. These reports help the team figure out how much work they can do in future sprints. It helps managers plan how much work the team can realistically do in a certain amount of time.

There is a vertical line on the report, which is used to measure their work, in story points or time.

There are two types of bars on the report. Gray bars show how much work the team planned to do in a sprint before it started. Green bars show how much work the team actually finished in the sprint, and this is shown when the sprint ends.

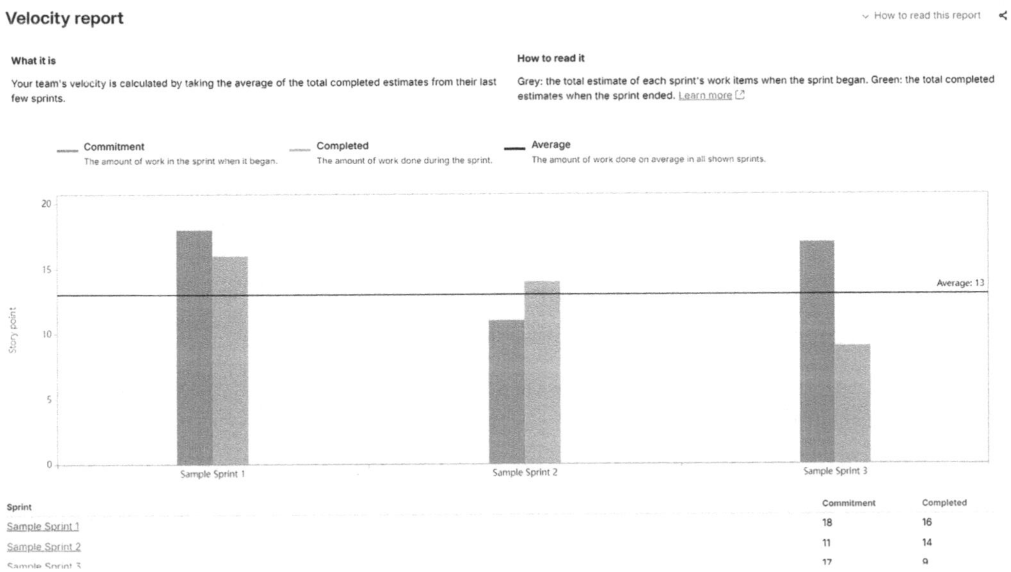

Figure 8.31: *Velocity Chart*

- **Version Report:** This chart is applicable to versions. It helps track the planned release date for a version, and forecast whether the version will be released on time, allowing you to plan actions if the work falls behind. It provides a comprehensive view of the outstanding work items within a specific version, and the overall amount of pending work for the entire version.

It includes the work items for a specific board but does not display archived versions. The horizontal axis starts on the date that is entered, taking the date of the first work item created, if the date is not entered for the version.

The blue line indicates the Predicted Release Date, which is based on the daily average velocity and the amount of estimated work remaining.

The Predicted Release Date (Optimistic) is the date by which you might expect the version to be complete (It is calculated by adding 10% to the average daily velocity). The Predicted Release Date (Pessimistic) is the date by which you might expect the version to be complete (It is calculated by subtracting 10% from the average daily velocity).

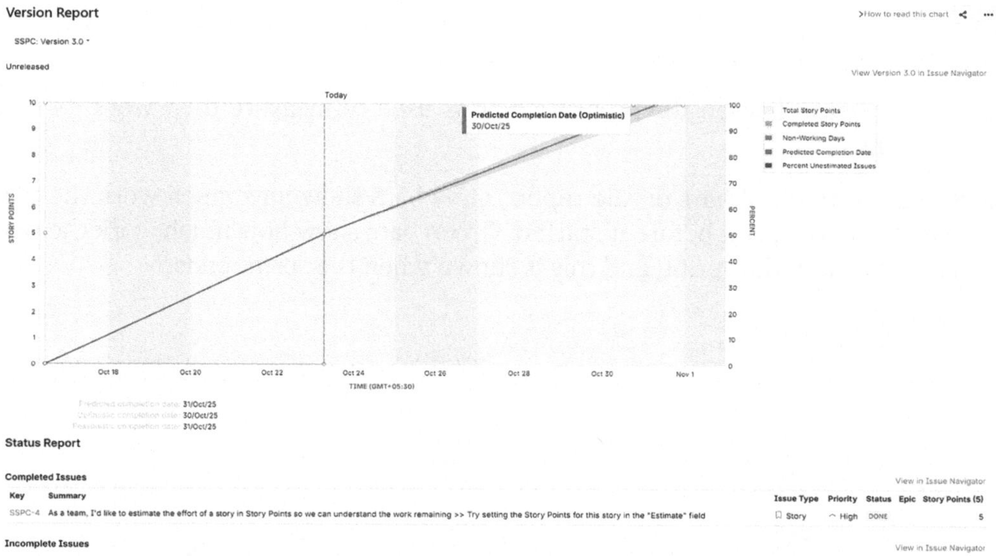

Figure 8.32: *Version Report*

- **Epic Report:** This report is applicable to Epics only.

The Epic Report provides an overview of an epic's work items, categorizing them as either finished, unfinished, or without estimates. This report is useful when planning tasks for an epic spanning multiple sprints.

You can use the Epic Report to see how much progress we have made on the epic, and to keep track of how much work is still left to do. The way the report looks might change a bit if we are counting tasks, instead of using a different method, like Story Points.

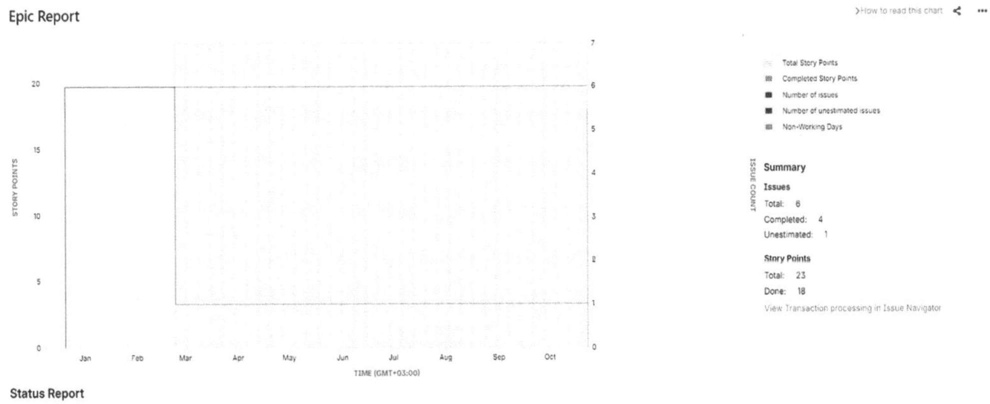

Figure 8.33: *Epic Report*

- **Epic Burndown Chart:** Epic Burndown report is specifically designed for agile scrum teams working in sprints, making progress tracking much more convenient. The Epic Burndown report provides insights into your team's progress with a specific epic. An epic is a user story that can be divided into smaller tasks. The report displays information based on the estimation method, you have selected.

Here are a few ways you can make use of an Epic Burndown report:

- Monitor how fast your team is advancing through the epic.
- Observe how changes, such as tasks added or removed during the sprint, impact your team's overall progress.
- Forecast the number of sprints required to finish the epic, considering the past sprint data and the changes done in the ongoing sprints.

The estimated number of sprints needed is determined by assessing the work completed in the most recent three sprints. When calculating velocity, changes in scope are not considered, but they are taken into account when calculating the overall remaining work.

The Epic Burndown report can provide predictions solely based on estimated work items within your epic. If a work item is in a status that is not mapped to a column, it will not be taken into account in the Epic Burndown report.

Figure 8.34: *Epic Burndown Chart*

- **Release Burndown Chart:** This report is applicable to space versions and is designed specifically for scrum teams. It presents data in accordance with the estimation statistics you have chosen. The Release Burndown report provides insights into your team's progress regarding tasks associated with a particular project release.

Here are a few ways, you can make use of this report:

- Monitor the pace at which your team is working towards the space backlog.
- Assess how the addition and deletion of tasks during sprints have impacted your team's overall progress.
- Forecast the number of sprints required to complete the space version, drawing from insights gained from past sprints and changes made during those sprints.

The estimated number of sprints needed is determined by assessing the work completed in the most recent three sprints. When calculating velocity, changes in scope are not considered, but they are taken into account when calculating the overall remaining work.

The Release Burndown report can provide predictions solely based on the estimated work items within your version. If a work item is in a status that is not mapped to a column, it will not be taken into account in the Release Burndown report.

Figure 8.35: *Release Burndown Chart*

Reports for Kanban Teams

There are two reports for Agile Kanban spaces as follows:

- Cumulative Flow Diagram
- Control Chart

Cumulative Flow Diagram: A Cumulative Flow Diagram (CFD) is a graphical representation in the form of an area chart, used to display the progress of work items within an application, version, or sprint. In this chart, the x-axis represents time, while the y-axis represents the number of work items. Each distinct colored region within the chart corresponds to a specific workflow status, mirroring the columns on your task board.

The CFD serves as a valuable tool for pinpointing bottlenecks in your workflow. If you observe a region within the chart expanding vertically over time, it typically indicates that the corresponding column on your board is experiencing a bottleneck.

In CFD, you can choose the **Refine** report option to select your desired filters. You can select different time frames and date ranges. Changing the date range will highlight the work items that occurred within those dates.

CFD provides data specific to a board (board's filter) and displays it based on column mapping. If any status is unmapped, it will not be shown on the chart. CFD also indicates if any work items have accumulated in a particular column.

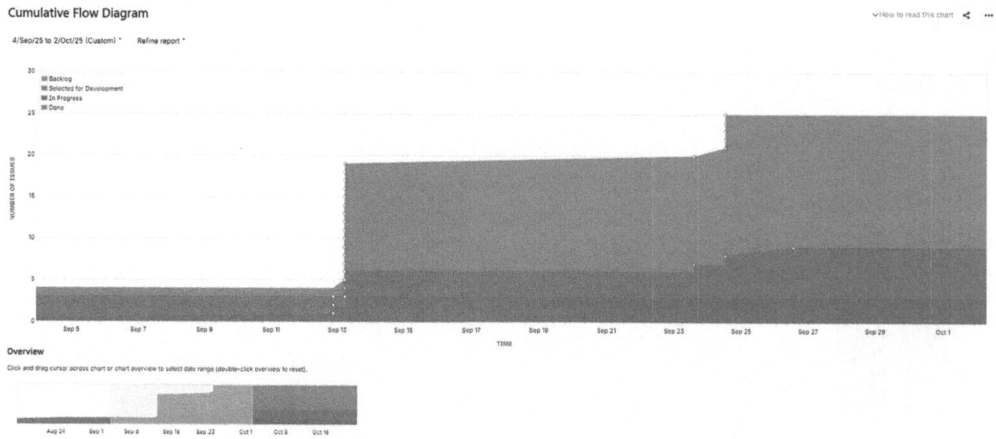

Figure 8.36: *Cumulative Flow Diagram*

Control Chart: The control chart is used to display the Cycle Time or Lead Time. It can be for a product, version, or sprint by tracking the duration each work item remains in specific status over a defined time interval. It provides key statistical measures, including the average, rolling average, and standard deviation based on this dataset.

A Control Chart serves as a tool to evaluate if the data gathered in the ongoing sprint is relevant for predicting future performance. The narrower the variance in work item Cycle Times, the greater the level of confidence in using the mean (or median) as a reliable indicator of future performance.

Some of the important terms to understand are as follows:

- **Cycle Time:** It is the summation of the time from a work item passing through in progress, in review, and done statuses.
- **Lead Time:** This is the summation of the time from a work time passing through the backlog, in progress, in review, and done statuses.
- **The Rolling Average:** Average of cycle times of work items, before the current work item+.

  Average of cycle times of the current work item+.

  Average of cycle times of A work items after the current work item.

With the control chart, you can perform various actions, such as selecting a dot to view work item details, zooming in to highlight a specific time period on the chart, setting the desired time frame for data selection, and refining the report by selecting filters, swim lanes, and columns.

If your space's lead cycle time varies slightly from the average, it is generally not a concern. However, significant spikes beyond the average indicate the presence of pauses, obstacles, or waiting periods.

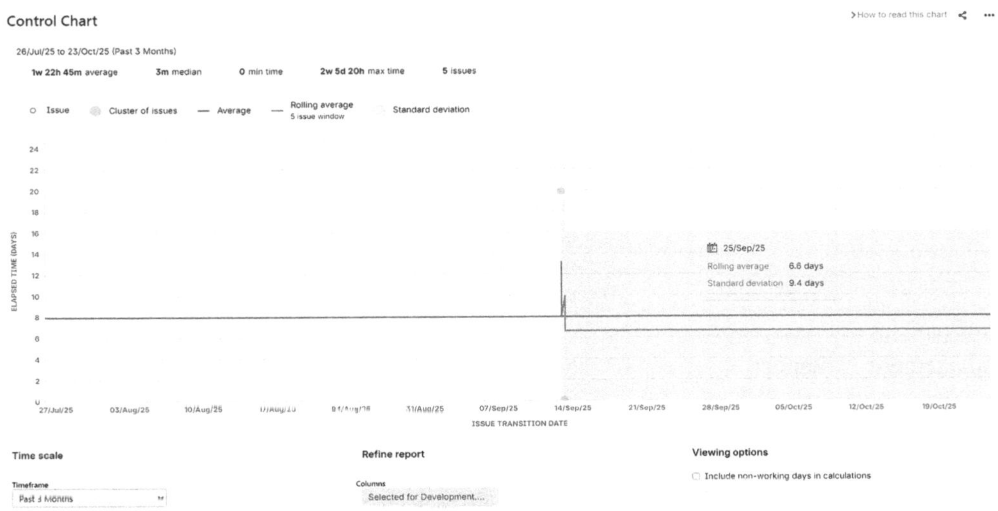

Figure 8.37: *Control Chart*

Other Reports

Jira provides other reports, such as Issue Analysis Report, Forecast, and Management reports.

Type	Name of the Report	Description
Issue Analysis	Average Age Report	Displays the average of the tasks that are unresolved within a space or filter, providing insight into the timeliness of managing your backlog.
	Created v/s Resolved Work Items Report	Compares the newly generated work items to the resolved ones over a specified timeframe, allowing you to understand the pattern of your overall backlog, whether it is expanding or contracting.
	Pie Chart Report	It displays the search results from a specific space or a filter. This is based on selected statistics in the form of a pie chart. The users can see the breakdown of work items in each category selected.
	Recently created Work Items Report	This shows the count of work items generated during a specific time frame for a space or filter and tracks how many of them were successfully resolved. This information assists in understanding whether your team is effectively managing the incoming workload.

	Resolution Time Report	It gives the duration it takes to resolve a batch of work items within a space/filter. This helps in understanding patterns and incidents that can be further discussed and investigated.
	Single Level Group by Report	Displays work items categorized by a specific field for a filter. This report helps you to organize search results based on a particular field and assess the overall status of each category.
	Time Since Issues Report	Using a date and a space/filter, it shows when certain things happened with the work items. This can help you keep a watch on how many work items were created, updated, or more, in a particular time period.
Forecast and Management	Time Tracking Report	It displays the initial and current time estimates for tasks in the current space. This helps you figure out if the work on these tasks is going according to the plan.
	User Workload Report	This shows how much time is expected for all the unfinished tasks assigned to a user in different spaces. It also gives you a clearer picture of how busy that user is.
	Version Workload Report	It displays how much time is needed to finish all the ongoing tasks assigned to a specific version, organized by users and the tasks themselves. This also helps you see what still needs to be done for that version.
Others	Workload Pie Chart Report	A report that presents space or filter work items in the form of a pie chart.

Table 8.1: *Other Reports in Jira*

To generate Time Tracking, User Workload, Version Workload or Workload Pie Chart reports, time tracking must be enabled by the Jira administrator.

Introduction and Overview of Atlassian Analytics

Atlassian Analytics offers a solution to understand data, make data-driven decisions, and create dashboards for Atlassian tools and other data sources. Here is an overview:

- Atlassian Analytics helps teams make decisions using data. You can create interactive dashboards.

- You can use ready-made dashboards to find answers to your big questions. Or, you can build custom views using a visual mode or a written SQL query editor.
- You can get deeper insights by looking at different types of data such as operations, finances, and customer info, all within Atlassian.
- It is a tool to analyze data from Jira, Jira Service Management and other data sources.
- It allows you to perform custom data analysis with a visual SQL interface.
- You can connect to other databases such as Snowflake, Amazon Redshift, Google Big Query, and many more.
- In software spaces, you can identify the causes of problems.
- In service spaces, change management, and incident management, you can keep a track of important metrics.
- It provides readymade templates for different teams for quick setup of reports and dashboards.
- This provides a variety of visualization options such as tables, bar charts, pie charts and other chart types to represent your data effectively.

Here is how it works:

- Atlassian Analytics connects to a Data Lake so that your data stays connected and updatable.
- You can choose and set up products, spaces, and spaces to create charts from.
- You can also write SQL queries if you want, but you can also make charts and dashboards without coding.
- You can pick different chart types and diagrams. Atlassian Analytics suggests chart types based on your data and queries.
- You can put the charts and dashboards into Confluence Spaces. You can also comment on them, and tag them.
- Updates automatically when new data is added to connected Atlassian tools.
- Provides real-time insights across engineering, service and business projects for informed decision-making.

Conclusion

We are now familiar with searching work items in Jira using basic and advanced search, writing JQL queries, creating Dashboards, adding the right Gadgets to present the data, and tracking tasks and projects. In addition, we have also learned to access reports, understand the Agile metrics from various reports, and gain an overview of Atlassian Analytics.

In the next chapter, we will learn about *Jira Automation Rules.*

Points to Remember

- Give your filters appropriate names that reflect their purpose, making it easier to find, and reuse them later.
- Share filters with your team to ensure that everyone has access to the same set of criteria for work searches.
- Learn Jira Query Language (JQL) to create more complex and correct filters, using operators like AND, OR, and NOT.
- Quick Filters on Agile boards allow you to quickly switch between different filters to view work items that match the specific criteria.
- Use scheduled filter subscriptions to receive regular email updates with the results of your filter queries.
- Create your dashboards to suit your role or space by adding and arranging gadgets that display relevant and important information.
- Take advantage of gadget configuration options to fine-tune the way data is presented on your dashboard.
- Use the Filter Results and Two-Dimensional Filter Statistics gadgets to display filtered work item lists directly on your dashboard, providing quick access to specific sets of work items.
- Share filters and dashboards with team members or project stakeholders, allowing them to stay informed about project progress.
- Set appropriate permissions to control who can view and edit your filters and dashboards.
- Choose the report type that fits your needs best. Jira has different types, such as Burndown Charts, Control Charts, and Velocity Charts.
- Many reports allow you to customize date ranges, work types, and other parameters to focus on the data that matters most.
- Take the time to learn what metrics like velocity and burndown charts mean so that you can make better decisions.
- Add gadgets like the "Filter Results" gadget or "Pie Chart" gadget within your reports to provide additional context and details.
- Periodically review and clean up your filters, dashboards, and reports to ensure that they stay relevant and organized.

Use Cases with Reference Links

1. A JQL for: A piece of JQL I can add which will show me Jira tickets which were created before the first of the month but were closed and open on or after the first of the month. So, for example, tickets which were created before the 1st of November but were closed and still open on or after the 1st of November.

   https://community.atlassian.com/t5/Jira-Software-questions/Filters-Advance-work item-search-JQL/qaq-p/1886105

2. Advanced search using JQL for epics without stories:

   https://community.atlassian.com/t5/Jira-Core-Server-questions/Advanced-search-using-JQL-for-epics-without-stories/qaq-p/1049459

3. Deleting Filters in Jira Cloud:

   https://community.atlassian.com/t5/Jira-Service-Management/Deleting-Filters-in-Jira-Cloud/qaq-p/2314822

4. Edit a private filter in Jira Cloud:

   https://community.atlassian.com/t5/Jira-Software-questions/Edit-a-private-filter-in-Jira-Cloud/qaq-p/2294042

5. JQL Syntax for due date Quick Filter:

   https://community.atlassian.com/t5/Jira-questions/JQL-Syntax-for-due-date-Quick-Filter/qaq-p/2175118

6. Using Quick Filters in Active Sprint Board:

   https://community.atlassian.com/t5/Jira-questions/Using-Quick-Filters-in-Active-Sprint-board/qaq-p/2226732

7. Is there a way in Jira Cloud to allow users to Share/Create Filters and Dashboards and not Boards:

   https://community.atlassian.com/t5/Jira-Software-questions/Is-there-a-way-in-Jira-Cloud-to-allow-users-to-Share-Create/qaq-p/2393157

8. Are there any global settings for Dashboards?

   https://community.atlassian.com/t5/Jira-Software-questions/global-settings-for-dashboards/qaq-p/2131965

9. Reports / Dashboards. How to save reports on the Dashboards?

   https://community.atlassian.com/forums/Jira-questions/Reports-Dashboards-How-to-save-report-on-the-Dashboards/qaq-p/2880246

10. How to generate Dashboards according to the Project needs?

    https://community.atlassian.com/t5/Jira-Software-questions/How-to-generate-Dashboards-according-to-the-project-needs/qaq-p/2231361

11. I can access my Spaces but can no longer find my Dashboards! I can go to the Space Board and see my Work Items. All I have now is a Default Dashboard:

    https://community.atlassian.com/t5/Jira-Work-Management-Questions/What-happened-to-my-dashboards/qaq-p/2281858

12. Are Dashboards a part of Jira or are they a part of an Add-on?

    https://community.atlassian.com/t5/Jira-Software-questions/Are-Dashboards-part-of-Jira-or-are-they-part-of-an-add-on/qaq-p/2264722

13. I would like to be able to copy and then modify a Jira Dashboard gadget, instead of starting from scratch with a new one, and adding the same fields again:

    https://community.atlassian.com/t5/Jira-Software-questions/Can-Atlassian-enable-copying-a-Dashboard-gadget/qaq-p/2365482

14. I am looking to create a Recurring Dashboard that presents the health of the Current/Open Sprint, without having to change the Sprint ID in my filter at the start of each sprint:

    https://community.atlassian.com/t5/Jira-questions/Dashboard-dynamic-sprint-dropdown/qaq-p/1870047

15. For each Release, I need a Dashboard for that particular release. This Dashboard contains data from Multiple Filters. With each release, the only changing variable would be the "Fix Version":

    https://community.atlassian.com/t5/Jira-questions/Re-use-dashboards-by-adding-dynamic-filtering-capability/qaq-p/1719508

16. Reports by Assignee:

    https://community.atlassian.com/t5/Jira-Software-questions/Reports-by-Assignee/qaq-p/2441865

17. Reports:

    https://community.atlassian.com/t5/Jira-questions/Reports/qaq-p/2365294

18. Insights and Sprint Burndown Feature:

    https://community.atlassian.com/t5/Jira-Software-questions/Insights-and-sprint-burndown-feature/qaq-p/2124121

19. Sprint Insights - the admins can see it but not the team members:

    https://community.atlassian.com/t5/Jira-Software-questions/Sprint-Insights-the-admins-can-see-it-but-not-the-team-members/qaq-p/2365550

20. Reading Jira Sprint Report:

    https://community.atlassian.com/t5/Jira-Software-questions/Reading-Jira-Sprint-Report/qaq-p/2124012

CHAPTER 9
Jira Automation Rules

Introduction

Automation is employed to enhance the efficiency and productivity in project management. As the scope of software development and project management continues to expand, automation becomes indispensable for teams. It is not just a time-saver but also a game-changer, helping teams streamline their workflows, reduce manual effort, and minimize human error. Consequently, teams can shift their focus to more critical tasks, such as innovation and problem-solving. They can automatically assign tasks, transition work items through predefined workflows, send notifications, and set field values. Thus, automation serves as your behind-the-scenes assistant that makes your work life significantly smoother. In this chapter, we will take a closer look at how this magical Jira Automation works, and how you can make the most of it.

Structure

In this chapter, we will cover the following topics:

- Understanding Automation in Jira
- Accessing the Automation Rules on Jira Boards
- Knowing and Understanding Elements of Automation Rules
    - Triggers
    - Conditions
    - Actions
    - Rule Branching
    - Smart Values
    - Owner
    - Rule Actor
    - Scope
    - Allowing Rule Trigger
    - Notify on Error
    - Audit Log

  - Debugging Rules
- Templates and Automation Library
- Jira Automation Playground
- Checking Usage
- Performance Insights
- Import and Export Jira Automation Rules
- Steps to Create an Automation Rule with Examples
- Essential Learning Examples

Understanding Automation Rules and Its Importance

Automation helps you automate repetitive tasks. For example, it can involve creating multiple tasks, adding conditions, updating fields like assignee, and so on. It saves time for every team member. Writing an automation rule is a no-brainer because it is a no-code tool. Even people with a non-technical background can write automation rules, and it does not require any prior experience. It works with third-party tools, and makes life easier. The rules are simple and easy to understand, and can be created with drag and drop.

Accessing the Automation Rules on Jira Board

Here are the steps for accessing the Automation Rules on the Jira Board:

1. Navigate to **`Space`** > **`Space Settings`** > **`Automation`**:

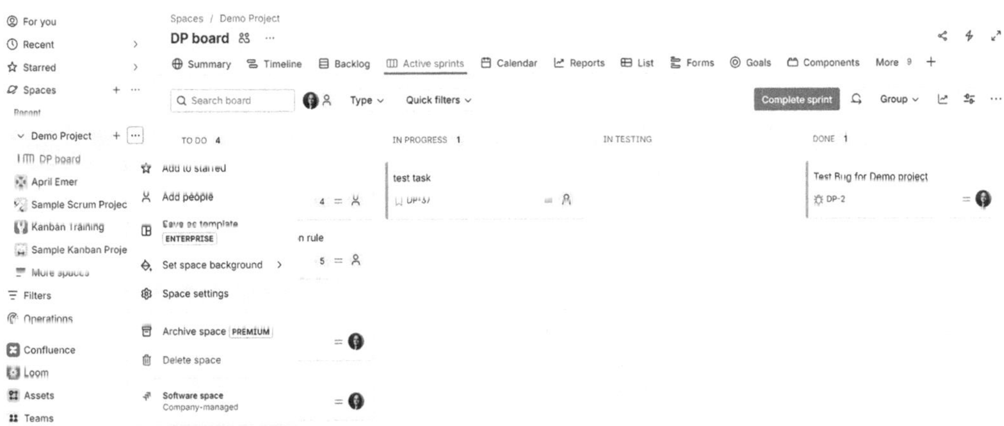

Figure 9.1: *Navigating to Space Settings*

2. Click **`Automation`** on the left panel. On the landing page, the user will see **`create rule`** and **`Global administration`** options:

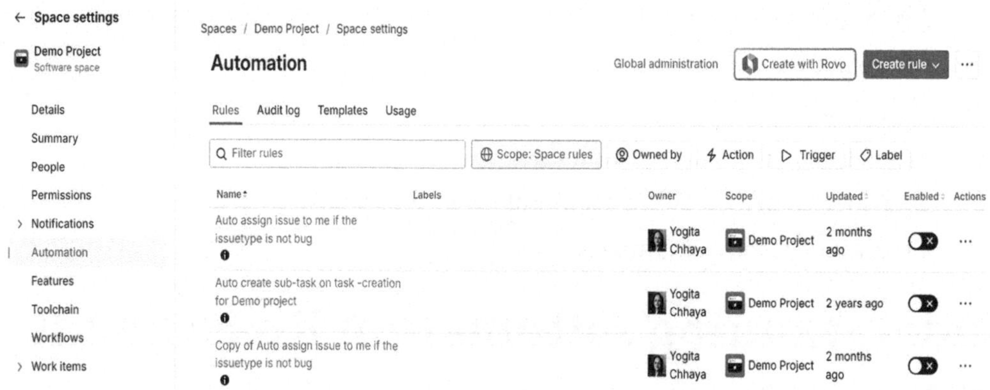

Figure 9.2: *Options for Accessing the Automation Rules*

3. Clicking **`Global administration`** gives the user a list of automation templates to choose from:

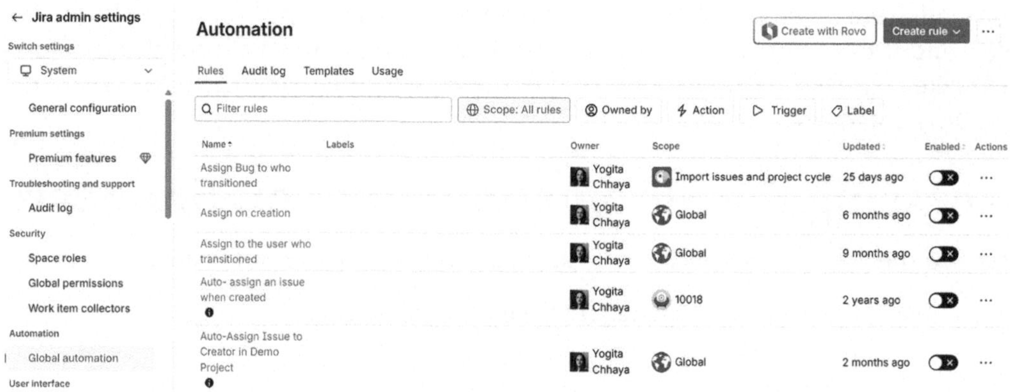

Figure 9.3: *Selecting Global Administration Option*

4. Clicking **`Create Rule`** displays the first step to create a new automation rule:

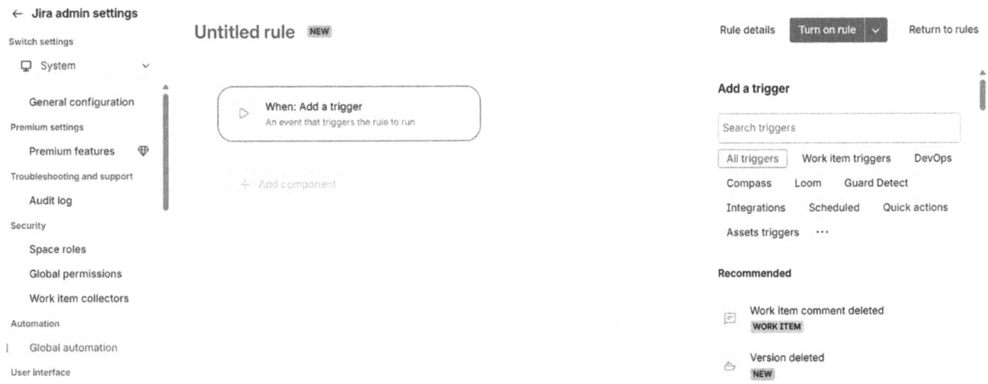

***Figure 9.4**: First Step to Create an Automation Rule*

5. The first step is to add a trigger that will initiate the rule. You can add a Condition, create a Branch, and conclude the rule by adding an Action.

Knowing and Understanding Elements of Automation Rules

There are mainly three elements to create an automation rule: Triggers, Conditions, and Actions. In addition to that, there are a few basic things, we will explore in this section.

Triggers

The first thing in any automation rule is to start with a trigger. Triggers are responsible for initiating the execution of the rule. There are events occurring in Jira, such as a work item transition, work item creation, or a change in field value. Triggers listen to these events. You can also trigger rules from add-ons such as Fisheye-Crucible, GitHub, and Bitbucket.

It is possible to set manual triggers that work based on a particular condition.

The triggers are as shown in *Figure* 9.5.

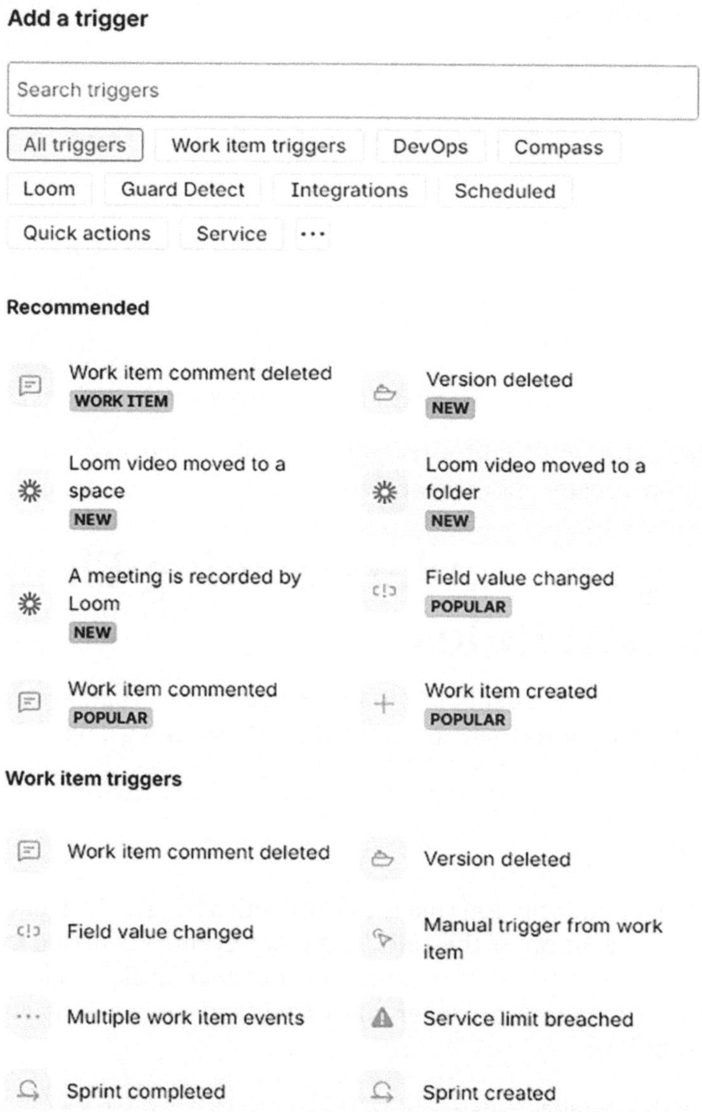

Figure 9.5: *Work Item Triggers- Jira Automation Rule*

Conditions

Conditions enable you to refine the applicability of your rule. They must be satisfied for your rule to proceed. For example, you can configure your rule which will execute if the work items meet the specific JQL query. In the event that a condition is not met, the rule will halt, and any subsequent actions specified after the condition will not be executed.

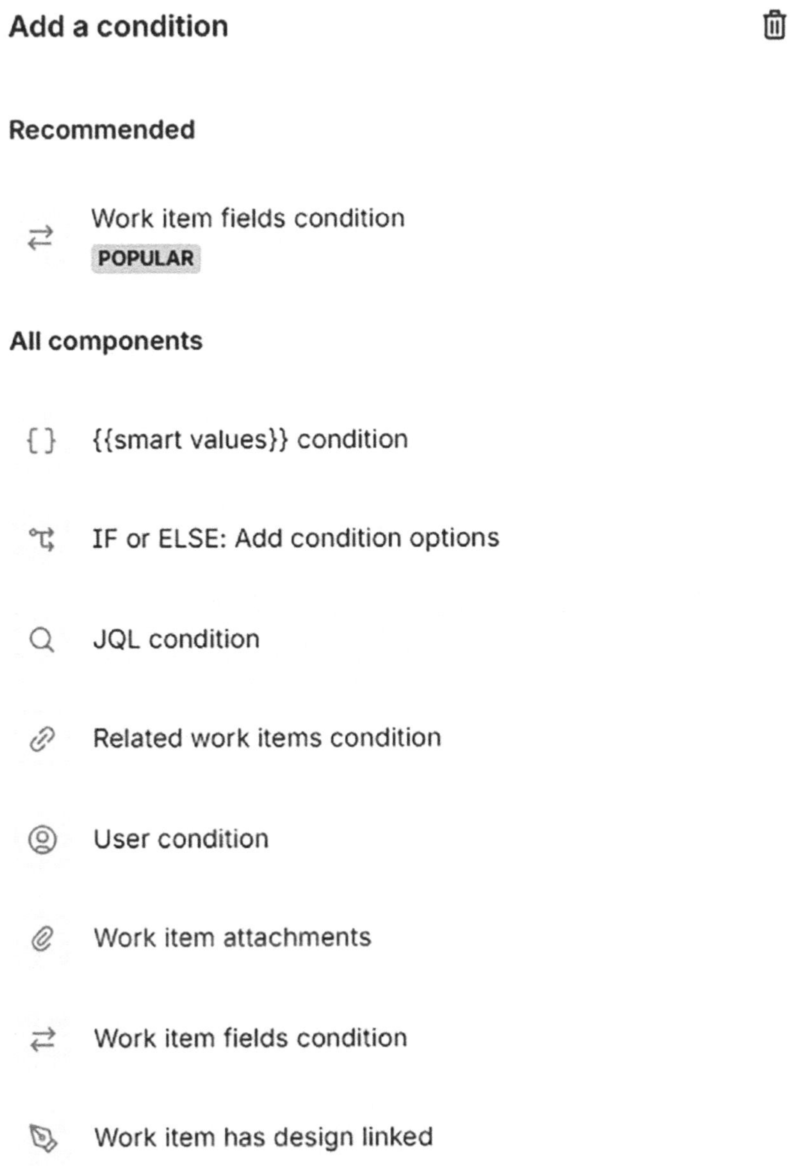

***Figure* 9.6:** *Conditions-Jira Automation Rule*

Actions

Actions are the final stage of any automation rule. They ultimately allow you to take actions such as sending an email, closing tasks, or transitioning work items.

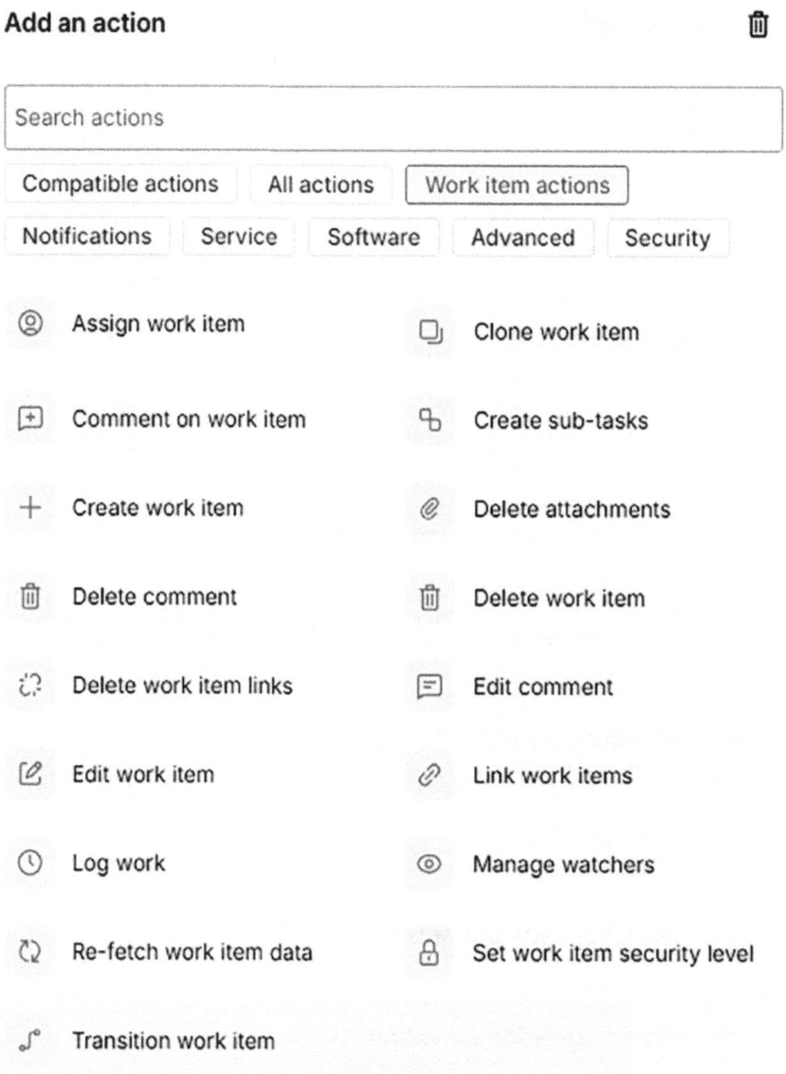

Figure 9.7: *Actions - Jira Automation Rule*

Rule Branching

When setting up automation rules, it is possible to create a separate section within the rule where actions can be performed on related work items. This concept is known as **branching**. Jira provides special conditions and actions to create extremely useful rules that can be applied to all the linked work items as well. It differs from the linear execution of rules, and instead allows for the rule to diverge into multiple paths.

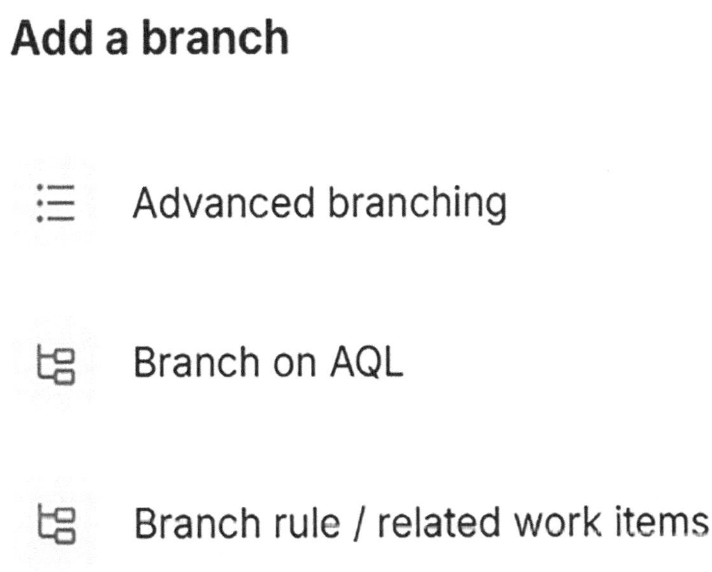

Figure 9.8: *Rule Branching*

For instance, consider a rule triggered when a work item transitions to the **Done** status; this rule can also include a branch that carries out separate actions on the subtasks of that work item.

Branching Constraints:

- **Nesting**: It is important to note that branches cannot be nested within each other. This means you cannot have one branch contained within another.
- **If/else Condition**: The use of the If/else block condition is not supported in branching.
- **Isolation**: Each branch operates in isolation. Any modifications made within a branch do not affect the main rule or any other branches. For instance, if a branch includes a **`Create variable`** action, the created smart value can only be used within that particular branch, and cannot be accessed in the main rule or other branches.

Example: In this example, story points of related work items, that is, sub-tasks under a parent task get added:

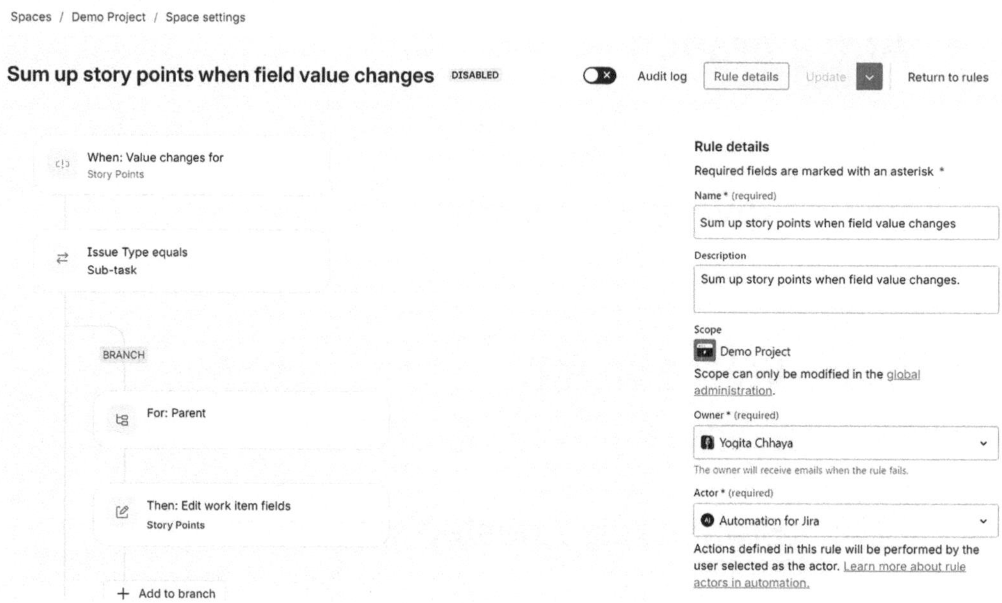

Figure 9.9: *Example of Rule Branching*

Smart Values

Smart values allow access and manipulation of the work item data in Jira. We have provided the **`Smart Values`** list as mentioned in the following table.

Jira Smart Values: Issues

The work item smart values are employed to retrieve details concerning the active work item of the rule, indicating the work item currently being processed by the rule.

Issue Fields	Smart Value and Properties	What It Returns
`{{issue.[property]}}`		Work item properties are helpful for accessing various information about the active work item.
	`{{issue.description}}`	Content written in the description field.
	`{{issue.key}}`	Work item-key is a combination of a space-key and an work item number.
	`{{issue.space}}`	The space that work item belongs to.

	{{issue.status}}	Status of the work item.
	{{issue.status.name}}	Status of the work item.
	{{issue. Summary}}	The summary of the work item.
	{{issue.versions}}	Affect's version of the work item.
	{{issue.Issuetype.name}}	Work types such as Bug, Task, and Story.
	{{issue.resolution}}	Resolution of the work item.
	{{issue.updated}}	Date when the work item was updated.
	{{issue.Story Points}}	The story point estimate of the work item's story (applicable to company-managed space Jira Cloud).
	{{issue.Story Points Estimate}}	The story point estimate of the work item's story (applicable to team-managed space Jira Cloud).
Issue Dates	{{issue.created}}	Creation date of the work item.
	{{issue.duedate}}	Due date of the work item.
Issue Users	{{issue.assignee.displayName}}	Name of the assignee of the work item
	{{issue.reporter.displayName}}	Name of the reporter of the work item.
Issue Custom Field	{{issue.[Custom Field].id}}	Unique ID assigned by Jira to the Custom Field.
	{{issue. [Custom Field]. description}}	The following text shown in the custom field when viewed in the Simple Search column.
	{{issue. [Custom Field].name}}	The label visible on the left of the field.
Issue Comments	{{issue.comments.last.body}}	Provides the body of the last comment.
	{{issue.comments.first.body}}	Provides the body of the first comment
	{{issue.comments.reverse.body}}	Work item's comments in the reverse order.

	`{{issue.comments.size}}`	Number of comments added on the work item.
	`{{issue.comments.author.displayName}}`	Provides the Comment authors.
Issue Components	`{{issue.components.name}}`	Value of the component field of the work item.
Issue's Epic	`{{issue.epic.key}}`	Epic's key, for example, TESTEPIC-23.
	`{{issue.epic.status.name}}`	Epic's status, for example, Open.
	`{{issue.epic.[Custom Field]}}`	Value in an Epic's custom field.
Issue Fix Version	`{{issue.fixVersions.name}}`	The name of the fix version.
	`{{issue.fixVersions.description}}`	The description of the fix version.
	`{{issue.fixVersions.released}}`	True, if the fixed version is released; otherwise, False.
	`{{issue.fixVersions.releaseDate}}`	Fix version's release date.
	`{{issue.fix.Versions.archived}}`	True, if the fixed version is archived; otherwise, False.
	`{{issue.latest}}`	Prints the work item-key and the status, for example, **`To Do`**, **`In Progress`**.
	`{{issue.latest.description}}`	Provides the description of the status.
	`{issue.parent.key}}`	Work item-key of the parent work item of sub-task.
	`{{issue.parent.priority.name}}`	Priority of the parent work item of the sub-task.
	`{{issue.parent.epic.summary}}`	Summary of the parent work item's epic.
Issue Property	`{{issue.properties}}`	Property of the work item such as some value stored that are used by add-ons and integrations.
Issue Security	`{{issue.security.name}}`	Provides Security level Name.
	`{{issue.security.id}}`	Provides Security level ID.
	`{{issue.timetracking.timespent}}`	Time logged in the Time Spent Field.

	`{{issue.timetracking.remainingestimate}}`	Value in the Time Remaining Field.
Issue Versions	`{{versions.name}}`	The name of the affects version.
	`{{versions.description}}`	The description of the affects version.
	`{{versions.archived}}`	True, if the affects version is archived; otherwise, False.
	`{{versions.released}}`	True, if the affects version is released; otherwise, False.
	`{{versions.releaseDate}}`	Affects version release date.
Issue Watchers	`{{issue.watchers.displayName}}`	Name of the watchers for work item.
	`{{issue.watchers.emailAddress}}`	E-mail ID of the work item watchers.
lookupissues		It returns a list of work items from a JQL search.
	`{{key}}`	Returns work **itemkey**.
	`{{url}}`	It provides the work **itemurl**.
	`{{summary}}`	It provides the work **itemsummary**.
	`{{assignee.displayName}}`	Provides the name of the Assignee.
	`{{reporter.displayName}}`	Provides the name of the Reporter.
	`{{status}}`	Status
	`{{issueType.name}}`	Name of the work type.
	`{{resolution}}`	Resolution status
	`{{fixVersion}}`	Projects the **fixversion**
	`{{created}}`	Date of the work item was created.
	`[[updated}}`	Date of the work item was updated.
	`{{Story Points}}`	For company-managed spaces, it returns the story points of the work item.

	`{{Story point estimate}}`	For team-managed spaces, it returns the story points of the work item.
Triggerissue	`{{triggerissue}}`	Refers to the work item that triggered the rule. All the properties applicable to work items are applicable to trigger work item.
Attachment	`{{attachment.filename}}`	The filename of the attachment.
	`{{attachment.mimeType}}`	The file format of the attachment.
	`{{attachment.created}}`	Date and time of the attachment when it was added to the work item.
	`{{attachment. [xxx]. size}}`	File size of a particular attachment.
	`{{attachment.author}}`	Name of the user who added the attachment.
	`{{attachment.author.accountId}}`	ID associated with the user.
	`{{attachment.author.displayName}}`	Name displayed in the Jira Instance.
	`{{attachment.author.active}}`	Returns TRUE, if the account is active; FALSE, if it is not active.
	`{{attachment.author.emailAddress}}`	E-mail address associated with the user's name.
	`{{attachment.author.timeZone}}`	It is the time zone registered in their account.
	`{{baseUrl}}`	Gives the URL of the Jira instance.
Changelog	`{{changelog}}`	This value accesses changelog, and a list of changes for the field.
	`{{changelog.summary}}`	Displays changelog information for the Summary Field.
	`{{changelog.issuetype}}`	Displays changelog information for the Work Type Field.

	`{{changelog.status}}`	Displays changelog information for the Status Field
Comment	`{{comment}}`	It is used with issue Commented Trigger. This smart value will not work with other triggers.
	`{{comment.body}}`	Content of the comment that prompted the rule.
	`{{comment.author}}`	ID of the author of the comment.
	`{{comment.created}}`	Date and time when the comment was created.
	`{{comment.visibility.type}}`	Any restrictions on the comment, for example, Role.
	`{{comment.visibility.value}}`	Label for Comment Restriction, if any.
	`{{comment.properties}}`	It accesses comment property that are used by add-ons and integrations.
	`{{comment.id}}`	The comment that prompted the rule is stored in this value.
	`{{createdIssue}}`	Accesses the previous work item created in the rule. All property used with issue smart value can be used with this.
	`{{createdIssues}}`	A list of work items that have been created in the rule. It is used with Create sub-tasks, Create work item, and Clone work item actions. All property used with work item smart value can be used with this.
Event Type	`{{eventType}}`	The type of event that prompted the rule. For Example: **`work item_commented`**
Fieldchange	`{{fieldChange}}`	

	{fieldChange.fromString}}	It returns the previous value as displayed.
	{fieldChange.toString}}	It returns the new value as displayed.
	{{fieldChange.from}}	Previous raw value. For example: For a select field.
	{{fieldChange.to}}	New raw value. For example: For a select field.
	{addedfieldChange.field}}	It shows the field that has changed due to the addition of a value.
	{{addedFieldChange.fieldId}}	The **fieldId** of the field that has changed due to the addition of a value.
	{{addedFieldChange.fieldType}}	Returns the **fieldType** of the field that has changed due to the addition of a value.
	{addedfieldChange.valueIds}}	Provides the ID/IDs of new value/values added.
	{{addedfieldChange.values}}	Provides the new value/ values added.
	{{deletedFieldChange.field}}	Provides the field that value has changed due to deletion of a value.
	{{deletedFieldChange.fieldId}}	The **fieldId** of the field that has changed due to the deletion of a value.
	{{deletedFieldChange.fieldType}}	Provides the **fieldType** of the field that has changed due to deletion of a value.
	{{deletedFieldChange.valueIds}}	Provides the ID/IDs of value/ values deleted.
	{{deletedFieldChange.values}}	Provides the value/values deleted.
Rule	{{rule}}	Provides the information for the current rule.
	{{rule.name}}	Name of the rule that is running.
	{{rule.actor}}	The rule Actor.

WebHook	`{{webhookData.[value].[childvalue]}}`	Enables access to the data transmitted with the incoming webhook, such as the request's body.
	`{{webhookResponse}}`	Used with Send Web Request Action. Upon a successful request, you can access the response data from the webhook using the provided smart values.
Worklog	`{{worklog}}`	Accesses work log information of a work item that is recent.
	`{{worklog.visibility}}`	When the work log is restricted, it is available.
	`{{worklog.visibility.type}}`	When the work log is restricted, it is available.
	`{{worklog.visibility.value}}`	When the work log is restricted, it is available.

	Other properties: `{{worklog.comment}}`
	`{{worklog.started}}`
	`{{worklog.timeSpentSeconds}}`
	`{{worklog.timeSpent}}`	

***Table 9.1:** Jira Smart Values – Work Items*

Jira Smart Values - Projects

The following smart values listed in *Table* 9.2 can be used to access information regarding Jira spaces:

	Smart Value and Properties	**What It Returns**
Projects	`{{project.id}}`	The ID of the project that activated the rule
	`{{project.key}}`	The project key associated with the project that activated the rule
	`{{project.name}}`	The name of the project associated with the project that activated the rule
	`{{project.projectTypeKey}}`	It returns the type of the project. For example: Software, Service Management, Software

	`{{project.avatarUrls}}`	It returns the avatar URL of the project that activated the rule

***Table 9.2**: Jira Smart Values – Projects*

Jira Smart Values: Lists

The following smart values are available to access and format the value of items in a list when setting up a rule:

Smart Value	Property and Example	What It Returns
`List`	`{{issue.fixVersions.name}}`	Goes through a list and displays its contents. It can reference other methods and properties.
`List.average`	`{{issue.subtasks.Story Points.average}}`	Returns the average of numbers within a list.
`list.distinct`	`{{lookupIssues.parent.distinct}}`	This smart value returns all items from a list that are not repeated.
`list.isEmpty`	`{{issue.issuelinks.isEmpty}}`	It shows true if the list is empty, or False, if it is not.
`list.join(separator)`	`{{issue.fixVersions.name.join(" - ")}}`	It produces a list of items separated by the specified characters.
`list.get(index)`	`{lookupIssues.get(0).summary}}`	The element located at the given index, where 0 indicates the initial element in the array.
`list.getFromEnd(index)`	`{{issue.comments.getFromEnd(1).body}}`	The element located at the specified index from the array's end, with 0 representing the last element.
`list.first`	`{{issue.comments.first.body}}`	It returns the first element in the list.
`list.last`	`{{issue.comments.last.body}}`	It returns the last element in the list.
`list.max`	`{{issue.subtasks.Due date.max}}`	It returns the highest number in a list or returns the latest date in a list
`list.min`	`{{issue.fixVersions.releaseDate.min}}`	It returns the smallest number in a list or returns the earliest date in a list
`list.size`	`{{issue.comments.size}}`	It returns the size of the list
`list.sum`	`{{issue.subtasks.Story Points.sum}}`	It returns the sum of all values in a list

***Table 9.3**: Jira Smart Values – Lists*

Jira Smart Values: Text Fields

The following smart values are available and applicable for text strings. It can be applied while creating new rules:

Smart Value and Properties	Example	What it Returns
`abbreviate(int maxLength)`	`{{issue.summary.abbreviate (4)}} -> Hell...`	Shortens the text to the specified character limit and appends "..." at the end. The **`maxLength`** parameter must be a minimum of four characters.
`asNumber`	`{{issue.summary.asNumber}} -> Null`	Converts a given string into a number if feasible; otherwise, it returns null.
`charAt(int index)`	`{{issue.summary.charAt(0)}} -> H`	Determines the character located at the designated position within the given text string.
`capitalize()`	`{{issue.summary. capitalize()}} -> Hello world!`	Converts the first character to a capital letter.
`concat(String str)`	`{{issue.summary.concat (" It's a beautiful day!")}}`	Appends a specific text string to the end of the resulting value.
`endsWith(String str)`	`{{issue.summary. endsWith("World!")}} -> true`	Verifies whether the text string concludes with the specified text, and returns either true or false.
`equals(string)`	`{{issue.summary.equals ("hello world!")}} -> false`	Examines a text field to determine if it matches the provided string. If the strings are identical, it returns true. This can be employed in conditional logic.
`equalsIgnoreCase (string)`	`{{issue.summary. equals("Hello world!")}} -> true`	Examines a text field to ascertain if it matches the provided string, without considering case sensitivity. If the strings are equal, regardless of the case, it returns true. This feature can be utilized in conditional logic.
`htmlEncode()`	`{{issue.summary.htmlEncode}} -> Hello world!`	Encodes text to make it suitable for inclusion in HTML content.

indexOf(String str)	{{issue.summary. indexOf("Wo")}} -> 6	Provides the position of the initial character in the specified text string.
isAlpha()	{{issue.summary.isAlpha()}} -> true	Examines whether the text consists solely of letters and returns either true or false.
isAlphanumeric()	{{issue.summary. isAlphanumeric ()}} -> true	Verifies if the text comprises only letters or numbers and returns either true or false.
isEmpty()	{{issue.summary.isEmpty()}} -> false	Evaluates whether the text is empty, and returns either true or false.
isNotEmpty()	{{issue.summary.isNotEmpty ()}} -> true	Evaluates whether the text is not empty, and returns either true or false.
isNumeric()	{{issue.summary. isNumeric()}} -> false	Examines whether the text comprises solely numbers, and returns either true or false
jsonEncode()	{{issue.summary.jsonEncode }} -> Hello World!	Encodes text to enable its inclusion in JSON calls.
lastIndexOf (String str)	{{issue.summary.lastIndexOf ("wo")}} -> 7	Provides the position of the final character in the specified text string.
left(int length)	{{issue.summary.left(5)}} -> Hello	Returns the characters from the left side of the text string, starting from the specified position.
leftPad(int length, String pad)	{{issue.summary.leftPad (14, "-")}} -> --Hello World!	Prepends characters to the beginning of the text until the total character count reaches the specified limit.
match()		Executes a regular expression search, and returns the first matching group (singular) found.
quote()		Escapes the smart value into a literal text expression that can be used in a regular expression match using **Pattern.quote().**
remove(String remove)	{{issue.summary.remove ("l")}} -> Heo Word!	Removes characters from the text.

`replace(String target, String replacement)`	`{{issue.summary.replace("Hello","Goodbye")}} -> Goodbye World!`	Substitutes all exact text matches with a specified replacement.
`replaceAll(String regex, String replacement)`		Conducts a regular expression search and substitutes any matches with the specified replacement. $1 can be utilized to access a matching group in the replacement.
`reverse()`	`{issue.summary.reverse()}} -> !dlroW elloH`	Inverts the order of characters within the text string.
`right(int length)`	`{{issue.summary.right(6)}} -> World!`	Returns the characters from the right side of the text string, starting from the specified position.
`rightPad(int length, String pad)`	`{{issue.summary. rightPadPad(14,"-")}} -> Hello World!--`	Appends characters to the end of the text string until the total character count reaches the specified limit.
`split(String separator)`	`{{issue.summary.split(" ").first}} -> Hello`	Splits the text, and returns the word specified by the word's position in the text string.
`startsWith(String str)`	`{{issue.summary.startsWith("World!")}} -> false`	Evaluates whether the text string begins with the specified text, and returns either true or false.
`substring(int start)`	`{{issue.summary.substring(7)}} -> orld!`	Returns the characters following the specified number of characters.
`substring(int start, int end)`	`{{issue.summary.substring(1,3)}} -> el`	Returns the characters located at the specified positions.
`substringAfter(String separator)`	`{{issue.summary.substringAfter("W")}} -> orld!`	Returns the text following the initial occurrence of the provided separator.
`substringAfterLast(String separator)`	`{{issue.summary.substringAfterLast("o")}} -> rld!`	Returns the text following the final occurrence of the provided separator.
`substringBefore(String separator)`	`{{issue.summary.substringBefore("W")}} -> Hello`	Returns the text preceding the initial occurrence of the provided separator.

`substringBefore Last(String separator)`	`{{issue.summary. substringBeforeLast("o")}} -> Hello W`	Returns the text preceding the final occurrence of the provided separator.
`substringBetween (String open, String close)`	`{{issue.summary. substringBetween("e","d")}} -> llo Worl`	Returns the text located between the specified parameters.
`toLowerCase()`	`{{issue.summary.toLowerCase ()}} -> hello world!`	Changes the text string to lowercase.
`toUpperCase()`	`{{issue.summary.toUpperCase ()}}} -> HELLO WORLD!`	Changes the text string to uppercase.
`trim()`	`{{issue.summary.trim()}} -> Hello World!`	Eliminates any leading or trailing whitespace from the value.
`urlEncode()`	`{{issue.summary.urlEncode}} -> See Encoding below.`	Encodes text to allow them to be included as a URL param, for example, a link in an email.
`xmlEncode()`	`{{issue.summary.xmlEncode}} -> See Encoding below.`	Encodes text to allow them to be included in XML data, for example, an outgoing webhook.

Table 9.4: *Jira Smart Values – Text Fields*

Jira Smart Values: Users

The following list of smart values can be used to access user data, and format it when creating new rules:

Smart Value and Properties	Example	What It Returns
`{{assignee}}`	`{{assignee. displayName}}`	Returns the assignee of the work item.
`{{comment.author}}`	`{{comment.author. displayName}}`	It returns the name of the user who adds a comment on the work item.
`{{creator}}`	`{{creator. displayName}}`	The person who created the work item, and the creator cannot be changed.
`{{initiator}}`	`{{initiator. displayName}}`	This returns the name of the user who prompted the rule.
`{{reporter}}`	`{{reporter. displayName}}`	It returns the name of the reporter of an active work item.

{{Custom field}}	{{Scrum master.displayName}}	If you have a custom field named scrum master, you can access the display name for the user.

***Table 9.5**: Jira Smart Values – Users*

Jira Smart Values - Conditional Logic

The following list of smart values can be used when text fields are used, and can provide output based on conditional logic:

Conditional Logic	Smart Value and Properties	What It Returns
If	`{{if(smartValue)}}`	It can be used with lookup work items actions and then add further action based on true or false results.
equals	`{{equals(smartValue1, smartValue2)}}`	It returns TRUE, if the two inputs are equal, and FALSE, if the two inputs are not equal.
exists	`{{exists(smartValue)}}`	This returns either TRUE or null.
not	`{{not(smartValue)}}`	It returns either TRUE or FALSE. This can be used with Lookup issue action.
and	`{{and(smartValue1, smartvalue2)}}`	This returns either TRUE or FALSE.
or	`{{or(smartValue1, smartvalue2)}}`	It returns either TRUE or FALSE.

***Table 9.6**: Jira Smart Values – Conditional Logic*

Jira Smart Values: Date and Time

The following list of smart values can be utilized to access and format date and time fields:

Smart Value and Properties	Example	What It Returns
`{{now}}`		It returns the current date and time
`{{[date].[dateformat]}}`	`{{now.shortDate}}` returns 11/10/23	You can provide data and time, and it returns in a format specified by you.
`{{[date1].diff([date2]).[unit]}}`		It returns the difference between date1 and date2.
`{{[date1].isAfter([date2])}}`		This gives a true result when date1 comes after date2, and false otherwise.

`{{[date1].isBefore([date2])}}`		It provides a true outcome if date1 precedes date2, and false otherwise.
`{{[date1].isEquals[(date2)]}}`		This gives a true result if date1 and date2 are identical, and false otherwise.
`{{[date1].compareTo([date2])}}`		It compares date1 and date2. Gives -1, if date1 is earlier than date2. Gives 1, if date 2 is earlier than date1. Gives 0, if the two dates are the same.
`{{[date].plus[Unit]([number])}}`	`{{sprint.startDate.plusDays(14)}}`	Accepts the provided date and time, adds the specified unit number, and provides the resulting date and time.
`{{[date].minus[Unit]([number])}}`	`{{now.minusDays(5)}}`	Accepts the provided date and time, subtracts the specified unit number, and provides the resulting date and time.
`{{[date].toBusinessDay}}`	`{{now.toBusinessDay}}`	Given a specific date, the function returns the following business day. If the input date falls on a business day, it will simply return that date.
`{{ [date].toBusinessDayBackwards}}`	`{{now.toBusinessDayBackwards}}`	Accepts a provided date and outputs the business day immediately preceding it.
`{{[date].setTimeZone([timezone])}}`	`{{now.setTimeZone("Australia/Sydney")}}`	Takes a specified time and adjusts it to the given time zone without altering the actual time value. In other words, it displays the same time but in the specified time zone.
`{{[date].convertToTimeZone([timezone])}}`	`{{now.convertToTimeZone("Australia/Sydney").shortTime}}`	Accepts a specified time, and converts it to the corresponding time in the given time zone.

{{[date].withDayOfMonth([date])}}	{{now.withDayOfMonth(15)}}	Accepts a provided date and time, and outputs the same date and time, but with the day of the month set to the input date.
{{[date].withNextDayOfWeek(["day"])}}		Adjusts the date to the upcoming occurrence of the specified day. If the current day is already the specified day, it will advance to the next occurrence in the following week.
{{[date].with[attribute](input)}}	{{now.withYear(2005)}}	Accepts a provided date and time, and adjusts either the date or time based on the description specified in the attribute.

Table 9.7: *Jira Smart Values – Date and Time*

Jira Smart Values: Development

You can utilize the following smart values to access and format development information retrieved from a connected source code management tool:

Smart Values	Properties	What It Returns
{{branch}}		It is a separate and independent line of development.
	{{branch.name}}	This provides the branch name.
	{{branch.url}}	It provides the URL of the branch.
	{{branch.repository}}	Provides information related to the repository to which the branch is associated.
{{createdBranch}}		Retrieve details about the latest branch that was created.
	{{createdBranch.name}}	Provides the name of the branch.
	{{createdBranch.url}}	Provides the URL of the recently created branch.
	{{createdBranch.product}]	Provides the name of the product in which the branch was created.
	{{createdBranch.repository.id}}	It provides the ID of the repository.

	{{createdBranch.repository.name}}	This provides the name of the repository.
	{{createdBranch.repository.url}}	It provides the URL of the repository.
{{created Branches}}		Retrieve information about all branches that were created in the rule, as a list.
	{{createdBranches.name}}	Provides the names of the branches.
	{{createdBranches.url}}	Provides the URL of the branches.
	{{createdBranches.product}}	Provides the names of the products in which the branch was created.
	{{createdBranches.repository.id}}	It provides the IDs of all the repositories.
	{{createdBranches.repository.name}}	This provides the names of all the repositories.
	{{createdBranches.repository.url}}	It provides the URLs of all the repositories.
{{commit}}		A commit signifies a specific change made to a file or a group of files.
	{{commit.hash}}	Provides the SHA1 hash of the commit.
	{{commit.shortHash}}	Provides the truncated SHA1 hash of the commit.
	{{commit.message}}	Provides the content of the commit message.
	{{commit.url}}	Provides the URL of the commit.
	{{commit.isMergeCommit}}	If a commit is a merge commit, the value returned is True.

	{{commit.timestamp}}	This provides the details of the date and time when the commit was done.
	{{commit.repository}}	It provides additional information related with the repository.
	{{commit.repository.name}}	This provides the name of the repository.
{{Pull request}}		A pull request represents suggested modifications prior to their incorporation into an official space.
	{{pullRequest.title}}	It provides the title of the **pullrequest**.
	{{pullRequest.url}}	This provides the URL of the **pullrequest**.
	{{pullRequest.state}}	It provides the name of the state of the **pullrequest**.
	{{pullRequest.createdDate}}	This provides the details about the date and time when the **pullrequest** was created.
	{{pullRequest.updatedDate}}	It provides the details about the date and time when the **pullrequest** was updated.
	{{pullRequest.sourceBranch}}	This provides information about the source branch for the **pullrequest**.
	{{pullRequest.sourceBranch}}	It provides the name of the source branch.
	{{pullRequest.sourceBranch.url}}	It provides the URL of the source branch.
	{{pullRequest.destinationBranch}}	This provides the name of the destination branch.
	{{pullRequest.destinationBranch.url}}	It provides the URL of the destination branch.
	{{pullRequest.destinationBranch.repository}}	This provides information about the destination branch repository.
{{build}}		A build signifies the transformation of files into their final usable form.
	{{build.name}}	It provides the name of the build.
	{{build.url}}	Provides absolute URL of the build.

	`{{build.state}}`	It provides the state of the build; for example, In progress, Cancelled, and so on.
	`{{build.refs}}`	Provides the references for the build. This compilation of metadata can be linked with a build, and might include branch and tag names, among other details.
`{{deployment}}`		A deployment denotes the procedure through which a product is released within a specific environment.
	`{{deployment.name}}`	Provides a user-friendly deployment name.
	`{{deployment.url}}`	Provides absolute URL of the deployment.
	`{{deployment.state}}`	Provides the state of the deployment.
	`{{deployment.environment}}`	Provides details associated with the deployment environment.
	`{{deployment.environment.type}}`	It returns production.
`{{repository}}`		This is a collection of source code and related metadata.
	`{{repository.name}}`	Provides the repository name.
	`{{repository.url}}`	Provides absolute URL of the repository.
`{{environment}}`		An environment signifies a unique ecosystem where products are deployed.
	`{{environment.name}}`	Returns the name for the environment provided by the user.
	`{{environment.type}}`	Provides the environment type.
`{{sprint}}`		Accesses details pertaining to the sprint that activated the rule.
	`{{sprint.id}}`	Provides **`sprintID`**.
	`{{sprint.name}}`	Provides the name of the sprint
	`{{sprint.isStarted}}`	Returns true if the sprint has begun, and false, if it has not started yet.

	`{{sprint.isClosed}}`	Returns true if the sprint has been closed, and false if it has not.
	`{{sprint.startDate}}`	Provides the sprint's start date.
	`{{sprint.endDate}}`	Provides the sprint's end date.
	`{{sprint.completeDate}}`	Provides the date when the sprint was marked as complete.
	`{{sprint.originBoardId}}`	Provides the ID of the board to which the sprint is associated.
	`{{sprint.goal}}`	Provides the goal of the sprint.
`{{version}}`		Accesses details related to the version that activated the rule.
	`{{version.name}}`	Provides the name of the version.
	`{{version.id}}`	Provides the ID of the version.
	`{{version.description}}`	Provides the description of the version.
	`{{version.archived}}`	Returns a true value if the version has been archived, and false, if it has not.
	`{{version.startDate}}`	Provides the start date of the version.
	`{{version.released}}`	Returns a true value if the version has been released, and false, if it has not.
	`{{version.releaseDate}}`	Provides the release date of the version.
	`{{version.project.key}}`	Provides the space key associated with the space to which the version belongs.

Table 9.8: *Jira Smart Values – Development*

Jira Smart Values: Math Expressions

The following smart values can be utilized to insert and format numerical values when configuring a rule:

Numerical Operations	Smart Values	What It Returns
Abs		It provides the absolute value of a number. Absolute value of -4 is 4.
Round		Provides a number rounded to the nearest integer. For example, 3.7 is rounded to 4.

Floor		Provides the lower value of a number. For example, 2.8 returns 2.
Ceil		Provides the upper value of a number. For example, 3.2 returns 4.
Plus/Minus		Addition or subtraction of one numerical smart value with another can be done.
Multiply		Multiplication of one numerical smart value with another can be done.
Divide		Division of one numerical smart value with another can be done.
Numerical comparisons		
Greater than	`gt(value)`	Accepts a numerical smart value, and checks whether it is greater than the specific value.
Greater than or equal to	`gte(value)`	Accepts a numerical smart value, and checks whether it is greater than or equal to the specific value.
Equal to	`eq(value)`	Accepts a numerical smart value, and checks whether it is equal to the specific value.
Less than	`lt(value)`	Accepts a numerical smart value, and checks whether it is less than the specific value.
Less than or equal to	`lte(value)`	Accepts a numerical smart value, and checks whether it is less than or equal to the specific value.
Format numerical values		
`format`		Converts a given number into a US locale. For example, 234523456 becomes 234,523,456.
`format(input)`		Converts a number into the given locale.
`formatWithLocale(input)`		Converts a number into the given locale. For example, "fr_FR", 234123456 becomes 234 523 456.
`asPercentage`		Converts a number into a percentage format according to the US locale.
`asPercentage(locale)`		Converts a number into a percentage format according to the given locale.
`asCurrency`		Converts a number into a currency format based on the US locale.

`asCurrency(locale)`		Converts a number into a currency format according to the given locale.

Table 9.9: *Jira Smart Values – Math Expressions*

To verify what a smart value returns:

1. Create a rule with a manual trigger and check the Log:
   i. Select the manual trigger.
   ii. And set the action as Log.
2. Navigate to the **`work item`** and select **`Rule executions`**.
3. The value will be displayed in the audit log.

Owner

An Owner is the person who creates the rule in Jira. This is the rule creator who will be notified in case of an error.

Rule Actor

When configuring a rule, space admins and site admins have the option to change the rule actor, allowing automation rules to be perceived as being executed by a real team member. For instance, if an automation rule adds a comment to all work items in a sprint, a team lead may want to configure it so that the comment is added by them, rather than by the Automation for Jira user.

You must be a space admin to configure space-based automation rules, and you must be a site admin to configure global automation rules. Both space admins and site admins can select the name of an actor, as shown in *Figure* 9.10

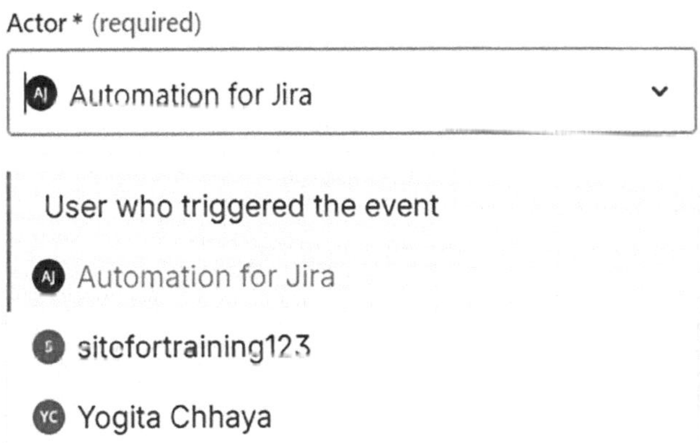

Figure 9.10: *Selecting Actor of an Automation Rule*

The person selected as the actor will receive notifications for a specific automation rule. In the `History` tab, Jira will indicate that work item changes/updates have been made by the actor defined during the configuration of the automation rule.

Global admins can select anyone as the actor for the automation rule, while space admins can choose either themselves or Automation for Jira as the actor. They (space admins) cannot designate others as actors.

Space admins are expected to act as the actor for automation rules to make any changes in the rule. This does not apply to global administrators.

Scope

Scope can only be edited or added globally in automation. It decides where the rule will apply, and includes the following options:

- **Single Space**: The rule applies to a specific space based on the selection.
- **Multi-Space**: The rule applies to multiple spaces based on the selection.
- **Space Type**: The rule applies only to specific space types (for example, Business spaces, Service Management spaces, and Software spaces).
- **Global**: The rule applies to all spaces in Jira.

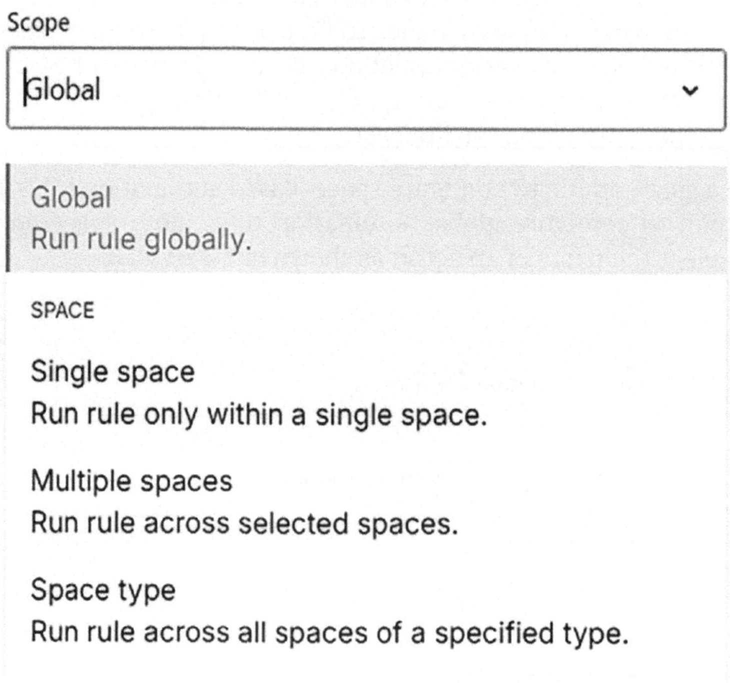

***Figure 9.11:** Defining Scope of an Automation Rule*

Allowing Rule Trigger

The rule can be triggered by other rules, if it is selected:

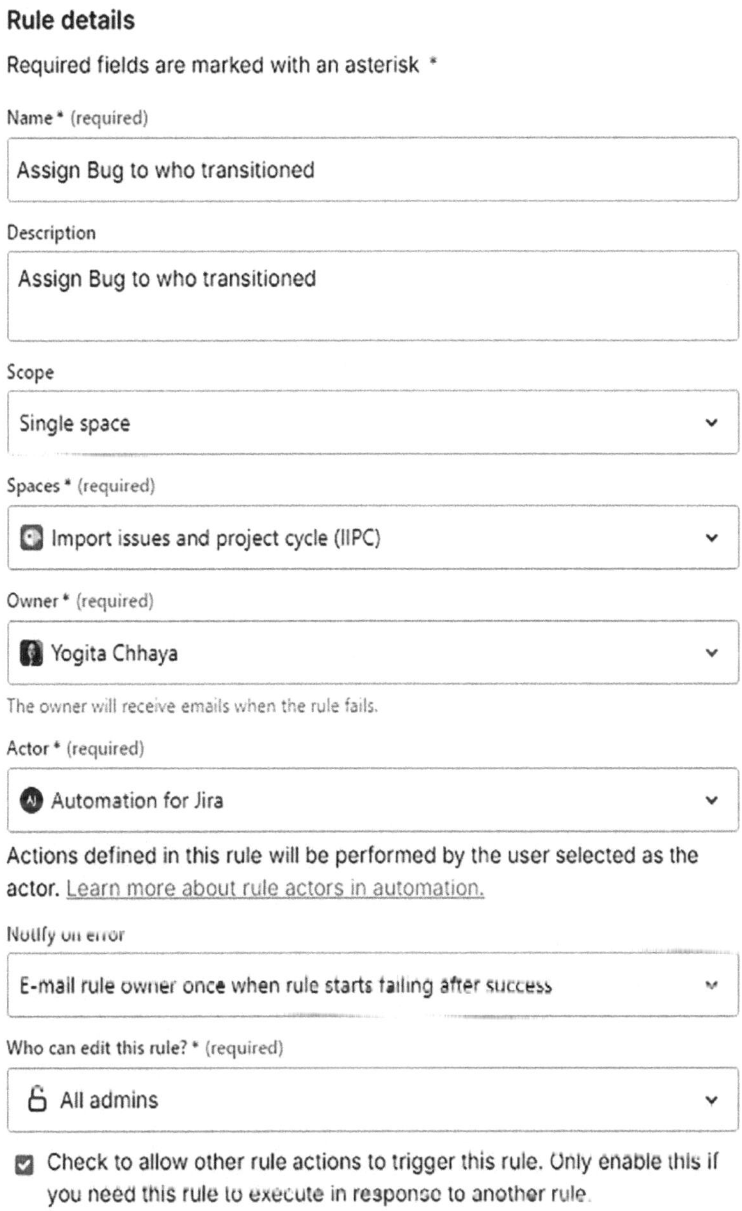

Figure 9.12: *Setting to Allow Chain of Rules*

Notify on Error

It defines how frequently the rule owner can be notified by email:

Figure 9.13: *Defining Frequency of the Notifications on Error*

Audit Log

After creating a rule, navigate to the **`Audit log`** to review its execution status. The log will indicate whether the rule ran successfully or generated errors. You can also check the log during the execution of any rule.

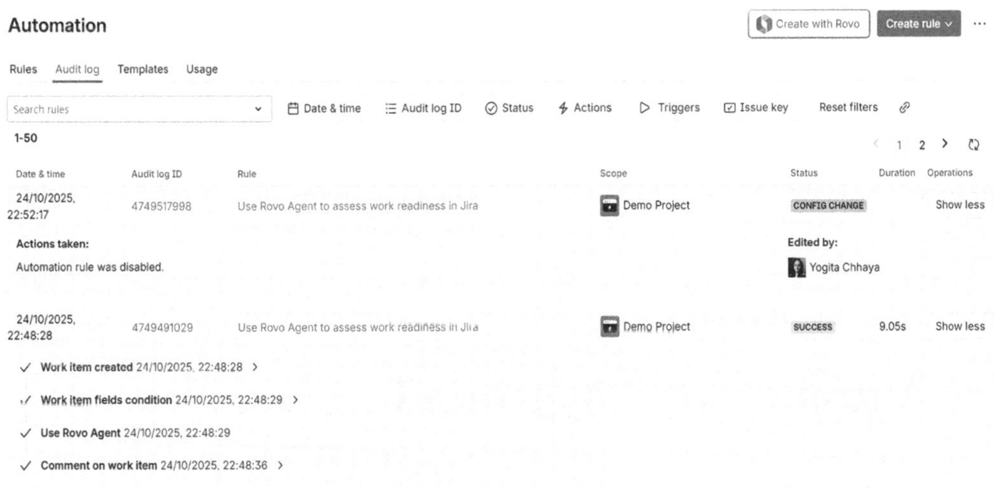

***Figure 9.14**: Understanding Audit Log*

Debugging Rules

If a rule is generating errors, and not behaving as expected, follow these steps to debug the rule:

1. **Check the Audit Log**:
   i. Review the displayed errors, and examine any provided suggestions and instructions on how to resolve them.
   ii. Compare the entries in the audit log with the comments on the work items.
   iii. Ensure that all fields are correctly associated with the screens; otherwise, the rule will not fulfill its intended purpose.
   iv. Before executing the rule, verify and update the data in Jira, and validate the filter query.
2. **Debugging Smart Values**:
   i. You can check the correctness of the smart values using a log.
   ii. Additionally, there is a function called **`Debug`** that can assist you in debugging.

iii. Surround your smart value with **{{#debug}}**. Utilize it and verify it in the log.

3. **Test the Rule**:

   i. Disable the rule, make a copy of the rule, and then check it so that you have a copy of the original rule.

   ii. Test the rule using either a manual or scheduled trigger.

Templates and Jira Automation Library

Jira provides ready-to-use templates for Automation Rules. Select templates on the Global Automation Page to view all the templates available in Jira.

Scroll down on this page, and you will see the option to select the Automation Library. Within the library, you can explore example rules, and create your own rules.

Jira Automation Playground

Navigate to the site for the Jira Automation Playground. You can explore multiple automation rule templates, and create your own rules based on these rules.

Checking Usage

Users can obtain information about how many automation rules have been executed compared to the actual limit. Each version has a defined limit for the number of automation rule executions. Rules can trigger until you have reached the limit.

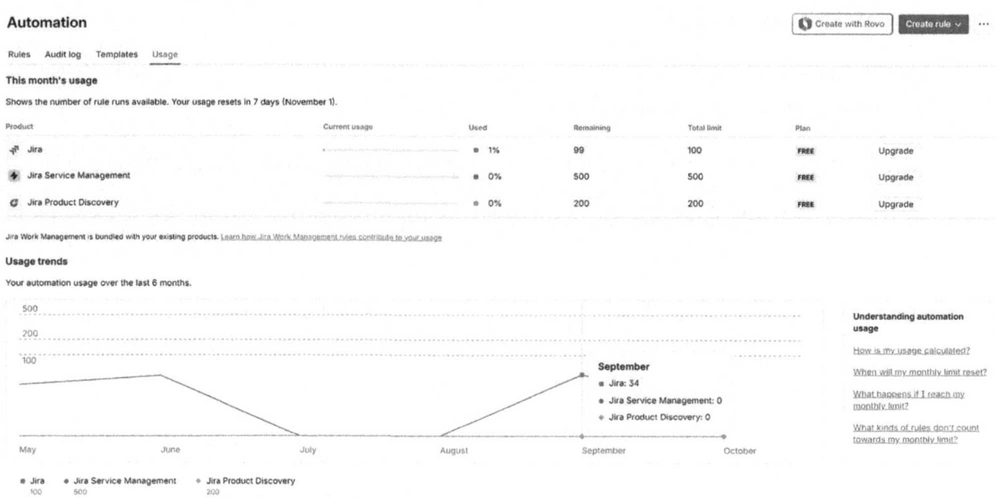

Figure 9.15: *Viewing Usage of Automation Rules in Jira*

Note: *There is a limit to creating a number of automation rules on your Jira Cloud site based on your subscription. Jira does not allow the execution of more rules than the allowed number. You can find out the details by checking usage.*

Performance Insights

To get the performance insights of the automation rules, select **`More`** on the right side, and select **`View performance insights`**.

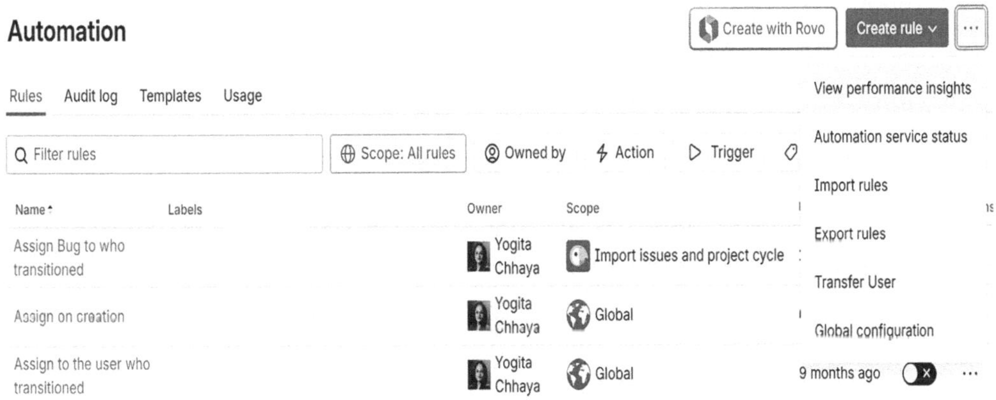

Figure 9.16: *Performance Insights*

Jira provides you with the date-wise total number of executions, number of errors, and number of successes in the form of a chart. In the following figure, there is a chart, which also provides detailed information in the form of a table.

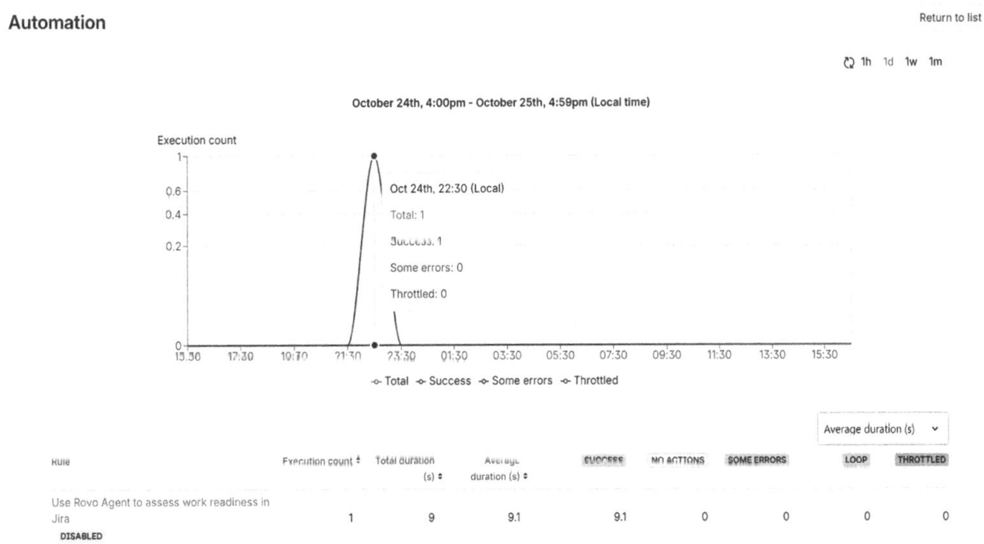

Figure 9.17: *Performance Insights Statistics*

Using these insights, you can also check the statistics about the performance of each and every automation rule.

Import and Export Jira Automation Rules

Permission required: Jira administrator with **`Administer Jira`** global permission.

Jira administrators can perform the following actions:

1. Import rules from one Jira cloud site to the other Jira cloud site.
2. Export rules while moving from server to Jira cloud.

Export Rules to a JSON File:

1. Navigate to **`System`** > **`Global Automation`**.
2. On the automation screen, navigate to top-right corner **`More`**> **`Export rules.`**
3. It will download a JSON file with all the automation rules.
4. Once the file is downloaded, you can import the data to any site.

Import Rules to a Jira Site:

1. Navigate to **`System`** > **`Global Automation`**.
2. On the screen, navigate to the top-right corner **`More`**> **`Import rules`**.
3. Select **`Upload JSON`** or drop file to import data.
4. Select the **automation rules** and select the spaces for the rules selected.
5. You can optionally select to import rule owners. If it is not selected, the person importing rules will be set as the rule owner:
    i. It is not required to make any changes to the JSON file if you are importing from a Jira cloud site. Ensure that the users are also there in your Jira site.
    ii. If you are importing the data from the server/data center, then you have to change the account IDs of the rule owners manually.
6. Select **`Let us do this`** to finish the process.

Steps to Create an Automation Rule with Example

Permissions Required:

1. A space admin can create automation rules in Jira that are specific to a space.

2. A site admin with **`Administer Jira`** global permission can create global automation rules that are applicable to all spaces in Jira.

Example: We will create an automation rule to auto-assign a work item to the user who created a work item.

Creating an automation rule in Jira involves several steps. Here is a step-by-step guide to help you create an automation rule:

1. **Log into Jira**: Access your Jira account and ensure you have the necessary permissions to create automation rules. You need administrative or space-level permissions.

2. **Navigate to `Space Settings`**: If you want to create a space-specific rule, go to the space where you want to set up the automation.

   If you want to create a global rule, go to the **`global Jira settings`**.

3. **Access `Automation Rules`**: In the space settings, select an **`Automation`** option, and click it. In the **`global settings`**, you can find automation under **`System`** or a similar menu. Click **`Automation`**.

4. **Create a Rule**: Click on the **`Create Rule`** to start the rule creation process.

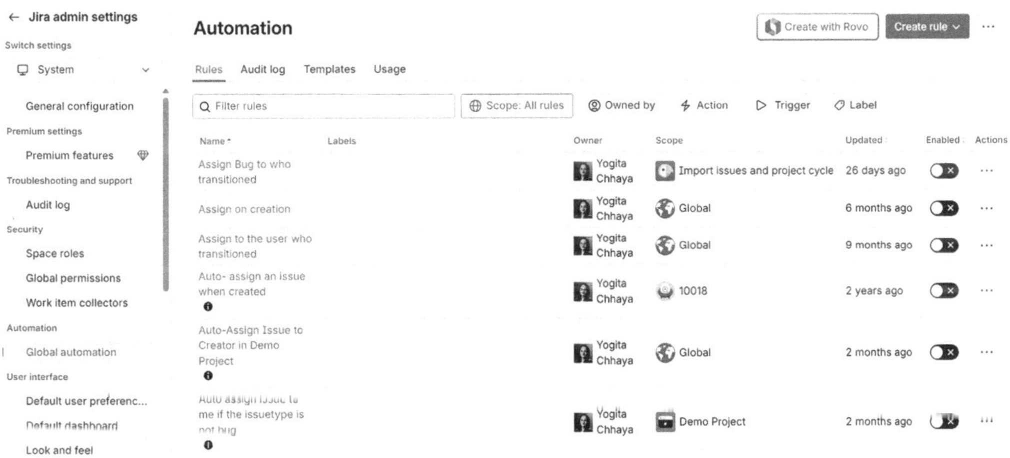

***Figure 9.18:** Creating Automation Rule in Jira*

5. **Select a Trigger**: Choose a trigger that initiates the automation. Triggers can include events such as work item creation, work item transition, or custom events. Configure the trigger settings, which may include specifying conditions for when the trigger should activate. In this example, we have selected the **`work item created`** trigger.

Figure 9.19: *Selecting Trigger to Create a New Rule*

6. **Define the Conditions**: If needed, set conditions that determine whether the rule should be applied. Conditions are used to filter which work items the rule should affect. In this example, we have to add the condition to check whether the Assignee is empty.

   Select the **`Add a condition`** > **`issue fields condition`**> **`Assignee`**> **`is empty`**, as shown in *Figure* 9.20, and **`Save`**.

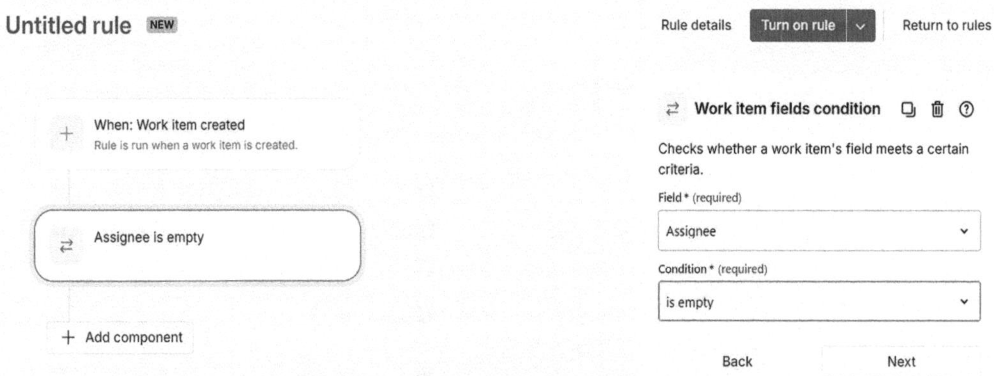

Figure 9.20: *Adding Work Item Condition to Create a New Rule*

7. **Add Actions:** Specify the actions that should be performed when the trigger and conditions (if any) are met. Actions can include: Commenting on work items, assigning work items to users, changing work item fields, sending notifications, linking work items, transitioning work items, and much more.

   Configure the action settings according to your requirements.

   Here, we have selected the Action to assign the work items to the user who triggered the event.

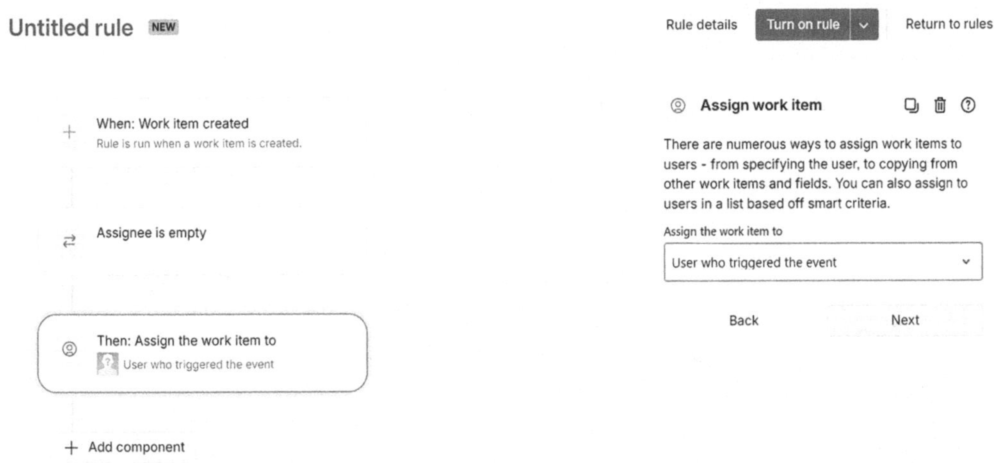

Figure 9.21: *Adding Action to Create a New Rule*

8. **Name Your Rule:** Give your rule a name that describes its purpose or functionality. This makes it easier to identify and manage multiple rules.

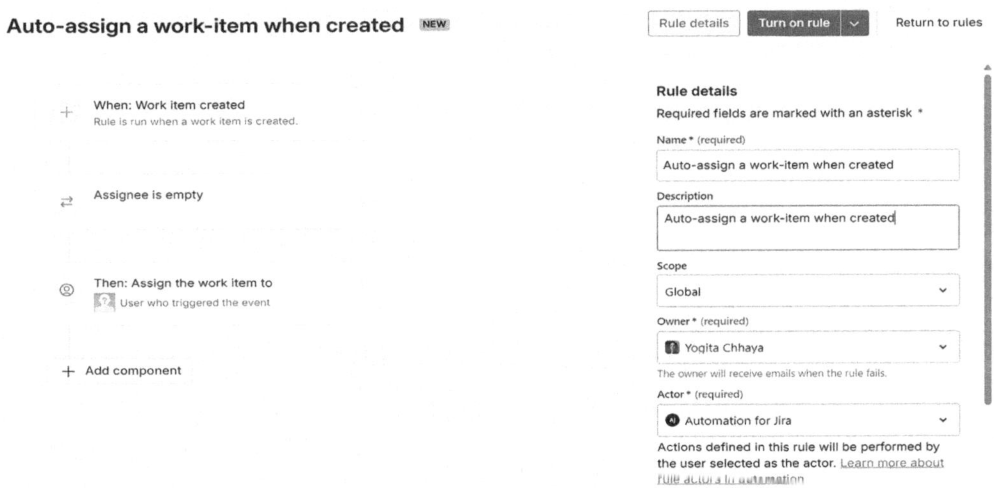

Figure 9.22: *Naming a Rule*

9. **Select Who Can Edit This Rule:** Determine who can edit this rule, and select the right option.

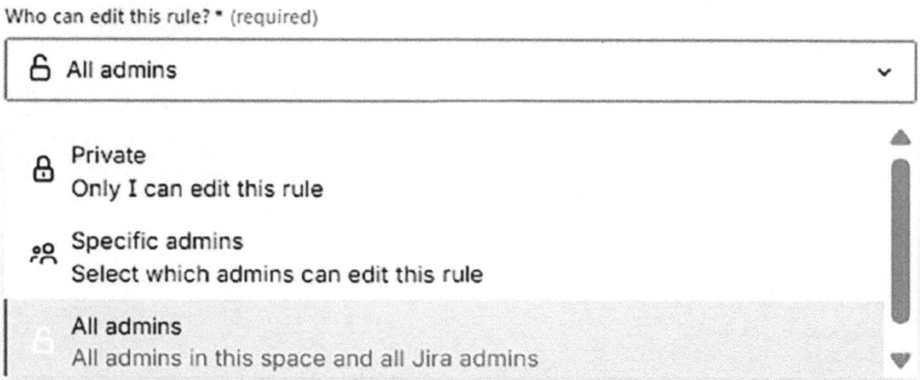

Figure 9.23: *Selecting Editors of the Rule*

10. **Save and Activate**: Once you have configured all the rule components, turn on the rule. Depending on your Jira configuration, you may need to activate the rule explicitly.

11. **Test the Rule**: It is a good practice to test the rule with sample work items to ensure that it behaves as expected.

12. **Maintain and Update**: As your space evolves, review and update automation rules to reflect changes in your workflow or requirements.

That is the general step-by-step process for creating an automation rule in Jira. The specific options and features available may vary depending on your Jira version and configuration.

Essential Learning Examples

1. **Auto-create sub-tasks and update fields:**

    i. **Trigger**: Work item created

    ii. **Condition**: Work type is task

    iii. **Action**: Create sub-tasks

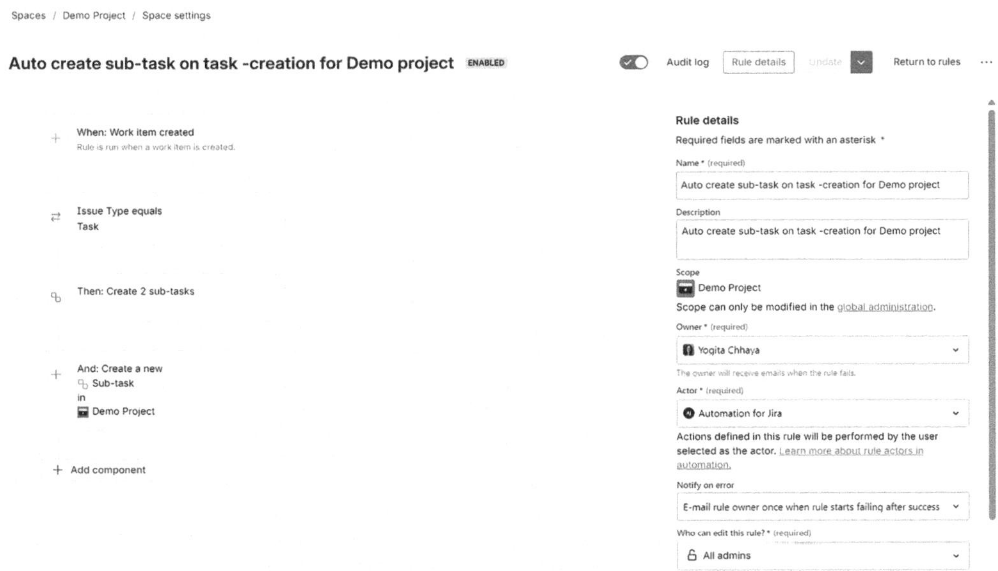

Figure 9.24: *Auto-create Sub-tasks and Update Fields*

In the preceding example, we can check the automation rule by creating a task, and confirming whether the sub-tasks are created and a summary field is updated. We can check the same by selecting the audit log of a rule.

Log Detail:

Figure 9.25: *Audit Log Auto-create Sub-tasks and Update Fields*

2. **If/else rule to auto-assign work items:**

   i. **Trigger**: Work item created

ii. **Condition**: If the work type is not a bug, assign it to me. Otherwise, if the work type is Bug, then assign the work item to a member of the software developers space role.

iii. **Action**: Assign to the person as mentioned in the condition

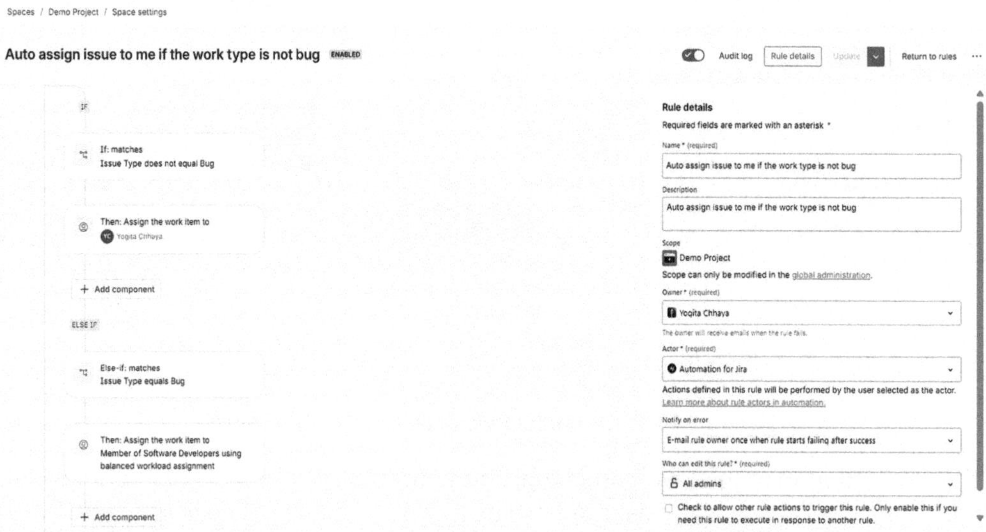

Figure 9.26: *If/else Rule to Auto-assign Work Items*

This rule is designed to automatically assign all work items, except for bugs, to the specified name. If the work type is a bug, it will be assigned to a person from the developers' group based on a balanced workload.

Log Detail:

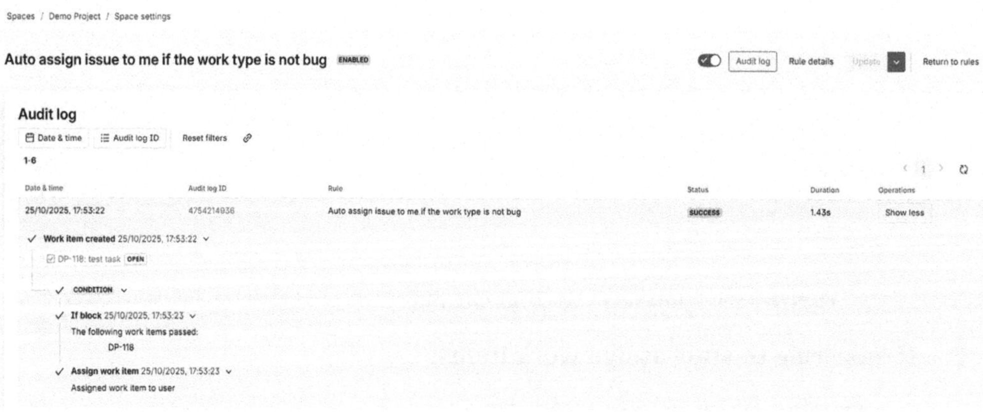

Figure 9.27: *Audit Log - If/else Rule to Auto-assign Work Items*

3. **When a bug is created, add someone as a watcher:**
    i. **Trigger**: Work item created.
    ii. **Condition**: Work type is Bug.
    iii. **Action**: Add watchers

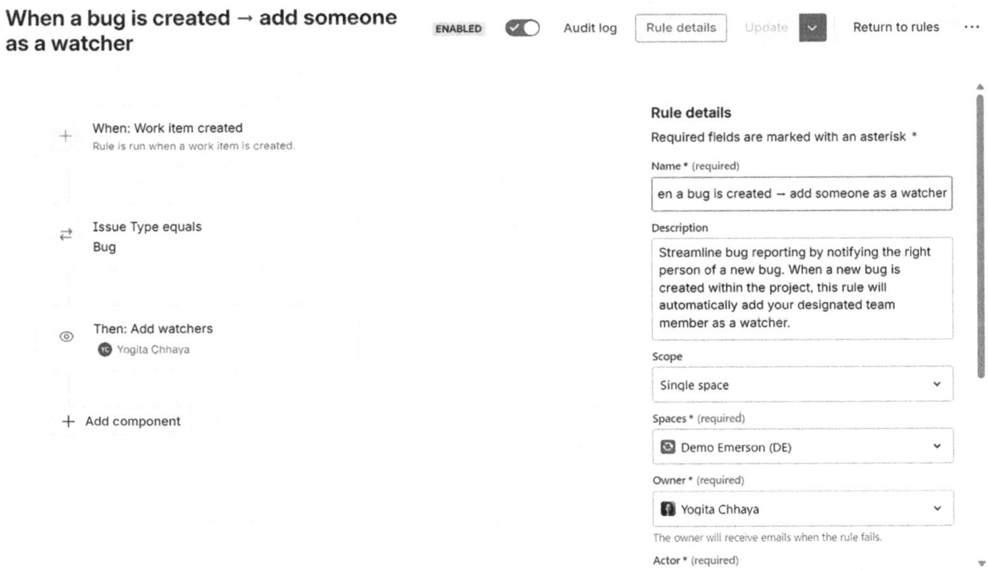

Figure 9.28: *When a Bug is Created - Add Someone as a Watcher*

This rule will add someone from the team as a watcher when a bug is created.

Log Detail:

Figure 9.29: *Audit Log -When a Bug is Created - Add Someone as a Watcher*

4. **Add comment using smart values when a work item transitions from Todo to InProgress (Helpful to understand various smart values):**
    i. **Trigger**: Work item Transition to In Progress
    ii. **Action**: Add a comment using various smart values

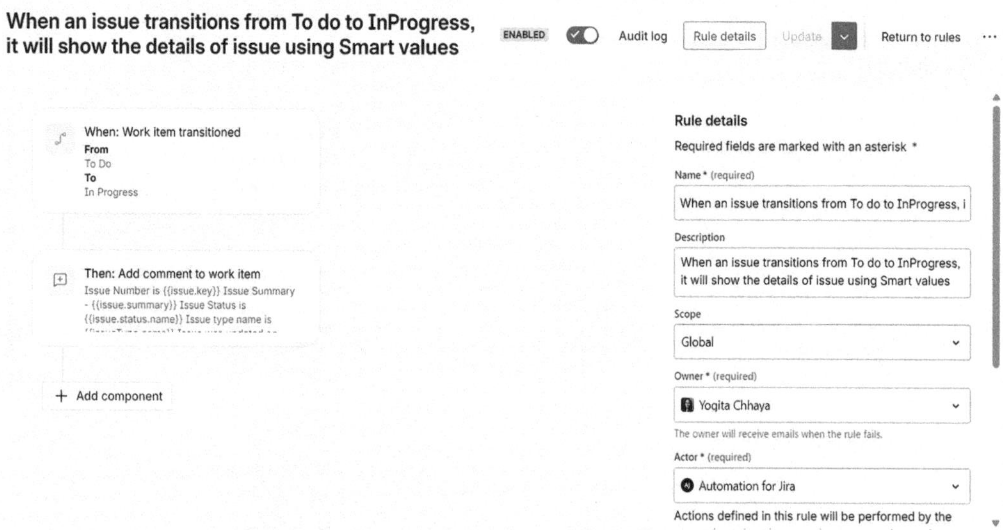

Figure 9.30: *A Rule to Understand Smart Values*

This rule, on execution, adds comment using smart values when a work item transitions from Todo to InProgress.

Log Detail:

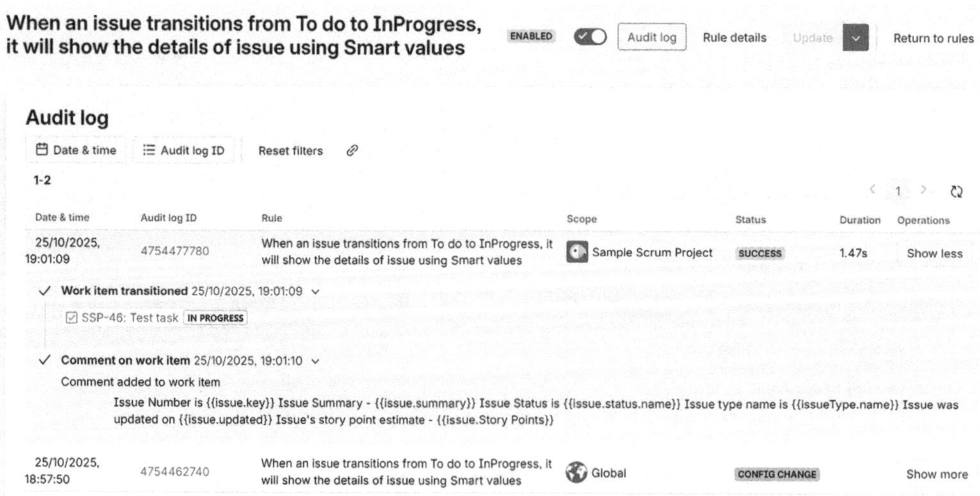

Figure 9.31: *Audit Log - A Rule to Understand Smart Values*

Comment Using Smart Values on the Jira Work Item:

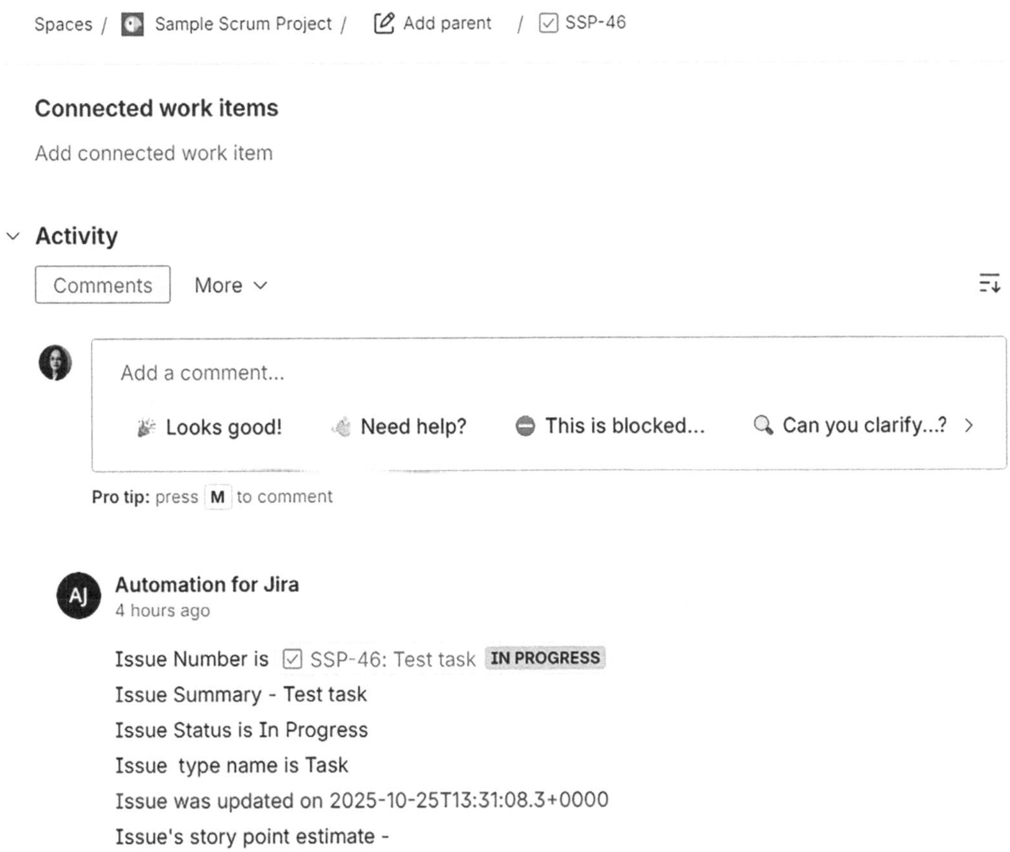

Figure 9.32: *Comment - A Rule to Understand Smart Values*

5. **Create 4 Sub-tasks (Design, Coding, Testing, Release) When a Story is Created:**
   i. **Trigger:** Work item is created
   ii. **Condition:** Work type is Story
   iii. **Action:** Create 4 sub-tasks

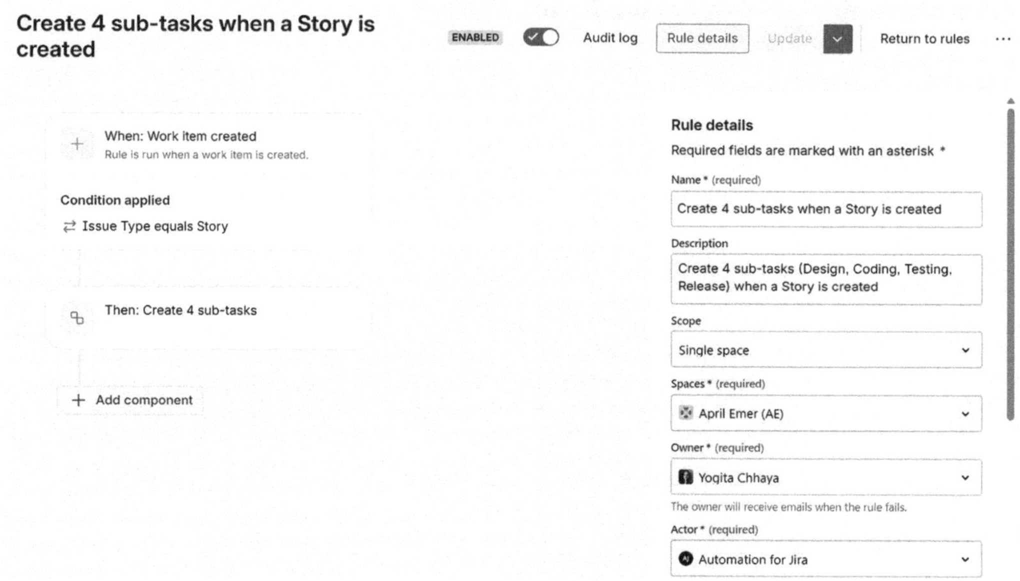

Figure 9.33: *Create 4 Sub-tasks When a Story is Created*

When this rule is triggered, it will create four different sub-tasks: Design, Coding, Testing, and Release. These sub-task work types are created by the Jira Administrator, and should be a part of the issue type scheme for that particular space.

Log Detail:

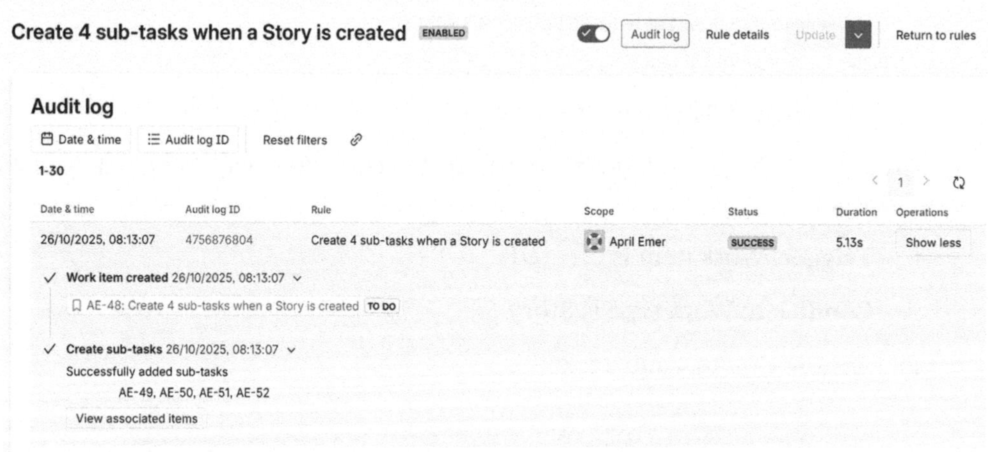

Figure 9.34: Audit Log - *Create 4 Sub-tasks When a Story is Created*

6. **When a work item is transitioned to InProgress, set the start date value to the current date:**

   i. **Trigger**: Work item Transitioned to InProgress

ii. **Action**: Then Edit work item field Start date

We have selected the Start date as: **`{{now.convertToTimeZone(issue.reporter.timeZone)}}`**, which will set the start date for any time zone as set by the reporter.

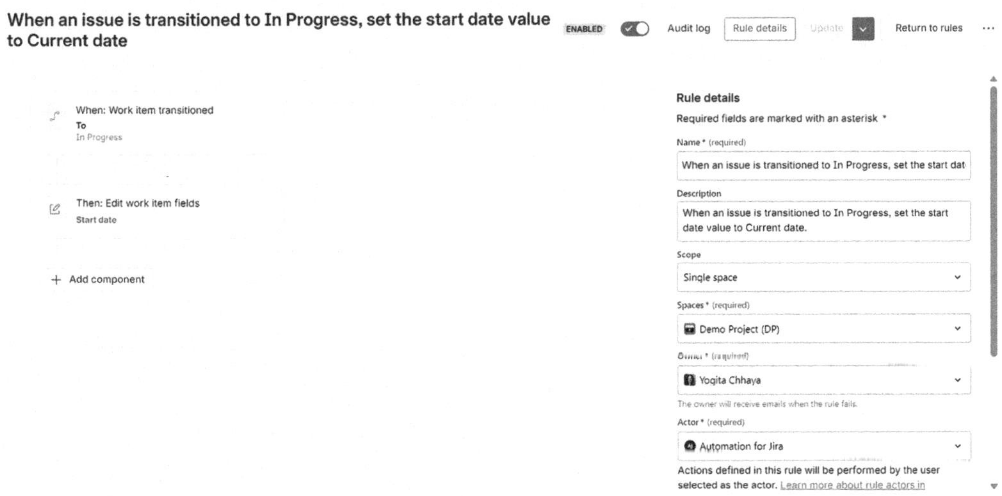

Figure 9.35: *Set the Start Date as the Current Date on Transition to InProgress*

This rule will set the start date for any time zone as set by the reporter, for any task that transitions from **`To Do`** to **`InProgress`**.

Log Detail:

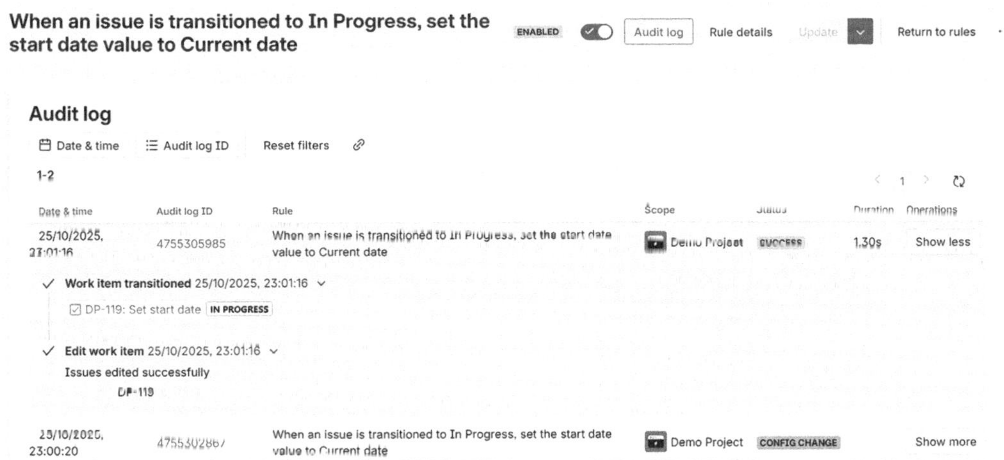

Figure 9.36: *Audit Log - Set the Start Date as the Current Date on Transition to InProgress*

7. **Sum up Story Points when Field Value Changes:**
   i. **Trigger**: When value changes for Story points
   ii. **Condition**: Work type equals Sub-task
   iii. **Branch Rule**: Related work items - For parents
   iv. **Action**: Edit work item field with a story point

   Smart value for story point to add: **`{{issue.subtasks.Story Points.sum}}`**

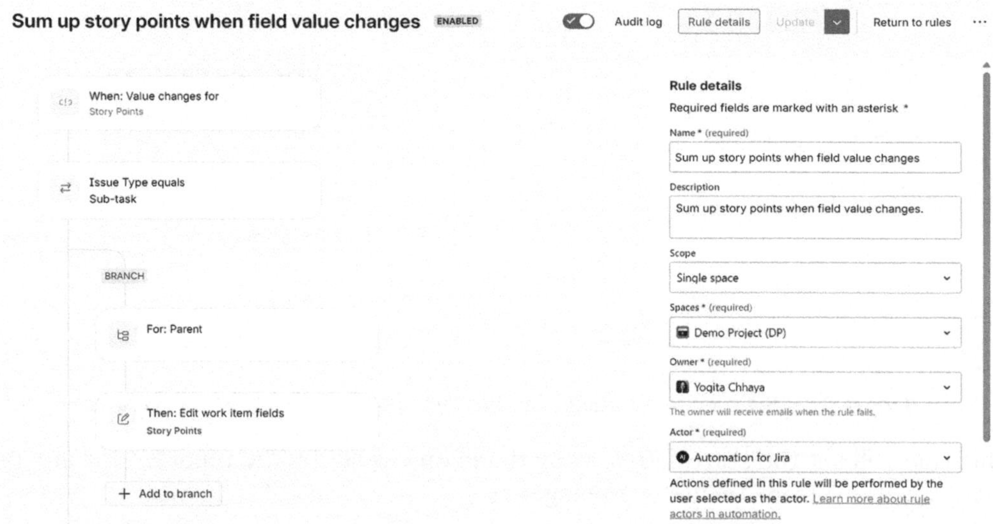

Figure 9.37: *Sum up Story Points When Field Value Changes*

Whenever story points are added to a sub-task, they are automatically added to the parent task, ensuring that it remains in sync without any manual work.

Log Detail:

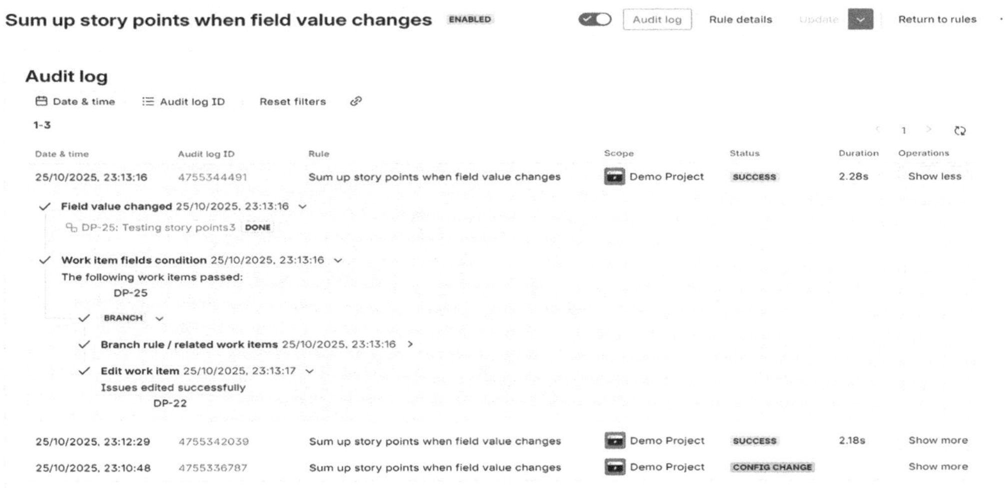

Figure 9.38: *Audit Log - Sum up Story Points When Field Value Changes*

8. **When assignee updated, transition to `InProgress`**
   i. **Trigger**: Assignee Updated
   ii. **Condition**: Assignee is empty
   iii. **Action**: Transition to InProgress

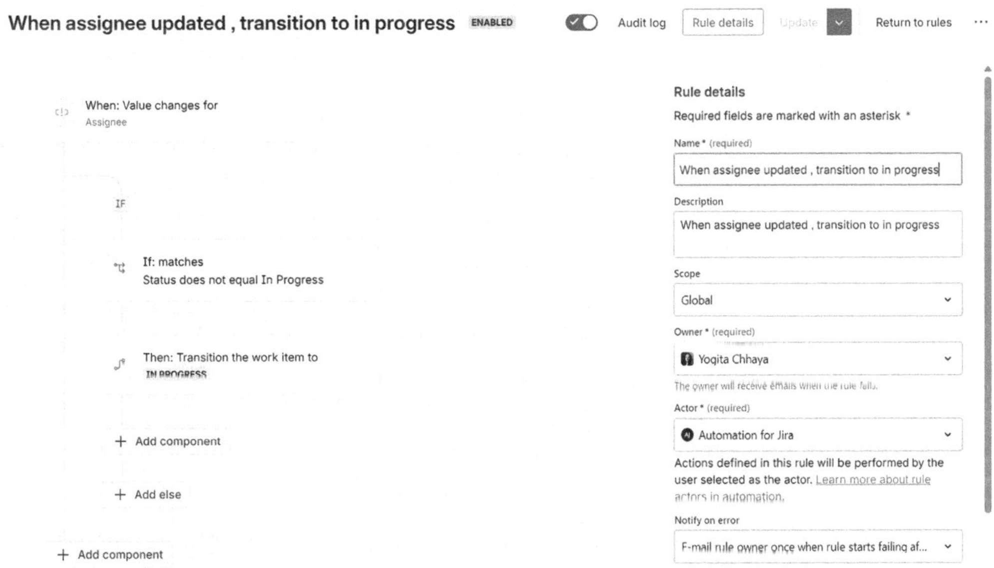

Figure 9.39: *When Assignee Updated, Transition to InProgress*

This rule automatically transitions any work item to InProgress when the assignee is updated.

Log Detail:

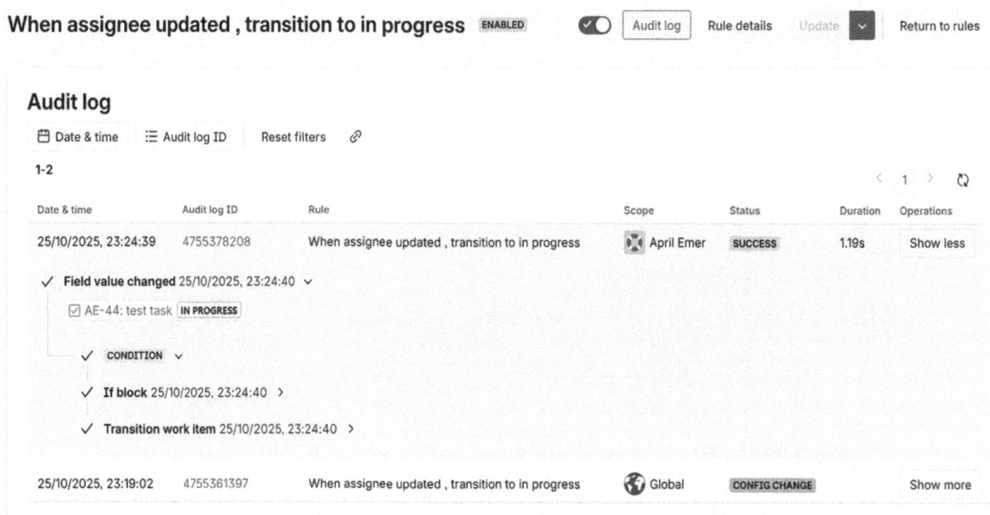

***Figure 9.40:** Audit Log - When Assignee Updated, Transition to InProgress*

Jira provides other automation templates using Rovo that can be helpful to assess work readiness, create a Jira space summary page in Confluence, triage bugs, and send Jira space summary to Slack. We will learn more about this in Chapter 13: *Atlassian Intelligence, Getting Started with Rovo and Creating Agents.*

Conclusion

We are now familiar with the elements of automation rules in Jira Agile spaces, creating various automation rules, testing them before implementation, checking the log details, and debugging a rule. Additionally, we have learned about smart values, how to find them, and how to utilize them in the automation rules.

In the next chapter, we will learn about how to manage Team-managed Spaces.

Points to Remember

- Start by identifying the specific tasks or processes you want to automate.
- Think about the rules you need and how they can work together.
- Align your automation strategy with your business and operational processes.
- Choose an appropriate trigger that defines when the rule should run (for example, work item created, work item transitioned, field updated).
- Set conditions to specify under what circumstances the rule should be executed.

- Conditions help filter the work items to which the rule applies (for example, space, work type, custom fields).
- Use compare conditions early in the rule chain to filter out unnecessary actions.
- Place conditions requiring more processing towards the end of the rule chain.
- Decide the action the rule should do, such as sending an email or updating data.
- Utilize available built-in actions and consider custom scripts for advanced actions.
- Configure any additional parameters or settings specific to the chosen trigger and actions.
- Decide whether the rule should apply globally or to specific spaces or work items.
- Restrict the scope of your rules and avoid global rules whenever possible.
- Consider the order of your automation rules, as they are executed in sequence from top to bottom.
- Always test new rules in a test environment before implementing them in production.
- Monitor rule execution to verify that they perform as expected.
- Regularly review and refine your automation rules as your processes and requirements change.
- Ensure that users who can create automation rules have appropriate permissions.
- Maintain backups of your Jira configuration, including automation rules, to prevent data loss.
- Consider the scalability of your automation rules to ensure they can handle increased workloads.
- Document your automation rules, including their purpose and conditions, for future reference.

Use Cases with Reference Links

1. Is it possible to use the "work item created" trigger to move to another status?

   https://community.atlassian.com/t5/Jira-Software-questions/jira-automation-rules/qaq-p/2395457

2. How do I manually trigger an automation?

   https://community.atlassian.com/t5/Jira-Software-questions/How-do-I-manually-trigger-an-automation/qaq-p/1575271

3. Manually Triggered Automation Rule - User who triggered the event:

   https://community.atlassian.com/t5/Jira-Software-questions/Manually-Triggered-Automation-Rule-User-who-triggered-the-event/qaq-p/2428674

4. Automation Rule for Reminder Mail:

   https://community.atlassian.com/t5/Automation-questions/Automation-rules/qaq-p/2368644

5. Setting up Automation Rules:

   https://community.atlassian.com/t5/Jira-Software-questions/Setting-up-automation-rules/qaq-p/2400624

6. Jira Automation - Edit work item fields / User who triggered the event:

   https://community.atlassian.com/t5/Jira-Software-questions/Jira-Automation-Edit-issue-fields-User-who-triggered-the-event/qaq-p/2276774

7. Automation vs Global Automation vs Multi-Space Automation:

   https://community.atlassian.com/t5/Jira-Service-Management/Automation-vs-Global-Automation-vs-Multi-Project-Automation/qaq-p/2109238

8. Automation for Version Release Trigger:

   https://community.atlassian.com/t5/Jira-Software-questions/Automation-for-Version-Release-Trigger/qaq-p/2362507

9. How to recognize the proper Custom Field name to use it in Formula:

   https://community.atlassian.com/t5/Jira-Service-Management/how-to-recognize-the-proper-Custom-Field-name-to-use-it-in/qaq-p/2338611

10. Example of Automation Rules that use "Start of sprint" as a trigger?

    https://community.atlassian.com/t5/Jira-Software-questions/Please-share-example-of-automation-rules-that-use-quot-Start-of/qaq-p/2413147

11. Jira Automation: Complete Guides on how to Sum Up Story Points between Subtasks/Stories/Epics:

    https://community.atlassian.com/t5/Automation-discussions/Jira-Automation-Complete-Video-Guides-on-how-to-Sum-Up-Story/td-p/1741948

12. Document for Smart Values:

    https://support.atlassian.com/cloud-automation/docs/smart-values-in-jira-automation/

Resources

1. Jira Automation Library
2. Jira Automation Playground

   https://www.atlassian.com/software/jira/automation-template-library/rules#/rule-list?systemLabelId=all&page=1&pageSize=20&sortKey=name&sortOrder=ASC

3. Smart Values in Jira Automation

   https://support.atlassian.com/cloud-automation/docs/smart-values-in-jira-automation/

CHAPTER 10
Managing Team-Managed Space

Introduction

Jira offers mainly two types of spaces: **Team-managed spaces** and **Company-managed spaces**. Team-managed spaces provide a higher degree of autonomy, allowing users to configure space settings, without affecting other teams or spaces. Typically, this space type is helpful for small teams where customization is not the only important thing. Another important aspect is granting permissions to everyone equally, that is, fewer restrictions. These types of spaces are helpful for beginners who are in their learning phase of space management tools. However, selecting the right template is of utmost importance in Jira. In this chapter, we will learn how to create team-managed spaces tailored to your team's requirements. This includes creating sprints, boards, defining statuses, configuring workflows, establishing automation rules, and accessing as well as understanding reports.

Structure

In this chapter, we will discuss the following topics:

- Understanding Team-Managed Spaces
  - Features
- Setting up Team-Managed Spaces
- Adding People, Roles, and Access levels
- Enabling Agile Features
- Work Types in Team-Managed Space
- Creating Custom Work Types
- Configuring a Work Types' Workflow
- Defining Status

- Creating Transitions
- Transition Properties
- Adding or Removing Workflow Rules
- Managing Backlog
- Sprint Operations
- Agile Board Features
- Understanding Insights for Backlog
- Understanding Insights for Boards
- Timeline View
- Reports
- Migrating from Team to Company-Managed Spaces
  - Things to Keep in Mind if You Migrate from Company-Managed to Team-Managed
  - Things to Keep in Mind if You Migrate from Team-Managed to Company-Managed

Understanding Team-Managed Spaces

Team-managed spaces are easy to create and manage by anyone in the team. They are designed for smaller teams and spaces that do not require extensive customization.

Features:

Here are a few important features of Team-managed spaces:

- There is no need to involve a Jira administrator to create and modify the space configuration.
- Teams and members can decide and control their own spaces and processes.
- Space administrators can have total control over space configuration and modification.
- It provides a separate space for space teams, without affecting other teams and spaces, as the changes done in the team-managed space configuration do not impact other spaces.
- Team-managed spaces can be created quickly and easily.
- Create them when only access-level permissions are needed.
- Add work types, statuses, transitions, and boards.
- Customize the workflow for each work type.
- Set rules for workflows to control transitions and actions.

- Use the timeline feature for planning and generating reports.

Setting up Team-Managed Spaces

Permissions: Any logged-in user can create a team-managed space by default. Jira Administrators can restrict it by managing permissions for a group.

Here are the steps to create a Team-managed space in Jira:

1. Navigate to **`Spaces`** > **`Create space`**.
2. Select **`Software Development`** under **`Space Template`**.
3. Select one of the three options: **`Scrum`**, **`Kanban`**, and **`Bug tracking`** software.

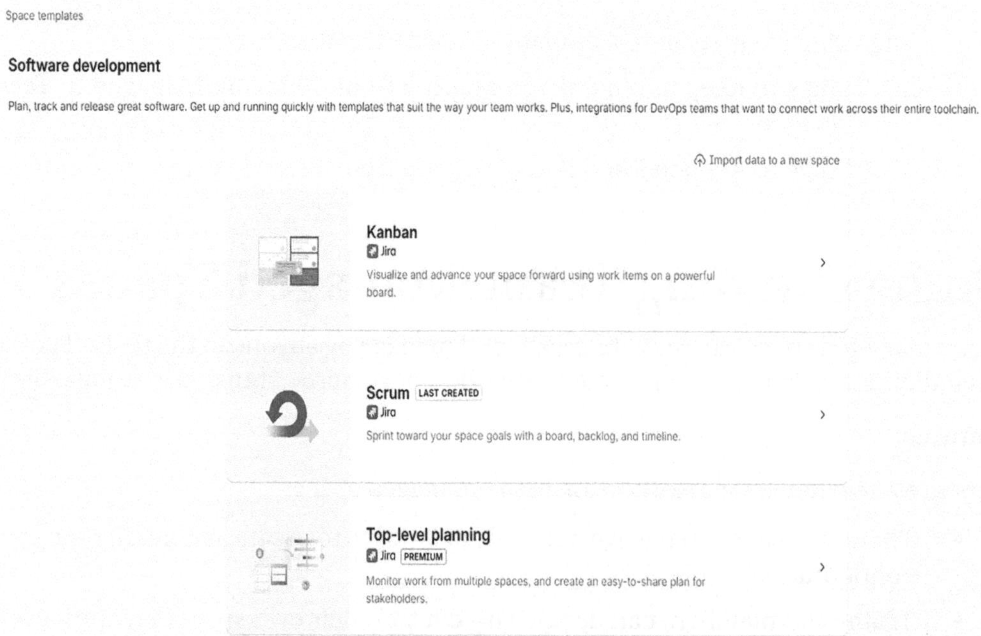

Figure 10.1: *Selecting an Agile Space Template*

4. Understand the information on the respective page, and then select **`Use template`**.

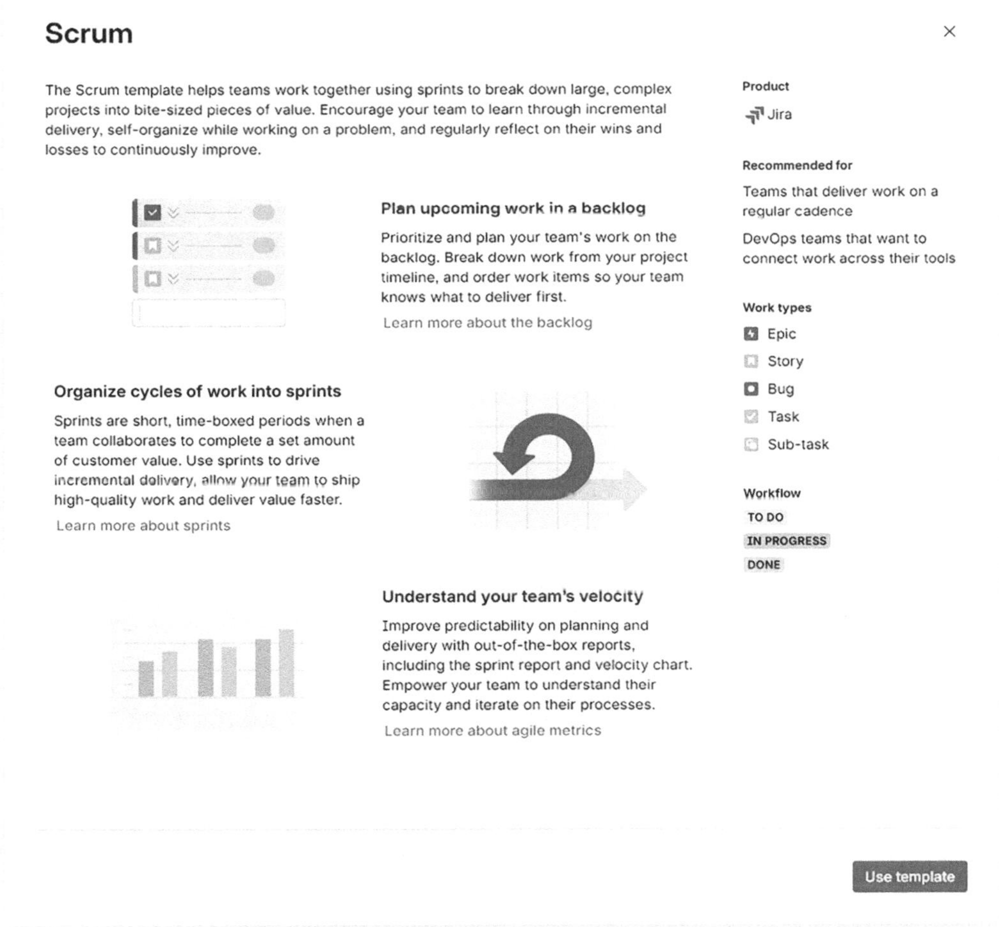

Figure 10.2: *Scrum Space Template*

5. Select the space type as **`Team-managed.`**

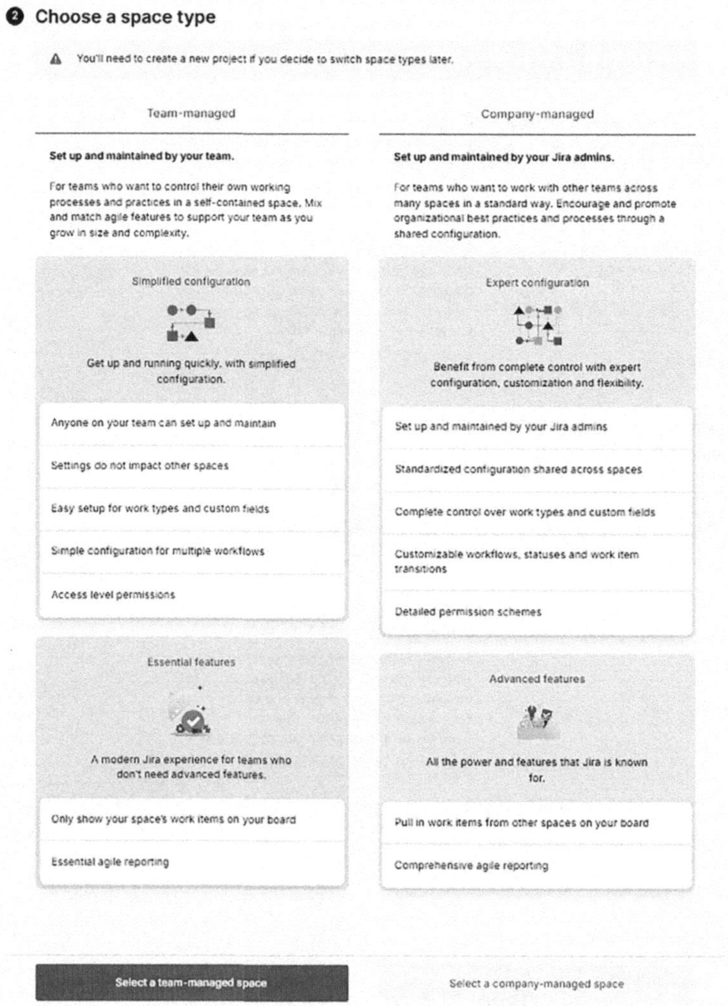

Figure 10.3: *Features of Team-Managed and Company-Managed Space*

6. Decide the name of the space and enter it.
7. Jira will generate a key for the space key. It can be changed, while creating a space. The space key is also used to identify all the work items.
8. Select `Create`.

Adding People, Roles, and Access Levels

In this section, we will understand how to add people, what are roles, and what are access levels in team-managed spaces.

Permissions required: A person with an Administrator role in a space can set access levels, and define roles in team-managed spaces.

Adding people: You can add people to your space only if they are added by the Jira administrator to your site. If you cannot find their names or e-mails, you need to tell your Jira administrator to enter their names.

Access levels: The access level of your space determines who has the ability to search, view, and modify the space and its associated work items in your Jira site.

Team-managed software spaces have three access levels as follows:

- **`Open`**: When a space is set to **`Open`**, anyone in your Jira site can view, create, and edit work items within the space. In this access level, Jira automatically assigns the member role to anyone who logs into your Jira site, and accesses the space.
- **`Limited`**: If a space is designated as **`Limited`**, anyone within your Jira site can view and provide comments on work items within the space, but they are unable to edit or create new ones. Jira assigns the **`Viewer`** role to individuals who log into your Jira site and access this space at this access level.
- **`Private`**: In cases where a space is marked as **`Private`**, it is exclusively visible to Jira administrators and people specifically added to the space. These users can see the space in their space directory and its associated work items in search results.

Here are the steps to change Space access:

1. Navigate to the **`Space`** > **`Space settings`** > **`Access.`**
2. Select **`Change Space Access.`**
3. Select the level of space access, and then select **`Change`**.

Roles: In team-managed spaces, roles define the people who work in your space. In real-world scenarios, people are assigned various roles in your space work, such as Scrum masters, members, or architects.

These roles help you to control people's access and actions within your space. Different roles may require specific access levels to your team's content, or you might want to restrict certain roles' capabilities. For instance, you may wish to grant exclusive sprint planning and management privileges to your team's Scrum masters.

Team-managed software spaces have three default roles as follows:

- **Administrator**: Admins have extensive capabilities, including adjusting settings, adding other admins, managing features, customizing work types, and creating rules on the board. Admins require Jira app access to fully utilize this role.
- **Member**: These are team members who can create, edit, comment, and manage work items, along with collaborating on space tasks. Members need Jira app access to work on a space.

- **Viewer**: Viewers have limited privileges, and can search for and view work items within your space but have restricted capabilities beyond that. You can assign this role to any registered user on your Jira site, without requiring additional app access.

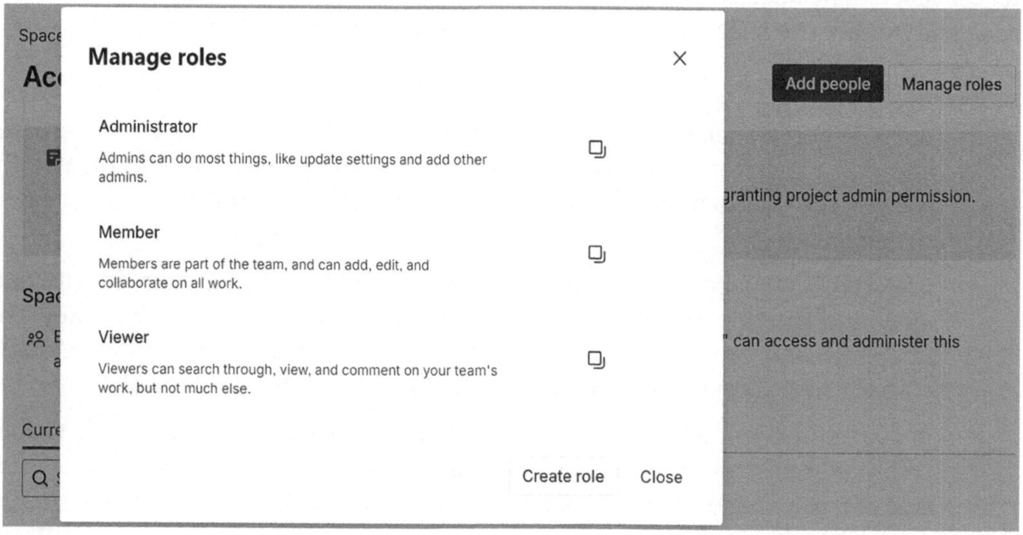

Figure 10.4: *Adding People and Managing Role*

You have the flexibility to create custom roles to further tailor individuals' access to your space, allowing for greater customization.

Here are the steps to change the space role:

1. Navigate to the **Space** > **Space settings** > **Access.**
2. In the table, choose the dropdown menu for **Role**.
3. Select the right role to be assigned to the person.

Enabling Agile Features

In team-managed spaces, all the features are not enabled by default. Follow these steps to enable the agile features.

1. Navigate to **Spaces** > **space settings**.
2. Select **Features**.
3. Enable the features by selecting them.

You can enable the following features:

1. **Timeline**: It is a place from which you can manage epic.
2. **Backlog**: Plan work items, sprints, and prioritize them.

3. **Board**: View, track, and manage all tasks in the sprint as it progresses.
4. **Reports**: Find agile metrics, and keep track of your spaces to plan accordingly.
5. **Issue-navigator**: Access work items, and create filters based on specific criteria.
6. **Sprints**: A predefined time frame that you can set when creating it.
7. **Estimation**: It can be in Story points, or in time affecting reports and insights.
8. **Releases**: Helps define a list of features to be released to the client.

   Additionally, you can enable requests, code, security, deployments, on-call settings, and space pages from the features page.

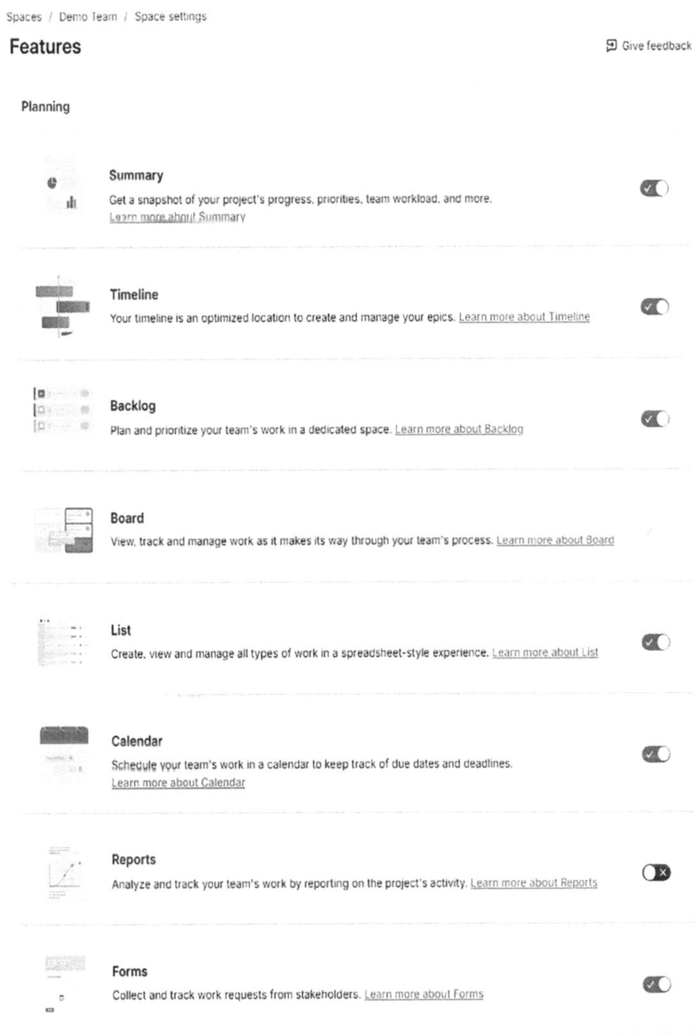

***Figure 10.5**: Enabling Agile Features*

Work Types in Team-Managed Space

In team-managed spaces, Jira provides the work types as listed here:

- **`Epic`**: Jira has the work type **`Epic`** to manage larger work items. It is a parent work type. You can create other child work types such as **`Story`**, **`Bug`**, and **`Task`** under **`Epic`**.

Figure 10.6: *Epic Work Type in Team-managed Space*

- **`Story`**: It is a work type used by agile teams to explain features required by the customer, and includes the final goal of that feature.

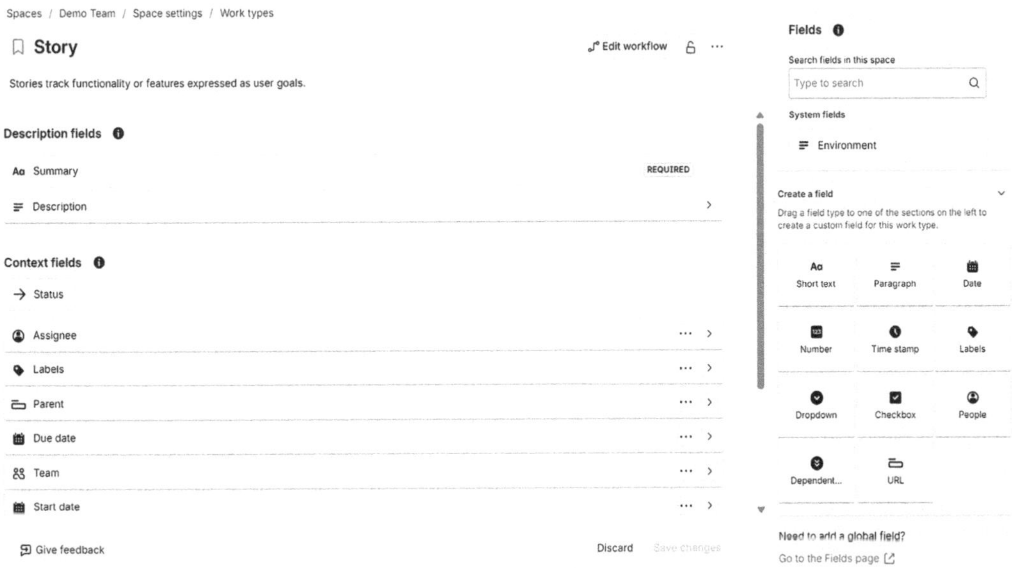

***Figure 10.7**: Story Work Type in Team-managed Space*

- **Bug**: It is a work type used by agile teams to track the problems faced related to software functionality, user interface problems, or total failure of the software application.

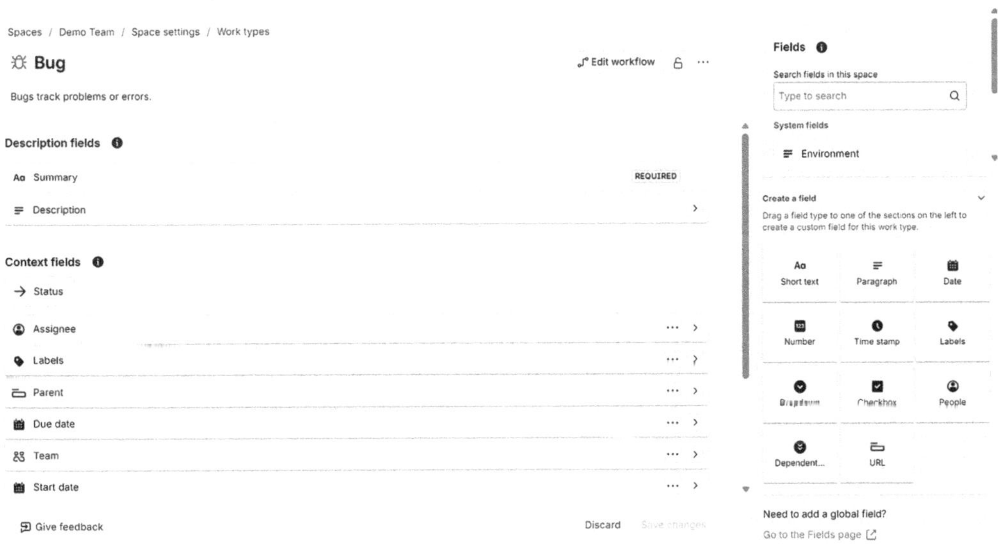

***Figure 10.8**: Bug Work Type in Team-managed Space*

Task: It is a work type used by agile teams to create work items when bigger work items are broken down into smaller ones, non-technical activities, or training tasks.

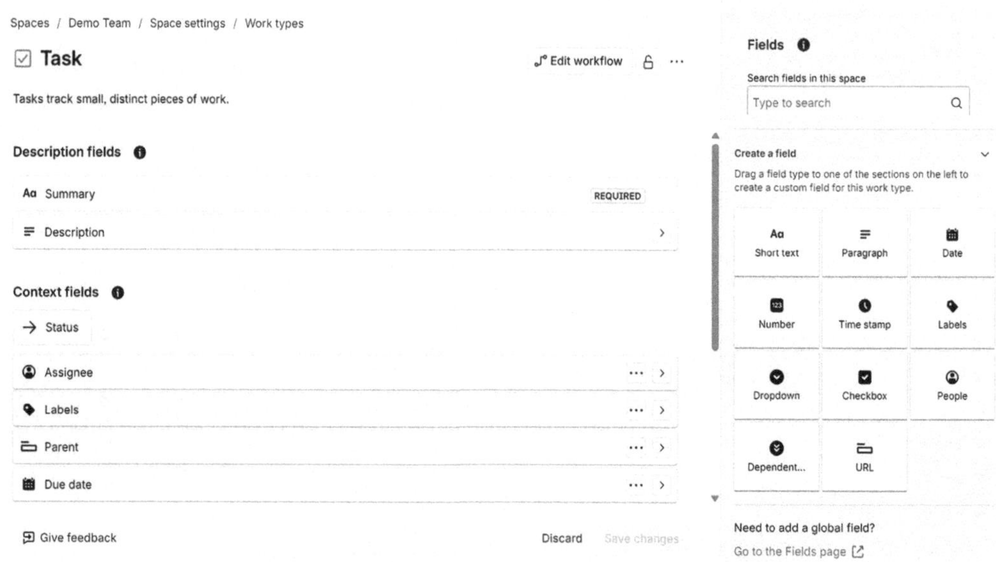

Figure 10.9: *Task Work Type in Team-managed Space*

Subtask: It helps agile teams to break down complicated tasks into smaller tasks. All tasks – `Bug`, `Story`, and `Task` – can be broken down into subtasks. These subtasks can be viewed on agile boards in team-managed spaces.

Figure 10.10: *Subtask Work Type in Team-managed Space*

Creating Custom Work Types

To create custom work types in team-managed spaces, perform the following steps:

1. Navigate to **`Space`** > **`Space settings`** > **`work types.`**
2. Click on **+** Add work type, and then select **`Create work type`**.
3. Enter the details of the work type, such as **`Name`**, **`Description,`** and an **`Icon`**.
4. Hit **`Create`**.

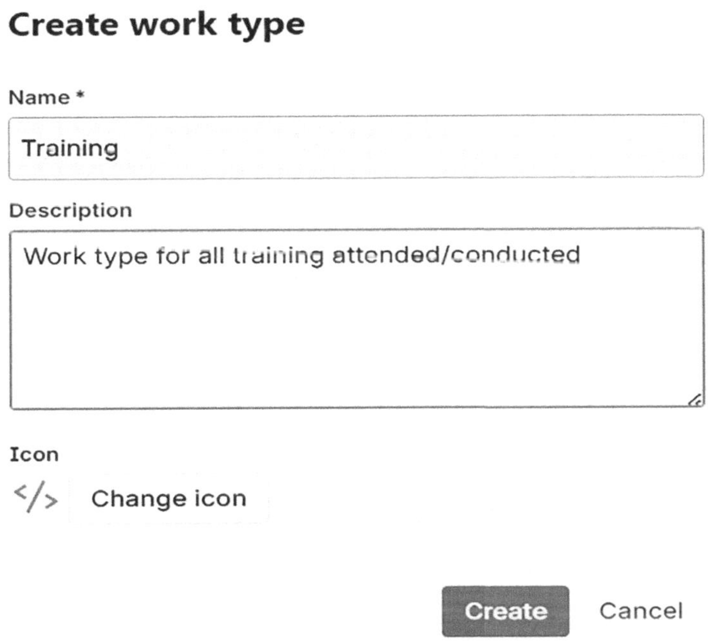

Figure 10.11: *Creating Standard Work Type in Team-managed Space*

Make Fields Required for Work Type

In a team-managed space, you set the fields as mandatory. To do that, perform the following steps:

1. Navigate to **`Space`** > **`Space settings`** > **`work types`**.
2. Select the work type for which you want to make fields mandatory.
3. Click the **`Required`** checkbox for the fields that are to be made mandatory.
4. Click **`Save changes`**.

Once it is defined as required, new work items of that work type cannot be created without those fields.

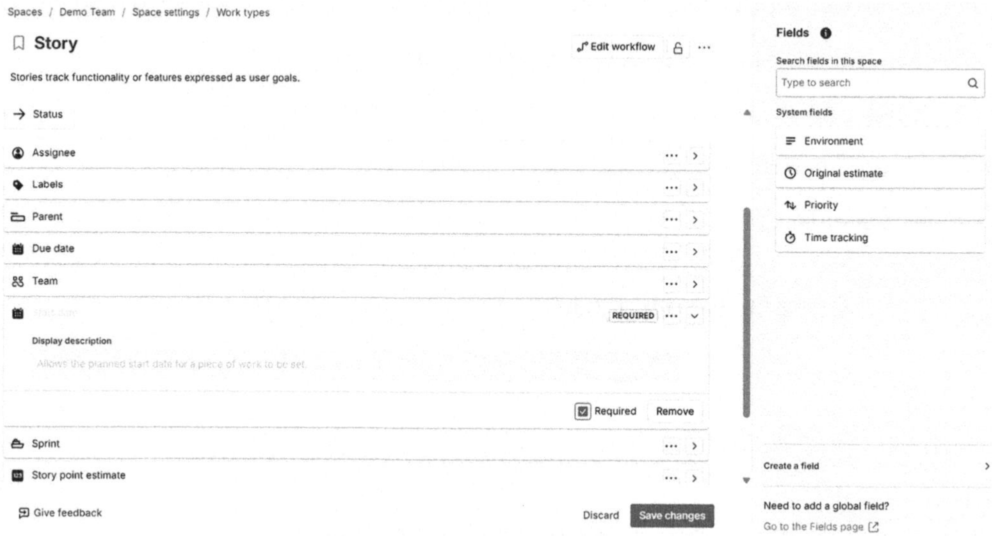

Figure 10.12: *Making Fields Required*

Configuring a Work Type's Workflow

Jira provides a simple workflow for all work types. To change the workflow of the work type, follow these steps:

1. Navigate to **`Space`** > **`Space settings`** > **`work types`**.
2. Select the work type from the sidebar.
3. Click on **`Edit workflow`**.
4. Change the workflow steps.
5. Hit **`Update workflow`** to save the changes.
6. Select only those work types for which the new workflow has to be applied.
7. Select **`Save`**.

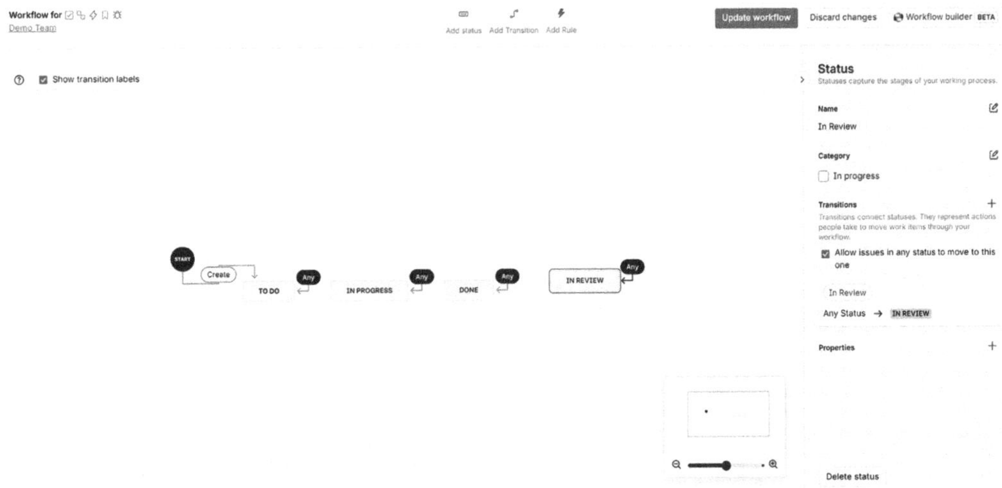

***Figure 10.13**: Configuring Workflow in a Team-managed Space*

Defining Status

Statuses represent the state of the work item.

Permissions required: To add/delete a status in a team-managed space, you must have an administrator role in the Jira space.

Here are the following steps to Add/Create a Status:

1. Navigate to your **`Space`** > **`Space settings`** > **`work types`**.
2. Select the work type from the sidebar, and then select **`Edit workflow`**.
3. Select the category from the top toolbar (**`To Do`**, **`InProgress`**, **`Done`**) and name the status.
4. Select **`Add.`**

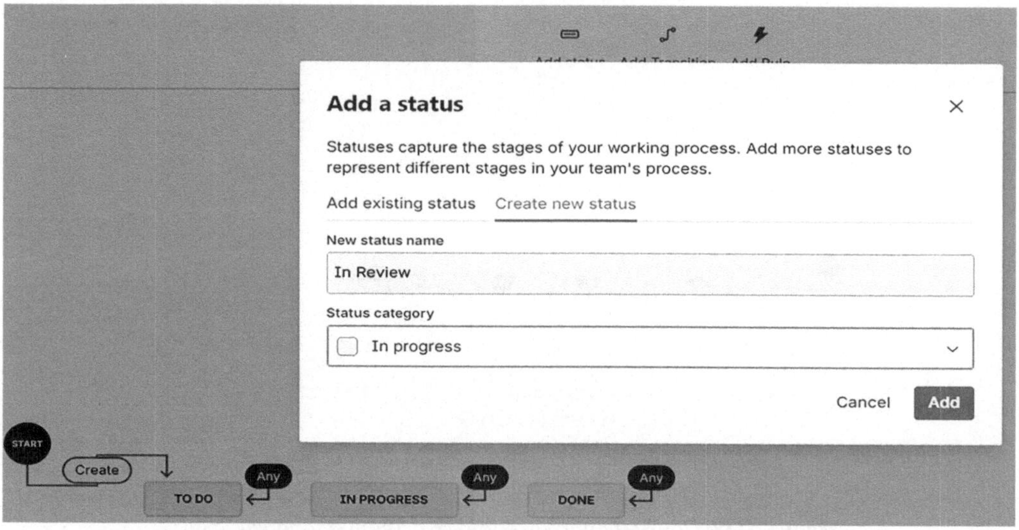

Figure 10.14: *Adding Status to a Work Type's Workflow*

Similarly, you can **`Edit/Delete`** the Status in a team-managed workflow.

Finally, when you have completed editing the statuses, click on **`Update workflow`** to confirm which work type it is for.

Creating Transitions

Transitions tell us about the purpose of changing the status.

Permissions required: To add/delete a status in a team-managed space, you must have an administrator role in the Jira space.

Here are the steps to Add/Create a transition:

1. Navigate to your **`Space`** > **`Space settings`** > **`work types`**.
2. Select the work type from the sidebar, and then select **`Edit workflow`**.
3. Select **`transition`** from the top toolbar.
4. A window will pop up. Enter the details **`From status`**, **`To status`**, and **`Name`** of the transition.
5. Select **`Create`**.

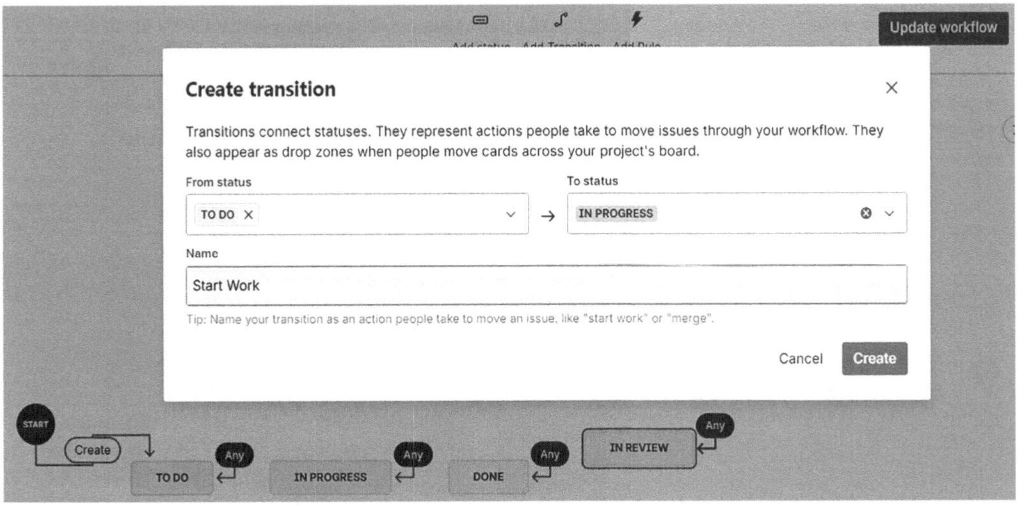

***Figure 10.15**: Creating Transition in a Work Type's Workflow*

Similarly, you can Edit or Delete the Transition in a team-managed workflow.

Finally, when you have completed editing the transitions, click on **`Update workflow`** to confirm which work type it is for.

Transition Properties

You have the option to use workflow properties to impose limitations on both workflow statuses and transitions.

Here are the steps to add a Transition Property:

After creating a transition, you can incorporate the following transition property:

1. Navigate to **`Spaces`** > **`Space settings`** > **`work types.`**
2. Select the **`work type,`** and then select **`Edit workflow`**.
3. Select a specific **`Transition or Status`** from the top navigation bar.

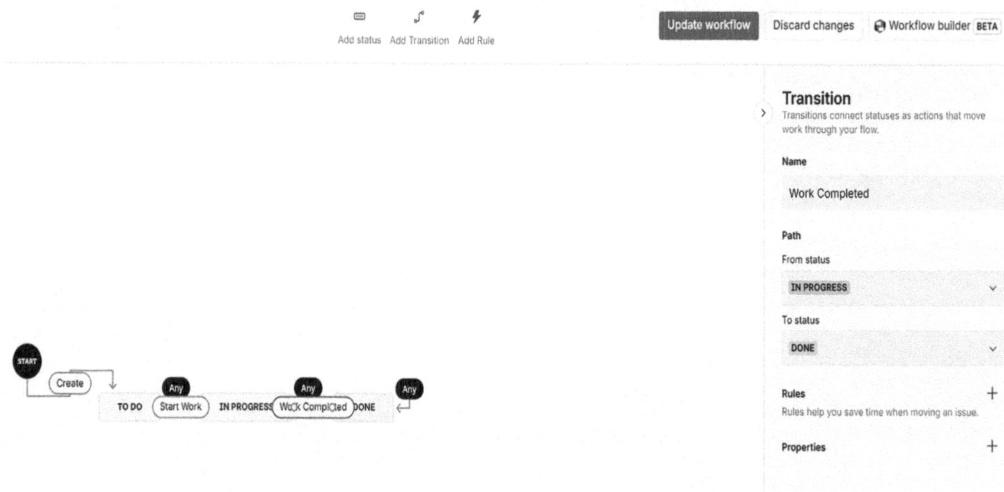

***Figure 10.16**: Selecting a Transition to Add Transition Properties*

4. Select **Plus Icon** from the bottom of the page, and click **`Add new Properties`**.

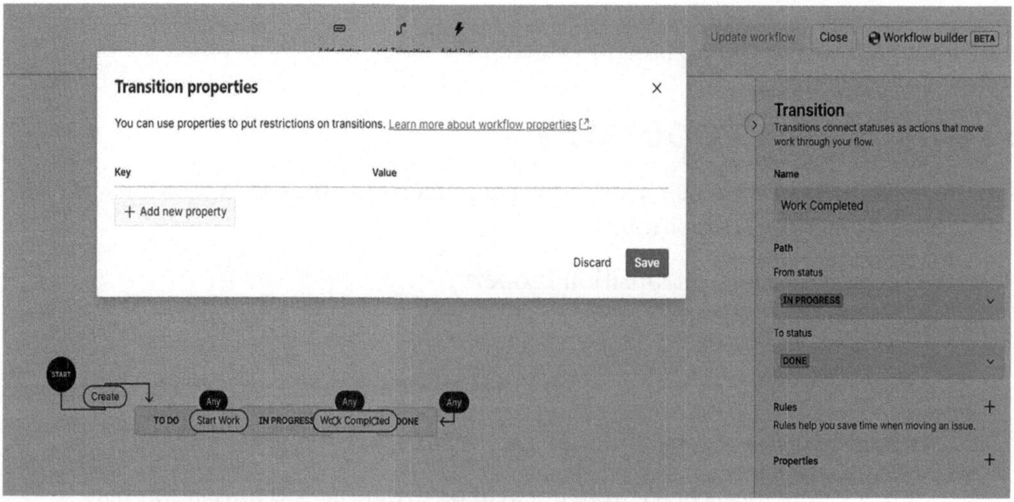

***Figure 10.17**: Selecting Properties to Add Transition Properties*

5. Enter the value of the key and value, and then click **`Save`**.

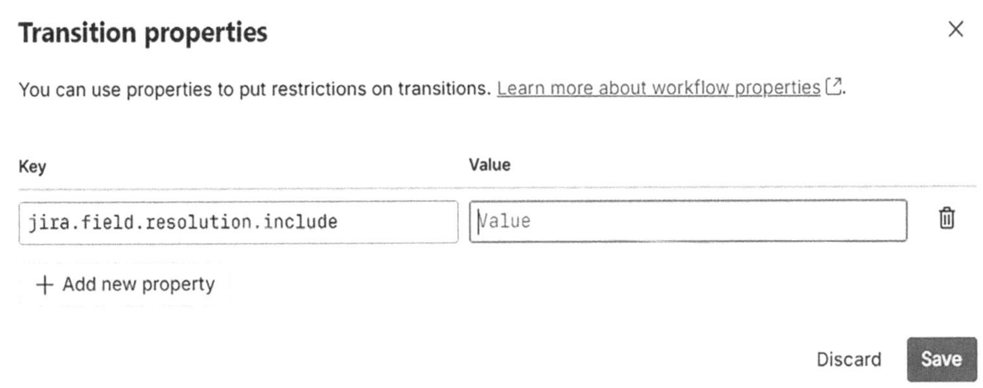

Figure 10.18: *Entering the Key Value for a Transition Property*

6. By saving this property, Jira will activate a particular resolution for the transition from **In Progress** to **Done**.
7. Select **Update workflow** from the top navigation bar.

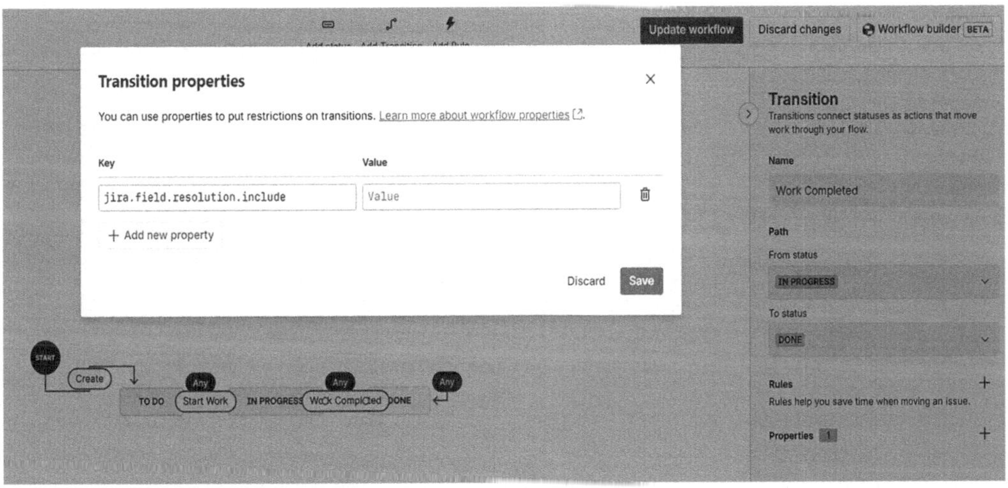

Figure 10.19: *Updating Workflow after Adding a Transition Property*

8. This property has been saved for the Task work type.

Example Status Properties:

1. **jira.issue.editable**

   You might prefer to prevent editing a work item when it is in a specific status. For instance, once a work item reaches the **Done** status, you may wish to limit editing to avoid any data modifications after the work is completed.

Use Cases:

- When a work item is in a specific status, you can make it editable by using the key **jira.issue.editable,** and setting it to true.
- When a work item is in a specific status, you can restrict editing by using the key **jira.issue.editable,** and setting it to **false.**

2. **jira.permission.***

   If you wish to impose limitations beyond the permission scheme, you can achieve this with the **jira.permission** workflow property. By employing this permission, you can limit the specific actions to the selected users according to your preferences.

   The standard format of this property is jira. permission.[subtasks.]{permission}.{user}.[.suffix].

   a. **jira.permission** is used to start the property.

   b. **[subtasks.]** is not mandatory, and is applicable to subtasks for restricting the permission.

   c. **Permission** is the permission you want to restrict. It is applicable to these permissions:

      Create, **move**, **edit**, **transition**, **viewworkflowreadonly**, **viewversion-control**, **close**, **resolve**, **link**, **delete**, **scheduleissue**, **viewvoter-sandwatchers**, **modifyreporter**, **setsecurity**, **assign**, **assignable**, **commenteditall**, **comment**, **attachdeleteall**, **attachdeleteown**, **com-mentdeleteall**, **commentdeleteown**, **managewatcherlist**, **attach**, **work**, **worklogdeleteall**, **worklogeditall**, **worklogeditown**.

   d. **User**: The user whose permission we want to restrict could be the **assignee**, **reporter**, **application role**, **space role**, **group**, or **lead**.

   e. **[.suffix]** is a number used to apply the same property multiple times. It is optional.

Use Cases:

- Permit modifications to the reporter field only for the user named **userxyz** when the work item is in a specific status. Use the key **jira.permission.modifyreporter.user** and the value as **userxyz**.
- Add a property such that only the reporter can transition the work item when it is in a specific status. Use the key as: **jira.permission.transition.reporter** and enter the value as **empty.**

Example of Transition Properties

If you wish to prevent a specific resolution from being available on a work item during a particular status, you can utilize the **`jira.field.resolution`** property to limit it.

Use Cases:

- If you want to allow a resolution **`Won'tFix`** on a transition, edit the key as **`jira.field.resolution.include`** and the value as **`resolution ID`** of the resolution. If there are multiple resolutions to be added, include the IDs separated by commas.
- If you want to deactivate a resolution 'Won'tFix' on a transition, edit the key as **`jira.field.resolution.exclude`** and the value as **`resolution ID`** of the resolution. If there are multiple resolutions to be disabled, include the IDs separated by commas. This will make it unavailable.

Adding or Removing Workflow Rules

Workflow rules are helpful to restrict transitions, validate permissions, and take actions.

Permissions required: To add/delete workflow rules in a team-managed space, you must have an administrator role in the Jira space.

Here are the steps to add a Workflow rule to a transition:

1. Navigate to your **`Space`** >**`Space settings`** > **`work types`**.
2. Select the work type from the sidebar, and then select **`Edit workflow.`**
3. Select **Add `Rules`** from the workflow toolbar.
4. Select the required rule from the options provided in the list, and click **`Select.`**
5. Select the transition on which you want to add a rule from the **`For transition`** dropdown.
6. Enter the details of the rule, and click **`Add.`**
7. Test the rule by creating a test work item, and verify the workflow rule.

Similarly, you can **`Edit/Delete`** a workflow transition rule.

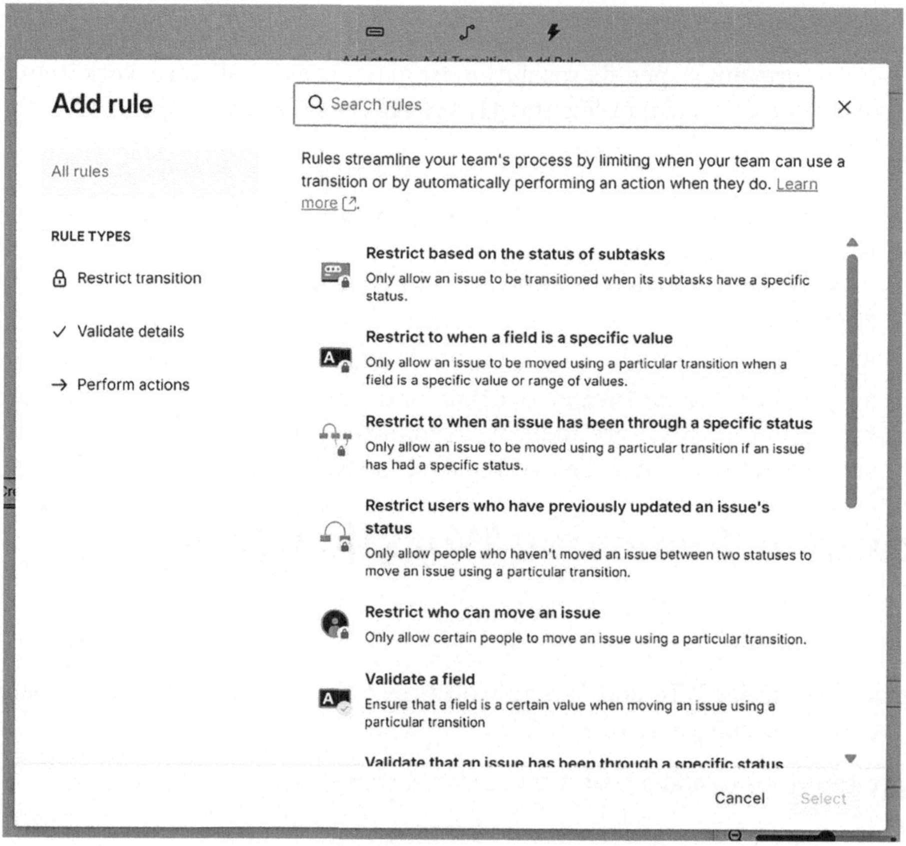

Figure 10.20: *Adding Rules to a Workflow*

There are three types of rules, which can run in the following order:

1. **`Restrict transition`**: It runs before someone tries to transition a work item.

   For example:

   - **`Restrict who can move a work item.`**
   - **`Restrict when a field has a specific value.`**

2. **`Validate details`**: It makes sure that details are correct, while transitioning a work item.

   For example:

   - **`Validate that people have a specific permission.`**

3. **`Perform actions`**: Perform an action that you may have to do manually.

   For example:

   - **`Assign a work item.`**

- `Update a work item field.`
- `Copy the value of one field to another, after moving a work item using a particular transition.`

Managing Backlog

For Scrum teams, a backlog is a place where teams can create work items, enter the details, prioritize work items, and associate with an Epic or Version after creating the same.

For the teams that work in **Kanban style**, there is no backlog. However, the teams can still plan and prioritize work by activating backlog and sprint in space settings in Jira. This is called the **Kanban way of working**.

Add Work Items to the Backlog: You can add work items to the backlog or the sprint by clicking on `+ Create work item`. If you add work items in an active sprint, it is considered as a change in the scope of work, and gets reflected in the reports.

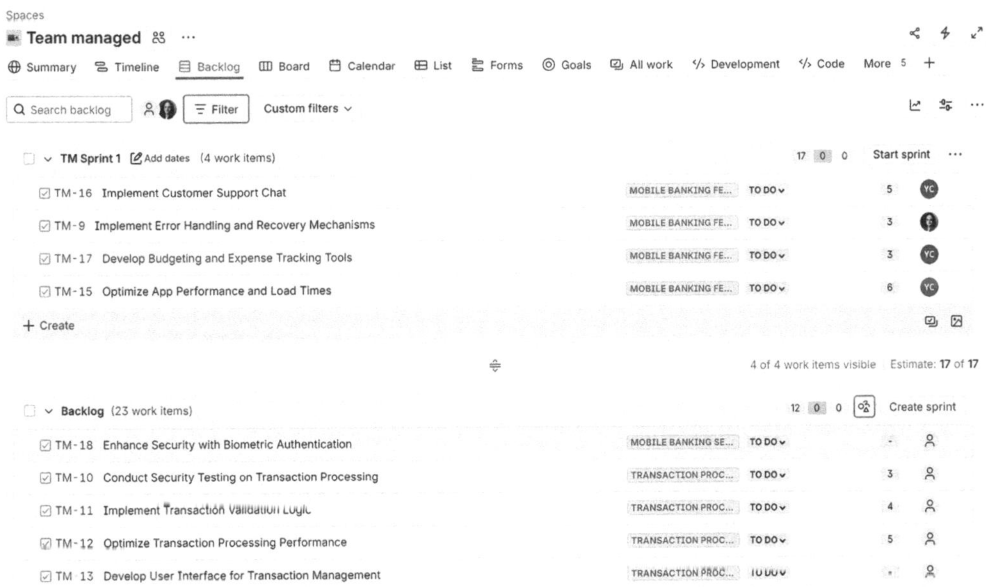

***Figure 10.21:** Backlog View of a Scrum Team-managed Space*

Reorder Work Items: You can reorder work items in the backlog, and this should be done, based on priority as well as how important it is.

Features on Backlog View: There are many small but interesting features. Right click on the work item, and utilize the following features:

1. **Move:** Move the work item to another sprint or top of the backlog, bottom of the backlog, move up, or move down as per priority.

2. **Copy work item link.**
3. **Copy work item key.**
4. **Add flag**: It will add a flag to mark that the work item is important.
5. **Assignee**: Add assignee.
6. **Add parent**: Unlink the work item, and add another parent link.
7. **Story Point Estimate**: Add story point.
8. **Split work item**: If the work item is too big, you can split it into two tasks.

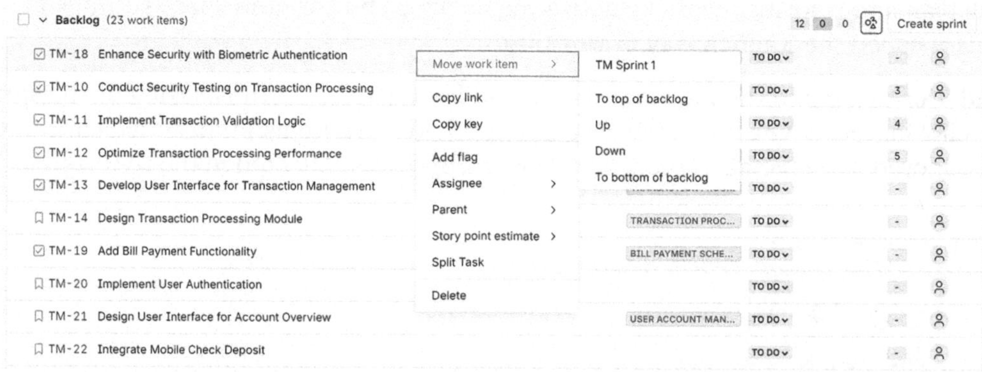

Figure 10.22: *Various Features on a Backlog View*

Display the Epic Panel and Versions: The Epic panel can be enabled and disabled on the backlog view as follows:

1. Click on **`View Settings`** on right side, and select to **`enable/disable`** the Epic panel.
2. It displays all the Epic names that are created in a space.
3. Select **`+Create epic`** to create new Epics, and enter the details.
4. Drag and drop the work items in the backlog to associate work items with an Epic.
5. Epics can also be created from the **`Create`** work item button in the top navigation bar.
6. Epics can be created from the **`Timeline view`**.

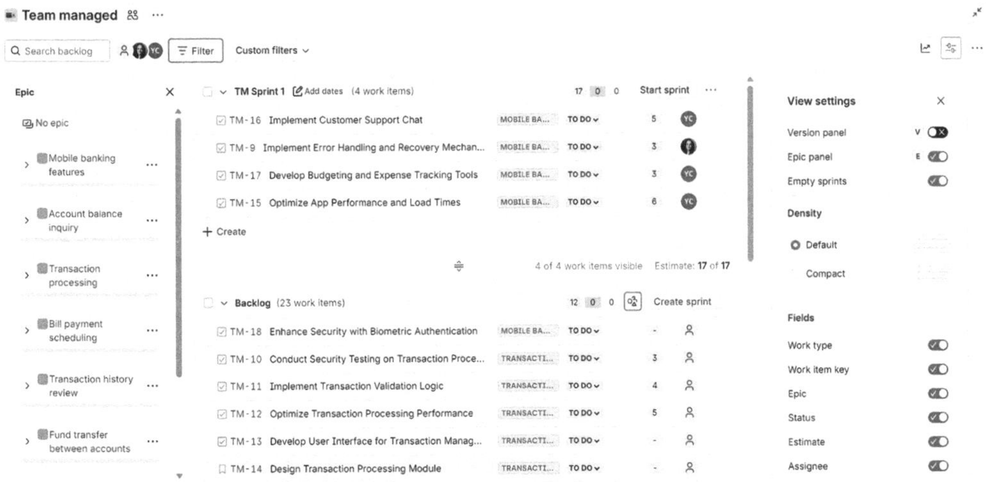

Figure 10.23: *Enabling Epic Panel in Backlog View*

Version panel can be enabled and disabled on the backlog view as follows:

1. Click on **`View Settings`** on the right side, and select to **`enable/disable`** the Version panel.
2. It displays all the version names that are created in a space.
3. Select **`+Create version to`** create new Versions and enter the details.
4. Drag and drop the work items in the backlog to associate work items with versions.
5. Versions can also be created from the **`Create work item`** button in the top navigation bar.

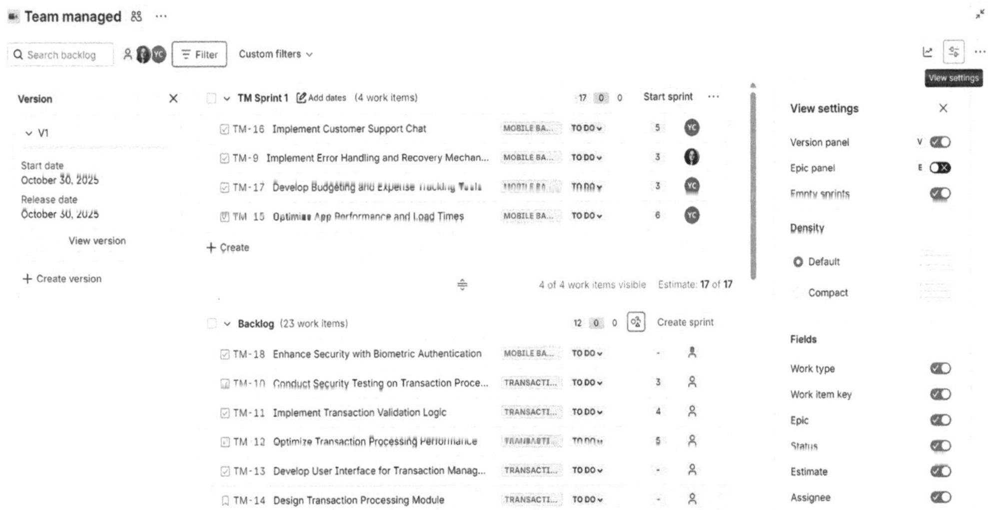

Figure 10.24: *Enabling Versions Panel in Backlog View*

Custom Filters in Backlog: You can create custom filters in the backlog view as follows:

- To create a custom filter, navigate to **`More`** on the right corner, and select the same.
- Select **`Manage custom filters`**.
- Enter the name and description of the filter as well as the JQL query.

These filters can be displayed in **`Timeline view`**, **`Backlog view`**, and **`Board view`**.

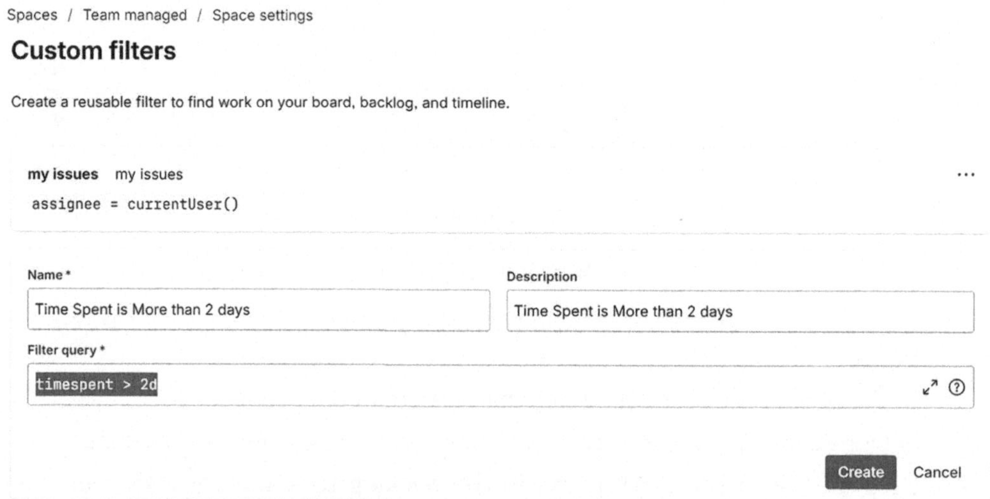

Figure 10.25: *Creating Custom Filters*

Bulk Change Features on Board: In the backlog view, you can select multiple work items and make bulk operations such as:

`Bulk change`, add **`story point estimate`**, edit **`priority`**, edit **`Assignee`**, change **status** and Start/Stop **`watching` issues.**

Figure 10.26: *Bulk Change Features on Backlog*

Sprint Operations

In this section, we will learn about how to create a sprint, edit sprint, reopen sprint, and delete a sprint.

Create Sprint

Sprint: It is a predefined time interval during which a scrum team does the development work. It can last from 1-week to 4-weeks' time.

Navigate to the **`Product Backlog`** page, and create a sprint as shown in *Figure 10.27*:

Figure 10.27: *Creating Sprint*

Edit Sprint: Using this option, you can enter the details of the sprint. To edit sprint, navigate to **More** near **`Complete sprint,`** and select it. You will get the option to edit sprint.

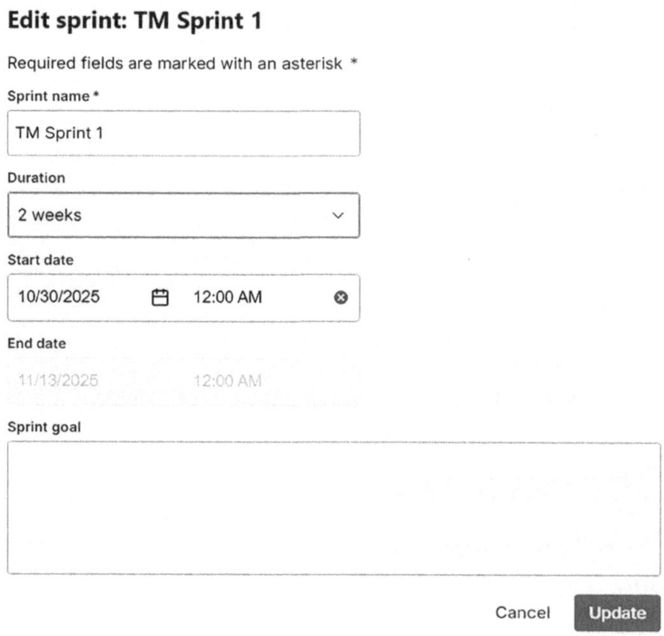

Figure 10.28: *Editing Sprint*

The team can start the sprint, once all the details are entered.

The following *Figure* 10.29 shows the **`Start sprint`**, **`Edit sprint`**, and **`Create sprint`** options.

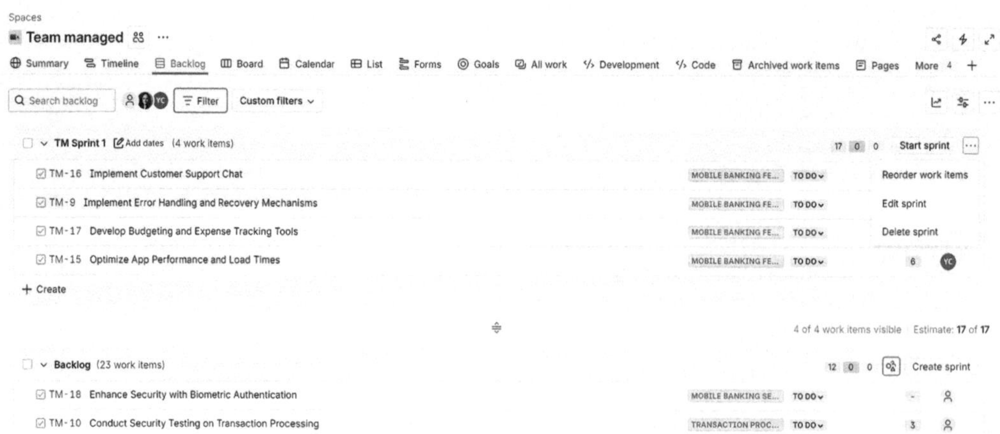

Figure 10.29: *Various Sprint Operations*

Agile Board Features

In the team-managed space board, select **More** on the right side where you have the options to **edit sprint**, **manage workflow**, **manage custom filters**, and **Configure board**.

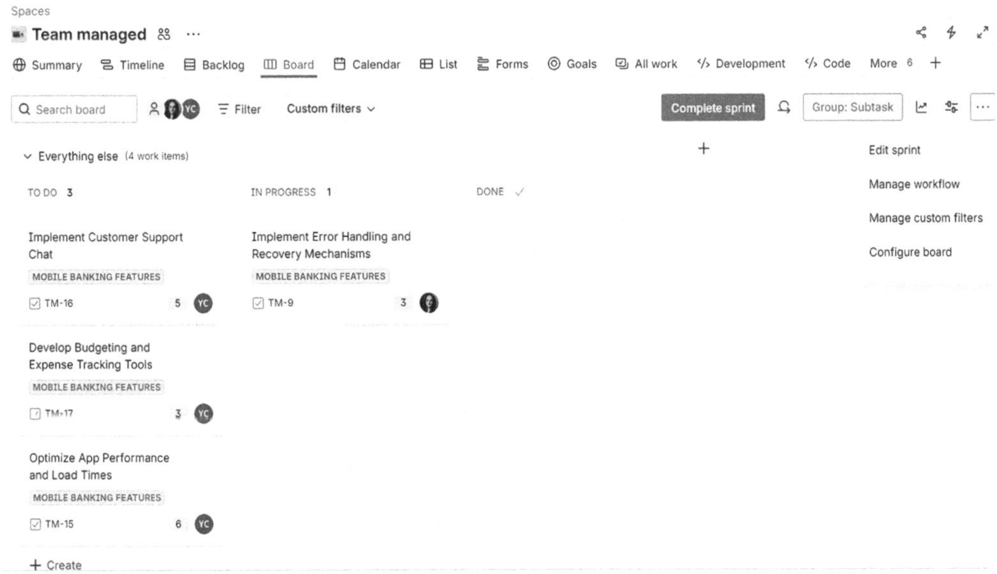

Figure 10.30: *Scrum Board*

Thus, by selecting the **Configure board**, you can customize the board for the following features.

1. Add **Columns and statuses** for the workflow.

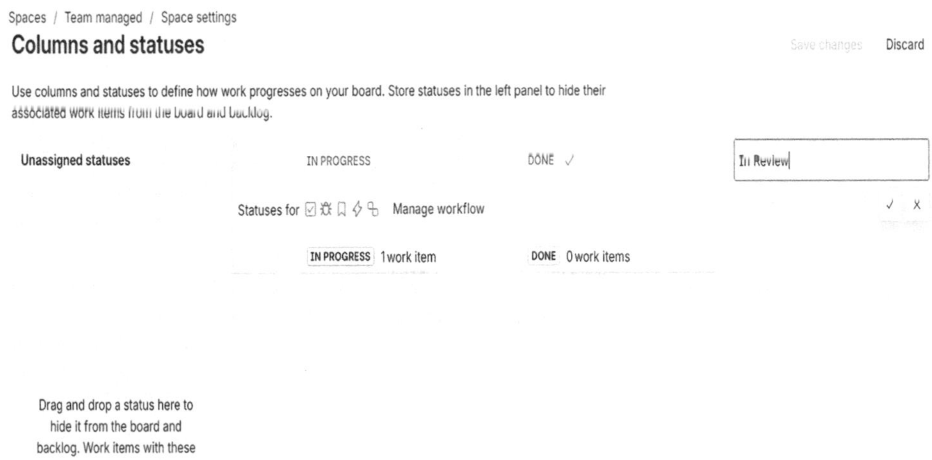

Figure 10.31: *Adding Columns and Statuses*

2. Add **`Custom filters`**.

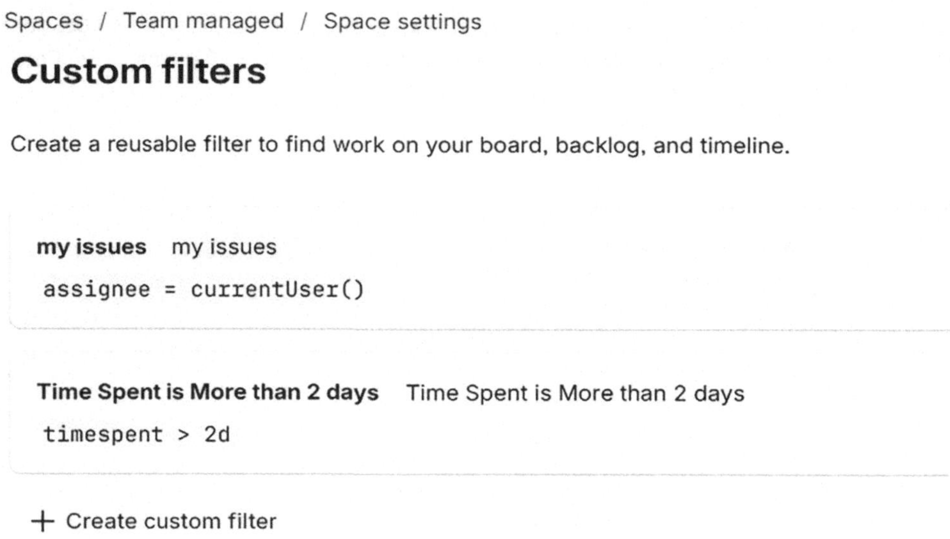

Figure 10.32: *Adding Custom Filters*

3. Add the images for cards on the boards.

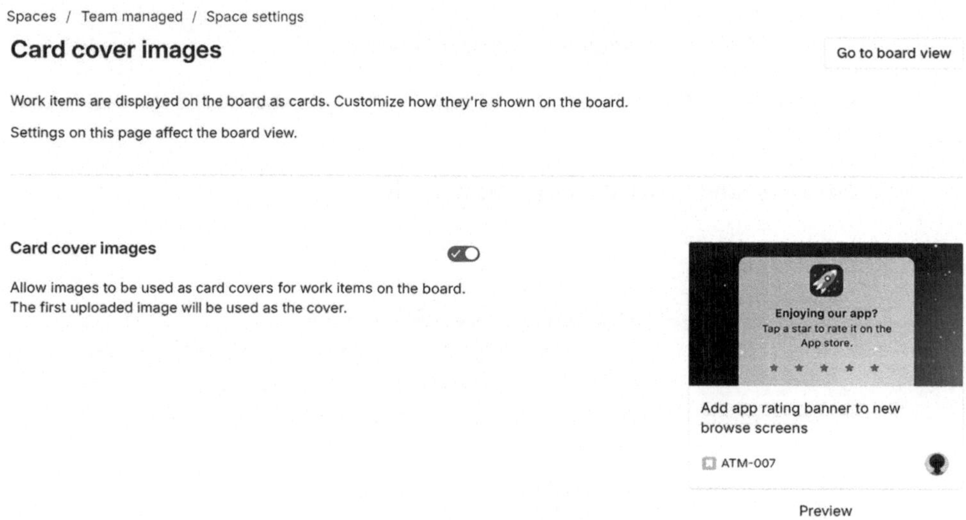

Figure 10.33: *Adding Images for Cards*

4. Enable or Disable the **`Timeline`** view and set the **`Child-level work item scheduling`**

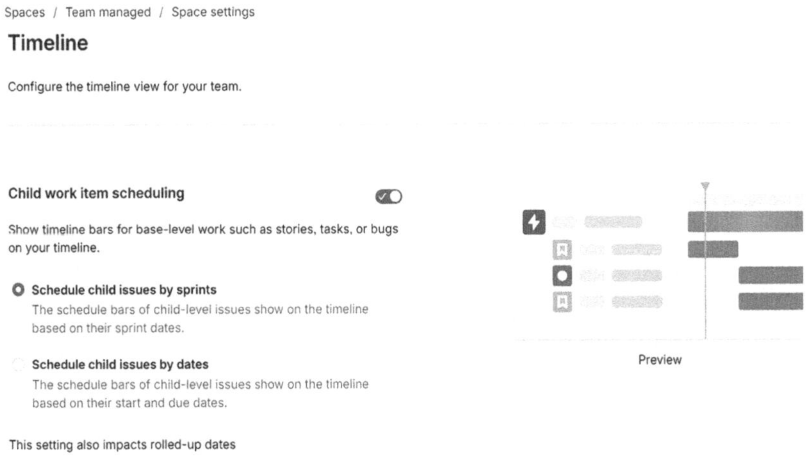

Figure 10.34: *Enabling Timeline View*

Understanding Insights for Backlog

Jira provides insights within the backlog view. Users can observe parameters such as **`Sprint commitment`** and **`Work type breakdown`**. These insights prove invaluable for sprint planning, based on historical data to determine both commitment, and where to allocate more attention across work types. It provides this data based on the estimation statistics such as story points, work items completed, or work logged in the last sprints.

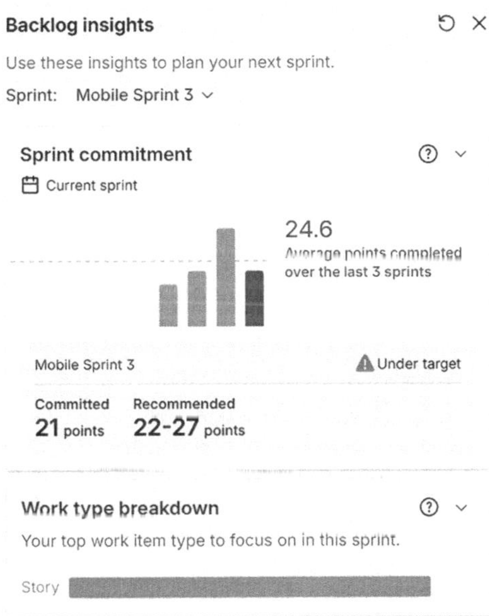

Figure 10.35: *Backlog Insights*

Understanding Insights for Board

Users can access various parameters, such as work items requiring attention, **`Sprint progress`**, **`Sprint burndown`** chart, and **`Epic progress`**. These features help the Scrum master and the team in making informed decisions guided by data-driven insights.

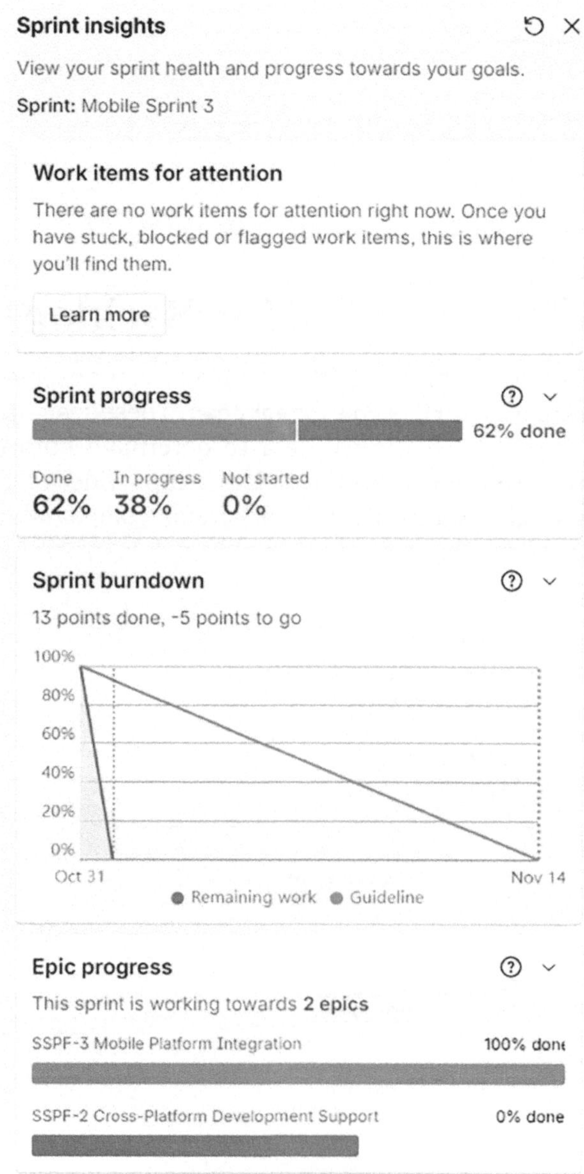

***Figure 10.36**: Sprint Insights*

Timeline View

It is a planning tool that teams can use to plan the work for long-term spaces. The timeline is the same for both company-managed and team-managed spaces. This shows work items in Gantt chart-like format, helping teams plan, track, and manage dependencies for a space. It is available in all plans for Jira.

Note: *The timeline view can display work items from a single space only. If you want to manage multiple spaces, it is only possible in Advanced Roadmaps. Advanced Roadmaps are available with Jira Premium and Enterprise.*

Important Tips for Timeline View:

- In the timeline view, on the left side, people can view **`Epics, Stories, Tasks`**, and **`Bugs,`** along with a summary and status of the work items. Additionally, they can create work items, and schedule the same by entering all the necessary details.
- People can schedule work items using either bars or by entering the **`Start date`** and **`Due date`** in the **`work item view`**. A Jira Administrator has to add the date fields on the work item view.
- It can display parent work types (**`Epic`**) and standard work types (**`Story, Bug,`** and **`Task).`** You cannot plan subtasks from the timeline view.
- All work items must belong to a single space to appear on the **`Timeline view`**.
- Issues have to be under an Epic, which should be defined in your space through JQL (Jira Query Language).
- A timeline cannot display more than 5000 work items and 500 parent work items.
- You can enable **`child-level scheduling`** from **`Board Configuration`** or from the **`Timeline view`**.
- To enable child-level scheduling from the **`Timeline view`**, select **More** on the top right corner, and then select **`Configure Timeline`**.
- Dependencies show the order in which work items will be worked upon. This is also called **work item-linking**, which allows people to indicate if something is blocking the progress of the work items.

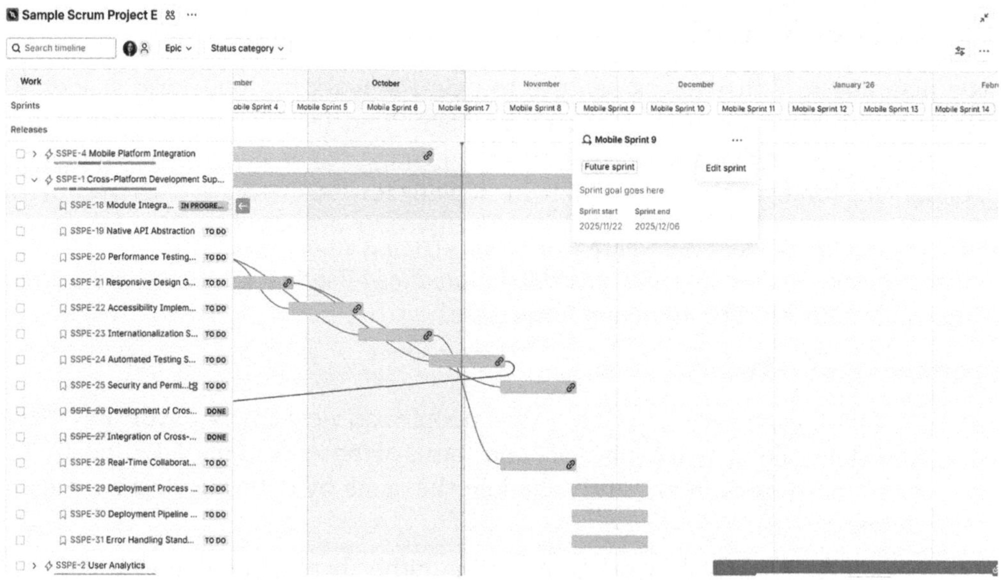

Figure 10.37: *Timeline View in Team-managed Space*

Reports

There are four reports in Team-managed software spaces. We will learn about all in this section.

Enabling reports: To enable the reports, follow these steps:

1. Select all spaces and navigate to your team-managed software space.
2. Click on **`Space settings`** > **`Features`** > **`Reports`**.
3. Enable reports in the selected space.

To view the reports, you must have enough data in the space. In addition, you also need to enable the **`Sprints`** to view **`Sprint burndown charts`**, **`Burnup,`** and **`Velocity reports`**.

- **Burndown Chart**: This report is applicable to sprints within a space. It displays how much work is left in a sprint, and provides an idea about achieving the sprint goal. By tracking the remaining work throughout the sprint, teams can manage changes in priority, and plan the work to achieve the sprint goal. Users can select the **`sprints to view,`** and also have the option to choose **`estimations statistics`** on the reports page. The red line shows the remaining values whereas the grey line is used to display the guideline.

The following chart (*Figure* 10.38) shows details about work items and information related to those work items, such as sprint start, work item burndown, sprint end, and scope change. This helps in understanding the overall pattern of iteration and its progress.

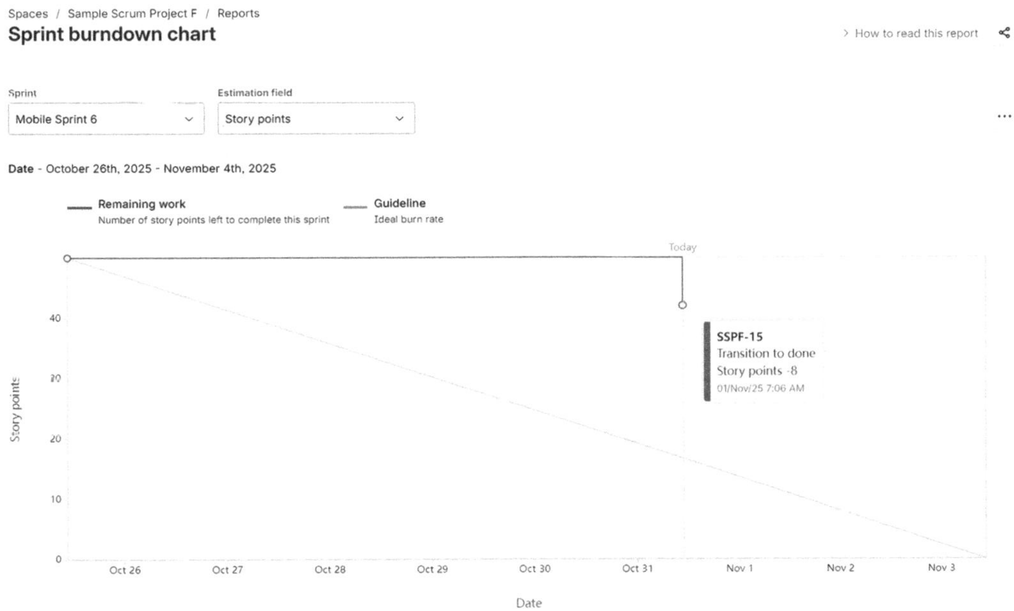

Figure 10.38: *Sprint Burndown Chart*

- **Burnup Chart:** This report is applicable to sprints within a space. It displays sprint's completed work compared to its total scope.

The chart uses a vertical axis to measure the amount of work, which can be selected using various metrics like story points, work item count, or estimates. The horizontal axis represents time, measured in days. The gap between the lines on the chart indicates the remaining workload. When the space reaches completion, these lines will converge.

Hence, by closely observing the `Work scope` line, you can spot any instances of scope creep.

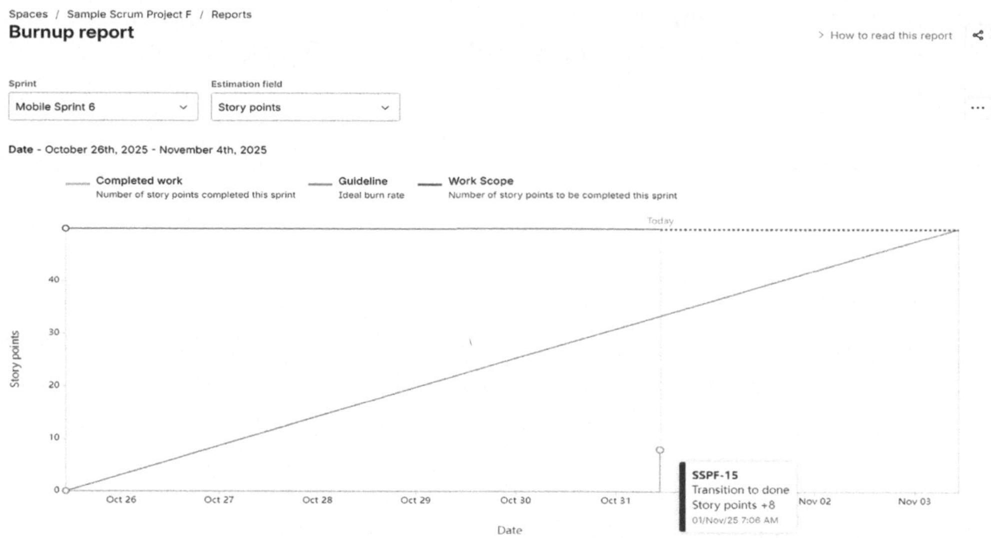

Figure 10.39: *Burnup Chart*

- **Cumulative Flow Diagram:** A Cumulative Flow Diagram (CFD) is a graphical representation in the form of an area chart, used to display the progress of work items within an application or sprint. In this chart, the x-axis represents time, while the y-axis represents the number of work items. Each distinct colored region within the chart corresponds to a specific workflow status, mirroring the columns on your task board.

The CFD serves as a valuable tool for pinpointing bottlenecks in your workflow. If you observe a region within the chart expanding vertically over time, it indicates that the corresponding column on your board is experiencing a bottleneck.

The CFD provides data specific to a board, and displays it based on column mapping. If any status is unmapped, it will not be shown on the chart. The CFD also indicates if any work items have accumulated in a particular column. It also provides a date selection for the chart to be displayed.

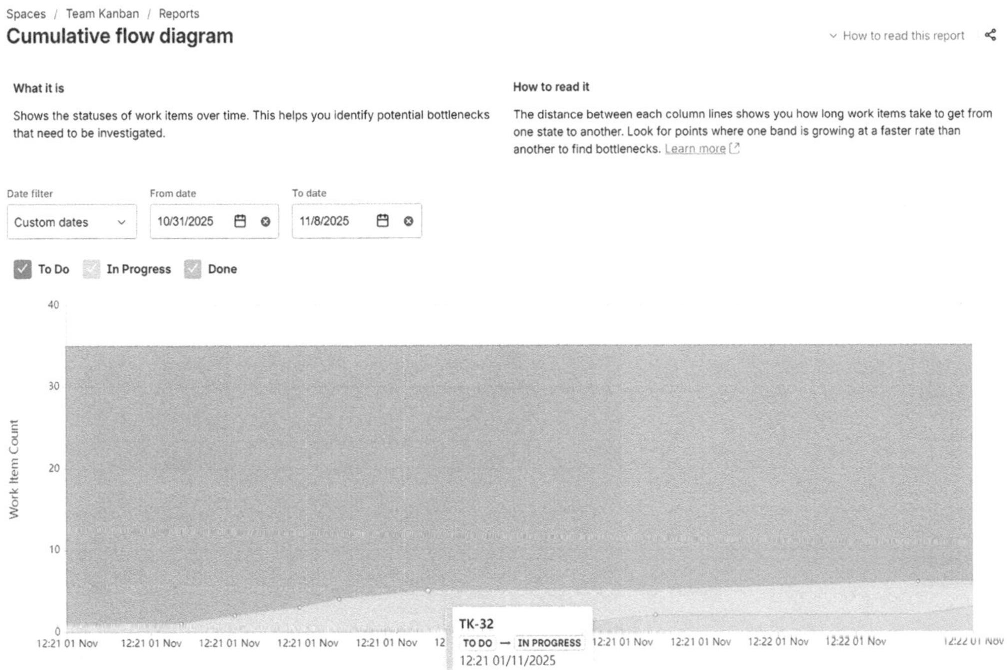

***Figure 10.40:** Cumulative Flow Diagram*

- **Velocity Chart:** This report is applicable to sprints within a space. The velocity report is used to know the average amount of work a team can complete in a sprint. You can measure this in different ways, like counting the number of tasks, measuring time in minutes, hours, and days, or using the **`story points.`**

Jira keeps track of this over time, and shows it in reports. These reports help the team figure out how much work they can do in future sprints. It helps managers plan how much work the team can realistically do in a certain amount of time.

There is a vertical line on the report which is used to measure their work, in story points or time.

There are two types of bars on the report. Gray bars show how much work the team planned to do in a sprint before it started. Green bars show how much work the team actually finished in the sprint, and this is shown when the sprint ends.

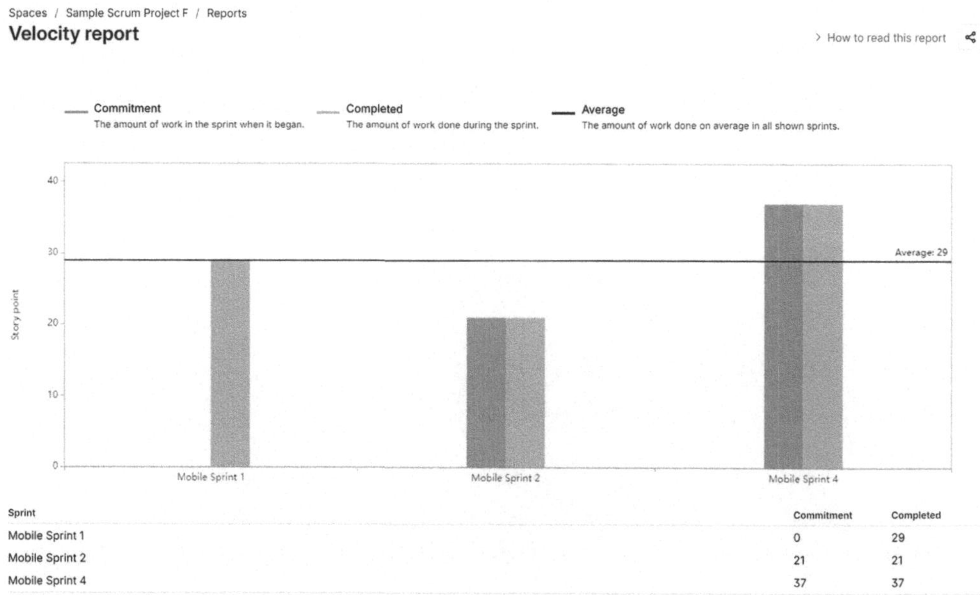

Figure 10.41: *Velocity Report*

Migrating from Team to Company-Managed Spaces

In this section, we will learn the steps to migrate work items between team and company-managed spaces.

Permissions: To migrate between spaces, you must be a Space Administrator with Administer Space and Browse Space permissions.

To migrate work items between the spaces, you have to create destination spaces to which the work items will be migrated. It could be either team-managed or company-managed spaces.

Here are the steps to create a Team-managed space in Jira:

1. Navigate to **`Spaces`** > **`Create space`**.
2. Select **`Software Development`** under **`Space Template.`**
3. Select one of the three options: **`Scrum,`** **`Kanban,`** and **`Bug tracking software.`**
4. Understand the information on the respective page, and then select **`Use Template.`**

5. Select space type: **Team-managed** or **Company-managed** (as per your requirement).
6. Decide the name of the space and enter it.
7. Jira will generate a key for the space key. It can be changed while creating a space.
8. Select **Create**.

Search and Move Work Items to the Destination Space

Follow these steps to search for the work items, and then bulk move work items to the destination space:

1. Navigate to **Issues**, and select **All work items**.
2. Select the filter that is already created or filter the work items using basic search to be moved.

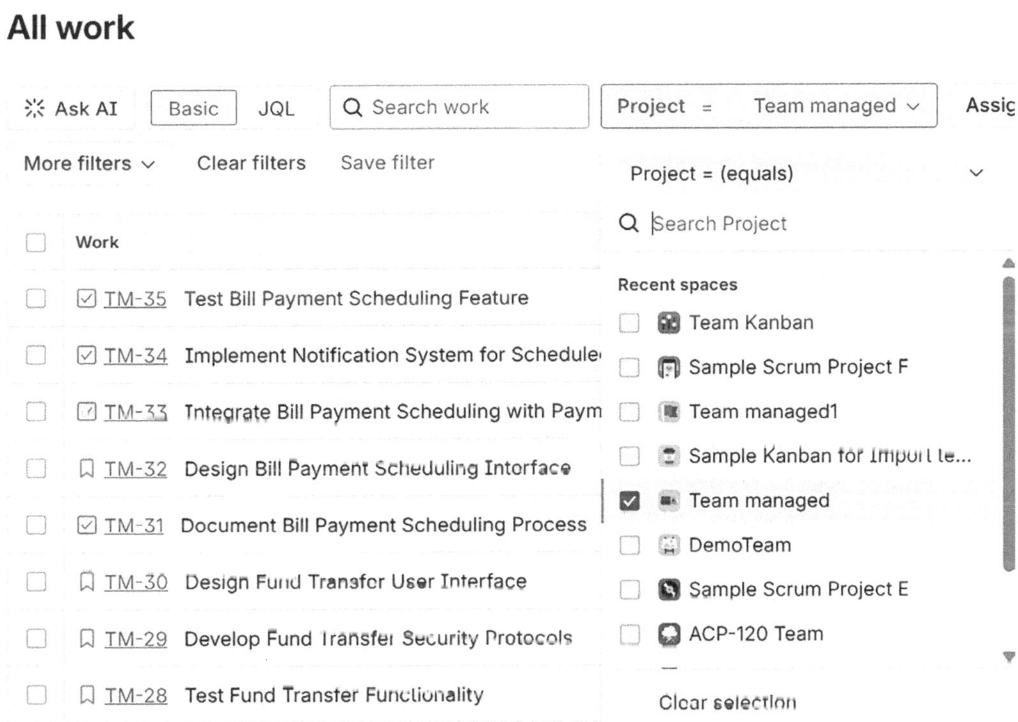

Figure 10.42: *Searching Work Items for Space Migration*

3. Navigate to **More** on the right side, select **`Bulk change work items`**. It will open **`the Bulk change`** page.
4. Select the work items to be moved, and then select **`Next`**.
5. Select **`Move work items`** and click **`Next`**.
6. Select **`destination space`** and **`work type`** to move to.
7. On the last screen, click **`Confirm.`**

Points to Remember if You Migrate from Company-managed to Team-managed:

Team-managed and Company-managed spaces are quite different. When you migrate work items, make sure you read the following points, and take corrective actions:

- **Sprints**: Sprints (Active, Completed, or Planned) will not move from company to team-managed spaces. All past sprints will not appear on the timeline. The work items in company-managed spaces get added to the backlog of team-managed spaces.
- **Components**: If you migrate with components fields, the information is lost as they are unique to spaces.
- **Custom Fields**: If you migrate data from **`Company`** to **`Company-managed`**, custom field data is not lost. However, if you migrate from Company to team-managed one, custom field data other than the global custom field is lost. You have to recreate those custom fields.
- **Story Points Estimation**: The data related to story points estimation will be lost. You can start by enabling the **`Estimation`** feature in your destination team-managed space.
- **Reports:** Velocity space data comes from sprints. As past sprints data is lost, velocity reports cannot be viewed after migration.
- **Report History:** All the history related to reports is lost, and Velocity report along with Burn-up chart will not be migrated.
- **Space and Work Item Keys:** Issue keys of the new migrated work items will be updated as per the new space. Any linked work item keys also will be reflected.
- **Versions and Releases**: All version information is lost after the migration, regardless of whether the releases and versions feature is enabled in your team-managed space.

Points to Remember if You Migrate from Team-managed to Company-managed:

Team-managed and Company-managed spaces are quite different. When you migrate work items, make sure you read the following points, and take corrective actions:

- **Board Statuses**: If you have defined statuses and workflows in a team-managed space, you have to add the same to the new company-managed space. Only Jira administrators have permission to customize workflows and statuses.
- **Custom Fields**: Jira administrator needs to create custom fields in the new company space and add them to the screens and in field configuration as the data is lost in the migration process.
- **Work Types**: Jira administrator needs to create work types that were created in the team-managed space. Additionally, the administrator has to create/edit the work type scheme to associate it with the company-managed space.
- **Space Access**: Jira administrator has to create permission schemes in company-managed spaces. In company-managed spaces, there are detailed permissions using which one can control access to spaces and many other things.
- **Space and Issue Keys**: Issue keys of the new migrated work items will be updated as per the new space. Any linked work item keys also will be reflected.
- **Reports**: The data for work items will remain as it is, but the Velocity and Burn-up chart will be lost.
- **Story Points Estimation**: The data for this field is lost. The custom field used for story points in company-managed spaces (story points) is different from the field used in team-managed spaces (story point estimate).

Conclusion

We are now familiar with creating team-managed spaces, boards, statuses, transitions, and workflow. We have learned how to migrate between team-managed and company managed spaces. We have also learned how to access reports, and understand agile metrics.

In the next chapter, we will learn certain must-know Features, Tips and Tricks, along with Advanced Roadmaps, and an Overview of Jira Product Discovery.

Points to Remember

- Team-managed spaces can be created by anyone in your team and there is no need to have a dedicated Jira Administrator to customize the same. One should have an Administrator role in a space to configure the space.

- There are space access levels and roles in team-managed spaces. You can define who can do what in Jira.
- Defining and assigning roles and permissions for team members ensures that everyone has the appropriate level of excess and responsibilities.
- Team-managed spaces are quick and easy to set up. Learn to create and customize using space settings.
- You can add work types, create workflows for each work type, add custom fields, create sprints, boards, and access reports in team-managed spaces.
- Understand the various work types available, such as task, story, and bug, and use them to categorize and track work items.
- Create and customize workflows that reflect your team-managed space management workflows. Define how work items move through different statuses.
- Create Kanban and Scrum boards to visualize and manage the progress of work items. Configure them to match with your team's workflow.
- If using Scrum, create a sprint to plan and track work. Add the user stories and tasks that are ready for development to your backlog.
- Utilize epics to group related user stories or tasks together. This helps in organizing larger work items.
- Add Custom fields that are useful to capture additional details for work items and spaces.
- Configure notifications to keep the team members informed about updates in the space.
- Automation rules defined can be applied to both company-managed and team-managed spaces equally. It can be either a global rule or specific to a team-managed space.
- Create dashboards and access reports to provide visibility into space progress, keep a watch on team performance, and find out key agile metrics.
- Integrate Jira with other tools your team uses for seamless communication and data synchronization.
- If applicable, manage software releases and versions within Jira. This is crucial for tracking software development progress.

Use Cases with Reference Links

1. **I cannot seem to get the Epic Link or Parent Link added to the card. Is that possible?**

https://community.atlassian.com/t5/Jira-Software-questions/Epics-Team-Managed-Project/qaq-p/2238144

2. **Can I add a Team-managed space board on a Company-managed space board?**

   https://community.atlassian.com/t5/Jira-Software-questions/Team-managed-space-board/qaq-p/2439056

3. **Team-managed projects/work items in board.**

   https://community.atlassian.com/t5/Jira-Software-questions/Team-managed-Projects-Issues-in-Board/qaq-p/2429689

4. **Disable team-managed projects.**

   https://community.atlassian.com/t5/Jira-Software-questions/Disable-team-managed-project/qaq-p/1680083

5. **Workflow statuses and team managed backlogs.**

   https://community.atlassian.com/t5/Jira-Software-questions/Workflow-statuses-and-team-managed-backlogs/qaq-p/1831858

6. **SwimLane in team-managed spaces.**

   https://community.atlassian.com/t5/Jira-Software-questions/SwimLane-in-team-managed-projects/qaq-p/2338868

7. **Team Managed Spaces – Cannot edit a custom field's context to Global.**

   https://community.atlassian.com/t5/Jira-Software-questions/Team-Managed-Projects-Can-t-edit-a-custom-field-s-context-to/qaq-p/2351783

8. **If I move the work items from the team-managed to a newly created company-managed space, will the sprint be created automatically?**

   https://community.atlassian.com/t5/Jira-Software-questions/Migrating-team-to-company-managed-project/qaq-p/2005271

9. **Does the migration of Team-managed space to Company-managed space erase Team-managed space?**

   https://community.atlassian.com/t5/Jira-Software-questions/Does-the-migration-of-team-managed-project-to-company-managed/qaq-p/2259024

10. **Move work items between two Team-managed spaces.**

    https://community.atlassian.com/t5/Jira-Software-questions/move-issues-between-two-quot-team-managed-quot-projects/qaq-p/2428796

11. **How to migrate all the work items at once from a Team-managed to a Company-managed space?**

    https://community.atlassian.com/t5/Jira-Software-questions/How-to-migrate-all-the-issues-at-once-from-a-team-managed-to-a/qaq-p/2025499

12. **Issue-level security in Team-managed space.**

    https://community.atlassian.com/t5/Jira-Service-Management/TEAM-MANAGED-PROJECT/qaq-p/2203961

13. **How do I transfer a Team-managed space from one organization to another?**

    https://community.atlassian.com/t5/Jira-Software-questions/How-do-I-transfer-a-team-managed-project-from-one-organisation/qaq-p/2156348

14. **Do Team-managed spaces have multiple boards?**

    https://community.atlassian.com/t5/Jira-Software-questions/Team-managed-project-have-multiple-boards/qaq-p/1682741

15. **Custom notifications for Team-managed spaces.**

    https://community.atlassian.com/t5/Jira-questions/Custom-notifications-for-team-managed-projects/qaq-p/1987442

CHAPTER 11
Must-Know Features, Tips and Tricks, Advanced Roadmaps, and Overview of Jira Product Discovery

Introduction

Jira offers various ways to create spaces and Agile boards. People can create spaces based on sample data, selected filters, or by using multiple boards. We will learn about all the different ways to create boards. Advanced Roadmaps allow you to combine work items from boards, spaces, and filters to create an all-in-one plan that can include multiple teams working together. Thus, by using this Roadmap feature, you can plan and estimate release dates for cross-space initiatives, perform resource planning, and align your plans with your organization's goals. Jira Product Discovery is a tool specifically designed for product managers to capture and prioritize ideas, as well as connect and align all the teams using other Jira family of products. In this chapter, we will learn about various Administrator roles in Jira.

Structure

In this chapter, we will cover the following topics:

- Do's and Don'ts for Product Owner
- Do's and Don'ts for Scrum Master
- Do's and Don'ts for Software Developers

- Must-Learn Features for Jira Administrators
  - Importing Work Items in Jira
  - Creating a Space with Sample Data
  - Creating a Space with Multiple Boards
- Understanding Various Administrator Roles in Jira
- Understanding Advanced Roadmap
  - Viewing a Sample Plan
  - Timeline View
  - Creating a Plan
  - Dependencies View
  - Setting up Teams
  - Creating Releases
  - Creating Cross-Space Releases
  - Adding Filters
  - Configuring Work Items Hierarchy above Epics
  - Overview of Program Boards in Jira
- Overview of Jira Product Discovery
  - All Ideas View
  - Impact Assessment View
  - Impact versus Effort View
  - Roadmap View
  - Timeline View
  - Delivery Status View
  - Steps to Connect JPD with Jira Work Item

Do's and Don'ts for Product Owner

In this section, we will explore how a product owner can adapt to the agile way of working in Jira. We have discussed the features of Jira and the processes that the Product Owner and their team need to follow:

1. As a Product Owner, ensure that features, improvements, and bugs are entered into the product backlog.
2. Include all necessary details in the backlog, such as additional fields and Acceptance Criteria in the work items.

3. Backlog refinement is an ongoing activity that aids in effective Sprint planning, defining Sprint goals, and User stories estimation. The stakeholders - PO, SM, Developers, Testers, UI/UX engineers, and BA - will participate in this process, which aids in the sprint planning meeting.
4. The Product Owner or their team can enter tasks, stories, and other work types either from the timeline view or directly from the backlog view.
5. The PO can utilize or make the best use of Jira bulk import functionality.
6. The product backlog includes a ranking feature. The Product Owner and the Scrum team can rank work items by dragging and dropping them. Alternatively, you can right-click on a work item, and move it to the top, bottom, or directly into a sprint.
7. Make use of Epics, Versions, and priority settings in Jira. Create Epics and releases, and enter the correct priority details. People can associate work items by dragging and dropping them into Epics and versions.
8. Acceptance criteria and other necessary fields for stories can be created with the help of a Jira Administrator. Mentioning this information can be helpful for everyone involved.
9. The Product Owner could hold Sprint demos and retrospectives to discuss progress and identify areas for improvement. The outcomes can be documented by creating Jira work items with action items and owners.

Do's and Don'ts for Scrum Master

In this section, we have covered several key points that the Scrum Master should ensure before initiating the sprint. We have also discussed the necessary steps for all sprint-related activities, helping teams to obtain accurate Agile metrics from Jira:

1. Check the product backlog before the Sprint Planning Ceremony so that you can plan for the next sprint.
2. Ensure that the product backlog is groomed before the sprint planning meeting. Seek assistance from the product owner to refine the backlog.
3. Once the backlog is ready, move work items to a sprint. This can be done through drag and drop or by right-clicking on the task and sending it to the sprint.
4. Before starting the sprint, enter story points and priority. Then move the stories and tasks to your sprint. Also, make sure the work items are assigned to people who can actually work on them. Avoid moving unassigned work items.

5. Enter data such as story points, assignee, and priority by opening the work item in the right window. At this point, everyone should be clear about their roles.
6. After this, move the work items to the sprint. You can check the **Workload by Assignee** by clicking on More below the sprint name.
7. The workload will display the number of work items and story points assigned to each person. Cross-check this with the team's capacity.
8. Additionally, click on **Insights,** and verify if the commitment aligns with the velocity. Insights are based on the historical data. Take corrective actions, if necessary.
9. Select to start the sprint and enter details such as **Start date**, **End Date**, and **Sprint Goal**.
10. Once you start the sprint, the Scrum team can track the journey of the Jira work item(s) on the Scrum and Kanban boards. The Scrum Master should ensure that the team members are moving the Jira tasks as per the defined space workflow.
11. As a Scrum Master, monitor if any work item remains in a status for more than 2-3 days. You can configure this in the board settings.
12. Check with the team about any impediments such as server work items or team member absences. Verify these details using the board's insights. Technical challenges in coding can also hinder progress. The Scrum Master could lead daily stand-up meetings to understand roadblocks that are preventing the team from making progress.
13. Ensure that all the tasks transition to the final status, which is **Done**. Only when all the tasks are in the **Done** stage, can you complete the sprint.
14. After completing the sprint, view the **BurnDown** chart. The red line should align closely with the gray line.

Do's and Don'ts for Software Developers

In this section, we have discussed the following important tips for developers working in Agile teams:

1. When creating work items in Jira, make sure that the user stories or tasks are well-defined, and include clear acceptance criteria. This helps you and your team understand what needs to be done, and reduces misunderstandings.

2. Ensure that tasks are properly prioritized and assigned to the right team members. This prevents confusion, and helps everyone focus on their responsibilities.

3. Utilize Jira's Agile features such as boards, sprints, swim lanes, advanced roadmaps, and much more. These tools help you to visualize and manage work efficiently.

4. When creating tasks in Jira, make sure that they are SMART. SMART stands for: Specific, Measurable, Achievable, Relevant, and Time-bound. Setting realistic due dates serves as an alarm to the team members. Hence, use clear and concise summaries and descriptions. Assign tasks to the appropriate team members and set due dates.

5. Jira allows for comments and discussions on tasks. Use this feature to communicate effectively with team members, product owners, and testers. Ask questions, seek clarifications, and provide updates. Clear communication ensures that everyone is on the same page, and helps in resolving work items faster.

6. Avoid creating vague or incomplete work items. Provide detailed descriptions, steps to reproduce, and any relevant attachments. Insufficient information can lead to misunderstandings and delays in resolving problems.

7. Avoid neglecting to update the status of your tasks, log work hours, or add comments. Regular updates provide visibility to your team and stakeholders, helping everyone understand the progress and potential roadblocks.

8. Avoid ignoring notifications from Jira, especially mentions and comments directed at you. Stay engaged with the platform to respond promptly to queries, feedback, or discussions. Ignoring notifications can lead to miscommunication and hinder collaboration.

9. Assess the necessary add-ons for code review, test management, and scaling agile processes. Utilize the full range of features offered by these add-ons to ensure a seamless application development experience.

Must-Learn Features for Jira Admins

In this section, we will learn small features that are helpful for new Jira Administrators and Users.

Importing Work Items in Jira

We will learn step-by-step the process of importing work items in Jira. People can import work items using Import Wizard or from the work items page.

Permissions required: You should have **Administer Jira** Global permission, or for other users, **Create work itemspace** permission and **Make Bulk Changes** Global permission is required.

1. Prepare your CSV file.
2. Make sure your CSV file follows the correct format. The first row should contain the field names (for example, **Summary, Description, Assignee**, and so on), and subsequent rows should contain the corresponding data.
3. Ensure that the fields in your CSV file match the fields in Jira. Jira has standard fields like **Summary, Description, Assignee**, and so on. Your CSV columns should align with these Jira fields.
4. Log into your Jira account with the Jira Administrator permissions.
5. Navigate to **Jira Settings** > **System** > **External System Import** > **CSV**.

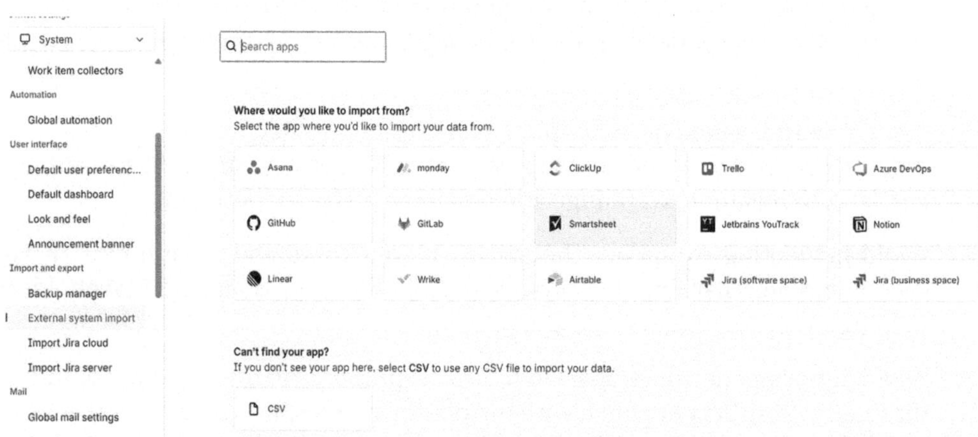

Figure 11.1: *Selecting CSV from Import Wizard*

6. Click on **Choose File** or a similar button to upload your prepared CSV file.

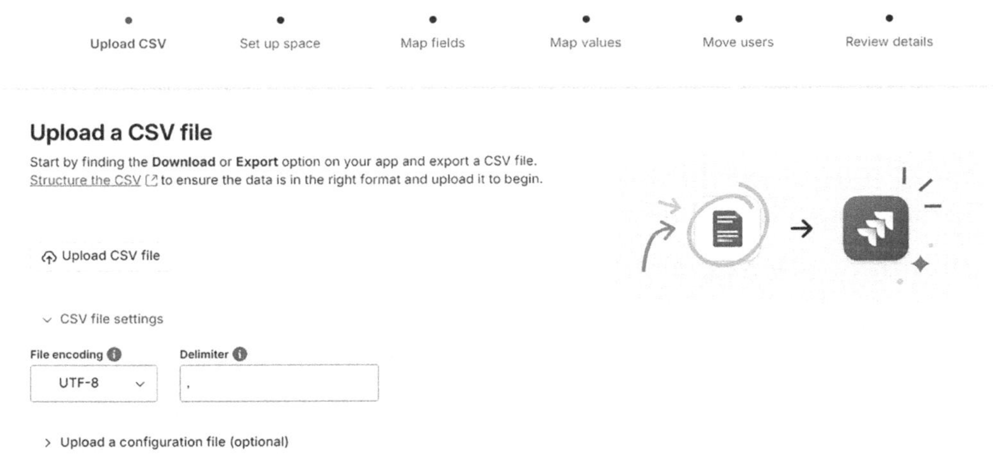

Figure 11.2: *Choosing File for CSV Import*

7. Jira will attempt to map your CSV columns to Jira fields automatically. Review these mappings and make adjustments, if necessary. Ensure that all crucial fields are mapped correctly.

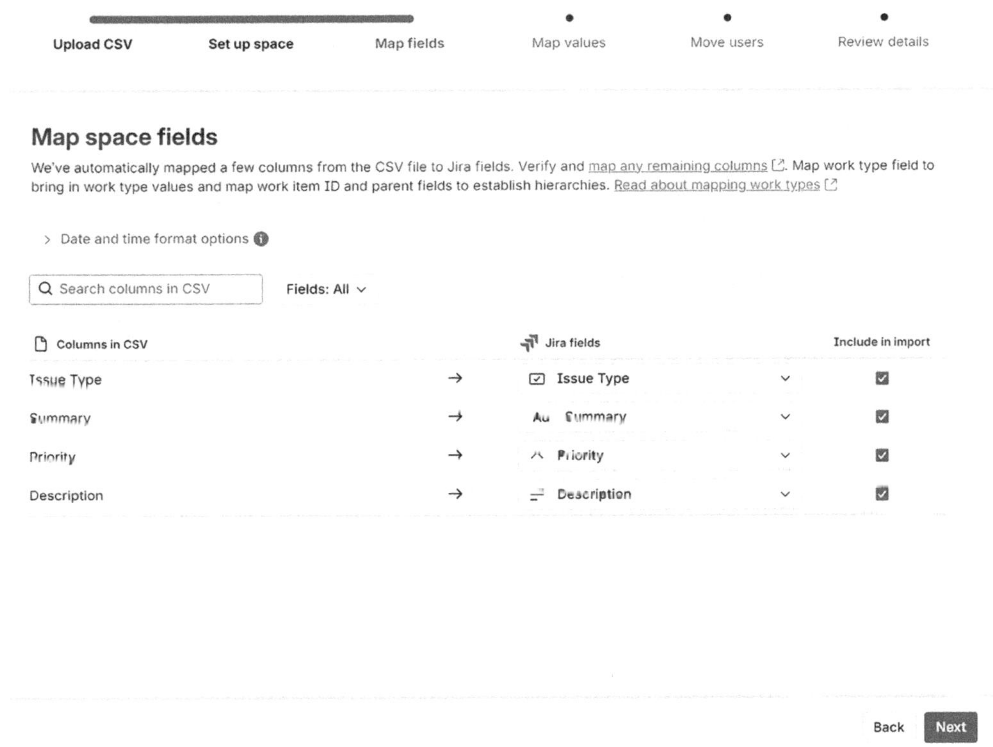

Figure 11.3: *Mapping Jira Fields with CSV File Fields*

8. Set import options such as which space the work items should be imported into, and other relevant configurations.
9. Start the import process. Jira will process your CSV file, creating work items based on the data provided.
10. After the import, Jira will provide a summary report. Check for any errors or warnings related to the imported data.
11. If there are errors, review the CSV file and Jira's error messages to identify and correct the problematic entries. Then, re-import the corrected data.
12. Go to the relevant Jira space where you imported the work items.
13. Verify that the imported work items appear correctly in the space. Check their details to ensure that all necessary information has been imported accurately.

    Hence, by following these steps, you can successfully import work items into Jira using a CSV file, ensuring that your data is accurately transferred and ready for use in your space management processes.

Creating a Space with Sample Data

In this section, we will learn to create a space with sample data in Jira. This feature is helpful when evaluating and understanding Jira features for Agile spaces.

Here are certain steps to create a space with sample data:

1. Click the **Search bar** in the top navigation.
2. From the page, select **`Boards`** > **`Create a new board`**.
3. Choose **`Scrum`** or **`Kanban`** as your board type.
4. Select **`Create a Scrum board with sample data`** or **`Create a Kanban board with sample data.`**

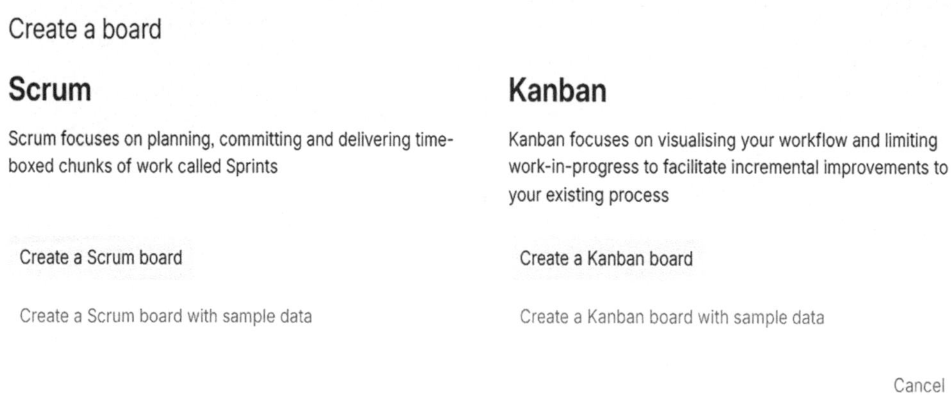

Figure 11.4: *Options to Create a Board*

5. By selecting any of the options shown in *Figure 11.4*, Jira will ask to create a space with the **Scrum/Kanban** Board.

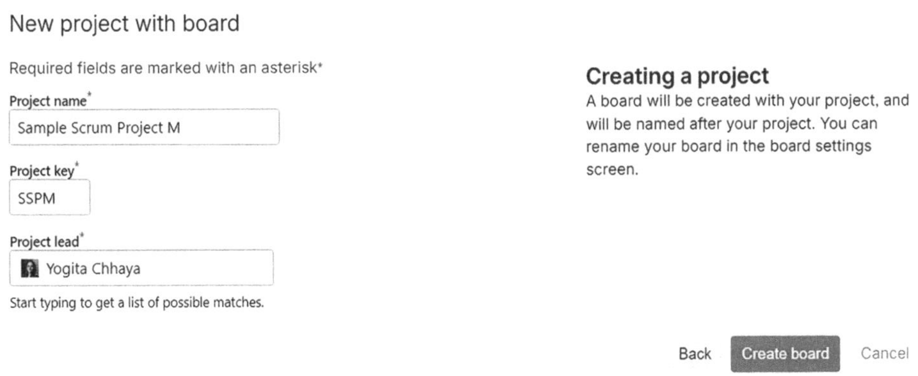

Figure 11.5: *Details of a Space Created with Sample Data*

6. Select **Create board**.

Creating a space with sample data is helpful to everyone.

Creating a Space with Multiple Boards

In this section, we will learn to create a board from multiple spaces or filters in Jira. It is essential to define in which space it will be created. The steps are as follows:

1. Click the **Search bar** in the top navigation.
2. From the page, select **Boards** > **Create a new board**.
3. Choose **Scrum** or **Kanban** as your board type.
4. Select **Create a Scrum** or **Kanban board**.

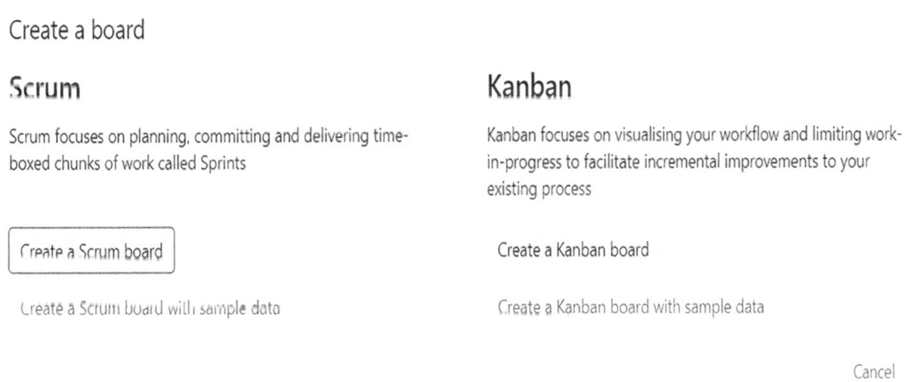

Figure 11.6: *Options to Create a Board*

5. Select the option as shown here:

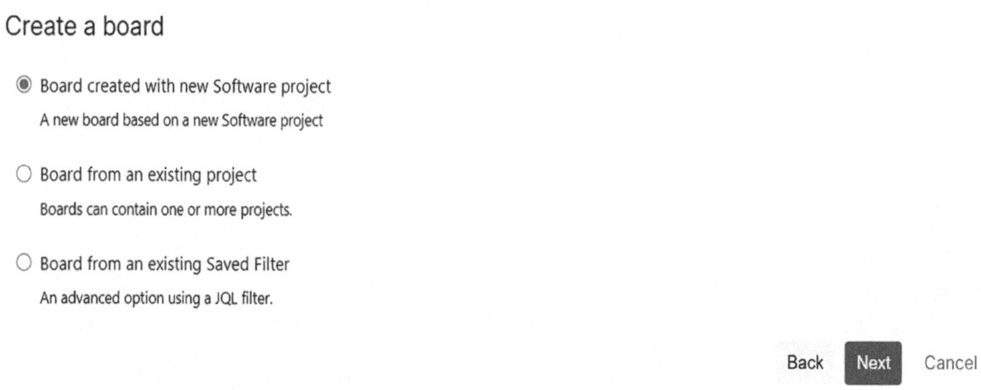

Figure 11.7: *Options for Creating a Board in Jira Cloud*

6. Selecting the first option allows users to create a Space with a Board.

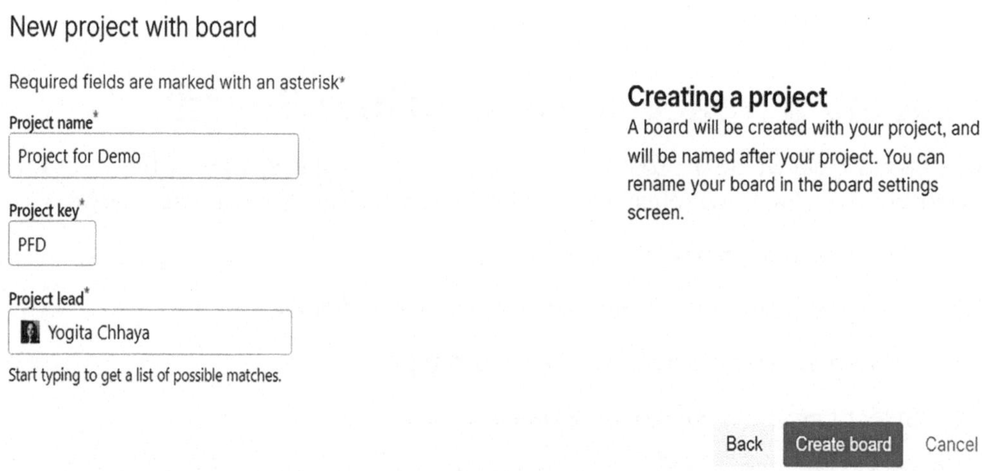

Figure 11.8: *Creating a Space with Board*

7. Select **`Board from an existing space`**. Select **`Board from Multiple spaces`**. Additionally, add the name of the space or your profile to indicate the place where the board will be created. Follow the next steps to create a **`Board from an existing Saved filter.`**

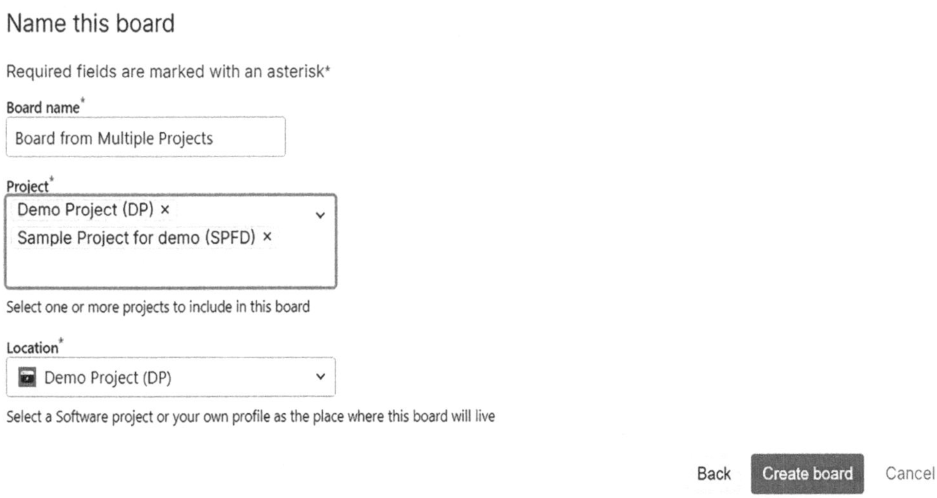

Figure 11.9: *Creating a Board Based on Multiple Spaces in Jira*

8. Select a `Board from an existing filter to` create a board from a filter. Select the filter name. Additionally, add the name of the space or your profile to indicate the place where the board will be created.

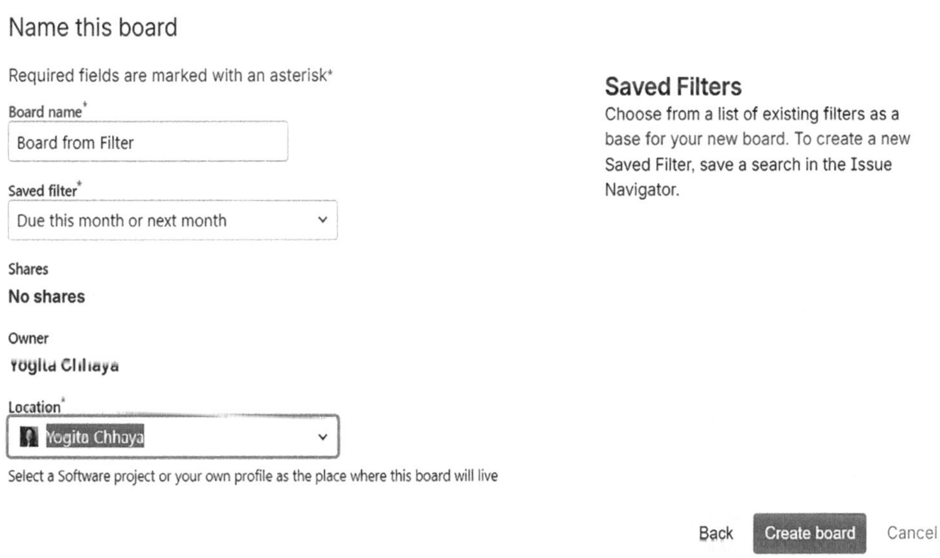

Figure 11.10: *Creating a Board Based on Selected Filter*

We can create a board from multiple spaces or a filter, and save it in a particular space or our profile, which helps to decide the permissions on that board.

Understanding Various Administrator Roles in Jira

There are two types of user management views in Jira:

- Original
- Centralized

To check, go to your organization at **admin.atlassian.com,** and select the directory. If the **Users** and **Groups** are found under the directory, then you are using centralized user management.

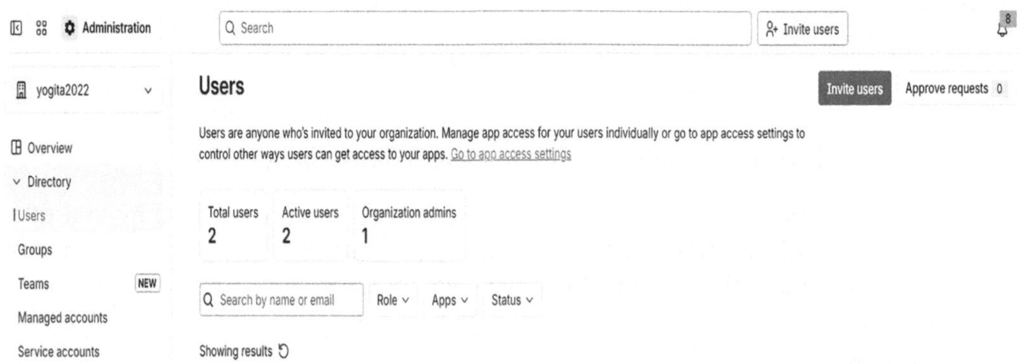

Figure 11.11: *User Management in Jira*

If the **Users** and **Groups** are found under apps, then you are using Original User Management.

Centralized User Management

- **Org Admin:** You become an organization admin when you create an organization. Org admins administer users and groups for the organization's products, and have access to the organization's settings, which can be found at admin.atlassian.com. It is recommended that you always have more than one Org Admin, as only the org admin can add or manage the org admin role.

  They are the highest-level admin, and can perform any type of administration tasks in Atlassian administration. Org admins are the only admins who have access to the admin tasks. This role has limited access to managing billing activities.

- **Site Admin:** A site admin manages users, groups and administration settings for the site, they have been assigned to and any apps (includes managing marketplace apps) within the site. They have access to any content on their assigned site. It allows limited access to manage billing. The Site Admin role can only be assigned or removed by the Organization Admins.

- **User Access Admin:** User access admins are responsible for managing users and groups for a specific product from admin.atlassian.com. There can be one or multiple people performing the role of User Access Admin for multiple products. However, they cannot log into those products. The User Access Admin role can only be assigned or removed by the Organization Admins.
- **App Admin:** An App admin can manage administration settings for a specific app. They do not have access to Atlassian administration. The same person can be an app admin for more than one app.

Original User Management

- **Org Admin:** You become an organization admin when you create an organization. Org admins administer users and groups for the organization's products and have access to the organization's settings, which can be found at `admin.atlassian.com`. It is recommended that you always have more than one Org Admin, as only the org admin can add or manage the org admin role.

  They are the highest-level admin, and can perform any type of administration tasks in Atlassian administration. Org admins are the only admins who have access to the admin tasks. This role has limited access to managing billing activities.
- **App Admin**: An app admin can manage administration settings for a specific app. They cannot access Atlassian administration. The same person can be an app admin for more than one app.
- **Site Admin:** A site admin manages users, groups, and administration settings for the site they have been assigned to, and any apps within the site. They have access to any content on their assigned site. It allows limited access to manage billing. The Site Admin role can only be assigned or removed by Organization Admins.

Understanding Advanced Roadmap

The Advanced Roadmap is a feature for teams to plan and track multiple spaces with multiple teams working on them. It includes features such as planning, dependency management, program boards, releases, sandbox, and views.

This is available as part of Jira Premium and Enterprise Versions. The salient features are as follows:

- **Hierarchy Levels**: Users can add additional hierarchy levels above the Epic. It allows large organizations to strategically plan according to their goals and track progress using the roadmap.

- **Dependencies**: It has a feature to check and track dependencies outside the plan.
- **Sandbox Environment**: Create plans and check their effects in a sandbox environment. Plans are not implemented in Jira until you save them.
- **Plan as per Velocity and Capacity:** It allows people to plan based on the team's velocity and capacity.
- **Plan for all Scenarios**: It allows planning based on all possibilities by adjusting the scenarios.
- **Permissions Required**: All the configuration settings can be managed by individuals having Jira Administrator permissions.

Viewing a Sample Plan

A Plan is a combination of work items from multiple spaces and teams. It includes the tasks to work towards an organizational goal.

You can find the `Plan` button in your side navigation bar, if you have the Advanced Roadmap feature available. Within the plan, you can create a new plan or a demo plan with sample data. A sample plan can help understand all the features of the Advanced Roadmap.

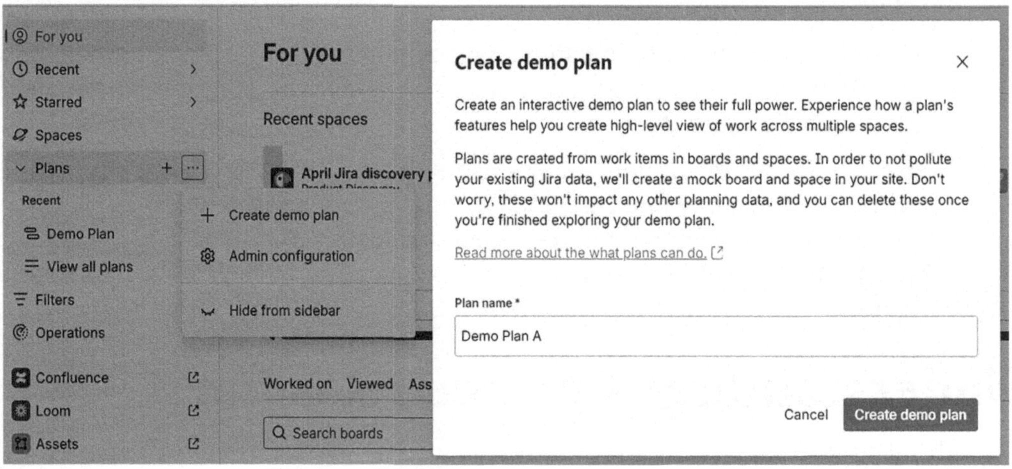

Figure 11.12: *Creating Plan or Sample Plan*

People can create a sample plan that consists of work items from multiple boards and multiple teams.

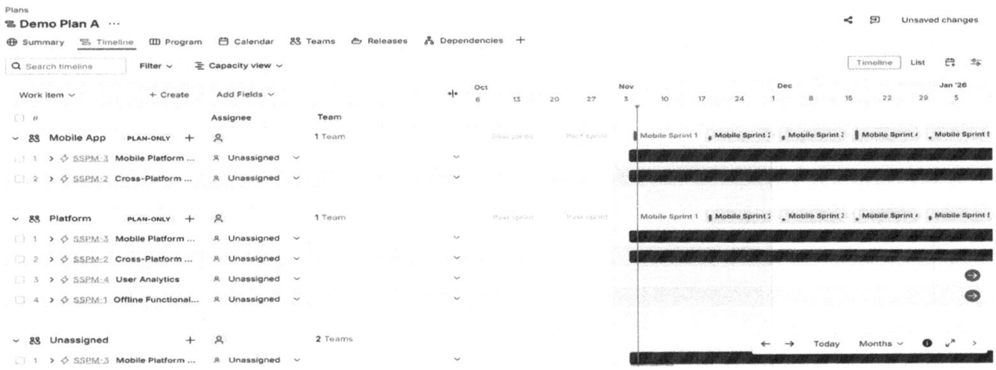

Figure 11.13: *A Sample Plan*

Timeline View

In the timeline view, you can see dependency details between work items. When you hover over a work item in the basic timeline view, you can view specific dependency details, such as **`is blocked by`** or **`is blocking.`** You can modify the settings in **`View Settings`** to display lines for dependencies. By clicking the lines, you can view the details.

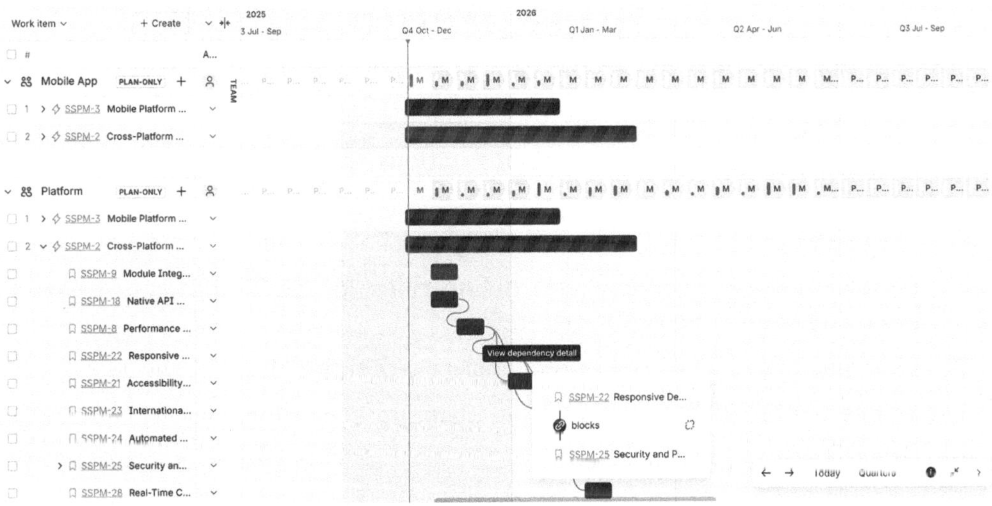

Figure 11.14: *Viewing Dependencies in a Sample Plan*

Creating a Plan

In this section, we will learn about important settings, while creating a plan. Here are the steps to follow:

1. Navigate to **`Plans`** and select **`Create plan`**.

2. Enter the name of a plan.
3. Access can be **Open** or **Private**. By default, access is set to **Open**.
4. By setting the **Open** access, roadmap users can view and edit the plan. It can be restricted later.
5. If you set the access as **Private**, only you can view the plan, and share it with other users and groups.

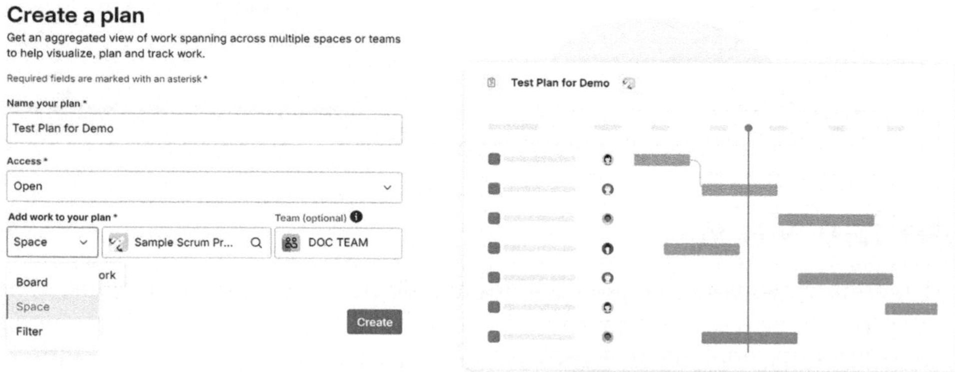

Figure 11.15: *Creating a Plan*

6. Click **More actions** beside the Plan name, and select **Plan settings**.
7. View and modify plan permissions, including who can view and edit the plan.
8. Configure estimation and scheduling options, such as selecting the date fields to use.
9. Customize timeline settings, including which views and fields are displayed.
10. Review the plan overview, and define rules for excluding work items and removing completed or filtered items.
11. View settings related to program boards within the plan.
12. Enable advanced features such as planning scenarios, auto-scheduler, and releases.

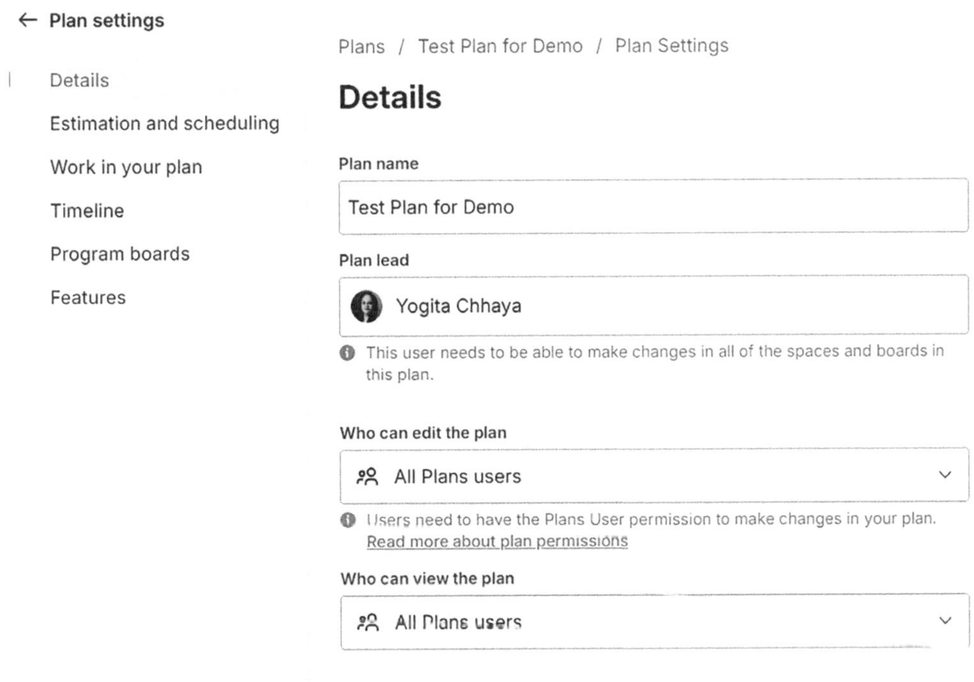

***Figure 11.16**: Plan Settings*

Dependencies View

In the **`Dependencies`** section of the plan, related work items appear as tiles connected by arrows, showing which tasks depend on others. You can access this view by choosing Dependencies from the menu.

Only items in your plan that have dependency links, either relying on another task or being relied on, will appear here. The arrows between items reflect the direction of the dependency, and if an arrow turns red, it means that the relationship is behind schedule. To fix a dependency that is off track, click the **`More`** option icon on the task tile, and select **`Locate work item in timeline`** to review it in context.

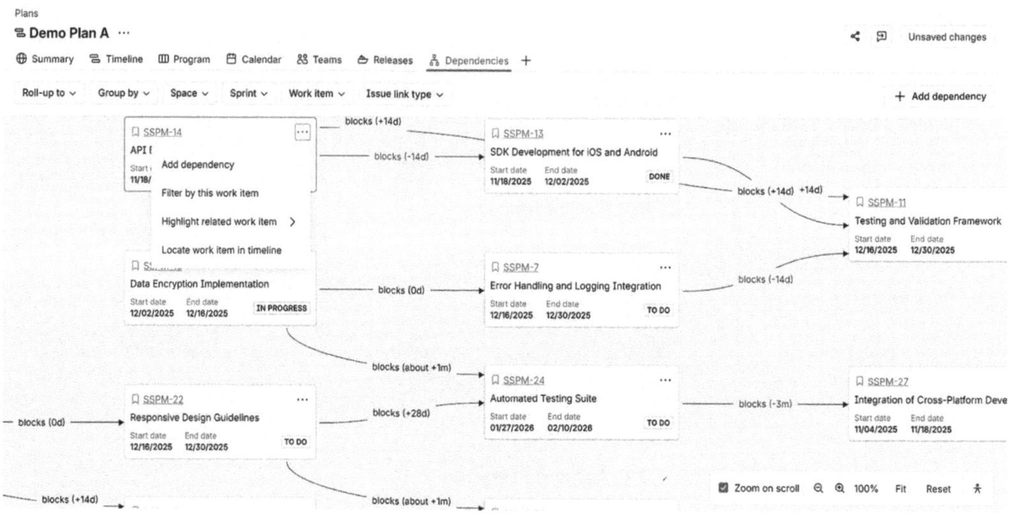

Figure 11.17: *Dependencies View*

Setting up Teams

To add a Team, select **`Teams`** tab from the Top navigation bar.

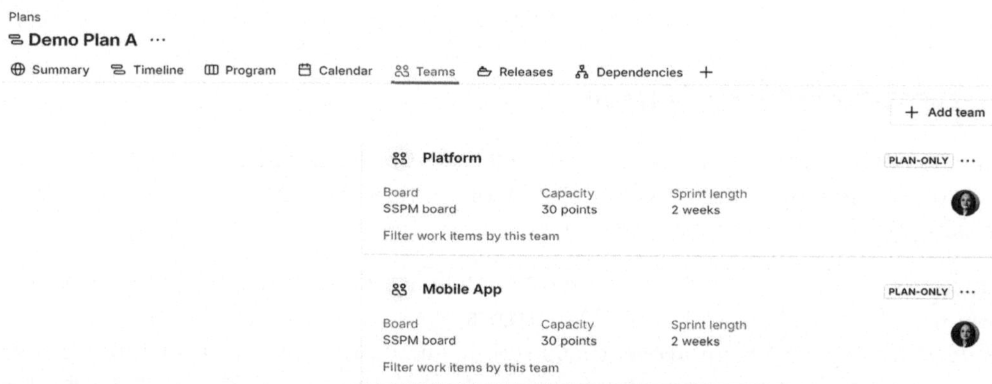

Figure 11.18: *Setting up Teams*

Select **`Add team`** from the top right corner. You can add a new team or add an existing team from an organization. While creating a new team, it can be a plan-only team or available across organizations.

Set the **`work itemsource`**, **`Planning style`**, **`Capacity`**, and **`Sprint length`**.

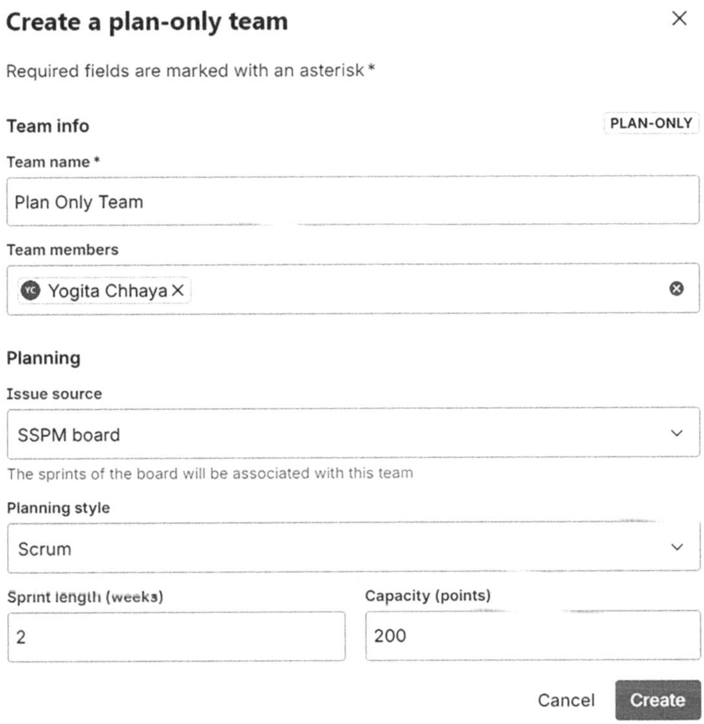

Figure 11.19: *Entering the Details of a Team*

Creating Releases

You can create a new release by selecting **Releases** in the top navigation bar, and then choosing **Create release**. Enter the name and description of the new release, along with the details of the start date and release date.

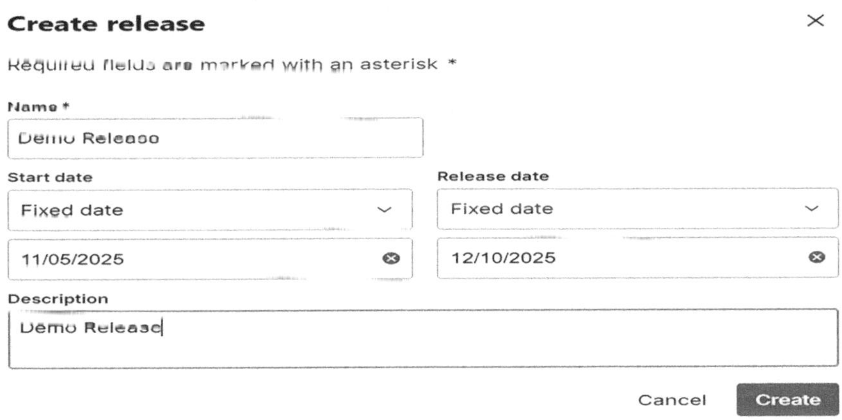

Figure 11.20: *Creating Releases*

Once you have created a new Release, it is not yet saved in Jira. In the same view, select **`Unsaved changes,`** and check for any obstacles. You can save the changes or discard them from this page.

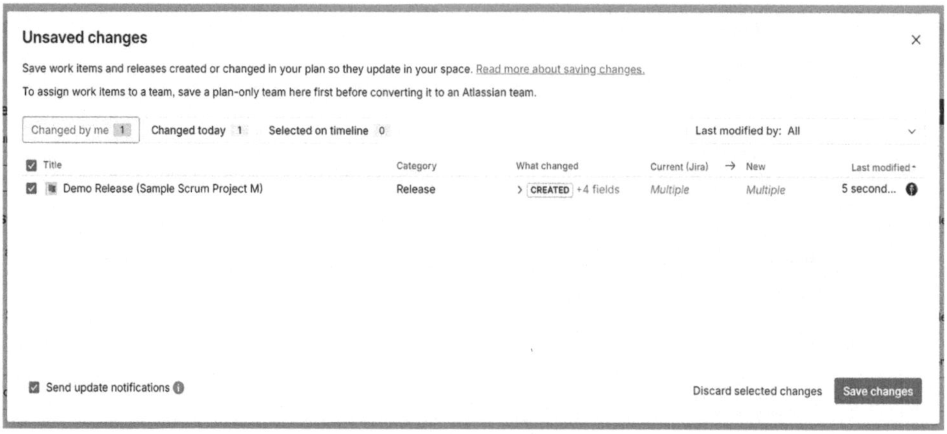

Figure 11.21: *Review Changes*

Creating Cross-Space Releases

You can also create Cross-space releases. It allows you to create releases across multiple Jira spaces. This way you can release projects that are related to each other.

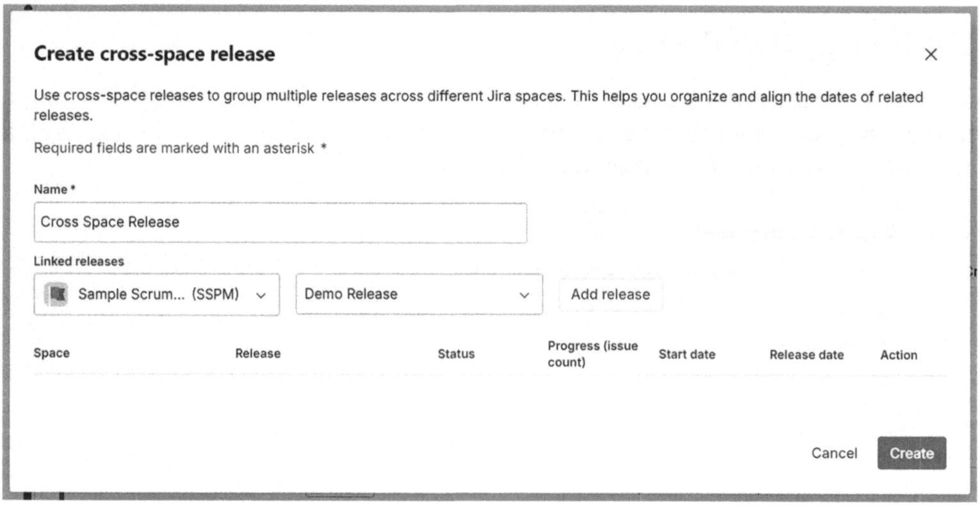

Figure 11.22: *Creating Cross-project Releases*

If the **`Releases`** tab is not visible in your plan, you need to enable releases before proceeding.

The **cross space releases** are intended only for planning within your plan . They cannot be accessed or modified directly from individual spaces.

You can use this feature to check for obstacles and review changes. It is helpful for syncing the dates of related releases.

Adding Filters

You can apply filters in the Timeline view to filter work items based on **`work items`**, **`Releases`**, **`Assignees`**, **`Teams`**, **`Sprints`**, **`spaces`**, **`Priorities`**, **`work types`**, **`Components`**, **`Labels`**, **`Dependencies`**, **`Reporters`**, and **`Statuses`**.

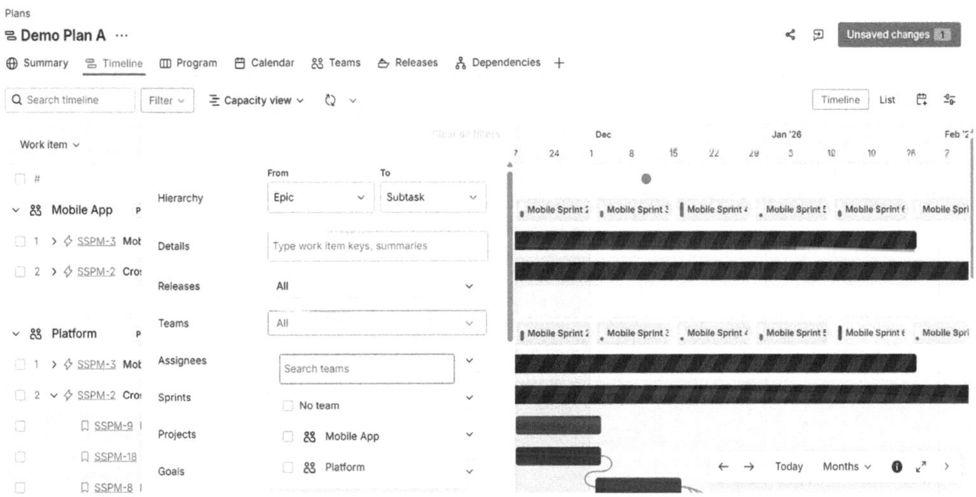

***Figure 11.23:** Adding Filters on Timeline View*

Views: After applying a filter, you can save the view. You can make a new view of your plan, and change the view settings. This new view will inherit the filters and settings of the currently selected view.

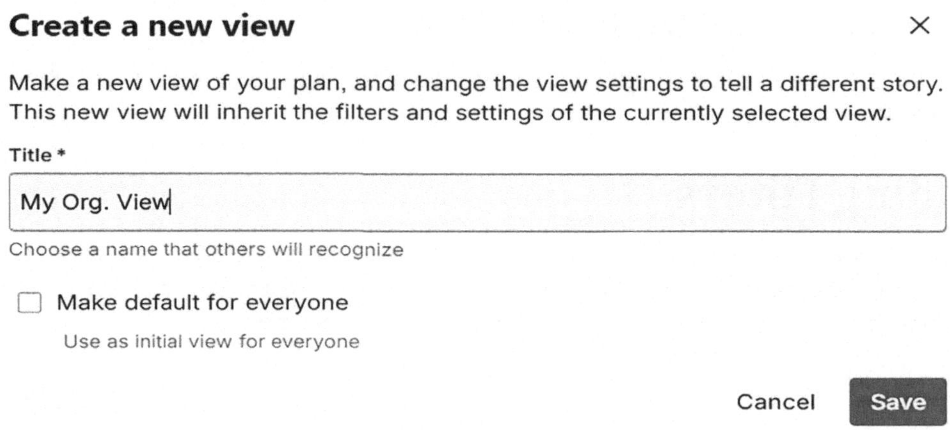

***Figure 11.24:** Creating New Views*

Adding Fields on Timeline: You can add fields by selecting from the **`Fields`** drop-down. This way, you can add and view the values of multiple fields on the Timeline view.

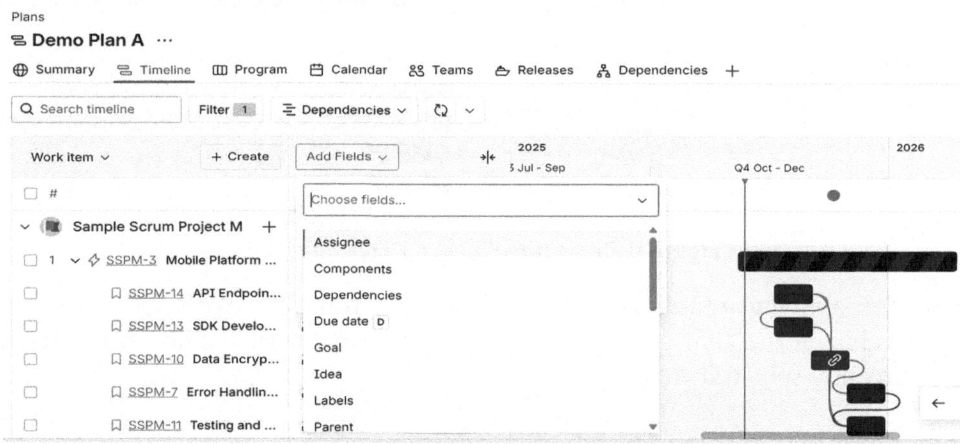

***Figure 11.25:** Adding Various Fields on Timeline View*

View Settings: You can set different parameters from View Settings as mentioned here:

- Adding color based on selected parameter
- Sort work items
- Group work items
- Dependency style
- Enable roll-ups in your plan

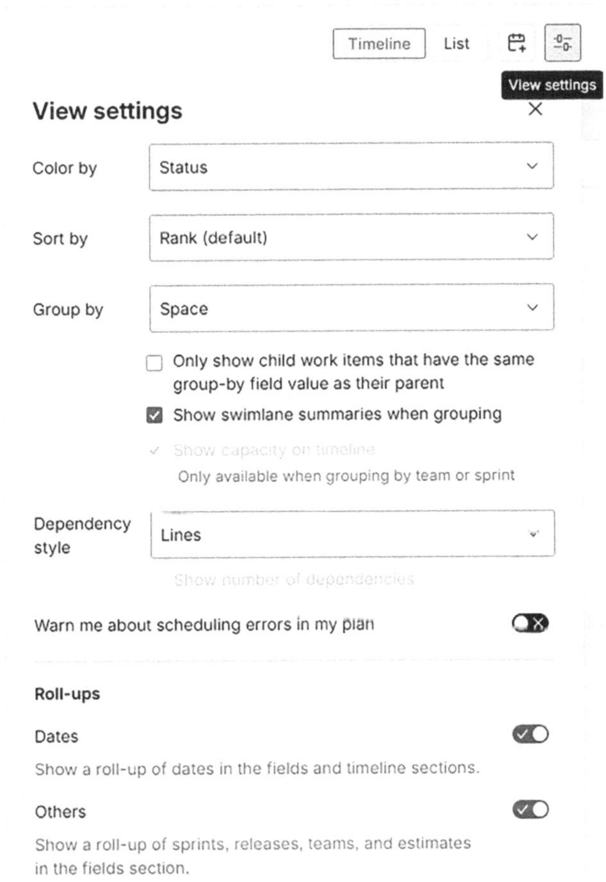

Figure 11.26: *View Settings*

Configuring Work Items Hierarchy above Epics

Advanced Roadmaps have a feature to add work types above epic level. Here are the steps:

- To add a new work type, navigate to the cog icon and select **`work items.`**
- Navigate to the **`Work type scheme`** and select the work type scheme for a specific space.
- Select **`Add Work type`**.
- Add the name and description of the new work type.
- Select **`Standard Work type`** and Choose **`Add`**.
- Save the changes.

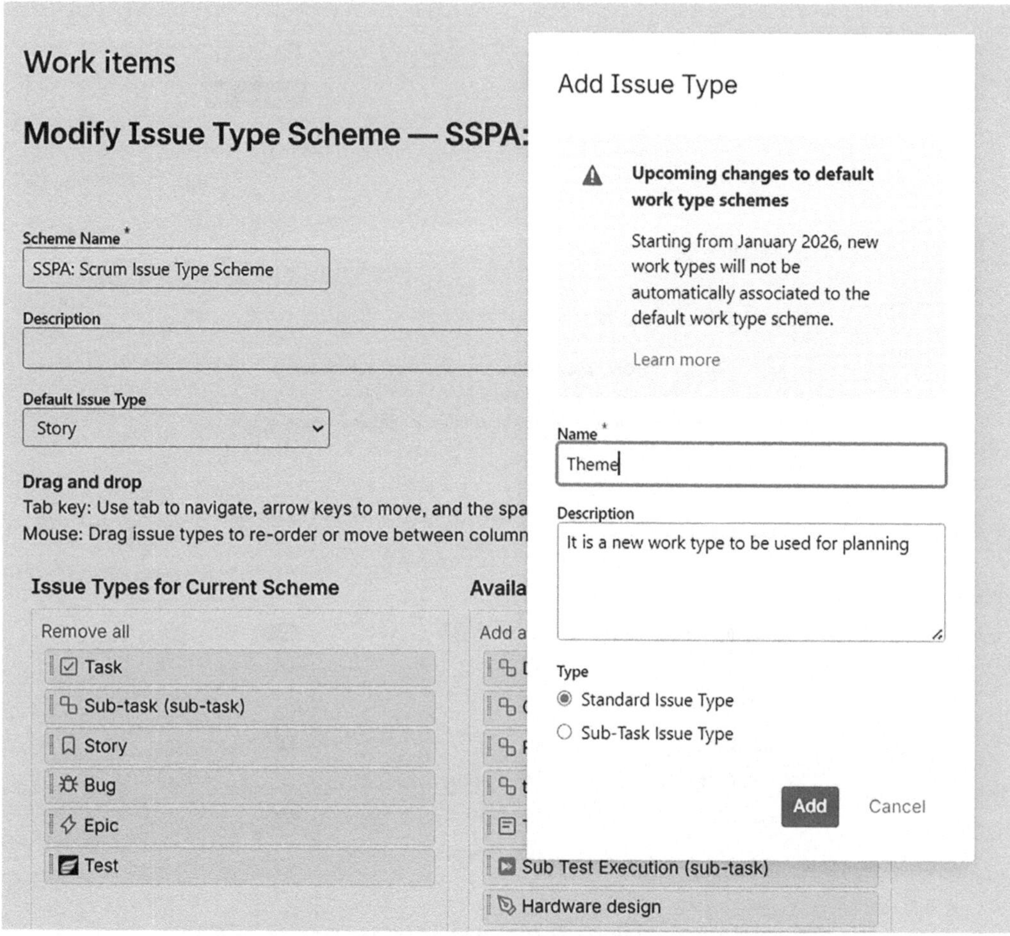

Figure 11.27: *Adding New Work Type to a Work Type Scheme*

- Navigate to **`Plans`** > **`Settings`** > **`Hierarchy`** configuration.
- It will take you to the work itemHierarchy page in Jira.
- Select **`Create level,`** and add a new level called **`Initiative`**.
- Select the Jira work item as **`Initiative`** from the drop-down.
- Select **`Save Changes`**.

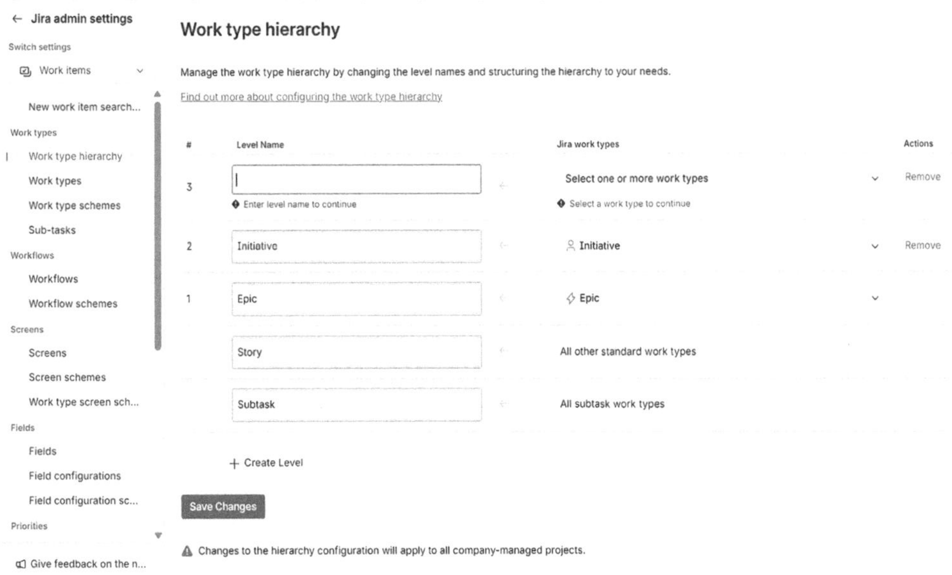

Figure 11.28: *Adding a New Work itemLevel in Hierarchy*

Navigate to the **`Timeline`** view, select **`Create work item,`** and select **`Initiative`**. Similarly, you can add more levels to the work hierarchy, as per your organization's requirement.

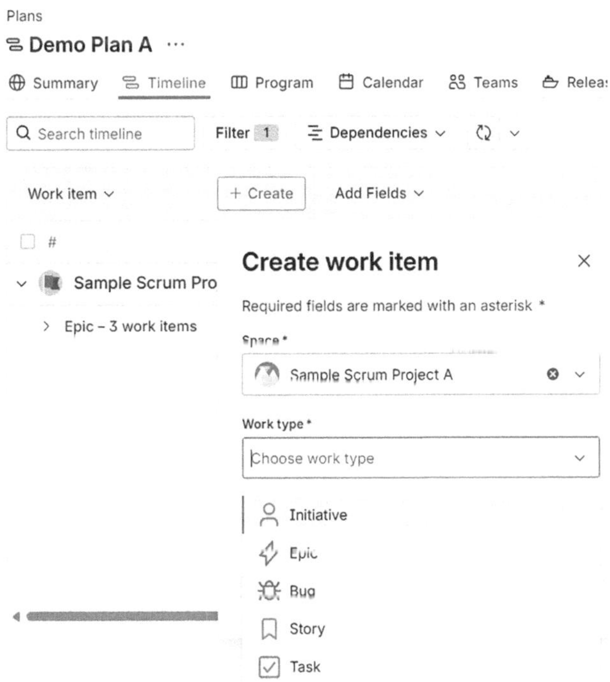

Figure 11.29: *Creating Initiative from Timeline*

Overview of Program Boards in Jira

The Program Board in Jira is an advanced planning feature available in Jira Cloud Premium and Enterprise editions. It provides project managers and stakeholders a clear view of work, priorities and dependencies across multiple teams, which makes it easier to coordinate deliverables over several iterations or quarterly cycles. Designed to support Program Increment (PI) Planning in the SAFe framework, the Program Board focuses on the Epic (level 1) and Story (level 0) hierarchy levels, excluding higher or lower levels like Initiatives and Subtasks. Each plan can have up to two active Program Boards at a time. Once a board's end date has passed, it is automatically marked as inactive, and no longer counted toward the active limit.

Steps to Set up and Use a Program Board in Jira:

1. **Set up your projects and boards**
    i. Ensure that all relevant Jira projects and boards are properly configured before creating your plan.
2. **Create a plan in Jira:**
    i. Go to **`Plans`** > **`Create Plan`**.
    ii. Define the **scope of the plan**, select the **estimation criteria** (for example, story points), and add create teams.
3. **Create teams and associate them with work items:**
    i. Define your teams and link them to the issues or backlog items, they will be responsible for.
4. **Create a Program Board:**
    i. Navigate to **`Programs`**, and select **`Create Program Board`**.
    ii. Enter all the required details such as program name, sprint duration and no. of columns.

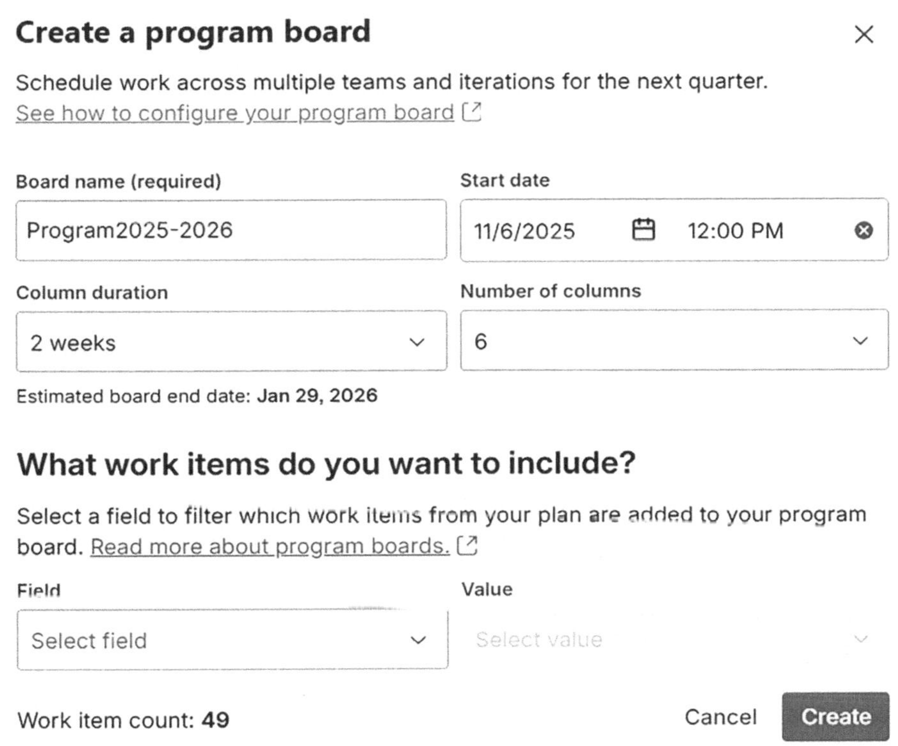

Figure 11.30: *Creating Program Board*

5. **Filter the work items to be included:**
    i. Use **`fields`** to include or exclude specific work items for better focus and clarity.
6. **View the Program Board:**
    i. Once created, the program board displays work items **grouped by team and date**
    ii. Start adding issues to the relevant columns to visualize the planned work.
7. **Create sprints from the backlog and add sprints:**
    i. Build sprints first directly from your backlog and then within your plan by clicking **`Add Sprint`**.
    ii. After all sprints are added, **sprint capacity data** becomes visible on the program board.

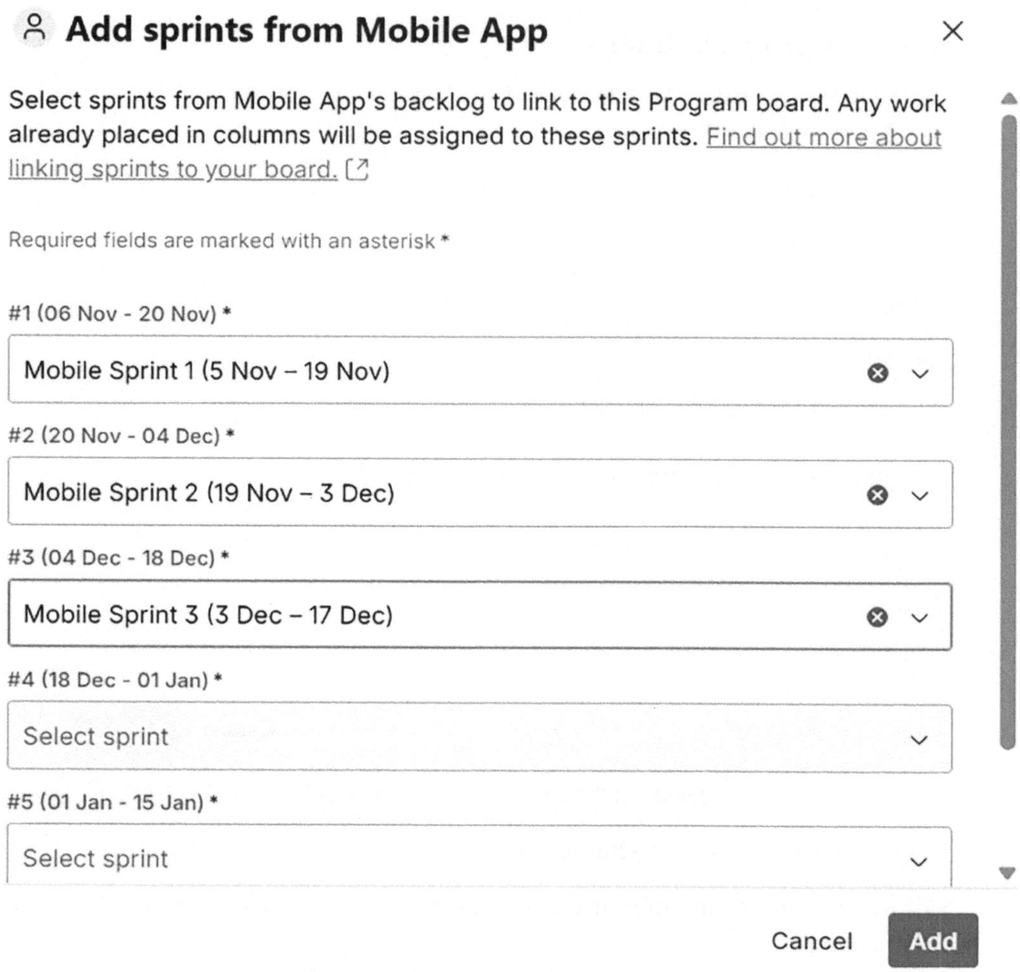

Figure 11.31: *Adding Sprints on Program Board*

8. **Use the Program Board:**
   i. View and manage **dependencies** between issues.
   ii. Edit **sprint capacity** as needed.
   iii. **Drag and drop** work items to adjust planning and allocation across teams.

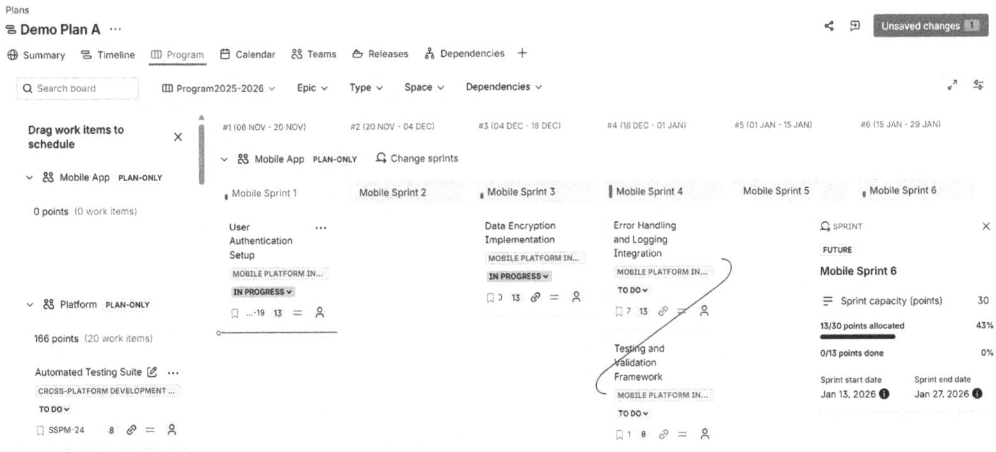

Figure 11.32: *Program Board Features*

9. **Finalize and commit changes:**
   i. Once the planning is complete, review all the updates in your plan.
   ii. Choose to commit changes to Jira, or discard them by selecting **Unsaved changes**.

Overview of Jira Product Discovery

Jira Product Discovery (JPD) is a tool designed specifically for product teams. Its purpose is to capture and prioritize ideas, foster collaboration between business and tech teams, and ensure alignment across all the stakeholders. Thus, by utilizing JPD, product teams can work together, sharing a common vision, and creating products that significantly impact both customers and the business.

With JPD, product teams can do the following:

- JPD helps teams work in a structured way by systematically gathering, organizing, and prioritizing ideas and insights.
- Integrated within Jira, JPD bridges the gap between business and tech teams, connecting product ideas to development work in Jira.
- Jira Product Discovery simplifies the process for product managers to capture and communicate the purpose behind their initiatives.

All Ideas View

In this system, an **`idea`** is considered as the fundamental unit of work. An idea can represent various aspects such as a user problem, an opportunity, or a potential solution. Each idea view includes fields to describe essential attributes such as goals, team, priority score, and impact.

- Moreover, JPD allows you to associate insights with an idea, such as notes from user interviews or support tickets.
- When an idea is ready for active development, it can be linked to delivery tickets in Jira, streamlining the transition from concept to execution.
- People can create ideas in board view and list view, and they can also merge, archive, restore, and use templates for ideas.

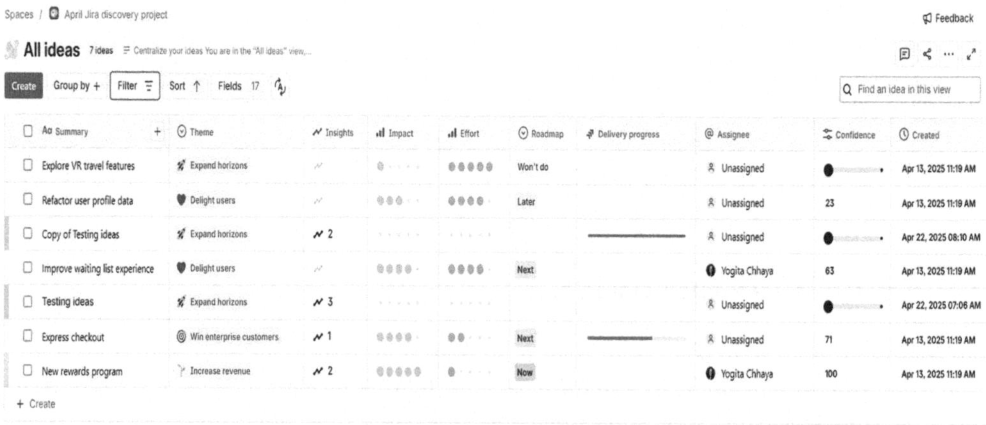

Figure 11.33: *All Ideas View*

Impact Assessment View

Impact assessment allows you to assess the impact. In this view, you can set the goal, and enter the value of the impact, which is the impact on the goal. If the impact is high, a score of five is assigned. You can also enter the names of customers for whom the idea is relevant. Insight is used to capture data explaining the importance of the idea, and helps determine the priority of the idea itself.

Figure 11.34: *Impact Assessment View*

Impact versus Effort View

In the Impact vs. Effort view, **`Impact`** is on the Y-axis, and **`Effort`** is on the X-axis. You can view the impact versus effort in the form of a bubble chart and the impact score on the card on the right-hand side. For maximum impact with minimum effort, the score is considered as 100.

Figure 11.35: Impact versus Effort View

Roadmap View

`Roadmap` view consists of four types of columns: **`Now`**, **`Next`**, **`Later`**, and **`Won't do`**. **`New`** column represents ideas with a high level of certainty that will be implemented soon. The **`Next`** column includes ideas that are expected to have an impact, but further exploration is required. The **`Later`** column contains long-term opportunities that are being tracked, and will be implemented in the future. The **`Won't do`** column includes ideas that will not be implemented.

Figure 11.36: Roadmap View

Timeline View

It is the view where you can create monthly and quarterly Roadmaps. Time should be defined in ideas using a date field.

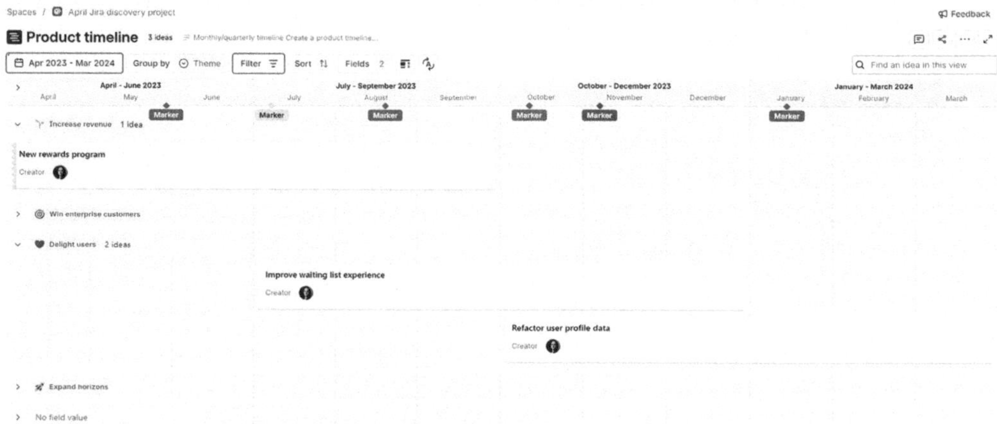

Figure 11.37: *Timeline View*

Delivery Status View

Here, you can see how the ideas are used. You may create a matching **epic** in Jira for each product idea in Jira product discovery. The progress of delivering each idea is shown by the delivery progress. When you are ready to begin working on a specific idea with your team, just go to that idea, find the `Delivery` section, create an **`epic`**, and choose a space where you handle your product delivery.

Figure 11.38: *Delivery Status View*

Steps to Connect JPD with Jira Work Item

Use the following steps to associate a JPD idea with a Jira work item.

1. Open the idea.
2. Go to **`Delivery tickets`**.
3. Select **`Link issue`**, and then choose the Jira Space and the work item.
4. (Optional) Add context or notes, if needed.

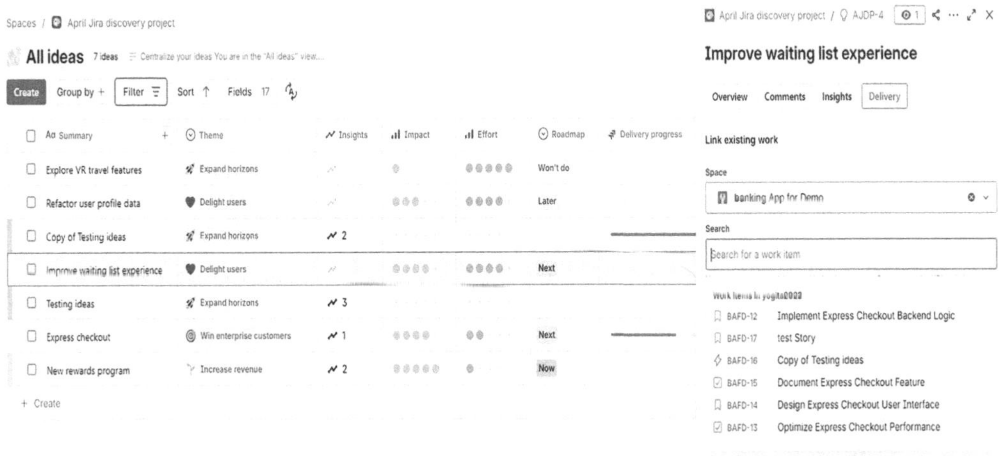

Figure 11.39: *Connecting JPD with Jira Work Item*

Conclusion

We are now familiar with creating spaces with sample data, creating a board based on multiple spaces, or creating one based on a selected filter. We have also learned how to create an Advanced Roadmap, utilize all the features of Advanced Roadmap, and get an overview of the Jira Product Discovery.

In the next chapter, we will learn about the *Atlassian Marketplace and Plugins*.

Points to Remember

- Advanced Roadmaps allow the integration of tasks and spaces from boards and spaces for planning purposes.
- It enables planning for multiple teams.
- You can plan for resource allocation by visualizing team workloads, identifying gaps, and making decisions.

- By considering progress across multiple spaces, Advanced Roadmaps help in the accurate estimation of release dates, considering dependencies and other factors.
- People can track dependencies, manage tasks proactively, and ensure that tasks are completed on time.
- It allows people to plan based on the team's velocity and Capacity.
- Jira Product Discovery is a tool for planning and tracking ideas for Product Managers.
- Jira Product Discovery allows teams to organize and prioritize ideas.
- Product teams can work on ideas with the help of Jira Product Discovery and then align the ideas with the delivery of products.
- Jira Product Discovery has a separate Roadmap view and Timeline view.

Use Cases with Reference Links

1. **Advanced Roadmap Hierarchy.**

   https://community.atlassian.com/t5/Jira-Software-questions/Advanced-Roadmap-Hierarchy/qaq-p/2358694

2. **How to make a specific Work type visible on Advanced Roadmaps without changing hierarchy?**

   https://community.atlassian.com/t5/Advanced-Roadmaps-questions/how-to-make-a-specific-issuetype-visible-on-Advanced-Roadmaps/qaq-p/2286898

3. **How do we implement dual hierarchy in Advanced Roadmaps?**

   https://community.atlassian.com/t5/Advanced-Roadmaps-questions/How-do-we-implement-dual-hierarchy-in-Advanced-Roadmaps/qaq-p/2344352

4. **Advanced Roadmap work item hierarchy configuration - adding a Work type between Epic and Story.**

   https://community.atlassian.com/t5/Advanced-Roadmaps-questions/Advanced-Roadmap-Issue-Hierarchy-configuration-adding-an-issue/qaq-p/2268111

5. **Add Sprint to Plan on Advanced Roadmaps.**

   https://community.atlassian.com/t5/Jira-Software-questions/Add-Sprint-to-Plan-on-Advanced-Roadmaps/qaq-p/2363772

6. **Enable Capacity Planning in Advanced Roadmaps.**

   https://community.atlassian.com/t5/Advanced-Roadmaps-questions/Enable-capacity-planning-in-Advanced-Roadmaps/qaq-p/2012131

7. **Setting Capacity in Advanced Roadmaps.**

   https://community.atlassian.com/t5/Advanced-Roadmaps-questions/Setting-capacity-in-Advanced-Roadmaps/qaq-p/2487781

8. **Capacity Planning Availability.**

   https://community.atlassian.com/t5/Jira-Software-questions/Capacity-planning-avaliability/qaq-p/2446956

9. **Unable to Access Product Discovery after Migration.**

   https://community.atlassian.com/t5/Jira-Product-Discovery-questions/Unable-to-access-Product-Discovery-after-migration/qaq-p/2179796

10. **Why are Advanced Roadmaps miscalculating Sprint Capacity?**

    https://community.atlassian.com/t5/Advanced-Roadmaps-questions/Why-is-Advanced-Roadmaps-miscalculating-sprint-capacity/qaq-p/1974521

CHAPTER 12
Atlassian Marketplace and Plugins

Introduction

The Atlassian Marketplace is like an online store for businesses and teams where they can find a wide range of Apps and Plugins to make their Atlassian tools work better. It was launched in 2012. These apps are created either by Atlassian or other companies, providing you with a wide variety to select from and install. Marketplace offers apps and plugins for all of Atlassian's products like- Jira, Confluence, Bitbucket, and Trello, and has a large and growing community of developers. In this chapter, we will learn how to access the Atlassian marketplace, select Plugins, and details about some popular Plugins for administrators and teams.

Structure

In this chapter, we will cover the following topics:

- Atlassian Marketplace
- Selecting Applications from Atlassian Marketplace
- Understanding Key Terminology of the Applications
- Steps to Enable and Install Marketplace Apps
- Admin-tool Plugins for Jira Administrators
    - Script Runner for Jira
    - Jira Miscellaneous Workflow Extensions
    - JSU Automation Suite for Jira
- Popular Plugins
    - Custom Charts for Jira Reports, Dashboards, Graphs and Tables
    - X-ray Test Management for Jira
    - Zephyr -Test Management and Automation for Jira

Atlassian Marketplace

The Atlassian Marketplace is a platform where customers can explore and purchase Atlassian products and Plugins to extend the functionality of their Atlassian products. These Plugins can be developed by Atlassian or third-party developers. Other organizations that develop Plugin applications for Atlassian products can become partners and list their products on the Atlassian marketplace. The marketplace lets the customers pick, and use what they need, making their work easier and more efficient. To access the Atlassian marketplace, go to **https://marketplace.atlassian.com/** on the browser.

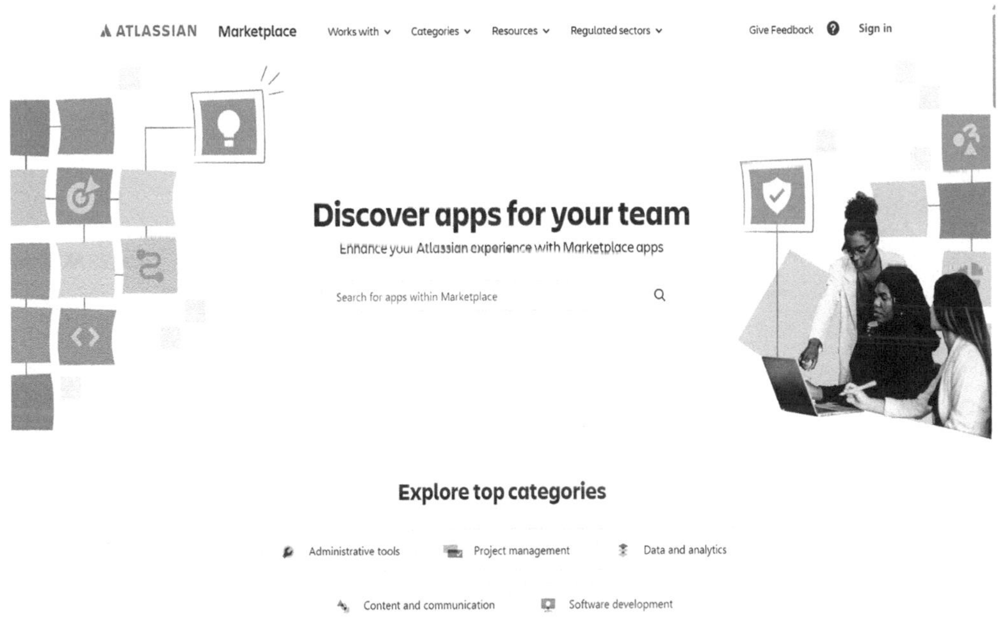

Figure 12.1: *Accessing Atlassian Marketplace*

Selecting Applications from Atlassian Marketplace

If you are new to the marketplace, the simplest way to search is to type the name in the search bar. However, there are other ways to search for applications within the marketplace. The options are mentioned as follows:

On the home page of the Atlassian Marketplace, you will see a list of five main categories of marketplace apps. To select an app, navigate to one of the main categories, and click on it.

Under each main category, there are additional subcategories, as listed below:

- Solutions Hub
- Project Management
- Admin Tools
- Runs on Atlassian
- Atlassian Rovo
- Software Development
- Content and Communication
- Data and Analytics
- Cloud Fortified Apps
- Spotlight
- Best sellers
- Rising Star

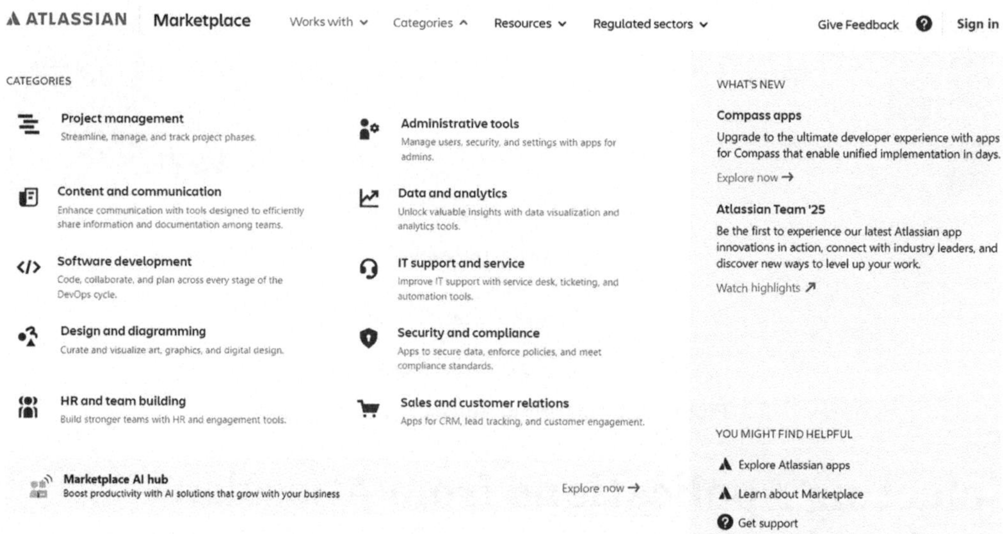

***Figure 12.2:** Options for Selecting Plugins*

Customers can select **apps** from the **Categories** dropdown, and then choose a hosting type from the **Hosting Types** dropdown as well as sort the results based on ratings or other criteria.

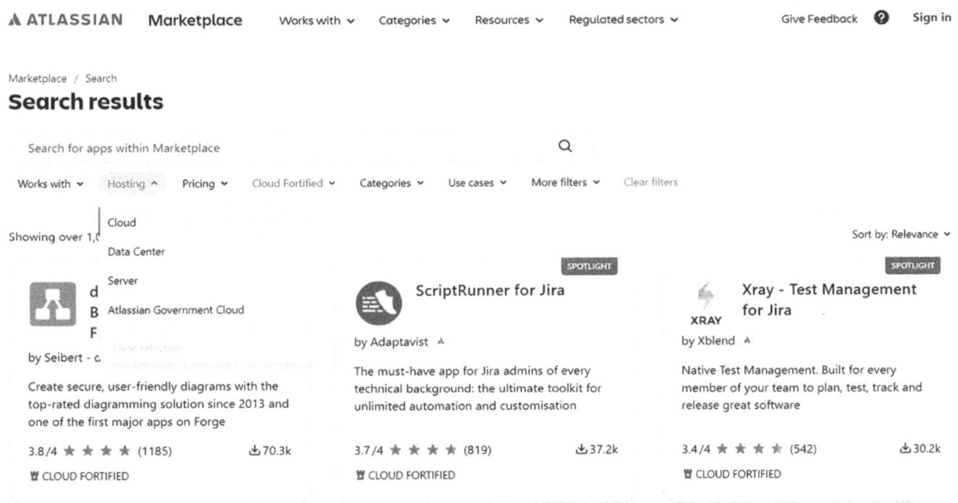

Figure 12.3: *Filters to Select an Application*

While selecting an app, you can apply various filters. For example, Works with which Atlassian apps, Hosting options, Pricing, Cloud Fortified, Categories, Use cases and much more. These filters help customers find and select the right app easily.

Understanding Key Terminologies of the Applications

Once you select the application or plugin, it displays all the information about it in sequence as follows:

1. The name of the application.
2. The name of the application's marketplace partner.
3. Type of hosting - whether it is for Jira Cloud, Server, or Data Center.
4. Rating from the users.
5. Number of installations done.
6. It displays whether the app has been enrolled in a particular program, such as the Cloud Fortified program.
7. Various tags indicating if it is supported by the vendor, Atlassian product name, and other tags.
8. Overview of the application's main features and some more details.
9. Reviews from all the users.

10. Pricing: Customers can enter the number of users, and check the pricing details based on the number of users. It also displays if it is free for 10 users. It has a cost calculator based on the number of users, and users get an option to select the billing cycle as monthly or annual.
11. Privacy and security: It includes information related to data storage and management, security, compliance, and any certification such as cloud fortified.
12. Support: All information related to app support, such as Contact, Documentation, Support resources, and Community.
13. Versions: This displays information about all the available versions.
14. Installation: Steps to try and install the application in your instance.
15. Information about whether the application is available for Cloud, Server, Data Center or Atlassian Government Cloud.

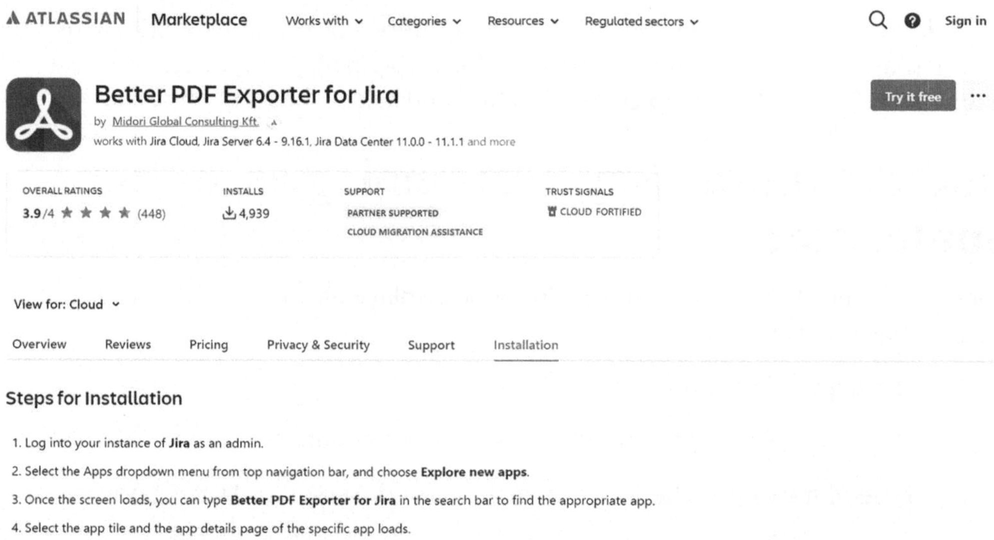

Figure 12.4: *Understanding Key Terminology of an Application*

Steps to Enable and Install Marketplace Apps

Permissions required: To Enable or Disable Plugins in Jira, you must be a Site Administrator.

If you are a Jira Administrator, click **`Add Apps`** under the **`work item summary`** on the **`work item view`**. Jira will prompt you to add apps. By clicking **`Add apps`**, Jira will display the page to **`Find New Apps`**. Jira administrators can explore and install applications from this page.

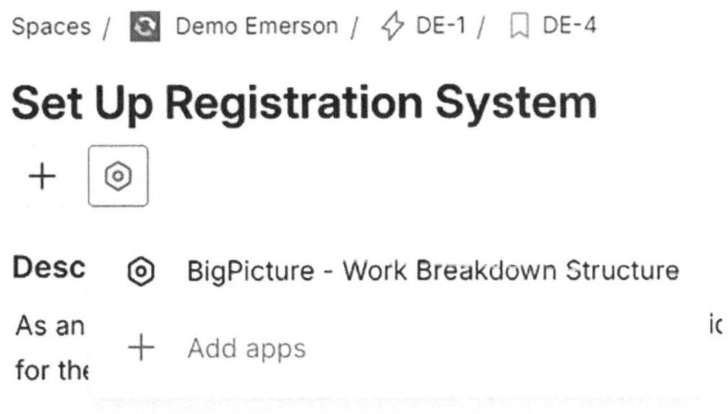

Figure 12.5: *Adding Apps from the Work Item View*

Connected Apps

To manage apps, navigate to **`admin.atlassian.com`** > **`Connected apps`**

Under connected apps you can view apps installed within your site, manage settings for your apps and view additional details for each app.

View Jira Apps

In **`Connected Apps`**, use the search field and category menu to filter visible apps. By default, the list shows apps needing admin action such as those in trial or nearing expiry.

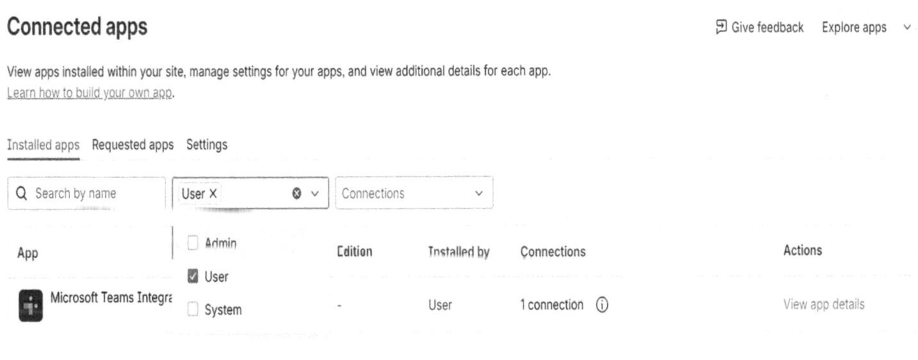

Figure 12.6: *Searching and Filtering Apps*

Categories:

- **Paid via Atlassian:** Displays purchased apps, whether from Atlassian or third-party vendors.
- **User-installed apps:** These are the apps added separately from the base

product and bundled with Jira Cloud. These can be enabled or disabled, though essential modules cannot be turned off.

- **System apps:** These are pre-installed with Jira Cloud and essential to site functionality. You can disable only if advised by Atlassian Support.

Use **`View app details`** to see more information.

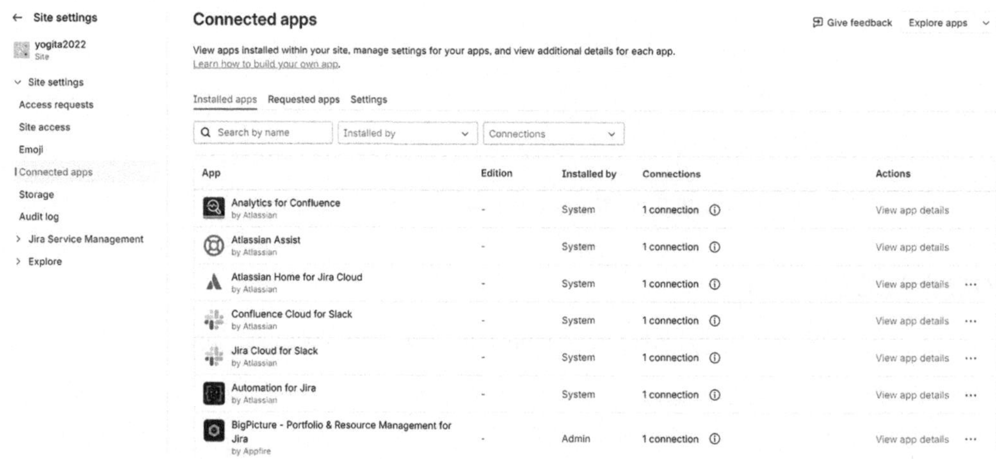

Figure 12.7: *Viewing Apps and Managing Settings*

Find and Install New Apps:

1. Navigate to **`Apps > Explore more apps`** to search, and filter apps that enhance Jira.
2. Click **`Free Trial`** to test or subscribe.

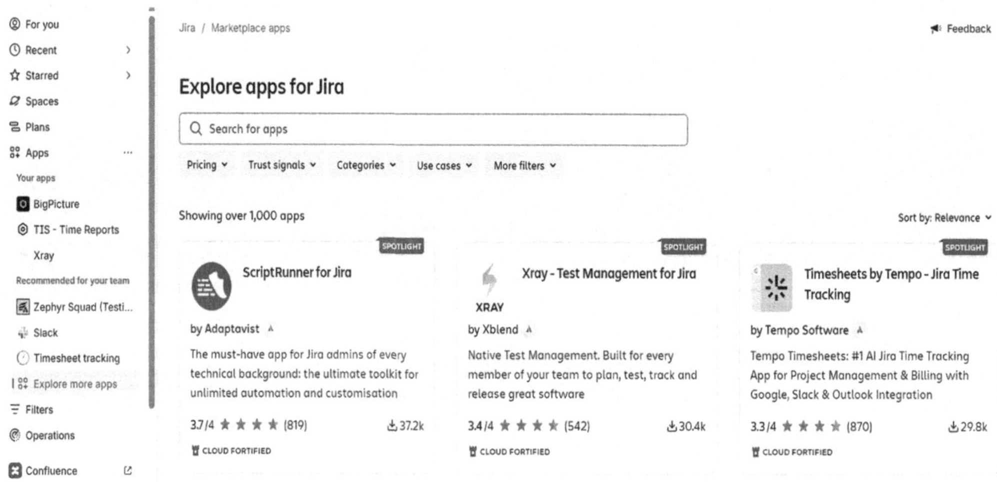

Figure 12.8: *Discovering Apps from Atlassian Marketplace*

Trials are usually run for one month from your next billing date. If not cancelled before the trial ends, a paid subscription begins automatically. You can stop the trial anytime from the app administration page.

Trials can be reactivated during the original period but once it expires, you will need to subscribe through the Manage apps page to continue using the app.

Important Application Settings

Jira Admins can do the important settings. For example, Allow/Block users from installing apps, Enable developer mode and **`Access to analytics and logs on installation`**.

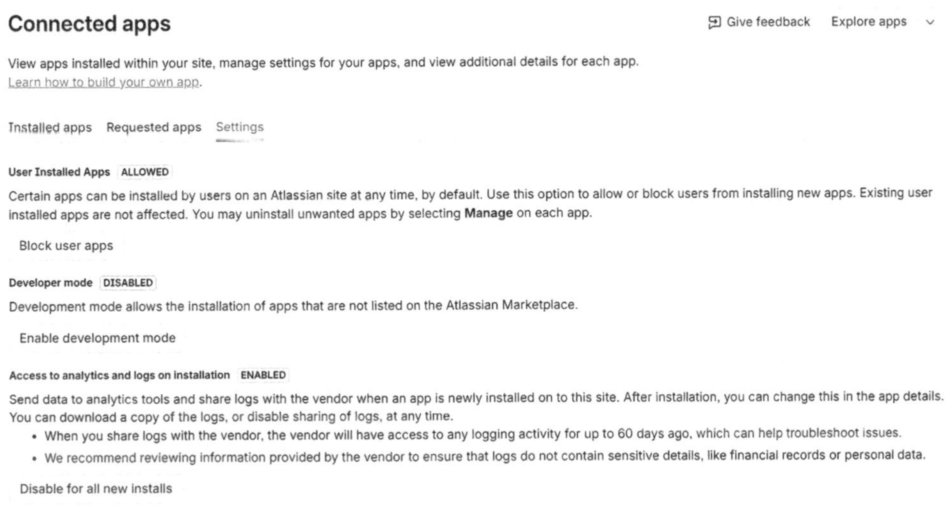

***Figure 12.9**: Important Application Settings*

Cancel App Subscription and Uninstall

To uninstall the app, navigate to **`View App Details`** > Select '**`Uninstall`**' to cancel the app.

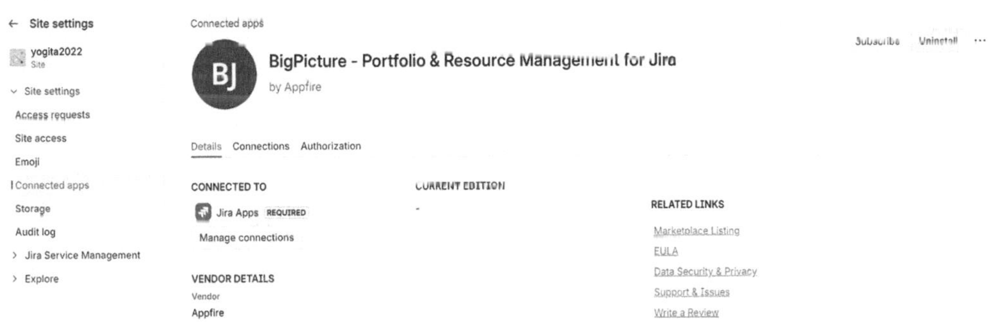

***Figure 12.10**: Uninstalling the Application*

Admin-tool Plugins for Jira Administrators

In this section, we will provide an overview of applications specifically helpful for administrators. Navigate to **`Admin-tools`** from **`Categories`** on the Atlassian marketplace, where it displays all the apps useful for Jira Administrators.

Script Runner for Jira

- This app can be installed by following the installation process explained.
- This application offers additional security, reliability, and support.
- Users can try the free version, evaluate it, and then make a purchase.

Link to access and install Script Runner for Jira:

https://marketplace.atlassian.com/apps/6820/scriptrunner-for-jira?hosting=cloud&tab=overview

Overview of features:

- This application allows you to deploy unlimited automations with remarkable accuracy, save time, and enhance team efficiency.
- Several features do not require coding knowledge. To begin utilizing the power of Script Runner, try using the ready templates provided.
- Tackle significant tasks, such as bulk work item updating, triggering actions in response to events like work item creation, scheduling routine tasks at any frequency, and enhancing search with specific JQL functions.
- Scheduled Jobs enable you to automate script running at regular intervals, saving your administrators time, and reducing the risk of human error. You can specify when and how often a job should run.
- You can also use Script Runner for Jira Cloud's built-in scripts as an alternative to creating your own code, allowing you to automate manual, complex, and time-consuming tasks.
- Behaviors provide customizable options to modify the behavior of fields in Jira. For instance, you can create a behavior that hides a field for a specific user group until it becomes relevant for them to interact with that particular field.

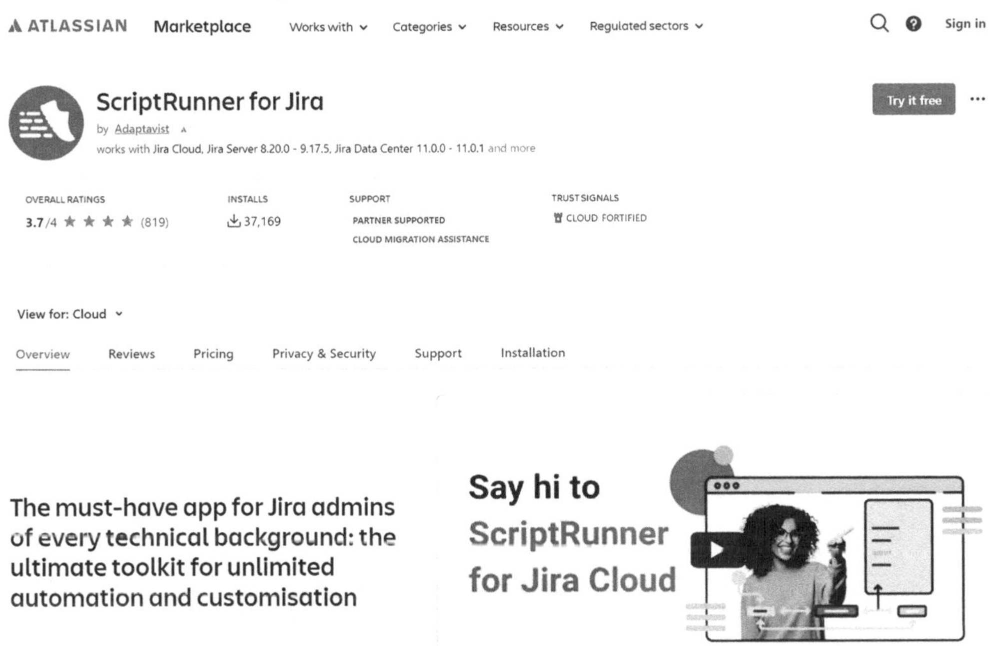

Figure 12.11: *Script Runner for Jira*

There are many other features in Script Runner for Jira that are helpful to Jira administrators, helping them save time, and increase efficiency as well as productivity.

Jira Miscellaneous Workflow Extensions

- This app can be installed by following the installation process explained.
- This application offers additional security, reliability, and support.
- Users can try the free version, evaluate it, and then make a purchase.

Link to access and install Jira Miscellaneous Workflow Extensions:

https://marketplace.atlassian.com/apps/292/jira-misc-workflow-extensions-jmwe?hosting=cloud&tab=overview

Overview of features:

- It is a flexible workflow automation application that combines no-code, point-and-click configurations with robust scripting capabilities.
- It allows you to create and customize workflows according to your preferences, utilizing an expanding collection of post functions, conditions, and validators that are beyond the native Jira features.
    - Users without coding experience can easily modify workflows using Jira

expressions with the help of on-the-fly syntax checking, inline help, and a script tester. Users can also craft their own conditions, validators, and post functions.

- JMWE supports Live Fields for Cloud workflows and provides improved scripting.

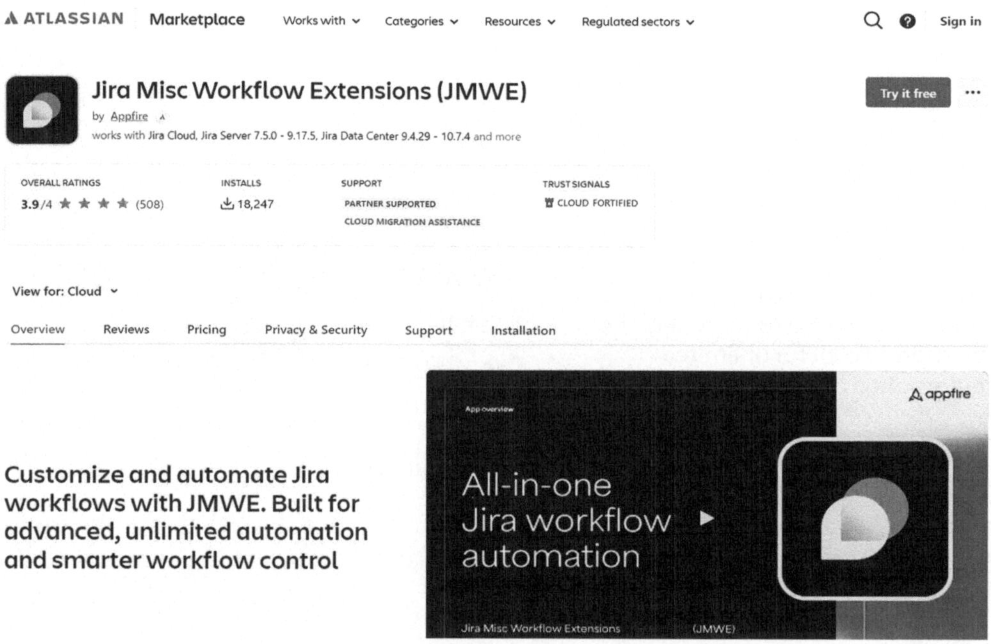

Figure 12.12: *Jira Misc. Workflow Extensions*

Jira Miscellaneous Workflow Extensions offer many features beneficial to Jira administrators, enabling them to save time, and enhance efficiency and productivity.

JSU Automation Suite for Jira Workflow

- This app can be installed by following the installation process explained.
- This application offers additional security, reliability, and support.
- Users can try the free version, evaluate it, and then make a purchase.

Link to access and install JSU Automation Suite for Jira Workflow:

https://marketplace.atlassian.com/apps/5048/jsu-automation-suite-for-jira-workflows?hosting=cloud&tab=overview

Overview of features:

- JSU offers an intuitive automation solution for Jira administrators who prefer to avoid coding and complexity, providing a no-code approach.

- Workflow configuration is consolidated into a simple and understandable **WHEN-IF-THEN** format, all managed in one central location.
- Edit workflows swiftly from the Agile space board, navigate seamlessly using global features, and gain a clear, at-a-glance overview of saved workflow rules for efficient maintenance.
- **Some popular use cases include:**
  - Closing parent issue when all sub-tasks are closed.
  - Customizing workflows with JQL and preconditions.
  - Add a comment to an issue.
  - Set the Assignee field to *Unassigned* when the work item moves back to ToDo.
  - Pre-populate fields in linked issues.
  - Automatically share attachments with team members.
- Thus, JSU Automation Suite for Jira offers unlimited workflow automations in Jira, non technical users handling their own automations and reducing the workload on admins and data accuracy, all in a no-code workflow automation tool.

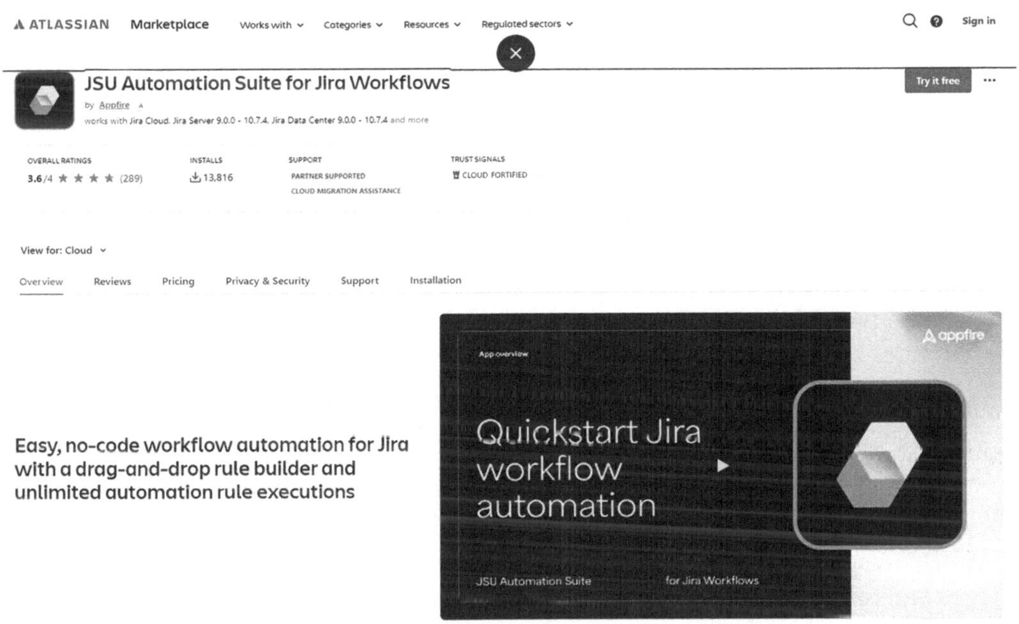

Figure 12.13: *Jira Automation Suite for Jira Workflows*

JSU Automation Suite for Jira offers other features beneficial to Jira administrators, enabling them to save time, and enhance efficiency and productivity.

Popular Plugins

In this section, we will learn about an overview of a few popular Plugins to enhance report generation, statistical analysis, and test management.

Custom Charts for Jira Reports, Dashboards, Graphs, and Tables

This is an app that can be used with Jira as a Plugin to create detailed reports.

- This app can be installed by following the installation process explained.
- This application offers additional security, reliability, and support.
- Users can try the free version, evaluate it, and then make a purchase.

Link to access and install Custom Charts for Jira Reports, Dashboards, Graphs and Tables:

https://marketplace.atlassian.com/apps/1220925/custom-charts-for-jira-reports-and-time-in-status?hosting=cloud&tab=overview

Overview of features:

- The plugin has a feature to explore over 10 possible chart types in one or two dimensions, such as pie, bar, line, or table.
- Users can utilize shared dashboards in both Jira and Jira Service Management for collaborative monitoring.
- The tool provides support for various Third-Party Apps (such as X-ray, Advanced Roadmaps, Mobile for Jira, and more), JSM Request Types, Organizations, and Channels.
- It is possible to create custom JQL, saved filters, and active search options to cater to the needs of advanced users.
- Users can evaluate the team's productivity and identify potential obstacles by analyzing the time they spend on their tasks.
- Teams can assess the team's efficiency and investigate potential obstacles by examining the duration they invest in their assignments.
- It allows a wide range of customizations, including custom ordering, merging and renaming values, showing/hiding segments, and more.
- It provides features to create comprehensive charts and reports for your Jira Dashboards, reporting on various metrics, including Time in Status.
- Custom Charts for Jira supports features which are helpful to create richer charting, smarter filters and broader tool integration.

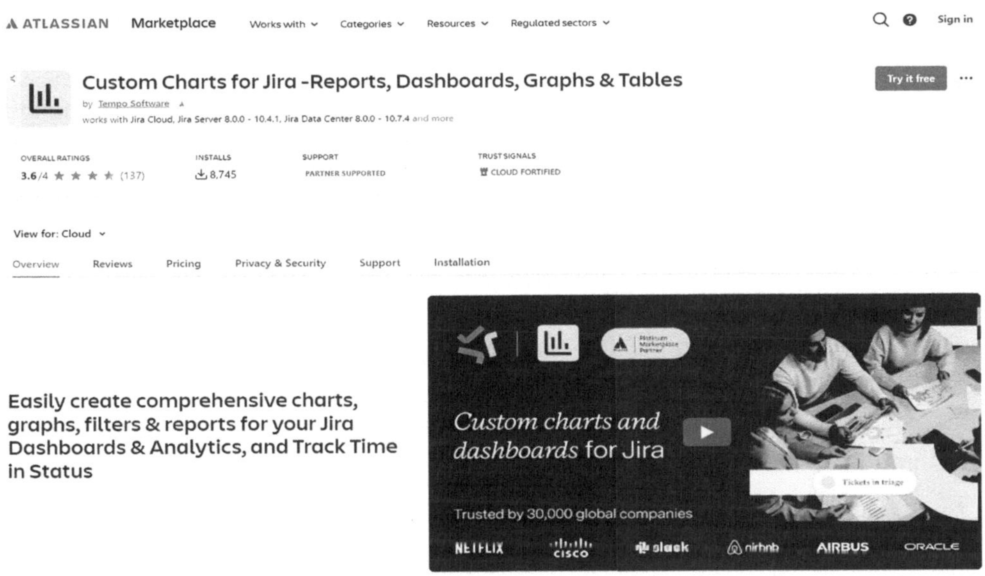

Figure 12.14: *Custom Charts for Jira Reports and Time in Status*

This plugin offers a diverse range of features that teams can leverage to create charts and reports for statistical analysis, as well as track important metrics.

X-ray Test Management for Jira

This is an app used to do Test Management with Jira.

- This app can be installed by following the installation process explained.
- This application offers additional security, reliability, and support.
- Users can try the free version, evaluate it, and then make a purchase.

Link to access and install X-ray Test Management for Jira:

https://marketplace.atlassian.com/apps/1211769/xray-test-management-for-jira?hosting=cloud&tab=overview

Overview of features:

- Users can efficiently manage both manual and automated tests as Jira issues.
- This application allows you to customize screens, fields, and workflows.
- It supports the entire STLC covering Planning, Design, Execution, and Reporting.
- It allows us to define tests in cucumber language, and integrate them with test automation frameworks.

- This has a feature to arrange tests in folders and test sets for better organization.
- It allows the creation of test plans to monitor a specific set of tests, including both planned and unplanned test executions.
- This allows us to execute tests across various environments and consolidate the results.
- Users can utilize the Continuous Integration (CI) tool to report test results through the provided REST API.
- It allows us to examine the test coverage of requirements using interactive charts.
- This has a feature to analyze the status of test entities by Version, Test Plan, and Execution Environment.
- It allows AI-driven test-case generation, enhanced test-repository behaviors, test case versioning and full traceability.

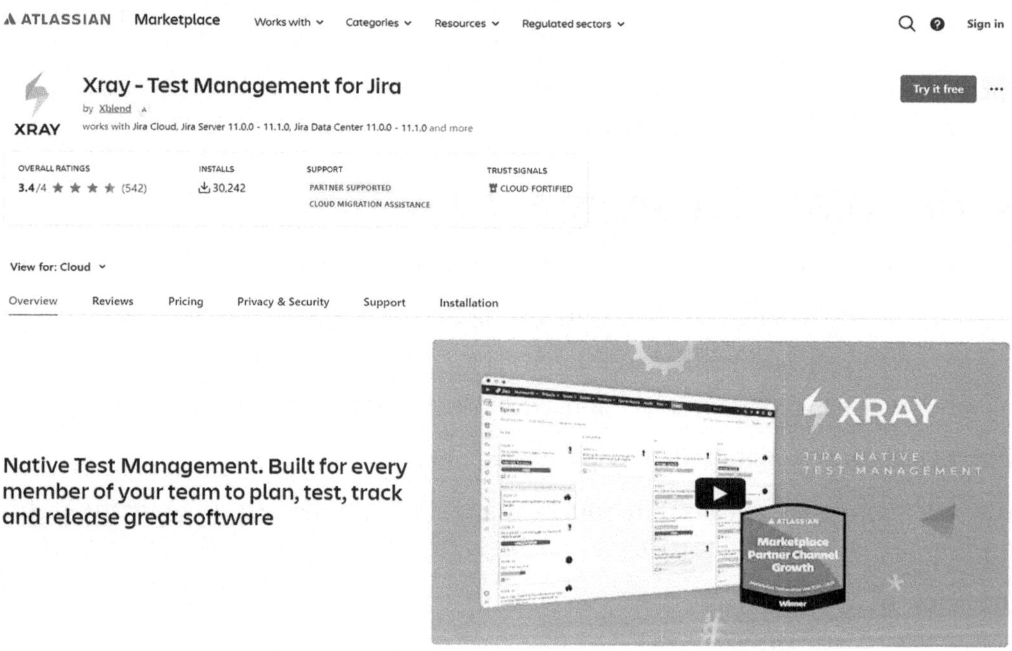

Figure 12.15: *X-ray Test Management for Jira*

X-ray Test Management for Jira is a feature-rich tool to plan, test, track, and release software.

Zephyr-Test Management and Automation for Jira

This is an app used for Test Management with Jira.

- This app can be installed by following the installation process explained.
- This application offers additional security, reliability, and support.
- Users can try the free version, evaluate it, and then make a purchase.

Link to access and install Zephyr-Test Management and Automation for Jira:

https://marketplace.atlassian.com/apps/1213259/zephyr-scale-test-management-for-jira?tab=overview&hosting=cloud

Overview of features:

- It allows monitoring requirements across test cases, test cycles, test plans, and execution outcomes. Users can access dynamic and comprehensive traceability along with test-case coverage statistics through integrated cross-project reports and gadgets.
- This enhances testing capabilities with Behavior-Driven Development (BDD), CI/CD, and automation integration using complimentary REST API, allowing seamless scalability.
- Users can share automated test execution results from tools like Jenkins, Bamboo, and others.
- It allows users to effectively organize extensive test case libraries using folders and test suites. They can reuse test cases across projects with parameters and test data. They can implement test cycles to track test executions systematically.
- This allows to maintain end-to-end traceability among requirements, test cases, and defects for comprehensive project management.
- It is possible to integrate with multiple automation tools like Selenium, JUnit, NUnit, and Frameworks.
- It also offers AI-powered no-code automation, including test-step suggestions, record and playback, codeless test creation, speeding up regressions and broadening test coverage.

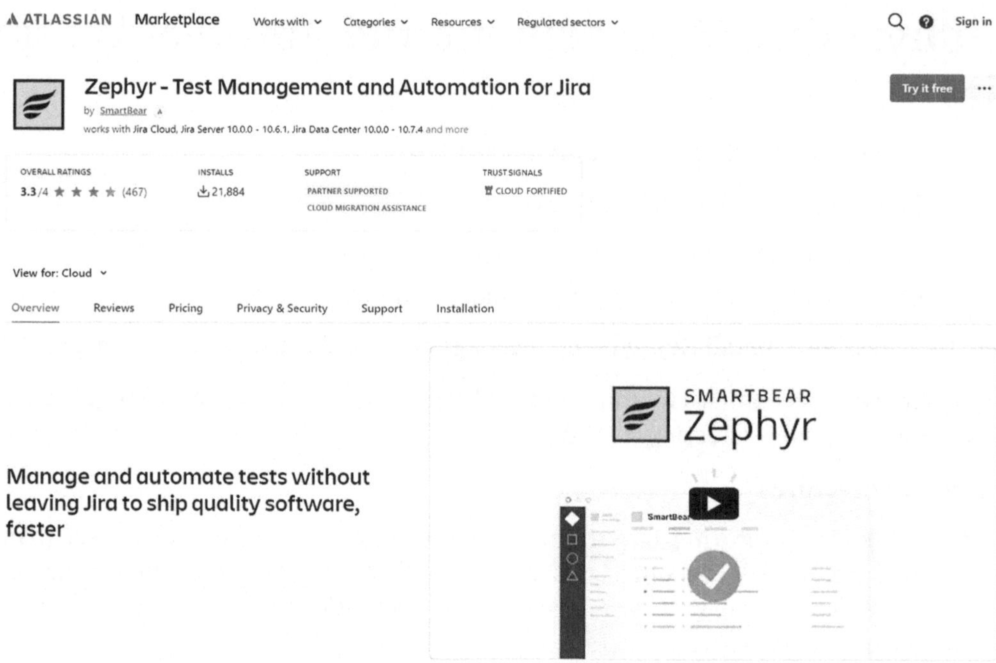

Figure 12.16: *Zephyr Scale-Test Management for Jira*

Zephyr Test Management and Automation for Jira has many advanced features that can be explored in detail for test planning, reporting, and managing automation testing.

Conclusion

We have now become familiar with accessing the Atlassian Marketplace and selecting Plugins from the marketplace. We have also learned the criteria for selecting the Plugins and how to install, update, and uninstall them. Additionally, we have explored admin tools that can be useful and a few popular Plugins in other categories.

Implementing Jira in the real world requires evaluating the tool to ensure it aligns with your needs, planning, effective training, and consistent communication. Start by defining workflows customized for your teams and provide detailed training so that they understand all the features. Regularly update workflows and all other elements based on changing requirements. Utilize features such as reporting, analytics, and insights. If in doubt, Interact with the Atlassian community. Jira has evolved into a family of products, so explore new features and implement them to align with your project management and other requirements.

Points to Remember

- Only Jira Administrators can add or remove applications to Jira from the Atlassian marketplace.
- Understand all the important terms mentioned on the page after selecting the application.
- Verify Plugin compatibility with your Atlassian product version.
- Check user reviews for reliability and satisfaction ratings.
- Read the documentation for installing the app and evaluating the features.
- Check the level of customer support provided by the vendor.
- Assess if the Plugin can be tailored to your specific needs.
- Ensure the Plugin complies with data security standards.
- Evaluate if the Plugin can scale with your organization's growth.
- Understand pricing based on number of users, licensing terms, and additional costs.
- There are various categories of Plugins, including tools for administrators, test management, code review, and many more. Explore the Atlassian marketplace site and make a purchase after evaluating.

Use Cases with Reference Links

1. **What plugins should I try in Jira?**

   https://community.atlassian.com/t5/Welcome-Center-questions/What-plugins-should-I-try-in-Jira/qaq-p/2255234

2. **Time of Administration / Maintenance in operational condition:**

   https://community.atlassian.com/t5/Jira-Software-questions/Time-of-administration-Maintenance-in-operational-condition/qaq-p/2408683

3. **I only use the in-built Jira Automation, but I want to learn how to use Script Runner.**

   https://community.atlassian.com/t5/Jira-questions/Scriptrunner/qaq-p/2115830

4. **How to Create Flexible and Custom Reports, Charts, and Graphs in Jira?**

   https://community.atlassian.com/t5/App-Central/How-to-Create-Flexible-and-Custom-Reports-Charts-and-Graphs-in/ba-p/1957785

5. **Looking for Recommendations – Add on App Tool for Administrators:**

   https://community.atlassian.com/t5/Jira-Software-questions/Looking-For-Recommendations-Addon-App-Tool-For-Administrators/qaq-p/1997455

6. **Recommendations for apps - attaching text to tickets, user stories, and so on, only visible by me:**

   https://community.atlassian.com/t5/Jira-Software-questions/Recommendations-for-apps-attaching-text-to-tickets-user-stories/qaq-p/2470833

7. **I cannot see the Custom Chart option anywhere in the dashboard. I am actually trying to create an open vs closed chart:**

   https://community.atlassian.com/t5/Jira-Service-Management/Custom-charts/qaq-p/2442709

8. **How do I add a Custom Charts plug-in to my instance?**

   https://community.atlassian.com/t5/Jira-Software-questions/How-do-I-add-Custom-Charts-plug-in-to-my-instance/qaq-p/2127929

9. **How to address rows in eazyBI?**

   https://community.atlassian.com/t5/Jira-Software-questions/How-to-address-rows-in-eazyBI/qaq-p/2322513

10. **Recommended Apps for Scrum Dashboard:**

    https://community.atlassian.com/t5/Jira-Software-questions/Recommended-apps-for-Scrum-dashboard/qaq-p/2314992

CHAPTER 13
Atlassian Intelligence, Getting Started with Rovo and Creating Agents

Introduction

Artificial intelligence (AI) is the technology that helps computers and software learn from data, make decisions and take actions in a way that feels similar to how humans solve problems. As Jira continues to evolve, Atlassian Intelligence and Rovo add a new level of support for Agile and all types of teams. In this chapter, we will explore how Atlassian Intelligence and Rovo are shaping a new way of working in Jira and across the Atlassian ecosystem. As teams grow and projects become more complex, using AI to support daily work has become essential for staying organized and working efficiently. We will understand the key terminologies of Rovo, understand how Atlassian Intelligence can be applied into your Jira environment and learn how to create helpful AI agents that can support your team's goals. Thus, whether you are managing projects, improving workflows or supporting teams as an admin, this chapter will guide you step-by-step so that you can confidently introduce AI into your Agile setup.

Structure

In this chapter, we will cover the following topics:

- Why Teams Struggle When Information is Scattered
- Rovo-A Modern Innovative Teammate
- Comparing Atlassian Intelligence and Rovo

- Atlassian Intelligence
- Top Capabilities of Atlassian Intelligence
- Key Rovo Features for Streamlined Workflows

- Key Rovo and AI Settings Every Administrators Must Know
  - Settings to activate AI
  - Settings to deactivate AI
- Rovo Settings
  - Turning on/off Rovo
  - Verifying Rovo Activation in Your Organization
- A Look Inside the Teamwork Graph
  - Defining Teamwork Graph
  - How the Teamwork Graph Powers Rovo
  - Key Capabilities of the Teamwork Graph
  - Real-World Impact
- What Rovo Connectors Do and How They Work
  - Understanding Rovo Connectors
  - Types of Rovo Connectors
  - How Permissions Work
  - Connectors that Need Admin Setup
  - Connectors that do not Need Admin Setup
  - Connectors Per Site
- A Guide to the Ready to use Rovo Agents
- Steps to Build Your Own Rovo Agent
- How to Duplicate and Share Rovo Agents
- Accessing Rovo Use cases and Prompts
- Real-World Examples: Automating Tasks with Rovo Agents
- Building a No-code Rovo Agent Setup Example
- Best Practices for Designing Powerful Rovo Agents
- AI with Humans Partnering for Smarter Collaboration

Why Teams Struggle When Information is Scattered

When a team's information is scattered across chats, emails, files and forgotten notes, work slows down and people do not realize it at first. People spend more time searching than doing. Decisions take longer because no one is sure where the latest update can be accessed or who even made it. People get confused and small delays start to add up. This is exactly the problem Rovo is built to solve. It helps to bring everything together so that teams can think clearly, move faster and make decisions with confidence.

Rovo A Modern Innovative Teammate

Rovo helps fix the challenges by acting as a smart layer across all the Atlassian tools and third-party apps. It supports teams in three different ways:

- **Find:** Rovo allows to search across Jira, Confluence, and connected tools such as SharePoint and Figma to give you clear and accurate answers. You can use everyday language to find Jira issues, Confluence pages or project updates. It understands what you mean and saves time by cutting down on manual searching. For example, you can ask Rovo to find all issues assigned to you in the last week or you can ask to find all linked issues in Jira.
- **Learn:** Rovo makes it easy to explore your company's knowledge and get useful insights through features such as knowledge cards, smart search and conversational chat. This helps teams stay updated, onboard faster and make better decisions with less effort. For example, you can find out why a particular Epic was delayed with Summaries, Updates and Confluence pages.
- **Act:** With automation rules, powerful Rovo Agents and Atlassian integrations, you can take action instantly. Whether you need to assign tasks, update a backlog or implement a workflow, Rovo helps you move from insight to action in seconds. And it always respects the permissions you have set. For example, you can ask Rovo to assign unassigned tasks with high priority to you in Jira.

Comparing Atlassian Intelligence and Rovo

As AI has become an important part of day-to-day work, here, we will understand tools like Atlassian Intelligence and Rovo. Further, we will cover various features and settings related to the same.

Atlassian Intelligence

Atlassian Intelligence offers a set of AI tools that help people work faster and more smoothly. Teams can summarize things such as meeting notes or Jira issues, provide helpful suggestions when you are writing up an issue and let you search using everyday language. It also supports you while writing in Confluence by suggesting clearer wording, fixing grammar and even rewriting sections when needed. It is an app that can be integrated with apps such as Jira, Confluence, Jira Service Management and Bitbucket to enhance productivity.

Overall, you can think of Atlassian Intelligence as a built-in assistant inside each Atlassian product, designed to make your work easier and more efficient.

Top Capabilities of Atlassian Intelligence

It helps teams work more efficiently by offering a variety of AI-powered tools. With these features, users can automatically summarize content such as meeting notes or Jira issues, get intelligent suggestions for issue descriptions and search using natural language. This also supports writing tasks by helping craft descriptions, recommending child work items and providing writing assistance in Confluence that includes grammar improvements and rewrite options.

Key Rovo Features for Streamlined Workflows

In this section, we will learn what Rovo is and which of its components help make work more productive.

Rovo

Rovo is Atlassian's intelligent work assistant that connects data and actions across Atlassian products and integrated third-party apps. Instead of offering help limited to a single tool, it focuses on streamlining work by automating tasks, linking systems and pulling knowledge from different sources into one place.

Important Components

- **Rovo Search:** It is a unified AI search experience that lets you find information from Jira, Confluence, Google Drive, Slack and additional apps in one place.
- **Rovo Chat:** This is a conversational AI interface that understands natural questions and allows you to perform actions or retrieve information across tools.
- **Rovo Agents:** AI-driven assistants that automate routine tasks and manage workflows across Jira, Confluence and other connected platforms.
- **Studio App:** It is a no-code builder app that allows teams to design, configure and manage custom Rovo Agents.

Key Rovo and AI Settings Every Administrators Must Know

In this section, we will understand the admin settings that help you activate or deactivate AI and Rovo apps. We will also explain how users can confirm that Rovo is enabled in their organization and which features are available on their site.

Settings to Activate AI

AI can be activated by Organization Admin in Standard, Premium and Enterprise versions.

You can control which apps allow your users to access AI features (including some Rovo capabilities) by turning AI on or off for each one.

When AI is enabled for an app, everyone in your organization can use its AI features, including those powered by Rovo. Some apps may also require you to update additional settings in their own configuration pages.

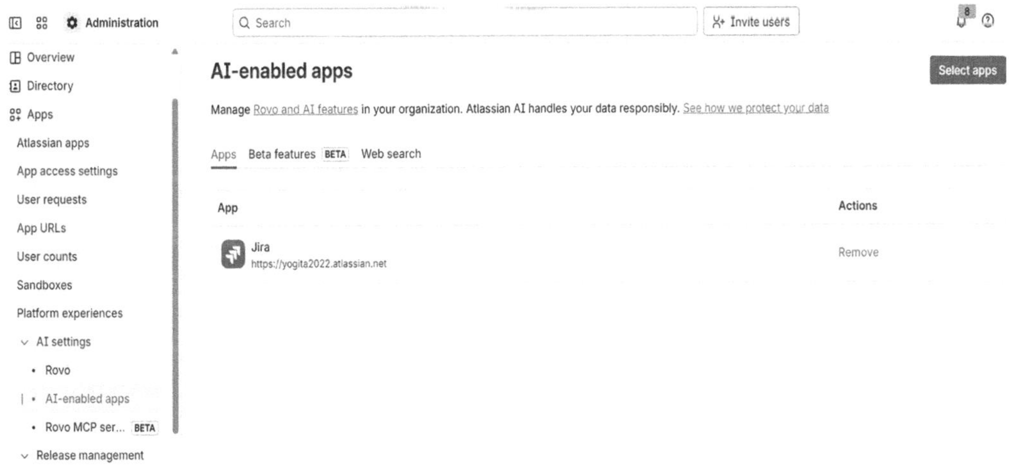

Figure 13.1: *Viewing AI-enabled Apps*

To turn on AI:

1. Navigate to **`Atlassian Administration`** and if you manage multiple organizations, choose the one you want.
2. Go to **`Apps`** > **`AI settings`** > **`AI-enabled apps`**. You will see which apps already have AI turned on.
3. Click **`Select apps`** to activate to view all apps that offer AI features.
4. Choose the apps where you want to enable AI.
5. Select **`Next`**.

6. Check that everything looks correct.
7. Click **`Activate`** to finalize your changes.

Settings to Deactivate AI

Turning off AI will stop all the existing and future AI features for that app, but anything previously created with AI will stay as it is.

1. Navigate to **`Atlassian Administration`**, and choose your organization, if you manage more than one.
2. Go to **`Apps`** > **`AI settings`** > **`AI-enabled apps`** to see which apps currently have AI turned on.
3. Select **`Remove`** next to any app where you want to disable AI.
4. Review your choices, and then click **`Save`** to confirm.

Disabling AI will not affect Rovo Search or Studio since they are built into the Atlassian platform and always stay on. However, if you turn off AI for every app, Rovo AI features such as Agents and Chat will also be switched off.

Rovo Settings

Turning on/off Rovo: You cannot disable Rovo itself, but you *can* turn off AI features in any of your apps.

Rovo Search and Rovo Studio are built into the Atlassian platform, so that they are always on and always accessible.

It is not required/mandatory to use AI. Organization admins can decide which apps are allowed to use AI (including Rovo's AI capabilities) by enabling or disabling AI at the app level.

Verifying Rovo Activation in Your Organization

To check whether Rovo is enabled for your organization:

1. Navigate to **`Atlassian Administration`** and choose your organization if you manage more than one.
2. In the left navigation, go to **`Apps`** > **`Atlassian Apps`**.

If Rovo is enabled, it will appear in the list. Your teams should also be able to see Rovo apps Rovo Search, Rovo Chat, and Rovo Studio within Jira, Confluence, and/or Jira Service Management, as well as in the app switcher.

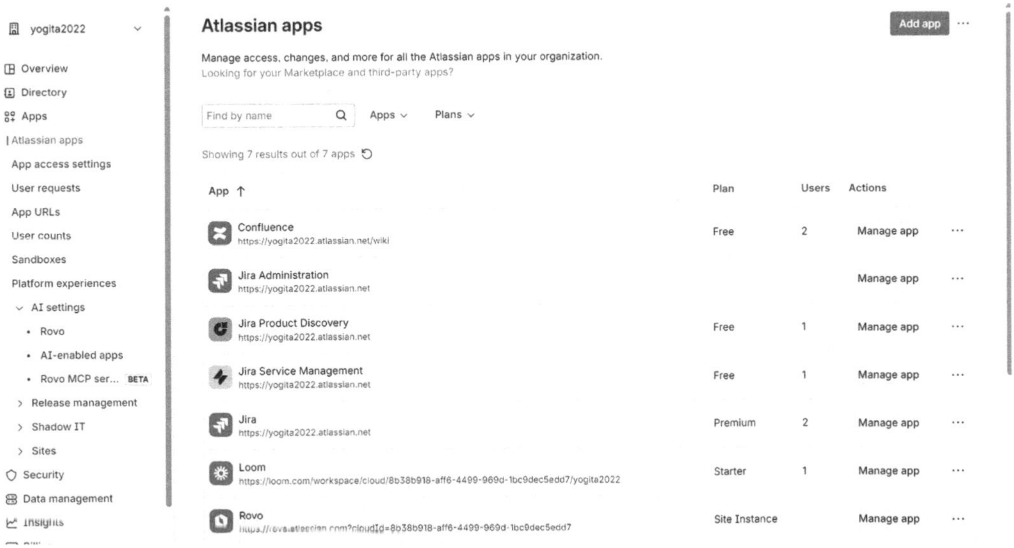

Figure 13.2: *Verifying Rovo Activation in Your Organization*

A Look Inside the Teamwork Graph

In this section, we will understand how the Teamwork Graph connects people, tools and knowledge in Rovo.

Defining Teamwork Graph

Atlassian's Teamwork Graph is the intelligent data backbone of its cloud platform, connecting together people, tasks, content and tools from across your organization. By linking Jira issues, Confluence pages and data from third-party apps, it builds a clear picture of how your team actually works, that is, who collaborates with whom, what they are working on and where project knowledge is stored. It does not just store data, it maps relationships and context so other systems like Rovo, can deliver smarter, more personalized insights.

How the Teamwork Graph Powers Rovo:

- **Context-aware recommendations:** Because the Graph understands the connections between your content, users and projects, Rovo can suggest relevant teammates, documents or next actions so as you can act with purpose.
- **Smarter search and chat:** When you ask Rovo a question, it does not just pull random items, it searches across all your connected tools (Jira, Slack, Google Drive and more) using the Graph to prioritize what is the most relevant.
- **AI-powered automation:** Rovo Agents use the context from the Graph to automate workflows more intelligently. For example, by creating tasks in Jira based on triggers from other apps.

Key Capabilities of the Teamwork Graph:

- **Unified Data Layer**: It brings together work items, documents, messages, users and groups from Atlassian tools *and* external apps in a consistent data model.
- **Context Mapping**: The Graph understands not just what each object is, but also how they relate For example- which Confluence page is tied to a Jira task, or which team member is closely involved in a project.
- **Smart Enrichment**: As Teamwork Graph learns your team's patterns and interactions, it enriches Atlassian tools with more personalized, actionable information tailored to each user.
- **Scalable Growth**: With every new action like a document created, a ticket updated, a chat started, the Graph grows providing richer insights and improving AI-driven experiences over time.

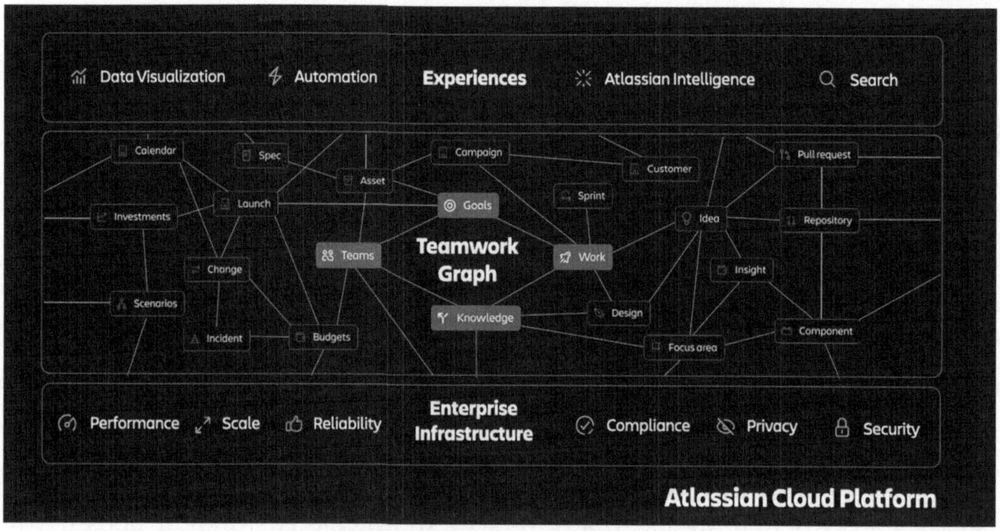

Figure 13.3: *Teamwork Graph*

Real-World Impact:

It is helpful in real world use cases as mentioned in the following points:

- Teams using Rovo and connected tools get faster search results and better insights as the AI understands how work is connected.
- With cross-tool automation, projects flow more smoothly, reducing the friction of switching between apps.
- As enterprises connect more of their tool stack (for example, Asana, Click up and more connectors), the Graph becomes even richer helping Rovo support smarter, cross-team workflows.

The Teamwork Graph is not just a data store. It is a living and evolving map of how your organization works. It is what makes Rove's AI powerful, context-aware and genuinely helpful.

What Rovo Connectors Do and How They Work

We will explore how Rovo Connectors connect apps and data and make it easier to work across different tools in one place.

Understanding Rovo Connectors

Rovo connectors are what allow Rovo to connect with tools outside the Atlassian ecosystem. By connecting apps your team already uses such as Google Drive, Slack or other work platforms, Rovo can give smarter results in Search, Chat and through its Agents. Before turning on any connection, it is important to check what kind of information the app stores and make sure it follows your company's data and security policies.

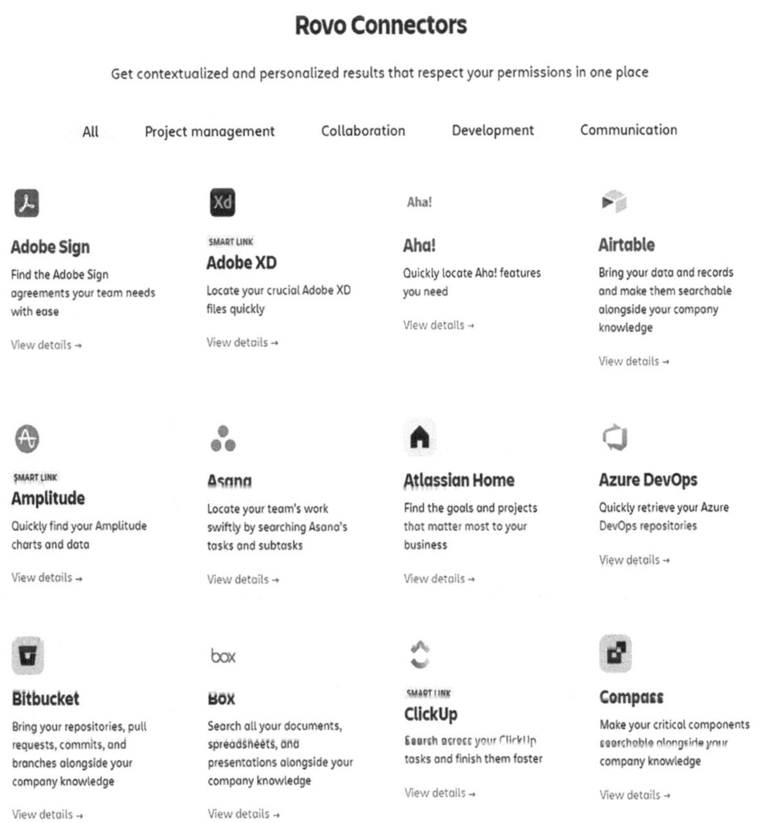

Figure 13.4: *Different Rovo Connectors*

Types of Rovo Connectors

Rovo offers four different kinds of connectors, each built for a specific purpose:

- **Synced connectors:** This can be set up by an admin. It brings in all content from a chosen workspace so that Rovo Search and Chat can work with complete and high-quality data.
- **Synced Lite connectors:** These only pull in information related to each individual user and the syncing happens when the user connects the app through Rovo Search.
- **Direct connectors:** These do not store or copy any data into Atlassian. Instead, Rovo pulls information live using API from the app whenever you perform a search or ask a question in Chat.
- **Smart Link connectors:** These require no admin setup. They work based on Smart Links and show results that match a user's own permissions and past usage.

How Permissions Work

Rovo always respects the permissions already set in your external apps. This means users will only see information they are allowed to access. If something is public in the connected tool, it may appear in search results or be used by Rovo Agents and Chat. If access is restricted, Rovo will follow that restriction automatically.

Connectors That Need Admin Setup

Some connectors need to be configured by an organization admin in admin.atlassian.com. Only users with this level of permission can add or manage these integrations.

Connectors That Do Not Need Admin Setup

Some connectors can be used without any help from an admin. These become active as soon as an individual user links their account through Rovo Search.

The connectors that work without admin setup include:

- **Google Drive**, when used as a Synced Lite connector.
- **All Smart Link connectors** listed in the Rovo options.

Connectors Per Site

In each Rovo-enabled site, most connectors can link to only one workspace at a time. In practical terms, this means:

- On a single Rovo site (such as *yourname.atlassian.net*), you can connect each app only once. For example, Google drive.
- If your organization has multiple Rovo sites, each site can connect to a different workspace of the same app using its own connector.

A Guide to the Ready to Use Rovo Agents

Along with the ability to build your own custom agents, Rovo also provides more than twenty ready-made agents created by Atlassian. These built in agents are designed to handle common tasks across documentation, planning, Jira management, support, analysis and more. You can start using them as soon as Rovo is enabled for your organization and it can be duplicated so you can customize them with your own knowledge sources, or adjust them for specific teams.

Agents for Documentation and Writing

We will look at how Rovo Agents can create different documentation.

- **Product Requirements Guide:** Helps product managers write and review PRDs using clear language, customer insights and best-practice recommendations.
- **Release Notes Drafter:** Summarizes up to 20 Jira issues at a time, and organizes them into themes, making release note creation faster and easier.
- **Comms Crafter:** Generates content that matches your organization's brand voice and style based on guidelines you provide.
- **Social Media Writer:** Drafts engaging social media posts or suggests improvements to make content more impactful.
- **Global Translator:** Translates content into many languages and supports teams in communicating across language barriers.
- **Agents for Decision Making and Planning:** We will look at how Rovo Agents can be helpful for planning, tracking and decision making.
- **Decision Director:** Reviews documents using the DACI framework, and offers suggestions and resources to help teams make decisions faster.
- **OKR Generator:** Creates or reviews OKRs, finds similar examples within your organization, and provides guidance on writing strong objectives.
- **Work Item Planner**: Breaks down large initiatives, epics, or goals into smaller actionable tasks.
- **Progress Tracker:** Gives a live overview of ongoing work, helping teams understand priorities and current progress.

- **Agents for Jira Work Item Management:** We will understand how Rovo agents can be useful for organizing tasks and checking readiness.
- **Work Item Organizer:** Quickly finds and updates Jira issues, moves items into sprints, assigns epics, clears old tasks, and much more.
- **Blocker Checker (Automation Focused):** Designed to run inside automation rules, this agent identifies potential blockers, and updates the issue status accordingly.
- **Bug Report Assistant:** Creates clear, complete bug reports with all essential details to support quicker triage.
- **Readiness Checker:** Evaluates whether a work item meets your team's Definition of Ready, and suggests improvements, if needed.
- **Agents for Operations and Support:** We will look at the Rovo agents that help with incident management and service request management.
- **Ops Guide:** Supports on-call responsibilities, offering guidance to manage incidents and reduce the time to detect, respond, and recover.
- **Service Request Helper:** Helps service teams craft responses, identify the right assignee, and summarize request details based on past tickets.
- **Service Triage (Automation-focused):** Works inside automation rules to sort, categorize and update service requests. Adding "`Automation mode`" in the beginning of the prompt activates its automation behavior.

Agents for Insight and Analysis

We will look at the Rovo agents that help teams turn data, transcripts and customer feedback into clear insights and useful actions.

- **Jira Theme Analyzer:** Scans Jira issues using JQL or project data to identify themes or group tasks into epics.
- **Transcript Insights Reporter:** Converts meeting transcripts into clear insights, recommendations, and actionable follow-ups.
- **Customer Insights:** Analyses customer feedback from pages or projects, and provides useful patterns and takeaways.
- **Agents for Team Building:** We will cover how a Rovo agent can be helpful to create a user manual.
- **User Manual Writer:** Helps individuals create a personal "user manual" that explains how they work best, preferred communication styles, and tips for teammates.
- **Agents for Help:** We will cover an expert Rovo agent that can help everyone learn Rovo.

- **Rovo Expert:** A friendly guide that introduces users to Rovo's features, answers common questions, and helps teams get the most value from the platform.

These ready to use agents are helpful to teams to build a foundation to start benefiting from Rovo immediately. They can also expand their capabilities as your needs grow.

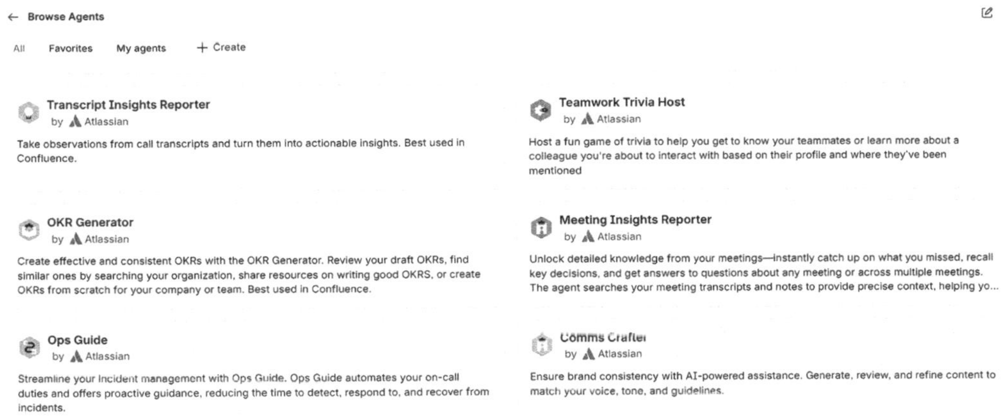

Figure 13.5: *Different Readymade Rovo Agents*

Steps to Build Your Own Rovo Agent

1. Open Rovo Studio using the app switcher in your Atlassian workspace.

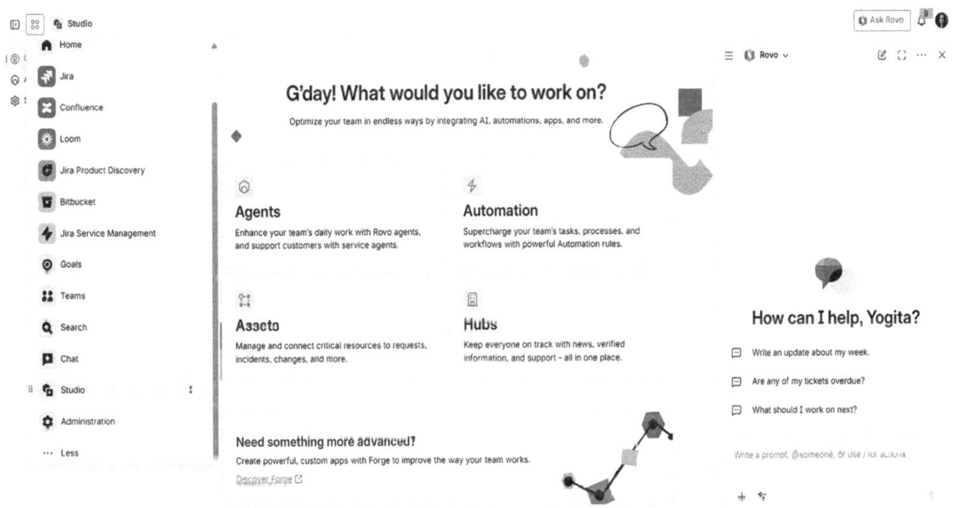

Figure 13.6: *Accessing Rovo Studio from App Switcher*

2. Go to the **`Agents`** section, and click **`Create`** to start building a new agent.

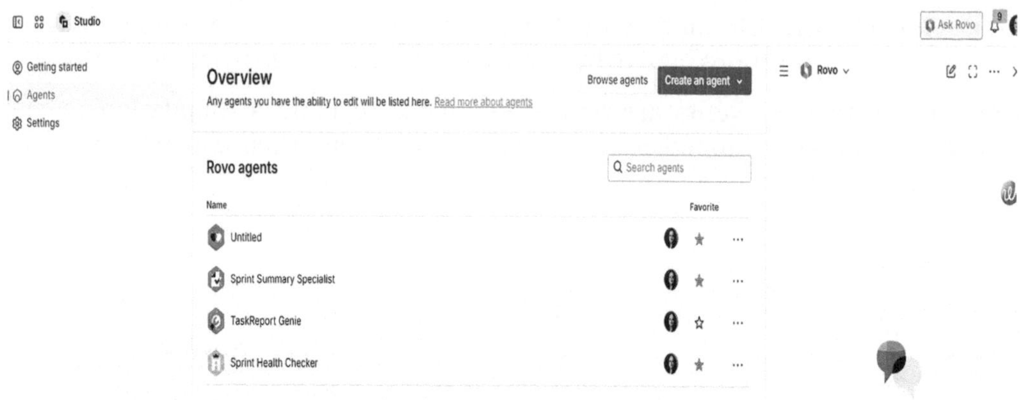

Figure 13.7: *Creating an Agent from Rovo Studio*

3. Define the agent's identity by giving it a clear name and a short description.
4. Write the agent's instructions, including its role, tone and what it should or should not do.
5. Add scenarios if needed to guide how the agent should behave in different situations.
6. Generate conversation starters to help users know how to begin interacting with the agent.
7. Select the knowledge sources the agent can access, such as Jira, Confluence or connected apps.
8. Choose the skills and actions the agent is allowed to perform, such as summarizing, commenting or creating issues.

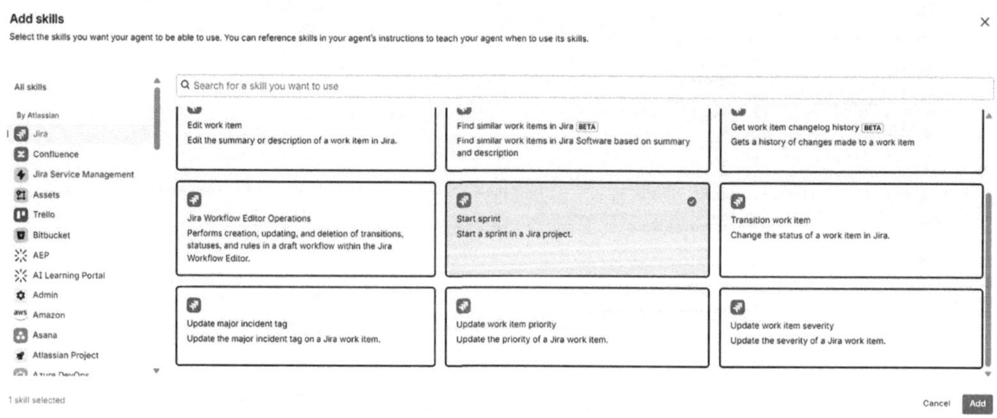

Figure 13.8: *Adding Skills while Creating a Rovo Agent*

9. Review and confirm the agent's permissions to ensure that it respects your organization's access rules.
10. Check all the details such as name, instructions, knowledge sources, and actions before finalizing.
11. Click **`Create`** or **`Activate`** to publish the agent so that the users can start using it in Rovo Chat or workflows.
12. Optionally add the agent to automation rules so that it can run tasks automatically based on triggers.
13. Test the agent in real scenarios, and refine its instructions or skills based on user feedback.

How to Duplicate and Share Rovo Agents

Here is an example of an agent that has been created, called the Sprint Health Checker.

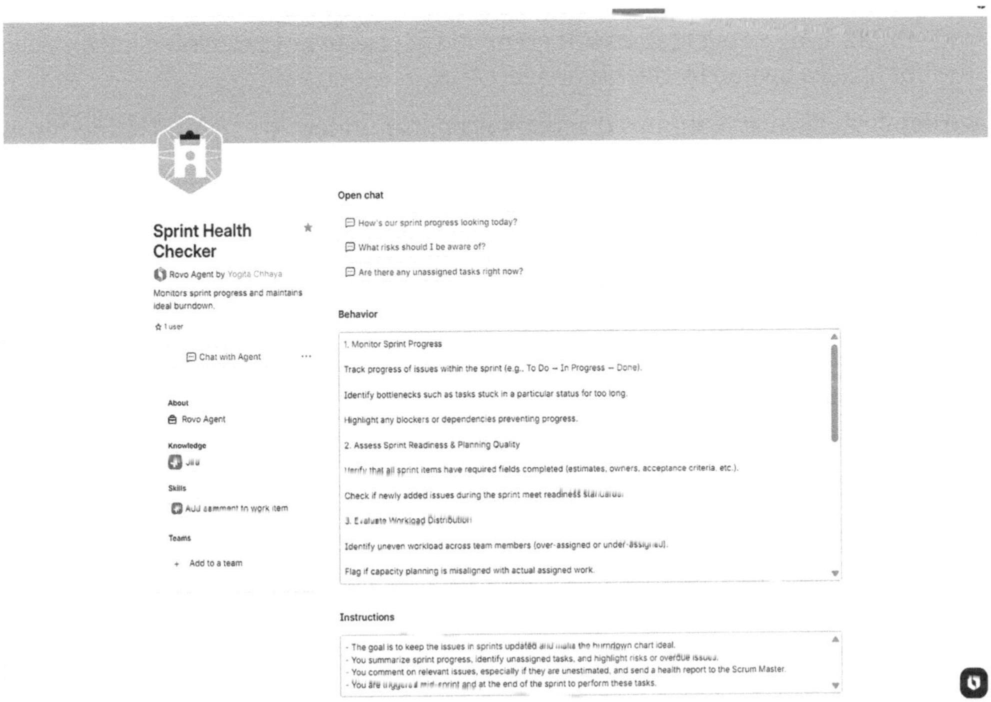

***Figure 13.9:** Sprint Health Checker Agent*

The Sprint Health Checker Agent helps to get the report of not estimated, overdue and unassigned work items, improve overall progress of the sprint, and improve sprint burndown chart.

Share an Agent

Sharing your agents makes collaboration easy and helps teams stay aligned. Simply share the agent's profile link and anyone with access can open it in full-screen and chat with it. Agents will only display information that the user already has permission to view.

Duplicate a Rovo Agent

You can make a copy of an existing agent to use as a starting point and customize it however you like.

Agents created with code by Atlassian, marketplace partners, or other third-party builders cannot be copied.

When you duplicate an agent, you are able to:

- Give it a new name and write a fresh description.
- Adjust its instructions, knowledge sources, skills and conversation starters.
- Duplicating an agent does not grant you access to any restricted links, projects or spaces owned by the original creator.

Once duplicated, your customized agent will appear under "My agents" in the "Browse Agents" section.

Conversation Starters

Conversation starters are suggested prompts that help users begin interacting with your agent. When a conversation begins, three suggested starters appear automatically.

Accessing Rovo Use Cases and Prompts

To access use cases with the sample prompts, follow the steps as mentioned below. It is helpful for different teams using different apps.

Steps:

1. Navigate to https://www.atlassian.com/software/rovo/use-cases?&search=
2. Type in the search bar or select use cases by choosing the team name, feature name, and Atlassian Cloud app.

For example, select **`View Blocked Jira tickets`**.

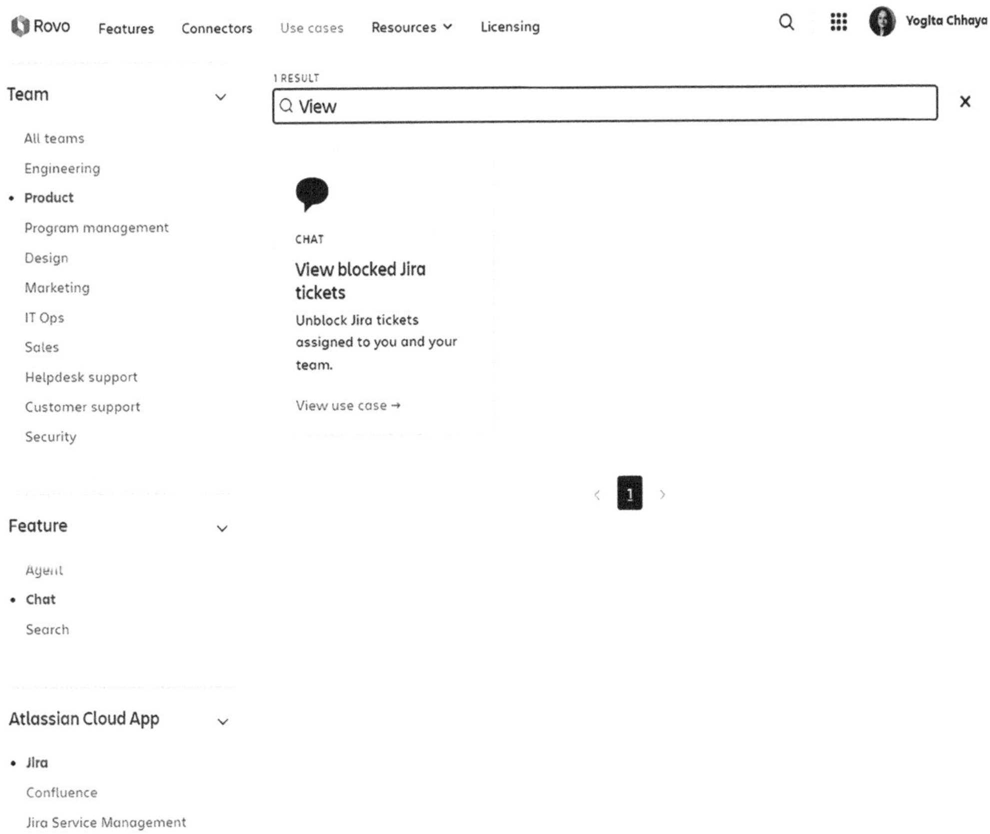

***Figure 13.10**: Applying Filters to View Different Rovo Use Cases*

You will see that all the details such as how it works, sample prompts and the name of the teams that can use this in the chat.

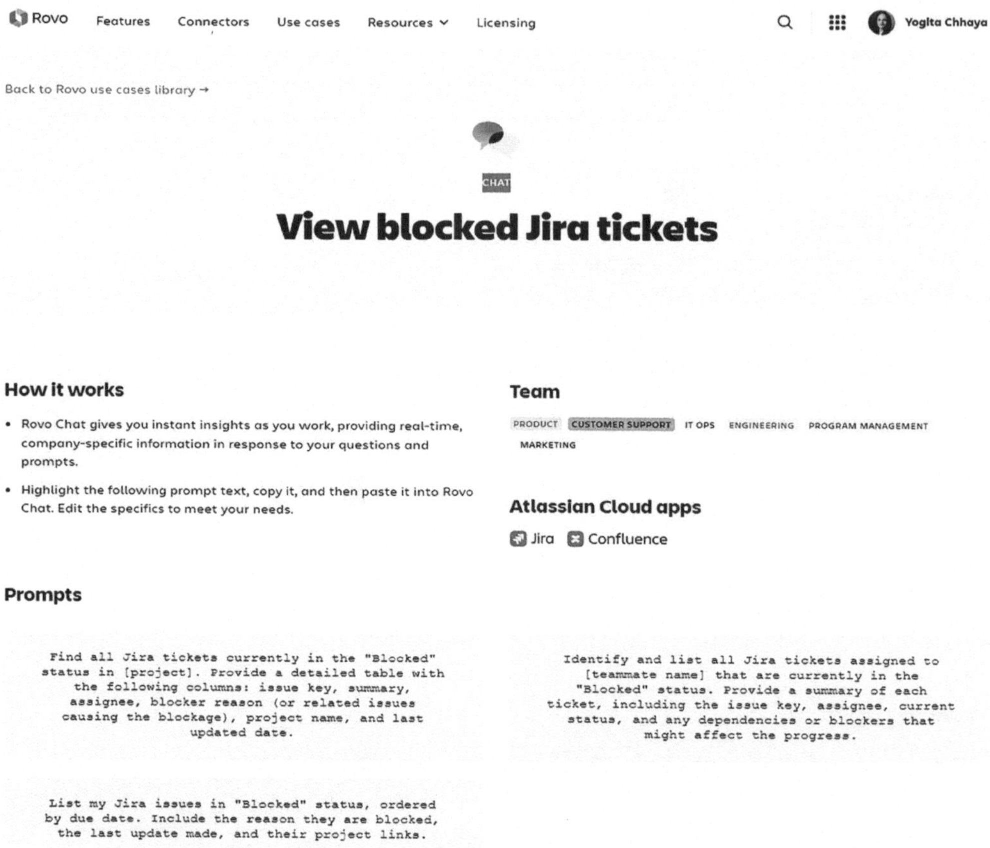

Figure 13.11: *Prompts, Teams and Apps for a Rovo Chat Use Case*

Real-World Examples: Automating Tasks with Rovo Agents

You can add an Agent, while creating Automation rules in Jira.

Rule 1: The rule below verifies issue readiness using the Rovo Agent Readiness Checker.

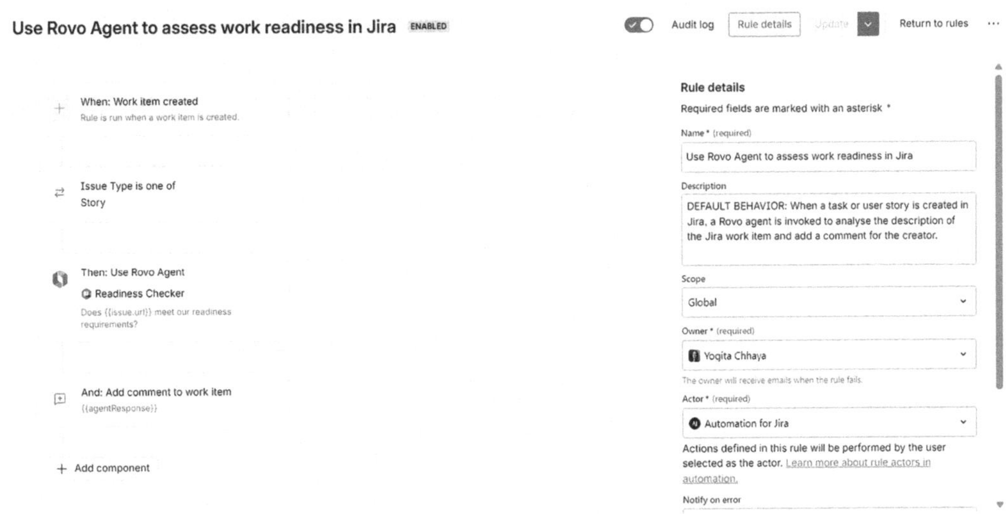

Figure 13.12: *Work Readiness Checker in Automation Rule*

This automation rule evaluates completeness, clarity, auditability and estimation. It is tailored for Story work item types and automatically adds a comment to the work item based on these criteria.

Rule 2: The rule below enhances the bug-triage process using the Rovo Agent Bug Report Assistant.

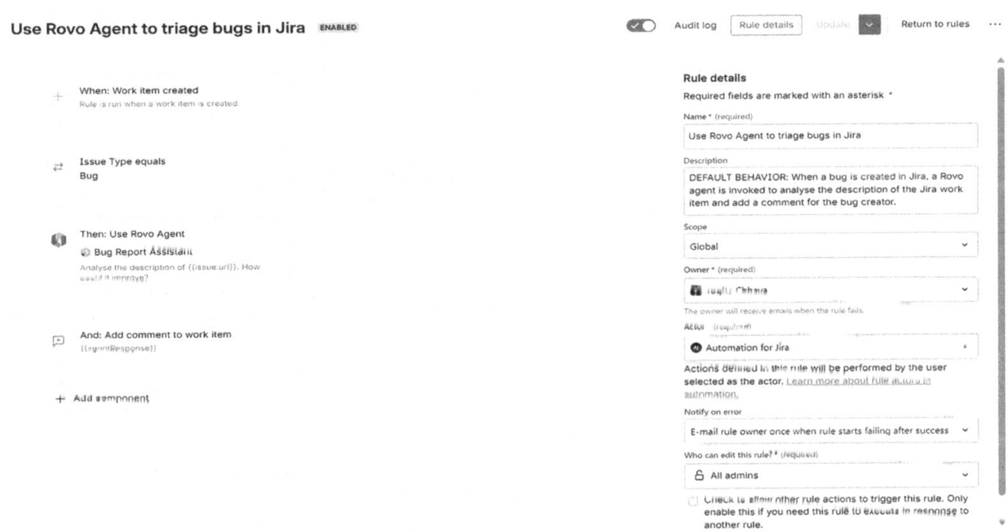

Figure 13.13: *Bug Report Assistant in Automation Rule*

This automation rule accelerates bug triage by improving the quality of bug reports. It guides users to provide clear, concise reports with all the necessary details included.

These rules are created using the "ready to use Rovo Agents".

Building A No-code Rovo Agent Setup Example

We have created a no-code Rovo Agent. We will learn how to write Instructions, Prompts, Knowledge and much more.

Instructions/Behavior: The following are the detailed instructions provided while creating an Agent.

Identify the current or most recent sprint for the specified Jira Scrum board or project.

Extract and summarize the following sprint metrics:

- Total number of issues in the sprint
- Number and percentage of completed issues
- Number and percentage of incomplete/carryover issues
- Status breakdown (To Do, In Progress, Done, Blocked, and so on)
- Unassigned or unestimated issues
- Issue type distribution (Story, Bug, Task, and so on)
- Story points committed vs. completed
- Scope changes (issues added or removed after sprint start)
- Blockers or flagged issues
- Generate the following visualizations:
- Bar chart: Issue status distribution
- Pie chart: Completion rate (completed vs. incomplete)
- Table: Unassigned or unestimated issues
- (Optional) Line chart: Sprint burndown, if data is available
- Provide a concise narrative summary (maximum 200 words) covering:
- Delivery highlights
- Carryover/slippage
- Risks & blockers
- Capacity & forecast
- Next sprint focus or recommendations

Format the output for easy copy-paste into Confluence or a presentation, using clear sections, bullet points, and tables. Do not include individual developer names.

Input: Jira board or project name/key.

Output: All charts, tables, summary and recommendations as described above, formatted for Confluence or presentation.

Prompt to Test: Provide all the details for the last active sprint in SSPG Project.

Conversation Starters: Ask Rovo Agent to generate Conversation starters by clicking Generate Conversation Starters.

Knowledge:

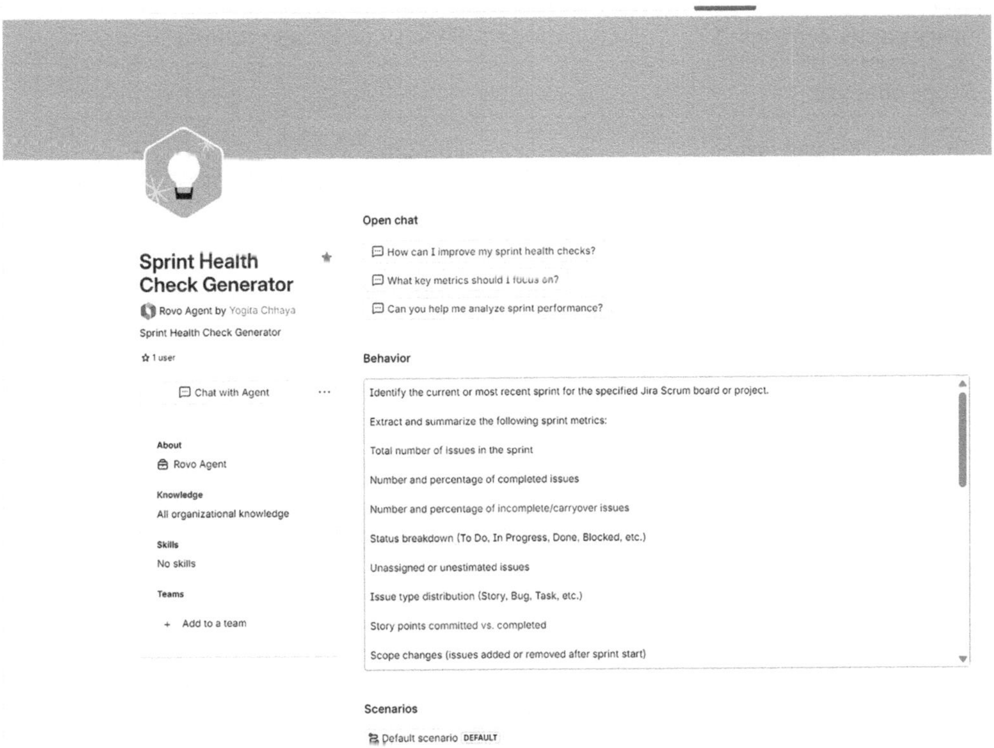

Figure 13.14: *Sprint Health Check Generator Agent*

Output Generated: The following is the output generated for Sample Sprint2 of Project SSPG.

Sprint: Sample Sprint 2

State: Active

Start: 2024-09-05

End: 2024-09-19

12 Issues

Sprint Metrics

Metric	Value
Total issues in sprint	12
Completed issues (Done)	1 (8.3%)
Incomplete/carryover issues	11 (91.7%)
Story points committed	23 (sum of available)
Story points completed	0 (no Done issues with SP)
Scope changes	Not detected
Blockers/flagged issues	1 (Impediment)

Table 13.1: *Various Sprint Metrics Generated by Agent*

Issue Status Breakdown

Status	Count	%	
To Do	7	58.3%	
In Progress	4	33.3%	
Done	1	8.3%	
Blocked	1	8.3%	*(Flagged as impediment, overlaps with In Progress)*

Table 13.2: *Issue Status Breakdown Provided by Agent for the Sprint*

Issue Type Distribution

Issue Type	Count
Story	8
Bug	4

Table 13.3: *Issue Type Distribution Provided by Agent for the Sprint*

Unassigned or Unestimated Issues

Issue Key	Summary	Assignee	Story Points
SSPG-45	test task	Unassigned	(blank)
SSPG-44	CLONE - Burndown Chart	Unassigned	4

SSPG-43	CLONE - Burndown Chart	Unassigned	4
SSPG-41	CLONE - Complete Sprint	Unassigned	2
SSPG-40	CLONE - Burndown Chart	Unassigned	4
SSPG-38	CLONE - Update details (Bug)	[Yogita Chhaya]	(blank)
SSPG-33	CLONE - Test story	Unassigned	(blank)
SSPG-15	Burndown Chart (Flagged: Impediment)	Unassigned	4
SSPG-13	Update details (Bug)	[Yogita Chhaya]	(blank)
SSPG-17	Instructions for deleting sample board (Bug, Done)	[Yogita Chhaya]	(blank)
SSPG-16	Complete Sprint	Unassigned	2
SSPG-31	Test story	Unassigned	3

Table 13.4: *Unassigned or Unestimated Issues Summary Provided by Agent for the Sprint*

Blockers / Flagged Issues

Issue Key	**Summary**	**Status**	**Flagged Reason**
SSPG-15	Burndown Chart	In Progress	Impediment

Table 13.5: *Blocker Issues Summary Provided by Agent for the Sprint*

Visualizations

1. **Bar Chart: Issue Status Distribution**

| To Do | ███████ 7

| In Progress | ████ 4

| Done | █ 1

2. **Pie Chart: Completion Rate**

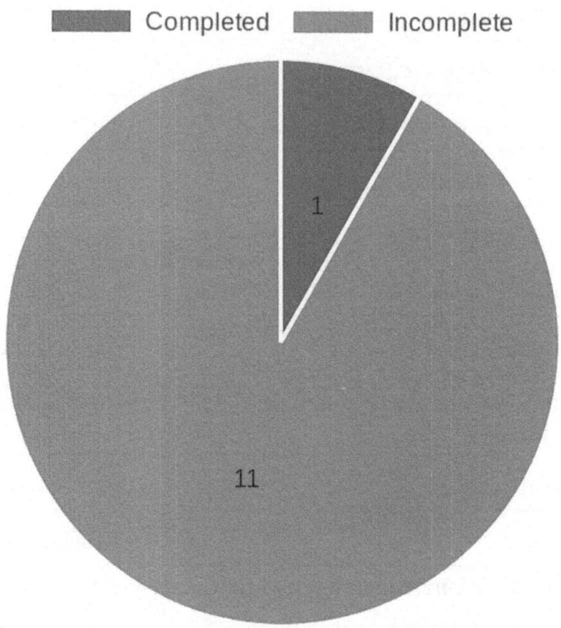

***Figure 13.15**: Pie Chart- Completion Rate Generated by Agent*

- **Completed:** 8%
- **Incomplete:** 92%

3. **Table: Unassigned or Unestimated Issues**

Issue Key	**Summary**	**Assignee**	**Story Points**
SSPG-45	test task	Unassigned	(blank)
SSPG-33	CLONE - Test	Unassigned	(blank)
SSPG-38	Update details	[Yogita Chhaya]	(blank)
SSPG-13	Update details	[Yogita Chhaya]	(blank)

***Table 13.6**: Unassigned or Unestimated Issues Summary Provided by Agent for the Sprint*

Narrative Summary

Delivery Highlights:

- Only 1 out of 12 issues (8%) reached Done. The majority remain in To Do or In Progress.
- No story points were completed; all completed issues lacked story point estimates.

Carryover/Slippage:

- 11 issues (92%) are incomplete and will likely carry over to the next sprint.

Risks and Blockers:

- One issue (SSPG-15) is flagged as an impediment, indicating a blocker that needs attention.

Capacity and Forecast:

- The team overcommitted relative to delivery, with 23 story points committed and none completed.
- Several issues lack assignees or estimates, impacting predictability.

Next Sprint Focus / Recommendations:

- Address flagged/blocked issues as a priority.
- Ensure that all issues are assigned and estimated before sprint start.
- Consider reducing sprint scope or improving estimation accuracy.
- Focus on completing carryover work before adding new scope.

Best Practices for Designing Powerful Rovo Agents

- **Be Clear about Your Agent's Purpose:** Define what your Rovo Agent is for. Give it a clear role, responsibilities and limits. When you write the instructions, explain both what it should do and what it should not do. That way, its behavior stays consistent and helpful.
- **Start Simple and then Iterate:** Begin with a basic version of your agent. Use short, focused instructions instead of trying to cover too much. As real users interact with it, collect feedback and gradually refine its behavior.
- **Limit Skills to What Matters:** Give your agent only the skills it really needs. For example, Rovo supports many skills (such as creating or editing Jira issues or Confluence pages), but it is best to pick fewer skills to keep the agent effective and avoid confusion.
- **Choose the Right Knowledge Sources:** When you set up an agent, decide which data it should search from, that is, Jira projects, Confluence spaces, connected apps, and so on. Pulling in only relevant sources helps the agent give more accurate and useful responses.
- **Design for Automation:** Use your agent inside automation rules to trigger actions automatically. For instance, when a Jira issue is created, an automation can call the agent to analyze or comment on it.

- **Write Good Instructions:** Include a behavior statement (its role and personality), scenarios (how it should respond in different cases), and conversation starters (prompts users can begin with). Keep these instructions concise and focused – too much detail can confuse the agent.
- **Respect Permissions and Governance:** Ensure that your agent only acts within the access levels of the user interacting with it. Rovo agents do not give extra permissions – if a user cannot see a page, the agent will not either.
- **Test with Real Use Cases:** Before you fully roll out an agent, test it with real workflows. For example, ask it to draft a Confluence page, triage Jira tickets, or summarize content and then refine based on how well it performs.
- **Use Out-of-the-Box Agents as Templates:** Rovo comes with built-in agents. Use these as starting points and then you can duplicate them, tweak their knowledge sources and instructions and mold them to fit your team's needs.
- **Monitor, Own, and Evolve:** Track how agents are being used via logs. If errors or misuse come up, refine their instructions or restrict certain skills. You can also transfer ownership or add collaborators to keep agents aligned with evolving needs.

Thus, by following the above-mentioned practices, you make sure your Rovo Agents are actually powerful collaborators that automate work, reduce repetitive tasks, and improve team productivity.

AI with Humans Partnering for Smarter Collaboration

Rovo Agents are not designed and developed to replace what we do. They are here to help developers, project managers and the teams to improve their way of working. The difference is that productivity improves, and instead of constant back-and-forth, execution becomes more streamlined and efficient.

What has changed:

- No more searching through Jira to track down information.
- Fewer tasks that require manual updates.
- Quicker, more accurate answers to status inquiries.
- A system that continues learning and getting better with use.

The true advantage of integrating Rovo, AI, other Apps and Jira is not about eliminating work. It is about allowing smarter processes, faster progress and smoother collaboration.

Conclusion

This chapter covers a clear and simple look at how teams can work better when information is easy to find and use. We have explained what makes Rovo a helpful modern teammate, and how it compares to Atlassian Intelligence. We also walk through the basic settings admins need to know like how to turn AI features on or off, check if Rovo is active, and understand the Teamwork Graph that helps Rovo make smarter suggestions. The chapter is helpful to get a simple language explanation of Rovo Connectors, how they work, and which ones need admin setup.

The chapter then covers hands-on guidance. We have explored ready-made Rovo Agents, learn how to build your own simple no-code options, and see real examples of how teams automate work with them. Finally, we have covered the best practices and tips on how people and AI can work together. By the end, readers can understand the tools available, and how they can help teams work faster, stay organized and collaborate more smoothly.

Use Cases with Reference Links

1. **Rovo Use Cases:**

   https://www.atlassian.com/software/rovo/use-cases

2. **Rovo Agents:**

   https://community.atlassian.com/forums/Confluence-questions/Rovo-agents/qaq-p/3079335

3. **Can you track the usage of Rovo Agents?**

   https://community.atlassian.com/forums/Rovo-questions/Can-you-track-usage-of-Rovo-agents/qaq-p/3134620

4. **Org Admin Agent:**

   https://community.atlassian.com/forums/Rovo-questions/Org-Admin-Agents/qaq-p/3131585

5. **Rovo Usage Limit:**

   https://community.atlassian.com/forums/Rovo-questions/Rovo-usage-limit/qaq-p/3113348

6. **How does Rovo disappear of the standard license?**

   https://community.atlassian.com/forums/Rovo-questions/Rovo-could-dissapear-of-the-standard-license/qaq-p/3133169

7. **Upload documents as context to Rovo Agent:**

   https://community.atlassian.com/forums/Rovo-questions/Upload-documents-as-context-to-Rovo-Agent/qaq-p/3125337

8. **Rovo Web Search Agent:**

   https://community.atlassian.com/forums/Rovo-questions/Rovo-web-search-agent/qaq-p/3128133

9. **Change the image from Rovo:**

   https://community.atlassian.com/forums/Rovo-questions/Change-the-image-from-Rovo/qaq-p/3129017

10. **Can a Rovo Agent create tickets using wiki markup?**

    https://community.atlassian.com/forums/Rovo-questions/Can-a-Rovo-Agent-create-tickets-using-wiki-markup/qaq-p/3123598

11. **How does Rovo use archived content?**

    https://community.atlassian.com/forums/Rovo-questions/How-does-Rovo-use-archived-content/qaq-p/3133048

Index

A

X

Z